2012

OCR Biology A2

Student Workbook

BIOZONE

OCR *Biology A2* 2012

Student Workbook

First edition 2010
Second edition 2012

ISBN 978-1-877462-83-2

Published by **BIOZONE International Ltd**

Printed by REPLIKA PRESS PVT LTD using paper produced from renewable and waste materials

About the Writing Team

Tracey Greenwood joined the staff of Biozone at the beginning of 1993. She has a Ph.D in biology, specialising in lake ecology, and taught undergraduate and graduate biology at the University of Waikato for four years.

Lissa Bainbridge-Smith worked in industry in a research and development capacity for eight years before joining BIOZONE in 2006. Lissa has a Masters degree in biology from Waikato University.

Kent Pryor has BSc from Massey University majoring in zoology and ecology. He was a secondary school teacher in biology and chemistry for 9 years before joining Biozone as an author in 2009.

Richard Allan has had 11 years experience teaching senior biology at Hillcrest High School in Hamilton, New Zealand. He attained a Masters degree in biology at Waikato University, New Zealand.

Purchases of this workbook may be made direct from the publisher:

BIOZONE **www.biozone.co.uk**

UNITED KINGDOM:

BIOZONE Learning Media (UK) Ltd.
Bretby Business Park, Ashby Road, Bretby,
Burton upon Trent, DE15 0YZ, **UK**
Telephone: 01283-553-257
FAX: 01283-553-258
E-mail: sales@biozone.co.uk

AUSTRALIA:

BIOZONE Learning Media Australia
P.O. Box 2841, Burleigh BC,
QLD 4220, **Australia**
Telephone: +61 7-5535-4896
FAX: +61 7-5508-2432
E-mail: sales@biozone.com.au

NEW ZEALAND:

BIOZONE International Ltd.
P.O. Box 13-034, Hamilton 3251, **New Zealand**
Telephone: +64 7-856-8104
FAX: +64 7-856-9243
E-mail: sales@biozone.co.nz

Preface to the 2012 Edition

This is the second edition of BIOZONE's workbook for OCR Biology A2. This edition has been updated and specifically written to meet the needs of students enrolled in **OCR GCE Biology**, in accordance with the OCR specification. OCR Biology A2 2012 builds on the successful features of the previous edition, while focusing on scientific literacy and learning within relevant contexts. Features of this workbook include:

- Content alignment. The organisation of this edition is aligned to the OCR specification. Concept maps divide the book into each of the three OCR A2 units. This organisation of content provides a more cohesive coverage of material within each unit, while retaining the flexible nature of the activity worksheet format. Extension material, and additional material for is provided on the **Teacher Resource CD-ROM** (for separate purchase).
- A contextual approach. We encourage students to become thinkers by applying their knowledge within appropriate contexts. Some chapters include an account examining a 'biological story' related to the theme of the chapter. This approach provides a context for the material and an opportunity to focus on the comprehension and the synthesis of ideas.
- Concept maps introduce each unit of the workbook, integrating the content across chapters to encourage linking of ideas.
- An easy-to-use chapter introduction comprising succinct learning objectives, a list of key terms, and a short summary of key concepts. The learning objectives are based on the learning outcomes of the OCR scheme, but in some cases include additional detail to assist with comprehension.
- There is an emphasis on acquiring skills in scientific literacy. Each chapter includes a comprehension and/or literacy activity, and the appendix includes references for works cited in the text.
- *Extension material* is identified with a E at the beginning of the activity code, e.g. ERA 3 = challenging extension activity requiring reading outside the page and application of knowledge.
- *Weblinks* and *Related activities* support the material provided on each activity page.
- This workbook will be regularly updated to keep abreast of new developments in biology and to reflect changes to the OCR course. Biozone continues to be committed to providing up-to-date, relevant, interesting, and accurate information.

A Note to the Teacher

This workbook is a student-centred resource, and benefits students by facilitating independent learning and critical thinking. This workbook is just that; a place for your answers notes, asides, and corrections. It is not a textbook and annual revisions are our commitment to providing a current, flexible, and engaging resource. The low price is a reflection of this commitment. Please do not photocopy the activities. If you think it is worth using, then we recommend that the students themselves own this resource and keep it for their own use. I thank you for your support. **Richard Allan**

Acknowledgements & Photo Credits

Royalty free images, purchased by Biozone International Ltd, are used throughout this workbook and have been obtained from the following sources: Corel Corporation from various titles in their Professional Photos CD-ROM collection; IMSI (International Microcomputer Software Inc.) images from IMSI's MasterClips® and MasterPhotosTM Collection, 1895 Francisco Blvd. East, San Rafael, CA 94901-5506, USA; ©1996 Digital Stock, Medicine and Health Care collection; ©Hemera Technologies Inc, 1997-2001; © 2005 JupiterImages Corporation www.clipart.com; ©Click Art, ©T/Maker Company; ©1994., ©Digital Vision; Gazelle Technologies Inc.; PhotoDisc®, Inc. USA, www.photodisc.com.

Biozone's authors also acknowledge the generosity of all those who have kindly helped or provided information and photographs for this first edition: • Gemma Conn and Denise Fort for their contributions to artwork • Sue FitzGerald, Mary McDougall, and Gwen Gilbert for their efficient handling of the office, • PASCO for their images of probeware • www.coastalplanning.net for the image of a marine quadrat • The three-spined stickleback image was originally prepared by Ellen Edmonson as part of the 1927-1940 New York Biological Survey. Permission for use granted by the New York State Department of Environmental Conservation • PIER digital library for the image of the coronary artery • Marc King for photographs of comb types in chickens • TechPool Studios, for their clipart collection of human anatomy: Copyright ©1994, TechPool Studios Corp. USA (some of these images were modified by Richard Allan and Tracey Greenwood) • Totem Graphics, for their clipart collection of plants and animals • Corel Corporation, for use of their eps clipart of plants and animals from the Corel MEGAGALLERY collection • Allan & Elaine Wilson • Beta Cell Biology Consortium • Bioengineering AG, Switzerland • Burkhard Budel • Cytogenetics Dept, Waikato Hospital • David Fankhauser, Uni. of Cincinnati, Clermont College • www.coastalplanning.net for the image of a marine quadrat • UC regents David campus • Dr David Wells, AgResearch • Dr D. Cooper, University of California, San Francisco • Ed Uthman • Genesis Research and Development Corp, Auckland • Georgetown University Hospital • Greenpeace • Han Knoll Institute, Germany • Karen Nichols (http://www.flickr.com/photos/camerar/) for the photo of the bee-wolf (also known as digger wasp), *Philanthus triangulum* • Kurchatov Inst • Leo Sanchez • NASA Earth Observatory • Pharmacia (Aust) PTY Ltd • Peter Halasz • Roslin Institute • Seoul National University • University of Waikato • Aptychus for the photo of the Tamil girl • Rita Willaert for the photo of the Nuba woman • Shirley Owens MSU • Jochen Wegner for the histological stain of fast and slow twitch muscle

We also acknowledge the photographers that have made their images available through Wikimedia Commons under Creative Commons Licences 2.5. or 3.0: : • Alan and Elaine Wilson (GFDL) • André Karwath (aka AKA) • Bruce Marlin • Dario U • Dirk Beyer • Indian Nomad • Jacoplane • Joel Mills (GFDL) • Lorax (GFDL) • Onno Zweers • Stephen Lea • UtahCamera • Ohio State university at Lima • VA Maryland Regional Veterinary College of Medicine (WMRCVM) • JPogi • Andreas Trepte • Stemonitis • it:Utente:Cits • Robert Scarth • ms-donna • HP R817 • Velela • D. Gordon E. Robertson • Mbz1 • Laitche • Janke • Mikrolit • Rasbak • Gina Mikel • Daderot • Jjron (John O'Neill) • William M. Gray • USDA • NYWTS (New York World-Telegram and the Sun, staff photographer, Al Aumuller)

Photos kindly provided by individuals or corporations identified by way of coded credits are as follows: **AKA**: André Karwath, **BH**: Brendan Hicks, **BOB**: Barry O'Brien (Uni. of Waikato), **CA**: Clipart.com, **CDC**: Centers for Disease Control and Prevention, Atlanta, USA, **CF**: Conan Fee, **EII**: Education Interactive Imaging, **HGSI**: Dena Borchardt at Human Genome Sciences Inc., **NASA**: National Aeronautics and Space Administration, **NIH**: National Institute for Health, **RA**: Richard Allan, **RCN**: Ralph Cocklin, **TG**: Tracey Greenwood, **WMU**: Waikato Microscope Unit.

Special thanks to all the partners of the Biozone team for their support.

Cover Photographs

Main photograph: The white tailed deer (*Odocoileus virginianus*), is a medium sized deer that shows tremendous genetic variation and is adaptable to a wide range of environments. Recent genetic studies indicate that there are actually fewer subspecies within the species range than the 30 to 40 subspecies described last century. PHOTO: Paul Tessier, iStock Photos www.istockphoto.com

Background photograph: Autumn leaves, Image ©2005 JupiterImages Corporation www.clipart.com

Contents

CODES: Δ Upgraded ☆ New activity ❑ to be done ✓ when completed

CONTENTS *(continued)*

CODES: Δ Upgraded ☆ New activity ❑ to be done ✓ when completed

CONTENTS *(continued)*

CODES: Δ **Upgraded** ☆ **New activity** ☐ **to be done** ☑ **when completed**

Getting The Most From This Resource

This workbook is designed as a resource to increase your understanding and enjoyment of biology. It is suitable for students in their A2 year of **OCR Biology**. The course guide on page 5 (or on the Teacher Resource CD-ROM) indicates where in this workbook the material in the specification is covered. This workbook will reinforce and extend the ideas developed by your teacher. It is **not a textbook**; its aim is to complement and reinforce the textbooks written for your course. Each topic in the workbook includes the following useful features:

Features of the Concept Map

Each major section of the workbook has a core theme:

- *Communication, Homeostasis, and Energy*
- *Control, Genomes, and Environment*
- *Practical Skills in Biology*

Encouraging Key Competencies

Thinking - bringing ideas together

Relating to others - communicating

Using language, symbols, and text

Managing self - independence

Participating and contributing

Chapter panels identify and summarise the material covered within each chapter.

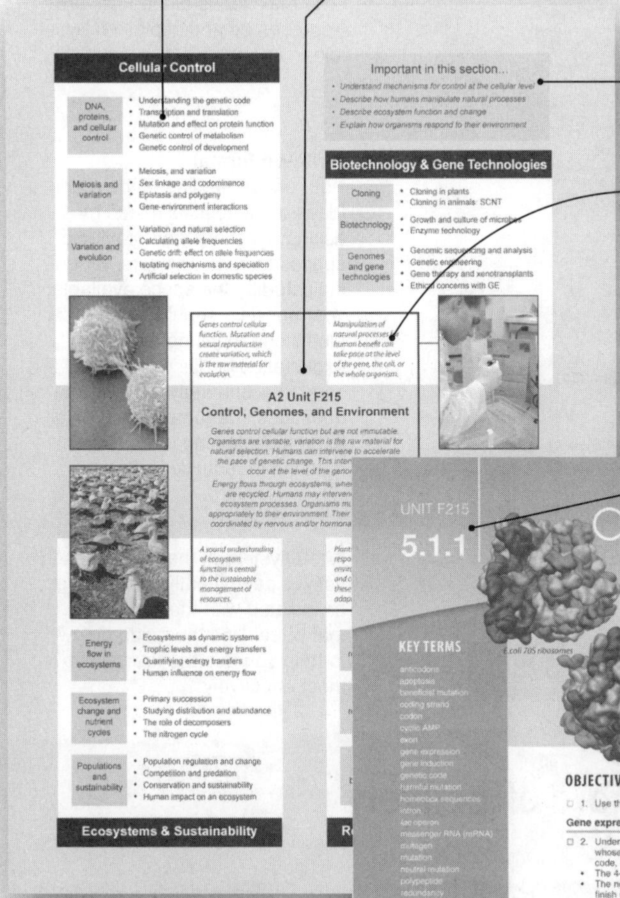

Each section of the workbook emphasises skills and knowledge to be gained.

A summary of why this material is important and where it fits into your understanding of your course content.

Features of the Chapter Topic Page

The part of the OCR scheme to which this chapter applies. Objectives can be assigned at the discretion of the teacher.

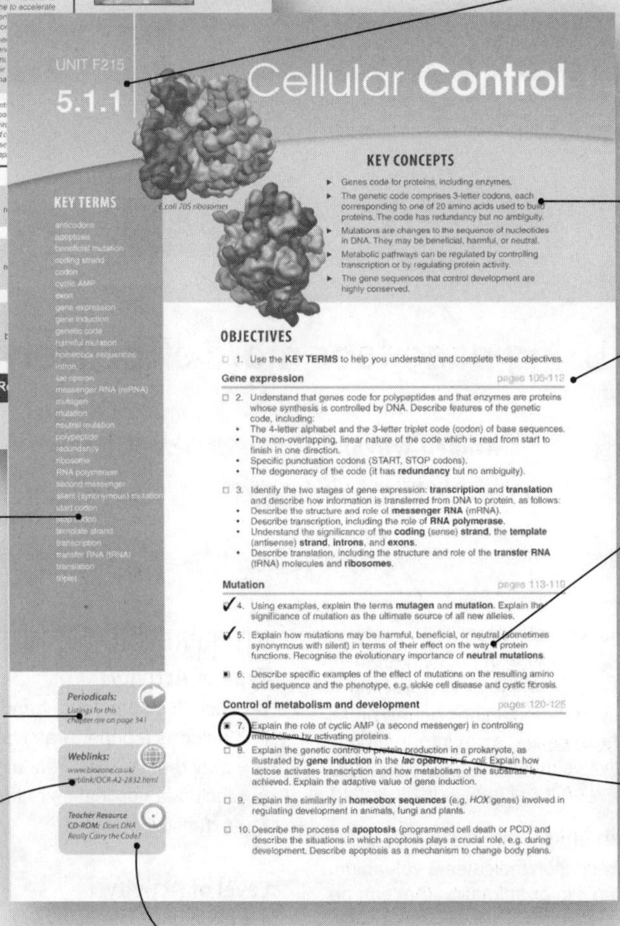

The important key ideas in this chapter. You should have a thorough understanding of the concepts summarised here.

The page numbers for the activities covering the material in this subsection of objectives.

The objectives provide a point by point summary of what you should have achieved by the end of the chapter. They are based on the content of the OCR specification but include some extra explanatory detail where this is important.

You can use the check boxes to mark objectives to be completed (a **dot** to be done; a **tick** when completed).

A list of key terms used in the chapter. These terms appear in the chapter's vocab activity and can be used to create a glossary for revision purposes. The list represents the minimum literacy requirement for the chapter.

Periodicals of interest are identified by title on a tab on the activity page to which they are relevant. The full citation appears in the **Appendix** on the page indicated.

The Weblinks on many of the activities can be accessed through the web links page at: *www.biozone.co.uk/weblink/OCR-A2-2832.html* See page 4 for more details.

Extra resources for this chapter are available on the Teacher Resource CD-ROM (for separate purchase).

Using the Activities

The activities make up most of the content of this book. Your teacher may use the activity pages to introduce a topic for the first time, or you may use them to revise ideas already covered by other means. They are excellent for use in the classroom, as homework exercises and topic revision, and for self-directed study and personal reference.

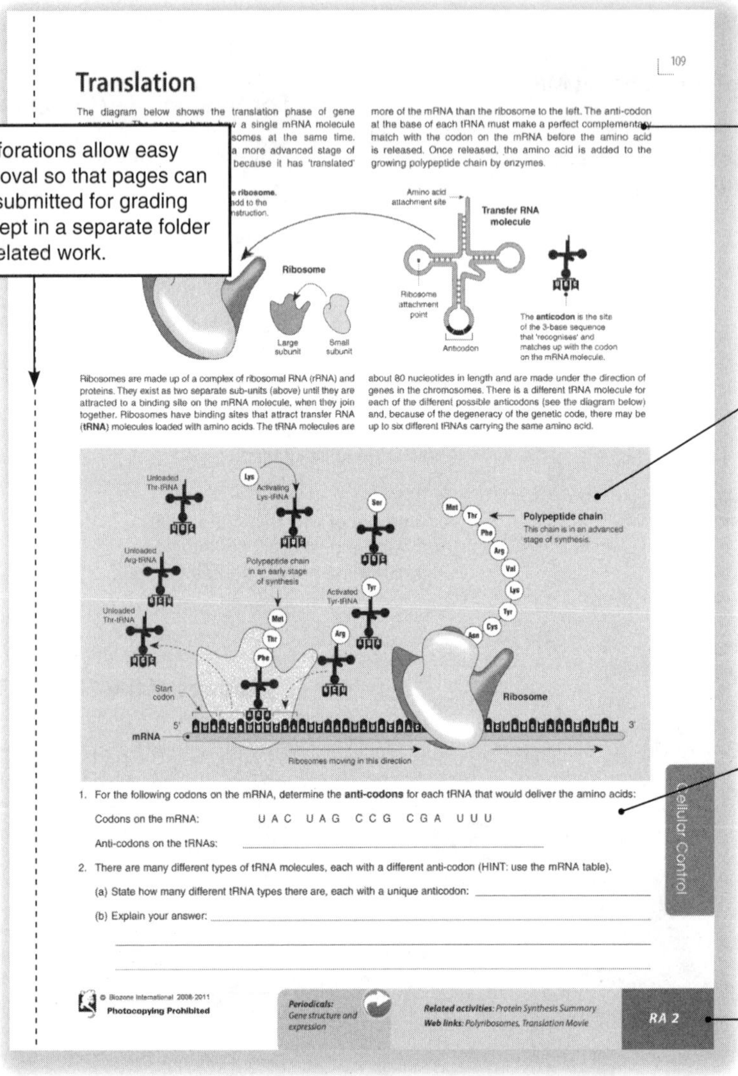

109

Translation

The diagram below shows the translation phase of gene ... w a single mRNA molecule ... somes at the same time. ... a more advanced stage of ... because it has 'translated' more of the mRNA than the ribosome to the left. The anti-codon at the base of each tRNA must make a perfect complementary match with the codon on the mRNA before the amino acid is released. Once released, the amino acid is added to the growing polypeptide chain by enzymes.

Ribosomes are made up of a complex of ribosomal RNA (rRNA) and proteins. They exist as two separate sub-units (above) until they are attracted to a binding site on the mRNA molecule, when they join together. Ribosomes have binding sites that attract transfer RNA (**tRNA**) molecules loaded with amino acids. The tRNA molecules are about 80 nucleotides in length and are made under the direction of genes in the chromosomes. There is a different tRNA molecule for each of the different possible anticodons (see the diagram below) and, because of the degeneracy of the genetic code, there may be up to six different tRNAs carrying the same amino acid.

1. For the following codons on the mRNA, determine the **anti-codons** for each tRNA that would deliver the amino acids:

   Codons on the mRNA: U A C U A G C C G C G A U U U

   Anti-codons on the tRNAs: ______________________

2. There are many different types of tRNA molecules, each with a different anti-codon (HINT: use the mRNA table).

   (a) State how many different tRNA types there are, each with a unique anticodon: ______________

   (b) Explain your answer: ______________________

Cellular Control

© Biozone International 2008-2011 Photocopying Prohibited

Periodicals: *Gene structure and expression*

Related activities: Protein Synthesis Summary
Web links: Polyribosomes, Translation Movie

RA 2

Perforations allow easy removal so that pages can be submitted for grading or kept in a separate folder of related work.

Introductory paragraph: The introductory paragraph provides essential background and provides the focus of the page. Note words that appear in bold, as they are 'key words' worthy of including in a glossary of terms for the topic.

Easy to understand diagrams: The main ideas of the topic are represented and explained by clear, informative diagrams.

Write-on format: Your understanding of the main ideas of the topic is tested by asking questions and providing spaces for your answers. Where indicated by the space available, your answers should be concise. Questions requiring more explanation or discussion are spaced accordingly. Answer the questions adequately according to the questioning term used (see the introduction).

A tab system at the base of each activity page identifies resources associated with the activity on that page. Use the guide below to help you use the tab system most effectively.

Using page tabs more effectively

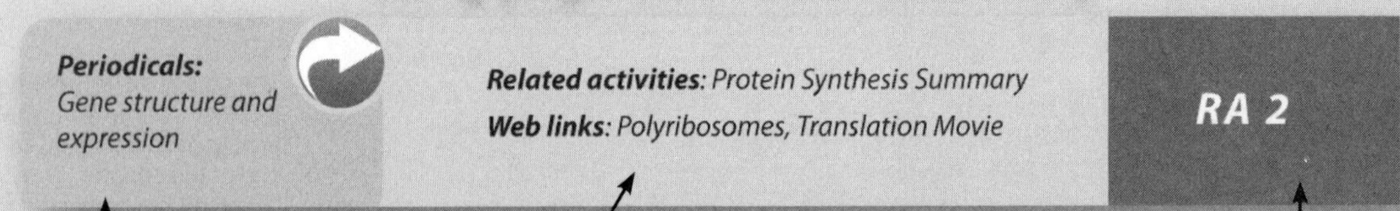

Students (and teachers) who would like to know more about this topic area are encouraged to locate the periodical cited on the **Periodicals tab**. Articles of interest directly relevant to the topic content are cited. The full citation appears in the Appendix as indicated at the beginning of the topic chapter.

Related activities

Other activities in the workbook cover related topics or may help answer the questions on the page. In most cases, extra information for activities that are coded R can be found on the pages indicated here.

Web links

This citation indicates a valuable video clip or animation that can be accessed from the web links page specifically for this workbook. www.biozone.co.uk/weblink/OCR-A2-2832.html

INTERPRETING THE ACTIVITY CODING SYSTEM

Type of Activity

D = includes some data handling or interpretation
P = includes a paper practical
R = *may* require extra reading (e.g. text or other activity)
A = includes application of knowledge to solve a problem
E = extension material

Level of Activity

1 = generally simpler, including mostly describe questions
2 = more challenging, including explain questions
3 = challenging content and/or questions, including discuss

Resources Information

Your set textbook should always be a starting point for information. There are also many other resources available, including scientific journals, magazine and newspaper articles, supplementary texts covering restricted topic areas, dictionaries, computer software and videos, and the internet.

A synopsis of some of the currently available resources is provided below. Access to the publishers of these resources can be made directly from Biozone's website through our resources hub: **www.biozone.co.uk/resource-hub.html**. Most titles are also available through www.amazon.co.uk. Please note that our listing any product in this workbook does not, in any way, denote Biozone's endorsement of that product.

OCR Specific Comprehensive Texts

Jones, M., 2008
Biology 2 for OCR
Publisher: Cambridge University Press
Pages: 304
ISBN: 978-052173299-4
Comments: *A new resource written for the 2008 OCR specification. Provides how science works themes and summaries. Interactive CD-ROM provides further resources.*

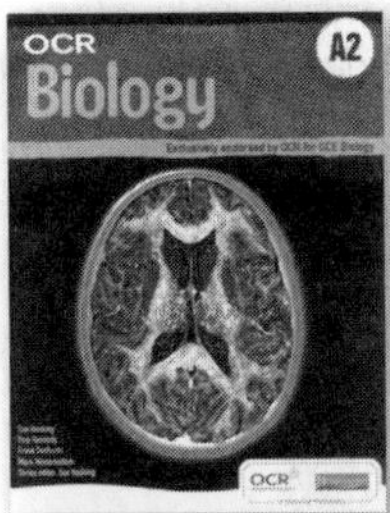

Hocking, S. 2008
OCR A2 Biology
Publisher: Heinemann
Pages: 312
ISBN: 978-0435691905
Comments: *A new book tailored for the new OCR specification. Includes an exam cafe CD-ROM with exam type questions and worked examples. This text is endorsed as an Official Publishing Partner for OCR Biology.*

Toole G. and S. Toole, 2004
Essential A2 Biology for OCR
Publisher: NelsonThornes
Pages: approx 170
ISBN: 0-7487-8518-3
Comments: *An appealing and student-friendly text written to meet the core A2 specifications for OCR. A comprehensive glossary is included.*

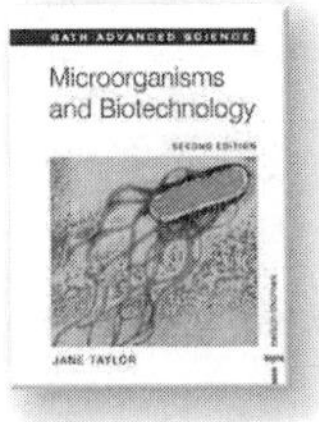

Taylor, J., 2001.
Microorganisms and Biotechnology, 192 pp.
ISBN: 0-17-448255-8
Comments: *Provides information for microbiology and biotechnology topics at A2 level. Other older titles in this series include Applied Genetics, 1990 (ISBN: 0174385110) and Biochemistry and Molecular Biology, 1994 (ISBN: 0174482078).*

Adds, J., E. Larkcom & R. Miller, 2004.
Genetics, Evolution, and Biodiversity, revised edition, 200 pp.
ISBN: 0-7487-7492-0
A range of topics including photosynthesis and the control of growth in plants, classification and quantitative field ecology, populations and pest control, conservation, Mendelian genetics and evolution, gene technology and human evolution.

Periodicals, Magazines and Journals

Biological Sciences Review (Biol. Sci. Rev.) *An excellent quarterly publication for teachers and students. The content is current and the language is accessible.* Subscriptions available from Philip Allan Publishers, Market Place, Deddington, Oxfordshire OX 15 OSE.
Tel. 01869 338652 **Fax**: 01869 338803
E-mail: sales@philipallan.co.uk

New Scientist: *Published weekly and found in many libraries. It often summarizes the findings published in other journals. Articles range from news releases to features.*
Subscription enquiries:
Tel. (UK and international): +44 (0)1444 475636. (US & Canada) 1 888 822 3242.
E-mail: ns.subs@qss-uk.com

Scientific American: *A monthly magazine containing mostly specialist feature articles. Articles range in level of reading difficulty and assumed knowledge.*
Subscription enquiries:
Tel. (US & Canada) 800-333-1199.
Tel. (outside North America): 515-247-7631
Web: www.sciam.com

Supplementary Texts

Indge, B., 2003
Data and Data Handling for AS and A Level Biology, 128 pp.
Publisher: Hodder Arnold H&S
ISBN: 1340856475
Comments: *Examples and practice exercises to improve skills in data interpretation and analysis.*

Morgan, S., 2002
Advanced Level Practical Work for Biology, 128 pp.
Publisher: Hodder and Stoughton
ISBN: 0-340-84712-3
Comments: *Caters for the investigative requirements of A level studies: experimental planning, techniques, observation and measurement, and interpretation and analysis.*

Biology Dictionaries

Clamp, A. **AS/A-Level Biology. Essential Word Dictionary**, 2000, 161 pp. Philip Allan Updates.
ISBN: 0-86003-372-4.
Carefully selected essential words for AS and A2. Concise definitions are supported by further explanation and illustrations where required.

Henderson, E. Lawrence. **Henderson's Dictionary of Biological Terms**, 2008, 776 pp. Benjamin Cummings. **ISBN**: 978-0321505798
This edition has been updated, rewritten for clarity, and reorganised for ease of use. An essential reference and the dictionary of choice for many.

Using Biozone's Website

The current internet address (URL) for the web site is displayed here. You can type a new address directly into this space.

Use Google to search for web sites of interest. The more precise your search words are, the better the list of results. EXAMPLE: If you type in "biotechnology", your search will return an overwhelmingly large number of sites, many of which will not be useful to you. Be more specific, e.g. "biotechnology medicine DNA uses".

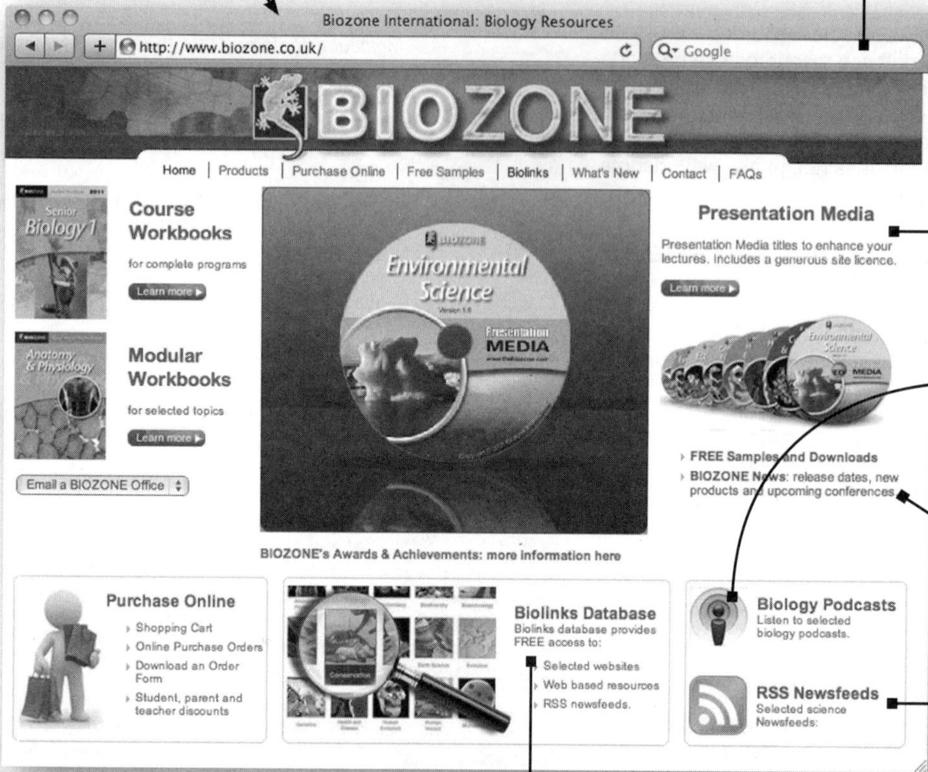

Find out about our superb **Presentation Media**. These slide shows are designed to provide in-depth, highly accessible illustrative material and notes on specific areas of biology.

Podcasts: Access the latest news as audio files (mp3) that may be downloaded or played directly off your computer.

News: Find out about product announcements, shipping dates, and workshops and trade displays by Biozone at teachers' conferences around the world.

RSS Newsfeeds: See breaking news and major new discoveries in biology directly from our web site.

Access the **BioLinks** database of web sites related to each major area of biology. It's a great way to quickly find out more on topics of interest.

Weblinks: www.biozone.co.uk/weblink/OCR-A2-2832.html

BOOKMARK WEBLINKS BY TYPING IN THE ADDRESS: IT IS NOT ACCESSIBLE DIRECTLY FROM BIOZONE'S WEBSITE

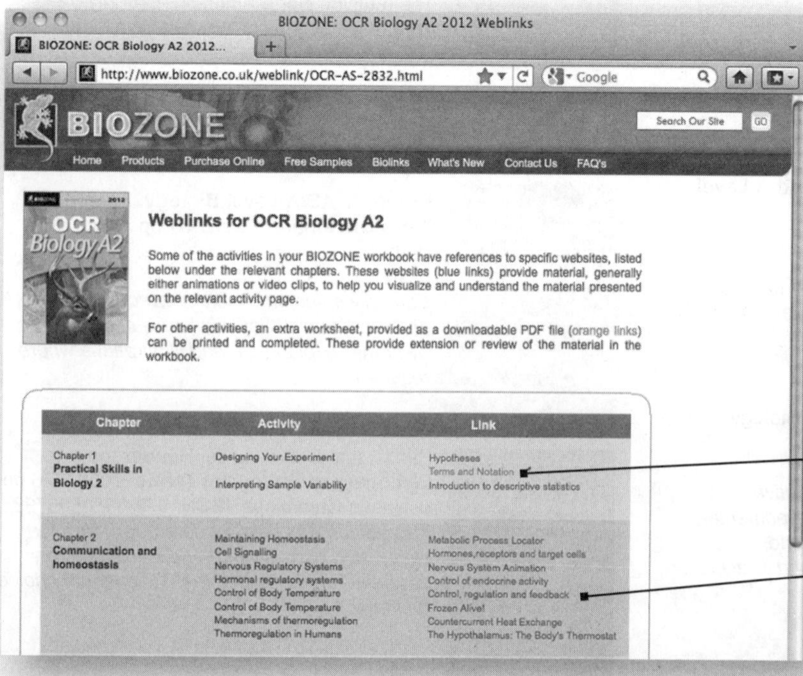

Throughout this workbook, some pages make reference to web links and periodicals that are particularly relevant to the activity on which they are cited. They provide great support to aid understanding of basic concepts:

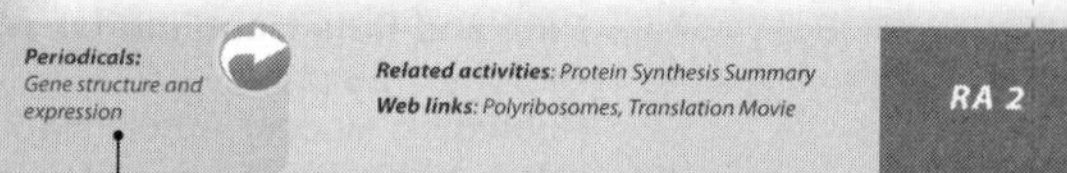

Periodicals: Full citations are provided in the Appendix for those that wish to read further on a topic.

Some are colour coded links to downloadable **Acrobat (PDF) files** which may provide an additional activity for revision or extension.

Web Link: Provides a link to an **external web site** with supporting information for the activity.

OCR Course Guide

Candidates taking the OCR A2 biology course are required to complete the prerequisite AS units (Units F211, F212 and F213), before commencing the OCR A2 Units F214, F215 and F216.

AS Content

Unit F211: Cells, Exchange and Transport	Topics in AS Workbook
Module 1: Cells	
1.1.1 Microscopy techniques & stains, organelle structure and function, protein secretion, eukaryote and prokaryote cells characteristics.	Cell Structure
1.1.2 Membrane structure and function. Membrane transport systems. Cell signalling and receptors. Osmosis and water potential.	Cell Membranes
1.1.3 Mitosis, homologous chromosomes. Stem cells, cell differentiation, and tissue organisation.	Cell Division & Organisation
Module 2: Exchange and Transport	
1.2.1 Surface area to volume ratio, diffusion. Mammalian lung & gas exchange system. Breathing in humans, measuring breathing.	Exchange Surfaces & Breathing
1.2.2 Animal transport systems, mammalian heart & the cardiac cycle. Structure and function of arteries, veins and capillaries, tissue fluid and lymph. Haemoglobin and oxygen binding.	Transport In Animals
1.2.3 Plant transport systems. Structure and function of transport tissues. Transpiration, translocation. Water potential, water movement.	Transport in Plants

Unit F212: Molecules, Biodiversity, Food and Health	Topics in AS Workbook
Module 1: Biological Molecule	
2.1.1 Water. Amino acids, peptide bonds. Structure and function of proteins, carbohydrates & lipids. Hydrolysis and condensation. Food testing methods.	Biological Molecules
2.1.2 Nucleic acids, structure of DNA, DNA replication, the basis of protein synthesis.	Nucleic Acids
2.1.3 Enzyme structure and function, mode of action, enzyme activity, inhibitors, cofactors.	Enzymes
Module 2: Food and Health	
2.2.1 Diet & nutrition, malnutrition & obesity, CHD. Importance of plants. Selective breeding, microbes & food production, increasing food production, food preservation.	Diet & Food Production
2.2.2 Health and disease, pathogens. Malaria, HIV, TB. Health effects of smoking. Immune system and the body's defences. Immunity and vaccination. New medicines.	Infectious Disease, Smoking: A Choice Against Health, Defence & the Immune System
Module 3: Biodiversity and Evolution	
2.3.1 Species, habitat and biodiversity. Sampling and measuring biodiversity.	Biodiversity & Classification
2.3.2 Classification systems. Features of the five kingdoms, identification keys.	Biodiversity & Classification
2.3.3 Darwin's theory of natural selection, speciation, variation. Mechanisms and evidence for evolution. Pesticide resistance. Antibiotic and other drug resistance.	Evolution
2.3.4 Conservation. Maintaining biodiversity, global climate change and biodiversity.	Maintaining Biodiversity

Unit F213: Practical Skills in Biology 1	Topics in AS Workbook
1. **Qualitative Task** Use of appropriate qualitative skills to perform a practical task. Safe techniques, accurate observation and recording.	Practical Skills in Biology 1, Cell Structure
2. **Quantitative Task** Use of appropriate quantitative skills to perform a practical task safely. Accurate measurements and use of the correct degree of precision.	Practical Skills in Biology 1
3. **Evaluative Task** Processing and recording results, evaluating trends and drawing conclusions. Identifying limitations. Reliability and validity of data.	Practical Skills in Biology 1

A2 Content

Unit F214: Communication, Homeostasis and Energy	Topics in A2 Workbook
Module 1: Communication and Homeostasis	
4.1.1 Communication systems in multicellular organisms: nervous and hormonal coordination, feedback, thermoregulation.	Communication & Homeostasis
4.1.2 Sensory receptors, neurones, action potentials, myelination, cholinergic synapses.	Nerves
4.1.3 Endocrine glands and chemical messengers, adrenal glands and pancreas, regulation of blood glucose, diabetes, control of heart rate.	Hormones
Module 2: Excretion	
4.2.1 Structure and roles of the liver and role of the kidneys. Control of urine output and composition, urinalysis, renal failure.	Excretion
Module 3: Photosynthesis	
4.3.1 Chloroplasts and basic photosynthesis. Photosynthetic pigments, light dependent stage, light independent stage, factors affecting photosynthetic rates.	Photosynthesis
Module 4: Respiration	
4.4.1 ATP, coenzymes in respiration, glycolysis and aerobic respiration, chemiosmosis, respiratory substrates, alcoholic and lactate fermentation.	Respiration

Unit F215: Control, Genomes and Environment	Topics in A2 Workbook
Module1: Cellular Control and Variation	
5.1.1 Genes and the genetic code, transcription, translation, mutation, Lac operon, apoptosis and genetic control of development.	Cellular Control
5.1.2 Meiosis and variation, genetic crosses, chi squared, sex linkage, codominance, epistasis. Continuous and discontinuous variation, genotype and environment.	Meiosis & Variation
Variation and selection, Hardy-Weinberg principle, calculation of allele frequencies, natural selection, genetic drift, isolation and speciation, species concept, artificial selection.	Variation & Evolution
Module 2: Biotechnology & Gene Technologies	
5.2.1 Reproductive and non-reproductive cloning, natural clones in plants, cloning in animals.	Cloning in Plants and Animals
5.2.2 Biotechnology, microorganisms in biotechnology, enzyme immobilisation, continuous and batch cultures, metabolites.	Biotechnology
5.2.3 Genome sequencing, genetic engineering DNA probes, transgenic organisms, gene therapy, GE xenotransplants, ethical issues.	Genomes & Gene Technologies
Module 3: Ecosystems and Sustainability	
5.3.1 Ecosystems: trophic structure, energy transfers, primary succession, measuring distribution and abundance, microbes recycling, and nitrogen cycle.	Ecosystems
5.3.2 Population growth, species interactions, conservation, preservation, and sustainable management. Human impact (Galápagos).	Populations & Sustainability
Module 4: Responding to the Environment	
5.4.1 Tropisms, phytohormones, gibberellins and auxins, commercial uses of plant hormones.	Plant Responses
5.4.2 Animal responses: brain and nervous system, autonomic nervous system and reflexes, muscle activity and movement, fight or flight responses.	Animal Responses
5.4.3 Innate behaviour, types of learning, sociality in primates, dopamine and behaviour.	Animal Behaviour

Unit F216: Practical Skills in Biology 2	Topics in A2 Workbook
1 Qualitative task 2 Quantitative task 3 Evaluative task	Practical Skills in Biology 2 Ecosystems

Command Words

Questions come in a variety of forms. Whether you are studying for an exam or writing an essay, it is important to understand exactly what the question is asking. A question has two parts to it: one part of the question will provide you with information, the second part of the question will provide you with instructions as to how to answer the question. Following these instructions is most important. Often students in examinations know the material but fail to follow instructions and do not answer the question appropriately. Examiners often use certain key words to introduce questions. Look out for them and be clear as to what they mean. Below is a description of terms commonly used when asking questions in biology.

Commonly used Terms in Biology

The following terms are frequently used when asking questions in examinations and assessments. Students should have a clear understanding of each of the following terms and use this understanding to answer questions appropriately.

Account for: Provide a satisfactory explanation or reason for an observation.

Analyse: Interpret data to reach stated conclusions.

Annotate: Add brief notes to a diagram, drawing or graph.

Apply: Use an idea, equation, principle, theory, or law in a new situation.

Appreciate: To understand the meaning or relevance of a particular situation.

Calculate: Find an answer using mathematical methods. Show the working unless instructed not to.

Compare: Give an account of similarities and differences between two or more items, referring to both (or all) of them throughout. Comparisons can be given using a table. Comparisons generally ask for similarities more than differences (see contrast).

Construct: Represent or develop in graphical form.

Contrast: Show differences. Set in opposition.

Deduce: Reach a conclusion from information given.

Define: Give the precise meaning of a word or phrase as concisely as possible.

Derive: Manipulate a mathematical equation to give a new equation or result.

Describe: Give a detailed account, including all the relevant information.

Design: Produce a plan, object, simulation or model.

Determine: Find the only possible answer.

Discuss: Give an account including, where possible, a range of arguments, assessments of the relative importance of various factors, or comparison of alternative hypotheses.

Distinguish: Give the difference(s) between two or more different items.

Draw: Represent by means of pencil lines. Add labels unless told not to do so.

Estimate: Find an approximate value for an unknown quantity, based on the information provided and application of scientific knowledge.

Evaluate: Assess the implications and limitations.

Explain: Give a clear account including causes, reasons, or mechanisms.

Identify: Find an answer from a number of possibilities.

Illustrate: Give concrete examples. Explain clearly by using comparisons or examples.

Interpret: Comment upon, give examples, describe relationships. Describe, then evaluate.

List: Give a sequence of names or other brief answers with no elaboration. Each one should be clearly distinguishable from the others.

Measure: Find a value for a quantity.

Outline: Give a brief account or summary. Include essential information only.

Predict: Give an expected result.

Solve: Obtain an answer using algebraic and/or numerical methods.

State: Give a specific name, value, or other answer. No supporting argument or calculation is necessary.

Suggest: Propose a hypothesis or other possible explanation.

Summarise: Give a brief, condensed account. Include conclusions and avoid unnecessary details.

In Conclusion

Students should familiarise themselves with this list of terms and, where necessary throughout the course, they should refer back to them when answering questions. The list of terms mentioned above is not exhaustive and students should compare this list with past examination papers / essays etc., and add any new terms (and their meaning) to the list above. The aim is to become familiar with interpreting the question and answering it appropriately.

Important in this section...

- *Develop your understanding of how science works*
- *Carry out experimental and investigative activities*
- *Analyse and interpret experimental data*
- *Evaluate methodology, evidence, and data*

ICT for Data Handling (TRC)

Descriptive statistics

- Entering data in *Excel®* for analysis
- Protocols for entering formulae
- Calculating descriptive statistics

Graphing using Excel®

- Choosing your graph type in *Excel®*
- Labelling axes and adding headings
- Plotting your data

Skills in Biology

Hypotheses

- Asking appropriate questions
- Making a sensible hypothesis

A qualitative practical task

- Procedures for qualitative work
- The limitations of qualitative data
- Presenting qualitative data

A quantitative practical task

- Procedures for quantitative work
- Reliability, accuracy, and precision
- Safety in practical work

Evaluating quantitative work

- Presenting data in graphs and tables
- Descriptive statistics
- Communicating your findings clearly
- Evaluating sources of error

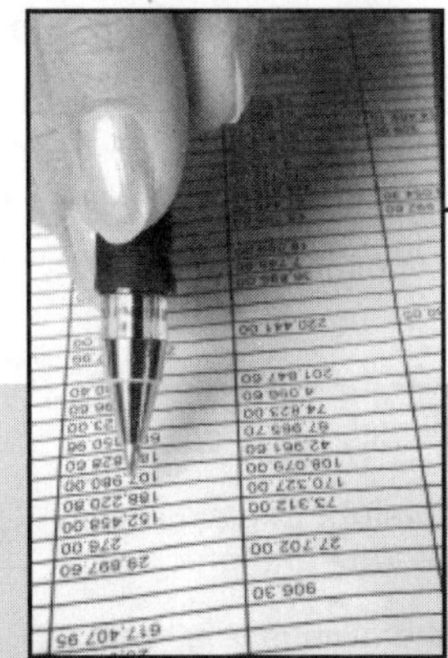

Used properly, computers can help to analyse your data more quickly and understand it better.

Developing skills in practical work and critical evaluation helps you understand how science works

A2 Unit F216 Practical Skills in Biology 2

Asking Questions, Finding Answers

The scientific method provides a framework for investigating the natural world.

Appropriate collection and analysis of data allows us to study biological systems objectively, and to attempt to understand them better.

Field work gives an appreciation of the complexity of community patterns.

Recognising and appreciating biodiversity is an essential part of all biology.

Planning a field study

- Practical considerations for field work
- Collecting and recording data
- Looking for trends and patterns

Population & community ecology

- Considerations for sampling
- Quadrat sampling
- Transect sampling

Ecological sampling is covered in context in the topic Ecosystems, but some aspects are introduced in this first chapter. Investigative skills can be applied appropriately to population and community studies.

Practical Skills in Field Work

Biodiversity

- Species' diversity
- Genetic diversity
- Ecosystem diversity

Classifying organisms

- Naming organisms
- Defining species

The classification of organisms is covered in OCR Biology AS (OCR F212, Module 3). An understanding of the nature of species as the basic unit of diversity is central to evolution and ecology.

Appreciating Diversity

UNIT

F216

Practical Skills in Biology 2

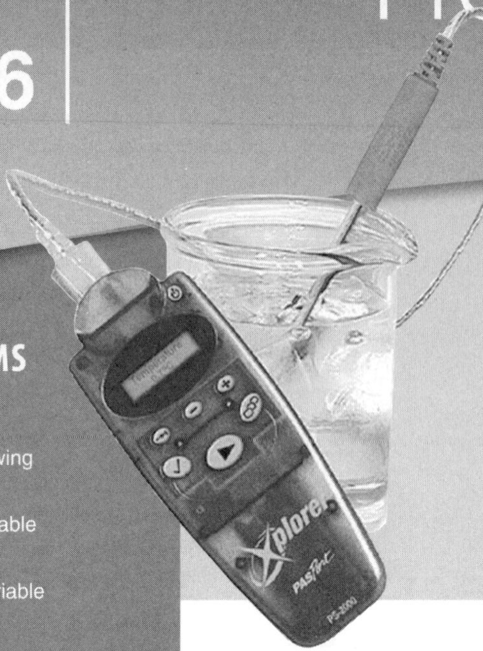

KEY TERMS

accuracy
biological drawing
control
controlled variable
data
dependent variable
graph
histogram
hypothesis
independent variable
mean
measurement
median
mode
observation
parameter
precision
qualitative data
quantitative data
raw data
sample
scientific method
statistic
table
transformation (of data)
trend (of data)
variable
X axis
Y axis

KEY CONCEPTS

- The basis of all science is observation, hypothesis, and investigation.
- Data may be quantitative or qualitative.
- Data can be analysed and presented in various ways, including in graphs and tables.
- Evaluation of quantitative data involves analysis of processed data and objective assessment of sources of error.

OBJECTIVES

☐ 1. Use the **KEY TERMS** to help you understand and complete these objectives.

Recall: Understanding the scientific method pages 9-12

☐ 2. Describe and explain the basic principles of the scientific method.

☐ 3. Explain the difference between **accuracy** and **precision**. Explain why it is important to make measurements that are both accurate and precise.

☐ 4. Demonstrate an ability to make accurate biological drawings, e.g. from prepared histological slides.

Qualitative practical tasks pages 13-14

☐ 5. Explain the difference between **qualitative data** and **quantitative data** and give examples of their appropriate use.

☐ 6. A qualitative practical task requires you to carry out a practical investigation for which you collect qualitative (categorical) data.

☐ 7. Describe an experiment or study for which qualitative data are collected and describe its outcome. Describe the limitations of qualitative data and explain why the collection of quantitative data is preferable in most scientific studies.

Quantitative practical tasks pages 15-24

☐ 8. You are required to carry out a quantitative investigation in the laboratory. Identify your **dependent** and **independent variables**, their range, and how you will measure them. Identify **controlled variables** and their significance. Describe an appropriate **control** for your experiment.

☐ 9. Demonstrate an ability to **systematically record** data. Evaluate the **accuracy** and **precision** of any recording or measurements you make.

☐ 10. Demonstrate an ability to process **raw data**. Calculate percentages, rates, and frequencies for raw data (as appropriate) and explain the reason for these manipulations.

☐ 11. Present your of data appropriately in a **table**, including any calculated values.

☐ 12. Recognise the benefits of graphing data and present your processed data appropriately in a **graph** format.

☐ 13. Considered and objective analysis of your **data** is an essential part of evaluating your quantitative study. Identify and explain the important features of your investigation including:
- trends in your processed data
- conclusions based on analysis of the data and the experimental aims
- discussion of the biological concepts involved
- evaluation, including erroneous results and sources of error

Periodicals:
Listings for this chapter are on page 340

Weblinks:
www.biozone.co.uk/weblink/OCR-A2-2832.html

Teacher Resource CD-ROM:
Spreadsheets and Statistics

Designing Your Experiment

The figure below provides an example of a basic experimental design aimed at investigating the effect of pH on the growth of a bog adapted plant species. It is not intended to represent a full methodology, but offers some points to consider. An appropriate analysis for this experiment would be a calculation of the mean for each treatment group, followed by a plot of the data with a calculated measure of spread (e.g. 95% confidence intervals). Depending on trends indicated by the plotted data, either a regression or an ANOVA would be an appropriate analysis (see the activities on measures of spread, regression, and ANOVA for more information on the use of these analyses).

Observation

Two students noticed an abundance of a common plant (species A) in a boggy area of land near their school. They tested the soil pH in the area and found it to be quite low (between 4 and 5). Garden soil was about pH 7.

Hypothesis

Species A is well adapted to grow at low pH and pH will influence the vigour with which this plant species grows.

Prediction

Species A will grow more vigorously (as measured by wet weight after 20 days) at pH 5 than at higher or lower pH.

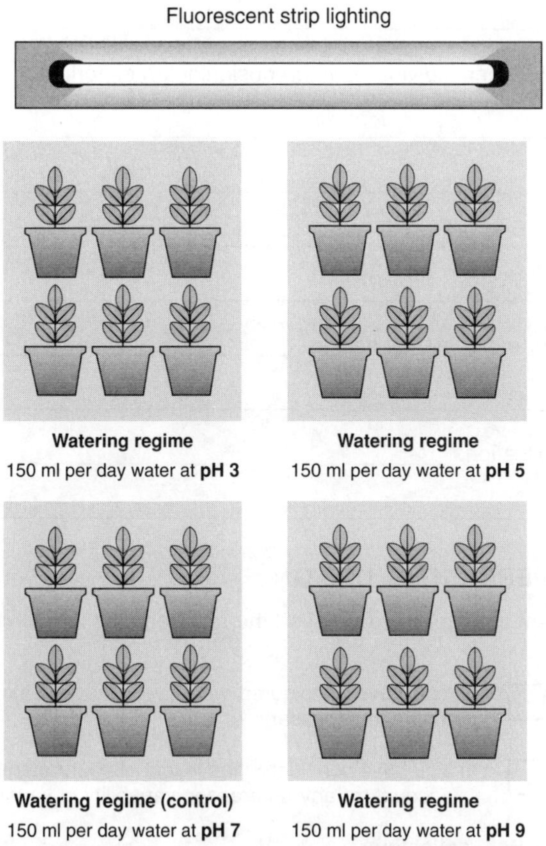

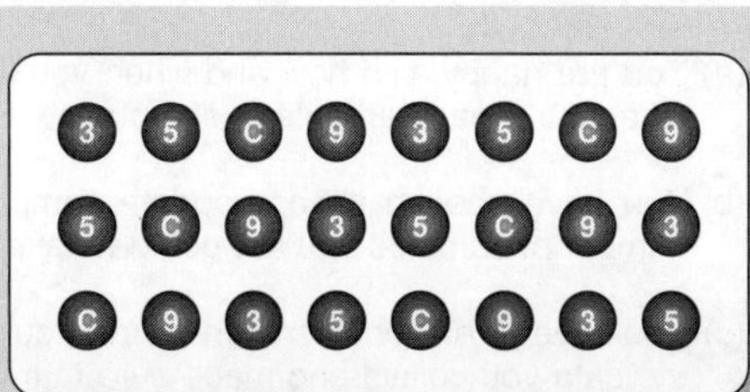

Plan view of the experimental layout. 3 = pH 3, 5 = pH 5, C = control (pH 7), 9 = pH 9. Note that in experiments with a large number of treatments and replication, it is important to randomise the arrangement of the treatments to account for any effects of location in the set-up.

Experiment

An experiment was designed to test the prediction that the plants would grow best at low pH. The design is shown here (it is not intended to be a full methodology).

Control of Variables

Fixed (controlled) variables: These are controlled and the same across all treatments.

- Lighting regime (quantity and quality).
- Age and history of plants.
- Soil type and volume.
- Pot size and type (dimensions, material).
- Watering regime (volume per day, frequency).

Dependent variable: The biological response.

- Plant growth rate (g day^{-1}) calculated from wet weight of entire plants (washed and blotted) after 20 days.

Independent variable: This is the factor that is being manipulated in the experiment.

- pH of the water provided to the plants.

Other variables: These are factors that you should be aware of but cannot control.

- Genetic variation between plants (uncontrollable but assessed by having six plants per treatment).
- Temperature (all plants received the same room temperature regime but this was not controlled).

Assumptions

Features of the experiment that you assume to be true but do not (or cannot) test.

- All plants are essentially no different to each other in their growth response at different pH levels.
- The soil mix, light quality and quantity, and temperature are adequate for healthy continued growth.
- Watering volume of 150 ml day^{-1} is an adequate volume. This could be tested with a trial experiment beforehand.
- A pH of 7 is a good indicator of the ideal growth pH for most non-acid adapted plants.

Replication in Experiments

Replication refers to the number of times you repeat your entire experimental design (including controls). True replication is not the same as increasing the sample size (n) although it is often used to mean the same thing. Replication accounts for any unusual and unforeseen effects that may be operating in your set-up (e.g. field trials of plant varieties where soil type is variable). Replication is necessary when you expect that the response of treatments will vary because of factors outside your control. It is a feature of higher level experimental designs, and complex statistics are needed to separate differences between replicate treatments. For simple experiments, it is usually more valuable to increase the sample size than to worry about replicates.

In this experiment of the effects of nutrient level on plant growth (above), the sample size is 5 ($n = 5$), there are three treatments (nutrient level) and four replicates (12 pots in all; not all are visible). The plot is randomised.

1. With reference to the experiment on the previous page, explain the importance of each of the following:

   (a) Only one plant in each pot: ______________________

   ____

   (b) The layout of treatments on the bench (see plan view of layout): ______________________

   ____

2. Explain the best way to take account of the natural variability between individuals when designing an experiment:

   ____

   ____

3. (a) Explain the purpose of replication in experiments: ______________________

   ____

   (b) Describe factors that would limit your ability to replicate your experimental design: ______________________

   ____

   (c) Suggest how you could compensate for the lack of true replication: ______________________

   ____

CHECKLIST FOR YOUR EXPERIMENTAL DESIGN

Check off the points on the checklist below when you are confident that you have satisfied the requirements in each case:

1. **Preliminary:**

   ☐ (a) Makes a hypothesis based on observation(s).

   ☐ (b) The hypothesis (and its predictions) are testable using the resources you have available (the study is feasible).

   ☐ (c) The organism you have chosen is suitable for the study and you have considered the ethical issue involved.

2. **Variables and assumptions:**

   ☐ (a) You are aware of any assumptions that you are making in your experiment.

   ☐ (b) You have identified all the variables in the experiment (fixed, manipulated, response, uncontrollable).

   ☐ (c) You have considered how you will control the variables you wish to remain fixed and what will be your control.

   ☐ (d) You have considered what preliminary treatment or trials are necessary.

   ☐ (e) You have considered the layout of your treatments to account for any unforeseen variability in your set-up.

3. **Data collection:**

   ☐ (a) You are happy with how and when you are going to take your measurements or samples.

   ☐ (b) You have chosen an appropriate sample size (the number of samples you are going to take).

   ☐ (c) You have given consideration to how you will analyse the data you collect and made sure that your design allows you to answer the questions you wish to answer.

Designing Your Field Study

The figure below provides an example and some ideas for designing a field study. It provides a framework which can be modified for most simple comparative field investigations. For reasons of space, the full methodology is not included.

Observation

A student read that a particular species of pill millipede (left) is extremely abundant in forest leaf litter, but a search in the litter of a conifer-dominated woodland near his home revealed only very low numbers of this millipede species.

Hypothesis

This millipede species is adapted to a niche in the leaf litter of oak woodlands and is abundant there. However, it is rare in the litter of coniferous woodland. The **null hypothesis** is that there is no difference between the abundance of this millipede species in oak and coniferous woodland litter.

Oak or coniferous woodland

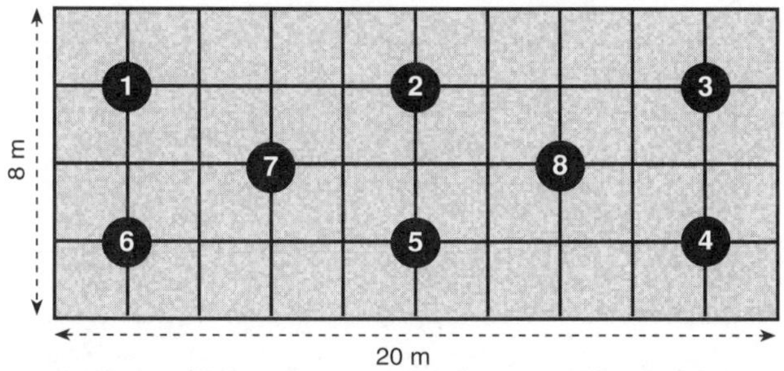

1 Sampling sites numbered 1-8 at evenly spaced intervals on a 2 x 2 m grid within an area of 20 m x 8 m.

Sampling equipment: leaf litter light trap

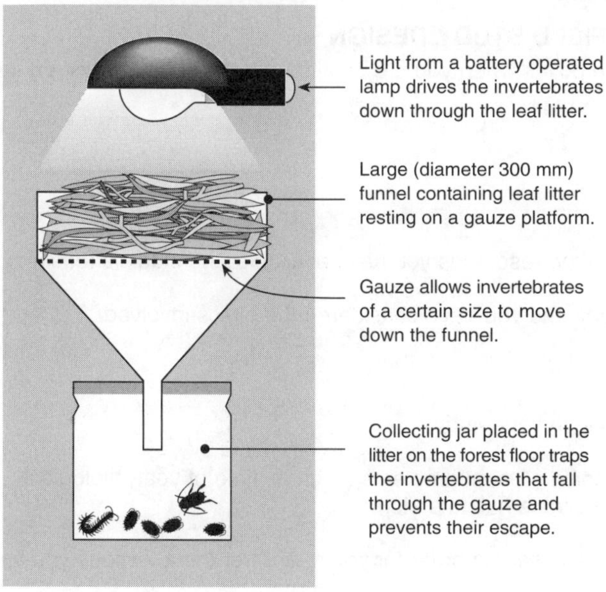

Notes on collection and analysis

- Mean millipede abundance was calculated from the counts from the eight sites. The difference in abundance at the sites was tested using a Student's *t* test.
- After counting and analysis of the samples, all the collected invertebrates were returned to the sites.

Sampling Programme

A sampling programme was designed to test the prediction that the millipedes are more abundant in the leaf litter of oak woodlands than in coniferous woodlands.

Equipment and Procedure

Sites: For each of the two woodland types, an area 20 x 8 m was chosen and marked out in 2 x 2 m grids. Eight sampling sites were selected, evenly spaced along the grid as shown.

- The general area for the study chosen was selected on the basis of the large amounts of leaf litter present.
- Eight sites were chosen as the largest number feasible to collect and analyse in the time available.
- The two woodlands were sampled on sequential days.

Capture of millipedes: At each site, a 0.4 x 0.4 m quadrat was placed on the forest floor and the leaf litter within the quadrat was collected. Millipedes and other leaf litter invertebrates were captured using a simple gauze lined funnel containing the leaf litter from within the quadrat. A lamp was positioned over each funnel for two hours and the invertebrates in the litter moved down and were trapped in the collecting jar.

- After two hours each jar was labelled with the site number and returned to the lab for analysis.
- The litter in each funnel was bagged, labelled with the site number and returned to the lab for weighing.
- The number of millipedes at each site was recorded.
- The numbers of other invertebrates (classified into major taxa) were also noted for reference.

Assumptions

- The areas chosen in each woodland were representative of the woodland types in terms of millipede abundance.
- Eight sites were sufficient to adequately sample the millipede populations in each forest.
- A quadrat size of 0.4 x 0.4 m contained enough leaf litter to adequately sample the millipedes at each site.
- The millipedes were not preyed on by any of the other invertebrates captured in the collecting jar.
- All the invertebrates within the quadrat were captured.
- Millipedes moving away from the light are effectively captured by the funnel apparatus and cannot escape.
- Two hours was long enough for the millipedes to move down through the litter and fall into the trap.

  Note that these last two assumptions could be tested by examining the bagged leaf litter for millipedes after returning to the lab.

Periodicals:
Fieldwork - sampling animals,
Fieldwork - sampling plants

Related activities: *Designing Your Experiment*

Sample Size

When designing a field study, the size of your sampling unit (in this case quadrat size) and the sample size (the number of samples you will take) should be major considerations. There are various ways to determine the best quadrat size. Usually, these involve increasing the quadrat size until you stop finding new species. For simple field studies, the number of samples you take (the sample size or *n* value) will be determined largely by the resources and time available to collect and analyse your data. It is usually best to take as many samples as you can, as this helps to account for any natural variability present and will give you greater confidence in your data. However, at some point (dependent on the data), more samples will not yield much more information.

1. Explain the importance of each of the following in field studies:

   (a) Appropriate quadrat size (or any equivalent sampling unit): ______________________

   ____

   (b) Recognising any assumptions that you are making: ______________________

   ____

   (c) Appropriate consideration of the environment: ______________________

   ____

   (d) Return of organisms to the same place after removal: ______________________

   ____

   (e) Appropriate size of total sampling area within which the sites are located: ______________________

   ____

2. Describe how you could test whether any given quadrat size was adequate to effectively sample the organism involved:

   ____

   ____

   ____

YOUR CHECKLIST FOR FIELD STUDY DESIGN

The following provides a checklist for a field study. Check off the points when you are confident that you have satisfied the requirements in each case:

1. **Preliminary:**

   ☐ (a) Makes a hypothesis based on observation(s).

   ☐ (b) The hypothesis (and its predictions) are testable using the resources you have available (the study is feasible).

   ☐ (c) The organism you have chosen is suitable for the study and you have considered the ethics involved.

2. **Assumptions and site selection:**

   ☐ (a) You are aware of any assumptions that you are making in your study.

   ☐ (b) You have identified aspects of your field design that could present problems (such as time of year, biological rhythms of your test organism, difficulty in identifying suitable habitats etc.).

   ☐ (c) The study sites you have selected have the features necessary in order for you to answer the questions you have asked in your hypothesis.

3. **Data collection:**

   ☐ (a) You are happy with the way in which you are going to take your measurements or samples.

   ☐ (b) You have considered the size of your sampling unit and the number of samples you are going to take (and tested for these if necessary).

   ☐ (c) You have given consideration to how you will analyse the data you collect and made sure that your study design allows you to answer the questions you wish to answer.

Qualitative Practical Work: Biological Drawings

Many observational studies made using microscopes will require you to make accurate representations of what you see. Although some observations will be made using relatively low power (X40) microscopy, some histological preparations require higher magnifications to identify the finer structure of the tissue. Your work in OCR A2 Biology may require you to make drawings of stained preparations of pancreatic and/or kidney tissue. Tissue sections will usually be provided as longitudinal (LS) or traverse sections (TS). When you have access to both TS and LS images from the same specimen it is also possible to visualise the three dimensional shape of the structure under view. Observational drawing from a microscope is a skill that must be developed. It requires relaxed viewing in which the image is viewed with one eye, while the other eye attends to the drawing being made. Attention should be given to the symmetry and proportions of the structure, accurate labelling, statement of magnification and sectioning, and stain used, if this is appropriate. In this activity, you will practise the skills required to translate what is viewed into a good biological drawing. The stages in creating a biological drawing of pancreatic tissue has been described to help you.

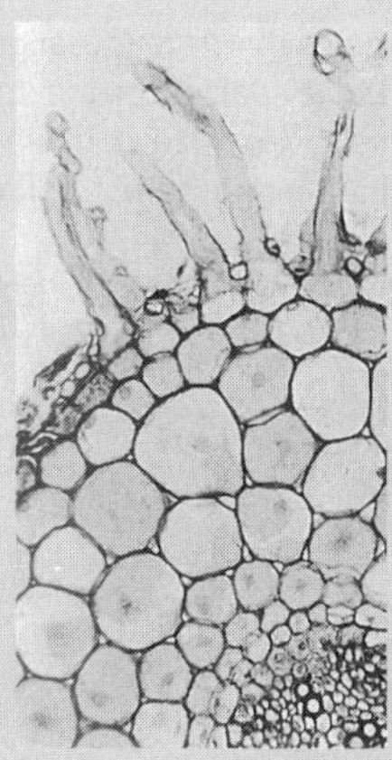

Above: Light micrograph TS through a *Ranunculus* root.
Left: Use one eye (the left for right handers) to view and the right eye to view and direct your drawing.

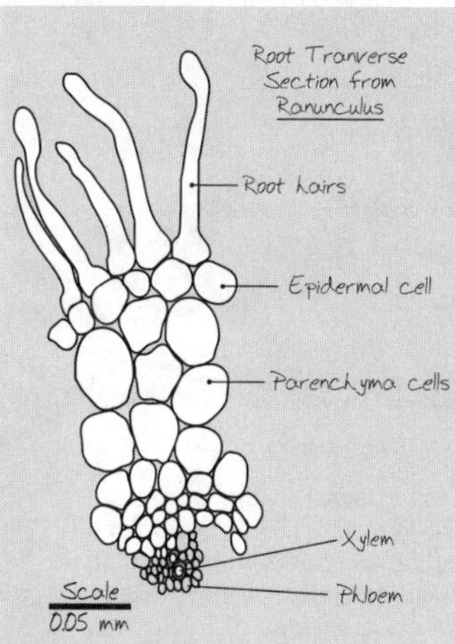

A biological drawing of the same section. A biological drawing is different from a diagram, which is idealised and may contain more structure than can be seen in one section.

Biological drawings should include as much detail as you need to distinguish different structures and types of tissue, but avoid unnecessary detail. Tissue preparations are rarely neat and tidy and there may be areas where it is difficult to distinguish detail and where cells will appear to overlie one another. In these cases you will need to infer detail where possible from adjacent cells. Avoid shading as this can smudge and obscure detail. Labelling involves interpretation based on your knowledge and labels should be away from the drawing with label lines pointing to the structures identified. Add a title and details of the image such as magnification.

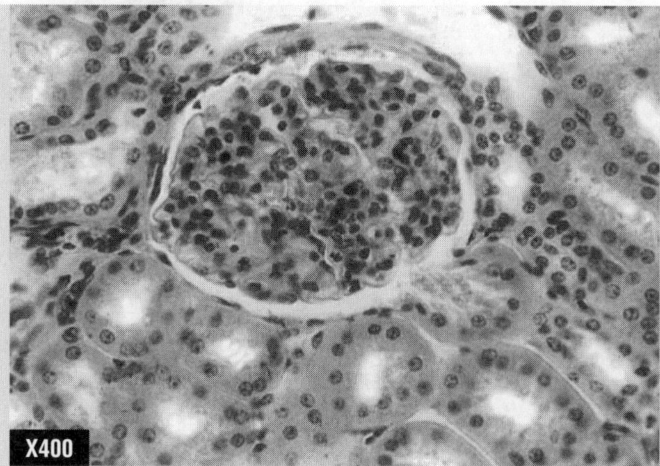

Light micrograph of a transverse section through a kidney nephron to show glomerulus and convoluted tubules.

TASK

Complete the biological drawing of a TS through a kidney nephron in the cortical region. The ovoid glomerular cluster of capillaries can be seen in the upper centre of the photograph, separated from the Bowman's capsule by a space. The capsule is lined with squamous epithelium and surrounded by tubules formed by cuboidal epithelial cells. You can infer this from the position and spacing of the cell nuclei. To assist you with the level of detail required, one kidney tubule has been completed for you.

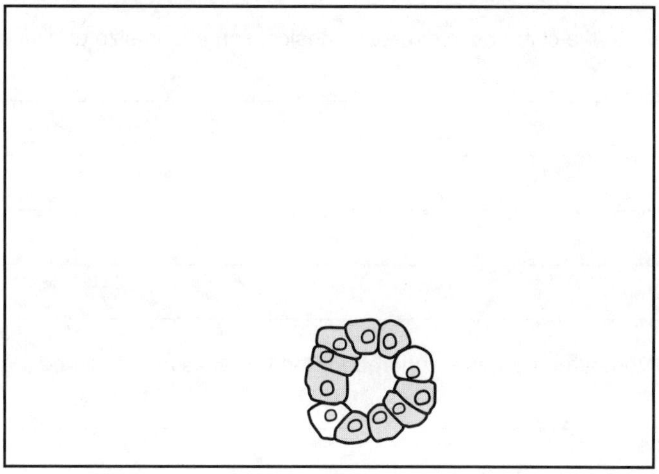

Qualitative Practical Work: Seaweed Zonation

Zonation patterns in the brown seaweeds of the genus *Fucus* provide an ideal opportunity to combine both quantitative and qualitative work. In determining patterns of distribution and abundance for *Fucus* species, it is also useful to make qualitative observations about the size, vigour, and degree of desiccation of specimens at different points on the shore. These observations provide biological information which can help you to explain the patterns of distribution and abundance you find. *Fucus* is a genus of marine brown algae, commonly called wracks, which are found in the midlittoral zone of rocky seashores (i.e. the zone between the low and high levels). Three *Fucus* species, together with another brown alga *Ascophyllum nodosum*, form the dominant seaweeds on rocky shores in Britain, where they form distinct zones along the shore. The species' distribution is governed by the extent to which each species is tolerant of exposure to air. This activity summarises a study of their ecology.

Andreas Trepte

A group of students made a study of a rocky shore dominated by three species of wrack: spiral wrack, bladder wrack, and serrated wrack.

Their aim was to investigate the distribution of three *Fucus* species in the midlittoral zone and relate this to the size and **vigour (V)** of the seaweeds and the degree of **desiccation (D)** evident.

Stemonitis

Stemonitis

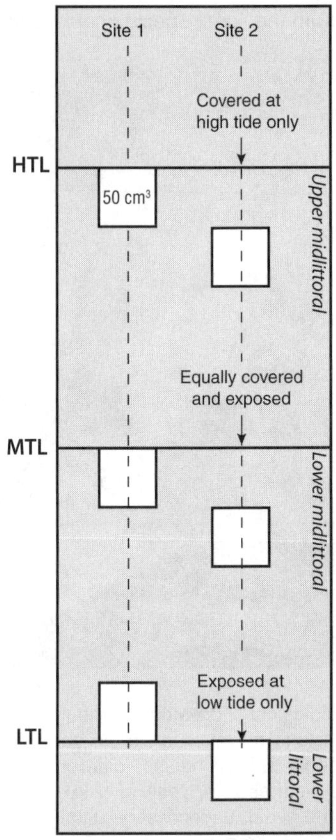

Procedure

Three 50 cm^3 quadrats were positioned from the LTL to the HTL at two locations on the shoreline as shown in the diagram (far right). An estimate of **percentage cover** (**C**) of each species of *Fucus* was made for each sample. Information on vigour and degree of desiccation was collected at the same time.

Qualitative data were collected as simple scores:

- \+ = vigorous with large thalli no evidence of dessication
- 0 = less vigorous with smaller thalli some evidence of dessication
- – = small, poorly grown thalli obvious signs of desiccation

1. (a) Describe the quantitative component of this study:

   (b) Describe the qualitative component of this study:

	SITE 1									SITE 2								
	HTL			MTL			LTL			HTL			MTL			LTL		
Species	C	D	V	C	D	V	C	D	V	C	D	V	C	D	V	C	D	V
Spiral wrack	50	0	+	0	na	na	0	na	na	30	+	0	0	na	na	0	na	na
Bladder wrack	15	–	–	80	+	+	20	+	0	50	0	–	70	+	+	0	na	na
Serrated wrack	0	na	na	0	na	na	75	+	+	0	na	na	10	–	–	80	+	+

2. The results of the quadrat survey are tabulated above. On a separate sheet, plot a column graph of the percentage coverage of each species at each position on the shore and at sites 1 and 2. Staple it to this page.

3. Relate the distribution pattern to the changes in degree of desiccation and in size and vigour of the seaweed thalli:

4. Suggest why the position of the quadrats was staggered for the two sites and describe a disadvantage of this design:

Related activities: Types of Graphs

A Quantitative Practical Task

The middle stage of any investigation (following the planning) is the practical work when the data are collected. Practical work may be laboratory or field based. Typical laboratory based experiments involve investigating how a biological response is affected by manipulating a particular **variable**, e.g. temperature. The data collected for a quantitative practical task should be recorded systematically, with due attention to safe practical techniques, a suitable quantitative method, and accurate measurements to an appropriate degree of precision. If your quantitative practical task is executed well, and you have taken care throughout, your evaluation of the experimental results will be much more straightforward and less problematic.

Carrying Out Your Practical Work

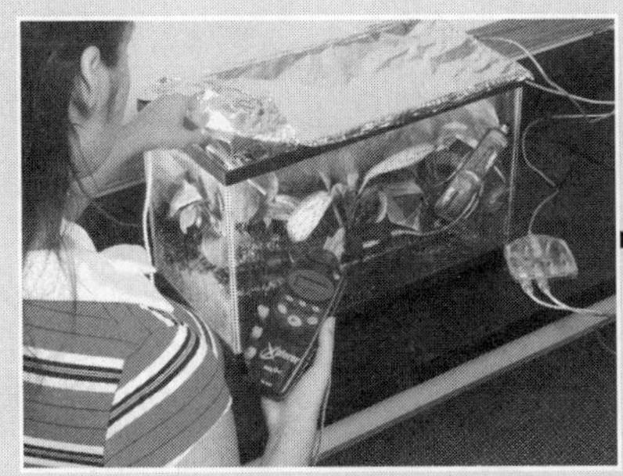

Preparation

Familiarise yourself with the equipment and how to set it up. If necessary, calibrate equipment to give accurate measurements.

Read through the methodology and identify key stages and how long they will take.

Execution

Know how you will take your measurements, how often, and to what degree of precision.

If you are working in a group, assign tasks and make sure everyone knows what they are doing.

Recording

Record your results systematically, in a hand-written table or on a spreadsheet.

Record your results to the appropriate number of significant figures according to the precision of your measurement.

Identifying Variables

A variable is any characteristic or property able to take any one of a range of values. Investigations often look at the effect of changing one variable on another. It is important to identify all variables in an investigation: independent, dependent, and controlled, although there may be nuisance factors of which you are unaware. In all fair tests, only one variable is changed by the investigator.

Dependent variable

- Measured during the investigation.
- Recorded on the y axis of the graph.
- Example: Rate of CO_2 production in yeast

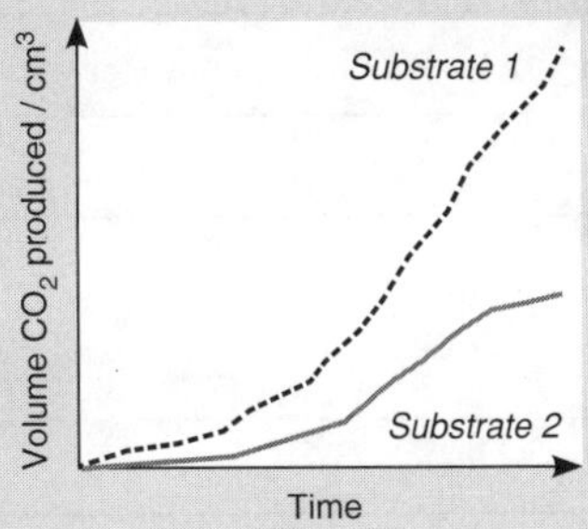

Controlled variables

- Factors that are kept the same or controlled.
- List these in the method, as appropriate to your own investigation.

Independent variable

- Set by the experimenter.
- Recorded on the graph's x axis.
- Example: Time

Assumptions

In any experimental work, you will make certain assumptions about the biological system you are working with.

Assumptions are features of the system (and your experiment) that you assume to be true but do not (or cannot) test.

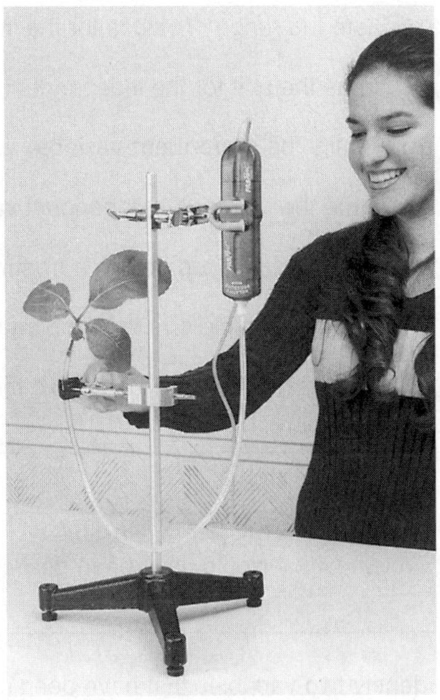

Examples of Investigations

Aim		Variables	
Investigating the effect of varying...	on the following...	Independent variable	Dependent variable
Temperature	Fermentation rate in yeast	Temperature	Volume of CO_2 produced
Temperature	Depth distribution of *Daphnia*	Temperature	Number at each depth
Soil pH	Plant height at age 6 months	pH	Plant height

Related activities: Evaluating Your Results

In order to write a sound method for your investigation, you need to determine how the independent, dependent, and controlled variables will be set and measured (or monitored). A good understanding of your methodology is crucial to a successful investigation. You need to be clear about how much data, and what type of data, you will collect. You should also have a good idea about how you will analyse the data. Use the example below to practise your skills in identifying this type of information.

Activity of yeast (*Saccharomyces cerevisiae*) on different carbohydrates

Brewer's (baker's) yeast is an facultative anaerobe that will preferentially use alcoholic fermentation when sugars are in excess. An experiment investigated the ability of yeast to ferment different carbohydrates.

A simple experimental set-up was used for the reactions, each one (pictured right) contained 1 cm^3 of 8% stock solution of active yeast and 9 cm^3 of a 10% solution of each of the test substrates (lactose, glucose, maltose, and sucrose). All test tubes were kept in a water bath at 24°C and all solutions were buffered to pH 4.5.

Activity was quantified for each substrate by measuring the cumulative volume of carbon dioxide produced at each 5 minute interval over a period of 30 minutes. As the yeast ferments, the carbon dioxide produced pushes the fluid down the pipette and the volume can be read off the pipette.

This experimental set-up is also easily scaled to larger volumes using Erlenmyer flasks to accommodate a larger volume of solution and a longer fermentation (reaction) time.

$$C_6H_{12}O_{6\,(l)} \longrightarrow C_2H_5OH_{\,(l)} + 2CO_{2\,(g)}$$

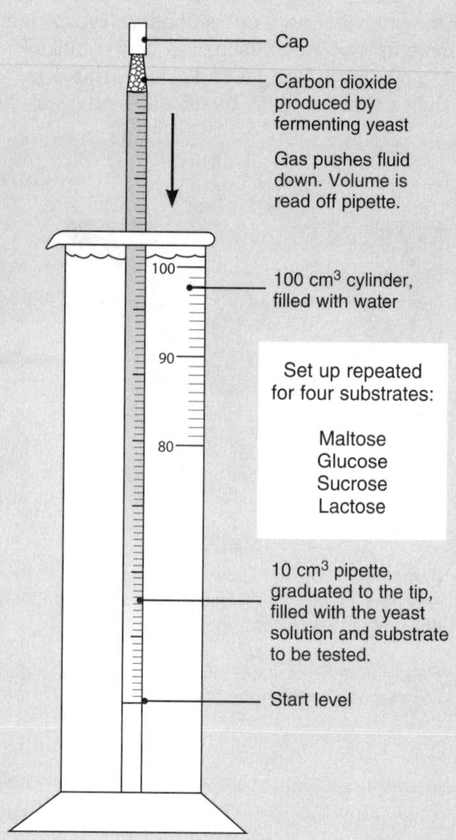

1. Write a suitable aim for this experiment: ______________________________

____

2. Write a suitable hypothesis for this experiment: ______________________________

____

3. (a) Identify the **independent variable**: ______________________________

   (b) State the range of values for the independent variable: ______________________________

   (c) Name the unit for the independent variable: ______________________________

4. (a) Identify the **dependent variable**: ______________________________

   (b) Name the unit for the dependent variable: ______________________________

5. (a) Each substrate represents a treatment/sample/trial (circle one):

   (b) State the sample size for each treatment: ______________________________

   (c) Suggest how you could improve the experimental design to account for any potential variability in the results:

   ____

   ____

6. Explain why it would have been desirable to have included an extra set up containing no substrate: ______________________________

____

7. Identify two variables that have been controlled in this experiment, and how they could have been monitored:

   (a) ______________________________

   (b) ______________________________

Transforming Raw Data

Data are often subjected to a mathematical manipulation as a first step in the initial data analysis. Some simple calculations, such as percentages and rates, can be useful by helping to highlight trends and make meaningful comparisons between data recorded over different periods or for different test subjects. Data transformations, including logs, are also used to convert data to a required standard (normal) form prior to a statistical test. Some simple data manipulations are outlined below.

Action	Explanation and rationale
Frequency table	A tally chart of the number of times a value occurs in a data set. It is a useful first step in data analysis as a neatly constructed tally chart can double as a simple histogram.
Total	The sum of all data values for a variable. Useful as an initial stage in data handling, especially in comparing replicates. Used in making other data transformations.
Percentages	Provide a clear expression of what proportion of data fall into any particular category. This relationship may not be obvious from the raw data values.
Rates	Expressed as a measure per unit time. Rates show how a variable changes over a standard time period (e.g. one second, one minute or one hour). Rates allow meaningful comparison of data that may have been recorded over different time periods.
Reciprocals	Reciprocals of time (1/data value) can provide a crude measure of rate in situations where the variable measured is the total time taken to complete a task, e.g. time taken for a colour change to occur in an enzyme reaction.
Relative values	Expression of data values relative to a standard value e.g. number of road deaths per 1000 cars or calorie consumption per gram of body weight. They allow data from different sample sizes or different organisms to be meaningfully compared. Sometimes they are expressed as a percentage (e.g. 35%) or as a proportion (e.g. 0.35).
Log_{10}	A log transformation is also called a transformation to linearity and it has the effect of normalising data. Useful for data where there is an exponential increase in numbers (e.g. cell growth). Log transformed data will plot as a straight line and the numbers are more manageable. To find the log10 of a number, e.g. 32, using a calculator, key in [log] [32] [=]. The answer should be 1.51.

1. Explain the general purpose of transforming data: ______________________________

____

2. For each of the following examples, state a suitable transformation, together with a reason for your choice:

(a) Determining relative abundance from counts of four plant species in two different habitat areas:

Suitable transformation: ______________________________

Reason: ______________________________

(b) Making a meaningful comparison between animals of different size in the volume of oxygen each consumed:

Suitable transformation: ______________________________

Reason: ______________________________

(c) Making a meaningful comparison of the time taken for chemical precipitation to occur in a flask at different pH values:

Suitable transformation: ______________________________

Reason: ______________________________

(d) Determining the effect of temperature on the production of carbon dioxide by respiring seeds:

Suitable transformation: ______________________________

Reason: ______________________________

3. Complete the transformations for each of the tables on the right. The first value is provided in each case.

(a) TABLE: ***Incidence of cyanogenic clover in different areas***

Working: 124 ÷ 159 = 0.78 = 78%

This is the number of cyanogenic clover out of the total.

Incidence of cyanogenic clover in different areas

Clover plant type	Frost free area		Frost prone area		Totals
	Number	%	Number	%	
Cyanogenic	124	78	26		
Acyanogenic	35		115		
Total	159				

(b) TABLE: ***Plant transpiration loss using a bubble potometer***

Working: (9.0 – 8.0) ÷ 5 min = 0.2

This is the distance the bubble moved over the first 5 minutes. Note that there is no data entry possible for the first reading (0 min) because no difference can be calculated.

Plant transpiration loss using a bubble potometer

Time */min*	Pipette arm reading */cm³*	Plant water loss */cm³ min⁻¹*
0	9.0	–
5	8.0	0.2
10	7.2	
15	6.2	
20	4.9	

(c) TABLE: ***Photosynthetic rate at different light intensities***

Working: 1 ÷ 15 = 0.067

This is time taken for the leaf to float. A reciprocal gives a per minute rate (the variable measured is the time taken for an event to occur).

NOTE: In this experiment, the flotation time is used as a crude measure of photosynthetic rate. As oxygen bubbles are produced as a product of photosynthesis, they stick to the leaf disc and increase its buoyancy. The faster the rate, the sooner they come to the surface. The rates of photosynthesis should be measured over similar time intervals, so the rate is transformed to a 'per minute' basis (the reciprocal of time).

Photosynthetic rate at different light intensities

Light intensity */%*	Average time for leaf disc to float */ min*	Reciprocal of time */ min⁻¹*
100	15	0.067
50	25	
25	50	
11	93	
6	187	

(d) TABLE: ***Frequency of size classes in a sample of eels***

Working: (7 ÷ 270) x 100 = 2.6 %

This is the number of individuals out of the total that appear in the size class 0-50 mm. The relative frequency is rounded to one decimal place.

Frequency of size classes in a sample of eels

Size class */mm*	Frequency	Relative frequency/ %
0-50	7	2.6
50-99	23	
100-149	59	
150-199	98	
200-249	50	
250-299	30	
300-349	3	
Total	270	

Data Presentation

Data can be presented in a number of ways. **Tables** provide an accurate record of numerical values and allow you to organise your data in a way that allows you to clarify the relationships and trends that are apparent. **Graphs** provide a visual image of trends in the data in a minimum of space. It is useful to plot your data as soon as possible, even during your experiment, as this will help you to evaluate your results as you proceed and make adjustments as necessary (e.g. to the sampling interval). The choice between graphing or tabulation in the final report depends on the type and complexity of the data and the information that you are wanting to convey. Usually, both are appropriate. Some of the basic rules for constructing tables and graphs are outlined below. Note that values for standard deviation and 95% confidence intervals are provided in these examples. Calculating these will help you to understand your data better and critically evaluate your results. Always allow enough space for a graph, e.g. one third to one half of an A4 page. The examples in this workbook are usually reduced for reasons of space.

Presenting Data in Tables

Tables should have an accurate, descriptive title. Number tables consecutively through the report.

Table 1: Length and growth of the third internode of bean plants receiving three different hormone treatments (data are given ± standard deviation).

Treatment	Sample size	Mean rate of internode growth / mm day $^{-1}$	Mean internode length / mm	Mean mass of tissue added / g day $^{-1}$
Control	50	0.60 ± 0.025	32.3 ± 2.3	0.36 ± 0.025
Hormone 1	46	1.52 ± 0.030	41.6 ± 3.4	0.51 ± 0.030
Hormone 2	98	0.82 ± 0.018	38.4 ± 0.9	0.56 ± 0.028
Hormone 3	85	2.06 ± 0.019	50.2 ± 1.4	0.68 ± 0.020

Independent variable in left column.

Control values (if present) should be placed at the beginning of the table.

Each row should show a different experimental treatment, organism, sampling site etc.

Heading and subheadings identify each set of data and show units of measurement.

Tables can be used to show a calculated measure of spread of the values about the mean (e.g. standard deviation or 95% confidence interval).

Show values only to the level of significance allowable by your measuring technique.

Columns that need to be compared should be placed alongside each other.

Organise the columns so that each category of like numbers or attributes is listed vertically.

Presenting Data in Graph Format

Fig. 1: Yield of two bacterial strains at different antibiotic levels (± 95% confidence intervals, n= 6)

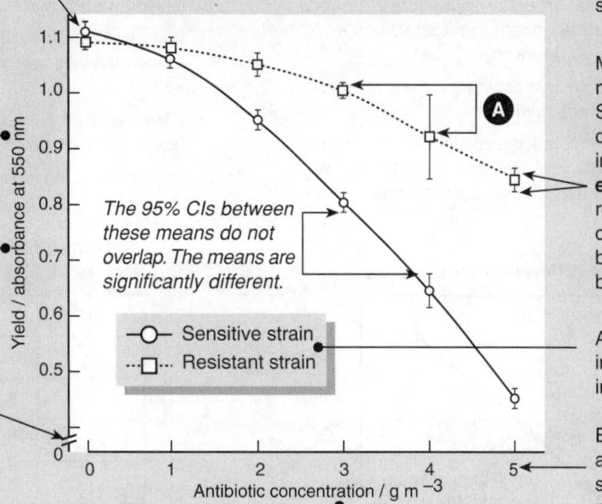

Plot points accurately. Different responses can be distinguished using different symbols, lines or bar colours.

Label both axes (provide SI units of measurement if necessary).

Place the dependent variable, e.g. biological response, on the vertical (y) axis (if you are drawing a scatter graph it does not matter).

A break in an axis allows economical use of space if there are no data in the "broken" area. A floating axis (where zero points do not meet) allows data points to be plotted away from the vertical axis.

Graphs (called figures) should have a concise, explanatory title. If several graphs appear in your report they should be numbered consecutively.

Measures of spread about the plotted mean value can be shown on the graph. Such measures include standard deviation and the 95% confidence intervals (CI). The values are plotted as **error bars** and give an indication of the reliability of the mean value. If the 95% confidence intervals do not overlap between points, then these means will be significantly different.

A key identifies symbols. This information sometimes appears in the title or the legend.

Each axis should have an appropriate scale. Decide on the scale by finding the maximum and minimum values for each variable.

Place the independent variable, e.g. treatment, on the horizontal (x) axis.

1. What can you conclude about the difference (labelled A) between the two means plotted above? Explain your answer:

2. Discuss the reasons for including both graphs and tables in a final report:

Periodicals:
It's a plot!
Descriptive statistics

Related activities: *Types of Graphs, Interpreting Sample Variability*

Types of Graphs

Graphs can be used to display data in a way that makes it easy to see trends or relationships between different variables. Before representing data graphically, it is important to identify the kind of data you have. Choosing the correct type of graph can help to clarify an otherwise complicated set of data. It may also highlight important aspects of a relationship between two measured variables. Choosing the wrong type of graph can obscure information and make data more difficult to interpret. Examples of the common types of graph, and the data that are appropriate to them, are provided here. Graphs appropriate for continuous data (line and scatter graphs) are illustrated on this page. Graphs for discontinuous data are illustrated on the next page.

Scatter Graph

In scatter graphs, there is no manipulated (independent) variable but the variables are usually *correlated* i.e. they vary together in some predictable way. The points on the graph need not be connected, but a line of best fit is often drawn through the points (this may be drawn be eye or computer generated).

- The data for this graph must be continuous for both variables
- Useful for determining the relationship between two variables

Relationship between body length and brood size in *Daphnia*

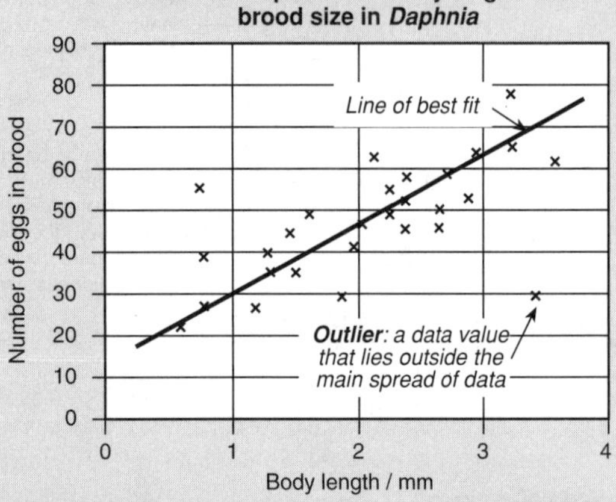

Line Graph

Line graphs are used when one variable (called the independent variable), affects another, the dependent variable. The independent variable is often time or the experimental treatment (controlled or manipulated variable). The dependent variable is usually the biological response.

- The data for line graphs must be continuous for both variables
- If extreme points are likely to be important, draw a line connecting the points. If there is an implied relationship in the data (e.g. growth increases), a line of best fit that excludes outliers is best.

Metabolic rate in a rat at different temperatures

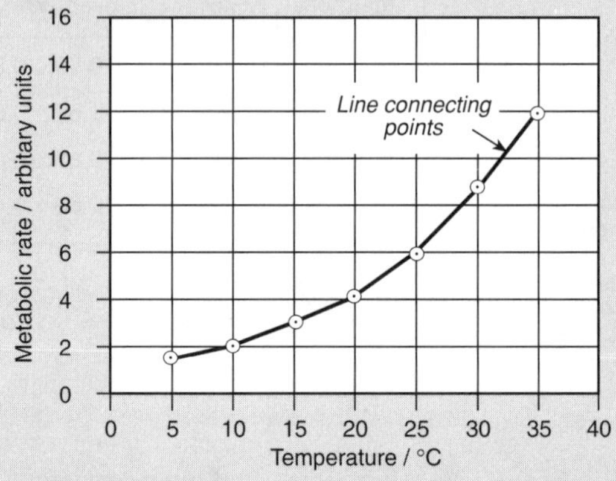

Line Graph with Measure of Spread

Line graphs may be drawn with **error bars**. These are calculated values and indicate the degree of spread (scatter) of the data about a mean. Error bars are used if there are calculated mean (average) values and a measure of data spread (e.g. standard deviation).

- Where error bars are large, the data are less consistent (more variable) than in cases where the error bars are small.
- Where no error value has been calculated, the scatter can be shown by plotting the individual data points vertically above and below the mean. By convention, bars are not used to indicate the range of raw values in a data set.

Growth rate in peas at different temperatures

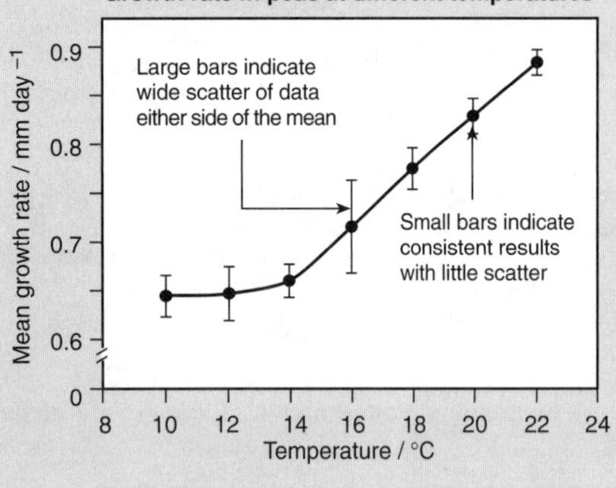

Line Graph: Two Curves Plotted Together

More than one curve can be plotted per set of axes. This is useful when you wish to compare two data sets together.

- If the two data sets use the same measurement units and a similar range of values use one scale and distinguish the two curves with a key
- If the two data sets use different units and/or have a very different range of values use two scales (see example below)
- Adjust scales if necessary to avoid overlapping plots

Transpiration and root uptake rates in peas at different relative humidity

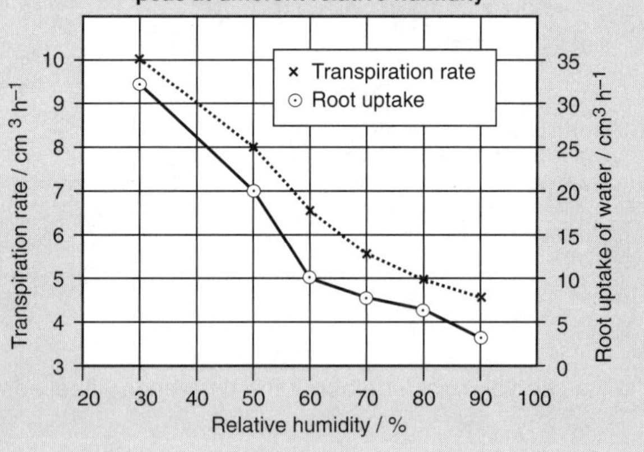

1. (a) Explain what is meant by an outlier: ______________________

   (b) Suggest how outliers might arise in a data set: ______________________

   ____

   (c) Suggest why outliers are sometimes excluded from an analysis of results: ______________________

   ____

Bar Graph

The data for this graph are non-numerical and **discrete** for at least one variable i.e. they are grouped into separate categories. There are no dependent or independent variables. Axes may be reversed to give graph with the categories on the x axis.

- The data are discontinuous, so the bars do not touch
- Data values may be entered on or above the bars
- Multiple data sets can be displayed using different coloured bars placed side by side within the same category

Size of various woodlands in Britain

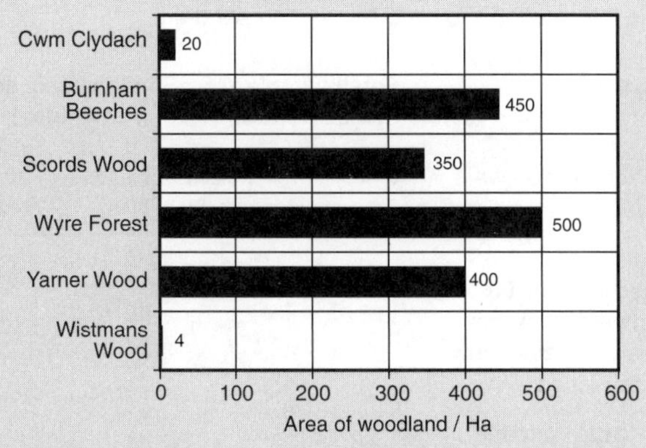

Histograms

Histograms are plots of **continuous** data, usually of some physical variable against frequency of occurrence. Column graphs are drawn to plot frequency distributions when the data are discrete, numerical values (1, 2, 3 etc.). In this case the bars do not touch.

- Histogram data are continuous so the bars touch
- The X-axis usually records the class interval. The Y-axis usually records the number of individuals in each class interval (frequency)

The frequency of different weight classes of animals in a population.

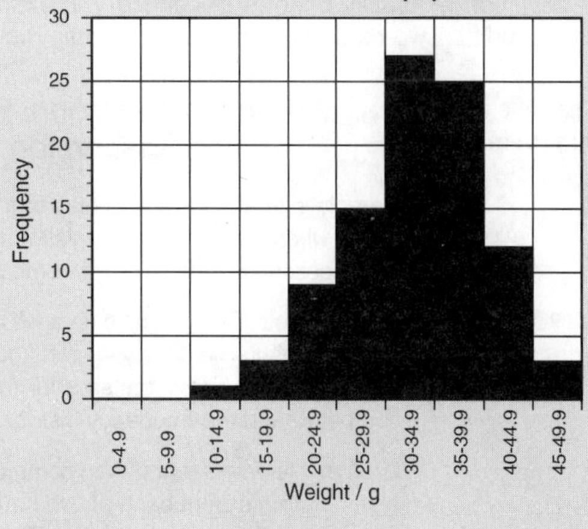

Pie Graph

As with bar graphs, pie graphs are used when the data for one variable are discrete (categories) and the data for the other variable are in the form of counts. A circle is divided according to the proportion of counts in each category. Pie graphs are:

- Good for visual impact and showing relative proportions
- Useful for six or fewer categories
- Not suitable for data sets with a very large number of categories

Average residential water use

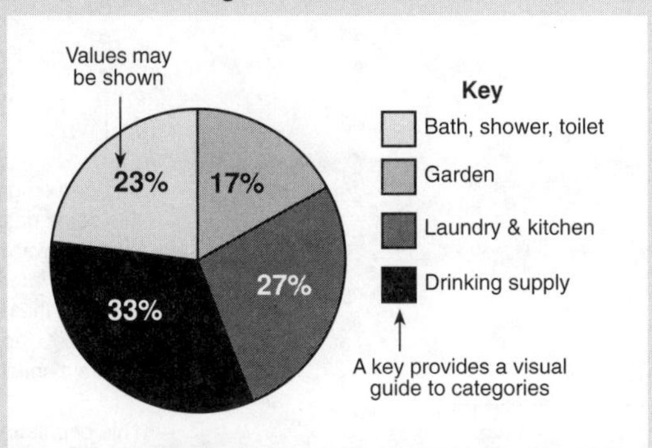

Kite Graph

Kite graphs are elongated figures drawn along a baseline. They can show species distribution across a landscape (or, in some cases, the distribution of one species at different times).

- Each kite represents species abundance across a landscape
- The actual abundance can be calculated from the kite width
- A single thin line on a kite graph represents species absence
- The axes can be reversed depending on preference

Species abundance along a rocky shoreline

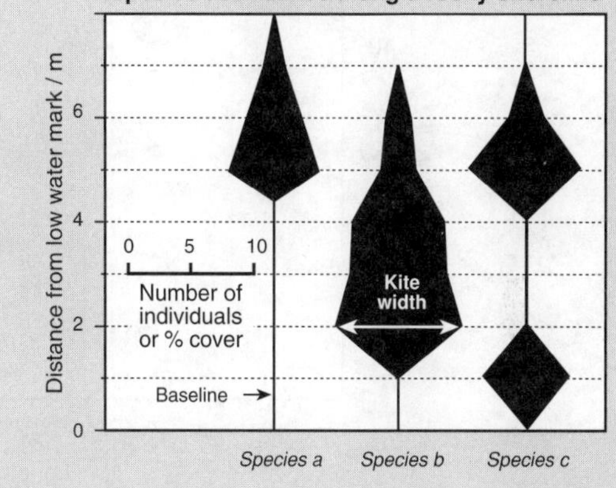

2. Decide which type of graph you would use to plot the data below and give a brief reason for your choice in each case:

Temperature/ °C	Oxygen content of water/ *mg dm⁻³*
5	9.0
15	7.0
25	5.8
35	5.0

Organism *(at sea level)*	RBC/ *millions cm⁻³ blood*
Man	5.00
Sheep	10.50
Rabbit	4.55
Vicuna	14.90

Size of leaf/ *mm*	Number of individuals
15 - 19	5
20 - 24	11
25 - 29	16
30 - 34	6

(a) Graph type: ______________________

Reason: ______________________

____

(b) Graph type: ______________________

Reason: ______________________

____

(c) Graph type: ______________________

Reason: ______________________

____

3. Explain why it is important to choose an appropriate class interval when constructing a histogram:

____

____

Interpreting Sample Variability

Measures of central tendency, such as mean, attempt to identify the most representative value in a set of data, but the description of a data set also requires that we know something about how far the data values are spread around that central measure. As we have seen in the previous activity, the **standard deviation** (*s*) gives a simple measure of the spread or **dispersion** in data. The **variance** (s^2) is also a measure of dispersion, but the standard deviation is usually preferred because it is expressed in the original units. Two data sets could have exactly the same mean values, but very different values of dispersion. If we were simply to use the central tendency to compare these data sets, the results would (incorrectly) suggest that they were alike. The assumptions we make about a population will be affected by what the sample data tell us. This is why it is important that sample data are unbiased (e.g. collected by **random sampling**) and that the sample set is as large as practicable. This exercise will help to illustrate how our assumptions about a population are influenced by the information provided by the sample data.

Random Sampling, Sample Size, and Dispersion in Data

Sample size and sampling bias can both affect the information we obtain when we sample a population. In this exercise you will calculate some descriptive statistics for some sample data.

The complete set of sample data we are working with comprises 689 length measurements of year zero (young of the year) perch (column left). Basic descriptive statstics for the data have bee calculated for you below and the frequency histogram has also been plotted.

Look at this data set and then complete the exercise to calculate the same statistics from each of two smaller data sets (tabulated right) drawn from the same population. This excercise shows how random sampling, large sample size, and sampling bias affect our statistical assessment of variation in a population.

Complete sample set
n = 689 (random)

Length in mm	*Freq*
25	1
26	0
27	0
28	0
29	0
30	0
31	0
32	2
33	3
34	3
35	4
36	5
37	10
38	23
39	22
40	33
41	39
42	41
43	41
44	36
45	49
46	32
47	14
48	32
49	27
50	25
51	24
52	17
53	18
54	27
55	21
56	20
57	11
58	18
59	16
60	22
61	13
62	8
63	10
64	5
65	7
66	2
67	3
68	3
69	1
70	0
71	1

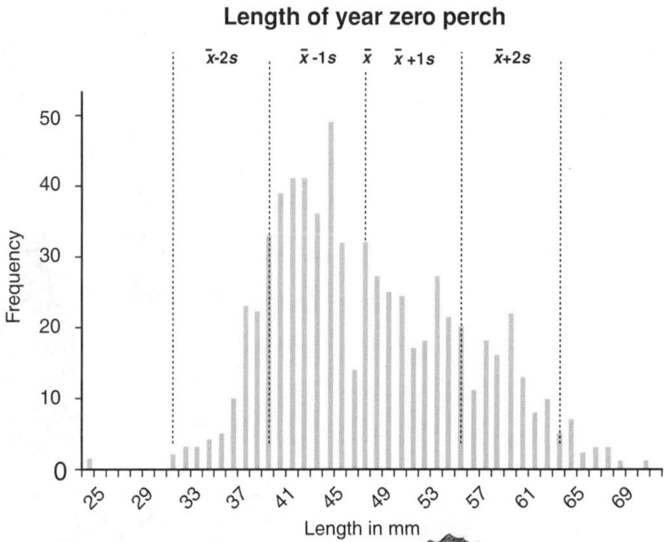

Descriptive statistics

MEAN	48
MEDIAN	47
MODE	45
VARIANCE	61.03
STANDARD DEVIATION	7.81

Small sample set
n = 30 (random)

Length in mm	*Freq*
25	1
26	0
27	0
28	0
29	0
30	0
31	0
32	0
33	0
34	0
35	2
36	0
37	0
38	3
39	2
40	1
41	3
42	0
43	0
44	0
45	0
46	1
47	0
48	2
49	0
50	0
51	1
52	3
53	0
54	0
55	0
56	0
57	1
58	0
59	3
60	2
61	2
62	0
63	0
64	0
65	0
66	0
67	2
68	1
	30

This population was sampled randomly to obtain this data set

This column records the number of fish of each size

Number of fish in the sample

Small sample set
n = 50 (bias)

Length in mm	*Freq*
46	1
47	0
48	0
49	1
50	0
51	0
52	1
53	1
54	1
55	1
56	0
57	2
58	2
59	4
60	1
61	0
62	8
63	10
64	13
65	2
66	0
67	2
	50

The person gathering this set of data was biased towards selecting larger fish because the mesh size on the net was too large to retain small fish

1. For the complete data set (*n* = 689) calculate the percentage of data falling within:

   (a) ± one standard deviation of the mean: ______________________

   (b) ± two standard deviations of the mean: ______________________

   (c) Explain what this information tells you about the distribution of year zero perch from this site: ______________________

   ____

2. Give another reason why you might reach the same conclusion about the distribution: ______________________

   ____

Web links: Descriptive Statistics

Periodicals: *Estimating the mean and standard deviation*

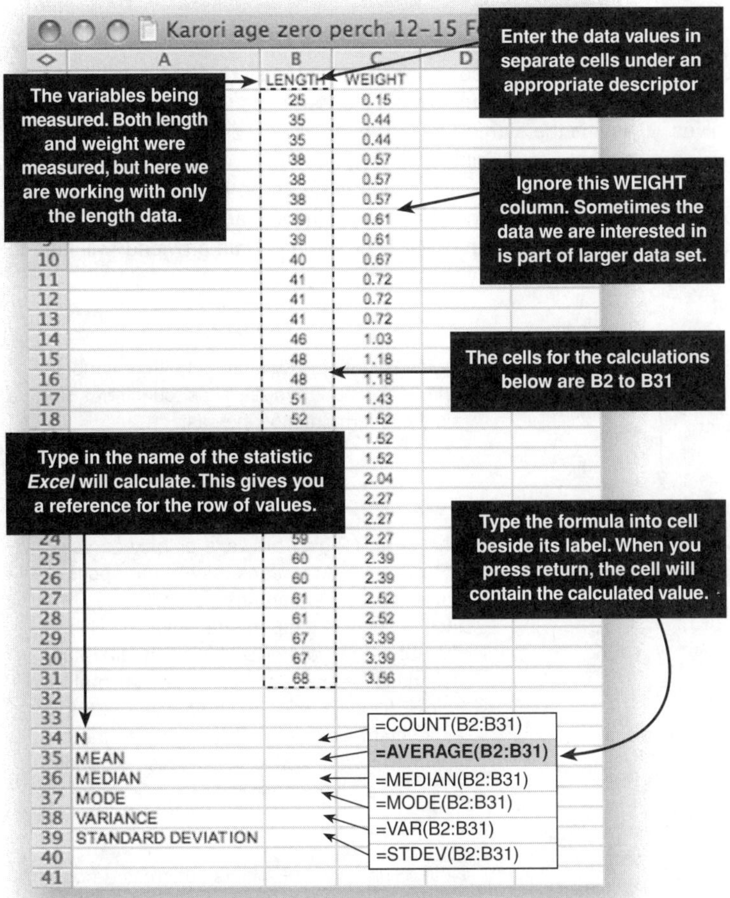

Calculating Descriptive Statistics Using *Excel*

You can use *Microsoft Excel* to easily calculate descriptive statistics for sample data. You should be familiar from you work in AS with the calculation of standard deviation from first principles. The purpose of this activity is not the calculation itself but the interpretion of the result.

In this first example, the smaller data set ($n = 30$) is shown as it would appear on an *Excel* spreadsheet, ready for the calculations to be made. Use this guide to enter your data into a spreadsheet and calculate the descriptive statistics as described.

When using formulae in *Excel*, = indicates that a formula follows. The cursor will become active and you will be able to select the cells containing the data you are interested in, or you can type the location of the data using the format shown. The data in this case are located in the cells B2 through to B31 (B2:B31).

3. For this set of data, use a spreadsheet to calculate:

   (a) Mean: ______

   (b) Median ______

   (c) Mode: ______

   (d) Sample variance: ______

   (e) Standard deviation: ______

   Staple the spreadsheet into your workbook.

4. Repeat the calculations for the second small set of sample data (n = 50) on the previous page. Again, calculate the statistics as indicated below and staple the spreadsheet into your workbook.

   (a) Mean: ______ (b) Median: ______ (c) Mode: ______

   (d) Variance: ______ (e) Standard deviation: ______

5. On a separate sheet, plot **frequency histograms** for each of the two small data sets. Label them $n = 30$ and $n = 50$. Staple them into your workbook. If you are proficient in *Excel* and you have the "Data Analysis" plug in loaded, you can use *Excel* to plot the histograms for you once you have entered the data.

6. Compare the descriptive statistics you calculated for each data set with reference to the following:

   (a) How close the median and mean to each other in each sample set: ______

   (b) The size of the standard deviation in each case: ______

   (c) How close each small of the sample sets resembles the large sample set of 689 values: ______

7. (a) Compare the two frequency histograms you have plotted for the two smaller sample data sets: ______

   (b) Explain why you think two histograms look so different: ______

Periodicals:
The variability of samples

Evaluating Your Results

Any practical investigation requires you to critically evaluate your results in the light of your own hypothesis and your biological knowledge. A critical evaluation of any study involves analysing, presenting, and discussing the results, as well as accounting for any deficiencies in your procedures and erroneous results. This activity describes an experiment comparing different carbohydrates for their effectiveness as substrates for fermentation. Brewer's yeast is a facultative anaerobe that will preferentially use alcoholic fermentation when sugars are in excess. One would expect glucose to be the preferred substrate, as it is the starting molecule in cellular respiration, but yeast are capable of utilising a variety of sugars, which may be isomers of glucose or disaccharides that can be broken down into their constituent monomers. Completing this activity, which involves a critical evaluation of the second-hand data provided, will help to prepare you for your own evaluative task.

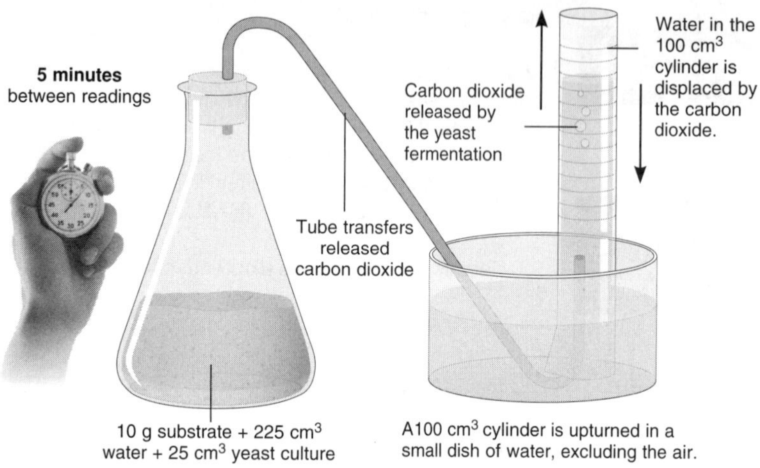

The Apparatus

In this experiment, all substrates tested used the same source culture of 30 g active yeast dissolved in 150 cm^3 of room temperature (24°C) tap water. For each substrate, 25 g of the substrate to be tested was added to 225 cm^3 room temperature (24°C) tap water buffered to pH 4.5. Then 25 cm^3 of source culture was added to the test solution. The control contained yeast solution but no substrate:

Substrate / Time / min	**Group 1**: Volume of carbon dioxide collected / cm^3				
	None	**Glucose**	**Maltose**	**Sucrose**	**Lactose**
0	0	0	0	0	0
5	0	0	0.8	0	0
10	0	0	0.8	0	0
15	0	0	0.8	0.1	0
20	0	0.5	2.0	0.8	0
25	0	1.2	3.0	1.8	0
30	0	2.8	3.6	3.0	0.5
35	0	4.2	5.4	4.8	0.5
40	0	4.6	5.6	4.8	0.5
45	0	7.4	8.0	7.2	1.0
50	0	10.8	8.9	7.6	1.3
55	0	13.6	9.6	7.7	1.3
60	0	16.1	10.4	9.6	1.3
65	0	22.0	12.1	10.2	1.8
70	0	23.8	14.4	12.0	1.8
75	0	26.7	15.2	12.6	2.0
80	0	32.5	17.3	14.3	2.1
85	0	37.0	18.7	14.9	2.4
90	0	39.9	21.6	17.2	2.6

Substrate / Time / min	**Group 2**: Volume of carbon dioxide collected / cm^3				
	None	**Glucose**	**Maltose**	**Sucrose**	**Lactose**
90	0	24.4	19.0	17.5	0

The Aim

To investigate the suitability of different mono- and disaccharide sugars as substrates for alcoholic fermentation in yeast.

Background

The rate at which brewer's or baker's yeast (*Saccharomyces cerevisiae*) metabolises carbohydrate substrates is influenced by factors such as temperature, solution pH, and type of carbohydrate available. The literature describes yeast metabolism as optimal in warm, slightly acid environments and this experiment was set up to investigate the pH optimum for the active yeast which is readily available at supermarkets.

Note: High levels of sugars suppress aerobic respiration in yeast, so yeast will preferentially use the fermentation pathway in the presence of excess substrate.

1. Write the equation for the fermentation of glucose by yeast:

 ____

2. Calculate the rate of carbon dioxide production per minute for each substrate in group 1's results:

 (a) None: ______________

 (b) Glucose: ______________

 (c) Maltose: ______________

 (d) Sucrose: ______________

 (e) Lactose: ______________

3. A second group of students performed the same experiment. Their results are summarised, below left. Calculate the rate of carbon dioxide production per minute for each substrate in group 2's results:

 (a) None: ______________

 (b) Glucose: ______________

 (c) Maltose: ______________

 (d) Sucrose: ______________

 (e) Lactose: ______________

Experimental design and results adapted from Tom Schuster, Rosalie Van Zyl, & Harold Coller, California State University Northridge 2005

4. What assumptions are being made in this experimental design and do you think they were reasonable?

5. Use the tabulated data to plot an appropriate graph of group 1's results on the grid provided:

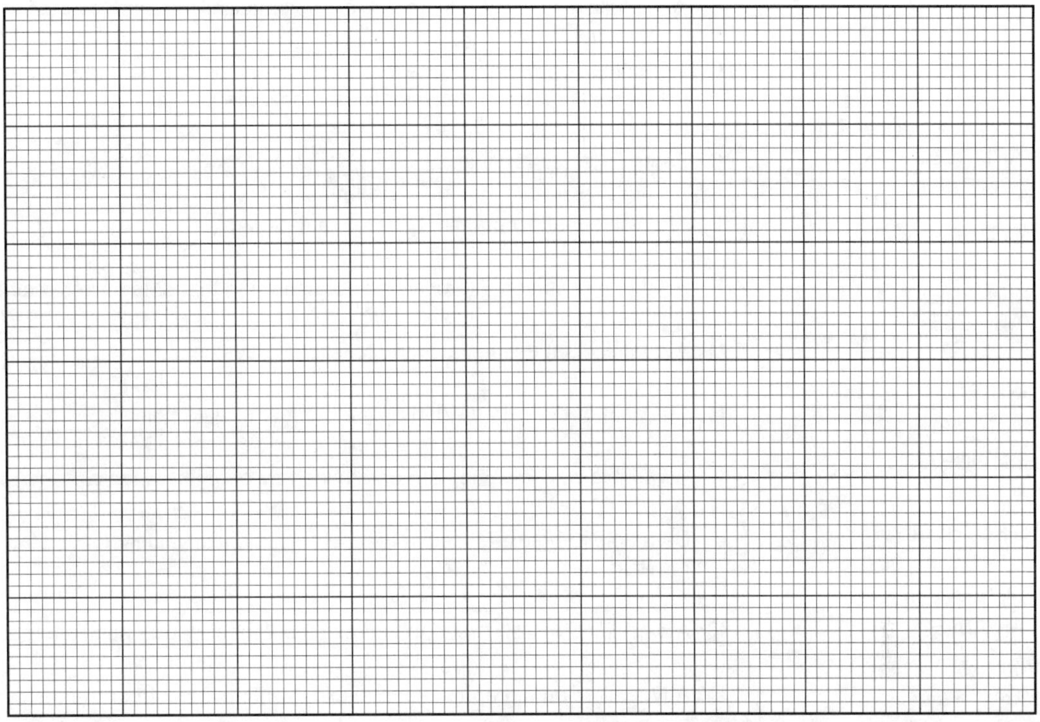

6. (a) Summarise the results of group 1's fermentation experiment:

(b) Explain the findings based on your understanding of cellular respiration and carbohydrate chemistry:

7. (a) Plot a column chart to compare the results of the two groups in the volume of CO_2 collected after 90 minutes for each substrate (axes have been completed):

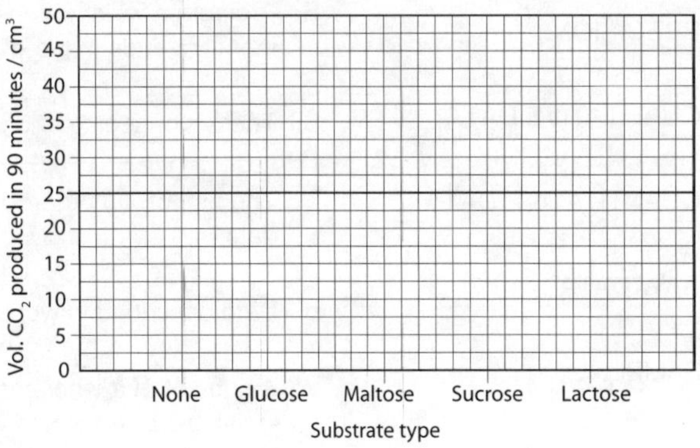

(b) Compare the results of the two groups:

(c) Provide a probable explanation for any differences in the results:

(d) Describe one improvement you could make to the experiment in order to generate more reliable data:

KEY TERMS: Mix and Match

INSTRUCTIONS: Test your vocabulary by matching each term to its definition, as identified by its preceding letter code.

- ACCURACY
- BIOLOGICAL DRAWING
- CONTROL
- CONTROLLED VARIABLES
- DATA
- DEPENDENT VARIABLE
- GRAPH
- HISTOGRAM
- HYPOTHESIS
- INDEPENDENT VARIABLE
- MEAN
- MEASUREMENT
- MEDIAN
- MODE
- OBSERVATION
- PARAMETER
- PRECISION
- QUALITATIVE DATA
- QUANTITATIVE DATA
- RAW DATA
- SAMPLE
- SCIENTIFIC METHOD
- STANDARD DEVIATION
- STATISTIC
- TREND (OF DATA)
- VARIABLE

A Factors in an experiment that are controlled or kept the same.

B A variable whose values are set, or systematically altered, by the investigator.

C A treatment or group in an experiment that is the same as the experimental group, except for the variable being manipulated by the experimenter.

D Facts collected for analysis.

E The value that occurs most often in a data set.

F A pattern observed in processed data showing that data values may be linked.

G A quantity that defines a characteristic of a system.

H The sum of the data divided by the number of data points.

I A variable whose values are determined by another variable.

J Data able to be expressed in numbers. Numerical values derived from counts or measurements.

K A calculated statistic used to express the variability of a population about the mean.

L A type of column graph used to display continuous data or frequency distributions.

M A tentative explanation of an observation, capable of being tested by experimentation.

N The central value in a sorted set of data.

O How close a measured value is to the true value.

P The sampling of an object or substance to record numerical data that describes some aspect of the it, e.g. length or temperature.

Q Data that has not been processed or summarised in any way.

R A diagram which often displays numerical information in a way that can be used to identify trends in the data.

S The act of seeing and noting an occurrence in the object or substance being studied.

T The use of an ordered, repeatable method to investigate, manipulate, gather, and record data.

U Data described in words or terms rather than by numbers.

V A sub-set of a whole used to estimate the values that might have been obtained if every individual or response was measured.

W A calculated measure of some attribute of a sample (e.g. the arithmetic mean).

X A clear and accurate representation of an observation of a biological specimen, made at the time of observation as a permanent record of what is actually seen.

Y A factor in an experiment that is subject to change.

Z The repeatability of a measurement.

Communication and Homeostasis

Homeostasis
- Responding to changing environments
- Negative feedback and stability
- Positive feedback and its role

Nerves
- The role of sensory receptors
- Sensory and motor neurones
- The action potential
- Synaptic transmission

Hormones
- Endocrine glands and target tissues
- Second messenger systems
- Structure and role of the pancreas
- Blood glucose regulation
- Control of heart rate

Important in this section...

- *Understand the body's internal communication systems*
- *Describe excretion in mammals by the liver and kidneys*
- *Describe the role of and processes in photosynthesis*
- *Describe the role of and processes in cellular respiration*

Excretion

Metabolic wastes
- The nature of metabolic wastes
- The structure and role of liver
- The ornithine cycle
- The role of the liver in detoxification

Kidneys and urine production
- The structure and role of the kidneys
- Urine formation in the nephron
- Control of urine volume
- Kidney failure and urine analysis

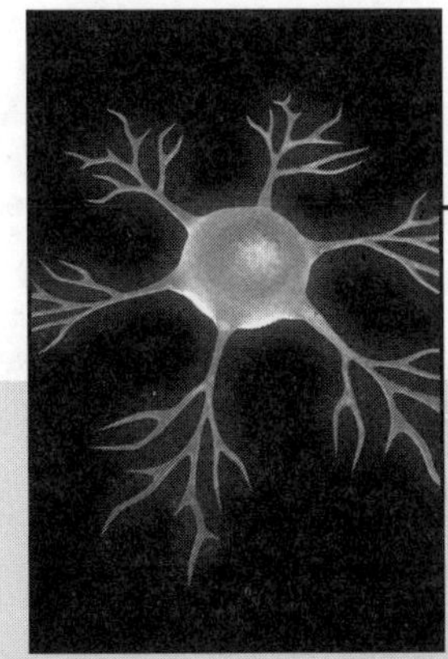

The responses of organisms to changes in their environment are controlled and coordinated by nerves and hormones.

Metabolism produces toxic waste products, which must be excreted. Excretion is the role of the lungs, kidneys, liver, and skin.

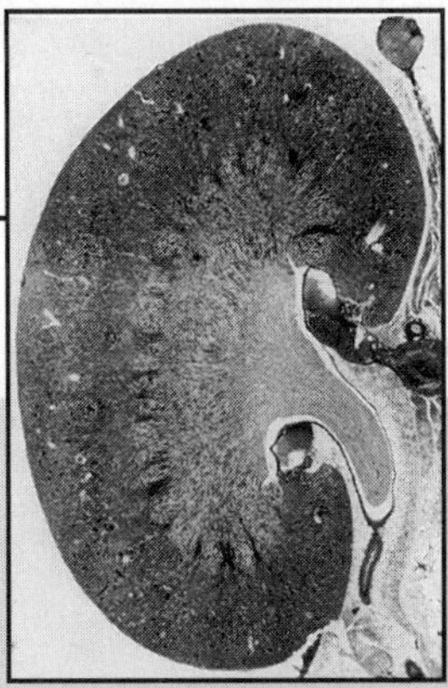

A2 Unit F214 Communication, Homeostasis, and Energy

Photosynthesis is an anabolic process using light energy to fix carbon in organic compounds. Cellular respiration is a catabolic process in which ATP is generated to fuel metabolism.

Nervous and hormonal communication systems regulate metabolism to achieve homeostasis . Negative feedback is central to this regulation. Metabolism produces waste products, which must be excreted by the kidneys, liver, lungs, and skin.

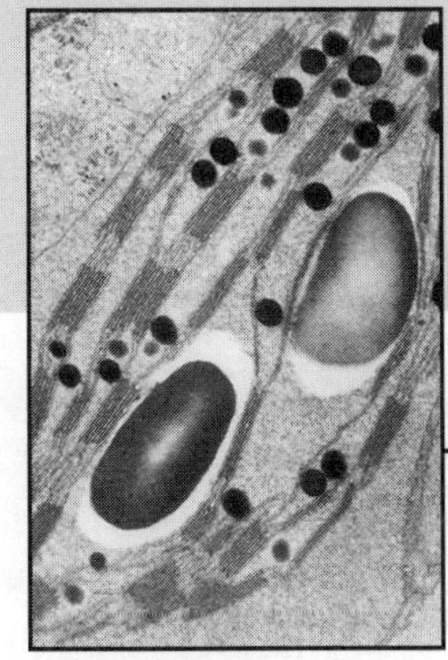

Photosynthesis sustains life on Earth; light energy is used to fix carbon in organic compounds. Oxygen is a product of this.

Cellular respiration is a fundamental process occurring in all cells and, as such, is part of the definition of life.

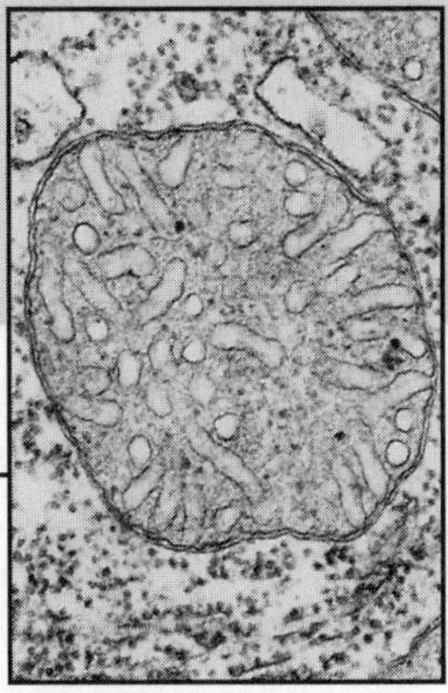

The role of photo-synthesis
- The nature and role of autotrophy
- Relationship between respiration and photosynthesis
- Heterotrophic dependence on producers

Chloroplasts and photo-synthesis
- Chloroplast structure
- Photosynthetic pigments
- Light capture in the thylakoid
- Production of ATP and NADPH
- Carbon fixation in the Calvin cycle

Photo-synthetic rates
- Effect of CO_2 level on photosynthetic rate and levels of intermediates
- Limiting factors for photosynthesis
- Investigating photosynthesis

Photosynthesis

The role of cellular respiration
- The need for cellular respiration
- The role of ATP in metabolism
- The role of coenzymes in respiration
- The structure of mitochondria

Glycolysis and the link reaction
- The processes involved in glycolysis
- Pyruvate as the end product
- The transition (link) reaction

Krebs cycle and the ETC
- Krebs cycle: reduction of NAD and FAD substrate level phosphorylation
- The ETC and oxidative phosphorylation
- ATP yield from aerobic respiration

Anaerobic pathways
- Lactic acid fermentation
- Alcoholic fermentation
- Yield from anaerobic pathways

Cellular Respiration

UNIT F214

4.1.1 Communication and Homeostasis

KEY TERMS

autonomic nervous system
cell signalling
chemoreceptors
ectotherm
effector
endocrine
endotherm
homeostasis
homeothermic
hypothalamus
mechanoreceptors
negative feedback
paracrine
photoreceptors
positive feedback
receptor
stimulus (pl. stimuli)
target cells
thermoreceptors
thermoregulation

KEY CONCEPTS

- Multicellular organisms require communication systems in order to regulate their metabolism.
- Homeostasis describes the constancy of the body's systems. It enables efficiency of function.
- Homeostasis is achieved through negative feedback mechanisms, which guard against excessive change.
- The nervous and endocrine systems work together, e.g in thermoregulation, to maintain homeostasis.

OBJECTIVES

☐ 1. Use the **KEY TERMS** to help you understand and complete these objectives.

Stimulus and communication

pages 29-30

☐ 2. Explain the need for communication systems in multicellular organisms. Identify internal and external stimuli and describe examples of sensory receptors that respond to these, as illustrated by: **mechanoreceptors**, **photoreceptors**, **chemoreceptors**, and **thermoreceptors**.

☐ 3. Explain how cells communicate by **cell signalling**. Recognise types of cell signalling in neuronal and hormonal systems, e.g. endocrine signalling in hormonal systems and paracrine signalling at synapses.

Principles of homeostasis

pages 31-36

☐ 4. Explain the role of **homeostasis** in providing independence from the fluctuating external environment.

☐ 5. Using examples, explain the principles of **negative feedback**, identifying how it stabilises systems against excessive change. Explain the role of **receptors**, **effectors**, and negative feedback in homeostasis.

☐ 6. Describe examples of **positive feedback** in biological systems, explaining how it has an amplifying effect to bring about a specific result. Explain how positive feedback is suppressed once a certain result has been achieved.

☐ 7. Explain how the structure of the nervous system enables reception and response to stimuli. Describe examples of negative feedback operating in nervous systems.

☐ 8. Describe the role of endocrine system in homeostasis. Explain how hormones act on **target cells** and why they have wide-ranging physiological effects. Explain the role of feedback mechanisms in regulating hormone levels. Contrast the speed of nervous and endocrine responses.

☐ 9. Recognise the interdependence and roles of the nervous and hormonal systems in maintaining homeostasis in mammals.

Thermoregulation

pages 37-42

☐ 10. Contrast **thermoregulation** in an **ectotherm** (e.g. a reptile) and in an **endothermic homeotherm** (e.g. a placental mammal). Describe the mechanisms involved in heat production, conservation, and loss, and identify the degree of tolerance to fluctuations in body temperature.

☐ 11. Describe the physiological and behavioural responses used to regulate body temperature, including:
(a) Hypothalamus (heat gain and heat loss centres).
(b) Autonomic nervous system and the role of effectors in skin and muscles.
(c) Thermoreceptors in the skin (hot/cold receptors).
(d) Voluntary activity such as changes in behaviour.

Periodicals:
Listings for this chapter are on page 340

Weblinks:
www.biozone.co.uk/weblink/OCR-A2-2832.html

Detecting Changing States

A stimulus is any physical or chemical change in the environment capable of provoking a response in an organism. Animals respond to stimuli in order to survive. Stimuli may be either external (outside the organism) or internal (within its body). Some of the stimuli to which animals respond are described below. The sense organs that detect and respond to these stimuli in humans are also described, together with some examples of sensory perception in other animal groups. Note that sensory receptors respond only to specific stimuli. The sense organs an animal possesses therefore determine how it perceives the world.

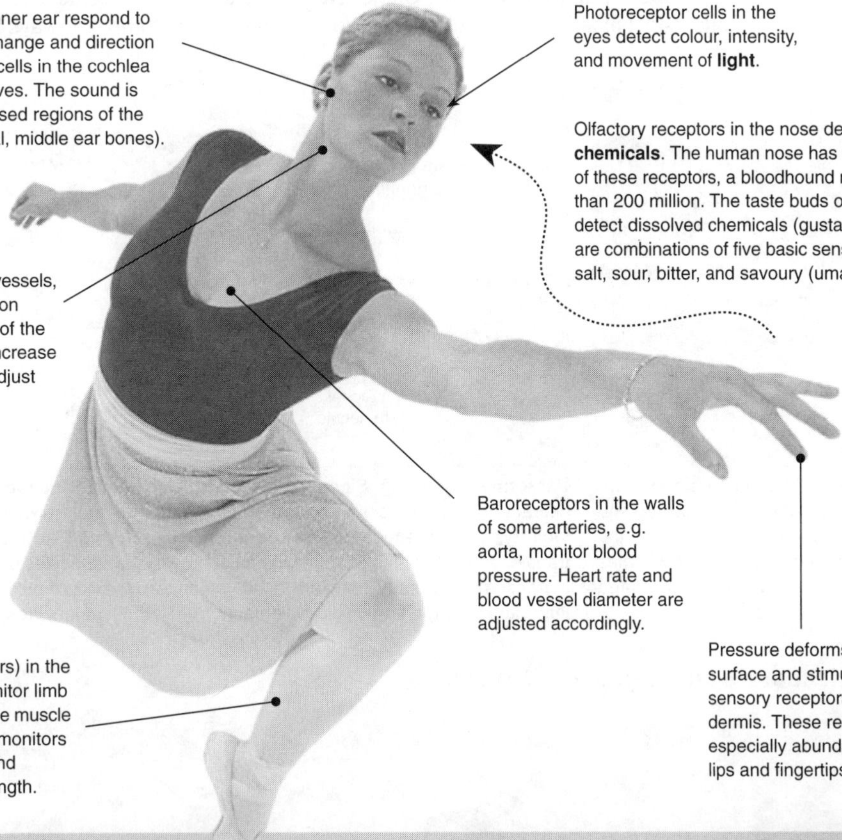

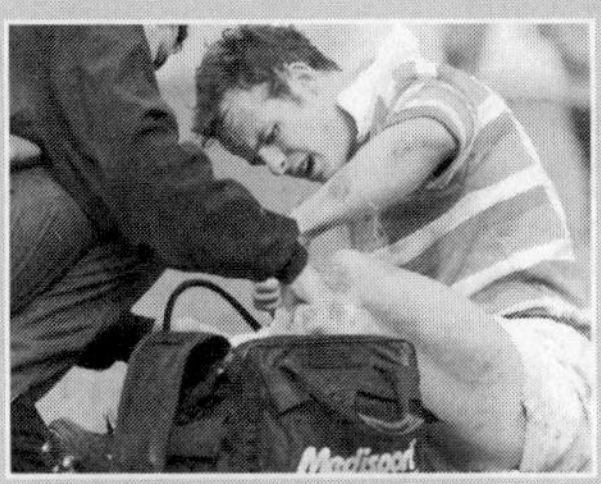
Pain and temperature are detected by simple nerve endings in the skin. Deep tissue injury is sometimes felt on the skin as referred pain.

Humans rely heavily on their hearing when learning to communicate; without it, speech and language development are more difficult.

The vibration receptors in the limbs of arthropods are sensitive to movement: either sound or vibration (as caused by struggling prey).

The chemosensory Jacobson's organ in the roof of the mouth of reptiles (e.g. snakes) enables them to detect chemical stimuli.

Breathing and heart rates are regulated in response to sensory input from chemoreceptors.

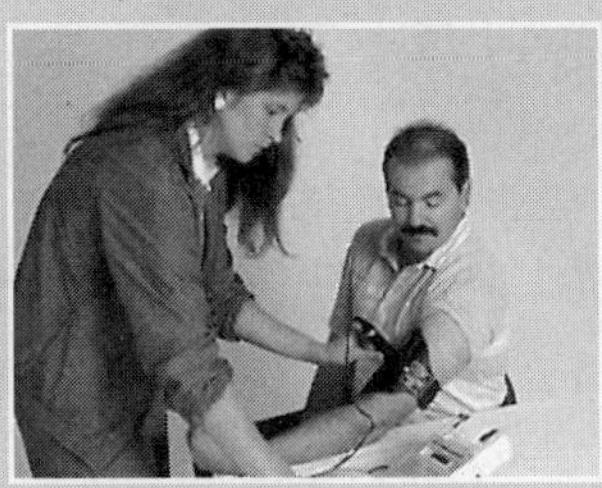
Baroreceptors and osmoreceptors act together to keep blood pressure and volume within narrow limits.

Many insects, such as these ants, rely on chemical sense for location of food and communication.

Jacobson's organ is also present in mammals and is used to detect sexual receptivity in potential mates.

1. Provide a concise definition of a stimulus: ______________________________

____

2. (a) Name one external stimulus and its sensory receptor: ______________________________

(b) Name one internal stimulus and its sensory receptor: ______________________________

Cell Signalling

Cells use **signals** (chemical messengers) to gather information about, and respond to, changes in their cellular environment and for communication between cells. The signalling and response process is called the **signal transduction pathway**, and often involves a number of enzymes and molecules in a **signal cascade** which causes a large response in the target cell. Cell signalling pathways are categorised primarily on the distance over which the signal molecule travels to reach its target cell, and generally fall into three categories. The **endocrine** pathway involves the transport of hormones over large distances through the circulatory system. During **paracrine** signalling, the signal travels an intermediate distance to act upon neighbouring cells. **Autocrine** signalling involves a cell producing and reacting to its own signal. These three pathways are described below.

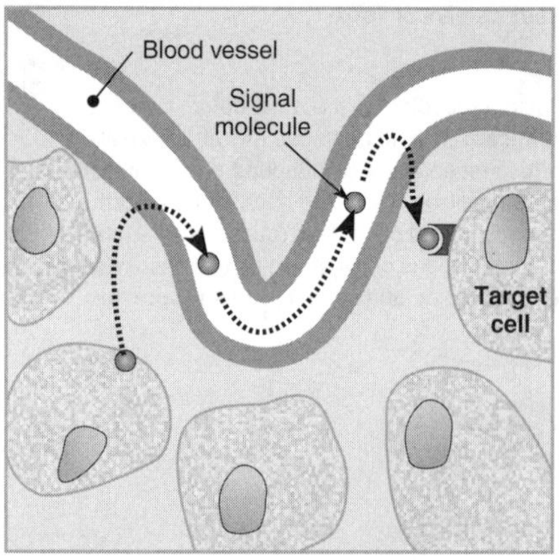

Endocrine signalling: Hormone signals are released by ductless endocrine glands and carried long distances through the body by the circulatory system to the target cells. Examples include sex hormones, growth factors and neurohormones such as dopamine.

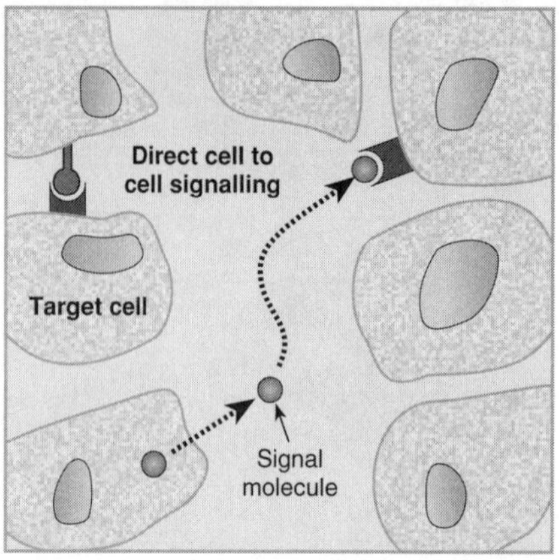

Paracrine signalling: Signals released from a cell act upon target cells within the immediate vicinity. The chemical messenger can be transferred through the extracellular fluid (e.g. at synapses) or directly between cells, which is important during embryonic development.

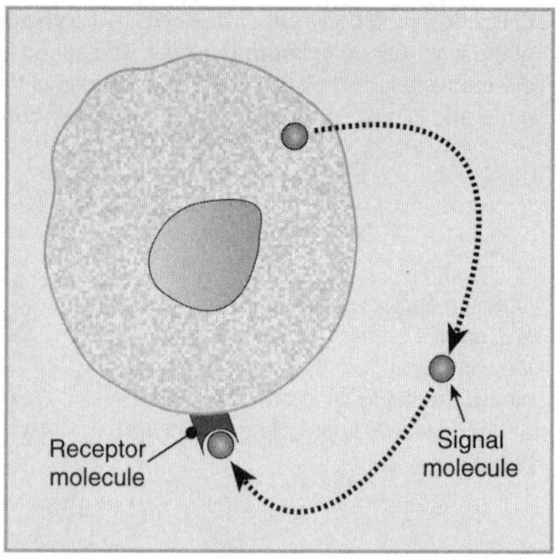

Autocrine signalling: Cells produce and react to their own signals. In vertebrates, when a foreign antibody enters the body, some T-lymphocytes produce a growth factor to stimulate their own production. The increased number of T-lymphocytes helps to fight the infection.

Signalling Receptors and Signalling Molecules

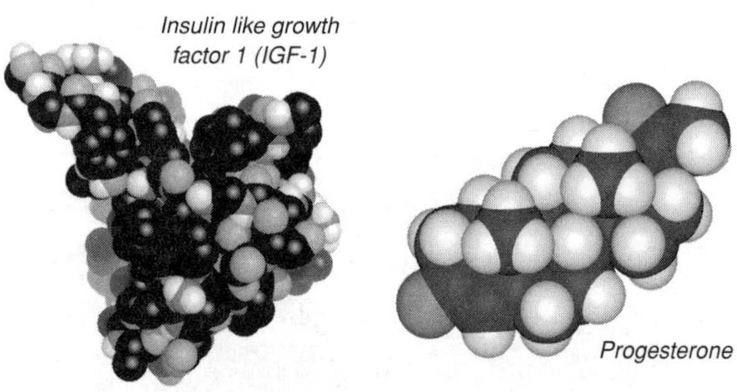

Examples of cell signalling molecules

The binding sites of cell receptors are very specific; they only bind certain **ligands** (signal molecules). This stops them from reacting to every signal bombarding the cell. Receptors fall into two main categories:

- **Cytoplasmic receptors**
Cytoplasmic receptors, located within the cell cytoplasm, bind ligands which are able to cross the plasma membrane unaided.

- **Transmembrane receptors**
These span the cell membrane and bind ligands which cannot cross the plasma membrane on their own. They have an extra-cellular domain outside the cell, and an intracellular domain within the cell cytosol. Ion channels, protein kinases and G-protein linked receptors are examples of transmembrane receptors (see diagram on right).

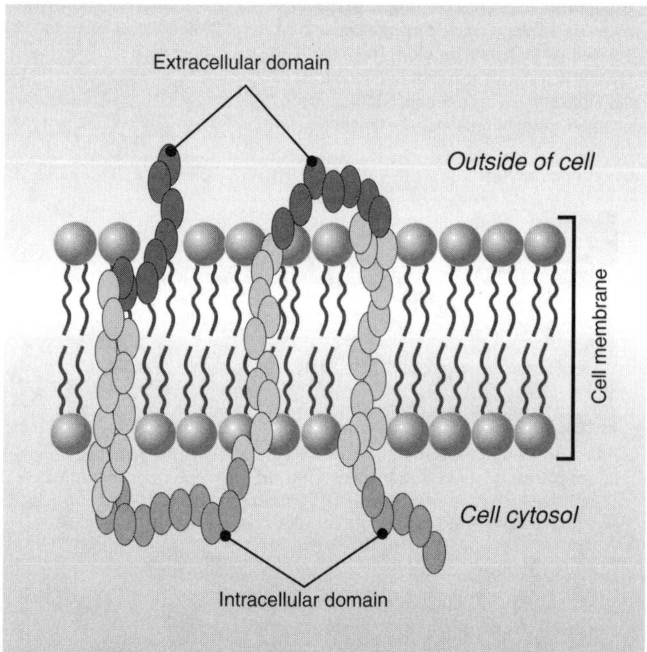

Structure of a transmembrane receptor

1. Briefly describe the three types of cell signalling:

(a) ______________________________

(b) ______________________________

(c) ______________________________

2. Identify the components that all three cell signalling types have in common: ______________________________

____

____

Principles of Homeostasis

Homeostasis the relative physiological constancy of the body, despite external fluctuations. Homeostasis of the internal environment is an essential feature of complex animals and it is the job of the body's **organ systems** to maintain it, even as they make necessary exchanges with the environment. Homeostatic control systems have three functional components: a receptor to detect change, a control centre, and an effector to direct an appropriate response. In **negative feedback** systems, movement away from a steady state triggers a mechanism to counteract further change in that direction. Using negative feedback systems, the body counteracts disturbances and restores the steady state. **Positive feedback** is also used in physiological systems, but to a lesser extent since positive feedback leads to the response escalating in the same direction.

Organ systems maintain a constant internal environment that provides for the needs of all the body's cells, making it possible for animals to move through different and often highly variable external environments. This representation of a mammal shows how organ systems permit exchanges with the environment. The exchange surfaces of organ systems are usually internal, but may be connected to the environment via openings on the body surface.

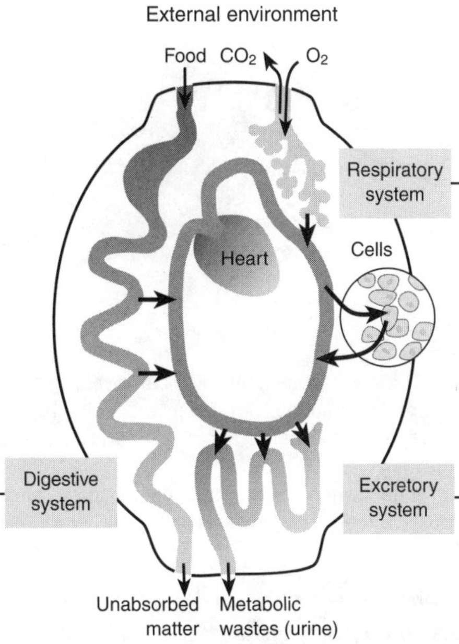

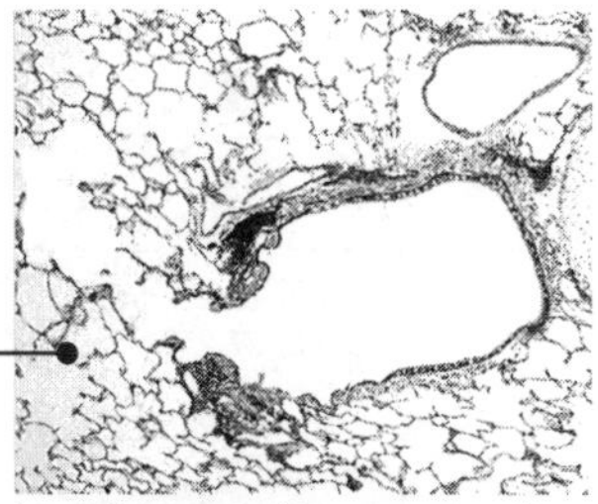

Lung tissue provides an expansive, moist surface for gas exchange.

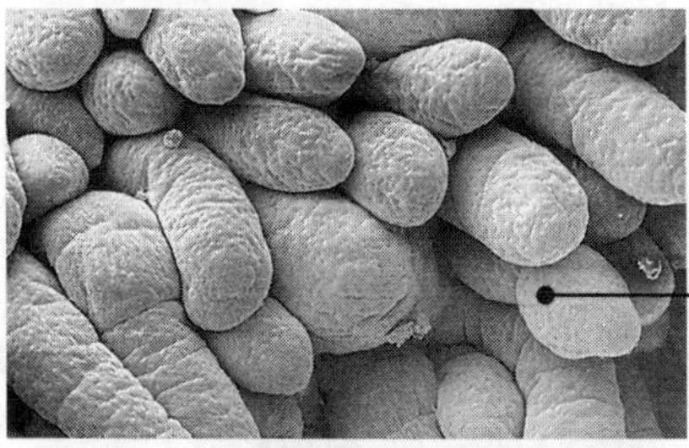

The finger-like villi of the small intestine greatly expand the surface area for nutrient absorption.

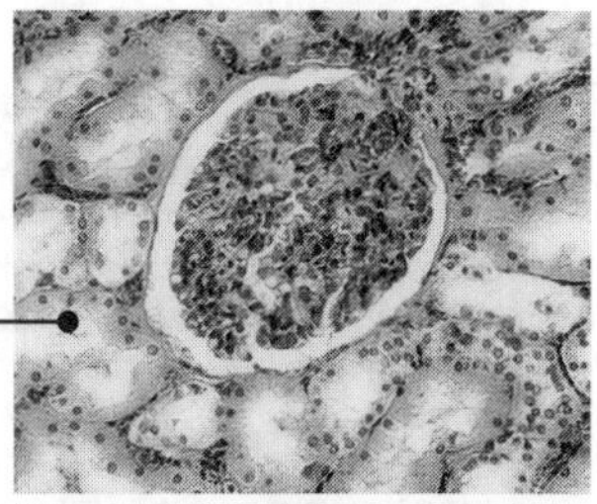

Kidney tubules exchange chemicals with the blood through capillaries.

All photos this page: EII

Negative Feedback and Control Systems

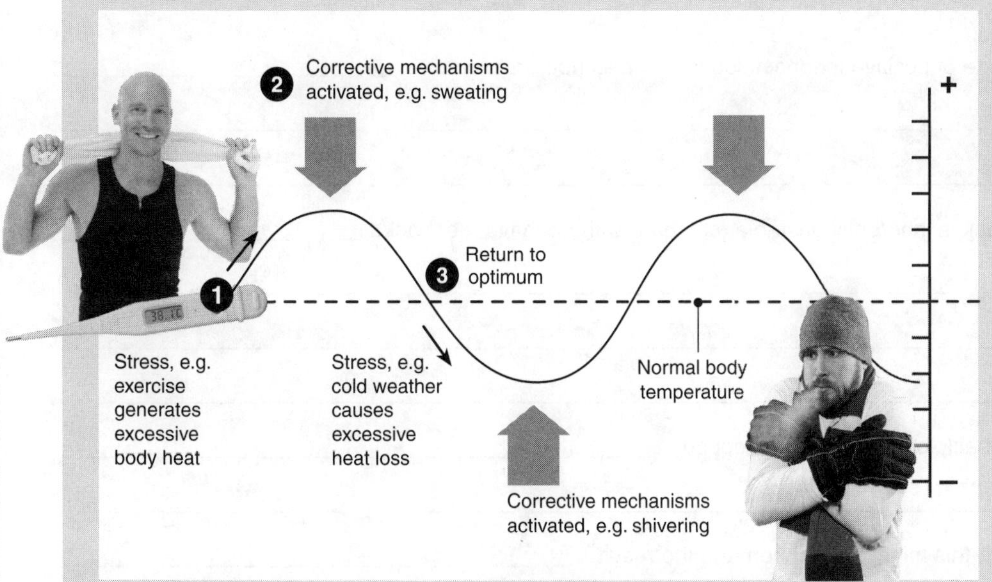

1. A stressor, e.g. exercise, takes the internal environment away from optimum.
2. Stress is detected by receptors and corrective mechanisms (e.g. sweating or shivering) are activated.
3. Corrective mechanisms act to restore optimum conditions.

Negative feedback acts to counteract departures from steady state. The diagram shows how stress is counteracted in the case of body temperature.

1. Describe the three main components of a regulatory control system in the human body: ____________________

____

____

2. Explain how negative feedback mechanisms maintain homeostasis in a variable environment: ____________________

____

____

____

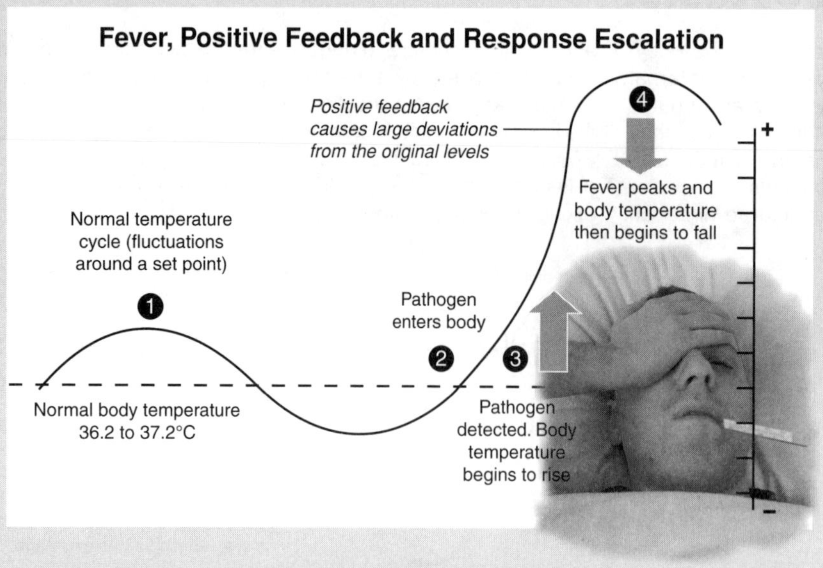

1. Body temperature fluctuates on a normal, regular basis around a narrow set point.
2. Pathogen enters the body.
3. The body detects the pathogen and macrophages attack it. Macrophages release interleukins which stimulate the hypothalamus to increase prostaglandin production and reset the body's thermostat to a higher 'fever' level by shivering (the chill phase).
4. The fever breaks when the infection subsides. Levels of circulating interleukins (and other fever-associated chemicals) fall, and the body's thermostat is reset to normal. This ends the positive feedback escalation and normal controls resume. If the infection persists, the escalation may continue, and the fever may intensify. Body temperatures in excess of 43°C are often fatal or result in brain damage.

Unlike negative feedback, positive feedback will push physiological levels out of the normal range. Positive feedback is inherently unstable, but it has a specific biological purpose. It will cause an escalation in response in order to achieve a particular result.

Normally, a positive feedback loop is ended when the natural resolution is reached. Labour is another example of where positive feedback plays an important role.

LABOUR: Positive feedback: oxytocin and uterine contraction. Result: delivery of infant. During childbirth (far right), the release of oxytocin intensifies the contractions of the uterus so that labour proceeds to its conclusion. The birth itself restores the system by removing the initiating stimulus.

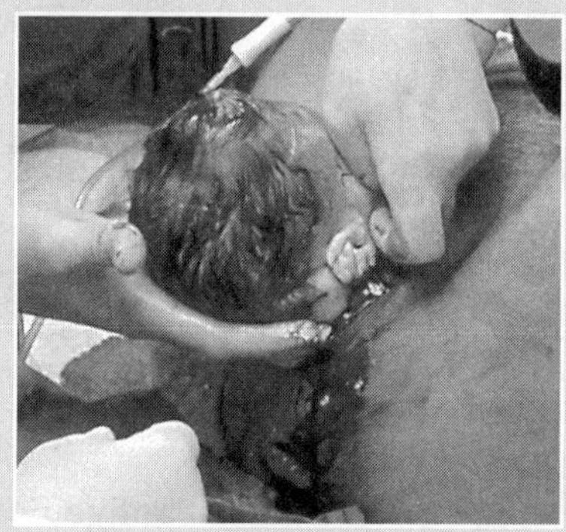

3. (a) Explain the biological purpose of positive feedback loops and describe an example:

(b) Explain why positive feedback is inherently unstable (compare with negative feedback):

(c) Explain how a positive feedback loop is normally stopped:

(d) Describe a situation in which this might not happen and the result:

4. Explain the value in having separate negative feedback mechanisms to control departures in different directions:

Maintaining Homeostasis

The various organ systems of the body act to maintain homeostasis through a combination of hormonal and nervous mechanisms. In everyday life, the body must regulate respiratory gases, protect itself against agents of disease (pathogens), maintain fluid and salt balance, regulate energy and nutrient supply, and maintain a constant body temperature. All these must be coordinated and appropriate responses made to incoming stimuli. In addition, the body must be able to repair itself when injured and be capable of reproducing (leaving offspring).

Regulating Respiratory Gases

Oxygen must be delivered to all cells and carbon dioxide (a waste product of cellular respiration) must be removed. **Breathing** brings in oxygen and expels CO_2, and the cardiovascular and lymphatic systems circulate these respiratory gases (the oxygen mostly bound to haemoglobin). The rate of breathing is varied according to oxygen demands (as detected by CO_2 levels in the blood).

Coping with Pathogens

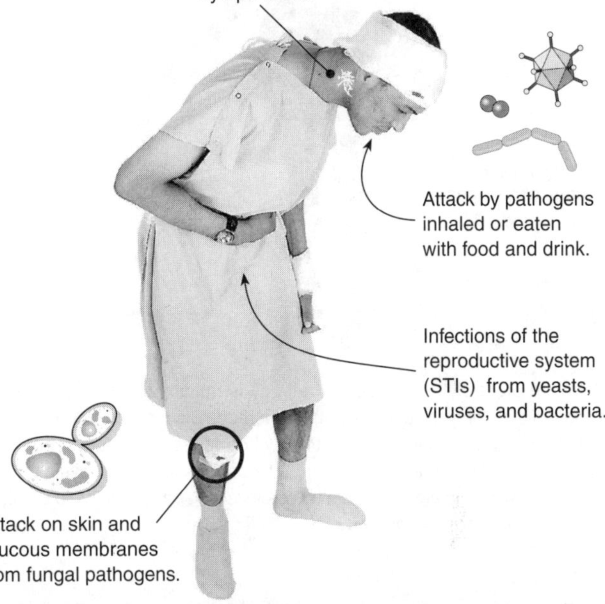

All of us are under constant attack from pathogens (disease causing organisms). The body has a number of mechanisms that help to prevent the entry of pathogens and limit the damage they cause if they do enter the body. The skin, the digestive system, and the immune system are all involved in the body's defence, while the cardiovascular and lymphatic systems circulate the cells and antimicrobial substances involved.

Maintaining Nutrient Supply

Food and drink must be taken in to maintain the body's energy supplies. The digestive system makes these nutrients available, and the cardiovascular system distributes them throughout the body. Food intake is regulated largely through nervous mechanisms while hormones control the regulation of cellular uptake of glucose.

Repairing Injuries

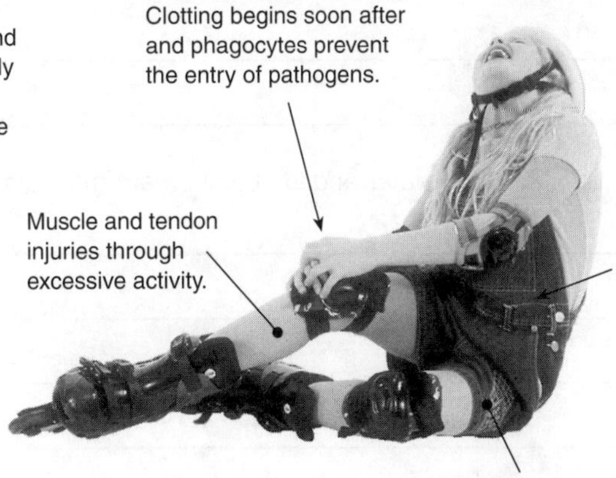

Damage to body tissues triggers the **inflammatory response** and white blood cells move to the injury site. The inflammatory response is started (and ended) by chemical signals (e.g. from histamine and prostaglandins) released when tissue is damaged. The cardiovascular and lymphatic systems distribute the cells and molecules involved.

Maintaining Fluid and Ion Balance

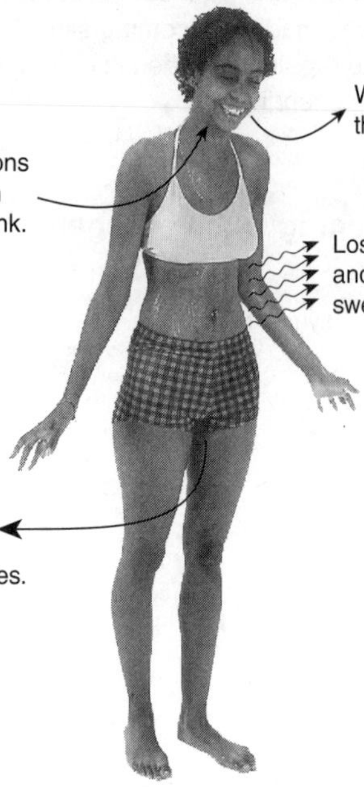

Fluid and electrolyte balance in the body is maintained by the kidneys (although the skin is also important). Osmoreceptors monitor blood volume and bring about the release of regulatory hormones; the kidneys regulate reabsorption of water and sodium from blood in response to levels of the hormones ADH and aldosterone. The cardiovascular and lymphatic system distribute fluids around the body.

Coordinating Responses

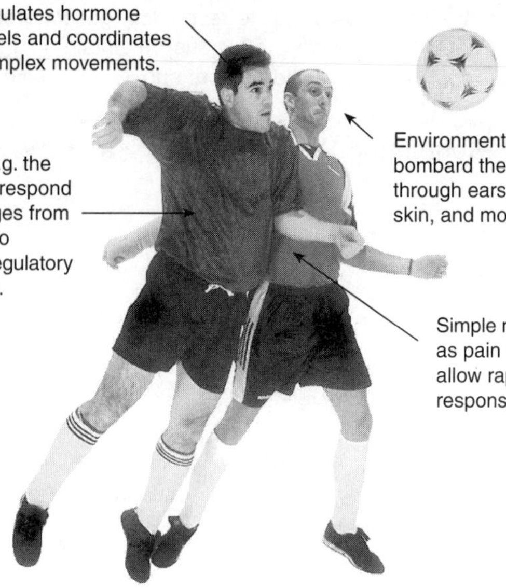

The body is constantly bombarded by stimuli from the environment. The brain sorts these stimuli into those that require a response and those that do not. Responses are coordinated via nervous or hormonal controls. Simple nervous responses (reflexes) act quickly. Hormones, which are distributed by the cardiovascular and lymphatic systems, take longer to produce a response and the response is more prolonged.

1. Describe two mechanisms that operate to restore homeostasis after infection by a pathogen:

   (a) ______________________________

   (b) ______________________________

2. Describe two mechanisms by which responses to stimuli are brought about and coordinated:

   (a) ______________________________

   (b) ______________________________

3. Explain two ways in which water and ion balance are maintained. Name the organ(s) and any hormones involved:

   (a) ______________________________

   (b) ______________________________

4. Explain two ways in which the body regulates its respiratory gases during exercise:

   (a) ______________________________

   (b) ______________________________

Nervous Regulatory Systems

An essential feature of living organisms is their ability to coordinate their activities. In multicellular animals, such as mammals, detecting and responding to environmental change, and regulating the internal environment (homeostasis) is brought about by two coordinating systems: the nervous and endocrine systems. Although these two systems are quite different structurally, they frequently interact to coordinate behaviour and physiology. The nervous system contains cells called neurones (or nerve cells). Neurones are specialised to transmit information in the form of electrochemical impulses (action potentials). Impulses can be transmitted over considerable distances and the response is very precise and rapid. Whilst it is extraordinarily complex, comprising millions of neural connections, its basic plan (below, left) is quite simple, structured around reception of sensory input, integration or processing of the information, and formulation of a response.

Coordination by the Nervous System

The vertebrate nervous system consists of the central nervous system (brain and spinal cord), and the nerves and receptors outside it (peripheral nervous system). Sensory input to receptors comes via stimuli. Information about the effect of a response is provided by feedback mechanisms so that the system can be readjusted. The basic organisation of the nervous system can be simplified into a few key components: the sensory receptors, a central nervous system processing point, and the effectors which bring about the response (below):

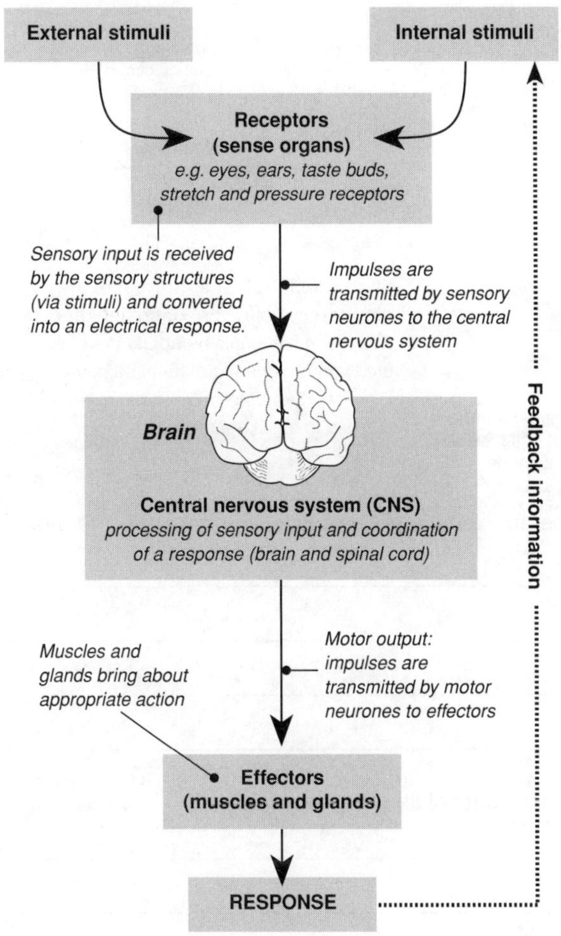

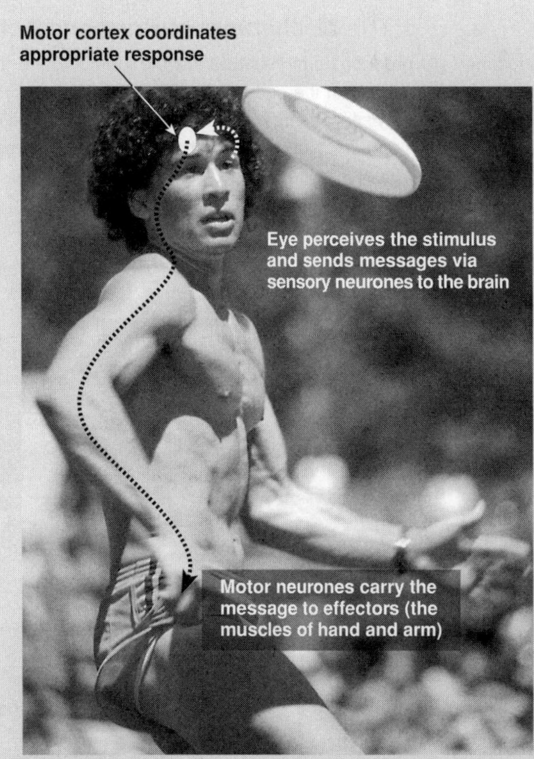

In the example above, the approach of the frisbee is perceived by the eye. The motor cortex of the brain integrates the sensory message. Coordination of hand and body orientation is brought about through motor neurones to the muscles.

Comparison of nervous and hormonal control

	Nervous control	Hormonal control
Communication	*Impulses across synapses*	*Hormones in the blood*
Speed	*Very rapid (within a few milliseconds)*	*Relatively slow (over minutes, hours, or longer)*
Duration	*Short term and reversible*	*Longer lasting effects*
Target pathway	*Specific (through nerves) to specific cells*	*Hormones broadcast to target cells everywhere*
Action	*Causes glands to secrete or muscles to contract*	*Causes changes in metabolic activity*

1. Identify the three basic components of a nervous system and explain how they function to maintain homeostasis:

(a) ____________________

(b) ____________________

(c) ____________________

2. Describe two differences between nervous control and endocrine (hormonal) control of body systems:

(a) ____________________

(b) ____________________

Related activities: *Hormonal Regulatory Systems*
Web links: *Nervous System Animation*

Hormonal Regulatory Systems

The endocrine system regulates the body's processes by releasing chemical messengers called **hormones** into the bloodstream. Hormones are potent chemical regulators: they are produced in minute quantities yet can have a large effect on metabolism. The endocrine system is made up of endocrine cells (organised into endocrine glands), and the hormones they produce. Unlike exocrine glands (e.g. sweat and salivary glands), endocrine glands are **ductless glands**, secreting hormones directly into the bloodstream rather than through a duct or tube. Some organs (e.g. the pancreas) have both endocrine and exocrine regions, but these are structurally and functionally distinct. The stimulus for hormone release may be **hormonal** (e.g. action of hypothalamic releasing hormones), a **humoral** trigger (such as high blood glucose), or **neural** (e.g. sympathetic nervous system stimulation). The basics of hormonal action and regulation are described below.

The Mechanism of Hormone Action

Endocrine cells produce hormones and secrete them into the bloodstream where they are distributed throughout the body. Although hormones are broadcast throughout the body, they affect only specific target cells. These target cells have receptors on the plasma membrane which recognise and bind the hormone (see inset, below right). The binding of hormone and receptor triggers the response in the target cell. Cells are unresponsive to a hormone if they do not have the appropriate receptors.

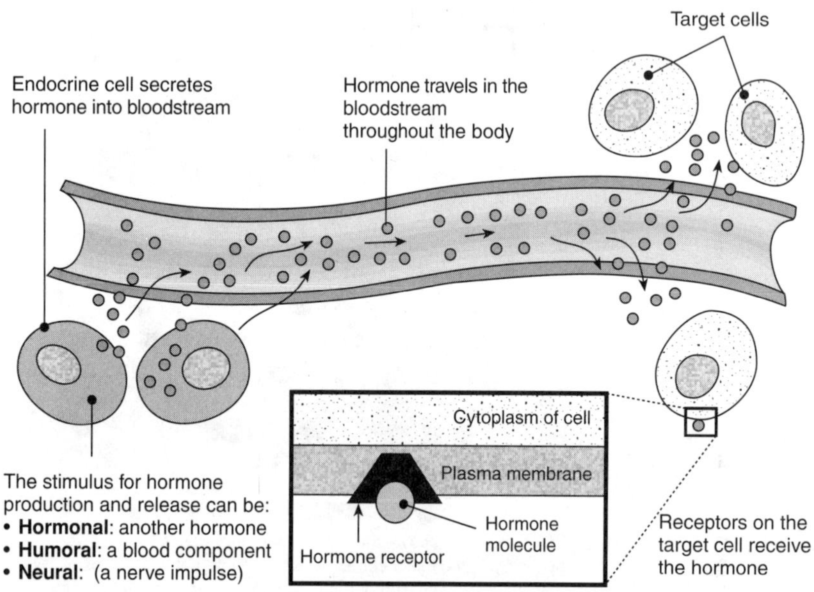

Antagonistic Hormones

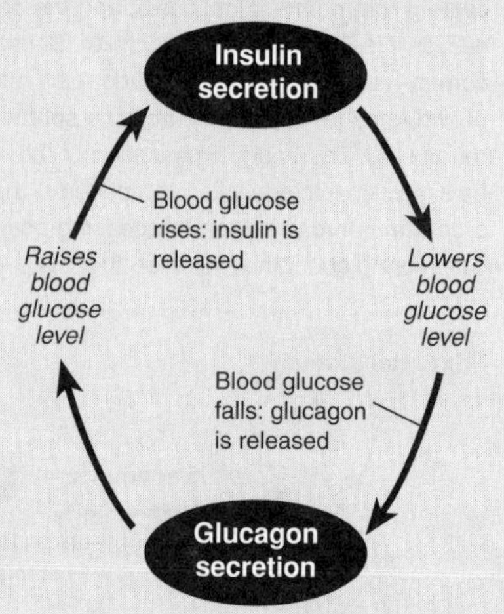

The effects of one hormone are often counteracted by an opposing hormone. Feedback mechanisms adjust the balance of the two hormones to maintain a physiological function. Example: insulin decreases blood glucose and glucagon raises it.

1. (a) Explain what is meant by **antagonistic hormones** and describe an example of how two such hormones operate:

   Example:

   (b) Explain the role of feedback mechanisms in adjusting hormone levels (explain using an example if this is helpful):

2. Explain how a hormone can bring about a response in target cells even though all cells may receive the hormone:

3. Explain why hormonal control differs from nervous system control with respect to the following:

   (a) The speed of hormonal responses is slower:

   (b) Hormonal responses are generally longer lasting:

Control of Body Temperature

The process of controlling body temperature is called thermoregulation. For many years, animals were classified as either homeotherms or homoiotherms (= constant body temperature) or poikilotherms (= variable body temperature). Unfortunately, these terms are not particularly accurate for many animals; for example, some mammals (typical homeotherms), may have unstable body temperatures. A more recent, thermal classification of animals is based on the source of the body heat: whether it is largely from the environment (**ectothermic**) or from metabolic activity (**endothermic**). This classification can be more accurately applied to most animals but, in reality, many animals still fall somewhere between the two extremes.

How Body Temperature Varies

Aquatic invertebrates like jellyfish are true poikilotherms: their temperature is the same as the environment.

Tuna and some of the larger sharks can maintain body temperatures up to 14°C above the water temperature.

Hibernating rodents and bats let their body temperature drop to well below what is typical for most mammals.

Most birds and mammals maintain a body temperature that varies less than 2°C: they are true homeotherms.

Increasingly homeothermic →

Poikilothermic

Body temperature varies with the environmental temperature. Traditionally includes all animals other than birds and mammals, but many reptiles, some large insects and some large fish are not true poikilotherms because they may maintain body temperatures that are different from the surrounding environment.

Homeothermic

Body temperature remains almost constant despite environmental fluctuations. Traditionally includes birds and mammals, which typically maintain body temperatures close to 37-38°C. Many reptiles are partially homeothermic and achieve often quite constant body temperatures through behavioural mechanisms.

Source of Body Heat

With a few exceptions, most fish are fully ectothermic. Unlike many reptiles they do not usually thermoregulate.

Snakes use heat energy from the environment to increase their body temperature for activity.

Some large insects like bumblebees may raise their temperature for short periods through muscular activity.

Mammals (and birds) achieve high body temperatures through metabolic activity and reduction of heat losses.

Increasingly endothermic →

Ectothermic

Ectotherms depend on the environment for their heat energy. The term ectotherm is often equated with poikilotherm, although they are not the same. Poikilotherms are also ectotherms but many ectotherms may regulate body temperature (often within narrow limits) by changing their behaviour (e.g. snakes and lizards).

Endothermic

Endotherms rely largely on metabolic activity for their heat energy. Since they usually maintain a constant body temperature, most endotherms are also homeotherms. As well as birds and mammals, some fast swimming fish, like tuna, and some large insects may also use muscular activity to maintain a high body temperature.

Daily Temperature Variations in Ectotherms and Endotherms

Ectotherm: Diurnal lizard (top right)

Body temperature is regulated by behaviour so that it does not rise above 40°C. Basking increases heat uptake from the sun. Activity occurs when body temperature is high. Underground burrows are used for retreat.

Endotherm: Human (bottom right)

Body temperature fluctuates within narrow limits over a 24 hour period. Exercise and eating increase body temperature for a short time. Body temperature falls during rest and is partly controlled by an internal rhythm.

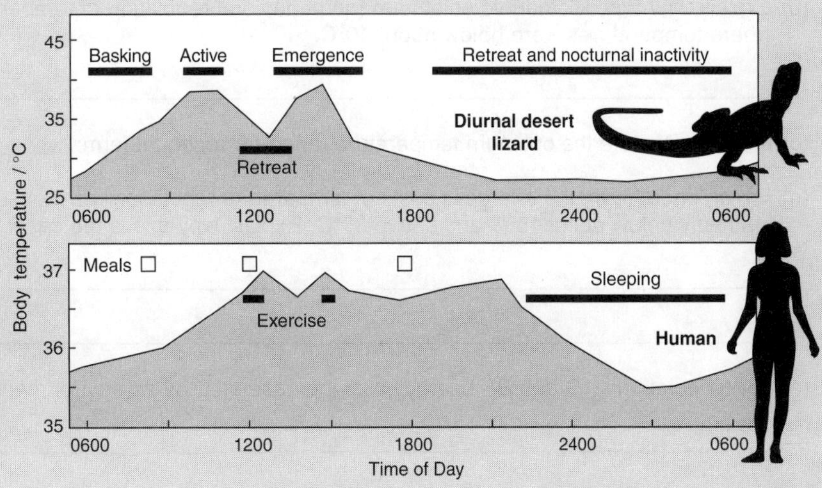

Related activities: *Mechanisms of Thermoregulation, Thermoregulation in Humans*
Web links: *Control, Regulation and Feedback, Frozen Alive!*

1. (a) Explain what is meant by a homeothermic endotherm:

(b) Explain why the term poikilotherm is not a good term for classifying many terrestrial lizards and snakes:

2. Ectotherms will often maintain high, relatively constant body temperatures for periods in spite of environmental fluctuations, yet they also tolerate marked declines in body temperature to levels lower than are tolerated by endotherms.
(a) Describe the advantages of letting body temperature fluctuate with the environment (particularly at low temperatures):

(b) Suggest why ectothermy is regarded as an adaptation to low or variable food supplies:

3. Some endotherms do not always maintain a high body temperature. Some, such as small rodents, allow their body temperatures to fall during hibernation. Explain the advantage of this behaviour:

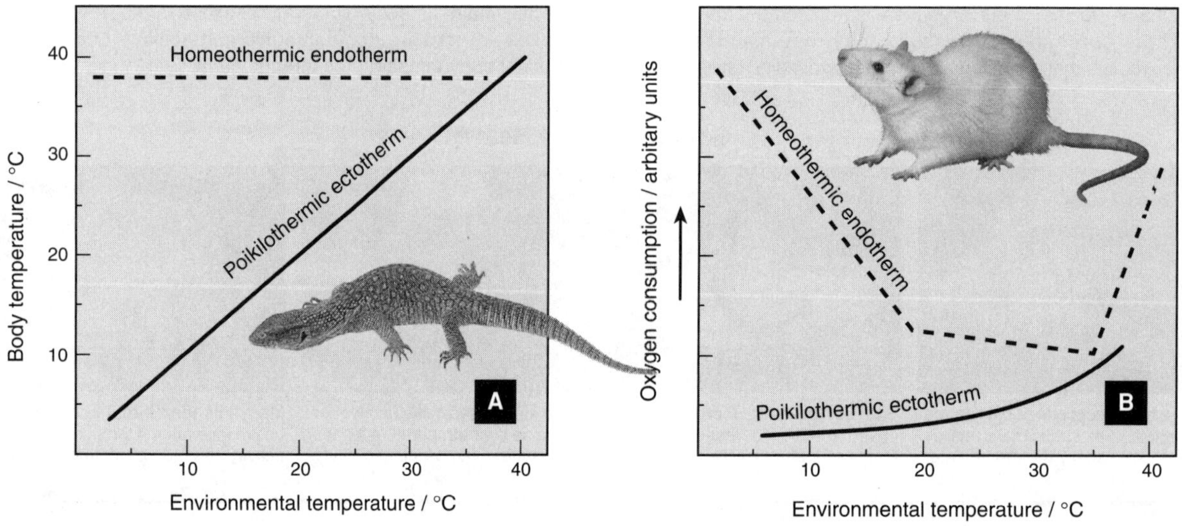

4. The two graphs above illustrate the differences in temperature regulation between a homeothermic endotherm and a poikilothermic ectotherm (such as a fish). Graph A shows change in body temperature with environmental temperature. Graph B shows change in oxygen consumption with environmental temperature. Use the graphs to answer the following:
(a) Explain how ectotherms and endotherms differ in their response to changes in environmental temperature (graph **A**):

(b) Explain why a poikilothermic ectotherm (no behavioral regulation of temperature) would be limited to environments where temperatures were below about 40°C:

(c) In graph **B**, state the optimum temperature range for an endotherm:

(d) For an endotherm, the energetic costs of temperature regulation (as measured by oxygen consumption) increase markedly below about 15°C and above 35°C. Explain why this is the case:

(e) For an ectotherm (Graph B), energy costs increase steadily as environmental temperature increases. Explain why:

Mechanisms of Thermoregulation

For a body to maintain a constant temperature heat losses must equal heat gains. Heat exchanges with the environment occur via three mechanisms: **conduction** (direct heat transfer), **radiation** (indirect heat transfer), and **evaporation**. The importance of each of these depends on environment. For example, there is no evaporative loss in water but such losses in air can be very high.

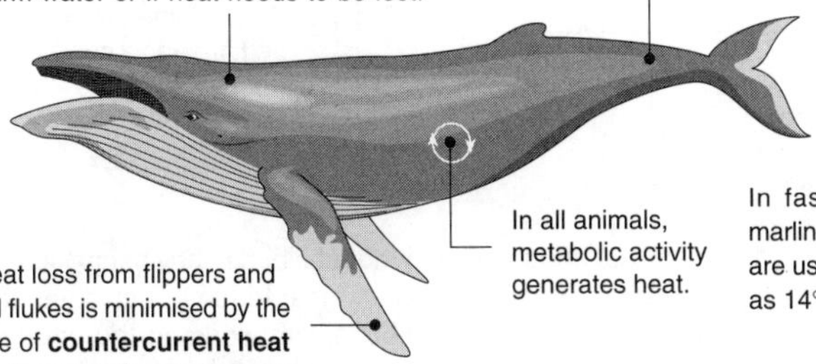

Water has a great capacity to transfer heat away from organisms; its cooling power can be more than 50 times greater than that of air. For most aquatic animals (with the exception of aquatic birds and mammals and a few fish) heat retention is impossible. Instead, they carry out their metabolic activities at the ambient temperature. For most marine organisms this does not fluctuate much.

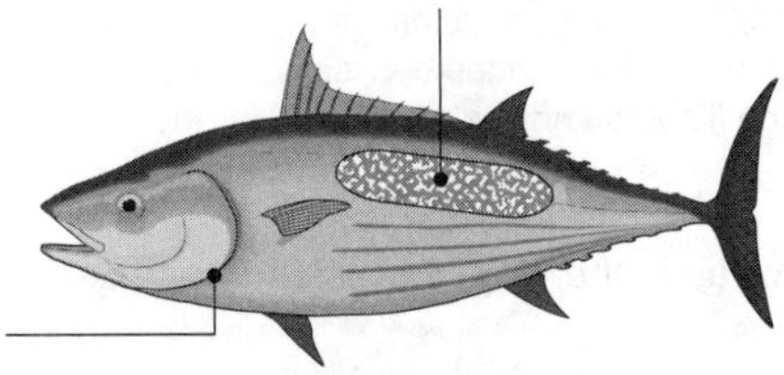

Temperature regulation mechanisms in water

- Low metabolic activity
- Heat generation from metabolic activity
- Insulation layer of blubber
- Changes in circulation patterns when swimming
- Large body size
- Heat exchange systems in limbs or high activity muscle

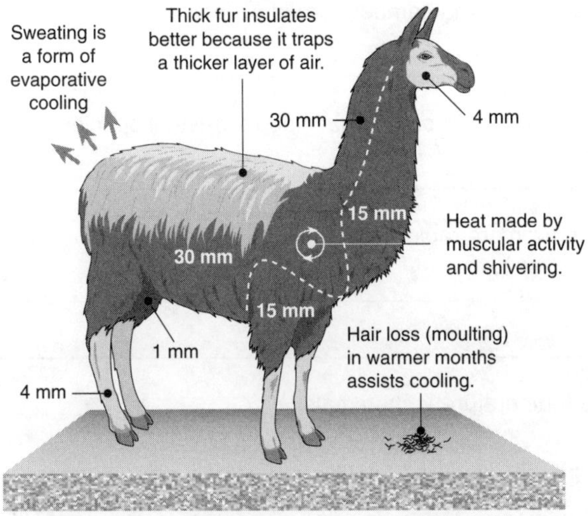

For most mammals, **fur thickness** varies around the body. Thermoregulation is assisted by adopting body positions that expose or cover areas of thin fur (figures above are for the llama-like *guanaco*).

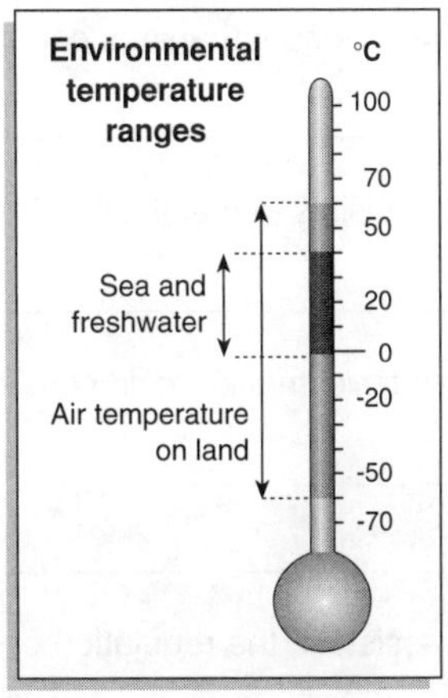

Temperature regulation mechanisms in air

- Behaviour or habitat choice
- Heat generation from metabolic activity
- Insulation (fat, fur, feathers)
- Changes in blood flow
- Large body size
- Sweating and panting
- Tolerance of fluctuation in body temperature

Animals adapted to temperature extremes (hot or cold) can often tolerate large fluctuations in their body temperature before they become stressed. In camels, the body temperature may fluctuate up to 7°C (34°C to 41°C) over a 24 hour period.

Panting to lose accumulated heat is important in dogs, which have sweat glands only on the pads of their feet.

Circulation changes slow heat loss in water and speed heat gain when basking on land in marine iguanas.

Thick blubber and large body size in seals and other marine mammals provide an effective insulation.

Mammals and birds in cold climates, like the musk oxen above, cluster together to retain body heat.

Behaviours to reduce heat uptake via conduction e.g. standing on two legs, are important in desert lizards.

Bumblebees can heat up their flight muscles by "shivering". Their thick fuzz helps conserve the heat they produce.

Thick hair, fur or wool traps air in a layer next to the skin. This insulating air layer reduces heat loss and slows heat gain.

The plumage of birds acts similarly to fur or hair in mammals. The feathers trap air which slows heat gain and loss.

Countercurrent Heat Exchange Systems

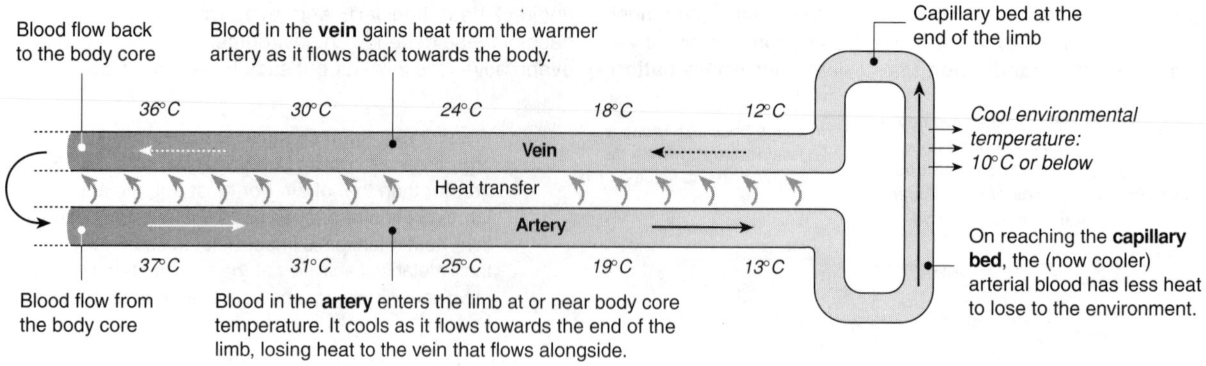

Countercurrent heat exchange systems occur in both aquatic and terrestrial animals as an adaptation to maintaining a stable core temperature. The diagram illustrates the general principle of countercurrent heat exchangers: heat is exchanged between incoming and outgoing blood. In the flippers and fins of whales and dolphins, and the legs of aquatic birds, they minimise heat loss. In some terrestrial animals adapted to hot climates, the countercurrent exchange mechanism works in the opposite way to prevent the head from overheating: venous blood cools the arterial blood before it supplies the brain.

1. (a) Explain how water differs from air in the way in which it transmits heat away from the body of an organism:

   (b) Name two ways in which a "warm bodied" animal can maintain its internal temperature in water:

   (c) Explain how a large body size assists in maintaining body temperature in both aquatic and terrestrial species:

   (d) Describe a way in which small terrestrial animals compensate for more rapid heat loss from a high surface area:

2. (a) Explain how thick hair or fur assists in the regulation of body temperature in mammals:

   (b) Explain why fur/hair thickness varies over different regions of a mammal's body:

   (c) Explain how you would expect fur thickness to vary between related mammal species at high and low altitude:

   (d) Explain how marine mammals compensate for lack of thick hair or fur:

3. (a) Suggest why fast swimming fish use countercurrent exchange mechanisms in their swimming muscles:

   (b) In some large sharks (e.g. white pointer and mako), countercurrent exchangers are used to maintain a higher temperature around the gut. Explain the advantage of this adaptation:

4. (a) Describe the role that group behaviour plays in temperature regulation in some animals:

   (b) Name an animal, other than musk oxen, that use this behaviour:

Thermoregulation in Humans

In humans and other placental mammals, the temperature regulation centre of the body is in the **hypothalamus**. In humans, it has a 'set point' temperature of 36.7°C. The hypothalamus responds directly to changes in core temperature and to nerve impulses from receptors in the skin. It then coordinates appropriate nervous and hormonal responses to counteract the changes and restore normal body temperature. Like a thermostat, the hypothalamus detects a return to normal temperature and the corrective mechanisms are switched off (negative feedback). Toxins produced by pathogens, or substances released from some white blood cells, cause the set point to be set to a higher temperature. This results in fever and is an important defence mechanism in the case of infection.

Counteracting Heat Loss

Heat promoting centre* in the hypothalamus monitors fall in skin or core temperature below 35.8°C and coordinates responses that generate and conserve heat. These responses are mediated primarily through the **sympathetic nerves** of the autonomic nervous system.

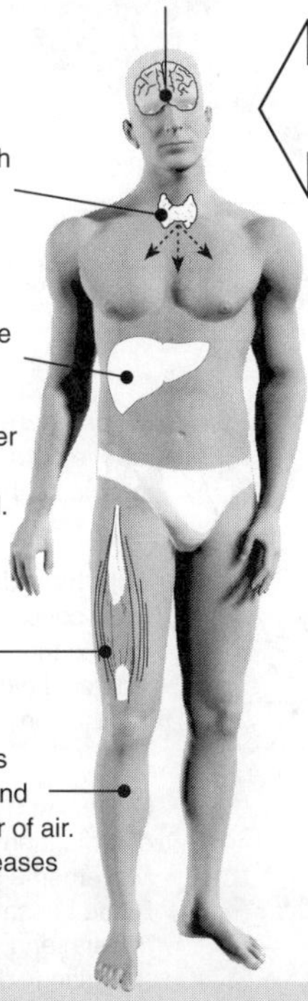

Thyroxine (together with adrenaline) **increases metabolic rate**.

Under conditions of *extreme* cold, adrenaline and thyroxine increase the energy releasing activity of the liver. Under normal conditions, the liver is thermally neutral.

Muscular activity (including **shivering**) produces internal heat.

Erector muscles of hairs contract to raise hairs and increase insulating layer of air. Blood flow to skin decreases (**vasoconstriction**).

Factors causing heat loss

- Wind chill factor accelerates heat loss through conduction.
- Heat loss due to temperature difference between the body and the environment.
- The rate of heat loss from the body is increased by being wet, by inactivity, dehydration, inadequate clothing, or shock.

Factors causing heat gain

- Gain of heat directly from the environment through radiation and conduction.
- Excessive fat deposits make it harder to lose the heat that is generated through activity.
- Heavy exercise, especially with excessive clothing.

**NOTE: The heat promoting centre is also called the "cold centre" and the heat losing centre is also called the "hot centre". We have used the terminology descriptive of the activities promoted by the centre in each case.*

Counteracting Heat Gain

Heat losing centre* in the hypothalamus monitors any rise in skin or core temperature above 37.5°C and coordinates responses that increase heat loss. These responses are mediated primarily through the **parasympathetic nerves** of the autonomic nervous system.

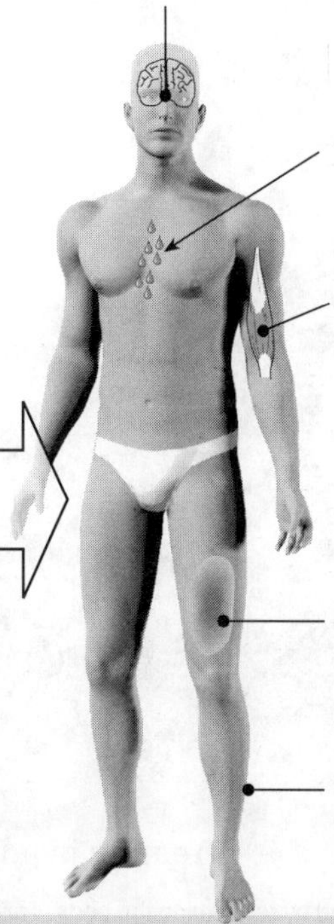

Sweating increases. Sweat cools by evaporation.

Muscle tone and **metabolic rate** are decreased. These mechanisms reduce the body's heat output.

Blood flow to skin (**vasodilation**) increases. This increases heat loss.

Erector muscles of hairs relax to flatten hairs and decrease insulating air layer.

The skin and thermoregulation

Thermoreceptors in the dermis (probably free nerve endings) detect changes in skin temperature outside the normal range and send nerve impulses to the hypothalamus, which mediates a response. Thermoreceptors are of two types: **hot thermoreceptors** detect a rise in skin temperature above 37.5°C while the **cold thermoreceptors** detect a fall below 35.8°C. Temperature regulation by the skin involves **negative feedback** because the output is fed back to the skin receptors and becomes part of a new stimulus-response cycle.

Note that the thermoreceptors detect the temperature change, but the hair erector muscles and blood vessels are the **effectors** for mediating a response.

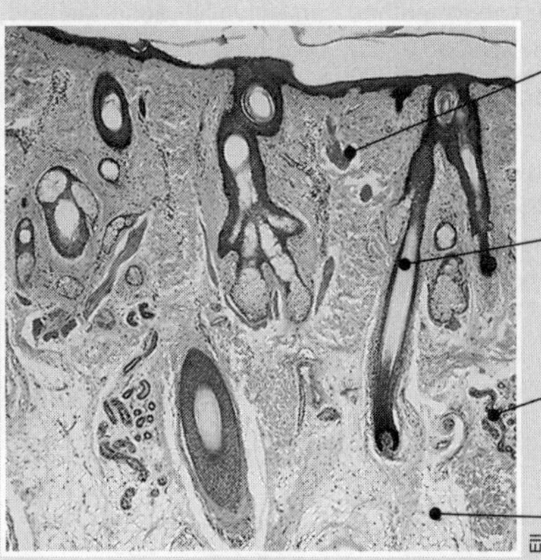

Cross section through the skin of the scalp.

Blood vessels in the dermis dilate (vasodilation) or constrict (vasoconstriction) to respectively promote or restrict heat loss.

Hairs raised or lowered to increase or decrease the thickness of the insulating air layer between the skin and the environment.

Sweat glands produce sweat in response to parasympathetic stimulation from the hypothalamus. Sweat cools through evaporation.

Fat in the subdermal layers insulates the organs against heat loss.

1. State two mechanisms by which body temperature could be reduced after intensive activity (e.g. hard exercise):

   (a) ______________________ (b) ______________________

2. Briefly state the role of the following in regulating internal body temperature:

   (a) The hypothalamus: ______________________

   (b) The skin: ______________________

   (c) Nervous input to effectors: ______________________

   (d) Hormones: ______________________

Related activities: *Control of Body Temperature, Hypothermia*
Web links: *The Hypothalamus: the Body's Thermostat*

Hypothermia

Hypothermia is a condition experienced when the core body temperature drops below 35°C. Hypothermia is caused by exposure to low temperatures, and results from the body's inability to replace the heat being lost to the environment. The condition ranges from mild to severe depending how low the body temperature has dropped. Severe hypothermia results in severe mental confusion, including inability to speak and amnesia, organ and heart failure, and death.

Maintaining a normal body temperature of around 37°C allows the body's metabolism to function optimally. At temperatures below 35°C, metabolic reactions begin to slow, resulting in a loss of coordination, difficulty in moving, and mental fatigue. Hypothermia can result from exposure to very low temperatures for a short time or to moderately low temperatures for a long time. Exposure to cold water (even just slightly cold) will produce symptoms of hypothermia far more quickly than exposure to the same temperature of air. This is because water is much more effective than air at conducting heat away from the body.

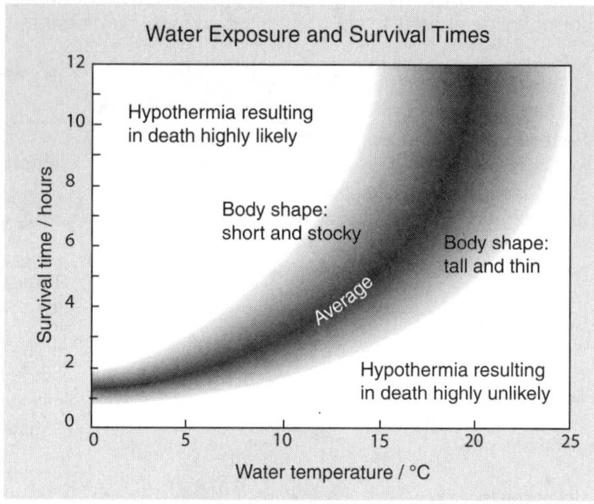

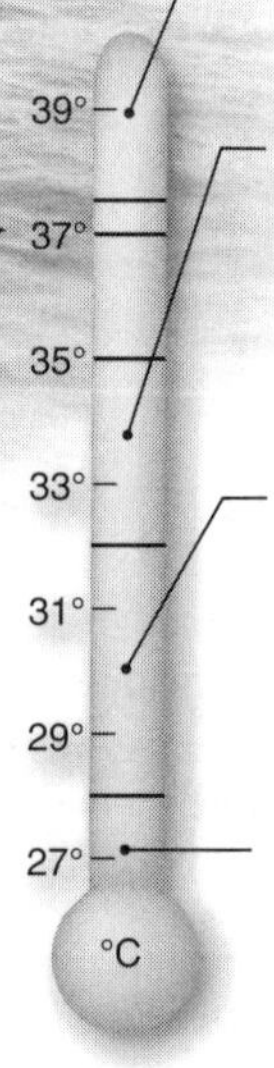

Hyperthermia: Body temperatures above normal cause metabolic problems that can lead to death.

Mild hypothermia: Shivering. Vasoconstriction reduces blood flow to the extremities. Hypertension and cold diuresis (increased urine production due to the cold).

Moderate hypothermia: Muscle coordination becomes difficult. Movements slow or laboured. Blood vessels in ears, nose, fingers, and toes constrict further resulting in these turning a blue colour. Mental confusion sets in.

Severe hypothermia: Speech fails. Mental processes become irrational, victim may enter a stupor. Organs and heart eventually fail resulting in death.

Treating hypothermia

Hypothermia is treated by rewarming the body. This must be done with extreme care because rewarming the body too quickly or with the wrong method can actually cause the body to attempt to remove the sudden excess of heat and so cause more heat loss and/or death.

Mild hypothermics can be rewarmed by **passive rewarming**, using their own body heat coupled with warm, dry, insulated clothing in a warm dry environment. Moderate hypothermia requires **active external rewarming**. This involves using warming devices such as hot water bottles or warm water baths. Severe hypothermics must be treated with **active internal** or **core warming**. Methods include delivery of warm intravenous fluids, inhaling warm moist air, or warming the blood externally by using a heart-lung machine.

1. Describe the conditions that may cause a person to become hypothermic: ______________________

2. (a) With reference to the graph (above), identify which body shape has best survival at 15°C: ______________________

   (b) Explain your choice: ______________________

3. Describe the methods used to rewarm hypothermics and the importance of using the correct methods.

KEY TERMS: Flash Card Game

The cards below have a keyword or term printed on one side and its definition printed on the opposite side. The aim is to win as many cards as possible from the table. To play the game.....

1) Cut out the cards and lay them definition side down on the desk. You will need one set of cards between two students.
2) Taking turns, choose a card and, BEFORE you pick it up, state your own best definition of the keyword to your opponent.
3) Check the definition on the opposite side of the card. If both you and your opponent agree that your stated definition matches, then keep the card. If your definition does not match then return the card to the desk.
4) Once your turn is over, your opponent may choose a card.

Cell signalling	Receptor	Thermo-receptors
Homeostasis	Endotherm	Autonomic nervous system
Negative feedback	Hypothalamus	Photoreceptor
Mechano-receptors	Ectotherm	Positive feedback
Stimulus	Homeothermic	Thermo-regulation
Effector	Paracrine	Endocrine

When you've finished the game keep these cutouts and use them as flash cards!

Sensory structures that detect changes in the skin temperature.	Specialised cells that detect stimuli and respond by producing a nerve impulse.	The mechanism by which cells use chemical messengers to gather information about their cellular environment and to communicate with other cells.
A branch of the peripheral nervous system that controls involuntary visceral functions.	An animal that relies on metabolic activity for its heat energy.	Regulation of the internal environment to maintain a constant, stable state.
A receptor that responds to light.	A region of the brain with an important role in linking the nervous and endocrine systems.	A mechanism in which the output of a system acts to oppose changes to the input of the system; the net effect is to stabilise the system and dampen fluctuations.
A destabilising mechanism in which the output of the system causes an escalation in the initial response.	An organism that is dependent on environmental (external) sources of energy to regulate body temperature.	A sensory receptor sensitive to mechanical energy, i.e. pressure, stretching, or bending.
An organism's regulation of body temperature to within certain boundaries, against external fluctuations.	An animal that maintains a constant body temperature despite environmental fluctuations.	A detectable change in the internal or external environment that is capable of eliciting a response in an organism.
A term describing control by hormones, which are carried through the body by the circulatory system to target cells.	Cell signalling in which the target cell is close to the cell producing the signal molecule.	A structure that responds to a stimulus to bring about a response in an organism.

UNIT F214

4.1.2 Nerves

KEY CONCEPTS

- Sensory receptors act as biological transducers.
- Neurones are electrically excitable cells capable of transmitting impulses over a considerable distance.
- Action potentials are discrete all-or-nothing impulses.
- Information about the stimulus is encoded in the stimulus frequency.
- Synapses are junctions across which action potentials are transmitted. Chemical synapses in mammals involve the diffusion of a neurotransmitter substance.

KEY TERMS

acetylcholine
action potential
biological transducer
cholinergic synapse
electrochemical gradient
motor neurone
myelin
myelinated neurone
neuromuscular junction
neurone
neurotransmitter
nodes of Ranvier
non-myelinated neurone
postsynaptic
presynaptic
refractory period
resting potential
saltatory conduction
Schwann cells
sensory neurone
sensory receptor
stimulus
synapse
synaptic integration

Periodicals:

Listings for this chapter are on page 340

Weblinks:

www.biozone.co.uk/weblink/OCR-A2-2832.html

OBJECTIVES

☐ 1. Use the **KEY TERMS** to help you understand and complete these objectives.

The basis of sensory reception

page 46

☐ 2. Using specific examples, describe the role of **sensory receptors** in mammals as **biological transducers**.

Neurone structure and function

pages 47-52

☐ 3. Describe **neurones** as electrically excitable cells. Using diagrams, describe the structure and functions of **sensory neurones** and **motor neurones**.

☐ 4. Explain how the **resting potential** of a neurone is established and maintained. Include reference to the differential permeability of the membrane to Na^+ and K^+, and the generation of an electrochemical gradient.

☐ 5. Explain how an **action potential** (nerve impulse) is generated. Explain the all-or-nothing nature of the impulse and the significance of the **refractory period** in producing discrete impulses.

☐ 6. Explain how an action potential is propagated along a myelinated nerve by **saltatory conduction**. Include reference to the voltage-gated ion channels and the roles of **myelin** and the **nodes of Ranvier**.

☐ 7. Interpret graphs of the voltage changes occurring during the generation and transmission of an action potential.

☐ 8. Explain the significance of the frequency of impulse conduction in encoding information about the stimulus strength.

☐ 9. Compare and contrast the structure and function of **myelinated** and **non-myelinated motor neurones**. Include reference to the role of supporting cells (e.g. Schwann cells) in motor neurone myelination. Describe factors affecting the speed of impulse conduction.

☐ 10. EXTENSION: Describe the structure and function of a simple reflex arc. Appreciate the adaptive value of reflex behaviours.

Synapses

pages 53-54

☐ 11. Describe the role of **synapses** in nervous systems, including their role in unidirectionality, and **integration** through summation and inhibition.

☐ 12. Describe the structure of a cholinergic synapse and recognise the neuromuscular junction as a specialised cholinergic synapse.

☐ 13. Explain the role of neurotransmitters in impulse transmission. Describe the events at a cholinergic synapse following arrival of an action potential at the presynaptic terminal. Include reference to the role of Ca^{2+} and acetylcholine, and the generation of the action potential in the postsynaptic neurone.

The Basis of Sensory Reception

Sensory receptors are specialised to detect stimuli and respond by producing an electrical (or chemical) discharge. In this way they act as **biological transducers**, converting the energy from a stimulus into an electrochemical signal. They can do this because the stimulus opens (or closes) ion channels and leads to localised changes in membrane potential called **receptor potentials**. Receptor potentials are graded and not self-propagating, but sense cells can amplify them, generating action potentials directly or inducing the release of a neurotransmitter. Whether or not the sensory cell itself fires action potentials, ultimately the stimulus is transduced into action potentials whose frequency is dependent on stimulus strength. The simplest sensory receptors consist of a single sensory neurone (e.g. nerve endings). More complex sense cells form synapses with their sensory neurones (e.g. taste buds). Sensory receptors are classified according to the stimuli to which they respond (e.g. photoreceptors respond to light).

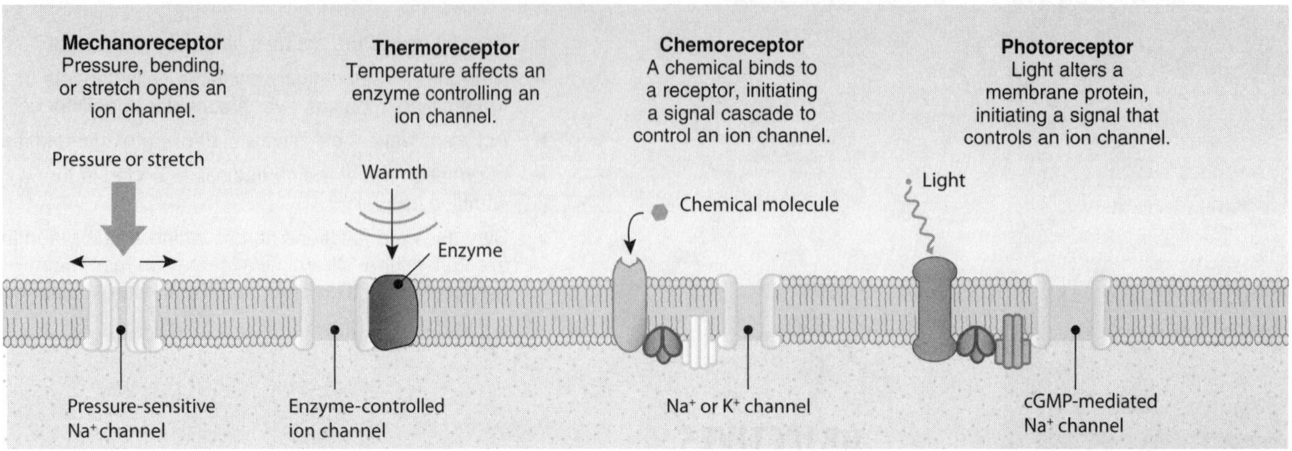

Signal Transduction

Sensory cells convert one type of stimulus energy (e.g. pressure) into an electrical signal by altering the flow of ions across the plasma membrane and generating receptor potentials. In many cases (as in the Pacinian corpuscle), this leads directly to action potentials which are generated in the voltage-gated region of the sensory cell.

In some receptor cells, the receptor potential leads to neurotransmitter release, which then leads directly or indirectly to action potentials in a post-synaptic cell.

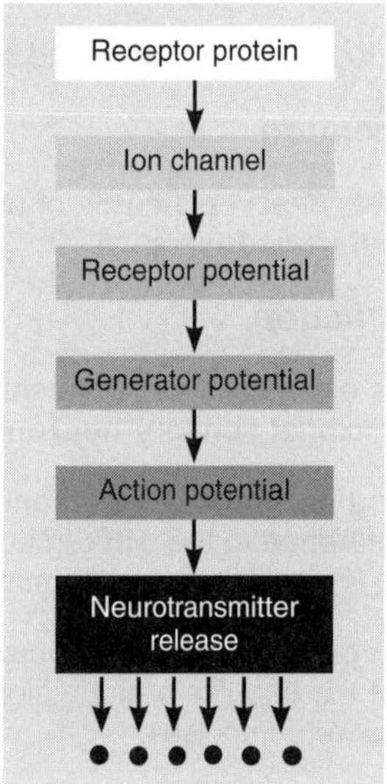

The Pacinian Corpuscle

Pacinian corpuscles are pressure receptors in deep subcutaneous tissues of the body. They are relatively large but structurally simple, consisting of a sensory nerve ending (dendrite) surrounded by a capsule of connective tissue layers. Pressure deforms the capsule, stretching the nerve ending and leading to a localised depolarisation called a **receptor potential**. Receptor potentials are graded and do not spread far, although they may sum together and increase in amplitude.

The sense cell converts the receptor potentials to action potentials in the spike generating zone at the start of the axon (where there are voltage-gated channels). The action potential is then propagated along the axon.

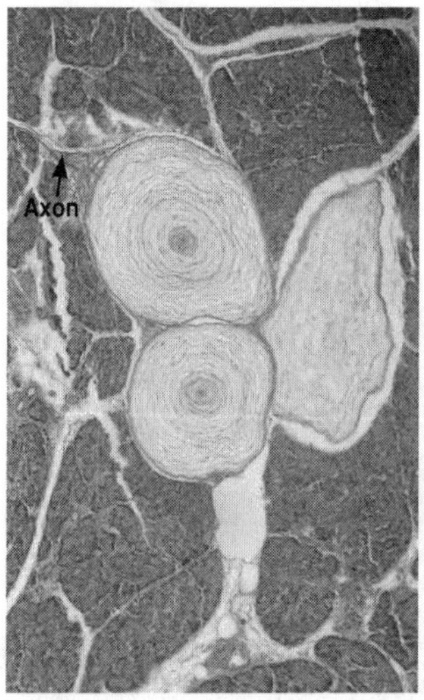

D. Fankhauser, University of Cincinnati, Clermont College

1. Explain why sensory receptors are termed 'biological transducers': ______________________

2. Identify one feature that all sensory receptors have in common: ______________________

3. Explain how a stimulus received by a sensory receptor is converted into an electrical response: ______________________

4. (a) Describe the properties of receptor potentials: ______________________

(b) Explain how summation of receptor potentials leads to an increased frequency of action potentials in the axon:

Neurone Structure and Function

As described earlier, homeostasis depends on the nervous system detecting, interpreting, and responding appropriately to both internal and external stimuli. Many of these responses are involuntary and are achieved through **reflexes**. Information, in the form of electrochemical impulses, is transmitted along nerve cells (**neurones**) from receptors to effectors. The speed of impulse conduction depends primarily on the axon diameter and whether or not the axon is **myelinated**. Within the tolerable physiological range, an increase in temperature also increases the speed of impulse conduction. In cool environments, impulses travel faster in endothermic than in ectothermic vertebrates. Neurones typically consist of a cell body, dendrites, and an axon (below). The principle behind increasing impulse speed through **saltatory conduction** is described overleaf.

Neurone Structure

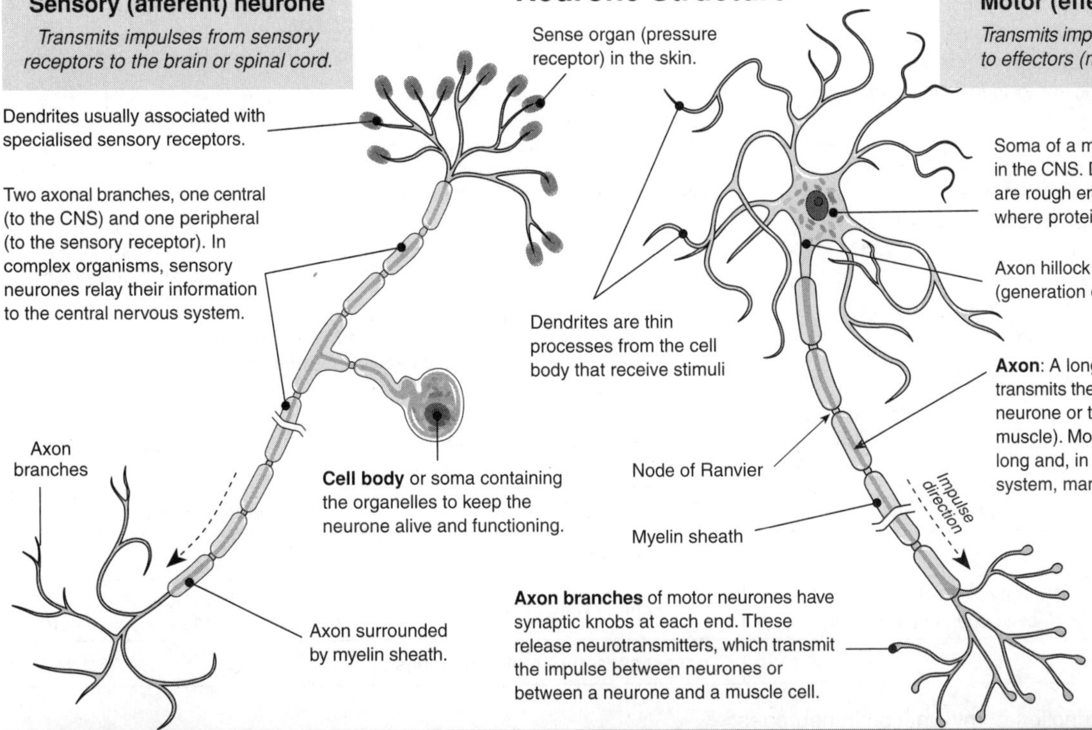

Where conduction speed is important, the axons of neurones are sheathed within a lipid and protein rich substance called **myelin**. Myelin is produced by **oligodendrocytes** in the central nervous system (CNS) and by **Schwann cells** in the peripheral nervous system (PNS). At intervals along the axons of myelinated neurones, there are gaps between neighbouring Schwann cells and their sheaths. These are called **nodes of Ranvier**. Myelin acts as an insulator, increasing the speed at which nerve impulses travel because it prevents ion flow across the neurone membrane and forces the current to "jump" along the axon from node to node.

Myelinated Neurones

Diameter: 1-25 µm
Conduction speed: 6-120 ms^{-1}

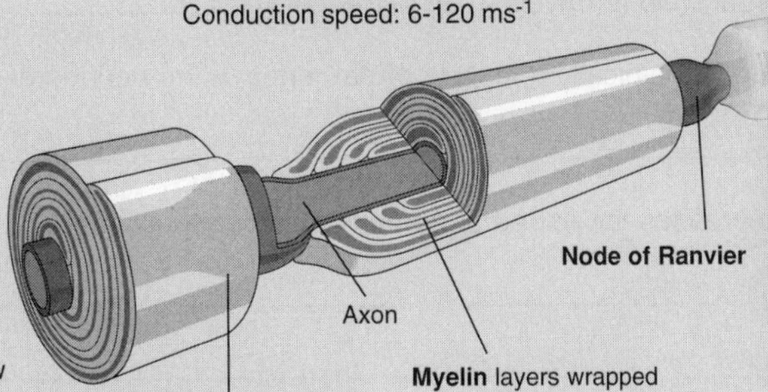

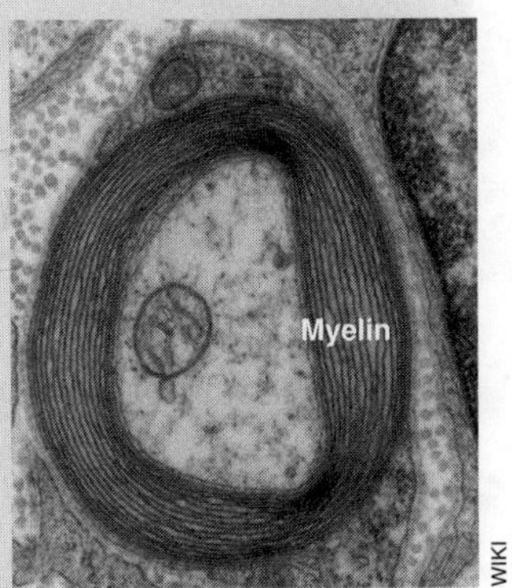

TEM cross section through a myelinated axon

Non-myelinated axons are relatively more common in the CNS where the distances travelled are less than in the PNS. Here, the axons are encased within the cytoplasmic extensions of oligodendrocytes or Schwann cells, rather than within a myelin sheath. The speed of impulse conduction is slower than in myelinated neurones because the nerve impulse is propagated along the entire axon membrane, rather than jumping from node to node as occurs in myelinated neurones. Conduction speeds are slower than in myelinated neurones, although they are faster in larger neurones (there is less ion leakage from a larger diameter axon).

Non-myelinated Neurones

Diameter: <1 µm in vertebrates
Conduction speed: 0.2-0.5 ms^{-1}

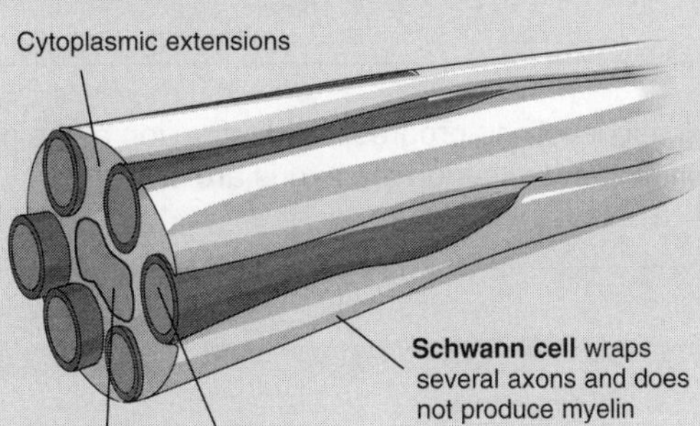

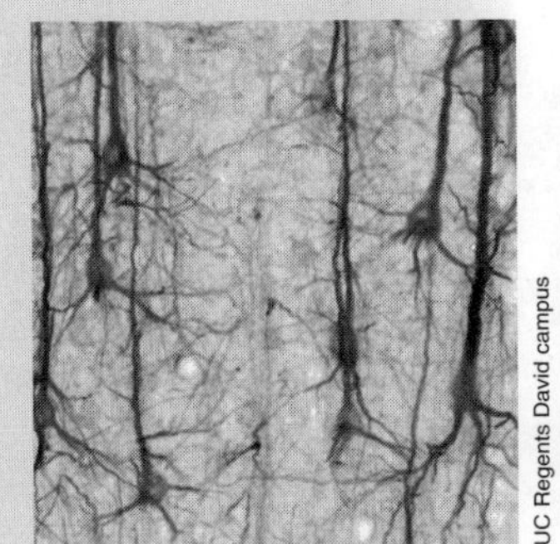

Unmyelinated pyramidal neurones of the cerebral cortex

Nerves

Axon myelination is a characteristic feature of vertebrate nervous systems and it enables them to achieve very rapid speeds of nerve conduction. Myelinated neurones conduct impulses by **saltatory conduction**, a term that describes how the impulse jumps along the fibre. In saltatory conduction, only the nodes of Ranvier are involved in action potential generation. In myelinated (insulated) regions, there is no leakage of ions across the neurone membrane and the action potential at one node is sufficient to trigger an action potential in the next node.

Apart from increasing the speed of the nerve impulse, the myelin sheath helps in reducing energy expenditure because the area of depolarisation is decreased (and therefore also the number of sodium and potassium ions that need to be pumped to restore the resting potential).

Saltatory Conduction in Myelinated Axons

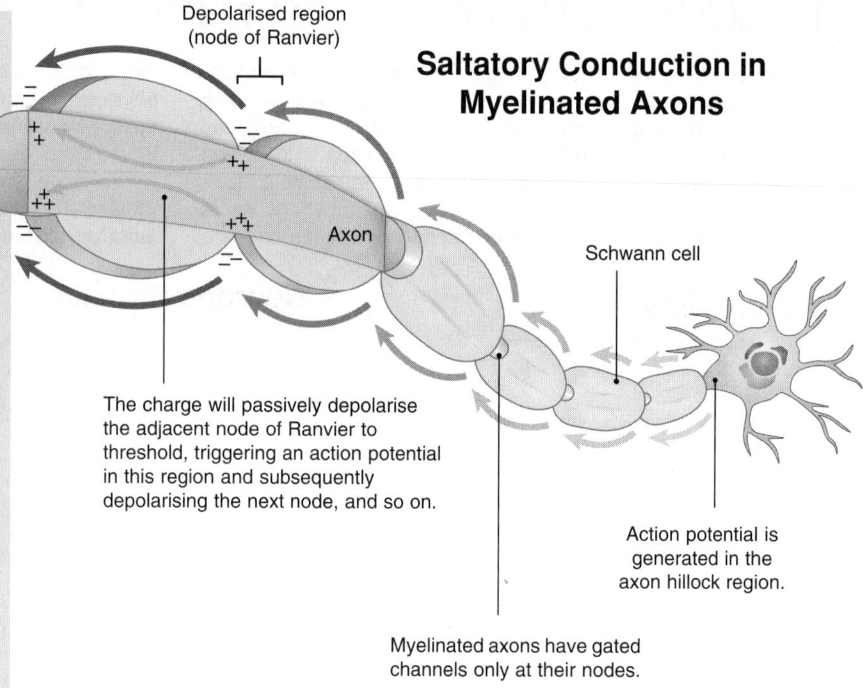

1. Complete the missing panels of the following table summarising structural and functional differences between neurones:

	Sensory neurone	Interneurone	Motor neurone
Structure		Short dendrites, long or short axon	
Location	Dendrites outside the spinal cord, cell body in spinal ganglion	Entirely within the CNS	Dendrites and cell body in the spinal cord; axon outside the spinal cord.
Function		Connect sensory & motor neurones	

2. (a) Explain the function of myelination in neurones:

(b) Name the cell type responsible for myelination in the CNS:

(c) Name the cell type responsible for myelination in the PNS:

(d) Explain why myelination is a typically a feature of neurones in the peripheral nervous system:

3. Explain how myelination increases the speed of nerve impulse conduction:

4. (a) Describe the adaptive advantage of faster conduction of nerve impulses:

(b) Suggest why increasing the axon diameter also increases the speed of impulse conduction:

5. Multiple sclerosis (MS) is a disease involving progressive destruction of the myelin sheaths around axons. Explain why MS impairs nervous system function even though the axons are still intact:

Action Potentials

The plasma membranes of cells, including neurones, contain **sodium-potassium ion pumps** which actively pump sodium ions (Na^+) out of the cell and potassium ions (K^+) into the cell. The action of these ion pumps in neurones creates a separation of charge (a potential difference or voltage) either side of the membrane and makes the cells **electrically excitable**. It is this property that enables neurones to transmit electrical impulses. The **resting state** of a neurone, with a net negative charge inside, is maintained by the sodium-potassium pumps, which actively move two K^+ into the neurone for every three Na^+ moved out (below left). When a nerve is stimulated, a brief increase in membrane permeability to Na^+ temporarily reverses the membrane polarity (a depolarisation). After the nerve impulse passes, the sodium-potassium pump restores the resting potential. The depolarisation is propagated along the axon by local current in non-myelinated fibres and by **saltatory conduction** in myelinated fibres. Impulses pass from neurone to neurone by crossing junctions called **synapses**.

The Resting Neurone

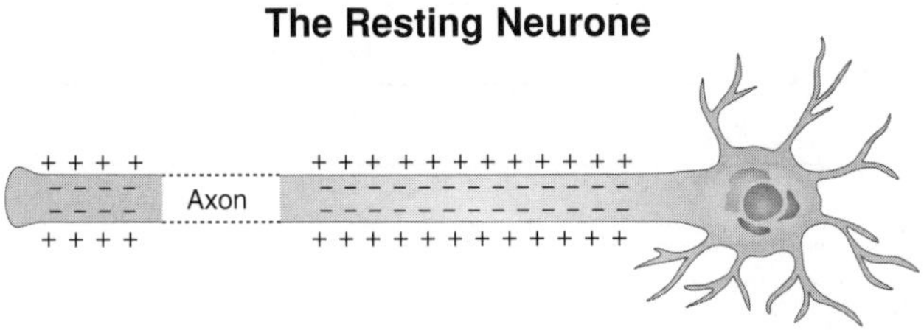

When a neurone is not transmitting an impulse, the inside of the cell is negatively charged relative to the outside and the cell is said to be electrically polarised. The potential difference (voltage) across the membrane is called the **resting potential**. For most nerve cells this is about -70 mV. Nerve transmission is possible because this membrane potential exists.

The Nerve Impulse

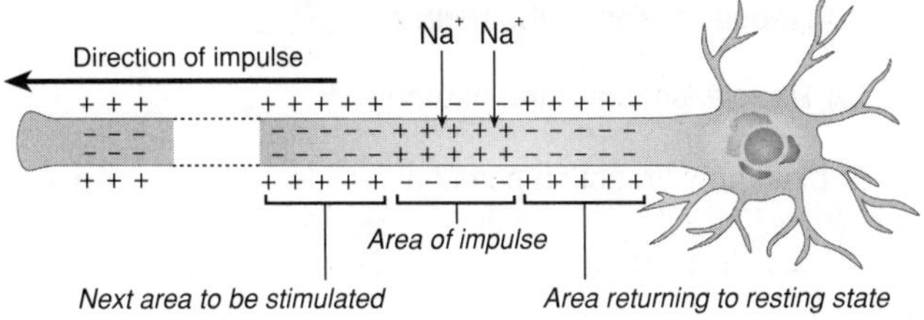

When a neurone is stimulated, the distribution of charges on each side of the membrane briefly reverses. This process of **depolarisation** causes a burst of electrical activity to pass along the axon of the neurone as an **action potential**. As the charge reversal reaches one region, local currents depolarise the next region and the impulse spreads along the axon.

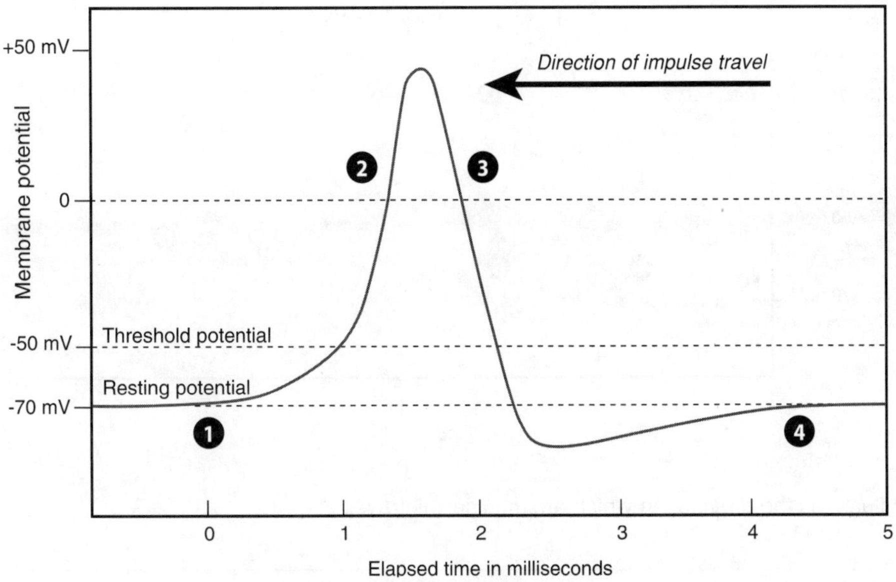

The depolarisation in an axon can be shown as a change in membrane potential (in millivolts). A stimulus must be strong enough to reach the **threshold potential** before an action potential is generated. This is the voltage at which the depolarisation of the membrane becomes unstoppable.

The action potential is **all or nothing** in its generation and because of this, impulses (once generated) always reach threshold and move along the axon without attenuation. The resting potential is restored by the movement of potassium ions (K^+) out of the cell. During this **refractory period**, the nerve cannot respond, so nerve impulses are discrete.

Voltage-Gated Ion Channels and the Course of an Action Potential

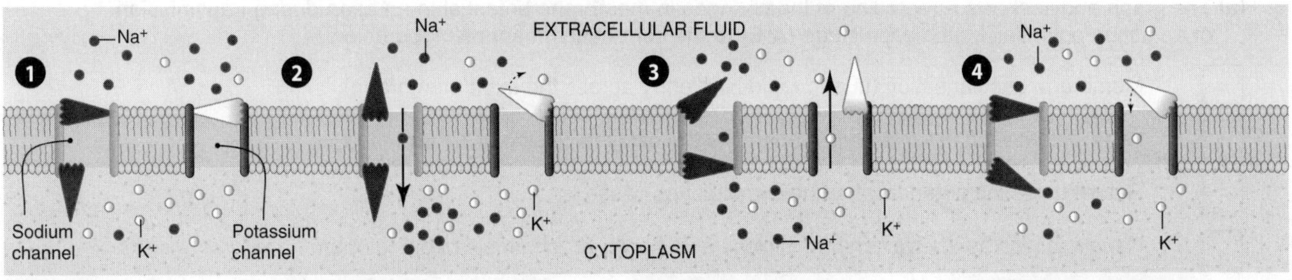

Resting state: Voltage activated Na^+ and K^+ channels are closed.

Depolarisation: Voltage activated Na^+ channels open and there is a rapid influx of Na^+ ions. The interior of the neurone becomes positive relative to the outside.

Repolarisation: Voltage activated Na^+ channels close and the K^+ channels open; K^+ moves out of the cell, restoring the negative charge to the cell interior.

Returning to resting state: Voltage activated Na^+ and K^+ channels close to return the neurone to the resting state.

1. In your own words, explain what an action potential is: ______________________________

____

2. (a) Describe a defining feature of neurones: ______________________________

____

(b) Explain how the supporting cells of nervous tissue (e.g. Schwann cells) differ from neurones: ______________________________

____

3. Describe the movement of voltage-gated channels and ion associated with: ______________________________

(a) Depolarisation of the neurone: ______________________________

(b) Repolarisation of the neurone: ______________________________

4. Explain how an action potential is able to pass along a neurone: ______________________________

____

____

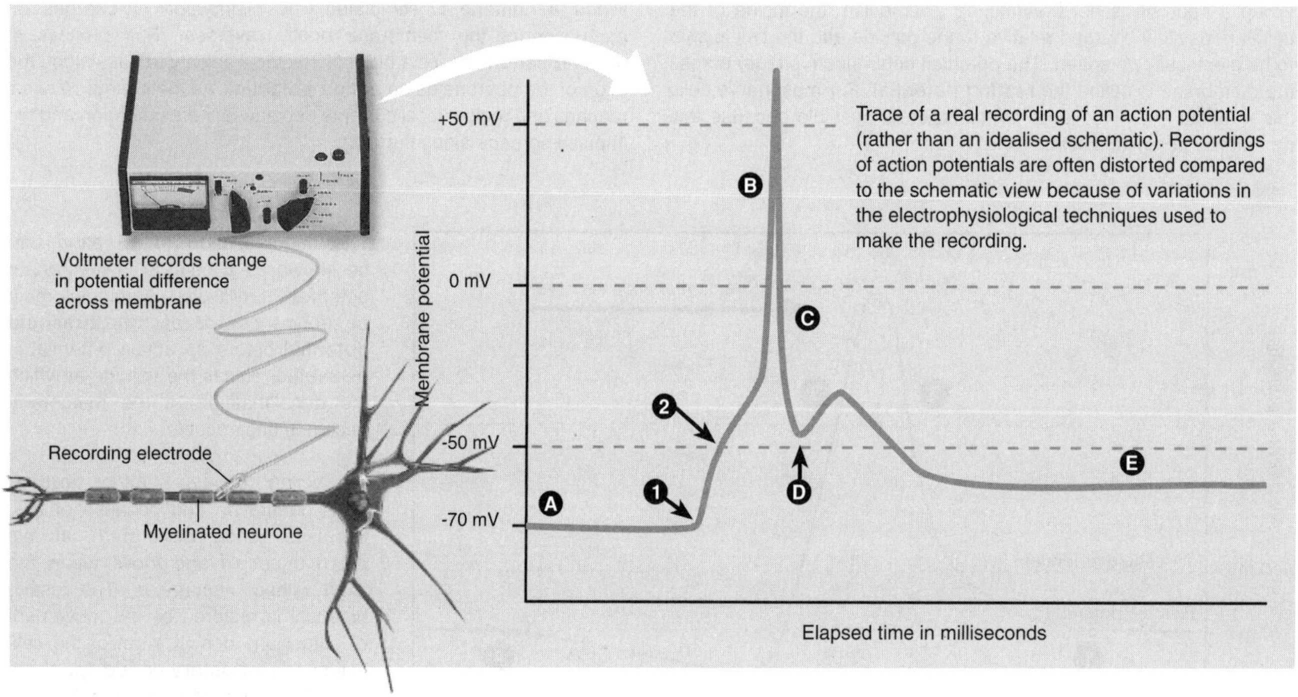

5. Explain how the refractory period influences the direction in which an impulse will travel: ______________________________

____

____

6. (a) The graph above shows a recording of the changes in membrane potential in an axon during transmission of an action potential. Match each stage (**A-E**) to the correct summary provided below.

☐ Membrane depolarisation (due to rapid Na^+ entry across the axon membrane).

☐ Hyperpolarisation (an overshoot caused by the delay in closing of K^+ channels).

☐ Return to resting potential after the stimulus has passed.

☐ Repolarisation as the Na^+ channels close and slower K^+ channels begin to open.

☐ The membrane's resting potential.

(b) Explain what is happening at point **1** on the graph: ______________________________

(c) Explain what is happening at point **2** on the graph: ______________________________

Encoding Information

A receptor must do more than simply record a stimulus. It is important that it also provides information about the stimulus strength. Action potentials obey the 'all or none law' and are always the same size, so stimulus strength cannot be encoded by varying the amplitude of the action potentials. Instead, the frequency of impulses conveys information about the stimulus intensity; the higher the frequency of impulses, the stronger the stimulus. This encoding method is termed **frequency modulation**, and it the way that receptors inform the brain about stimulus strength. In the Pacinian corpuscle, described below and earlier in this chapter, frequency modulation is possible because a stronger pressure produces a larger receptor potential, which depolarises the first node of Ranvier to threshold more rapidly and results in a more rapid volley of action potentials. Sensory receptors also show **sensory adaptation** and will cease responding to a stimulus of the same intensity.

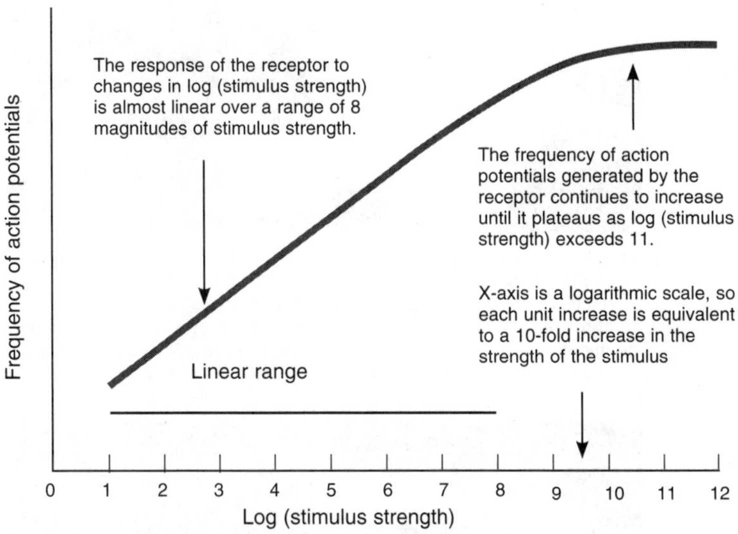

Receptors can use variation in action potential frequency to encode stimulus strengths that vary by nearly 11 orders of magnitude.

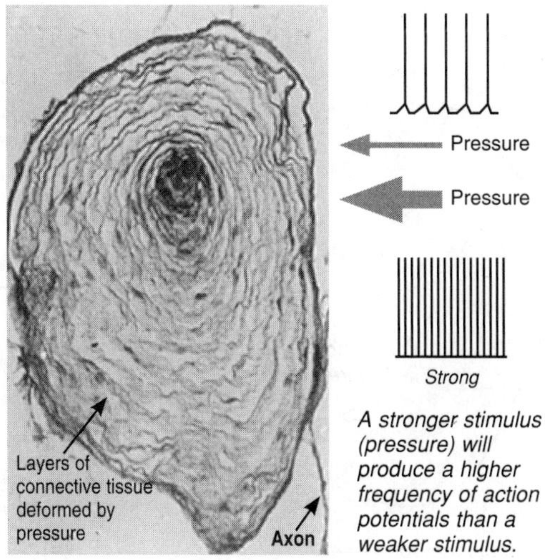

A stronger stimulus (pressure) will produce a higher frequency of action potentials than a weaker stimulus.

A Pacinian corpuscle (above), illustrating the many layers of connective tissue. Pacinian corpuscles are rapidly adapting receptors; they fire at the beginning and end of a stimulus, but do not respond to unchanging pressure.

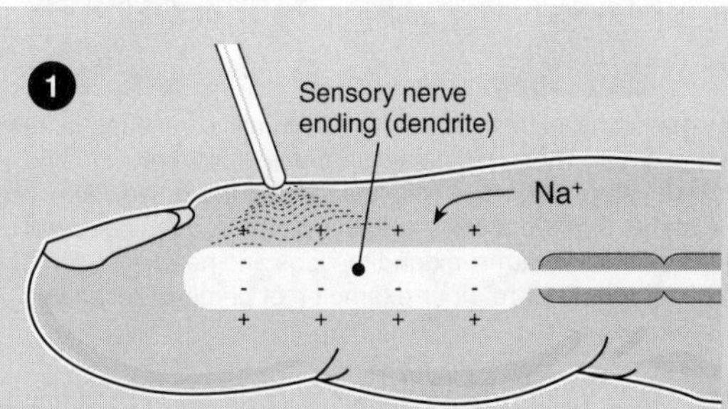

Deforming the corpuscle leads to an increase in the permeability of the nerve to sodium. Na^+ diffuses into the nerve ending creating a localised depolarisation. This depolarisation is called a **receptor potential**.

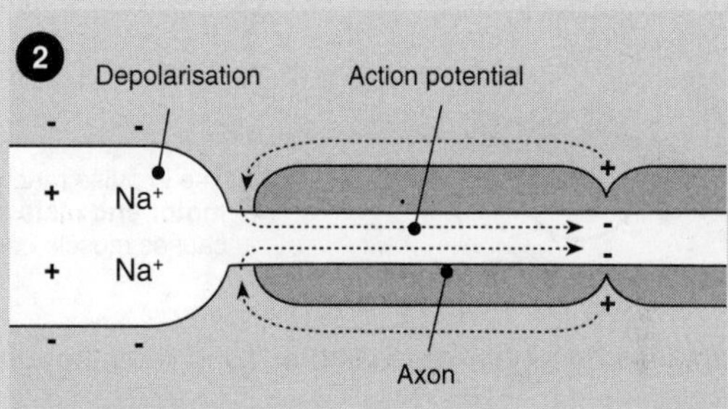

The receptor potential spreads to the first node of Ranvier, which is the first region with voltage-gated Na+ channels. It depolarises the node to threshold and generates an action potential, which propagates along the axon.

1. (a) Explain how the strength of a stimulus is encoded by the nervous system: ___

   (b) Explain the significance of encoding information in this way: ___

2. Using the example of the Pacinian corpuscle, explain the physiological mechanism by which stimulus strength is linked to frequency of action potentials:

3. Explain the physiological importance of sensory adaptation:

Nerves

Reflexes

A reflex is an automatic response to a stimulus involving a small number of neurones and a central nervous system (CNS) processing point (usually the spinal cord, but sometimes the brain stem). This type of circuit is called a **reflex arc**. Reflexes permit rapid responses to stimuli and are highly adaptive in that they provide a mechanism for immediate protective behaviour. They are classified according to the number of CNS synapses involved; **monosynaptic reflexes** involve only one CNS synapse (e.g. knee jerk reflex), whereas **polysynaptic reflexes** involve two or more (e.g. pain withdrawal reflex). Both are spinal reflexes. The pupil reflex (opening and closure of the pupil) is an example of a cranial reflex. In some invertebrates, reflex escape behaviours such as the caridoid tail flip, bypass the main neural system controlling locomotion and are controlled by giant neurones.

Pain Withdrawal: A Polysynaptic Reflex Arc

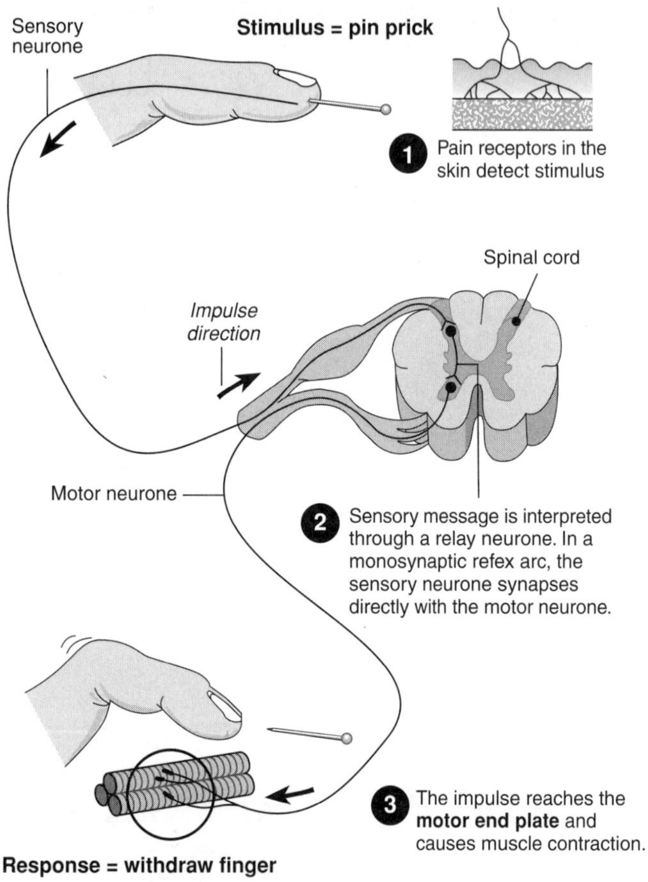

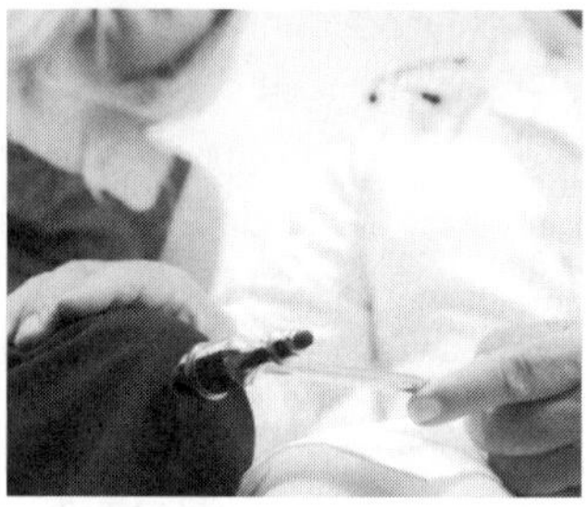

The patella (knee jerk) reflex is a simple deep tendon reflex that is used to test the function of the femoral nerve and spinal cord segments L2-L4. It helps to maintain posture and balance when walking.

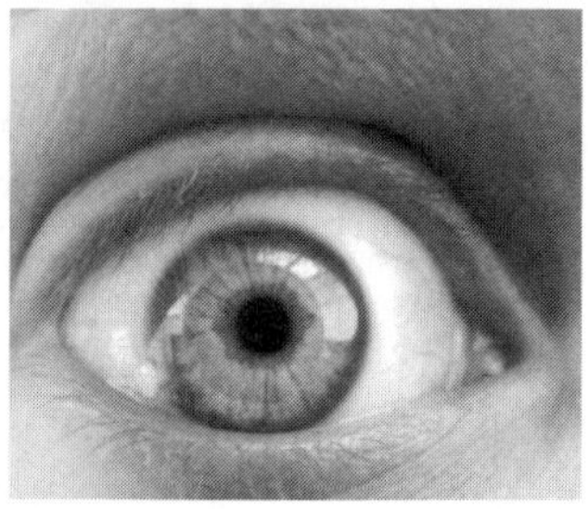

The pupillary light reflex refers to the rapid expansion or contraction of the pupils in response to the intensity of light falling on the retina. It is a polysynaptic cranial reflex and can be used to test for brain death.

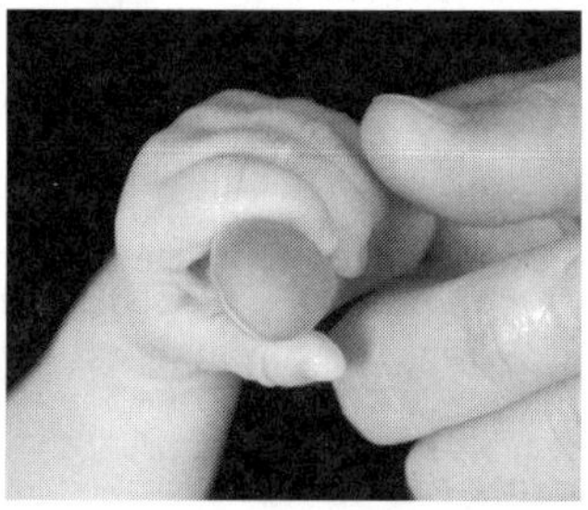

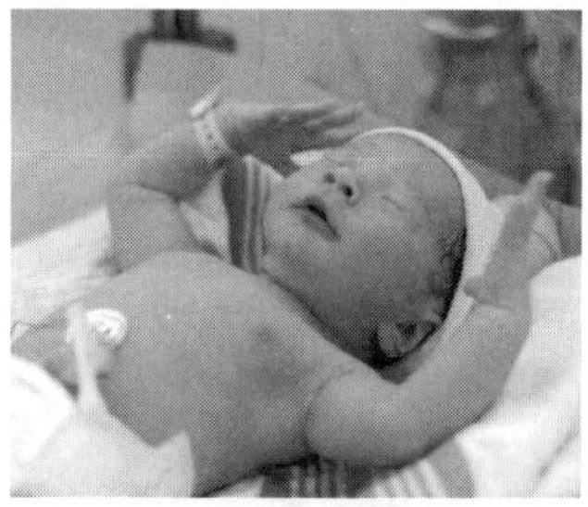

Normal newborns exhibit a number of primitive reflexes in response to particular stimuli. These reflexes disappear within a few months of birth as the child develops. Primitive reflexes include the grasp reflex (above left) and the startle or Moro reflex (right) in which a sudden noise will cause the infant to throw out its arms, extend the legs and head, and cry. The rooting and sucking reflexes are other examples of primitive reflexes.

1. Explain why higher reasoning or conscious thought are not necessary or desirable features of reflex behaviours:

2. Distinguish between a spinal reflex and a cranial reflex and give an example of each:

3. (a) Distinguish between a monosynaptic and a polysynaptic reflex arc and give an example of each:

   (b) Given similar length sensory and motor pathways, identify which would produce the most rapid response and why:

4. (a) With reference to specific examples, describe the adaptive value of primitive reflexes in newborns:

   (b) Explain why newborns are tested for the presence of these reflexes:

The Cholinergic Synapse

Action potentials are transmitted between neurones across **synapses**: junctions between the end of one axon and the dendrite or cell body of a receiving neurone. Electrical synapses, where cells are electrically coupled through gap junctions between cells, occur in heart muscle and in the retina, but they are relatively uncommon elsewhere. Most synapses in the nervous system are **chemical synapses**. In these, the axon terminal is a swollen knob, and a small gap, the **synaptic cleft**, separates it from the receiving neurone. The synaptic knobs are filled with tiny packets of chemicals called **neurotransmitters**.

Nerve transmission involves the diffusion of the neurotransmitter across the cleft, where it interacts with the receiving membrane and causes an electrical response. The response of a receiving (post-synaptic) cell to the arrival of a neurotransmitter depends on the nature of the cell itself, on its location in the nervous system, and on the neurotransmitter involved. Synapses that release acetylcholine (ACh) are termed **cholinergic**. In the example below, ACh results in membrane depolarisation and an action potential (an excitatory response). Unlike electrical synapses, transmission at chemical synapses is always unidirectional.

The Structure of a Cholinergic Synapse

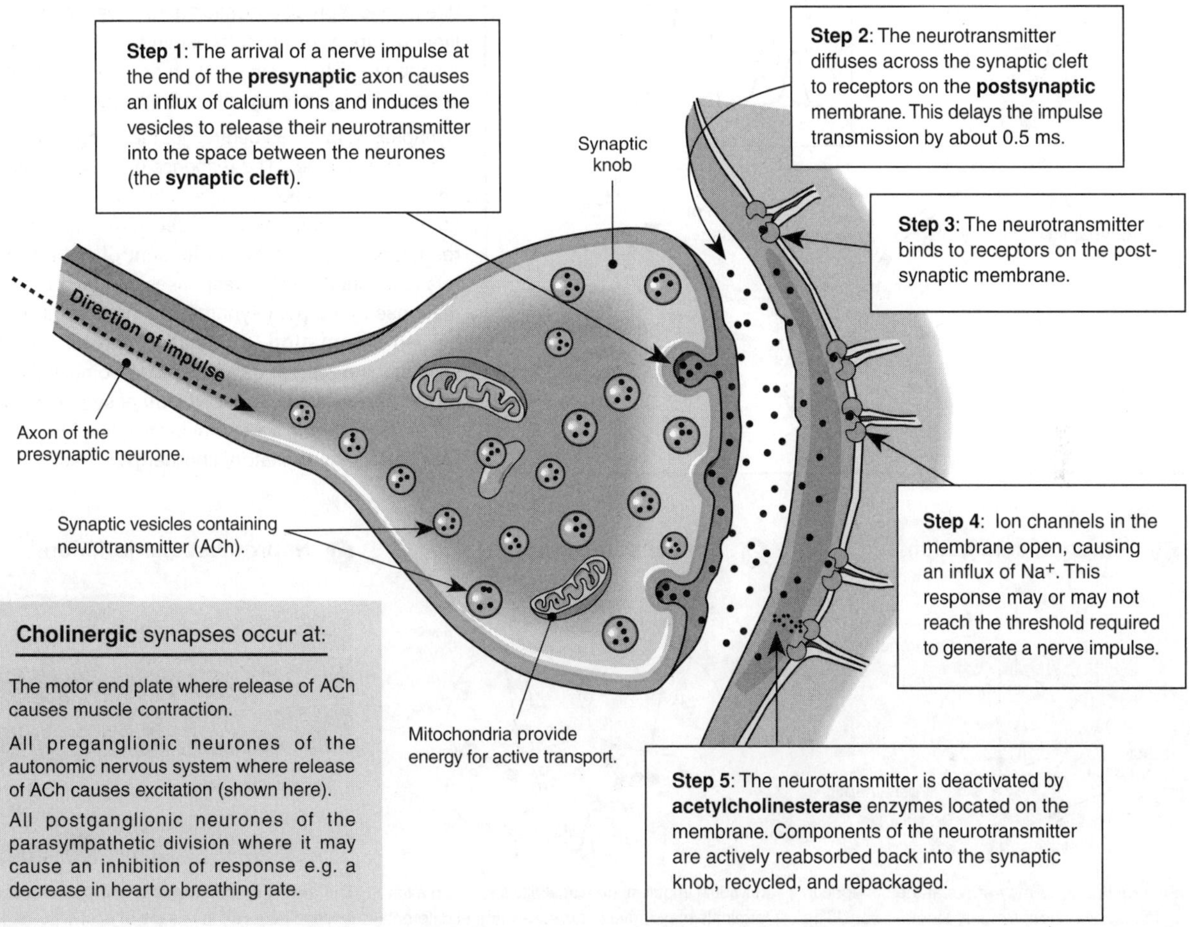

Cholinergic synapses occur at:

- The motor end plate where release of ACh causes muscle contraction.
- All preganglionic neurones of the autonomic nervous system where release of ACh causes excitation (shown here).
- All postganglionic neurones of the parasympathetic division where it may cause an inhibition of response e.g. a decrease in heart or breathing rate.

1. Explain what is meant by a **synapse**: ________________

2. Explain what causes the release of neurotransmitter into the synaptic cleft: ________________

3. State why there is a brief delay in transmission of an impulse across the synapse: ________________

4. (a) State how the neurotransmitter is deactivated: ________________

   (b) Explain why it is important for the neurotransmitter substance to be deactivated soon after its release:

5. Consult a reference source to identify one function of acetylcholine in the nervous system: ________________

6. Suggest one factor that might influence the strength of the response in the receiving cell: ________________

Nerves

Integration at Synapses

Synapses play a pivotal role in the ability of the nervous system to respond appropriately to stimulation and to adapt to change. The nature of synaptic transmission allows the **integration** (interpretation and coordination) of inputs from many sources. These inputs need not be just excitatory (causing depolarisation). Inhibition results when the neurotransmitter released causes negative chloride ions (rather than sodium ions) to enter the postsynaptic neurone. The postsynaptic neurone then becomes more negative inside (hyperpolarised) and an action potential is less likely to be generated. At synapses, it is the sum of **all** inputs (excitatory and inhibitory) that leads to the final response in a postsynaptic cell. Integration at synapses makes possible the various responses we have to stimuli. It is also the most probable mechanism by which learning and memory are achieved.

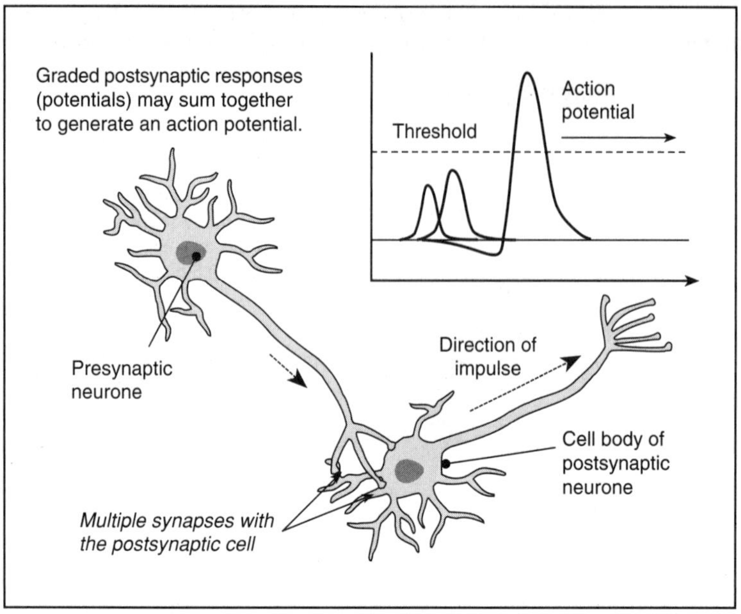

Synapses and Summation

Nerve transmission across chemical synapses has several advantages, despite the delay caused by neurotransmitter diffusion. Chemical synapses transmit impulses in one direction to a precise location and, because they rely on a limited supply of neurotransmitter, they are subject to fatigue (inability to respond to repeated stimulation). This protects the system against overstimulation.

Synapses also act as centres for the **integration** of inputs from many sources. The response of a postsynaptic cell is often graded; it is not strong enough on its own to generate an action potential. However, because the strength of the response is related to the amount of neurotransmitter released, subthreshold responses can sum to produce a response in the post-synaptic cell. This additive effect is termed **summation**. Summation can be **temporal** or **spatial** (below left and centre). A neuromuscular junction (photo below) is a specialised form of synapse between a motor neurone and a skeletal muscle fibre. Functionally, it is similar to any excitatory cholinergic synapse.

1 Temporal summation

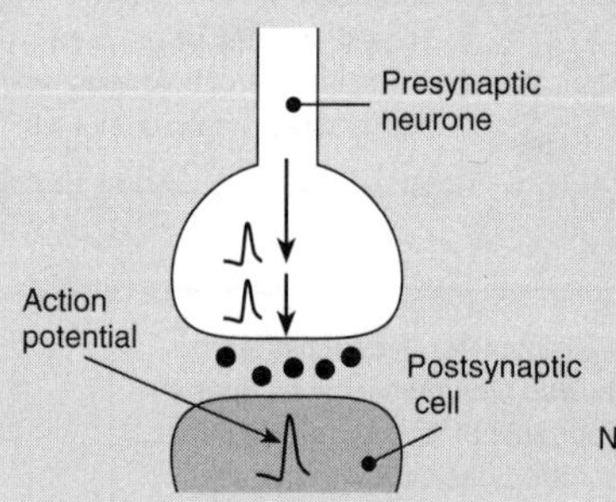

Several impulses may arrive at the synapse in quick succession from a single axon. The individual responses are so close together in time that they sum to reach threshold and produce an action potential in the postsynaptic neurone.

2 Spatial summation

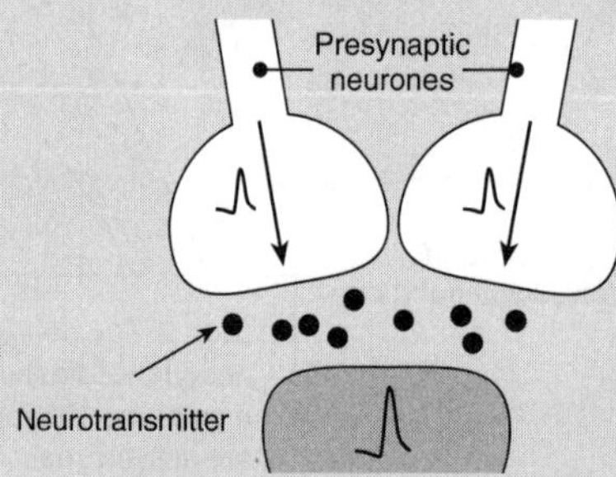

Individual impulses from spatially separated axon terminals may arrive **simultaneously** at different regions of the same postsynaptic neurone. The responses from the different places sum to reach threshold and produce an action potential.

3 Neuromuscular junction

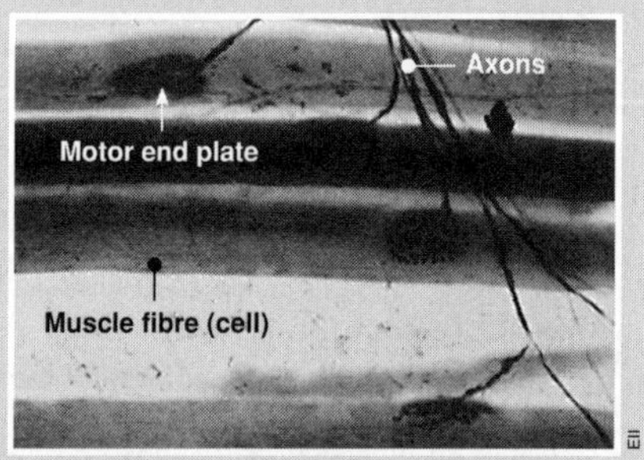

The arrival of an impulse at the neuromuscular junction causes the release of acetylcholine from the synaptic knobs. This causes the muscle cell membrane (sarcolemma) to depolarise, and an action potential is generated in the muscle cell.

1. Explain the purpose of nervous system integration: ____________________

2. (a) Explain what is meant by **summation**: ____________________

   (b) In simple terms, distinguish between temporal and spatial summation: ____________________

3. Describe two ways in which a neuromuscular junction is similar to any excitatory cholinergic synapse:

   (a) ____________________

   (b) ____________________

KEY TERMS: Mix and Match

INSTRUCTIONS: Test your vocabulary by matching each term to its definition, as identified by its preceding letter code.

ACETYLCHOLINE

ACTION POTENTIAL

BIOLOGICAL TRANSDUCERS

CHOLINERGIC SYNAPSE

ELECTROCHEMICAL GRADIENT

MOTOR NEURONE

MYELIN

MYELINATED NEURONE

NEUROMUSCULAR JUNCTION

NEURONE

NEUROTRANSMITTER

NODES OF RANVIER

NON-MYELINATED NEURONE

POSTSYNAPTIC

PRESYNAPTIC

REFRACTORY PERIOD

RESTING POTENTIAL

SALTATORY CONDUCTION

SCHWANN CELLS

SENSORY NEURONE

SENSORY RECEPTOR

STIMULUS

SYNAPSE

SYNAPTIC INTEGRATION

A A nerve cell, typically consisting of a cell body, dendrites, and an axon.

B Any physical or chemical change in the environment capable of provoking a response in an organism.

C The gradient across a membrane formed as a result of the movement of an ion or other solute.

D A neurone on the receiving side of a synapse.

E A nerve cell that carries impulses away from the central nervous system to an effector (muscle or gland). May be non-myelinated or myelinated.

F The propagation of action potentials along myelinated axons by 'jumping' from one node of Ranvier to the next.

G A specialised cell that detects stimuli and responds by producing an electrical discharge.

H The site at which an axon terminal contacts a muscle cell.

I A neurone whose axon is supported by cytoplasmic extensions of oligodendrocytes, rather than wrapped in a myelin sheath.

J The potential difference across the cell membrane of a neurone when there is no impulse passing.

K A nerve cell concerned with transmitting impulses from sensory receptors to other neurones.

L Structures, notably sensory receptors, that convert physical or chemical stimuli into electrical or chemical signals which can be processed by the organism.

M A chemical messenger released by axon terminals in response to an action potential.

N The junction between two neurones or between a neurone and an effector.

O The period during a nerve impulse when the sodium channels are inactivated and the neurone cannot respond.

P A neurone with an axon that is encased within a myelin sheath.

Q A neurone on the transmitting side of a synapse.

R Self propagating rapid depolarisation of a neuronal membrane, generated by voltage-gated ion channels.

S The interpretation and coordination of inputs from many neurones by a single neurone, resulting in the production of a new signal.

T A synapse that releases acetylcholine.

U A lipid-rich substance that surrounds and insulates the axons of some neurones.

V The gaps occurring at intervals along the myelin sheath.

W Glial cells in the PNS which forms the fatty sheath around myelinated nerve fibres.

X A neurotransmitter in both the CNS and PNS, notably at the neuromuscular junction.

Hormones

Insulin monomer

KEY TERMS

adrenal glands
adrenal medulla
adrenaline
catecholamines
cyclic AMP (cAMP)
endocrine gland
exocrine gland
first messenger
glucagon
gluconeogenesis
glycogenolysis
glycogenesis
hormone
insulin
islets of Langerhans
medulla (aka medulla oblongata)
noradrenaline
pancreas
second messenger
signal transduction pathway
stem cell therapy
target tissue
Type 1 diabetes mellitus
Type 2 diabetes mellitus

KEY CONCEPTS

- Negative feedback is important in regulating the nervous and hormonal responses that maintain homeostasis.
- Blood glucose levels are regulated through the activities of insulin and glucagon.
- The liver has a central role in carbohydrate metabolism.
- Diabetes mellitus is a disorder of blood glucose regulation.
- Heart rate is controlled through the autonomic nervous system and by hormones from the adrenal medulla.

OBJECTIVES

☐ 1. Use the **KEY TERMS** to help you understand and complete these objectives.

Chemical signalling

pages 57-60

☐ 2. Understand the terms **endocrine gland**, **hormone**, and **target tissue**. Distinguish between endocrine and **exocrine glands**. Outline the structure of the endocrine system, including reference to the location and function of the **pancreas** and the **adrenal glands**.

☐ 3. Recall how hormones exert their effects and the role of negative feedback in the control of hormone release.

☐ 4. Recall the role of cell signalling in cellular communication. Using **adrenaline** and **cyclic AMP** (cAMP) as examples, explain the role of first and second messengers in a **signal transduction pathway**.

Control of blood glucose

pages 61-66

☐ 5. Describe the gross structure, histology, and function of the pancreas. Outline its role as an organ with both endocrine and exocrine functions.

☐ 6. Using diagrams, describe the pancreatic **islets of Langerhans**, and outline the endocrine role of the pancreas in regulating blood glucose levels.

☐ 7. BACKGROUND: Identify the normal range over which blood glucose levels fluctuate and describe the factors that lead to variation in blood glucose levels.

☐ 8. Explain the regulation of blood glucose in humans, including reference to negative feedback, insulin and glucagon, and the role of the liver in glucose-glycogen conversions (glycogenesis, glycogenolysis, and gluconeogenesis).

☐ 9. Explain how the secretion of insulin from beta cells is controlled, with reference to the role of potassium and calcium channels.

☐ 10. Compare and contrast the causes of **Type 1** and **Type 2 diabetes mellitus**.

☐ 11. Discuss treatment of Type 1 diabetes mellitus with reference to insulin production using genetically modified bacteria. Discuss the potential role of **stem cell therapy** in the future treatment of diabetes mellitus.

Control of heart rate

pages 67-68

☐ 12. Recall that the **intrinsic heart rate** is set by the sinoatrial node, but that this is influenced by hormones and by the autonomic nervous system.

☐ 13. Describe the extrinsic regulation of heart rate through the autonomic nervous system (**vagus** and **cardiac nerves**). Identify the role of the cardiovascular centre in the **medulla**, **baroreceptors**, and **chemoreceptors** in mediating the response of the heart to changing demands (e.g. exercise, trauma).

☐ 14. Recall the function of the adrenal glands. Explain the role of **adrenaline** and **noradrenaline** (from the adrenal medulla) in regulating heart rate.

Periodicals:
Listings for this chapter are on page 340

Weblinks:
www.biozone.co.uk/weblink/OCR-A2-2832.html

Teacher Resource CD-ROM:
Hormones of the Pituitary

The Endocrine System

The nervous and endocrine systems interact to regulate the body's activities. The endocrine system comprises **endocrine glands** and their **hormones**. Endocrine glands, are **ductless glands** (compare with **exocrine glands** which deliver secretions via a duct) and are distributed throughout the body, frequently associated with the organs of other body systems. Under appropriate stimulation they secrete **hormones**, which are carried in the blood to exert a specific effect on target cells, before being broken down and excreted. Hormones may be amino acids, peptides, proteins (often modified), fatty acids, or steroids. Some basic features of the human endocrine system are explained below. The hypothalamus, although part of the brain and not strictly an endocrine gland, contains neurosecretory cells, and links the nervous and endocrine systems. The hypothalamus, together with the pituitary, adrenal, and thyroid glands, form a central axis of endocrine control that regulates much of the body's metabolic activity.

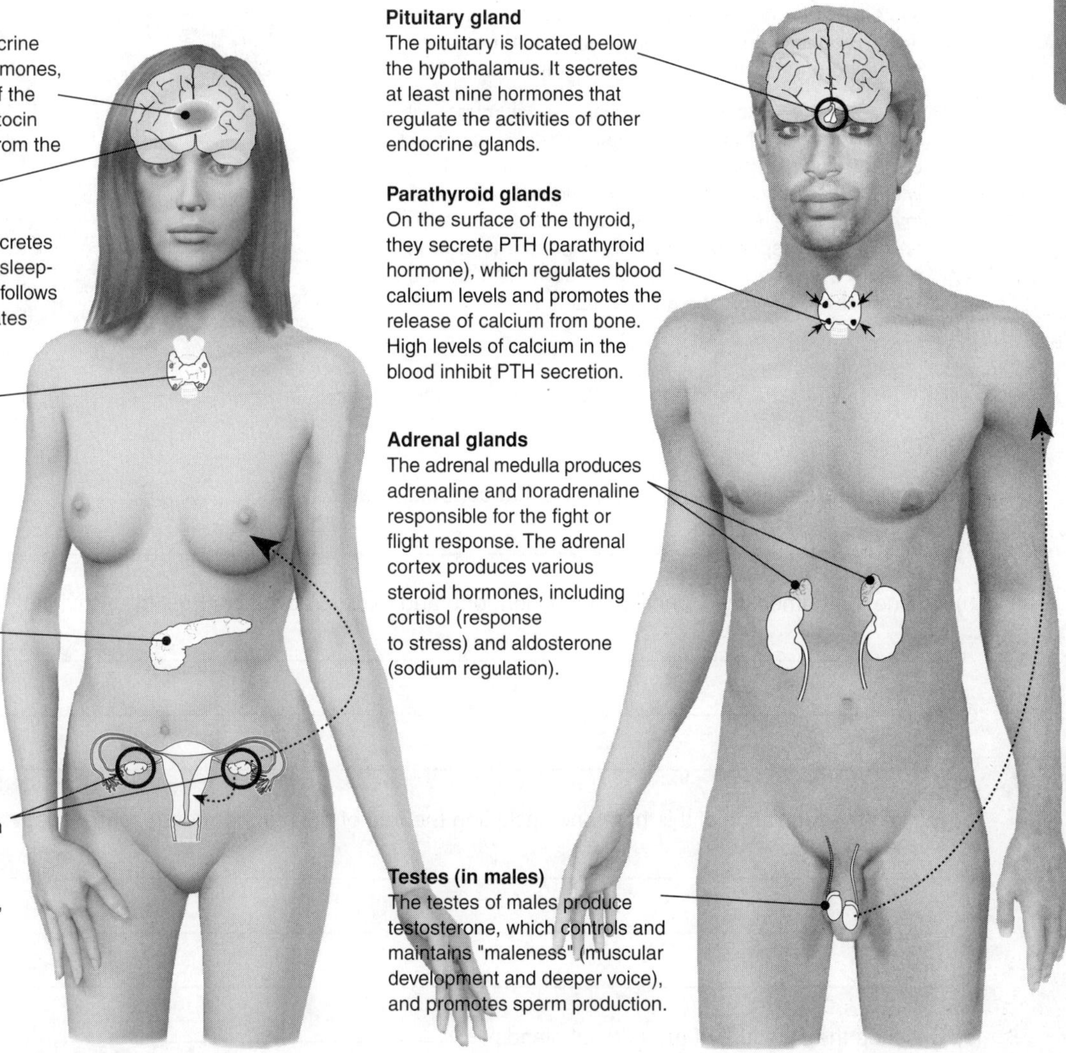

Hypothalamus
Coordinates nervous and endocrine systems. Secretes releasing hormones, which regulate the hormones of the anterior pituitary. Produces oxytocin and ADH, which are released from the posterior pituitary.

Pineal
This small gland in the brain secretes melatonin, which regulates the sleep-wake cycle. Melatonin secretion follows a circadian rhythm and coodinates reproductive hormones too.

Thyroid gland
Secretes thyroxine, an iodine containing hormone needed for normal growth and development. Thyroxine stimulates metabolism and growth via protein synthesis.

Pancreatic islets
Specialised α and β endocrine cells in the pancreas produce glucagon and insulin. Together, these control blood sugar levels.

Ovaries (in females)
The ovaries produce oestrogen and progesterone. These hormones control and maintain female characteristics, stimulate the menstrual cycle, maintain pregnancy, and prepare the mammary glands for lactation.

Pituitary gland
The pituitary is located below the hypothalamus. It secretes at least nine hormones that regulate the activities of other endocrine glands.

Parathyroid glands
On the surface of the thyroid, they secrete PTH (parathyroid hormone), which regulates blood calcium levels and promotes the release of calcium from bone. High levels of calcium in the blood inhibit PTH secretion.

Adrenal glands
The adrenal medulla produces adrenaline and noradrenaline responsible for the fight or flight response. The adrenal cortex produces various steroid hormones, including cortisol (response to stress) and aldosterone (sodium regulation).

Testes (in males)
The testes of males produce testosterone, which controls and maintains "maleness" (muscular development and deeper voice), and promotes sperm production.

1. Explain how a hormone is different from a neurotransmitter: ____________________

____

2. Using ruled lines, connect each of the following endocrine glands with its correct role in the body

(a) Pituitary gland	The hormone from this gland regulates the levels of calcium in the blood
(b) Ovaries	Master gland secreting at least nine hormones, including growth hormone and TSH
(c) Pineal gland	Produces hormones involved in the regulation of metabolic rate
(d) Parathyroid glands	Secretes melatonin to regulate sleep patterns and cycles of reproductive hormones
(e) Thyroid	Produce estrogen and progesterone in response to hormones from the pituitary

3. Review the three types of stimuli for hormone release and describe a specific example of each:

(a) Hormonal stimulus: ____________________

(b) Humoral stimulus: ____________________

(c) Neural stimulus: ____________________

The Adrenal Glands

The **adrenals** sit above the superior tip of the kidneys. Each adrenal gland has two structurally and functionally distinct regions; an outer cortex and an inner medulla.

- The **adrenal medulla** releases two catecholamine hormones: **adrenaline** and **noradrenaline**. Their release is controlled by the sympathetic nervous system and they are responsible for the 'fight or flight' response to stress, which includes increased breathing and heart rates, and paling of skin.
- The **adrenal cortex** produces a number of **corticosteroid hormones**. Glucocorticoids (e.g. cortisol) have effects on carbohydrate metabolism, while mineralocorticoids, (e.g. aldosterone) are involved in ion regulation. Glucocorticoids are also secreted in response to long term stress. Hormone release from the adrenal cortex is controlled by the hormone ACTH from the anterior pituitary gland.

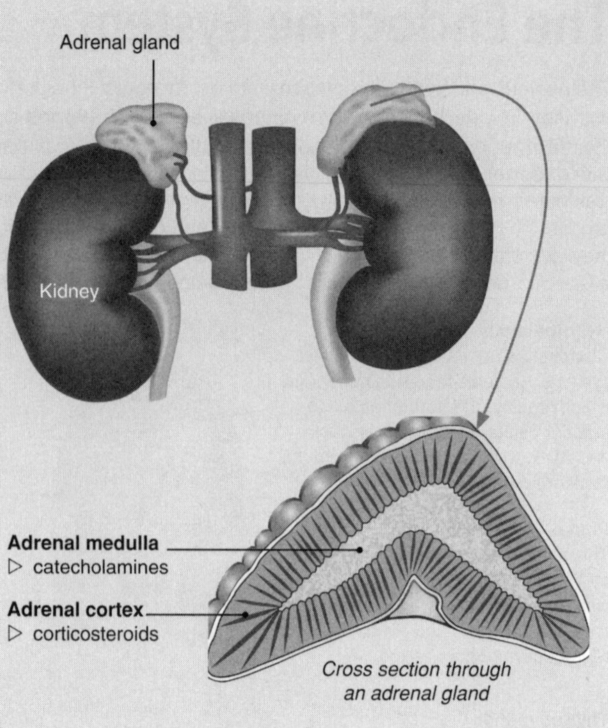

Cross section through an adrenal gland

4. (a) Identify a **target tissue** and a hormone that controls its activity: ____________________

(b) Outline the homeostatic function of this hormone and explain how it controls the activity of the target tissue:

(c) Explain the regulation of this hormone, including the role of nerves, hormones, and negative feedback as appropriate:

5. (a) Describe the structure of the adrenal glands: ____________________

(b) Relate the structural differentiation of the adrenal glands to the functional role of each distinct region:

(c) Explain the relationship between the pituitary gland and the adrenals: ____________________

(d) Explain the relationship between the sympathetic nervous system and the adrenals: ____________________

The Hypothalamus and Pituitary

The **hypothalamus** is located below the thalamus, just above the brain stem and the pituitary gland, with which it has a close structural and functional relationship. Information comes to the hypothalamus through sensory pathways from sensory receptors. On the basis of this information, the hypothalamus controls and integrates many basic physiological activities (e.g. temperature regulation, food and fluid intake, and sleep), including the reflex activity of the **autonomic nervous system**.

One of the most important functions of the hypothalamus is to link the nervous system to the endocrine system (via the pituitary). The hypothalamus contains **neurosecretory cells**. These are specialised secretory neurons, which are both nerve cells and endocrine cells. They produce hormones (usually peptides) in the cell body, which are packaged into droplets and transported along the axon. At the axon terminal, the **neurohormone** is released into the blood in response to nerve impulses.

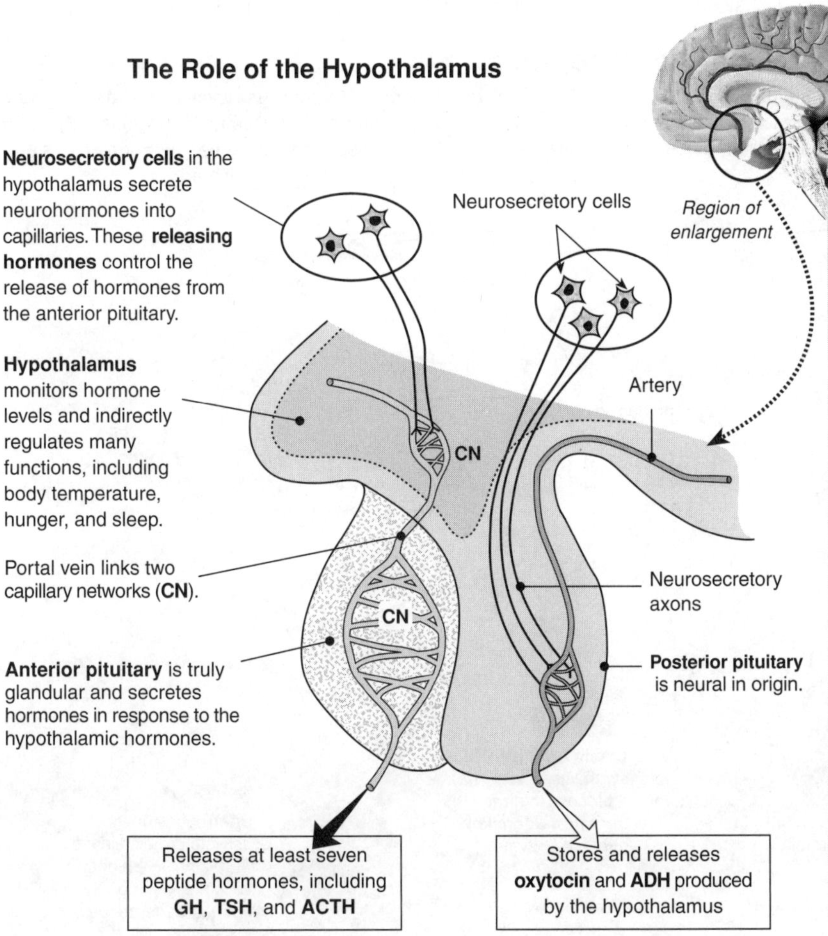

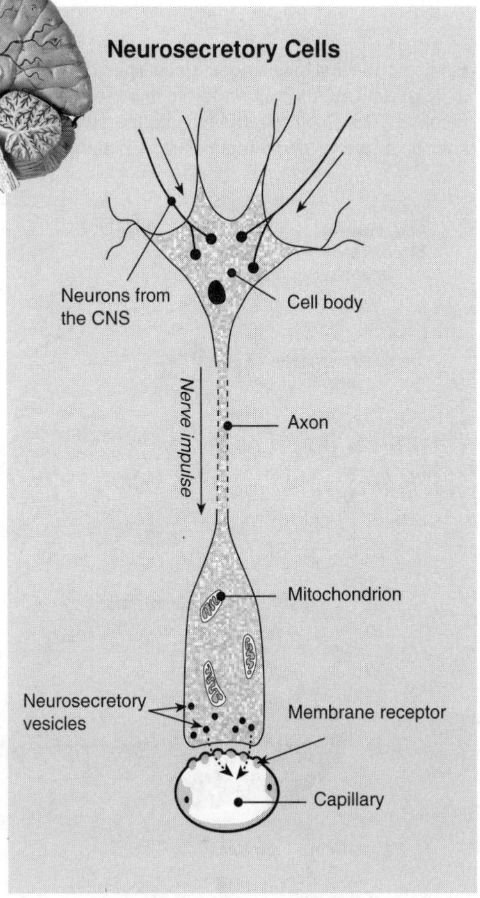

1. (a) Explain how the anterior and posterior pituitary differ with respect to their relationship to the hypothalamus:

(b) Explain how these differences relate to the nature of the hormonal secretions for each region:

2. Describe the role of the neurohormones released by the hypothalamus:

3. Explain why the adrenal and thyroid glands atrophy if the pituitary gland ceases to function:

4. Although the anterior pituitary is often called the master gland, the hypothalamus could also claim that title. Explain:

Signal Transduction

Once a hormone signal is released, it is carried in the blood to target cells that respond specifically to that hormone. For example, **adrenaline** binds to a family of membrane receptors called G protein-coupled receptors. Once the adrenaline has bound, the G protein becomes activated and regulates an array of activities, many involved with the flight or fight response of the body. There are two main groups of adrenergic receptors; α and β receptors. In both instances the adrenaline acts as a **first messenger**. It does not cross the plasma membrane, but binds and activates a transmembrane receptor to produce a **second messenger**. In the case of α receptors, the activated G protein reacts directly with an enzyme to cause a cellular response. When β receptors are activated, the G protein interacts with an intermediate enzyme, **adenylate cyclase** which produces cyclic AMP **(cAMP).** This in turn interacts with and regulates other proteins and enzymes to initiate a cellular response. Once the target cells respond, the response is recognised by the hormone-producing cell through a feedback signal and the hormone is degraded.

Adrenergic Receptors

Binding of the first messenger, adrenaline, to α type adrenergic receptors (below) activates the G protein component of the G protein-coupled receptor. The G protein travels into the cell cytoplasm where it binds specific enzymes and alters cellular function.

Beta (β) adrenergic receptors (below) use cyclic AMP as a second messenger to link the hormone to the cellular response. Cellular concentration of cAMP increases markedly once a hormone binds and the cascade of enzyme-driven reactions is initiated.

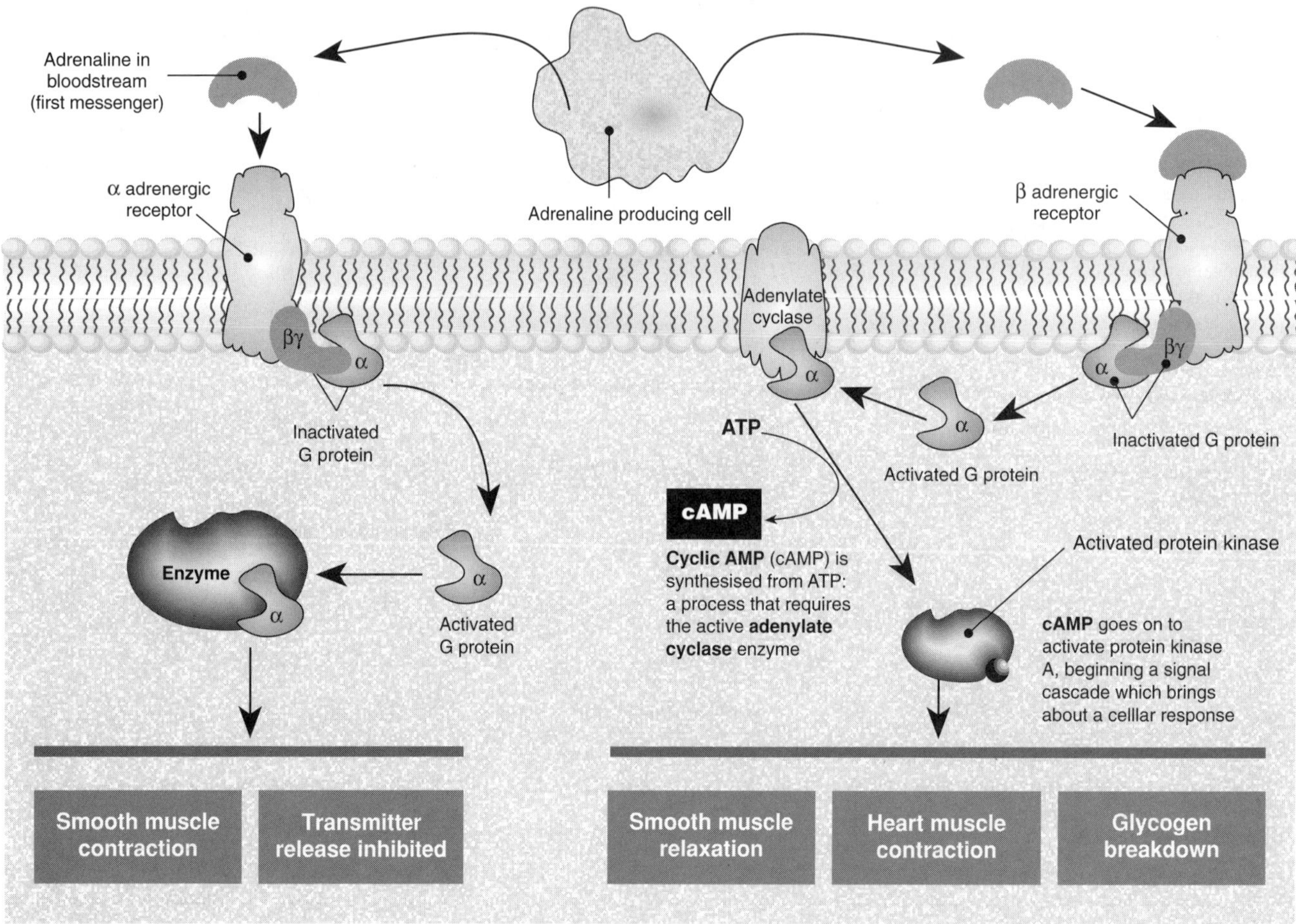

1. Explain how differences in the membrane receptor are related to how adrenaline brings about its intracellular effects:

2. Explain how a very small amount of hormone is able to exert a disproportionately large effect on a target cell:

3. Explain how the binding of a hormone to a target cell can be likened to an enzyme-substrate reaction:

***Related activities:** Cell Signalling* ***Web links:** Signal Transduction, Adrenaline Action, Peptide Hormone Action, First and Second Messenger System*

Pancreatic Histology

The **pancreas** is a diffuse organ, which lies alongside the stomach. For many years, the pancreas was thought to be only an exocrine gland, with a role in producing digestive secretions, but in 1869 Paul Langerhans discovered some unusual ductless cell clusters within the pancreatic tissue. These came to be called the **islets of Langerhans**, and were found to have an endocrine function in the regulation of blood glucose. The pancreas is now often described as an **organ gland,** because of its dual roles. The histology of the pancreas, and the functions of its endocrine and exocrine regions are described below.

The Pancreas

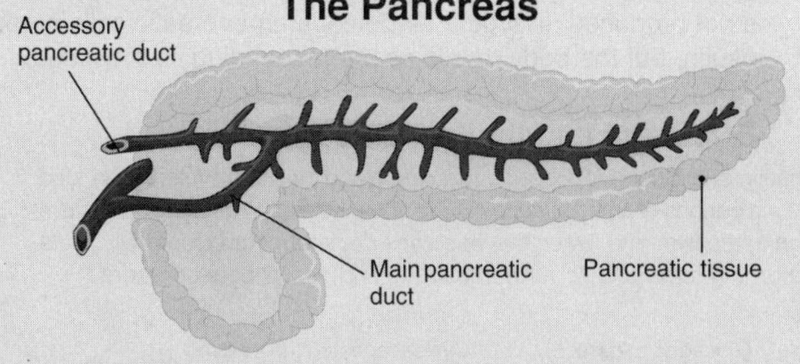

Gross structure of the human pancreas

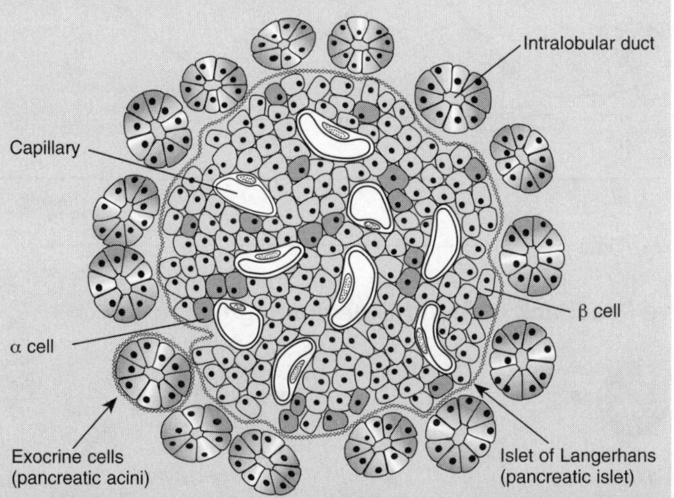

Diagram of pancreatic tissue

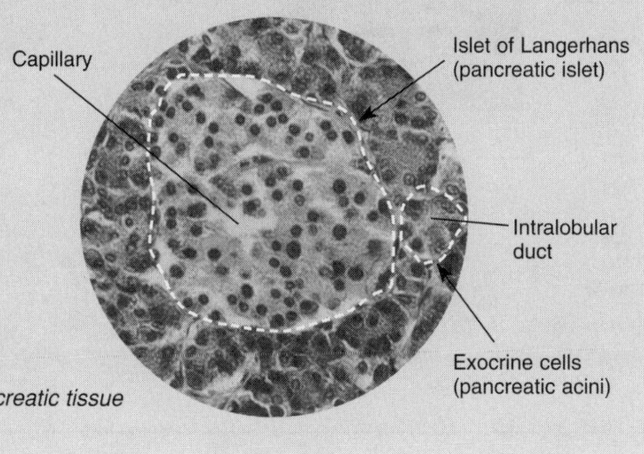

LM of pancreatic tissue

Endocrine Function

The islets of Langerhans are distinctive areas containing the endocrine cells of the pancreas. They make up 1-2% of the total mass of the pancreas.

There are five types of endocrine cells. The alpha (α) cells and beta (β) cells make up the majority of the islet cell mass (15% and 65% of the total respectively). The main homeostatic role of the pancreas is to regulate blood sugar levels.

- The α cells secrete **glucagon**, which elevates blood glucose levels if they become too low.
- The β cells secrete **insulin**, which lowers blood glucose by promoting its cellular uptake. The two hormones work together to maintain blood glucose at a constant level.

The remaining endocrine cells have the following roles:

- Delta (δ) cells: produce the hormone **somatostatin** which affects neurotransmission and cell proliferation.
- PP-cells: control self regulation of pancreatic secretions.
- Epsilion (ε) cells: produce ghrelin, an appetite stimulant.

Islet cells are not readily distinguishable by routine staining techniques. Special stains are required to differentiate them.

Exocrine Function

The bulk of the pancreas is composed of pancreatic exocrine cells, which are arranged in clusters called **acini** (singular acinus). The cells contain **bicarbonate ions** and precursor digestive enzymes which are secreted into the duodenal region of the small intestine to aid digestion of food. Secretion from the acini is via a series of small intralobular ducts which drain into the major pancreatic duct, and from there into the duodenum.

The enzymes (in their active form) are as follows:

- Trypsin and chymotrypsin: digestion of protein
- Pancreatic lipase: digestion of lipid (fats)
- Pancreatic amylase: digestion of carbohydrates

The role of the bicarbonate ions is to neutralise the acidic **chyme** entering the small intestine from the stomach. The increase in pH allows the digestive enzymes of the small intestine to function.

1. Discuss the statement: "The exocrine and endocrine regions of the pancreas are structurally and functionally distinct":

Control of Blood Glucose

The endocrine portion of the **pancreas** produces the hormones that regulate blood glucose. Two hormones, insulin and glucagon, maintain blood glucose at a steady state through **negative feedback**. Insulin promotes a decrease in blood glucose synthesising glycogen and promoting cellular uptake of glucose. Glucagon promotes an increase in blood glucose through the breakdown of glycogen and the synthesis of glucose from amino acids. When normal blood glucose levels are restored, negative feedback stops hormone secretion. Regulating blood glucose to within narrow limits allows energy to be available to cells as needed. Extra energy is stored, as glycogen or fat, and is mobilised to meet energy needs as required. The liver is pivotal in these carbohydrate conversions. One of the consequences of a disruption to this system is the disease **diabetes mellitus**. In type 1 diabetes, the insulin producing β cells of the pancreatic tissue are destroyed as a result of autoimmune activity and insulin is not produced. In type 2 diabetes, the pancreatic cells produce insulin, but the body's cells cease responding its message.

Effects of Insulin and Glucagon

The hormones insulin and glucagon together regulate blood glucose levels. When food is unavailable for long periods of time, glucose can be obtained firstly from the metabolism of stored glycogen in the liver and, when this becomes depleted, from stored fats. Data are based on a morning meal with no further food (fasting) for 12 hours or more.

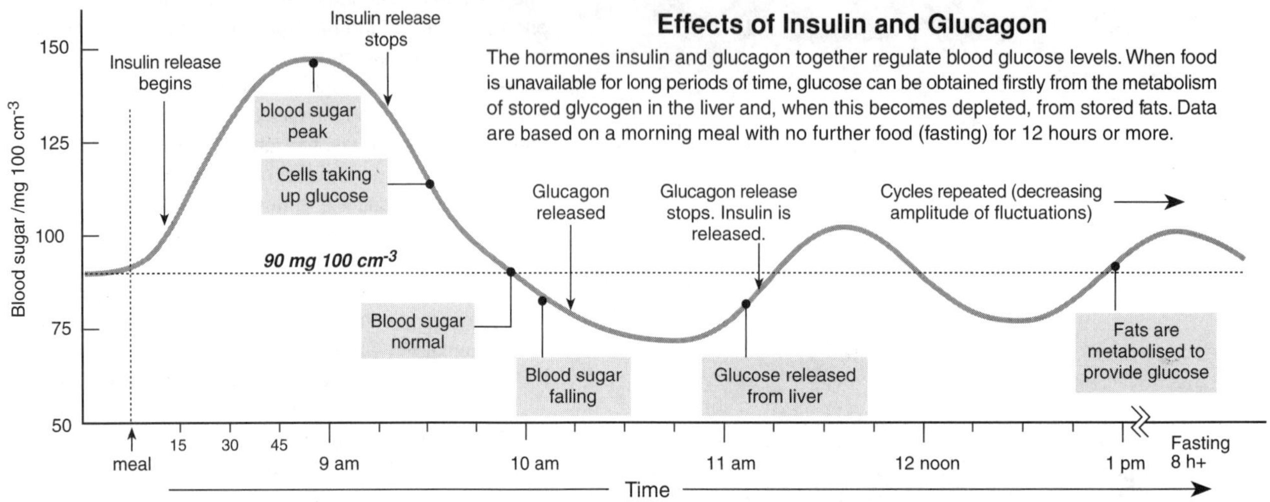

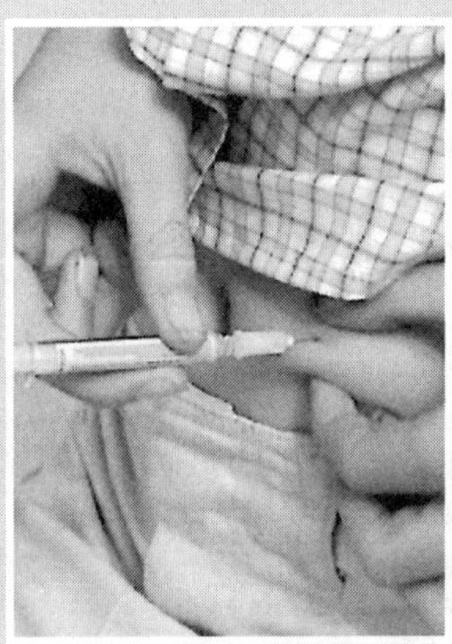

In type 1 diabetes mellitus, the β cells of the pancreas are destroyed and insulin must be delivered to the bloodstream by injection. Type 2 diabetics produce insulin, but their cells do not respond to it.

Negative Feedback in Blood Glucose Regulation

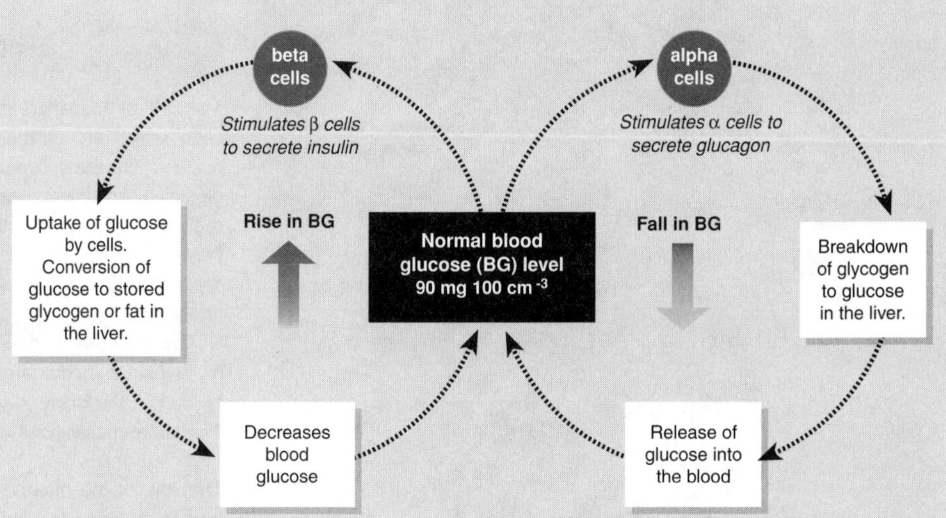

1. (a) Identify the stimulus for the release of insulin: ______

   (b) Identify the stimulus for the release of glucagon: ______

   (c) Explain how glucagon brings about an increase in blood glucose level: ______

   (d) Explain how insulin brings about a decrease in blood glucose level: ______

2. Outline the role of negative feedback in the control of blood glucose: ______

3. Explain why fats are metabolised after a long period without food: ______

The Liver in Carbohydrate Metabolism

The liver has a central role in carbohydrate metabolism, specifically the production of glucose from non-carbohydrate sources, and the interconversion of glucose and glycogen (a glucose polysaccharide). These processes ensure that carbohydrate is stored or made available to cells as required and are regulated by hormones, principally insulin and glucagon, but also adrenaline and glucocorticoids.

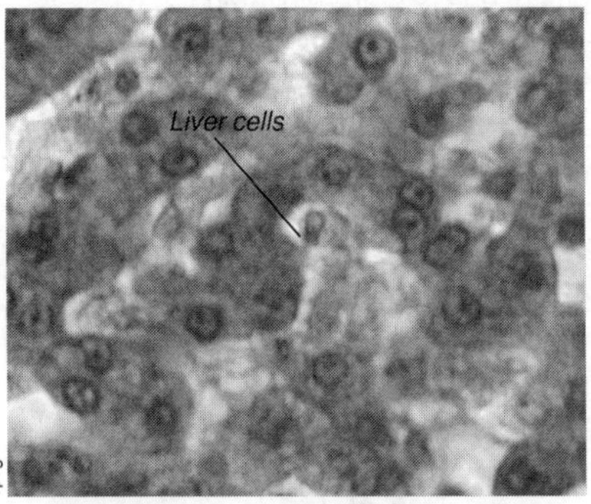

Glycogen is stored within the liver cells. Glucagon stimulates its conversion to glucose.

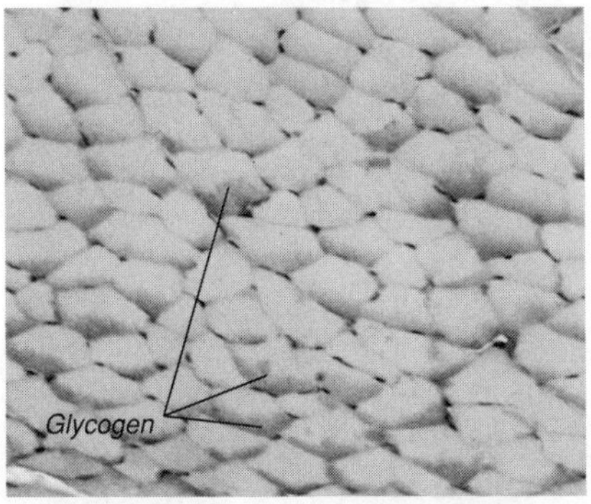

Glycogen is also stored in muscle, where it is squeezed out to the periphery of the cells.

- **Glycogenesis**
  Excess glucose in the blood is converted to **glycogen**. **Insulin** stimulates glycogenesis in response to high blood glucose. Glycogen is stored in the liver and muscle tissue.

- **Glycogenolysis**
  Conversion of stored glycogen to glucose (glycogen breakdown). The free glucose is released into the blood. The hormones **glucagon** and adrenaline stimulate glycogenolysis in response to low blood glucose.

- **Gluconeogenesis**
  Production of glucose from non-carbohydrate sources (e.g. glycerol, pyruvate, lactate, and amino acids). Adrenaline and glucocorticoid hormones (e.g. cortisol) stimulate gluconeogenesis in response to fasting, starvation, or prolonged periods of exercise when glycogen stores are exhausted. It is also part of the general adaptation syndrome in response to stress.

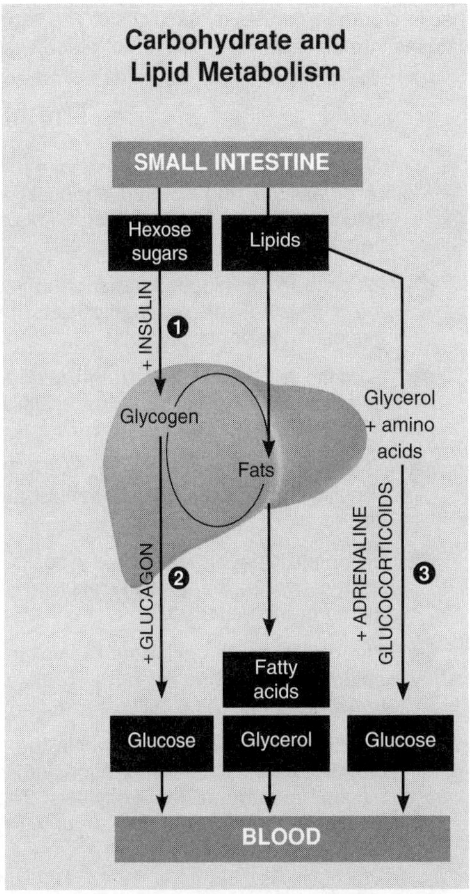

1. Explain the three important processes of carbohydrate metabolism in the liver, including how these are regulated:

   (a) ______________________________

   (b) ______________________________

   (c) ______________________________

2. Identify the processes occurring at each numbered stage on the diagram above, right:

   (a) Process occurring at point 1: ______________________________

   (b) Process occurring at point 2: ______________________________

   (c) Process occurring at point 3: ______________________________

3. Explain why it is important that the body can readily convert and produce different forms of carbohydrates:

   ____

Mechanism of Insulin Secretion

The release of insulin from the pancreatic beta cells is a complex multi-stage process involving selective entry of glucose into the cells and intracellular metabolism of the glucose to trigger the activation of voltage-gated calcium channels and export of insulin-storage granules by exocytosis. The exported insulin then diffuses into the extensive network of blood vessels surrounding the pancreatic islets. Insulin release occurs in two phases. The insulin initially released when glucose is taken up into the cell depends on the amount in storage. Once this is depleted, a second phase of longer duration occurs, during which insulin must be synthesised, processed, and secreted for the period of time over which blood glucose levels are elevated.

The Mechanism of Insulin Secretion

The diagram below summarises the role of potassium and calcium channels in insulin secretion from a pancreatic islet beta cell.

1. Glucose in the blood is transported into the β cells (of the pancreatic islets) by glucose transporter proteins.
2. Glucose is phosphorylated and used to generate ATP, increasing the intracellular ATP levels.
3. The ATP/ADP ratio increases, and ATP-sensitive potassium (K^+) channels are closed.
4. Increased K^+ levels lead to rise in positive charge inside the β cell, resulting in membrane depolarisation.
5. The depolarisation activates the voltage gated Ca^{2+} channels, and Ca^{2+} is transported into the β cell.
6. The increased Ca^{2+} levels within the β cell initiates insulin transportation across the cell membrane by exocytosis. The insulin is then transported around the body via the bloodstream.

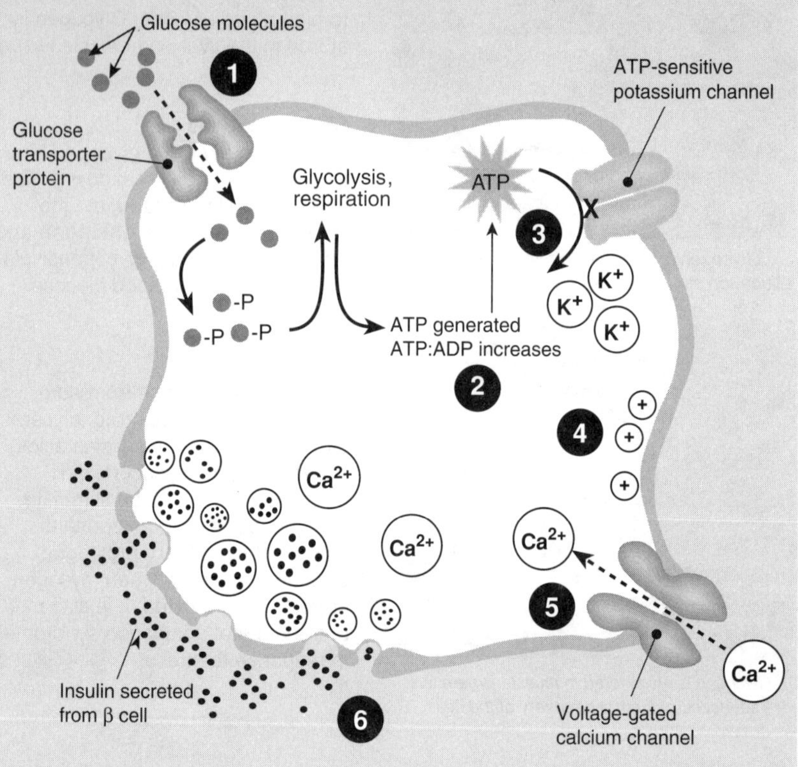

Adapted from Beta Cell Biology Consortium

1. Explain the role the following steps play in insulin secretion from a pancreatic beta cell:

   (a) The glucose transporter protein: ____

   (b) Increased intracellular ATP levels: ____

   (c) Membrane depolarisation: ____

   (d) Activation of the voltage-gated Ca^{2+} channels: ____

2. Explain the importance of the pancreatic islets being surrounded in an extensive network of blood vessels:

3. Explain the adaptive value of a two phase insulin release: an initial, large rapid release after eating, followed by a slower, longer lasting phase of insulin secretion:

Diabetes Mellitus

Diabetes is a general term for a range of disorders sharing two common symptoms: production of large amounts of urine and excessive thirst. **Diabetes mellitus** is the most common form of diabetes and is characterised by **hyperglycemia** (high blood sugar). **Type 1** diabetics lack insulin and usually develop the disease in childhood, while **type 2** diabetes is more typically a disease of older, overweight people whose cells develop a resistance to insulin. Both types are chronic, incurable conditions but they are managed differently. Type 1 is treated primarily with injection of insulin (now produced using genetic modification of microbes), whereas type 2 diabetics manage their disease through diet and exercise in an attempt to limit the disease's long term effects, which include kidney and retinal damage, cardiovascular disease, persistent ulcers, and gangrene.

In **type 1 diabetes mellitus**, the beta (β) cells are destroyed (probably in an autoimmune response following viral infection). No insulin is produced and blood glucose is elevated.

In **type 2 diabetes mellitus**, the body still produces insulin, but the body's cells do not respond properly to it. Cellular uptake of glucose is impaired and glucose enters the bloodstream.

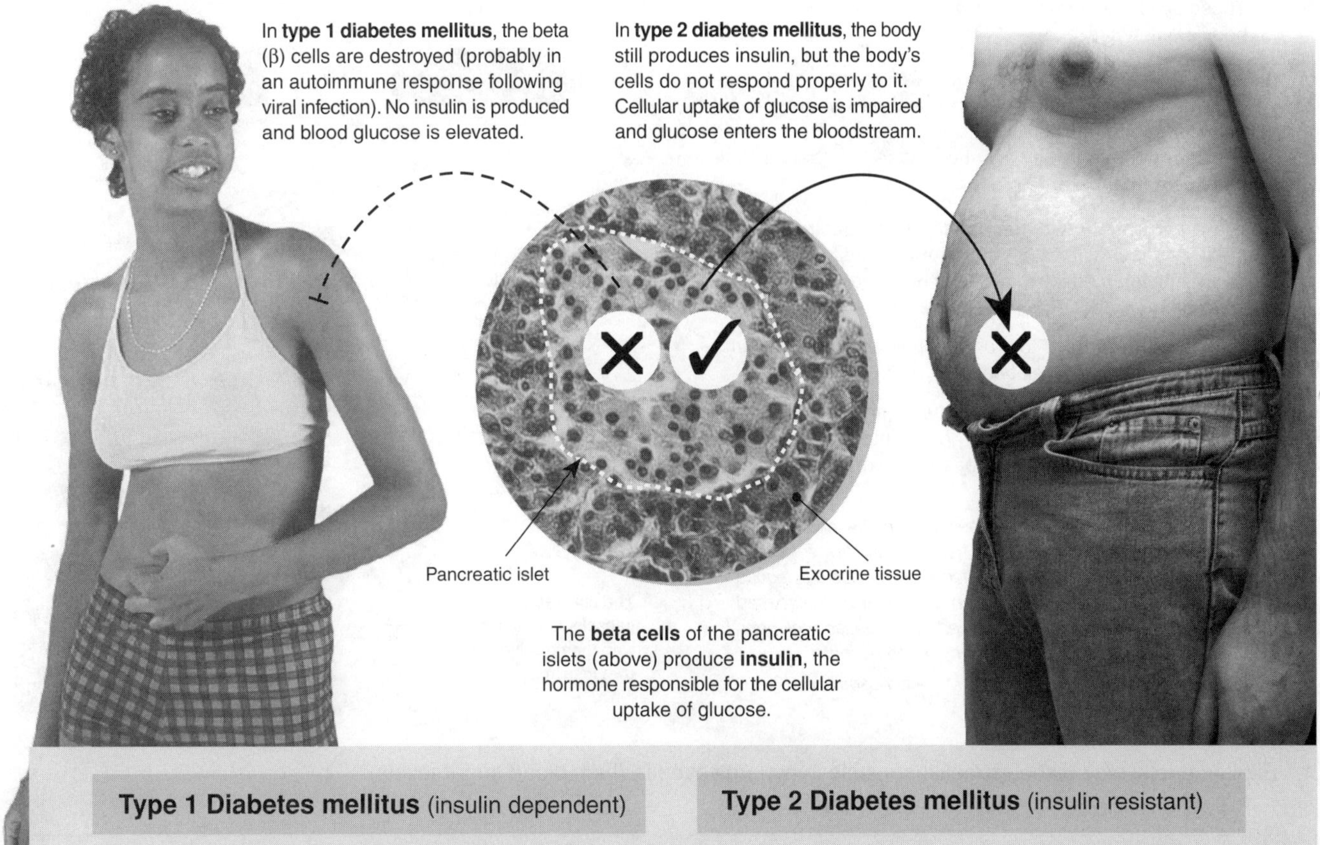

The **beta cells** of the pancreatic islets (above) produce **insulin**, the hormone responsible for the cellular uptake of glucose.

Type 1 Diabetes mellitus (insulin dependent)

The body does not produce insulin

Age at onset: Early in life; often in childhood (type 1 diabetes mellitus is often called juvenile onset diabetes).

Cause: Absolute deficiency of insulin due to lack of insulin production (pancreatic β cells are destroyed in an autoimmune reaction). There is a genetic component but usually a childhood viral infection triggers the development of the disease. Mumps, coxsackie, and rubella are implicated.

Treatment: Blood glucose is monitored regularly and insulin injections combined with dietary management have been used to keep blood sugar levels stable. New therapies involving transplants of insulin-producing islet cells have been used with varying degrees of success. In the future, the option of **gene therapy**, where the gene for insulin production is inserted into the patient's cells, may be possible.

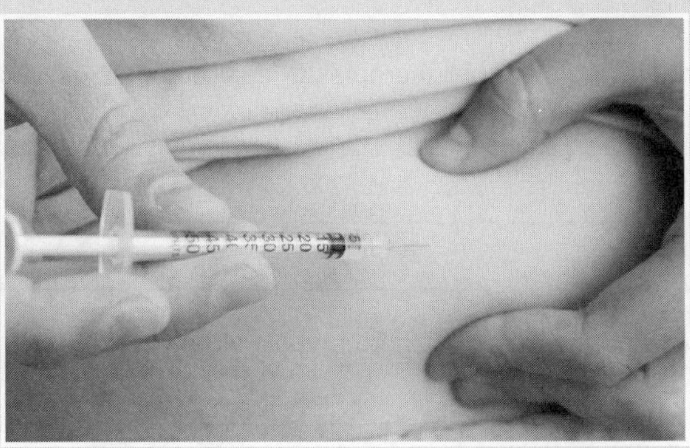

Type 2 Diabetes mellitus (insulin resistant)

The body fails to respond to insulin

Age at onset: Historically, type 2 diabetes mellitus has usually occurred in adults over the age of 40, but its incidence is increasing in younger adults and obese children.

Cause: Type 2 diabetes may have a genetic component (in susceptibility), but it occurs most commonly as a result of lifestyle factors. Obesity (BMI > 27), a sedentary lifestyle, hypertension, high blood lipids, and a poor diet all contribute to make a person more susceptible to developing type 2 diabetes. Ethnicity may also be a contributing factor.

Treatment: Increasing general physical activity, losing weight (especially abdominal fat), and improving diet may be sufficient to control type 2 diabetes in many cases. The use of prescribed anti-diabetic drugs and insulin therapy (injections) may be required if lifestyle changes are insufficient on their own.

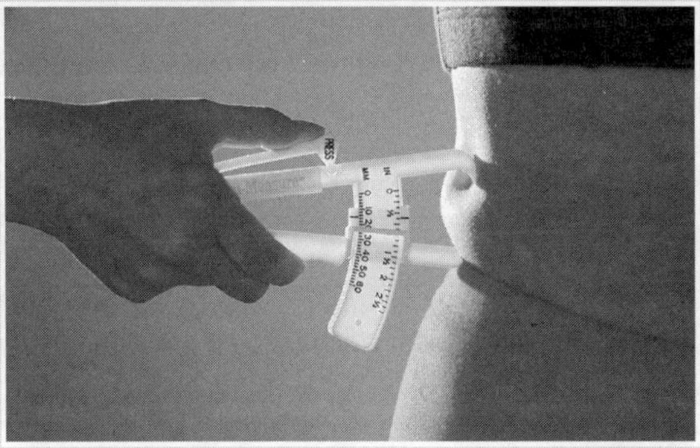

Treating Diabetes Mellitus Using Stem Cell Therapy

Shortages of donors for pancreatic transplants have prompted researchers to explore **stem cell therapies** as an alternative to donor tissue. Insulin-secreting pancreatic islet cells produced *in vitro* can be transplanted into diabetic patients, where they produce insulin naturally. Such treatments start with a supply of stem cells, either:

- Embryonic stem cells from blastocysts (5 day old embryos). These cells are pluripotent and can give rise to any of the body's cell types.
- Adult stem cells from bone marrow or cord blood. These cells can normally give rise to a limited number of cell types (they are **multipotent**). Under appropriate culturing conditions though, they may be induced to change their developmental path.

There are currently two approaches to producing insulin-secreting cells *in vitro*. With both approaches, the cultured cells are transplanted into a recipient in the hope that enough insulin will be produced to regulate blood glucose.

1. Use **growth factors** to promote their differentiation into insulin producing β islet cells.
2. Use **recombinant DNA techniques** (genetic engineering) to insert an insulin producing gene into the stem cells, and produce a culture of cells that express the gene.

This therapy has met with some success. In one trial, recently diagnosed type 1 diabetics were treated using transplants of stem cells from bone marrow. This technique (called autologous haematopoietic stem cells transplantation or AHST) increased beta cell function in all but one patient and induced prolonged insulin independence in the majority of the patients.
(Source: Journal of the American Medical Association, 2007)

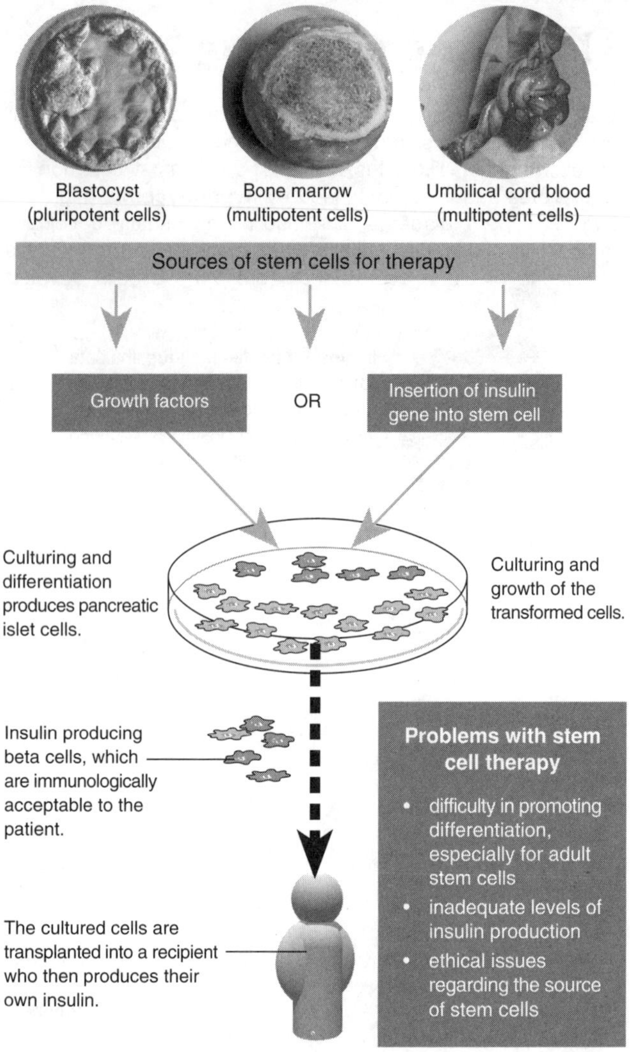

1. Explain briefly why diabetes mellitus results in hyperglycaemia (high blood sugar levels): ______

2. Discuss the differences between type 1 and type 2 diabetes, including causes and treatments: ______

3. Explain why the increase in type 2 diabetes is considered epidemic in the developed world: ______

4. (a) Describe some of the technical difficulties encountered when using stem cell therapies to treat diabetes mellitus: ______

   (b) Explain why adult stem cell therapies are less controversial than therapies using embryonic stem cells: ______

Control of Heart Rate

The origin of the heartbeat is **myogenic**; the contractions arise as an intrinsic property of the cardiac muscle itself. The heartbeat is regulated by a conduction system consisting of specialised muscle cells called the pacemaker (sinoatrial node) and a tract of conducting Purkyne fibres. The pacemaker initiates the cardiac cycle by spontaneously generating action potentials. It sets a basic rhythm for the heart, but the rate is influenced by higher brain function and by the cardiovascular control centre in the medulla in response to sensory information. Changes in the rate and force of heart contraction alter the **cardiac output**, i.e. the amount of blood pumped by the heart. When the body needs to prepare for physical exertion, cardiac output increases to meet the greater demand for gas exchange. Both nervous and endocrine controls are involved in regulating these changes.

Hormonal Control of Heart Rate

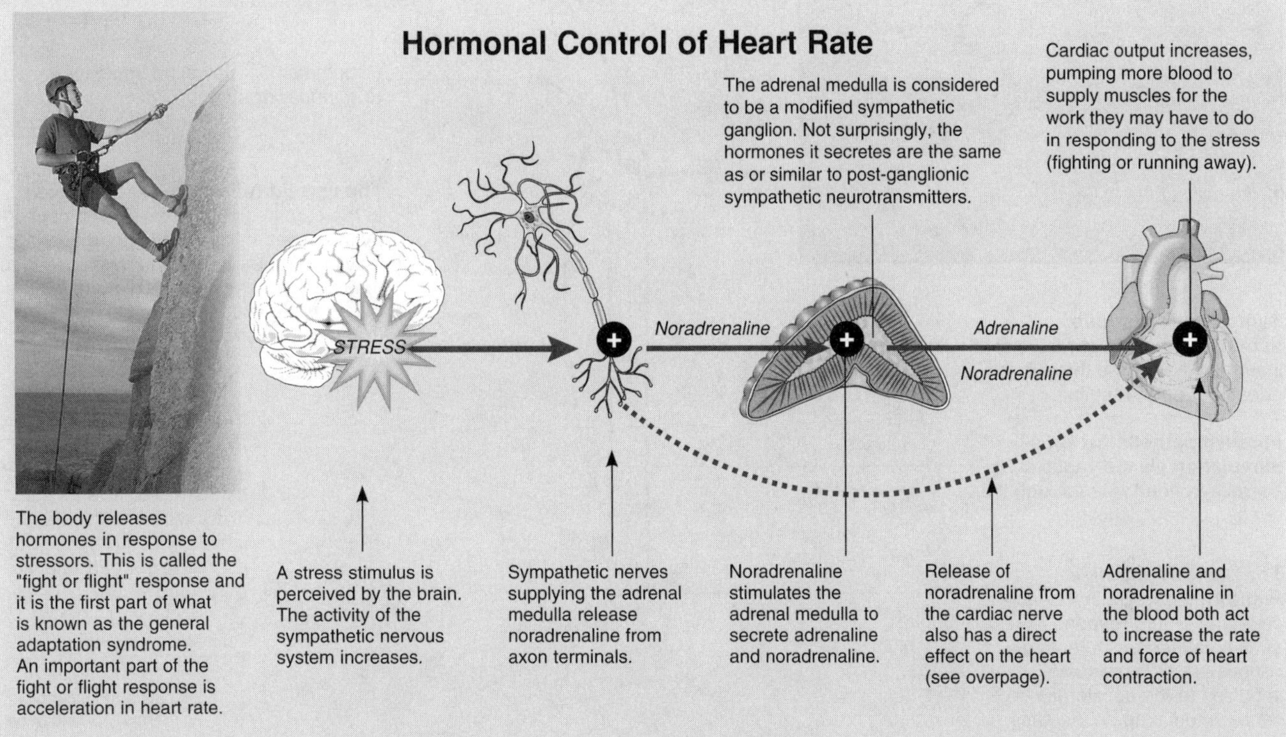

1. With respect to the heart beat, explain what is meant by **myogenic**: ______

2. Describe the role of the sinoatrial node in heart function: ______

3. Explain the role of noradrenaline as both a neurotransmitter and a hormone in the regulation of heart rate:

4. Explain the adaptive value of an elevated heart rate during the 'flight or fight' response: ______

5. (a) Describe the location of the cardiovascular control centre and its two basic components: ______

   (b) Explain the general role of the cardiovascular control centre in regulating heart rate: ______

Nervous control of heartbeat is controlled by sympathetic and parasympathetic pathways with opposing effects. Of these, sympathetic stimulation via the cardiac nerve is the predominant influence. The diagram below gives an overview of how the autonomic nervous system controls heart rate. The effector, which brings about the action in each case, is the heart muscle.

Autonomic Nervous System Control of Heart Rate

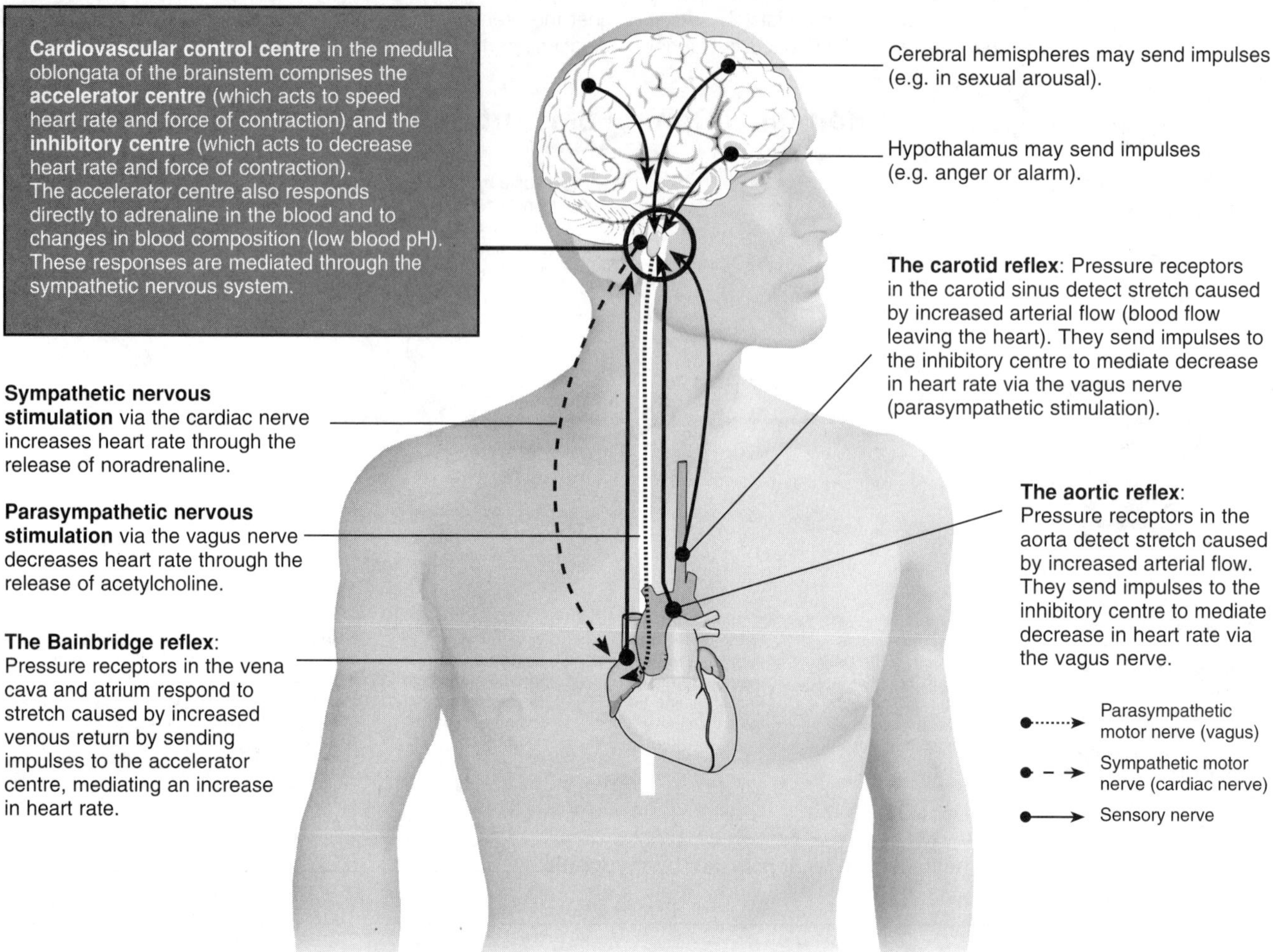

6. Describe the overall effect of the following on heart rate:

   (a) Sympathetic nervous system: ______

   (b) Parasympathetic nervous system: ______

7. (a) Describe a stimulus for a decrease in heart rate: ______

   (b) Explain how this change in heart rate is brought about: ______

   ______

8. Identify two locations of pressure receptors involved in control of heart rate and state what they respond to:

   (a) ______

   (b) ______

9. Guarana is a chemical which is found in many energy drinks. A group of students designed an experiment to test whether guarana stimulates a cardiovascular response. The test subjects had their pulses recorded before and after drinking an energy drink containing a known amount of guarana.

   (a) Suggest two reasons why the test subjects may respond in different ways: ______

   ______

   (b) Describe a suitable control for this experiment: ______

   ______

   ______

KEY TERMS: Word Find

Use the clues below to find the relevant key terms in the WORD FIND grid

X	T	M	F	X	V	T	A	D	R	E	N	A	L	G	L	A	N	D	S	D	X	P	A	E
B	H	A	H	M	P	A	U	F	I	R	S	T	M	E	S	S	E	N	G	E	R	M	Q	X
W	L	O	Y	U	K	U	X	U	G	N	O	R	A	D	R	E	N	A	L	I	N	E	C	G
S	I	G	N	A	L	T	R	A	N	S	D	U	C	T	I	O	N	P	A	T	H	W	A	Y
F	K	L	Z	X	I	S	T	E	M	C	E	L	L	T	H	E	R	A	P	Y	W	W	N	A
G	E	N	D	O	C	R	I	N	E	G	L	A	N	D	W	T	M	U	W	H	H	O	C	L
G	L	U	C	O	N	E	O	G	E	N	E	S	I	S	K	S	E	D	W	B	G	Z	C	A
Y	R	S	H	Q	G	N	T	P	A	N	C	R	E	A	S	P	D	C	Y	A	E	I	Y	Z
H	B	A	N	D	A	D	R	E	N	A	L	I	N	E	T	F	U	X	C	X	P	B	C	Q
N	A	D	R	E	N	A	L	M	E	D	U	L	L	A	T	H	L	U	B	M	H	B	L	H
W	I	H	K	U	S	D	I	A	B	E	T	E	S	M	E	L	L	I	T	U	S	V	I	O
N	N	E	X	O	C	R	I	N	E	G	L	A	N	D	M	G	A	C	L	B	P	D	C	R
Y	S	H	I	F	V	X	V	C	A	T	E	C	H	O	L	A	M	I	N	E	S	Z	A	M
X	U	Z	A	S	N	K	S	E	C	O	N	D	M	E	S	S	E	N	G	E	R	Z	M	O
K	L	C	V	S	B	O	L	B	B	G	L	Y	C	O	G	E	N	E	S	I	S	K	P	N
D	I	I	S	L	E	T	S	O	F	L	A	N	G	E	R	H	A	N	S	F	F	T	J	E
W	N	C	E	A	A	G	L	Y	C	O	G	E	N	O	L	Y	S	I	S	D	E	L	P	S

Chemical messengers produced by endocrine glands.

A ductless gland secreting hormones directly into the blood. (2 words)

The hormone that lowers blood glucose, primarily through the cellular uptake of glucose, but also by promoting storage of glucose as glycogen.

An abdominal organ with both endocrine and exocrine functions.

Excess blood glucose is converted into glycogen.

Conversion of stored glycogen to glucose (glycogen breakdown). The free glucose is released into the blood.

A hormone involved in the flight or fight response of the body.

The hormone that brings about the physiological processes to elevate blood glucose levels if they fall too low.

An important second messenger derived from ATP (2 words).

Ductless cell clusters found within pancreatic tissue, which have an endocrine function in the regulation of blood glucose (3 words).

The production of glucose from non-carbohydrate sources (e.g. glycerol, pyruvate, lactate, and amino acids).

A mechanism that converts a mechanical or chemical stimulus into a specific cellular response (3 words).

A gland that delivers secretions via a duct (2 words).

A disease caused by the body's inability to produce or react to insulin (2 words).

The lower half of the brainstem, below the pons. It regulates the reflex responses that control breathing, heart beat, blood pressure, and other essential involuntary functions.

Fight or flight hormones released by the adrenal glands in response to stress.

Endocrine glands located on top of the kidneys. They play a function in regulating metabolism, water balance, and stress (2 words).

A hormone and neurotransmitter produced by the adrenal gland.

The inner region of the adrenal gland. It produces the catecholamine hormones adrenaline and noradrenaline.

A substance which does not cross the plasma membrane, but binds and activates a transmembrane receptor to produce a second messenger (2 words).

An intracellular substance that relays signals from receptors on the cell surface to target molecules inside the cell (2 words).

The process of introducing stem cells into a person in order to treat a disease or injury (3 words).

UNIT F214

4.2.1

Excretion

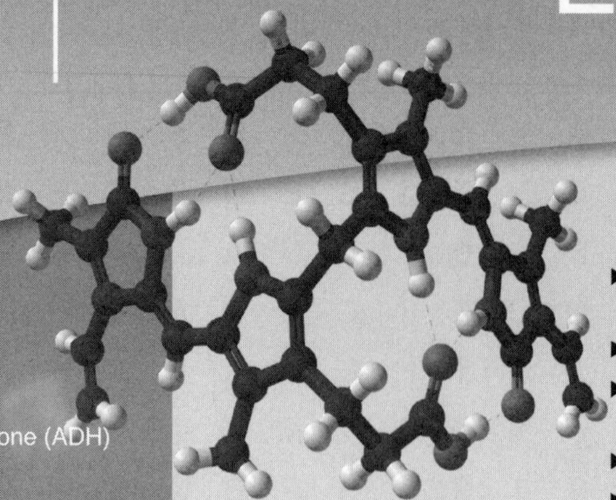

Bilirubin: a product of haemoglobin breakdown

KEY CONCEPTS

- Cellular metabolism creates metabolic waste products which must be excreted.
- Excretion is the job of the kidneys, liver, and the skin.
- Excess amino acids are metabolised in the liver through the ornithine cycle to form urea.
- The kidneys excrete urea and toxins from the body.
- Urine formation involves ultrafiltration and selective reabsorption. It is regulated through negative feedback.
- Renal failure is treated through dialysis and transplants.

KEY TERMS

anabolic steroids
antidiuretic hormone (ADH)
collecting duct
deamination
detoxification
distal convoluted tubule
excretion
glomerulus
hepatocyte
hypothalamus
kidney
kidney failure
kidney transplant
liver
liver lobule
loop of Henle
ornithine cycle
osmoreceptors
proximal convoluted tubule
renal dialysis
secretion
selective reabsorption
transamination
ultrafiltration
urea
urine
urine analysis

OBJECTIVES

□ 1. Use the **KEY TERMS** to help you understand and complete these objectives.

Disposing of wastes

pages 71

□ 2. Explain what is meant by **excretion**. Explain why organisms must regulate water and ion balances and dispose of the waste products of metabolism.

□ 3. Identify the major waste products excreted from the body and name the organs involved in their disposal.

The liver and homeostasis

pages 72-74

□ 4. Describe the gross structure and histology of the **liver**. Include reference to: liver lobule, hepatocytes, portal triad, Kupffer cells, sinusoids, central vein.

□ 5. Describe the role of the liver in protein metabolism: **deamination**, **transamination**, and formation of urea. Include an outline of the **ornithine cycle**.

□ 6. Describe the various roles of the liver in **detoxification**.

The urinary system

pages 75-81

□ 7. Describe the structure of the human urinary system, including kidneys, ureters, bladder, and urethra. Recognise the kidney as a major organ of homeostasis. Describe two main functions of the kidney in regulating the composition of body fluids.

□ 8. Describe the gross structure of the mammalian kidney to include the cortex, medulla, and renal pelvis. Interpret features of the histology of the kidney from sections viewed with a light microscope.

□ 9. Using a labelled diagram, describe the structure and arrangement of a nephron and its associated blood vessels in relation to its function in producing urine. Include reference to **glomerulus**, proximal and distal **convoluted tubules**, and **collecting duct**.

□ 10. Explain how the kidney nephron produces urine. Include reference to:
(a) Glomerular ultrastructure and the process of **ultrafiltration**.
(b) **Selective reabsorption** in the proximal convoluted tubule.
(c) The role of the loop of Henle and the counter-current multiplier system in creating and maintaining the ionic (salt) gradient in the kidney.
(d) The role of the ionic gradient in the kidney in concentrating the urine.

□ 11. Explain the regulation of water and solute content of the blood, including the role of **osmoreceptors** in the **hypothalamus**, and the role of **antidiuretic hormone** (ADH) from the posterior pituitary.

□ 12. Describe the consequences of kidney failure. Discuss **renal dialysis** and **kidney transplants** as options for treating kidney failure. Include reference to the basis of each procedure and problems associated with their use.

□ 13. Describe the use of **urine analysis** for medical and diagnostic purposes, e.g. to detect pregnancy and the illegal use of **anabolic steroids**.

Periodicals:
Listings for this chapter are on page 340

Weblinks:
www.biozone.co.uk/weblink/OCR-A2-2832.html

Waste Products in Humans

Excretion refers to the elimination from the body of the waste products of metabolism. It should not be confused with the elimination or egestion of undigested and unabsorbed food material from the gut. In humans and other mammals, a number of organs are involved in excretion: mainly the kidneys, liver, lungs, and skin. The liver is particularly important in processing wastes, particularly in detoxifying poisons, breakdown of haemoglobin, and formation of **urea** from ammonia. Note that the breakdown products of haemoglobin are excreted in bile and pass out with the faeces, but they are not the result of digestion.

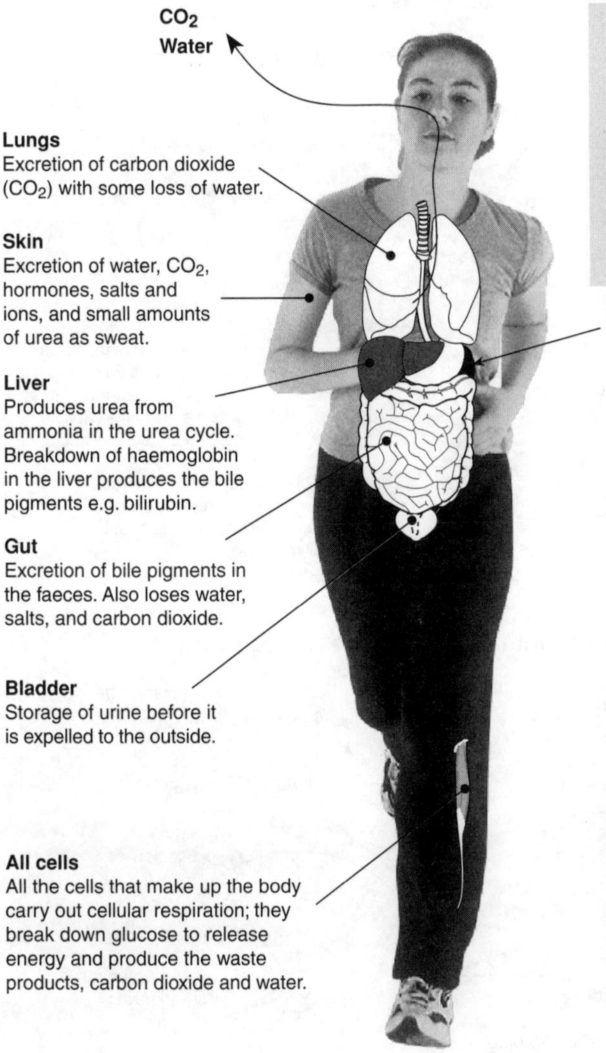

Excretion in Humans

In mammals, the kidneys are the main organs of excretion, although the liver, skin, and lungs are also important. As well as ridding the body of nitrogenous wastes, the kidneys also regulate pH and excrete many toxins that are taken in from the environment. Many toxic substances, such as alcohol, are rendered harmless by detoxification in the liver, but the kidneys can also eliminate some by actively secreting them into the urine.

Substance	Origin*	Organ(s) of excretion
Carbon dioxide		
Water		
Bile pigments		
Urea		
Ions (K^+, HCO_3^-, H^+)		
Hormones		
Poisons		
Drugs		

* Origin refers to from where in the body each substance originates

1. Explain the need for excretion: ______________________________

2. Complete the table above summarising the origin of excretory products and the main organ(s) of excretion for each.

3. Explain the role of the liver in excretion, even though it is not primarily an organ of excretion:

4. Suggest why ammonia is converted to urea to be excreted despite the fact that there is a high energy cost in doing so:

5. In people suffering renal failure, the kidneys cease to produce filtrate. Based on your knowledge of the central role of the kidneys in fluid and electrolyte balance, as well as nitrogen excretion, describe the typical symptoms of kidney failure:

***Related activities**: The Liver's Homeostatic Role, The Physiology of the Kidney,*

The Structure of the Liver

The liver the largest homeostatic organ. It is located just below the diaphragm and makes up 3-5% of body weight. It performs a vast number of functions including production of bile, storage and processing of nutrients, and detoxification of poisons and metabolic wastes. The liver receives a dual blood supply from the hepatic portal vein and hepatic arteries, and up to 20% of the total blood volume flows through it at any one time. This rich vascularisation makes it the central organ for regulating activities associated with the blood and circulatory system. In spite of its many functions, the liver tissue and the liver cells themselves are structurally relatively simple. Features of liver structure and function are outlined below.

Homeostatic Functions of the Liver

The liver is one of the largest and most complex organs in the body. It has a central role as an organ of homeostasis and performs many functions, particularly in relation to the regulation of blood composition. General functions of the liver are outlined below. Briefly summarised, the liver:

- Secretes bile, important in emulsifying fats in digestion.
- Metabolises amino acids, fats, and carbohydrates.
- Synthesises glucose from non-carbohydrate sources when glycogen stores are exhausted (gluconeogenesis).
- Stores iron, copper, and some vitamins (A, D, E, K, B_{12}).
- Converts unwanted amino acids to urea (ornithine cycle).
- Manufactures heparin and plasma proteins (e.g. albumin).
- Detoxifies poisons or turns them into less harmful forms.
- Some liver cells phagocytose worn-out blood cells.
- Synthesises cholesterol from acetyl coenzyme A.

The Gross Structure of the Liver

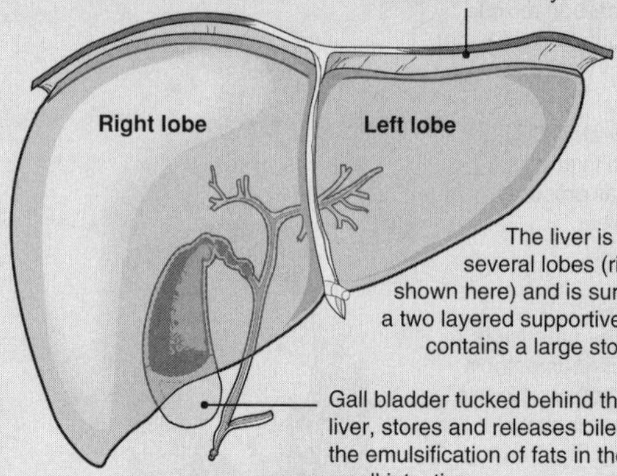

The Internal Structure of the Liver

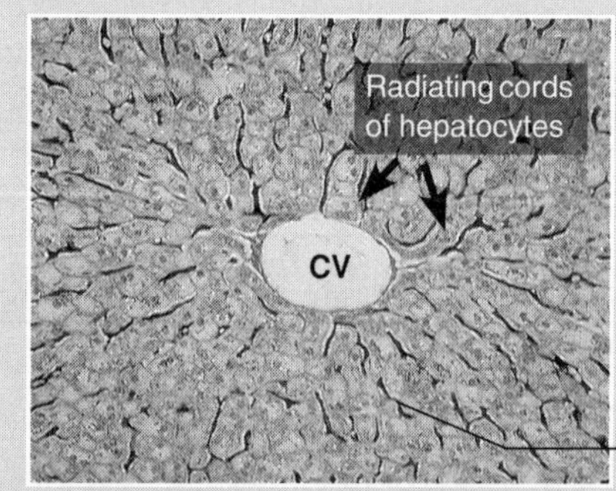

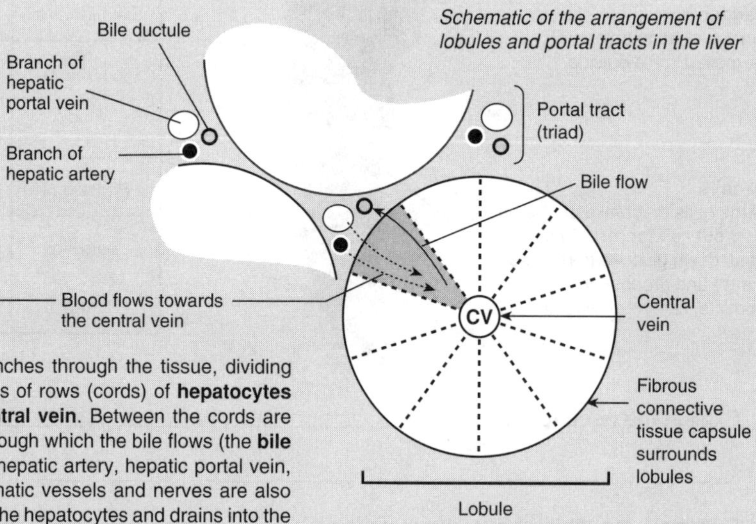

The connective tissue capsule covering the liver branches through the tissue, dividing it into functional units called **lobules**. A lobule consists of rows (cords) of **hepatocytes** (liver cells) arranged in a radial pattern around a **central vein**. Between the cords are blood spaces called **sinusoids** and small channels through which the bile flows (the **bile canaliculi**). Between the lobules are branches of the hepatic artery, hepatic portal vein, and bile duct. These form a portal tract (triad). Lymphatic vessels and nerves are also found in this area (not shown). The bile is produced by the hepatocytes and drains into the bile ductules and eventually into the bile duct. The photograph above shows the histology of a liver lobule, with the central vein, cords of liver cells, and sinusoids (dark spaces).

1. Identify the cells that produce bile: __________

2. Describe the components of a portal triad: __________

3. Describe one function of the liver under each of the following classifications:

   (a) Vascular functions: __________

   (b) Metabolic functions: __________

   (c) Secretory and excretory functions: __________

The Histology of the Liver

The functional repeating unit of the liver is the lobule, which comprises tightly packed rows of liver cells radiating from a central vein and surrounded by small blood vessels called sinusoids. Branches of the hepatic artery and the hepatic portal vein supply the lobules. This highly vascular structure is a reflection of the liver's important role as dynamic blood reservoir, able to both store and release blood as required. More than half of the 10-20% of the total blood volume normally in the liver resides in the sinusoids. Sinusoids are similar to capillaries but have a more porous endothelium. The increased permeability of the sinusoids allows small and medium-sized proteins, such as albumin, to readily enter and leave the bloodstream.

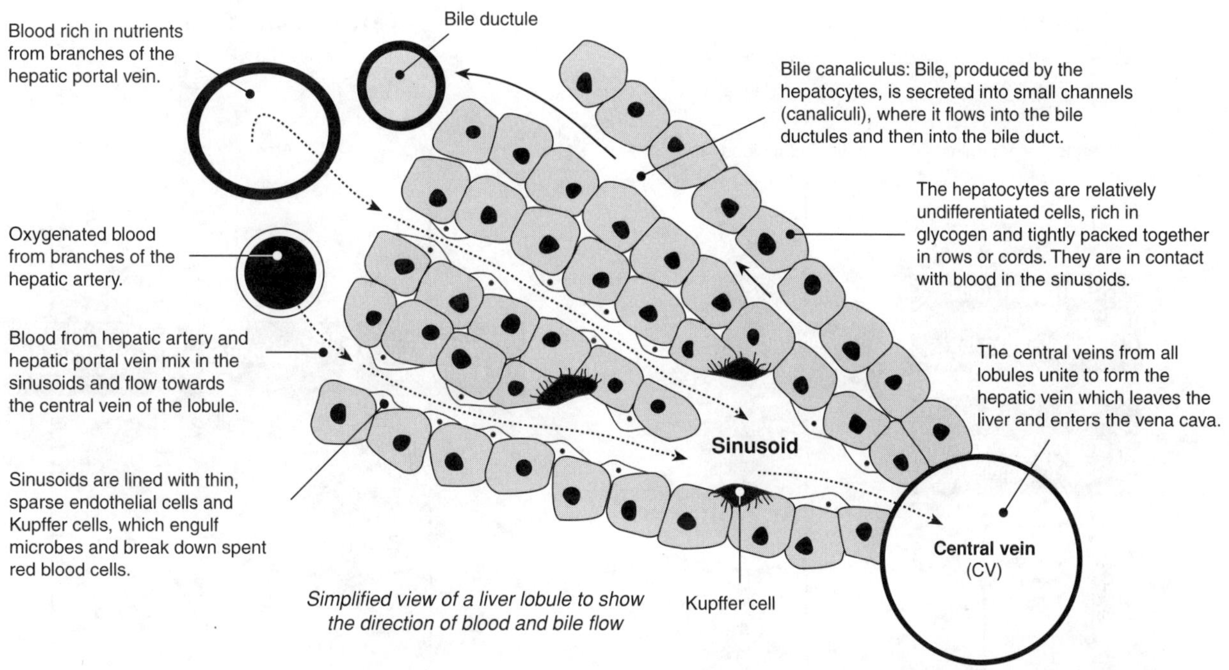

Simplified view of a liver lobule to show the direction of blood and bile flow

1. State the two sources of blood supply to the liver, describing the primary physiological purpose of each supply:

   (a) Supply 1: ____________________ Purpose: ____________________

   (b) Supply 2: ____________________ Purpose: ____________________

2. Briefly describe the role of the following structures in liver tissue:

   (a) Bile canaliculi: ____________________

   (b) Phagocytic Kupffer cells: ____________________

   (c) Central vein: ____________________

   (d) Sinusoids: ____________________

3. Explain the significance of the venous supply to the liver through the hepatic portal system: ____________________

4. Describe how the histology of the liver contributes to its considerable ability to serve as a blood storage organ:

5. Explain the significance of the leaky endothelium of the sinusoids: ____________________

The Liver's Role in Protein Metabolism

The liver has a crucial role in the metabolism of proteins and the storage and detoxification of hormones and ingested or absorbed poisons (including alcohol). The most critical aspects of protein metabolism occurring in the liver are deamination and transamination of amino acids, removal of ammonia from the body by synthesis of urea, and synthesis of non-essential amino acids. Hepatocytes are responsible for synthesis of most of the plasma proteins, including albumins, globulins, and blood clotting proteins. Urea formation via the ornithine cycle occurs primarily in the liver. The urea is formed from ammonia and carbon dioxide by condensation with the amino acid ornithine, which is recycled through a series of enzyme-controlled steps.

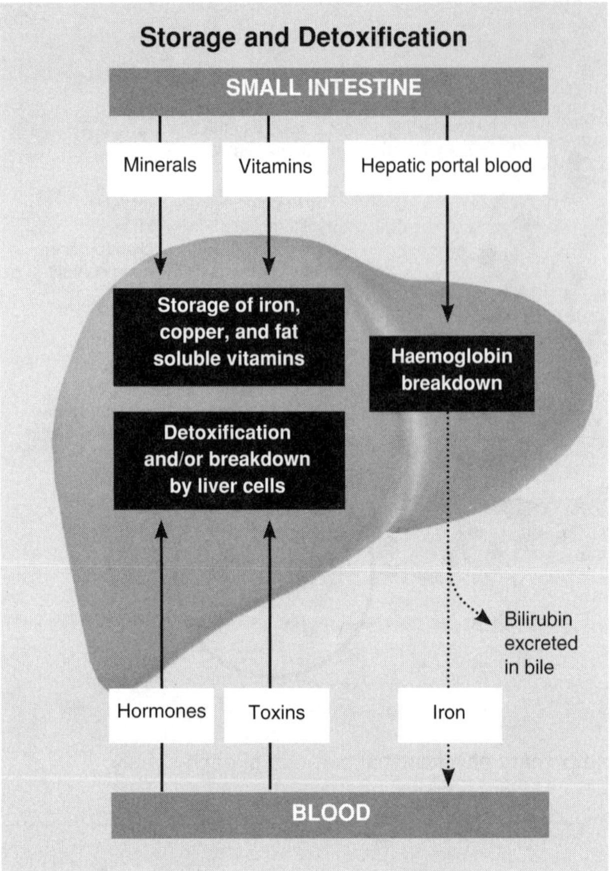

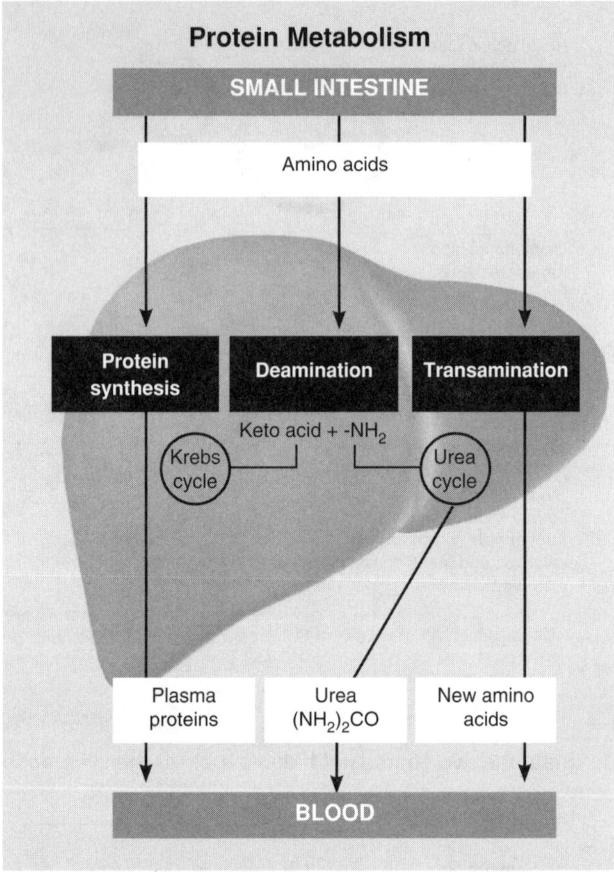

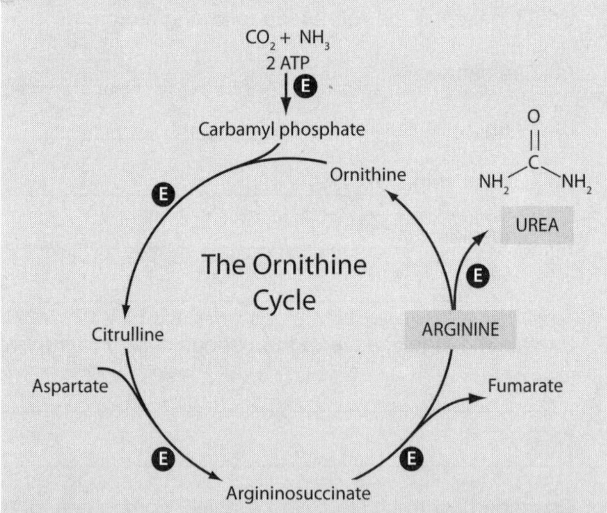

Ammonia (NH_3), the product of protein metabolism, is toxic in even small amounts and must be removed. It is converted to the less toxic urea via the ornithine cycle and is excreted from the body by the kidneys. The liver contains a system of carrier molecules and enzymes (E) which quickly convert the ammonia (and CO_2) into urea. One turn of the cycle consumes two molecules of ammonia (one comes from aspartate) and one molecule of CO_2, creates one molecule of urea, and regenerates a molecule of ornithine.

1. Explain three aspects of protein metabolism in the liver:

   (a) ____________________

   ____

   (b) ____________________

   ____

   ____

   (c) ____________________

   ____

2. Identify the waste products arising from deamination of amino acids and describe their fate:

   ____

   ____

3. An X-linked disorder of the ornithine cycle results in sufferers lacking the enzyme to convert ornithine to citrulline. Suggest what the symptoms and the prognosis might be:

   ____

   ____

   ____

The Urinary System

The mammalian urinary system consists of the kidneys and bladder, and their associated blood vessels and ducts. The kidneys have a plentiful blood supply from the renal artery. The blood plasma is filtered by the kidneys to form urine. Urine is produced continuously, passing along the ureters to the bladder, a hollow muscular organ lined with smooth muscle and stretchable epithelium. Each day the kidneys filter about 180 dm^3 of plasma. Most of this is reabsorbed, leaving a daily urine output of about 1 dm^3. By adjusting the composition of the fluid excreted, the kidneys help to maintain the body's internal chemical balance. The ability of the kidneys to concentrate the urine improves with maturity. It is less efficient in infants and young children, who produce relatively larger amounts of dilute urine and are also more susceptible to dehydration.

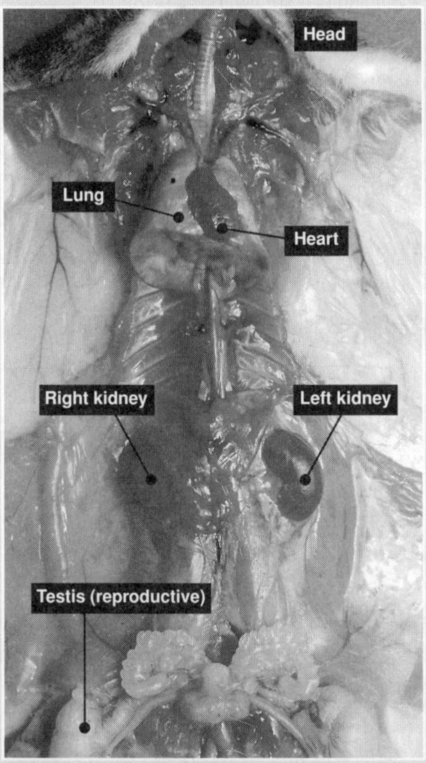

The kidneys of **rats** (above), humans, and other mammals are distinctive, bean shaped organs that lie at the back of the abdominal cavity to either side of the spine. The kidneys lie outside the peritoneum of the abdominal cavity and are partly protected by the lower ribs. Each kidney is surrounded by three layers of tissue. The inner-most renal capsule is a smooth fibrous membrane that acts as a barrier against trauma and infection. The two outer layers comprise fatty tissue and fibrous connective tissue. These act to protect the kidney and anchor it firmly in place.

The Human Urinary System

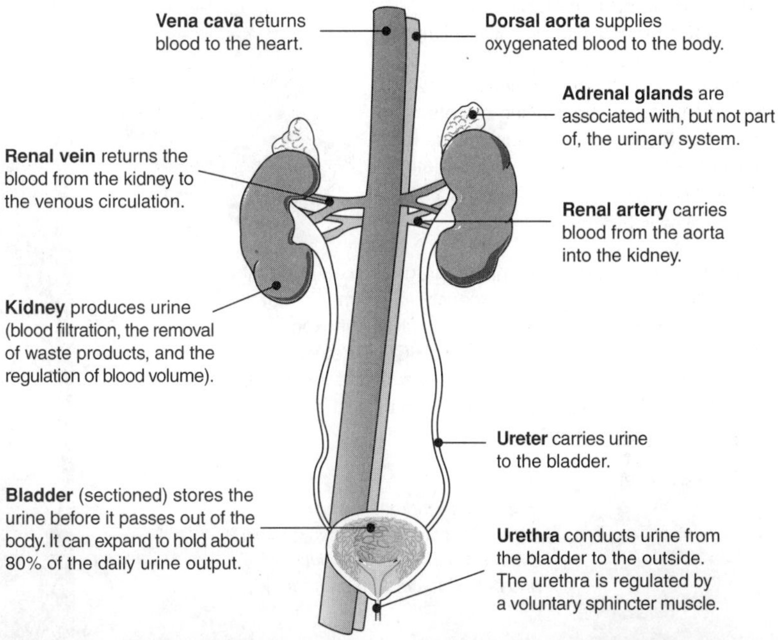

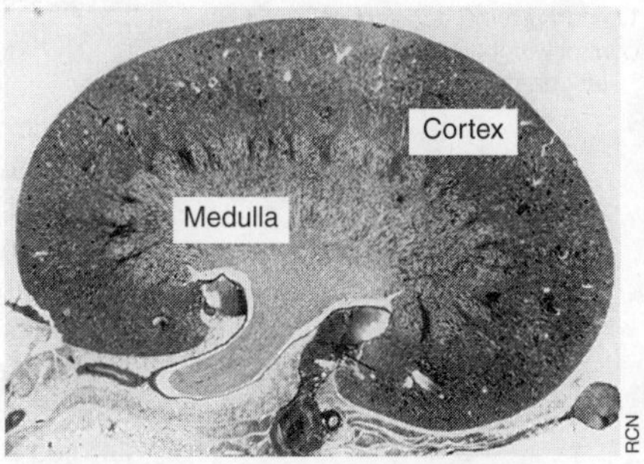

The very precise alignment of the nephrons (the filtering elements of the kidney) and their associated blood vessels gives the kidney tissue a striated appearance, as seen in this cross section.

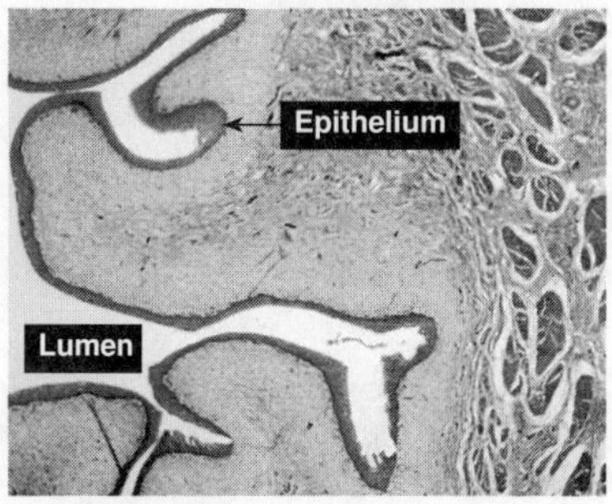

Transitional epithelium lines the bladder. This type of epithelium is layered, or stratified, and can be stretched without the outer cells breaking apart from each other.

1. Identify the components of the urinary system and describe their functions: ______________________

____

____

____

2. Calculate the percentage of the plasma reabsorbed by the kidneys: ______________________

3. The kidney receives blood at a higher pressure than other organs. Suggest why this is the case: ______________________

____

____

4. Explain why the kidneys are surrounded by fatty connective tissue: ______________________

____

Related activities: *The Physiology of the Kidney, Control of Kidney Function*

Urine Analysis

Urine is the liquid waste product of the body. It contains water, electrolytes, and other waste metabolites which are filtered out of the blood by the kidneys. **Urine analysis** (urinalysis) is used as a medical diagnostic tool for a wide range of metabolic disorders. In addition, urine analysis can be used to detect the presence of illicit (non-prescription) drugs and for diagnosing pregnancy.

Pregnancy Testing

Pregnancy testing determines whether or not a woman is pregnant. Obstetric ultrasonography can be used to detect pregnancy, but the most frequently used methods involve detecting **chemical markers** in urine or blood.

The hormone **human chorionic gonadotropin** (HCG) is the chemical marker used to confirm pregnancy. HCG is released from the placenta where it accumulates in the bloodstream before being excreted into the urine. Blood tests can quantify the level of HCG, and reveal additional information about the pregnancy, but urine test kits reveal only if HCG is present.

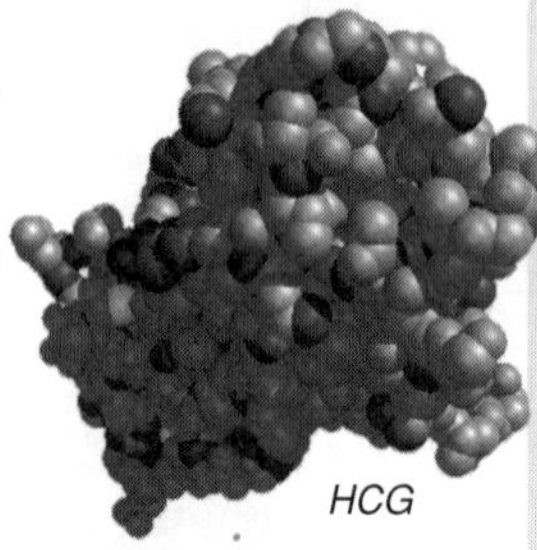

HCG

Blood tests can be used to confirm pregnancy 48 hours after fertilisation, but they are very expensive and time consuming. By comparison, urine analyses are quick and inexpensive. If used correctly they are 97% accurate. HCG is detectable only after implantation has occurred (6-12 days after fertilisation), so false negative results can be obtained if the test is performed too early in the pregnancy.

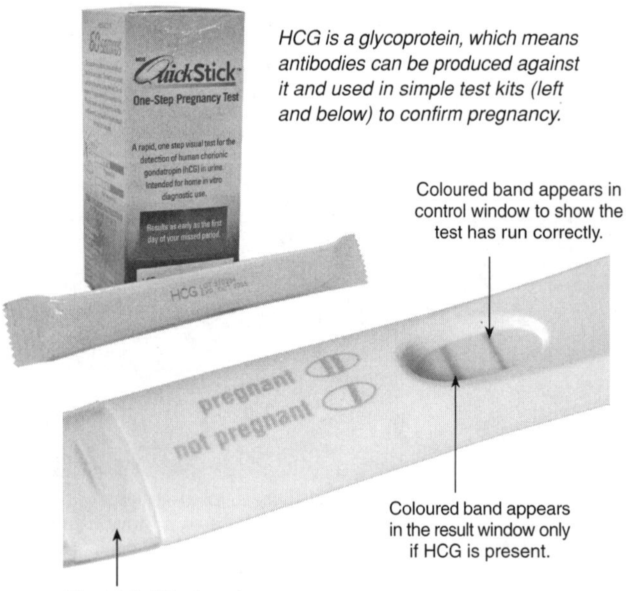

HCG is a glycoprotein, which means antibodies can be produced against it and used in simple test kits (left and below) to confirm pregnancy.

Testing For Anabolic Steroids

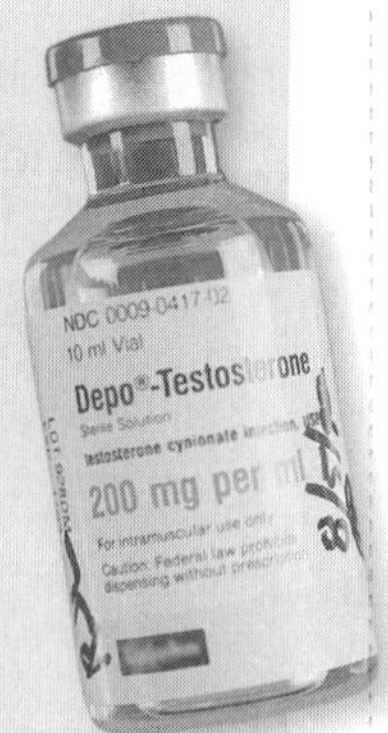

Anabolic steroids are synthetic steroids related to the male sex hormone **testosterone** (right). They work by increasing protein synthesis within cells, causing tissue, especially skeletal muscle, to build mass. They are used legitimately in medicine to stimulate bone growth and appetite, induce male puberty, and treat chronic wasting conditions. Misuse of anabolic steroids can have many adverse effects including elevated blood pressure, cardiovascular disease, and alteration of cholesterol ratios.

Steroids increase muscle mass and physical strength, and are used illegally by some athletes to gain an unfair advantage over their competitors. Anabolic steroid use is banned by most major sporting bodies, but many athletes continue to use them illegally. Athletes are routinely tested for **performance enhancing drugs**, including anabolic steroids.

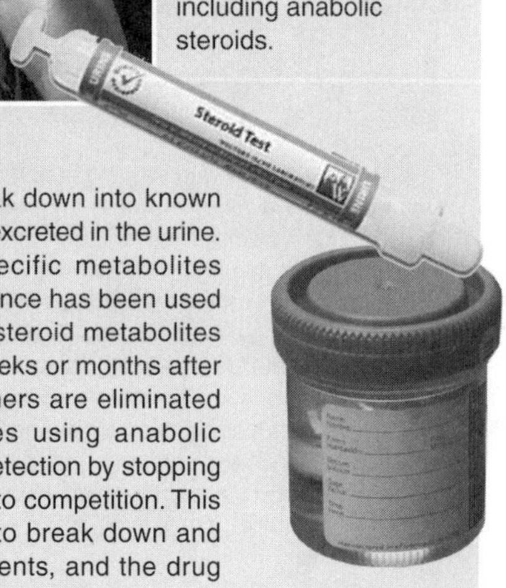

Anabolic steroids break down into known metabolites which are excreted in the urine. The presence of specific metabolites indicates which substance has been used by the athlete. Some steroid metabolites stay in the urine for weeks or months after being taken, while others are eliminated quite rapidly. Athletes using anabolic steroids can escape detection by stopping use of the drugs prior to competition. This allows the body time to break down and eliminate the components, and the drug use goes undetected.

1. (a) Explain the biological basis of a home-based pregnancy test: ______________________________

   (b) Explain potential errors with the use of such home-based pregnancy tests: ______________________________

2. (a) Explain the role of anabolic steroid testing in competitive sports: ______________________________

   (b) Explain why athletes exploiting illegal drugs might withhold them for a period before competition: ______________________________

The Physiology of the Kidney

The functional unit of the kidney, the **nephron**, is a selective filter element, comprising a renal tubule and its associated blood vessels. Filtration, i.e. forcing fluid and dissolved substances through a membrane by pressure, occurs in the first part of the nephron, across the membranes of the capillaries and the glomerular capsule. The passage of water and solutes into the nephron and the formation of the glomerular filtrate depends on the pressure of the blood entering the afferent arteriole (below). If it increases, filtration rate increases; when it falls, glomerular filtration rate also falls. This process is so precisely regulated that, in spite of fluctuations in arteriolar pressure, glomerular filtration rate per day stays constant. After formation of the initial filtrate, the **urine** is modified through secretion and tubular reabsorption according to physiological needs at the time.

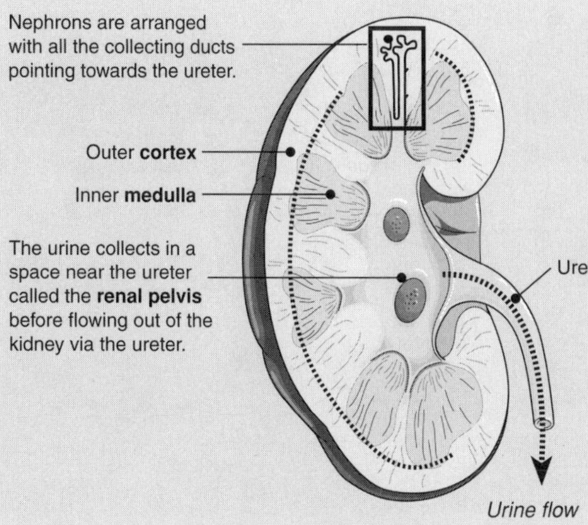

Internal Structure of the Human Kidney

Human kidneys are about 100-120 mm long and 25 mm thick. The functional unit of the kidney is the **nephron**. The other parts of the urinary system are primarily passageways and storage areas. The inner tissue of the kidney appears striated, because the nephrons and their surrounding blood vessels are aligned. It is this precise alignment of the nephrons in the kidney that makes it possible to fit in all the filtering units required.

Each kidney contains more than 1 million nephrons. They are **selective filter elements**, which regulate blood composition and pH, and excrete wastes and toxins. The initial urine is formed by **filtration** in the glomerulus. Plasma is filtered through three layers: the capillary wall, and the basement membrane and epithelium of Bowman's capsule. The epithelium comprises very specialised epithelial cells called **podocytes**. The filtrate is modified as it passes through the tubules of the nephron and the final urine passes out the ureter.

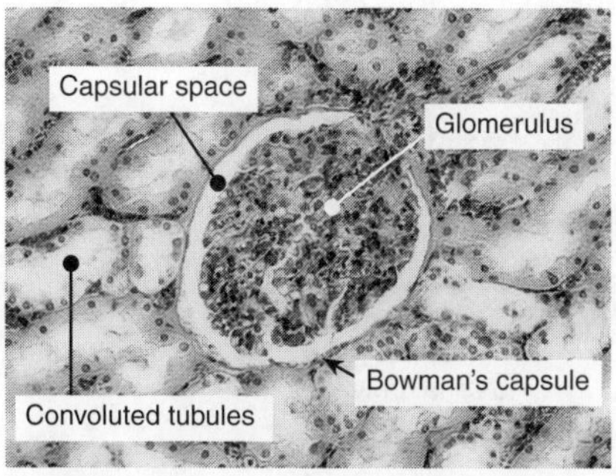

EII

Bowman's capsule is a double walled cup, lying in the cortex of the kidney. It encloses a capillary network called the **glomerulus**. The capsule and its enclosed glomerulus form a **renal corpuscle**.

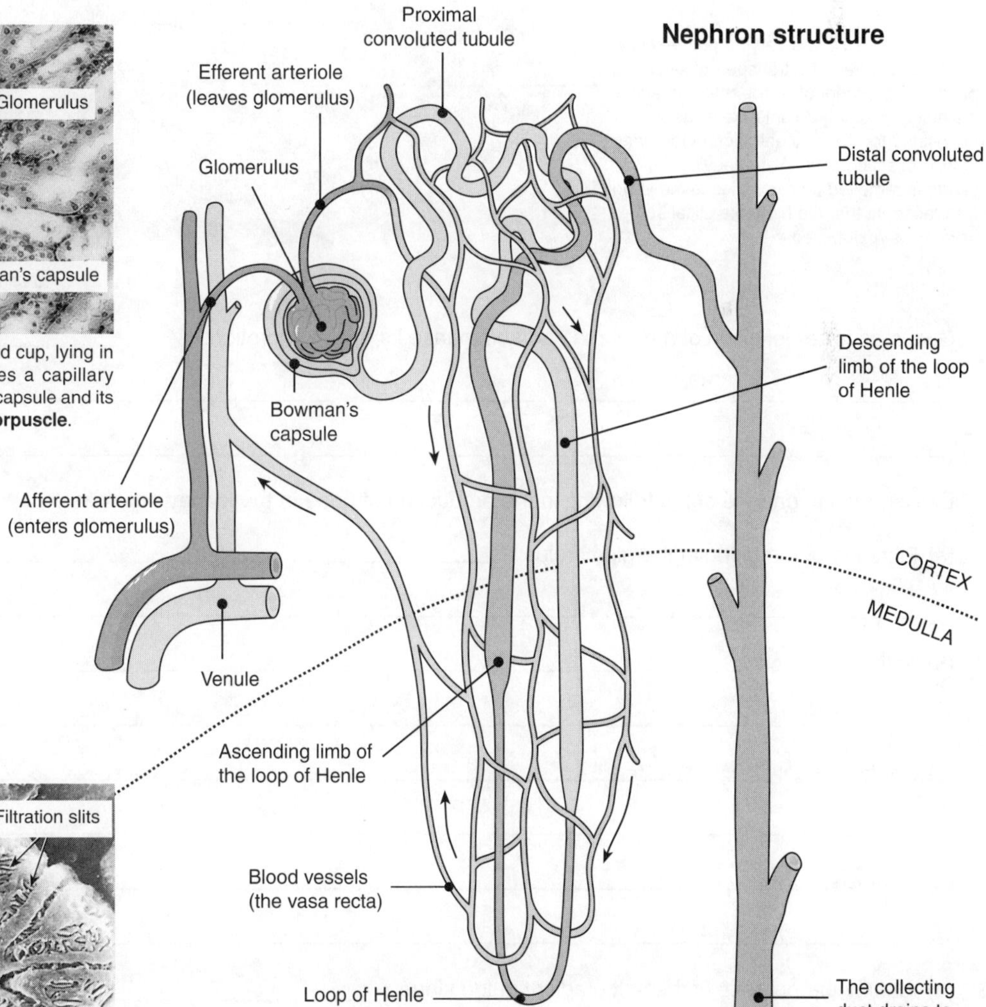

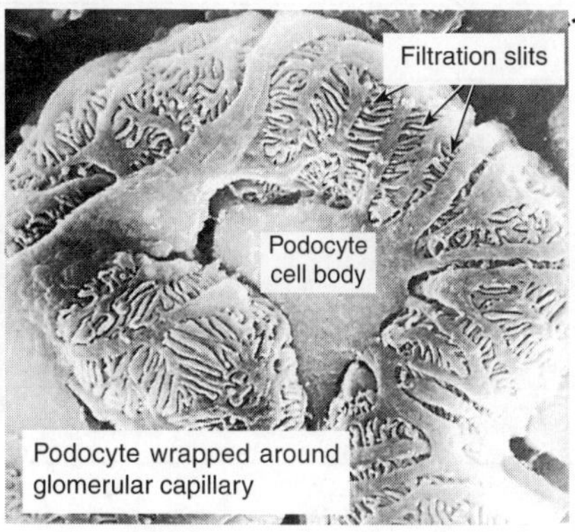

Dr D. Cooper: University of California San Francisco

The epithelium of Bowman's capsule is made up of specialised cells called **podocytes**. The finger-like cellular processes of the podocytes wrap around the capillaries of the glomerulus, and the plasma filtrate passes through the filtration slits between them.

Periodicals: *The kidney, Counter-current exchange mechanisms*

Related activities: *The Urinary System* *Web links:* *Interactive Kidney Quiz, Kidney Vascular System, The Juxtaglomerular Apparatus*

Summary of Activities in the Kidney Nephron

Urine formation begins by **ultrafiltration** of the blood, as fluid is forced through the capillaries of the glomerulus, forming a filtrate similar to blood but lacking cells and proteins. The filtrate is then modified by **secretion** and **reabsorption** to add or remove substances (e.g. ions). The processes involved in urine formation are summarised below for each region of the nephron: glomerulus, proximal convoluted tubule, loop of Henle, distal convoluted tubule, and collecting duct.

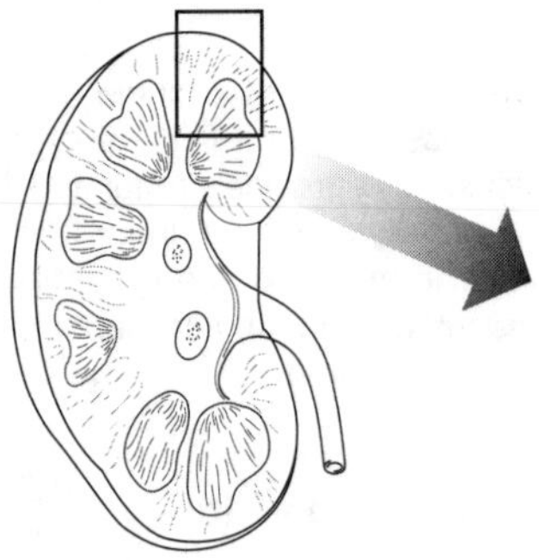

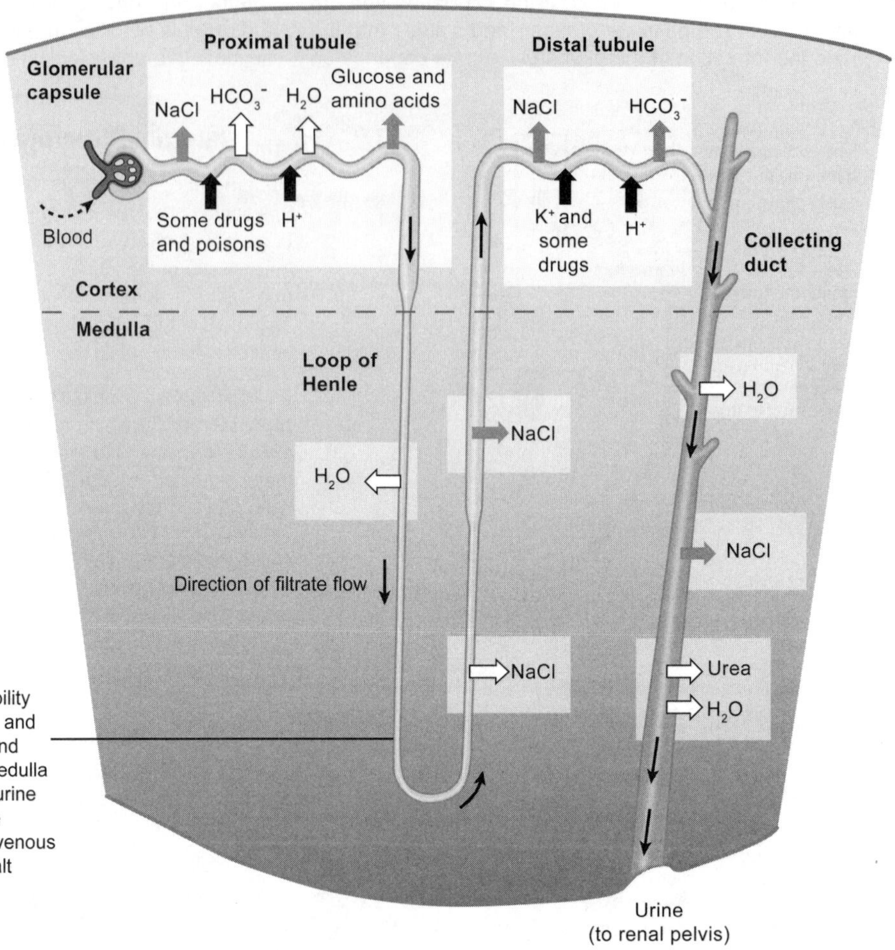

Filtrate
- H_2O
- Salts (e.g. NaCl)
- HCO_3^- (bicarbonate)
- H^+
- Urea
- Glucose, amino acids
- Some drugs

Reabsorption
- Active transport
- Passive transport
- Secretion (active transport)

The loop of Henle has varying permeability to salt and water. The transport of salts and passive movement of water establish and maintain the salt gradient across the medulla necessary for the concentration of the urine in the collecting duct. Water leaving the filtrate is removed by capillaries to the venous circulation so that the high interstitial salt gradient is maintained.

1. Give a concise definition of a nephron and summarise its role in excretion: ______

2. Explain the importance of the following in the production of urine in the kidney nephron:

   (a) Filtration of the blood at the glomerulus: ______

   (b) Active secretion: ______

   (c) Reabsorption: ______

   (d) Osmosis: ______

3. (a) Identify the purpose of the salt gradient in the kidney: ______

   (b) Explain how this salt gradient is produced: ______

Control of Urine Output

Variations in salt and water intake, and in the environmental conditions to which we are exposed, contribute to fluctuations in blood volume and composition. The primary role of the kidneys is to regulate blood volume and composition (including the removal of nitrogenous wastes), so that homeostasis is maintained. This is achieved through varying the volume and composition of the urine. Two hormones, **antidiuretic hormone** (ADH) and **aldosterone**, are involved in the process.

Control of Urine Output

Osmoreceptors in the **hypothalamus** detect a fall in the concentration of water in the blood. They stimulate **neurosecretory cells** in the hypothalamus to synthesise and secrete the hormone **ADH** (antidiuretic hormone).

ADH passes from the hypothalamus to the posterior pituitary where it is released into the blood. ADH increases the permeability of the kidney collecting duct to water so that more water is reabsorbed and urine volume decreases.

Factors inhibiting ADH release

- High water potential (less negative)
  - High blood volume
  - Low blood sodium levels
- High fluid intake
- Alcohol consumption

ADH levels decrease → Water reabsorption decreases. Urine output increases.

Factors causing ADH release

- Low water potential (more negative)
  - Low blood volume
  - High blood sodium levels
- Low fluid intake
- Nicotine and morphine

ADH levels increase → Water reabsorption increases. Urine output decreases.

Factors causing release of aldosterone

Low blood volumes also stimulate secretion of aldosterone from the adrenal cortex. This is mediated through a complex pathway involving the hormone renin from the kidney.

Aldosterone → Sodium reabsorption increases, water follows, blood volume restored.

1. (a) *Diabetes insipidus* is a type of diabetes, caused by a lack of ADH. Based on what you know of the role of ADH in kidney function describe the symptoms of this disease:

____

____

(b) Suggest how this disorder might be treated: ____

____

2. Explain why alcohol consumption (especially to excess) causes dehydration and thirst:

____

____

3. (a) State the effect of aldosterone on the kidney nephron: ____

(b) Explain the net result of this effect: ____

4. Explain how negative feedback mechanisms operate to regulate blood volume and urine output:

____

____

____

Kidney Transplants

Kidney failure (also called renal failure) arises when the kidneys fail to function adequately and filtrate formation decreases or stops. In cases of renal failure, normal blood volume levels and electrolyte balances are not maintained, and waste products build up in the body. Kidney failure is classified as **acute** (rapid onset) or **chronic** (developing over a period of months or years). There are many causes of kidney failure including decreased blood supply, drug overdose, chemotherapy, infection, and poorly controlled diabetic or hypertensive conditions. Recovery from acute renal failure is possible, but chronic renal damage can not be reversed. If kidney deterioration is ignored, the kidneys will fail completely. In some cases diet and medication can be used to treat kidney failure, but when the damage is extensive, **kidney dialysis** or a **kidney transplant** is required to keep the patient alive.

Renal Failure

Kidney (renal) failure is indicated by levels of **serum creatinine**, as well as by kidney size on ultrasound and the presence of anaemia (chronic kidney disease generally leads to anaemia and small kidney size). Creatinine is a break-down product of creatine phosphate in muscle, and is usually produced at a fairly constant rate by the body (depending on muscle mass). It is chiefly filtered out of the blood by the kidneys, although a small amount is actively secreted by the kidneys into the urine. A rise in blood creatinine levels is observed only when there is marked damage to functioning nephrons.

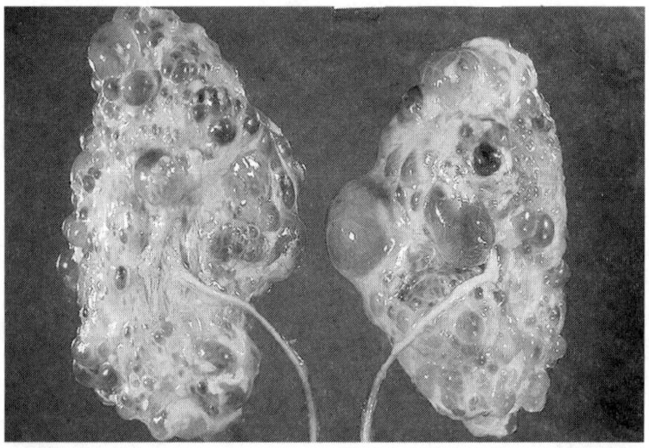

Acute renal failure (ARF) is characterised by decreased urine production (<400mL per day), and commonly arises because of low blood volume (blood loss), dehydration, or widespread infection. In contrast, **chronic renal failure**, which develops over months or years, is commonly the result of poorly controlled diabetes, poorly controlled high blood pressure, or **polycystic kidney disease**, a genetic disorder characterised by the growth of numerous cysts in the kidneys (above).

Kidney Transplants

Transplantation of a healthy kidney from an organ donor is the preferred treatment for end-stage kidney failure. The organ is usually taken from a person who has just died, although kidneys can also be taken from living donors. The failed organs are left in place and the new kidney transplanted into the lower abdomen. If recipients comply with medical requirements (e.g. correct diet and medication) more than 85% of kidney transplants are successful.

There are two major problems associated with kidney transplant technology: lack of donors and tissue rejection. Cells from donor tissue have different antigens to that of the recipient, and are not immunocompatible. Tissue-typing and the use of immunosuppressant drugs helps to decrease rejection rates. In the future, **xenotransplants** of genetically modified organs from other species may help to solve both the problems of supply and immune rejection.

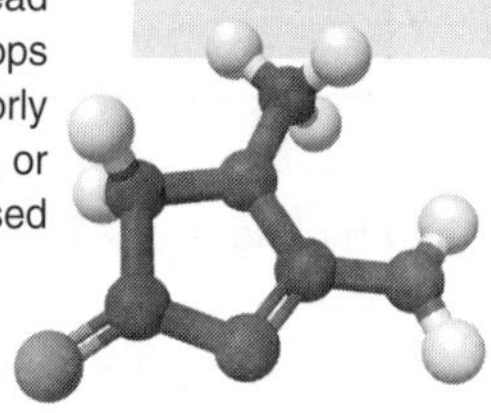

Creatinine

Creatinine levels in both blood and urine is used to calculate the creatinine clearance (CrCl), which reflects the glomerular filtration rate (GFR). The GFR is a clinically important measurement of renal function and more accurate than serum creatinine alone, since serum creatinine only rises when nephron function is very impaired.

1. Distinguish between acute and chronic renal failure and contrast their causes: ________________

2. (a) Explain why a rise in blood (serum) levels of creatinine would indicate a failure of nephron function:

   (b) Explain why a creatinine clearance is a more accurate indicator of renal function than a serum creatinine test alone:

3. Describe some of the advantages and disadvantages of kidney transplantation over a life-time of kidney dialysis:

Renal Dialysis

A dialysis machine is a machine designed to remove wastes from the blood. It is used when the kidneys fail, or when blood acidity, urea, or potassium levels increase much above normal. In kidney dialysis, blood flows through a system of tubes composed of partially permeable membranes. Dialysis fluid (dialysate) has a composition similar to blood except that the concentration of wastes is low. It flows in the opposite direction to the blood on the outside of the dialysis tubes. Consequently, waste products like urea diffuse from the blood into the dialysis fluid, which is constantly replaced. The dialysis fluid flows at a rate of several 100 cm^3 per minute over a large surface area. For some people dialysis is an ongoing procedure, but for others dialysis just allows the kidneys to rest and recover from injury or the effects of drugs or other metabolic disturbance.

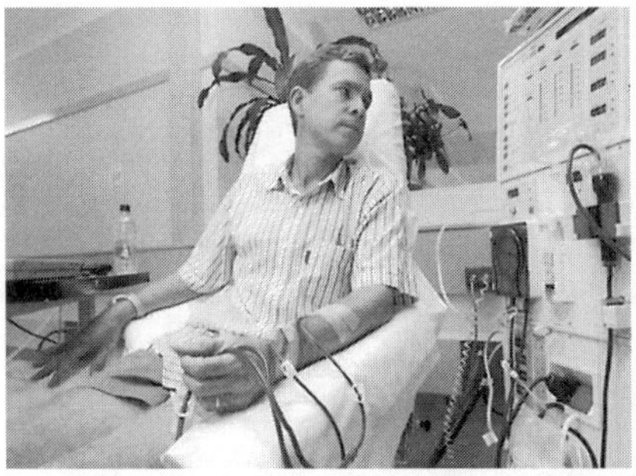

A patient undergoing kidney dialysis at a hospital.

Principles of Kidney Dialysis

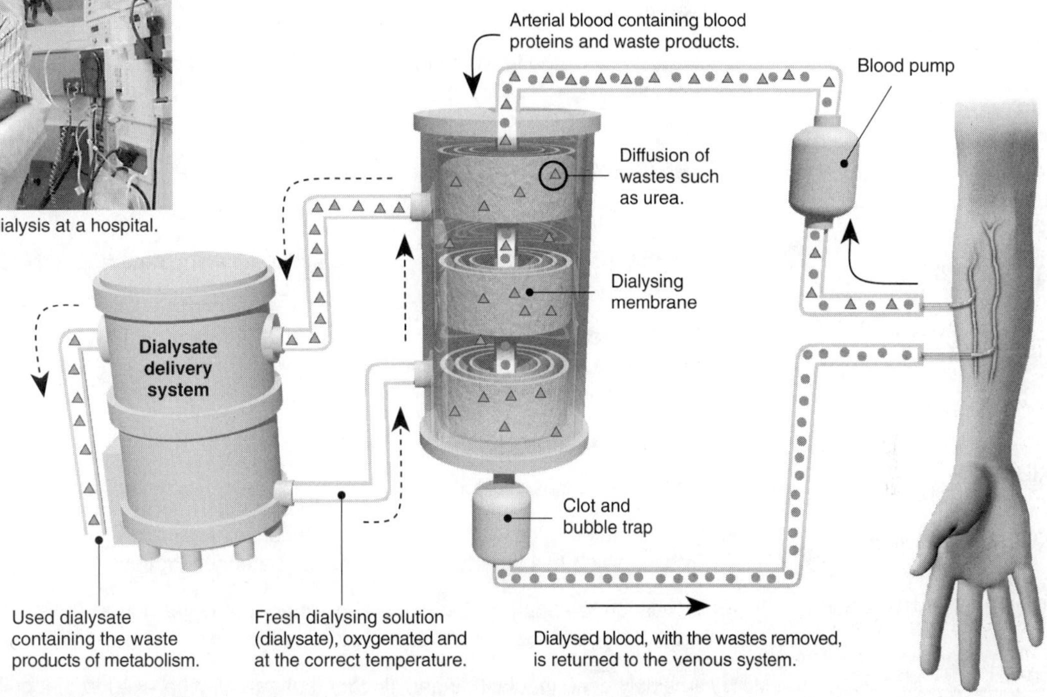

1. In kidney dialysis, explain why the dialysing solution is constantly replaced rather than being recirculated:

2. Explain why ions such as potassium and sodium, and small molecules like glucose do not diffuse rapidly from the blood into the dialysing solution along with the urea:

3. Explain why the urea passes from the blood into the dialysing solution:

4. Describe the general transport process involved in dialysis:

5. Give a reason why the dialysing solution flows in the opposite direction to the blood:

6. Explain why a clot and bubble trap is needed after the blood has been dialysed but before it re-enters the body:

KEY TERMS: Mix and Match

INSTRUCTIONS: Test your vocabulary by matching each term to its definition, as identified by its preceding letter code.

ANABOLIC STEROIDS

ANTIDIURETIC HORMONE

COLLECTING DUCT

DEAMINATION

DETOXIFICATION

DISTAL CONVOLUTED TUBULE

EXCRETION

GLOMERULUS

HEPATOCYTES

HYPOTHALAMUS

KIDNEY

KIDNEY FAILURE

KIDNEY TRANSPLANT

LIVER

LIVER LOBULE

LOOP OF HENLE

ORNITHINE CYCLE

OSMORECEPTOR

PROXIMAL CONVOLUTED TUBULE

RENAL DIALYSIS

SECRETION

SELECTIVE REABSORPTION

TRANSAMINATION

ULTRAFILTRATION

UREA

URINE

URINE ANALYSIS

A A knot of capillaries in the kidney bound within the Bowman's capsule..

B The portion of the kidney nephron located between the loop of Henle and the collecting duct. It is partly responsible for the regulation of sodium, potassium, calcium, and pH.

C The body's largest homeostatic organ. It produces bile, stores and processes nutrients, and detoxifies poisonous substances and metabolic wastes.

D A medical procedure involving the transplantation of a healthy kidney from an organ donor into a patient suffering end-stage kidney failure.

E Medical condition in which the kidneys fail to adequately filter toxins and waste products from the blood. Results in oedema and disruption of pH and electrolyte balance, and leads to anaemia in the long term.

F The removal of amino groups from a molecule; this occurs primarily in the liver.

G Drugs that mimic the effect of the male sex hormone testosterone.

H A bean shaped organ in vertebrates used to concentrate and remove metabolic wastes from the blood.

I The process by which a substance is passed through the plasma membrane of a cell to the outside, as occurs in glandular cells. May also refer to release of a substance through a duct (as from an organ).

J Elimination (by an organism) of waste products of metabolism.

K Relatively nontoxic and soluble nitrogenous waste excreted by mammals and amphibians.

L The hormone released in response to low blood volumes, high sodium levels, and low fluid intake, which has the effect of increasing the concentration of urine.

M In relation to nephron function, the movement of water and salts from the initial renal filtrate back into the blood capillaries surrounding the kidney nephron.

N A widely used medical diagnostic tool, but can also be used to detect illicit drug use, and to diagnose pregnancy.

O Part of the kidney nephron between the proximal convoluted tubule and the distal convoluted tubule. Its function is to create a gradient in salt concentration through the medullary region of the kidney.

P The region of the brain that coordinates the nervous and endocrine systems via the pituitary gland.

Q The transfer of amino groups to produce new amino acids; this process occurs in the liver.

R A medical process in which wastes are removed from the blood when the kidneys are not performing their physiologically function adequately.

S The process of metabolising or converting toxic substances to less toxic substances.

T The arrangement of hepatocytes around a central vein; the functional unit of the liver.

U Process in which hydrostatic pressure forces a liquid against a partially-permeable membrane to form a filtrate of water and low molecular weight solutes. It occurs in the nephron to form the renal filtrate.

V Fluid containing metabolic wastes that collects in the urinary bladder.

W Tubule in the kidney nephron where urine is concentrated as water leaves the tubule by osmosis.

X The metabolic cycle in which the ammonium ion formed during amino acid breakdown is converted to urea for excretion. Also called the urea cycle.

Y The portion of the kidney nephron located between the glomerulus and the loop of Henle. It is partly responsible for regulating pH and absorbing glucose and amino acids.

Z The primary type of cell in the liver, found in tightly packed cords.

AA A sensory organ that detects changes in osmotic pressure.

UNIT F214

4.3.1

Photosynthesis

KEY CONCEPTS

- Photosynthesis supports heterotrophic life.
- In photosynthesis, carbon dioxide (CO_2) is fixed as complex organic molecules.
- Photosynthesis is a two stage process occurring in the chloroplasts of green plants.
- The light dependent reactions produce ATP and NADPH, which are used in the Calvin cycle to reduce carbon dioxide to triose phosphate.
- Given sufficient water, photosynthetic rate is limited by availability of light and CO_2, and by temperature.

KEY TERMS

accessory pigments
ATP
autotroph
carbon dioxide
carotenoids
chlorophyll
chloroplast
chromatography
cyclic phosphorylation
glycerate 3-phosphate
ribulose bisphosphate
grana
heterotroph
lamellae
light-dependent reactions
light-independent reactions
NADPH
non-cyclic phosphorylation
photophosphorylation
photosynthesis
photosynthetic pigments
producers
Rubisco
stroma
thylakoids
triose phosphate

OBJECTIVES

☐ 1. Use the **KEY TERMS** to help you understand and complete these objectives.

Plants as producers page 84

☐ 2. Define the terms **autotroph** and **heterotroph**. Describe the ecological role and importance of plants as **producers**.

☐ 3. Describe the overall reaction of **photosynthesis**, including the role of **light energy**, and the source and fate of the products of photosynthesis.

☐ 4. Explain that respiration in plants and animals depends on the products of photosynthesis.

☐ 5. Describe photosynthesis as a two stage process occurring in **chloroplasts**. Identify the location of these organelles in plants.

Chloroplasts pages 85-88

☐ 6. With the help of diagrams and electron micrographs, describe the structure of a chloroplast, identifying the **stroma**, **grana**, **lamellae** (**thylakoids**), and location of the **chlorophylls** and other pigments. Describe how its structure relates to its functional role in photosynthesis.

☐ 7. Describe the role of the **photosynthetic pigments**, chlorophyll a and b, and **accessory pigments** (e.g. **carotenoids**) in light capture. Explain what is meant by the terms **absorption spectrum** and **action spectrum** with respect to the light absorbing pigments.

☐ 8. PRACTICAL EXTENSION: Make a qualitative investigation of chloroplast pigments using chromatography.

Photosynthesis in C_3 plants pages 89-92

☐ 9. Describe the **light-dependent reactions** of photosynthesis. Describe how light energy is trapped by chlorophyll pigments in chloroplasts, and converted into chemical energy (**ATP**) and reducing power (**NADPH**). Include reference to **cyclic** and **non-cyclic phosphorylation** and role of water.
Note that cyclic/non-cyclic phosphorylation are more correctly termed cyclic/non-cyclic **photophosphorylation** to recognise the role of light energy.

☐ 10. Explain how the products of the light-dependent phase are used in the **light-independent reactions** (the **Calvin cycle**) to reduce carbon dioxide to **triose phosphate** (TP). Include reference to the roles of carbon dioxide, glycerate 3-phosphate (GP), ribulose bisphosphate (RuBP), and Rubisco. Explain how RuBP is regenerated. Note that triose phosphate is also called glyceraldehyde 3-phosphate in many source references.

☐ 11. Identify the molecules made from TP and describe their biological roles.

☐ 12. Describe the effect of changes in CO_2, light intensity, and temperature on photosynthetic rate and on the levels of GP, RuBP, and TP. Discuss limiting factors in photosynthesis with reference to these three abiotic factors.

☐ 13. Describe how you would investigate the factors affecting photosynthetic rate.

Periodicals:
Listings for this chapter are on page 340

Weblinks:
www.biozone.co.uk/weblink/OCR-A2-2832.html

Teacher Resource CD-ROM:
Events in Biochemistry

Plants as Producers

Life on Earth is solar-powered; it runs on energy from the sun. Plants, algae, and some bacteria capture this solar energy and convert it into sugars. They achieve this through a process called **photosynthesis**. Each year these organisms produce more than 200 billion tonnes of food. The chemical energy stored in this food fuels the reactions that sustain life (metabolism). Producers are **autotrophs** (self-feeding). Organisms that cannot make their own food are **heterotrophs** and rely on producers either directly or indirectly for their energy. The photosynthesis that occurs in the oceans is vital to the Earth's functioning, providing oxygen and absorbing carbon dioxide. The oceans cover nearly three quarters of the globe. The evaporation from oceans provides most of the Earth's rainfall and ocean temperatures have a major effect on the world's climate. Despite its importance, humans have harvested the ocean heavily and used it to dump waste. Only in recent years have we realised the consequences of

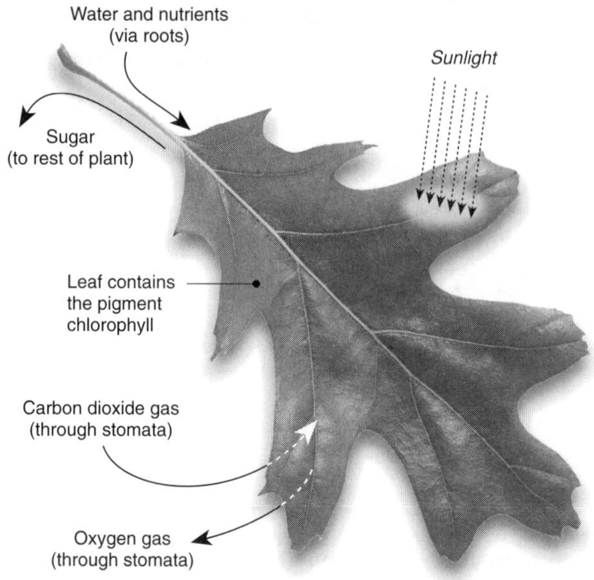

Requirements for Photosynthesis

In order to produce their own food, plants need only a few raw materials, light energy from the sun, and the pigment chlorophyll, which is contained in chloroplasts (in the leaves and stems of higher plants). Photosynthesis is summarised in the chemical equation below. It is important to note that this equation is a deceptively simple summary of a more involved process. Photosynthesis is not a single process but two complex processes (the light dependent and light independent reactions) each with multiple steps.

$$6CO_2 + 12H_2O \xrightarrow[\text{Chlorophyll}]{\text{Light}} C_6H_{12}O_6 + 6O_2 + 6H_2O$$

- $6CO_2$: 6 carbon dioxide molecules
- $12H_2O$: 12 water molecules
- Light / Chlorophyll: Chlorophyll and sunlight must be present
- $C_6H_{12}O_6$: 1 glucose molecule
- $6O_2$: 6 oxygen molecules
- $6H_2O$: 6 water molecules

The photosynthesis of marine algae supplies a substantial portion of the world's oxygen. The oceans also act as sinks for the absorption of large amounts of carbon dioxide.

Macroalgae, like this giant kelp, are important marine producers. Algae living near the ocean surface get access to light used in photosynthesis (the red wavelength).

On land, vascular plants (such as trees with transport vessels) are the main producers of food. Plants at different levels in a forest receive different intensity and quality of light.

1. Write the overall chemical equation for photosynthesis using:

   (a) Words: ____________________

   (b) Chemical symbols: ____________________

2. Describe three things of fundamental biological importance provided by photosynthesis:

   (a) ____________________

   (b) ____________________

   (c) ____________________

3. Explain how light limits the distribution of algae in the ocean: ____________________

4. Predict one probable effect of deforestation on the Earth's climate and/or level of the gases oxygen and carbon dioxide:

   ____

Energy in Cells

A summary of the flow of energy within a plant cell is illustrated below. Animal cells have a similar flow except the glucose is supplied by ingestion rather than by photosynthesis. The energy not immediately stored in chemical bonds is lost as heat. Note the role of ATP; it is made in cellular respiration and provides the energy for metabolic reactions, including photosynthesis.

Energy Transformations in a Photosynthetic Plant Cell

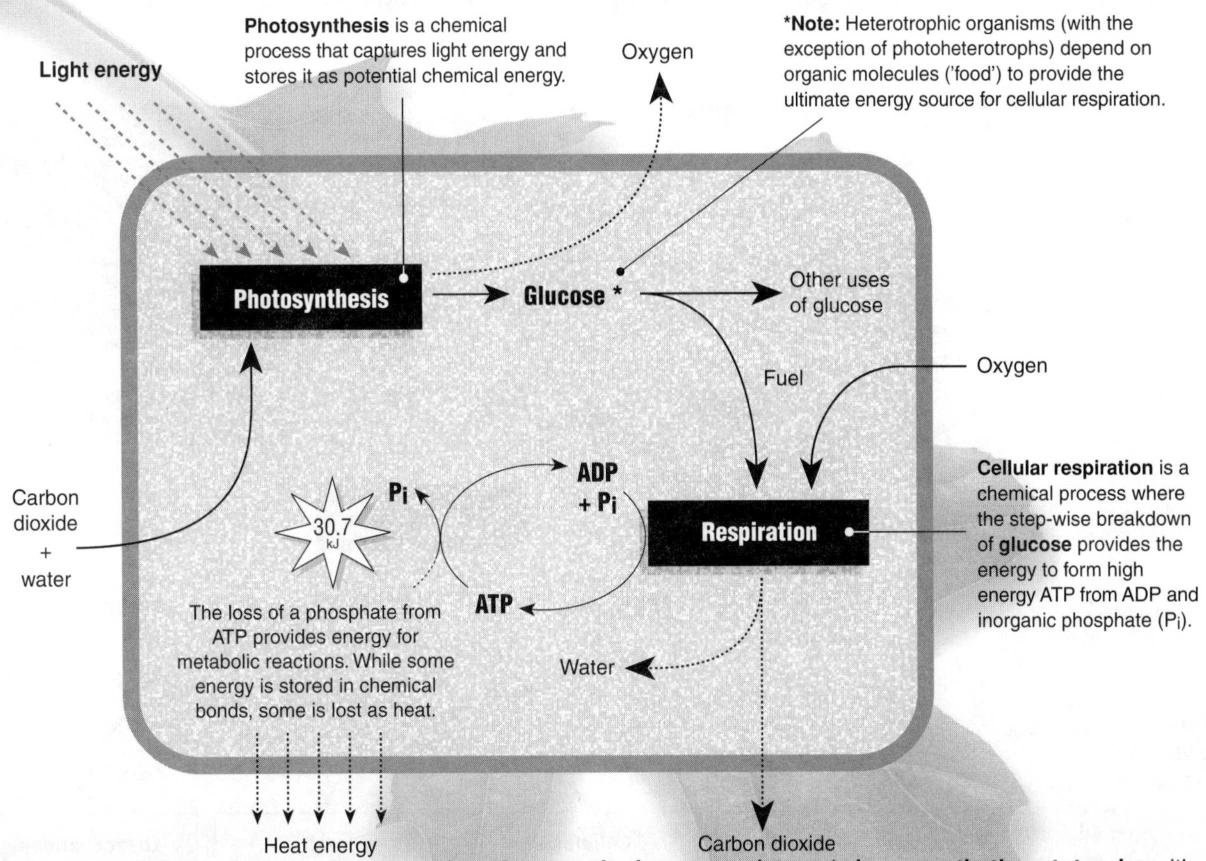

1. Discuss the differences between **heterotrophs**, **photosynthetic autotrophs**, and **chemosynthetic autotrophs** with respect to how these organisms derive their source of energy for metabolism:

2. In 1977, scientists working near the Galapagos Islands in the equatorial eastern Pacific found warm water spewing from cracks in the mid-oceanic ridges 2600 metres below the surface. Clustered around these hydrothermal vents were strange and beautiful creatures new to science. The entire community depends on sulfur-oxidising bacteria that use hydrogen sulfide dissolved in the venting water as an energy source to manufacture carbohydrates. This process is similar to photosynthesis, but does not rely on sunlight to provide the energy for generating ATP and fixing carbon:

   (a) Explain why a community based on photosynthetic organisms is not found at this site:

   (b) Name the ultimate energy source for the bacteria:

   (c) This same chemical that provides the bacteria with energy is also toxic to the process of cellular respiration; a problem that the animals living in the habitat have resolved by evolving various adaptations. Explain what would happen if these animals did not possess adaptations to reduce the toxic effect on cellular respiration:

   (d) Name the energy source classification for these sulfur-oxidising bacteria:

Summary of Photosynthesis

Photosynthesis is of fundamental importance to living things because it transforms sunlight energy into chemical energy stored in molecules, releases free oxygen gas, and absorbs carbon dioxide (a waste product of cellular metabolism). Photosynthetic organisms use special pigments, called **chlorophylls**, to absorb light of specific wavelengths and thereby capture the light energy.

Visible light is a small fraction of the total **electromagnetic radiation** reaching Earth from the sun. Of the visible spectrum, only certain wavelengths (red and blue) are absorbed for photosynthesis. Other wavelengths, particularly green, are reflected or transmitted. The diagram below summarises the process of photosynthesis.

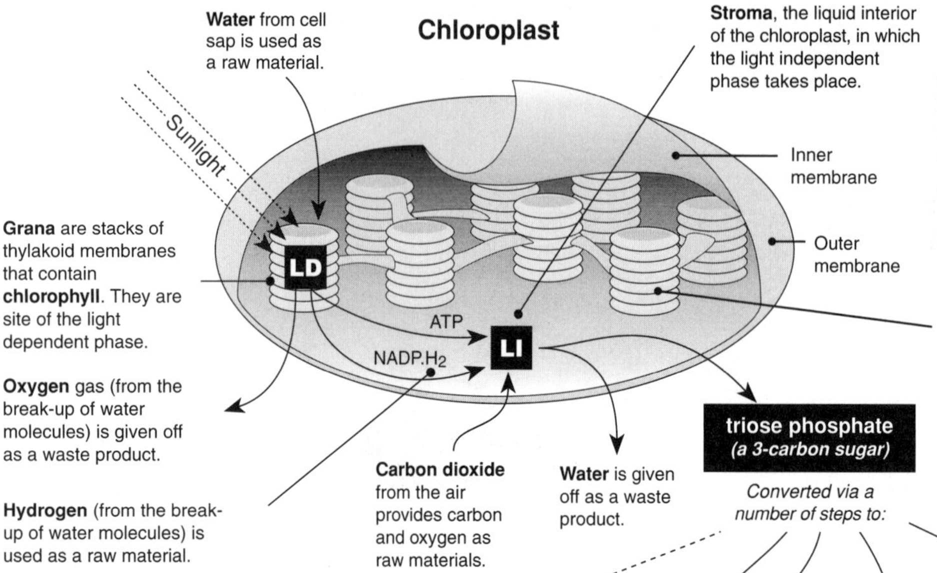

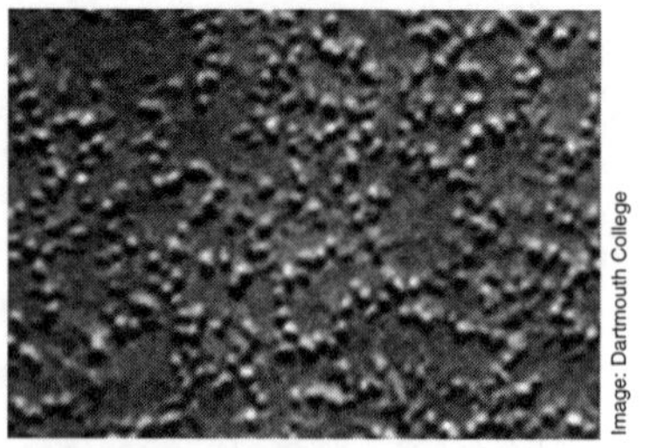

The **thylakoid** membranes contain thousands of embedded proteins and chlorophyll pigments, as revealed in the freeze fracture TEM image above.

triose phosphate
(a 3-carbon sugar)

Converted via a number of steps to:

Lipids and amino acids

Monosaccharides
Glucose is the fuel for cellular respiration and supplies energy for metabolism. Glucose can be converted to fructose.

Cellulose
Glucose is used as a building block for creating cellulose, a component of plant cell walls.

Starch
Stored as a reserve supply of energy in starch granules, to be converted back into glucose when required.

Disaccharides
Monosaccharides join to form disaccharides, e.g. fructose and glucose form sucrose, found in sugar cane.

LD = **Light dependent phase**
Process: *Energy capture* via photosystems I and II

LI = **Light independent phase**
Process: *Carbon fixation* via the Calvin cycle

1. Distinguish between the two different regions of a chloroplast and describe the biochemical processes that occur in each:

   (a) ______

   (b) ______

2. State the origin and fate of the following molecules involved in photosynthesis:

   (a) Carbon dioxide: ______

   (b) Oxygen: ______

   (c) Hydrogen: ______

3. Suggest how scientists might have determined the fate of these molecules: ______

4. Discuss the potential uses for the end products of photosynthesis: ______

Chloroplasts

Chloroplasts are the sites of photosynthesis in plants. They are a type of **plastid**. They are large disk shaped organelles (4-6 μm in diameter). A mesophyll leaf cell will contain between 50-100 chloroplasts. The chloroplasts are generally aligned so that their broad surface runs parallel to the cell wall to maximise the surface area available for light absorption. Chloroplasts have a complicated internal structure, characterised by a system of membrane structures called **thylakoids** arranged into stacks called **grana**. Plants use special pigments, called **chlorophylls** and **carotenoids** to absorb light of specific wavelengths and thereby capture the light energy. Chlorophylls give leaves their green colour.

The Structure of a Chloroplast

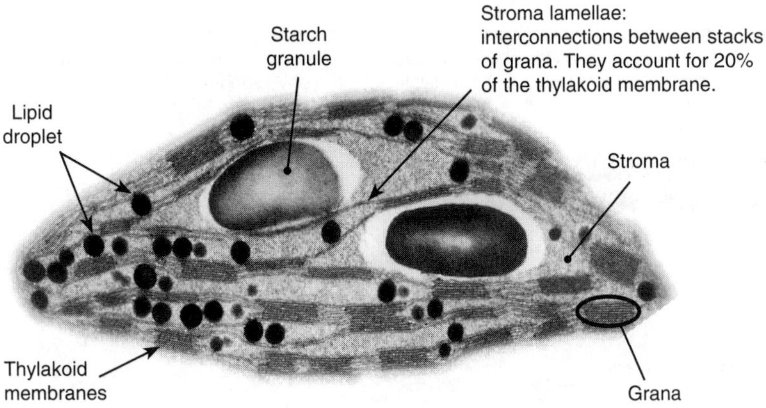

TEM image of a single chloroplast

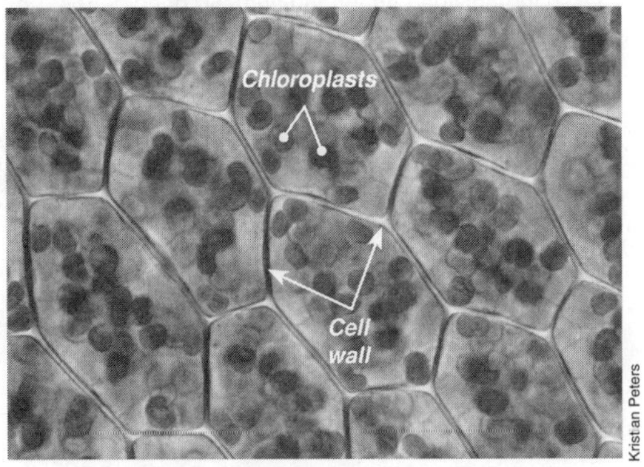

Chloroplasts visible in plant cells

1. Label the transmission electron microscope image of a chloroplast below:

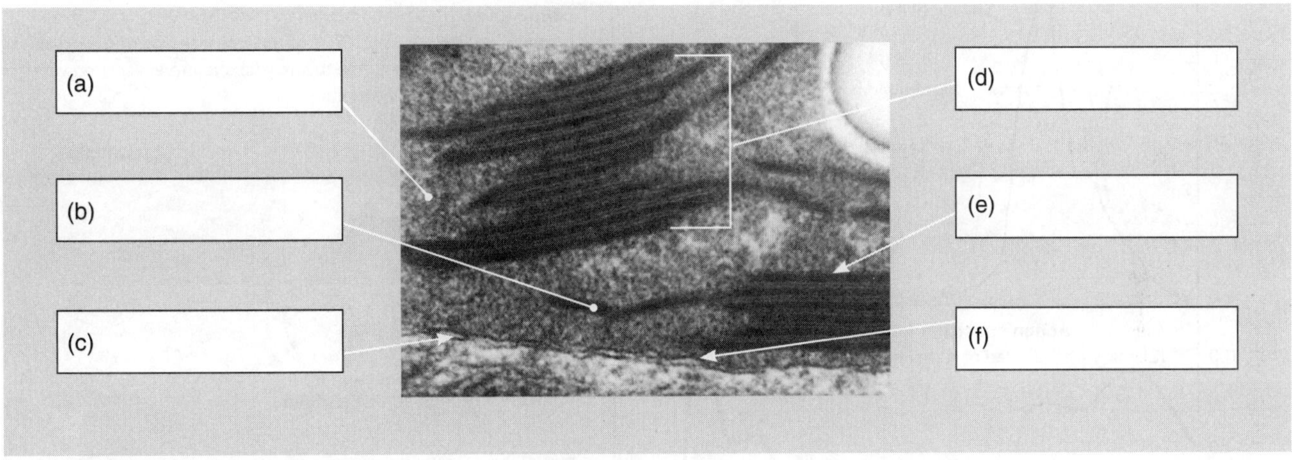

2. (a) Describe where chlorophyll is found in a chloroplast: ____________________

____

(b) Explain why chlorophyll is found there: ____________________

____

____

3. Explain how the internal structure of chloroplasts helps absorb the maximum amount of light: ____________________

____

____

____

4. Explain why plant leaves appear green: ____________________

____

____

Pigments and Light Absorption

As light meets matter, it may be reflected, transmitted, or absorbed. Substances that absorb visible light are called **pigments**, and different pigments absorb light of different wavelengths. The ability of a pigment to absorb particular wavelengths of light can be measured with a spectrophotometer. The light absorption vs the wavelength is called the **absorption spectrum** of that pigment. The absorption spectrum of different photosynthetic pigments provides clues to their role in photosynthesis, since light can only perform work if it is absorbed. An **action spectrum** profiles the effectiveness of different wavelength light in fuelling photosynthesis. It is obtained by plotting wavelength against some measure of photosynthetic rate (e.g. CO_2 production). Some features of photosynthetic pigments and their light absorbing properties are outlined below.

The Electromagnetic Spectrum

Light is a form of energy known as electromagnetic radiation. The segment of the electromagnetic spectrum most important to life is the narrow band between about 380 and 750 nanometres (nm). This radiation is known as visible light because it is detected as colours by the human eye (although some other animals, such as insects, can see in the ultraviolet range). It is the visible light that drives photosynthesis.

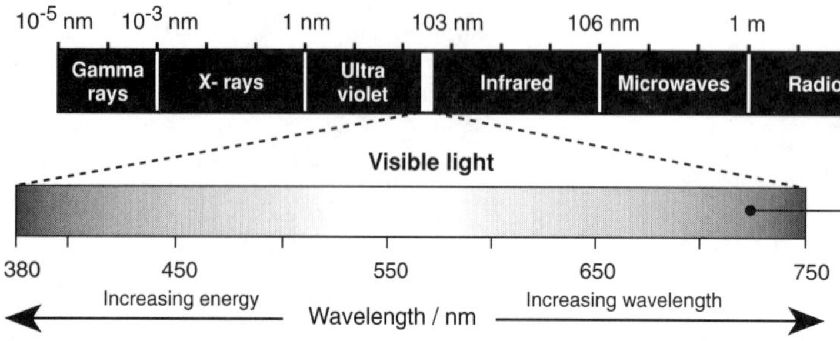

Electromagnetic radiation (EMR) travels in waves, where wavelength provides a guide to the energy of the photons; the greater the wavelength of EMR, the lower the energy of the photons in that radiation.

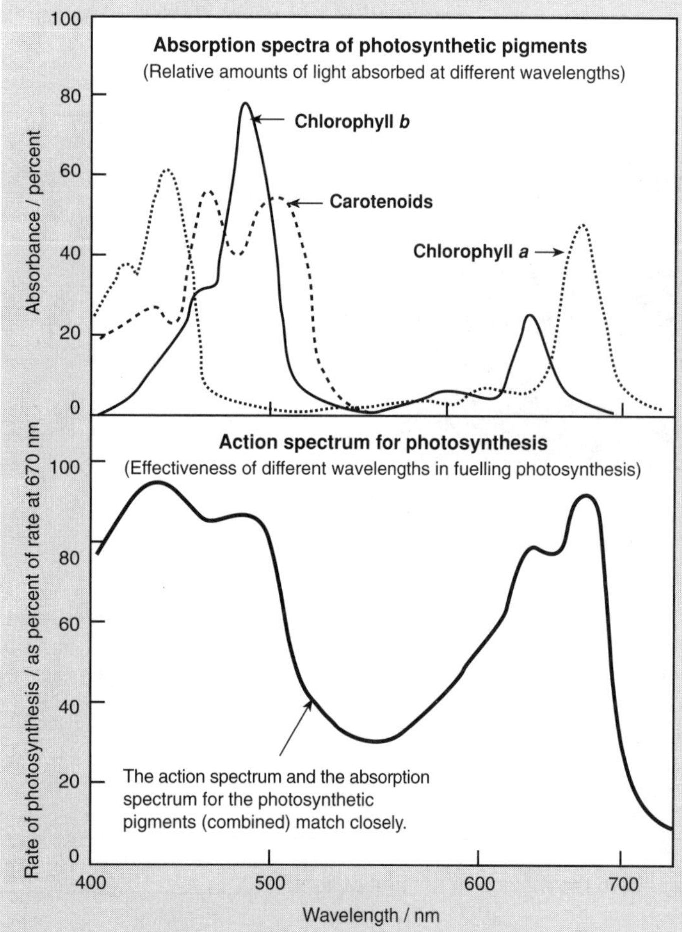

The Photosynthetic Pigments of Plants

The photosynthetic pigments of plants fall into two categories: **chlorophylls** (which absorb red and blue-violet light) and **carotenoids** (which absorb strongly in the blue-violet and appear orange, yellow, or red). The pigments are located on the chloroplast membranes (the thylakoids) and are associated with membrane transport systems.

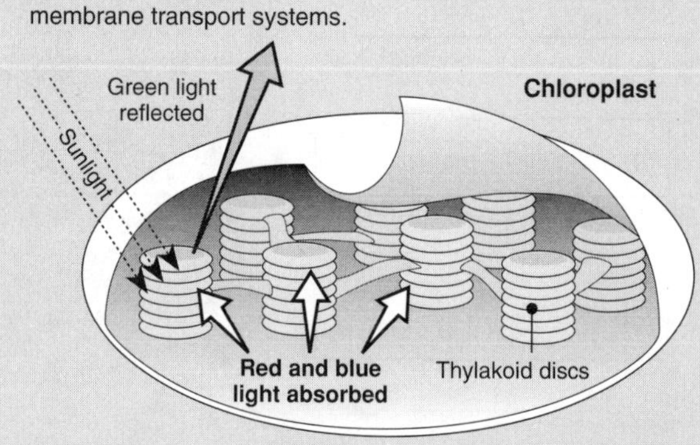

The pigments of chloroplasts in higher plants (above) absorb blue and red light, and the leaves therefore appear green (which is reflected). Each photosynthetic pigment has its own characteristic **absorption spectrum** (left, top graph). Although only chlorophyll *a* can participate directly in the light reactions of photosynthesis, the **accessory pigments** (chlorophyll *b* and carotenoids) can absorb wavelengths of light that chlorophyll *a* cannot. The accessory pigments pass the energy (photons) to chlorophyll *a*, thus broadening the spectrum that can effectively drive photosynthesis.

Left: Graphs comparing absorption spectra of photosynthetic pigments compared with the action spectrum for photosynthesis.

1. Explain what is meant by the absorption spectrum of a pigment:

2. Explain why the action spectrum for photosynthesis does not exactly match the absorption spectrum of chlorophyll *a*:

Light Dependent Reactions

Like cellular respiration, photosynthesis is a redox process, but in photosynthesis, water is split and electrons, together with hydrogen ions, are transferred from water to CO_2, reducing it to sugar. The electrons increase in potential energy as they move from water to sugar. The energy to do this is provided by light. Photosynthesis consists of two phases. In the **light dependent reactions**, light energy is converted to chemical energy (ATP and reducing power). In the **light independent reactions** (**Calvin cycle**), the chemical energy is used to synthesise carbohydrate. The light dependent phase most commonly operates by **non-cyclic phosphorylation**, which produces ATP and NADPH in roughly equal quantities. In **cyclic phosphorylation**, the electrons lost from photosystem II are replaced by those from photosystem I. ATP is generated, but not NADPH.

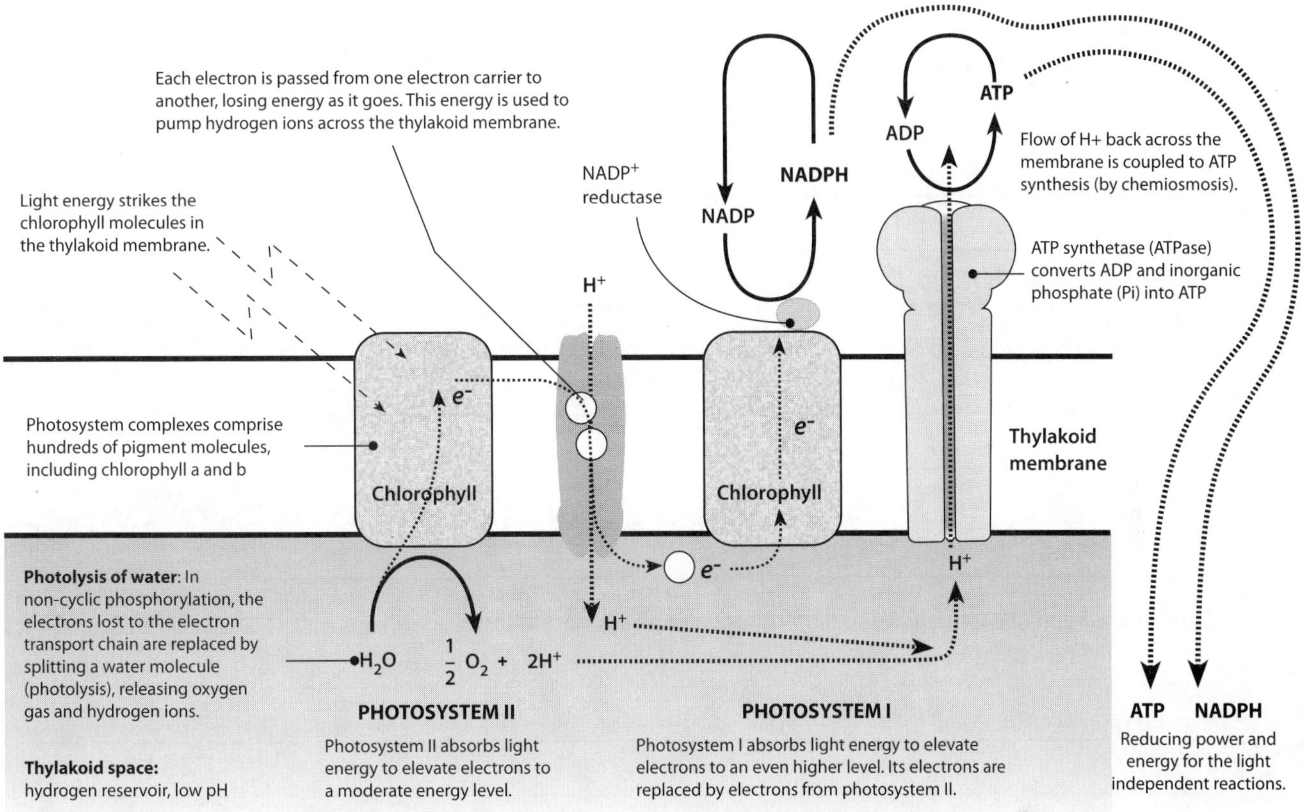

Non-cyclic phosphorylation (above)

Non-cyclic phosphorylation involves both photosystem I and II. The flow of electrons is coupled to generation of both ATP and NADPH (reducing power). The electrons lost by the system are replaced by the photolysis of water. The ATP and NADPH are used in the Calvin cycle to make carbohydrates.

Cyclic phosphorylation (right)

Cyclic phosphorylation only involves photosystem I, which is able to act independently of photosystem II. NADPH is not generated.

During **cyclic phosphorylation,** electrons from photosystem I are shunted back to the electron carriers in the membrane. This pathway produces ATP only. The Calvin cycle uses more ATP than NADPH, so cyclic phosphorylation makes up the difference. It is activated when NADPH levels build up, and remains active until enough ATP is generated to meet demand.

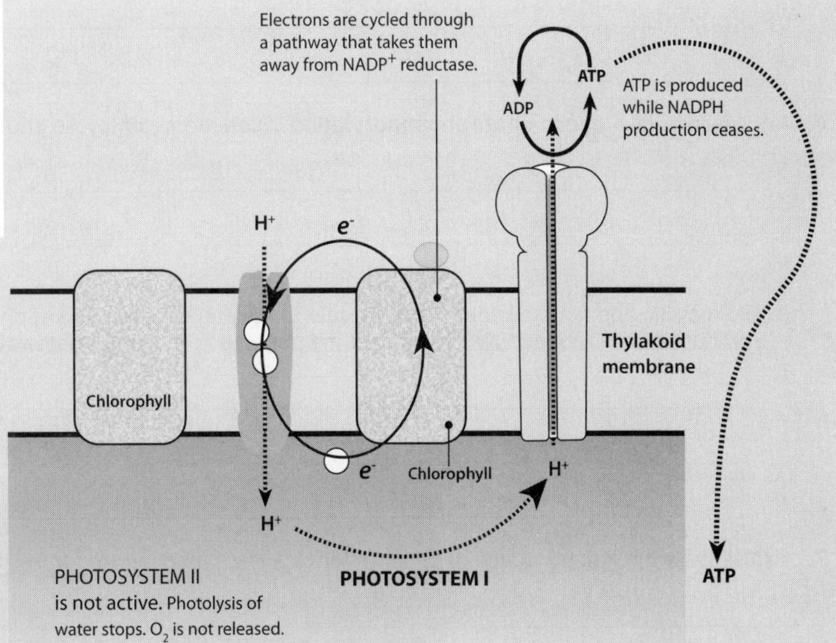

1. Describe the role of the carrier molecule **NADP** in photosynthesis:

2. Explain the role of chlorophyll molecules in photosynthesis:

3. Summarise the events of the light dependent reactions and identify where they occur:

4. Describe how ATP is produced as a result of light striking chlorophyll molecules during the light dependent phase:

5. (a) Explain what you understand by the term **non-cyclic phosphorylation**:

   (b) Suggest why this process is also known as non-cyclic **photo**phosphorylation:

6. (a) Describe how **cyclic photophosphorylation** differs from non-cyclic photophosphorylation:

   (b) Both cyclic and noncyclic pathways operate to varying degrees during photosynthesis. Since the non-cyclic pathway produces both ATP and NAPH, explain the purpose of the cyclic pathway of electron flow:

7. Explain how the independence of photosystem I gives a mechanism for evolution of the photosynthetic pathway:

Light Independent Reactions

The **light independent reactions** of photosynthesis (the **Calvin cycle**) take place in the stroma of the chloroplast, and do not require light to proceed. Here, hydrogen (H^+) is added to CO_2 and a 5C intermediate to make carbohydrate. The H^+ and ATP are supplied by the light dependent reactions. The Calvin cycle uses more ATP than NADPH, but the cell uses cyclic phosphorylation (which does not produce NADPH) when it runs low on ATP to make up the difference.

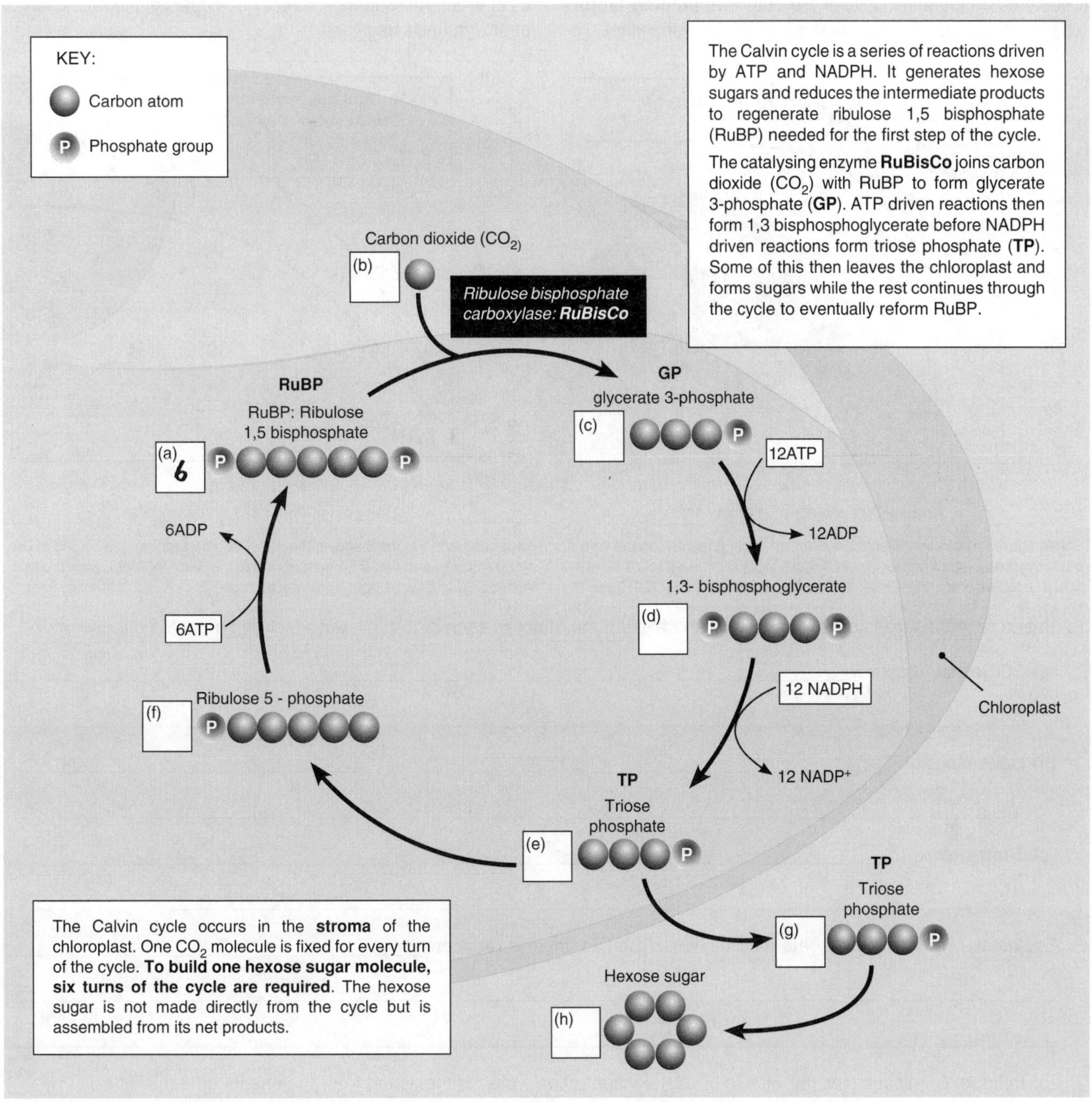

The Calvin cycle is a series of reactions driven by ATP and NADPH. It generates hexose sugars and reduces the intermediate products to regenerate ribulose 1,5 bisphosphate (RuBP) needed for the first step of the cycle.

The catalysing enzyme **RuBisCo** joins carbon dioxide (CO_2) with RuBP to form glycerate 3-phosphate (**GP**). ATP driven reactions then form 1,3 bisphosphoglycerate before NADPH driven reactions form triose phosphate (**TP**). Some of this then leaves the chloroplast and forms sugars while the rest continues through the cycle to eventually reform RuBP.

The Calvin cycle occurs in the **stroma** of the chloroplast. One CO_2 molecule is fixed for every turn of the cycle. **To build one hexose sugar molecule, six turns of the cycle are required**. The hexose sugar is not made directly from the cycle but is assembled from its net products.

1. In the boxes on the diagram above, write the number of molecules formed at each step during the formation of **one hexose sugar molecule**. The first one has been done for you:

2. Explain the importance of RuBisCo in the Calvin cycle: ______________________________

____

3. Identify the actual end product on the Calvin cycle: ______________________________

4. Write the equation for the production of one hexose sugar molecule from carbon dioxide: ______________________________

____

5. Explain why the Calvin cycle is likely to cease in the dark for most plants, even though it is independent of light:

____

Factors Affecting Photosynthesis

The rate at which plants make carbohydrate (the photosynthetic rate) is dependent on environmental factors, the most important of which are the availability of **light** and **carbon dioxide** (CO_2). Temperature is important, but its influence is less clear because it depends on the availability of the other two **limiting factors** (CO_2 and light) and the temperature tolerance of the plant. The effect of these factors can be tested experimentally by altering one of the factors while holding the others constant (a controlled experiment). In reality, a plant in its natural environment is subjected to variations in many different environmental factors, all of which will influence, directly or indirectly, the rate at which photosynthesis can occur.

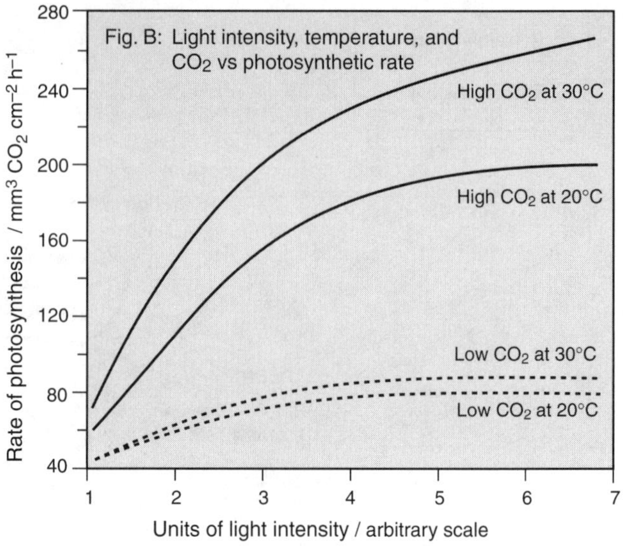

These figures illustrate the effect of different limiting factors on the rate of photosynthesis in cucumber plants. Figure A shows the effect of different light intensities when the temperature and carbon dioxide (CO_2) level are kept constant. Figure B shows the effect of different light intensities at two temperatures and two CO_2 concentrations. In each of these experiments, either CO_2 level or temperature was changed at each light intensity in turn.

1. Based on the figures above, summarise and explain the effect of each of the following factors on photosynthetic rate:

   (a) CO_2 concentration: ______

   (b) Light intensity: ______

   (c) Temperature: ______

2. Explain why photosynthetic rate declines when the CO_2 level is reduced: ______

3. (a) In figure B, explain how the effects of CO_2 concentration were distinguished from the effects of temperature:

   ______

   (b) Identify which factor (CO_2 or temperature) had the greatest effect on photosynthetic rate: ______

   (c) Explain how you can tell this from the graph: ______

4. Explain how glasshouses can be used to create an environment in which photosynthetic rates are maximised:

   ______

5. Design an experiment to demonstrate the effect of temperature on photosynthetic rate. You should include a hypothesis, list of equipment, and methods. Staple your experiment to this page.

***Related activities**: Summary of Photosynthesis*

KEY TERMS: Mix and Match

INSTRUCTIONS: Test your vocabulary by matching each term to its definition, as identified by its preceding letter code.

ACCESSORY PIGMENTS ....

ATP ....

AUTOTROPH ....

CARBON DIOXIDE ....

CAROTENOIDS ....

CHLOROPHYLL ....

CHLOROPLAST ....

CHROMATOGRAPHY ....

CYCLIC PHOSPHORYLATION ....

GLYCERATE 3-PHOSPHATE ....

GRANA ....

HETEROTROPH ....

LAMELLAE ....

LIGHT-DEPENDENT REACTIONS ....

LIGHT-INDEPENDENT REACTIONS ....

NADPH ....

NON-CYCLIC PHOSPHORYLATION ....

PHOTO-PHOSPHORYLATION ....

PHOTOSYNTHESIS ....

PHOTOSYNTHETIC PIGMENTS ....

PRODUCERS ....

RIBULOSE BISPHOSPHATE ....

RUBISCO ....

STROMA ....

THYLAKOIDS ....

TRIOSE PHOSPHATE ....

A The organelle found in the cells of all green plants and where photosynthesis takes place. It contains the green pigment chlorophyll and other pigments involved with photosynthesis.

B A phase of photosynthesis that uses energy from light to initiate photochemical reactions, which result in the production of ATP and NADPH.

C The process in photosynthesis where ATP is formed using the energy from light.

D Plant pigments that absorb wavelengths of light that chlorophyll a does not absorb.

E An organism occupying the first trophic level. Usually gains energy via photosynthesis or chemosynthesis.

F An orange, yellow, or red plant pigment that absorbs blue-violet light.

G A three-carbon phosphorylated sugar.

H A photosynthetic pigment, which absorbs red and blue-violet light strongly and appears green in colour.

I The liquid interior of the chloroplast where the light independent phase of photosynthesis takes place.

J Membrane bound compartments in chloroplasts. They are the site of the light dependent reactions of photosynthesis.

K A phase in photosynthesis that takes place in the stroma of chloroplasts and in which inorganic carbon is incorporated into organic molecules.

L A type of photophosphorylation in which light energy is used to generate both ATP and $NADPH_2$.

M Organisms that obtain their energy from other living organisms or their dead remains.

N An organism that manufactures its own food from simple inorganic substances.

O The name given to the stacks of thylakoid membranes where the light dependent phase of photosynthesis takes place.

P The reduced form of NADP.

Q A technique to separate compounds from a mixture on the basis of their chemistry.

R The major carbon fixing enzyme in photosynthesis.

S A three carbon molecule, which is a metabolic intermediate in both glycolysis and the Calvin cycle.

T An extension of a thylakoid within a chloroplast, interlinking stacks of grana.

U Pigments that capture light energy required for photosynthesis.

V A gas produced as a waste product of metabolism.

W The biochemical process that uses light energy to convert carbon dioxide and water into glucose molecules and oxygen.

X A nucleotide comprising a purine base, a ribose sugar, and three phosphate groups, which acts as the cell's energy carrier.

Y The primary CO_2 acceptor in photosynthesis.

Z A type of photophosphorylation in which light energy is used to produce ATP but not reducing power. It adjusts for the fact that the Calvin cycle uses more ATP than NADPH.

UNIT F214

4.4.1 Respiration

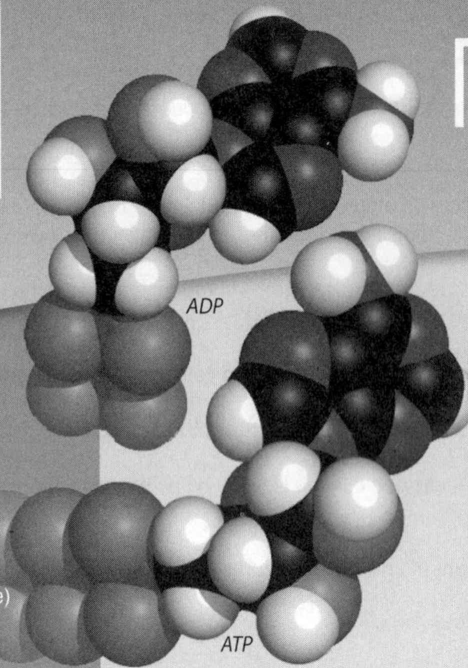

KEY CONCEPTS

- Glucose is the main respiratory substrate in cells.
- ATP has a universal role in metabolism, providing an immediate source of energy for biological processes.
- Glycolysis is the first stage of cellular respiration and occurs in the cytoplasm.
- The Krebs cycle and generation of ATP through oxidative phosphorylation take place in the mitochondria.
- In aerobic respiration, oxygen is the final electron acceptor. Anaerobic pathways involve a terminal electron acceptor other than oxygen and the ATP yield is low.

KEY TERMS

acetyl coenzyme A
aerobic respiration
alcoholic fermentation
anaerobic respiration
ATPsynthase (ATPase)
cellular respiration
chemiosmosis
chemiosmotic theory
coenzyme
cristae
electron acceptor
electron transport chain
FAD
glucose
glycolysis
Krebs cycle
lactic acid fermentation
link reaction
matrix
mitochondria
NAD
oxaloacetate
oxidative phosphorylation
proton gradient
pyruvate
respiratory substrate
substrate level phosphorylation
triose phosphate

Periodicals:
Listings for this chapter are on page 341

Weblinks:
www.biozone.co.uk/weblink/OCR-A2-2832.html

OBJECTIVES

☐ 1. Use the **KEY TERMS** to help you understand and complete these objectives.

The role of ATP
pages 96-97

☐ 2. Explain why organisms need to **respire**. Describe the universal role of **ATP** in metabolism, as illustrated by specific examples, e.g. active transport.

☐ 3. Describe the structure of ATP and its synthesis from **ADP** and **inorganic phosphate**. Explain how ATP stores and releases its energy.

Cellular respiration
pages 98-102

☐ 4. Explain the role of the coenzymes **NAD** and **coenzyme A** in respiration.

☐ 5. Describe mitochondrial structure, and relate its structure to its functional role.

☐ 6. Identify the stages in **cellular respiration** and their specific location.

☐ 7. Recognise **glycolysis** as the first stage in cellular respiration and the major anaerobic pathway in cells. Describe glycolysis as the phosphorylation of glucose and the subsequent splitting of a 6C sugar into two **triose phosphate** molecules, and further oxidation to two **pyruvate** molecules. State the small net yield of ATP and reduced NAD ($NADH_2$) from glycolysis. Appreciate that the subsequent metabolism of pyruvate depends on the availability of oxygen.

☐ 8. Describe the decarboxylation of pyruvate in the **link** (=transition) **reaction**, occurring in the mitochondrial matrix.

☐ 9. Describe the oxidation of glucose to CO_2, including:
- The conversion of pyruvate to **acetyl-coenzyme A** (the link reaction).
- Entry of acetyl CoA into the **Krebs cycle** by combination with **oxaloacetate**.
- The Krebs cycle in the **mitochondrial matrix** and the role of NAD and FAD.
- ATP synthesis by **oxidative phosphorylation** in the **electron transport chain**.
- Role of oxygen as the terminal electron acceptor and the formation of water.
- The net yield of ATP from aerobic respiration.

☐ 10. Outline the **chemiosmotic theory** of ATP generation, with reference to the role of the electron transport chain, **proton gradients** and **ATPsynthase**. Evaluate the experimental evidence for chemiosmotic theory.

☐ 11. Explain why the theoretical maximum yield of ATP per molecule of glucose is rarely achieved in aerobic respiration.

☐ 12. Describe situations in which the pyruvate formed in glycolysis is not completely oxidised. Compare and contrast **lactic acid fermentation** in mammalian muscle and **alcoholic fermentation** in yeast. *Note that fermentation is often used synonymously with anaerobic respiration, but they are not the same. Respiration always involves hydrogen ions passing down a chain of carriers to a terminal acceptor, which in anaerobic respiration is a molecule other than oxygen. This does not occur in fermentation.*

☐ 13. Explain the term **respiratory substrate**. Understand the relative energy values of carbohydrate, lipid, and protein as respiratory substrates.

ATP in Metabolism

All organisms require energy to be able to perform the metabolic processes required for them to function and reproduce. This energy is obtained by **cellular respiration**, a set of metabolic reactions which ultimately convert biochemical energy from 'food' into the nucleotide **adenosine triphosphate** (**ATP**). The details of this process are provided in the exercise "*Cellular Respiration*". ATP is considered to be a universal energy carrier, transporting chemical energy within the cell for use in metabolic processes such as biosynthesis, cell division, cell signalling, thermoregulation, cell mobility, and active transport of substances across membranes.

Adenosine Triphosphate (ATP)

The ATP molecule consists of three components; a purine base (**adenine**), a pentose sugar (**ribose**), and **three phosphate groups** which attach to the 5' carbon of the pentose sugar. The three dimensional structure of ATP is described below.

ATP acts as a store of energy within the cell. The bonds between the phosphate groups are **high-energy bonds**, meaning that a large amount of free energy is released when they are hydrolysed. Typically, this hydrolysis involves the removal of one phosphate group from the ATP molecule resulting in the formation of adenosine diphosphate (ADP).

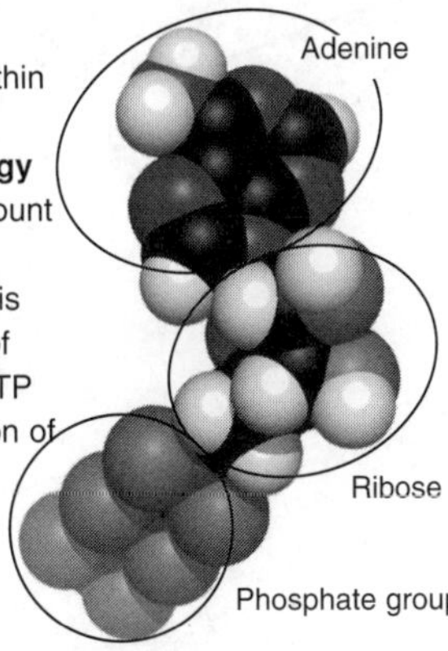

The Mitochondrion

Cellular respiration and ATP production occur in the mitochondria. A mitochondrion is bound by a double membrane. The inner and outer membranes are separated by an intermembrane space, compartmentalising the regions of the mitochondrion in which the different reactions of cellular respiration take place.

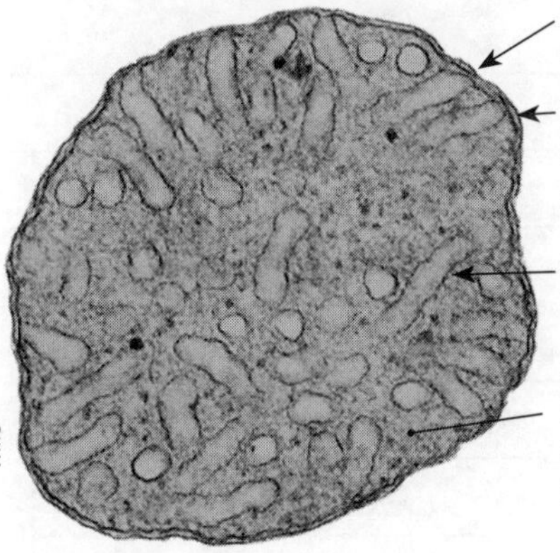

ATP Powers Metabolism

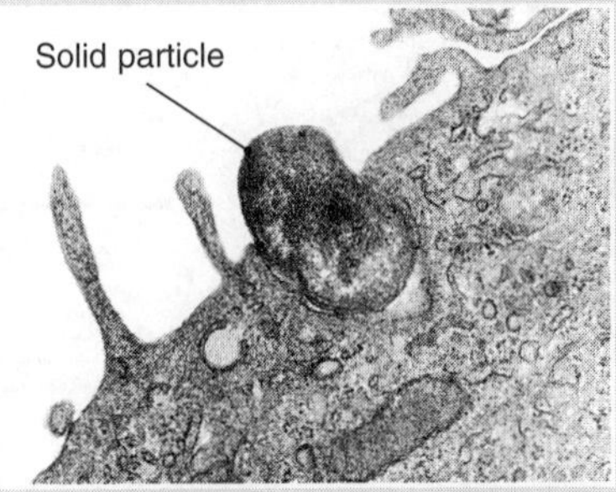

The energy released from the removal of a phosphate group of ATP is used to actively transport molecules and substances across the cellular membrane. **Phagocytosis** (left), which involves the engulfment of solid particles, is one such example.

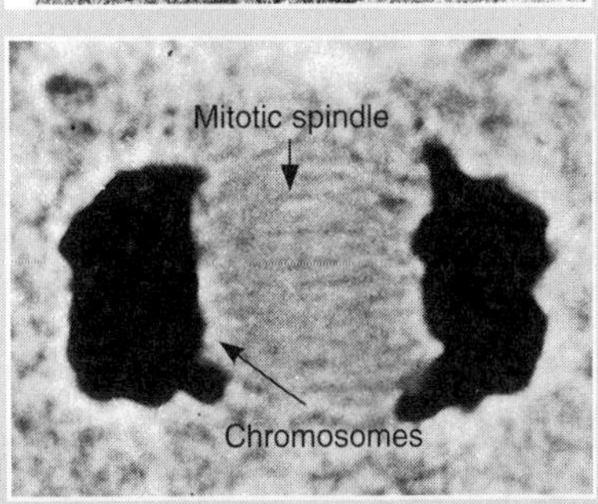

Cell division (mitosis), as observed in this onion cell left, requires ATP to proceed. Formation of the mitotic spindle and chromosome separation are two aspects of cell division which require energy from ATP hydrolysis to occur.

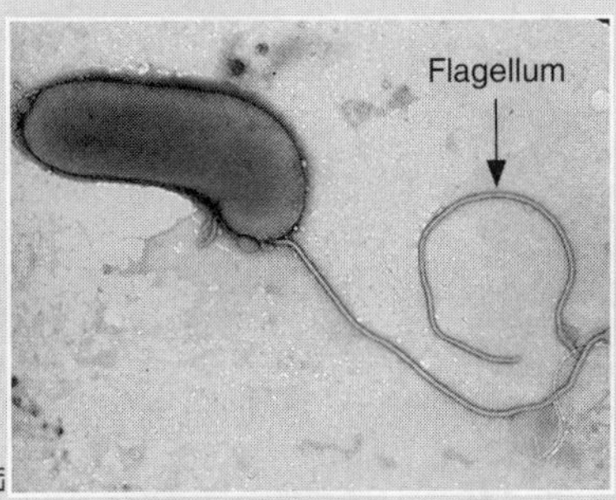

The hydrolysis of ATP provides the energy for motile cells to achieve movement via a tail-like structure called a flagellum. For example, the bacterium, *Helicobacter pylori* (left), is motile. Likewise, mammalian sperm must be able to move to the ovum to fertilise it.

The maintenance of body temperature requires energy. To maintain body heat, muscular activity increases (e.g. shivering, erection of body hairs). Cooling requires expenditure of energy too. For example, sweating is an energy requiring process involving secretion from glands in the skin.

1. Explain why organisms need to respire: ______________________________

____

2. (a) Describe the general role of mitochondria in cellular respiration: ______________________________

____

(b) Explain the importance of compartmentalisation in the mitochondrion: ______________________________

____

3. Explain why thermoregulation is associated with energy expenditure: ______________________________

____

____

Periodicals:
The double life of ATP

Related activities: *The Role of ATP in Cells, Cellular Respiration*

The Role of ATP in Cells

The molecule **ATP** (adenosine triphosphate) is the universal energy carrier for the cell. ATP can release its energy quickly; only one chemical reaction (hydrolysis of the terminal phosphate) is required. This reaction is catalysed by the enzyme ATPase. Once ATP has released its energy, it becomes ADP (adenosine diphosphate), a low energy molecule that can be recharged by adding a phosphate. This requires energy, which is supplied by the controlled breakdown of respiratory substrates in **cellular respiration**. The most common respiratory substrate is glucose, but other molecules (e.g. fats or proteins) may also be used.

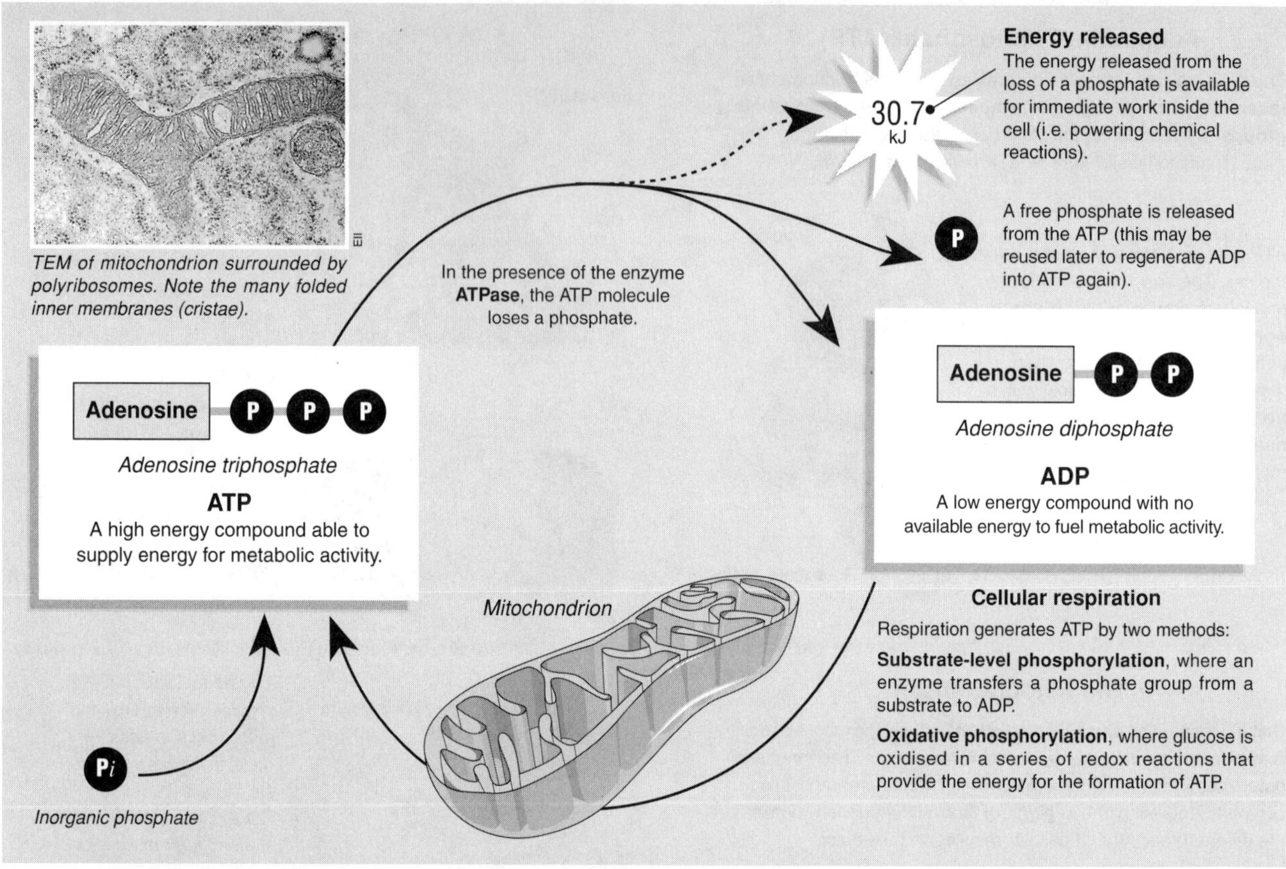

1. Describe how ATP acts as a supplier of energy to power metabolic reactions: ____________________

2. Name the immediate source of energy used to reform ATP from ADP molecules: ____________________

3. Name the process of re-energising ADP into ATP molecules: ____________________

4. Name the ultimate source of energy for plants: ____________________

5. Name the ultimate source of energy for animals: ____________________

6. Explain in what way the ADP/ATP system can be likened to a rechargeable battery: ____________________

7. In the following table, use brief statements to contrast photosynthesis and respiration in terms of the following:

Feature	Photosynthesis	Cellular respiration
Starting materials		
Waste products		
Role of hydrogen carriers: NAD, NADP		
Role of ATP		
Overall biological role		

Cellular Respiration

Cellular respiration is the process by which organisms break down energy rich molecules (e.g. glucose) to release the energy in a useable form (ATP). All living cells respire in order to exist, although the substrates they use may vary. **Aerobic respiration** requires oxygen. Forms of cellular respiration that do not require oxygen are said to be **anaerobic**. Some plants and animals can generate ATP anaerobically for short periods of time. Other organisms use only anaerobic respiration and live in oxygen-free environments. For these organisms, there is some other final electron acceptor other than oxygen (e.g. nitrate or Fe^{2+}).

An Overview of Cellular Respiration

Respiration involves three metabolic stages, summarised below. The first two stages are the catabolic pathways that decompose glucose and other organic fuels. In the third stage, the electron transport chain accepts electrons from the first two stages and passes these from one electron acceptor to another. The energy released at each stepwise transfer is used to make ATP. The final electron acceptor in this process is molecular oxygen.

1. **Glycolysis**. This occurs in the cytoplasm and involves the breakdown of glucose into two molecules of pyruvate.
2. **The Krebs cycle**. This occurs in the mitochondrial matrix, and decomposes a derivative of pyruvate to carbon dioxide.
3. **Electron transport and oxidative phosphorylation**. This occurs in the inner membranes of the mitochondrion and accounts for almost 90% of the ATP generated by respiration.

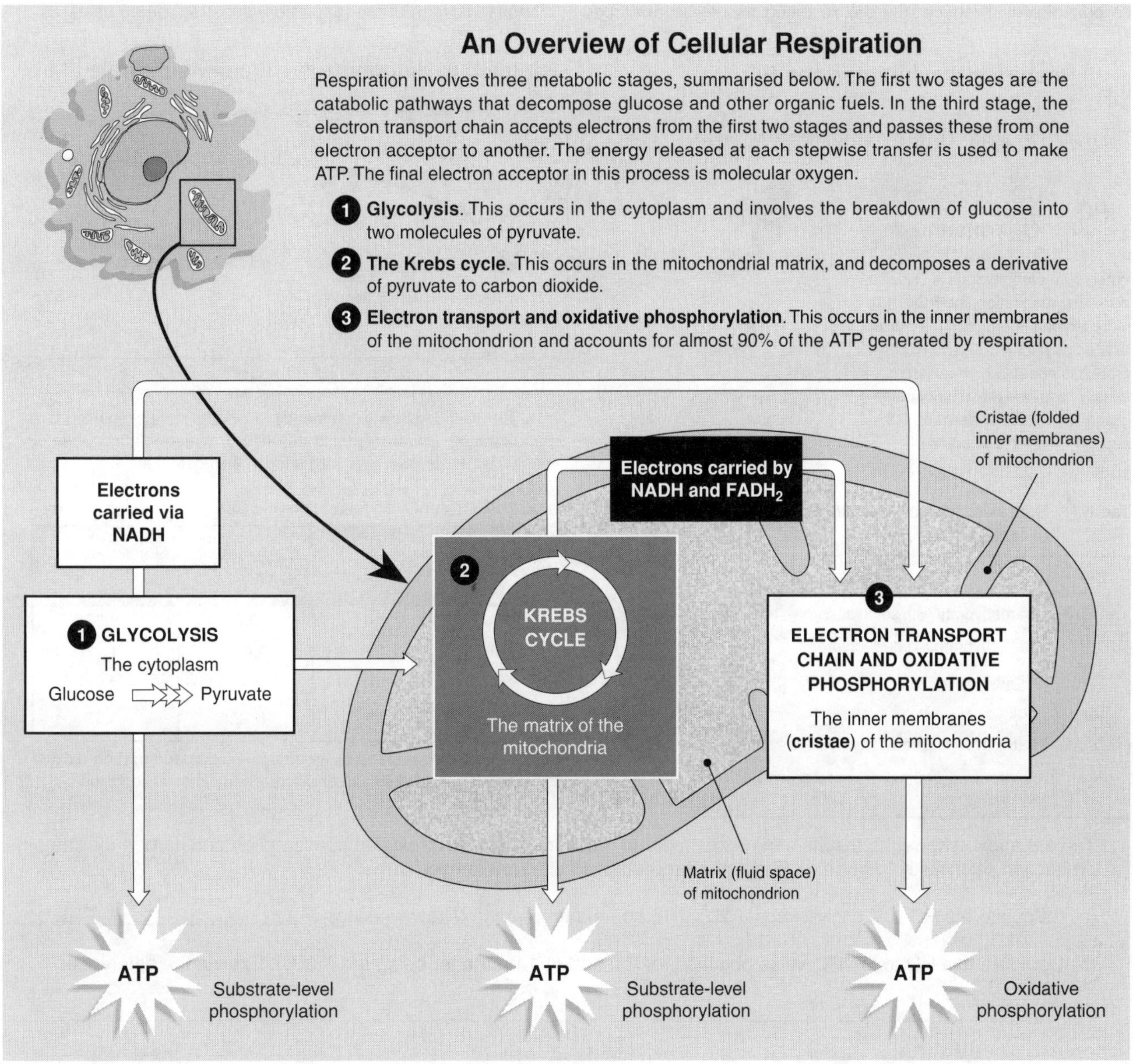

1. Describe precisely in which part of the cell the following take place:

   (a) Glycolysis: ______

   (b) Krebs cycle reactions: ______

   (c) Electron transport chain: ______

2. Provide a clear explanation of what is involved in each of the following processes:

   (a) Substrate-level phosphorylation: ______

   (b) Oxidative phosphorylation: ______

Measuring Respiration

Cellular respiration requires a **respiratory substance** to proceed. Carbohydrates, proteins, and fats (or mixtures of), can all be utilised as respiratory substances. In small animals or germinating seeds, the rate of cellular respiration can be measured using a simple respirometer: a sealed unit where the carbon dioxide produced by the respiring tissues is absorbed by soda lime and the volume of oxygen consumed is detected by fluid displacement in a manometer. Germinating seeds are also often used to calculate the **respiratory quotient** (RQ): the ratio of the amount of carbon dioxide produced during cellular respiration to the amount of oxygen consumed. RQ provides a useful indication of the respiratory substrate being used.

Respiratory substrates and RQ

The respiratory quotient (RQ) can be expressed simply as:

$$RQ = \frac{CO_2 \text{ produced}}{O_2 \text{ consumed}}$$

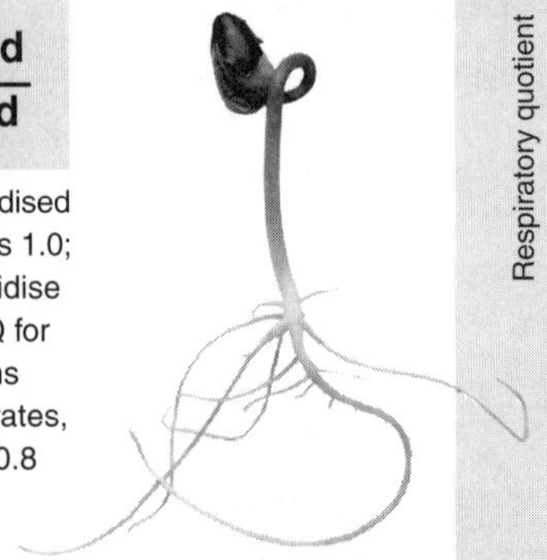

When pure carbohydrate is oxidised in cellular respiration, the RQ is 1.0; more oxygen is required to oxidise fatty acids (RQ = 0.7). The RQ for protein is about 0.9. Organisms usually respire a mix of substrates, giving RQ values of between 0.8 and 0.9 (see table 1, below).

Table 1: RQ values for the respiration of various substrates

RQ	Substrate
> 1.0	Carbohydrate with some anaerobic respiration
1.0	Carbohydrates, e.g. glucose
0.9	Protein
0.7	Fat
0.5	Fat with associated carbohydrate synthesis
0.3	Carbohydrate with associated organic acid synthesis

Using RQ to determine respiratory substrate

Fig. 1: RQ in relation to germination stage in wheat

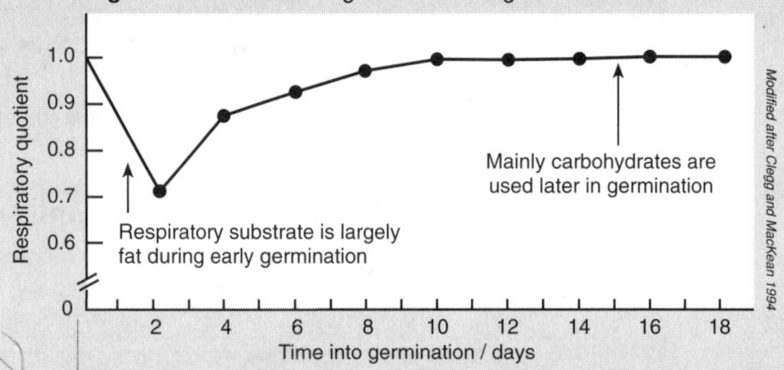

Fig. 1, above, shows how experimental RQ values have been used to determine the respiratory substrate utilised by germinating wheat seeds (*Triticum sativum*) over the period of their germination.

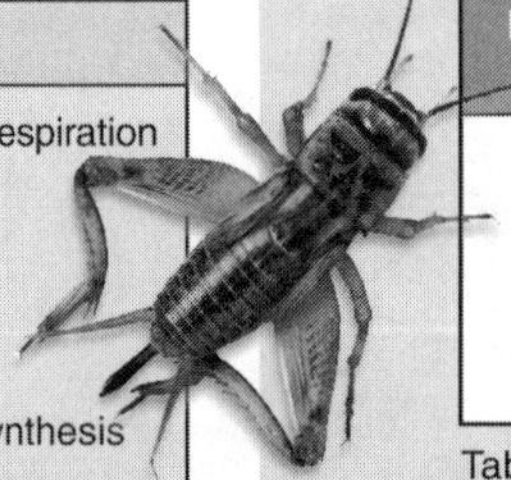

Table 2: Rates of O_2 consumption and CO_2 production in crickets

Time after last fed/ h	Temperature/ °C	Rate of O_2 consumption/ $mlg^{-1}h^{-1}$	Rate of CO_2 production/ $mlg^{-1}h^{-1}$
1	20	2.82	2.82
48	20	2.82	1.97
1	30	5.12	5.12
48	30	5.12	3.57

Table 2 shows the rates of oxygen consumption and carbon dioxide production of crickets kept under different experimental conditions.

1. Table 2 above shows the results of an experiment to measure the rates of oxygen consumption and carbon dioxide production of crickets 1 hour and 48 hours after feeding at different temperatures:

   (a) Calculate the RQ of a cricket kept at 20°C, 48 hours after feeding (show working): ______________

   (b) Compare this RQ to the RQ value obtained for the cricket 1 hour after being fed (20°C). Explain the difference:

   ____

   ____

2. The RQs of two species of seeds were calculated at two day intervals after germination. Results are tabulated to the right:

   (a) Plot the change in RQ of the two species during early germination:

   (b) Explain the values in terms of the possible substrates being respired:

   ____

   ____

   ____

   ____

   ____

   ____

   ____

Days after germination	RQ	
	Seedling A	Seedling B
2	0.65	0.70
4	0.35	0.91
6	0.48	0.98
8	0.68	1.00
10	0.70	1.00

The Biochemistry of Respiration

Cellular respiration is a catabolic, energy yielding pathway. The breakdown of glucose and other organic fuels (such as fats and proteins) to simpler molecules is **exergonic** and releases energy for the synthesis of ATP. As summarised in the previous activity, respiration involves glycolysis, the Krebs cycle, and electron transport. The diagram below provides a more detailed overview of the events in each of these stages. Glycolysis and the Krebs cycle supply electrons (via NADH) to the electron transport chain, which drives **oxidative phosphorylation**. Glycolysis nets two ATP, produced by **substrate-level phosphorylation**.

The conversion of pyruvate (the end product of glycolysis) to **acetyl CoA** links glycolysis to the Krebs cycle. One "turn" of the cycle releases carbon dioxide, forms one ATP by substrate level phosphorylation, and passes electrons to three NAD^+ and one FAD. Most of the ATP generated in cellular respiration is produced by oxidative phosphorylation when NADH and $FADH_2$ donate electrons to the series of electron carriers in the electron transport chain. At the end of the chain, electrons are passed to molecular oxygen, reducing it to water. Electron transport is coupled to ATP synthesis by **chemiosmosis** (see next page).

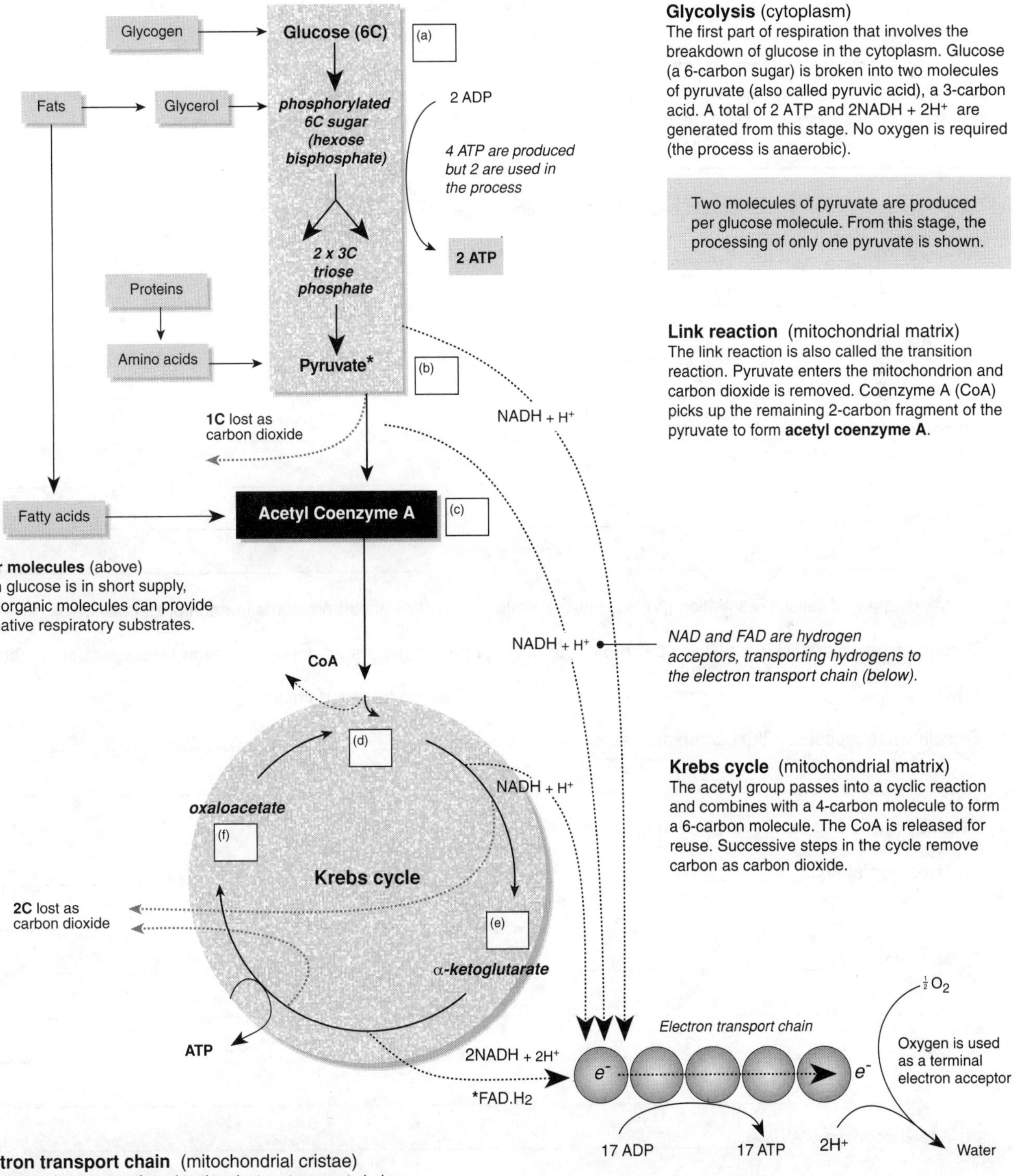

Glycolysis (cytoplasm)
The first part of respiration that involves the breakdown of glucose in the cytoplasm. Glucose (a 6-carbon sugar) is broken into two molecules of pyruvate (also called pyruvic acid), a 3-carbon acid. A total of 2 ATP and 2NADH + $2H^+$ are generated from this stage. No oxygen is required (the process is anaerobic).

Two molecules of pyruvate are produced per glucose molecule. From this stage, the processing of only one pyruvate is shown.

Link reaction (mitochondrial matrix)
The link reaction is also called the transition reaction. Pyruvate enters the mitochondrion and carbon dioxide is removed. Coenzyme A (CoA) picks up the remaining 2-carbon fragment of the pyruvate to form **acetyl coenzyme A**.

Other molecules (above)
When glucose is in short supply, other organic molecules can provide alternative respiratory substrates.

NAD and FAD are hydrogen acceptors, transporting hydrogens to the electron transport chain (below).

Krebs cycle (mitochondrial matrix)
The acetyl group passes into a cyclic reaction and combines with a 4-carbon molecule to form a 6-carbon molecule. The CoA is released for reuse. Successive steps in the cycle remove carbon as carbon dioxide.

Electron transport chain (mitochondrial cristae)
Hydrogen pairs are transferred to the electron transport chain, a series of hydrogen and electron carriers, located on the membranes of the **cristae**. The hydrogens or electrons are passed from one carrier to the next, losing energy as they go. The energy released in this stepwise process is used to produce ATP. Oxygen is the final electron acceptor and is reduced to water.
***Note** FAD enters the electron transport chain at a lower energy level than NAD, and only 2ATP are generated per $FAD.H_2$.

Total ATP yield per glucose
Glycolysis: 2 ATP, *Krebs cycle*: 2 ATP, *Electron transport*: 34 ATP

Respiration

Glycolysis and Fermentation	Aerobic Respiration
Occurs in the cytoplasm of the cell.	Occurs in the mitochondria of eukaryotic cells.
Oxygen is not required.	Oxygen is required.
Glycolysis: glucose is converted to pyruvic acid with a net production of 2ATP molecules (a very low energy yield).	Pyruvic acid is converted to carbon dioxide, water, and a further 36 ATP molecules from the Krebs cycle and electron transport chain (a high energy yield per glucose molecule).
Very inefficient production of energy.	An energy efficient process.
In the absence of oxygen, pyruvic acid cannot enter the mitochondrion. It is converted to ethanol and carbon dioxide in plants, and lactic acid in animals.	When oxygen is present, pyruvic acid can be oxidised further via the Krebs cycle and electron transport chain.

1. Summarise the events occurring in each of the following stages of cellular respiration:

   (a) Glycolysis: ____________________

   (b) Transition reaction: ____________________

   (c) Krebs cycle: ____________________

   (d) Electron transport chain: ____________________

2. On the diagram of cellular respiration (previous page), state the number of carbon atoms in each of the molecules (a)-(f):

3. Determine how many ATP molecules **per molecule of glucose** are generated during the following stages of respiration:

   (a) Glycolysis: ________ (b) Krebs cycle: ________ (c) Electron transport chain: ________ (d) Total: ________

4. Explain what happens to the carbon atoms lost during respiration: ____________________

5. Describe the role of each of the following in cellular respiration:

   (a) Hydrogen atoms: ____________________

   (b) NAD and FAD: ____________________

   (c) Oxygen: ____________________

   (d) Acetyl coenzyme A: ____________________

6. Explain what happens when the supply of glucose for cellular respiration is limited: ____________________

Chemiosmosis

Chemiosmosis is the process in which electron transport is coupled to ATP synthesis. It takes place in the membranes of the mitochondria of all eukaryotic cells, the chloroplasts of plants, and across the plasma membrane of bacteria. Chemiosmosis involves the establishment of a proton (hydrogen) gradient across biological membranes (shown below for cellular respiration). The concentration gradient is a form of potential energy, which in chemiosmosis is used to generate ATP. Chemiosmosis has two key components: an **electron transport chain** (ETC) sets up a proton gradient as electrons pass along it to a final electron acceptor, and an enzyme called **ATP synthase** which uses the proton gradient to catalyse ATP synthesis In cellular respiration, electron transport carriers on the inner membrane of the mitochondrion oxidise NADH + H^+ and $FADH_2$. Energy from this process forces protons to move, against their concentration gradient, from the mitochondrial matrix into the space between the two membranes. The protons then flow back into the matrix via ATP synthase molecules in the membrane. As the protons flow down their concentration gradient, energy is released and ATP is synthesised. In the chloroplasts of green plants, the process is similar as ATP is produced when protons pass from the thylakoid lumen to the chloroplast stroma via ATP synthase.

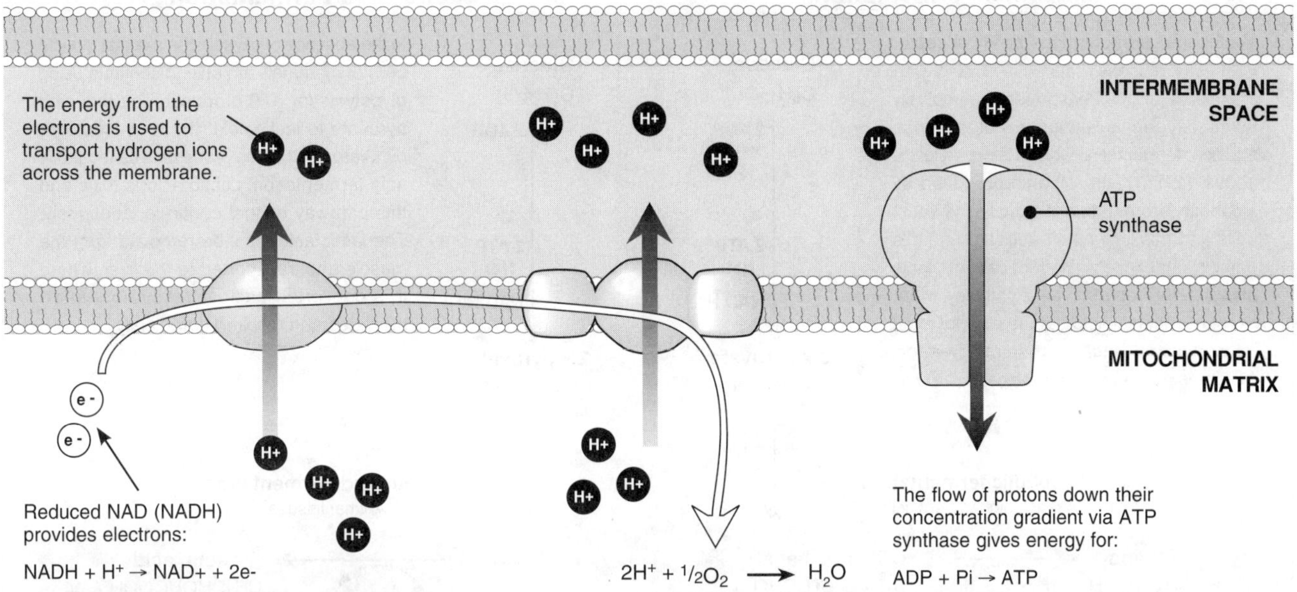

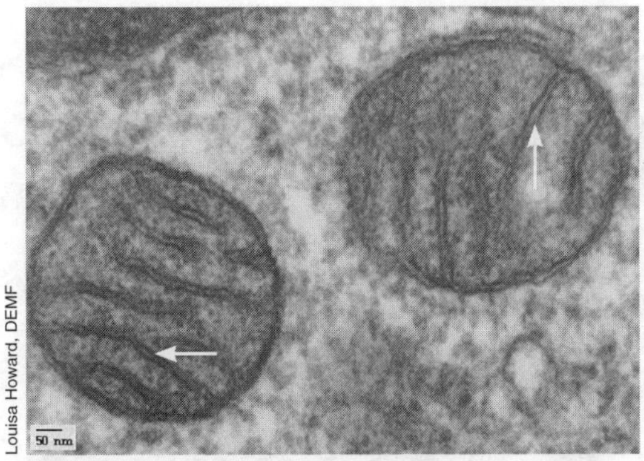

The intermembrane spaces can be seen (arrows) in this transverse section of miotchondria.

The Evidence for Chemiosmosis

The British biochemist Peter Mitchell proposed the chemiosmotic hypothesis in 1961. He proposed that, because living cells have membrane potential, electrochemical gradients could be used to do work, i.e. provide the energy for ATP synthesis. Scientists at the time were skeptical, but the evidence for chemiosmosis was extensive and came from studies of isolated mitochondria and chloroplasts. Evidence included:

- The outer membranes of mitochondria were removed leaving the inner membranes intact. Adding protons to the treated mitochondria increased ATP synthesis.
- When isolated chloroplasts were illuminated, the medium in which they were suspended became alkaline.
- Isolated chloroplasts were kept in the dark and transferred first to a low pH medium (to acidify the thylakoid interior) and then to an alkaline medium (low protons). They then spontaneously synthesised ATP (no light was needed).

1. Briefly summarise the process of chemiosmosis: ____________________

2. Explain why adding protons to the treated mitochondria increased ATP synthesis: ____________________

3. Explain why the suspension of isolated chloroplasts became alkaline when illuminated? ____________________

4. (a) Explain the purpose of transferring the chloroplasts first to an acid then to an alkaline medium: ____________________

   (b) Explain why ATP synthesis occurred spontaneously in these treated chloroplasts: ____________________

Respiration

Anaerobic Pathways

All organisms can metabolise glucose anaerobically (without oxygen) using glycolysis in the cytoplasm, but the energy yield from this process is low and few organisms can obtain sufficient energy for their needs this way. In the absence of oxygen, glycolysis soon stops unless there is an alternative acceptor for the electrons produced from the glycolytic pathway. In yeasts and the root cells of higher plants this acceptor is ethanal, and the pathway is called **alcoholic fermentation**. In the skeletal muscle of mammals, the acceptor is pyruvate itself and the end product is **lactic acid**. In both cases, the duration of the fermentation is limited by the toxic effects of the organic compound produced. Although fermentation is sometimes called anaerobic respiration, this is not correct. Respiration always involves hydrogen ions passing down a chain of carriers to a terminal acceptor, and this does not occur in fermentation. In anaerobic respiration, the final H^+ acceptor is a molecule other than oxygen, e.g. Fe^{2+} or nitrate.

Alcoholic Fermentation

In alcoholic fermentation, the H^+ acceptor is ethanal which is reduced to ethanol with the release of CO_2. Yeasts respire aerobically when oxygen is available but can use alcoholic fermentation when it is not. At levels above 12-15%, the ethanol produced by alcoholic fermentation is toxic to the yeast cells and this limits their ability to use this pathway indefinitely. The root cells of plants also use fermentation as a pathway when oxygen is unavailable but the ethanol must be converted back to respiratory intermediates and respired aerobically.

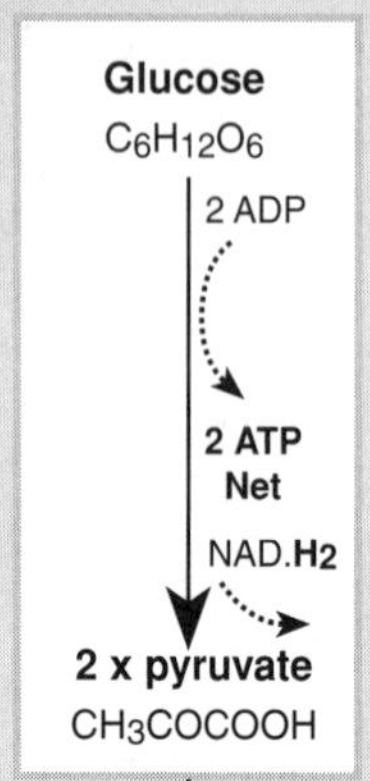

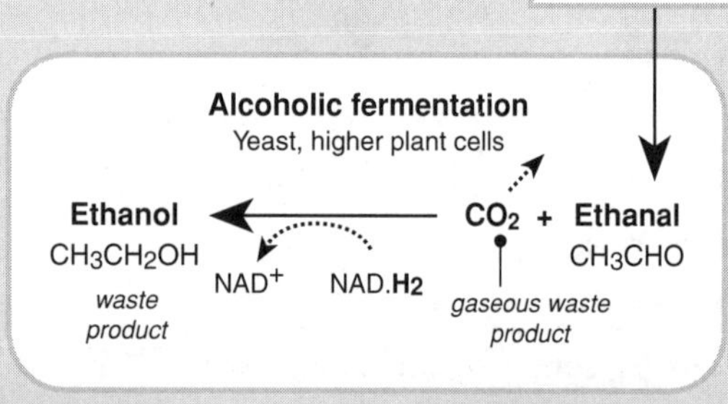

Lactic Acid Fermentation

In the absence of oxygen, the skeletal muscle cells of mammals are able to continue using glycolysis for ATP production by reducing pyruvate to lactic acid (the H^+ acceptor is pyruvate itself). This process is called lactic acid fermentation. Lactic acid is toxic and this pathway cannot continue indefinitely. The lactic acid must be removed from the muscle and transported to the liver, where it is converted back to respiratory intermediates and respired aerobically.

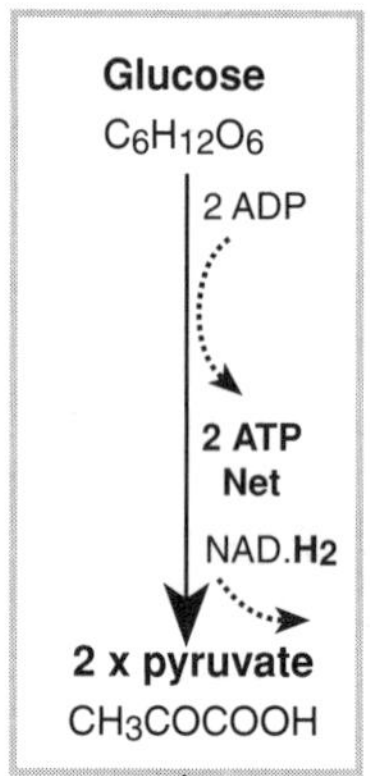

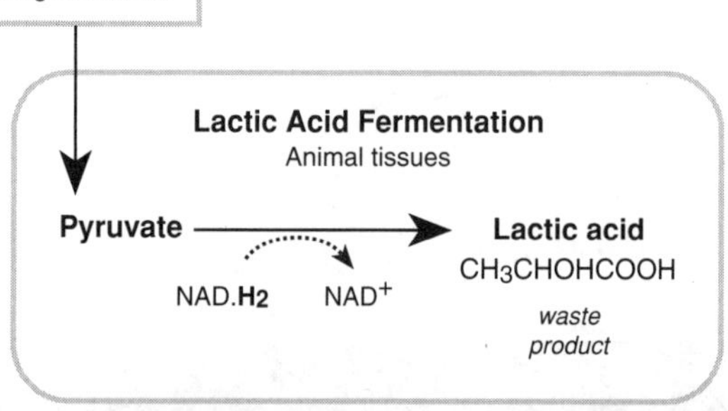

CDC

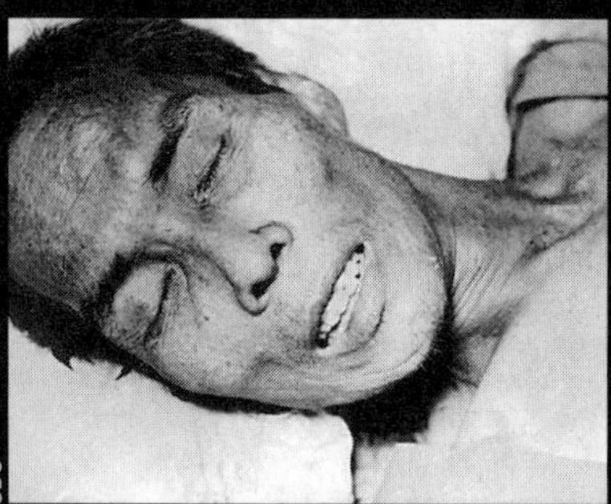

Some organisms respire only in the absence of oxygen and are known as **obligate anaerobes**. Many of these organisms are bacterial pathogens and cause diseases such as tetanus (*above*), gangrene, and botulism.

Vertebrate skeletal muscle is **facultatively anaerobic** because it has the ability to generate ATP for a short time in the absence of oxygen. The energy from this pathway comes from glycolysis and the yield is low.

The products of alcoholic fermentation have been utilised by humans for centuries. The alcohol and carbon dioxide produced from this process form the basis of the brewing and baking industries.

1. Describe the key difference between aerobic respiration and fermentation: ______________________

____

____

2. In simple terms, explain why the efficiency of anaerobic pathways is so low compared to aerobic pathways:

____

____

3. Explain why fermentation cannot go on indefinitely: ______________________

____

KEY TERMS: Mix and Match

INSTRUCTIONS: Test your vocabulary by matching each term to its definition, as identified by its preceding letter code.

ACETYL COENZYME A ....

AEROBIC RESPIRATION ....

ALCOHOLIC FERMENTATION ....

ANAEROBIC RESPIRATION ....

ATP SYNTHASE (ATPASE) ....

CELLULAR RESPIRATION ....

CHEMIOSMOSIS ....

CHEMIOSMOTIC THEORY ....

COENZYME ....

CRISTAE ....

ELECTRON ACCEPTOR ....

ELECTRON TRANSPORT CHAIN ....

FAD ....

GLUCOSE ....

GLYCOLYSIS ....

KREBS CYCLE ....

LACTIC ACID FERMENTATION ....

LINK REACTION ....

MATRIX ....

MITOCHONDRIA ....

NAD ....

OXALOACETATE ....

OXIDATIVE PHOSPHORYLATION ....

PROTON GRADIENT ....

PYRUVATE ....

RESPIRATORY SUBSTRATE ....

SUBSTRATE LEVEL PHOSPHORYLATION ....

TRIOSE PHOSPHATE ....

A The folds of the inner mitochondrial membrane.

B A form of respiration that occurs without oxygen.

C An intermediary molecule, which transfers carbon atoms within the acetyl group to the Krebs cycle to be oxidised for energy production.

D An organic molecule that acts as a cofactor in an enzyme reaction but is only loosely bound to the enzyme.

E A sugar found in all living cells. The main substrate for cellular respiration.

F Chain of enzyme based redox reactions which pass electrons from high to low redox potentials. The energy released is used to pump protons across a membrane and produce ATP.

G The process in cellular respiration where an enzyme transfers a phosphate group from a substrate to ADP.

H A three-carbon phosphorylated sugar.

I A product of glycolysis. An important intermediate in many metabolic pathways.

J The process in which the synthesis of ATP is coupled to electron transport and the movement of protons.

K A dinucleotide coenzyme found in all living cells where it acts as a hydrogen acceptor.

L A four-carbon intermediate in the Krebs cycle.

M Respiration requiring oxygen as the terminal electron acceptor.

N The process in cellular respiration which involves the oxidation of glucose by a series of redox reactions that provide the energy for the formation of ATP.

O The inner region of the mitochondrion enclosed by the inner mitochondrial membrane.

P A theory proposed to describe how ATP synthesis is coupled to the establishment of a proton gradient across a biological membrane.

Q A substance required for cellular respiration to derive energy through oxidation. Examples are carbohydrates (especially glucose), fats, and proteins.

R An enzyme which uses the proton gradient generated in the electron transport chain to catalyse the synthesis of ATP.

S Also known as the citric acid cycle. Part of a metabolic pathway involved in the chemical conversion of carbohydrates, fats and proteins to CO_2 and water to generate a form of usable energy (ATP).

T A molecule that accepts electrons.

U A flavin cofactor involved in many important metabolic redox reactions.

V An anaerobic pathway where ethanal acts as the electron acceptor, and the end product is ethanol.

W The catabolic process in which the chemical energy in complex organic molecules is coupled to ATP production.

X A gradient of hydrogen ions (protons) established across a biological membrane.

Y The stage in cellular respiration where pyruvate enters the mitochondrion and carbon dioxide is removed.

Z A series of reactions that convert glucose into pyruvate. The energy released is used to produce ATP.

AA An anaerobic pathway occurring in the skeletal muscle of mammals. Pyruvate is reduced to lactic acid.

BB Organelles responsible for producing the cell's ATP. They appear oval in shape with an outer double membrane and a convoluted interior membrane.

Respiration

Cellular Control

DNA, proteins, and cellular control
- Understanding the genetic code
- Transcription and translation
- Mutation and effect on protein function
- Genetic control of metabolism
- Genetic control of development

Meiosis and variation
- Meiosis, and variation
- Sex linkage and codominance
- Epistasis and polygeny
- Gene-environment interactions

Variation and evolution
- Variation and natural selection
- Calculating allele frequencies
- Genetic drift: effect on allele frequencies
- Isolating mechanisms and speciation
- Artificial selection in domestic species

Important in this section...
- *Understand mechanisms for control at the cellular level*
- *Describe how humans manipulate natural processes*
- *Describe ecosystem function and change*
- *Explain how organisms respond to their environment*

Biotechnology & Gene Technologies

Cloning
- Cloning in plants
- Cloning in animals: SCNT

Biotechnology
- Growth and culture of microbes
- Enzyme technology

Genomes and gene technologies
- Genomic sequencing and analysis
- Genetic engineering
- Gene therapy and xenotransplants
- Ethical concerns with GE

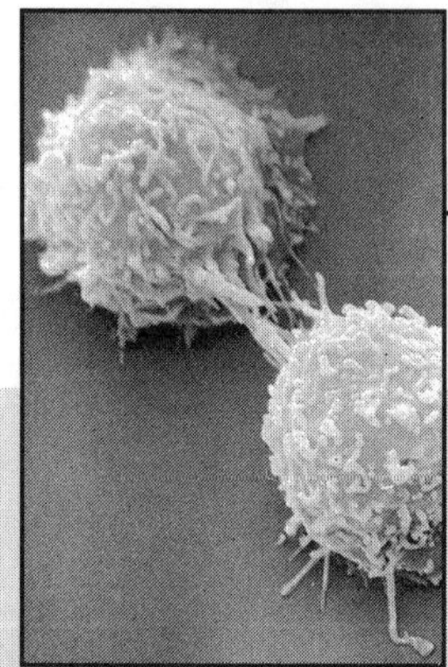

Genes control cellular function. Mutation and sexual reproduction create variation, which is the raw material for evolution.

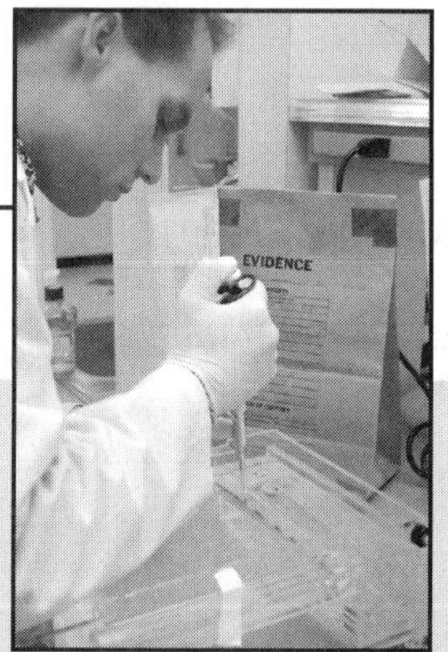

Manipulation of natural processes for human benefit can take place at the level of the gene, the cell, or the whole organism.

A2 Unit F215
Control, Genomes, and Environment

Genes control cellular function but are not immutable. Organisms are variable; variation is the raw material for natural selection. Humans can intervene to accelerate the pace of genetic change. This intervention may occur at the level of the genome.

Energy flows through ecosystems, whereas nutrients are recycled. Humans may intervene in these ecosystem processes. Organisms must respond appropriately to their environment. Their responses are coordinated by nervous and/or hormonal mechanisms

A sound understanding of ecosystem function is central to the sustainable management of resources.

Plants and animal respond to environmental stimuli and coordinate these responses in an adaptive way.

Energy flow in ecosystems
- Ecosystems as dynamic systems
- Trophic levels and energy transfers
- Quantifying energy transfers
- Human influence on energy flow

Ecosystem change and nutrient cycles
- Primary succession
- Studying distribution and abundance
- The role of decomposers
- The nitrogen cycle

Populations and sustainability
- Population regulation and change
- Competition and predation
- Conservation and sustainability
- Human impact on an ecosystem

Ecosystems & Sustainability

Plant responses
- Plant responses to environment
- Tropisms and the role of auxin
- The role of plant hormones

Animal responses
- Animal responses to environment
- Nervous system structure and function
- Muscle structure and function
- Nervous and endocrine influences

Animal behaviour
- Innate behaviour
- Reflexes, taxes, and kineses
- Types of learned behaviour
- Social behaviour in primates
- Dopamine and human behaviour

Responding to the Environment

UNIT F215

5.1.1

Cellular **Control**

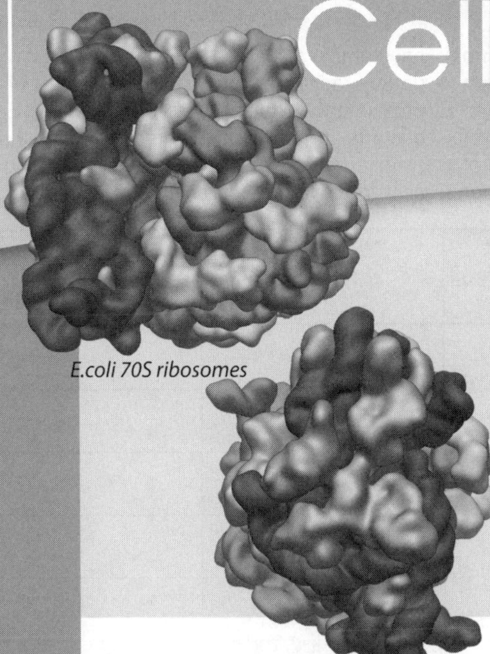

E.coli 70S ribosomes

KEY CONCEPTS

- Genes code for proteins, including enzymes.
- The genetic code comprises 3-letter codons, each corresponding to one of 20 amino acids used to build proteins. The code has redundancy but no ambiguity.
- Mutations are changes to the sequence of nucleotides in DNA. They may be beneficial, harmful, or neutral.
- Metabolic pathways can be regulated by controlling transcription or by regulating protein activity.
- The gene sequences that control development are highly conserved.

KEY TERMS

anticodons
apoptosis
beneficial mutation
coding strand
codon
cyclic AMP
exon
gene expression
gene induction
genetic code
harmful mutation
homeobox sequences
intron
lac operon
messenger RNA (mRNA)
mutagen
mutation
neutral mutation
polypeptide
redundancy
ribosome
RNA polymerase
second messenger
silent (synonymous) mutation
start codon
stop codon
template strand
transcription
transfer RNA (tRNA)
translation
triplet

OBJECTIVES

☐ 1. Use the **KEY TERMS** to help you understand and complete these objectives.

Gene expression — pages 105-112

☐ 2. Understand that genes code for polypeptides and that enzymes are proteins whose synthesis is controlled by DNA. Describe features of the genetic code, including:
- The 4-letter alphabet and the 3-letter triplet code (codon) of base sequences.
- The non-overlapping, linear nature of the code which is read from start to finish in one direction.
- Specific punctuation codons (START, STOP codons).
- The degeneracy of the code (it has **redundancy** but no ambiguity).

☐ 3. Identify the two stages of gene expression: **transcription** and **translation** and describe how information is transferred from DNA to protein, as follows:
- Describe the structure and role of **messenger RNA** (mRNA).
- Describe transcription, including the role of **RNA polymerase**.
- Understand the significance of the **coding** (sense) **strand**, the **template** (antisense) **strand**, **introns**, and **exons**.
- Describe translation, including the structure and role of the **transfer RNA** (tRNA) molecules and **ribosomes**.

Mutation — pages 113-119

☐ 4. Using examples, explain the terms **mutagen** and **mutation**. Explain the significance of mutation as the ultimate source of all new alleles.

☐ 5. Explain how mutations may be harmful, beneficial, or neutral (sometimes synonymous with silent) in terms of their effect on the way a protein functions. Recognise the evolutionary importance of **neutral mutations**.

☐ 6. Describe specific examples of the effect of mutations on the resulting amino acid sequence and the phenotype, e.g. sickle cell disease and cystic fibrosis.

Control of metabolism and development — pages 120-125

☐ 7. Explain the role of cyclic AMP (a second messenger) in controlling metabolism by activating proteins.

☐ 8. Explain the genetic control of protein production in a prokaryote, as illustrated by **gene induction** in the ***lac* operon** in *E. coli.* Explain how lactose activates transcription and how metabolism of the substrate is achieved. Explain the adaptive value of gene induction.

☐ 9. Explain the similarity in **homeobox sequences** (e.g. *HOX* genes) involved in regulating development in animals, fungi and plants.

☐ 10. Describe the process of **apoptosis** (programmed cell death or PCD) and describe the situations in which apoptosis plays a crucial role, e.g. during development. Describe apoptosis as a mechanism to change body plans.

Periodicals:
Listings for this chapter are on page 341

Weblinks:
www.biozone.co.uk/weblink/OCR-A2-2832.html

Teacher Resource CD-ROM: *Does DNA Really Carry the Code?*

The Genetic Code

The genetic information that codes for the assembly of amino acids is stored as three-letter codes, called **codons**. Each codon represents one of 20 amino acids used in the construction of polypeptide chains. The **mRNA-amino acid table** (bottom of page) can be used to identify the amino acid encoded by each of the mRNA codons. Note that the code is **degenerate** in that for each amino acid, there may be more than one codon. Most of this degeneracy involves the third nucleotide of a codon. The genetic code is **universal**; all living organisms on Earth, from viruses and bacteria, to plants and humans, share the same genetic code (with a few minor exceptions representing mutations that have occurred over the long history of evolution).

Amino acid	Codons that code for this amino acid	No.	Amino acid	Codons that code for this amino acid	No.
Ala Alanine	GCU, GCC, GCA, GCG	4	**Leu** Leucine		
Arg Arginine			**Lys** Lysine		
Asn Asparagine			**Met** Methionine		
Asp Aspartic acid			**Phe** Phenylalanine		
Cys Cysteine			**Pro** Proline		
Gln Glutamine			**Ser** Serine		
Glu Glutamic acid			**Thr** Threonine		
Gly Glycine			**Try** Tryptophan		
His Histidine			**Tyr** Tyrosine		
Iso Isoleucine			**Val** Valine		

1. Use the **mRNA-amino acid table** (below) to list in the table above all the **codons** that code for each of the amino acids and the number of different codons that can code for each amino acid (the first amino acid has been done for you).

2. (a) State how many amino acids could be coded for if a codon consisted of just two bases: ____________

   (b) Explain why this number of bases is inadequate to code for the 20 amino acids required to make proteins:

   ____

   ____

3. Describe the consequence of the degeneracy of the genetic code to the likely effect of a change to one base in a triplet:

   ____

   ____

mRNA-Amino Acid Table

How to read the table: The table on the right is used to 'decode' the genetic code as a sequence of amino acids in a polypeptide chain, from a given mRNA sequence. To work out which amino acid is coded for by a codon (triplet of bases) look for the first letter of the codon in the row label on the left hand side. Then look for the column that intersects the same row from above that matches the second base. Finally, locate the third base in the codon by looking along the row from the right hand end that matches your codon.

Example: Determine **CAG**

C on the left row, A on the top column, G on the right row
CAG is Gln (**glutamine**)

Read second letter here / Read first letter here / Read third letter here

First Letter	Second Letter: U	C	A	G	Third Letter
U	**UUU** Phe	**UCU** Ser	**UAU** Tyr	**UGU** Cys	U
U	**UUC** Phe	**UCC** Ser	**UAC** Tyr	**UGC** Cys	C
U	**UUA** Leu	**UCA** Ser	**UAA** STOP	**UGA** STOP	A
U	**UUG** Leu	**UCG** Ser	**UAG** STOP	**UGG** Try	G
C	**CUU** Leu	**CCU** Pro	**CAU** His	**CGU** Arg	U
C	**CUC** Leu	**CCC** Pro	**CAC** His	**CGC** Arg	C
C	**CUA** Leu	**CCA** Pro	**CAA** Gln	**CGA** Arg	A
C	**CUG** Leu	**CCG** Pro	**CAG** Gln	**CGG** Arg	G
A	**AUU** Iso	**ACU** Thr	**AAU** Asn	**AGU** Ser	U
A	**AUC** Iso	**ACC** Thr	**AAC** Asn	**AGC** Ser	C
A	**AUA** Iso	**ACA** Thr	**AAA** Lys	**AGA** Arg	A
A	**AUG** Met	**ACG** Thr	**AAG** Lys	**AGG** Arg	G
G	**GUU** Val	**GCU** Ala	**GAU** Asp	**GGU** Gly	U
G	**GUC** Val	**GCC** Ala	**GAC** Asp	**GGC** Gly	C
G	**GUA** Val	**GCA** Ala	**GAA** Glu	**GGA** Gly	A
G	**GUG** Val	**GCG** Ala	**GAG** Glu	**GGG** Gly	G

The Simplest Case: Genes to Proteins

The traditionally held view of genes was as specific sections of DNA encoding proteins (including **enzymes**). This simple definition was revised as the one gene-one polypeptide hypothesis in recognition of the fact that several polypeptide chains may contribute to the functional protein. Even more recently, geneticists have discovered that genes also encode functional RNAs that have regulatory roles in the cell. Much of the nonprotein-coding DNA there fore has a purpose and is not "junk" DNA as was previously assumed. Although our concept of what constitutes a gene is changing rapidly and now encompasses all those segments of DNA that are transcribed (to RNA), the concept of one gene-one polypeptide is still useful. This activity considers this simplest scenario: that in which the gene codes for a functional protein. The **nucleotides** are read as **triplets**, which are equivalent to **codons** on the mRNA. Punctuation codons mark the start and end points for the gene. The genes required to form a functional end-product (in this case, a functional protein) are collectively called a **transcription unit**.

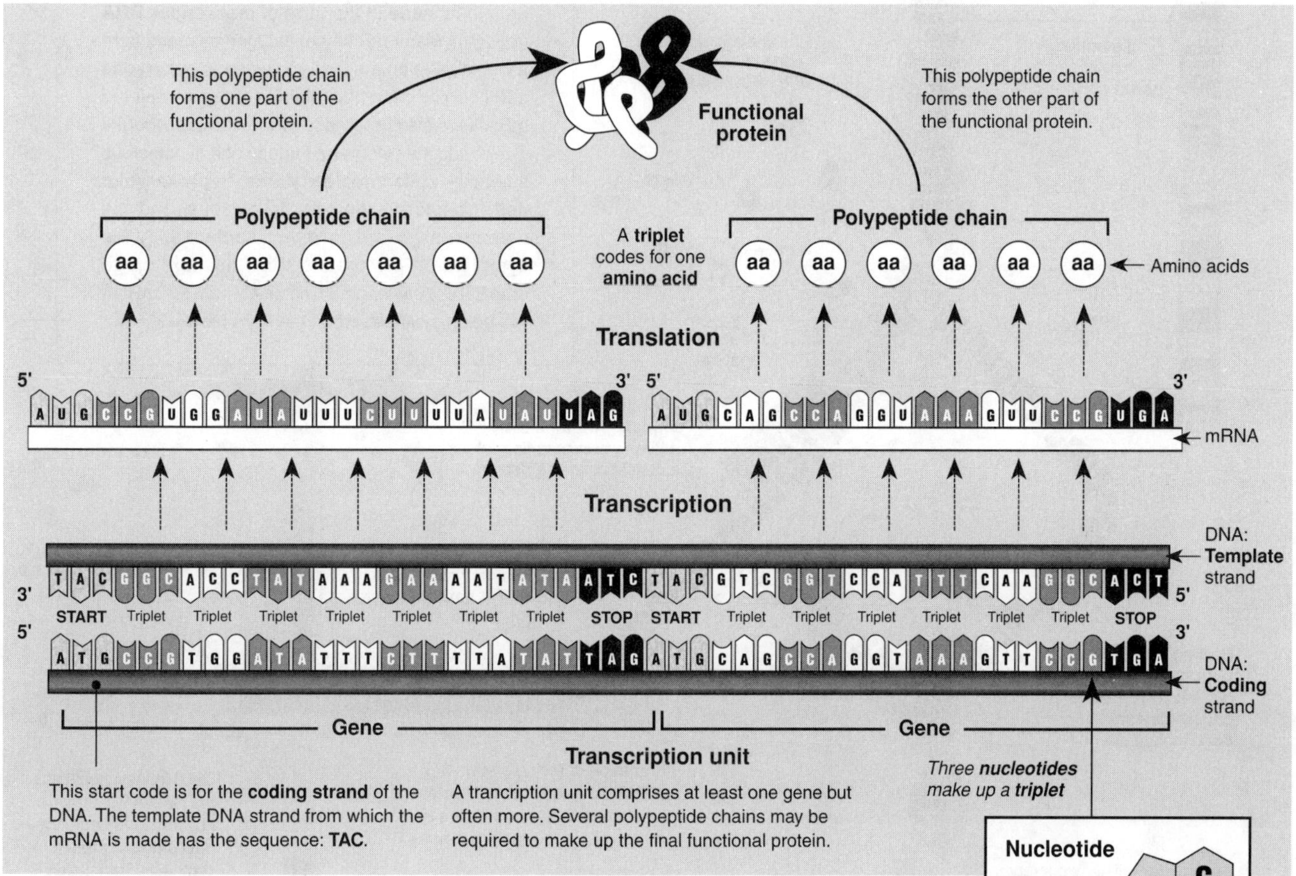

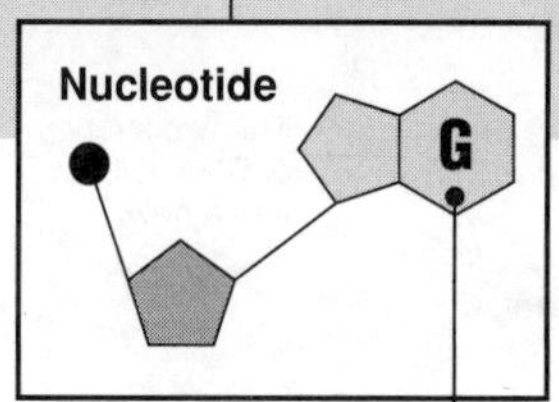

In models of nucleic acids, nucleotides are denoted by their base letter. (In this case: **G** is for guanine)

1. Describe the purpose of the start and stop codons on a strand of DNA:

____

____

____

____

2. (a) The mRNA strand is transcribed from which DNA strand? _______________________

   (b) Explain how the bases differ between the DNA strand and the mRNA strand that results from transcription:

   ____

3. Describe the steps involved in forming a functional enzyme comprising two polypeptide chains: ______________

____

____

4. Recall the anti-parallel nature of DNA, with the strands orientated in opposite directions. Explain its significance:

____

____

Transcription

Transcription is the process by which the code contained in the DNA molecule is transcribed (rewritten) into a **mRNA** molecule. Transcription is under the control of the cell's metabolic processes which must activate a gene before this process can begin. The enzyme that directly controls the process is RNA polymerase, which makes a strand of mRNA using the single strand of DNA (the **template strand**) as the template (hence the term). The enzyme transcribes only a gene length of DNA at a time and therefore recognises start and stop signals (codes) at the beginning and end of the gene. Only RNA polymerase is involved in mRNA synthesis; it causes the unwinding of the DNA as well. It is common to find several RNA polymerase enzyme molecules on the same gene at any one time; this allows a high rate of mRNA synthesis to occur.

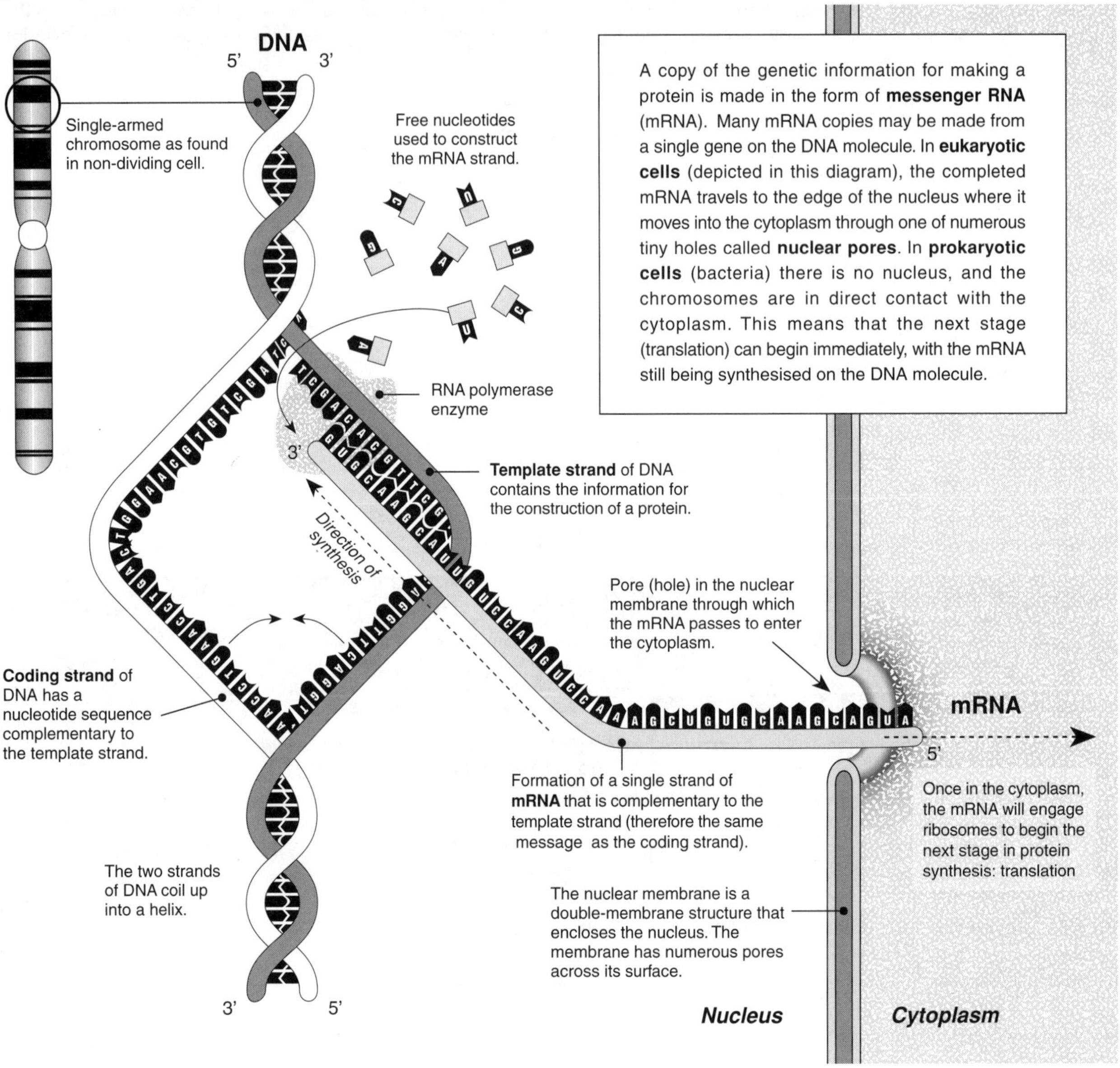

A copy of the genetic information for making a protein is made in the form of **messenger RNA** (mRNA). Many mRNA copies may be made from a single gene on the DNA molecule. In **eukaryotic cells** (depicted in this diagram), the completed mRNA travels to the edge of the nucleus where it moves into the cytoplasm through one of numerous tiny holes called **nuclear pores**. In **prokaryotic cells** (bacteria) there is no nucleus, and the chromosomes are in direct contact with the cytoplasm. This means that the next stage (translation) can begin immediately, with the mRNA still being synthesised on the DNA molecule.

1. Explain the role of messenger RNA in protein synthesis: ________________

____

____

2. The genetic code contains punctuation codons to mark the starting and finishing points for synthesis of polypeptide chains and proteins. Consult the mRNA amino acid table earlier in this workbook and state the codes for:

   (a) Start codon: ________________ (b) Stop (termination) codons: ________________

3. For the following triplets on the DNA, determine the **codon** sequence for the mRNA that would be synthesised:

   (a) Triplets on the DNA: T A C T A G C C G C G A T T T

   Codons on the mRNA: ________________

   (b) Triplets on the DNA: T A C A A G C C T A T A A A A

   Codons on the mRNA: ________________

Related activities: *The Simplest Case: Genes to Proteins, The Genetic Code*
Web links: *Transcription in Prokaryotes, Animation of Transcription, Transcription Movie*

Translation

The diagram below shows the translation phase of gene expression. The scene shows how a single mRNA molecule can be 'serviced' by many ribosomes at the same time. The ribosome on the right is in a more advanced stage of constructing a polypeptide chain because it has 'translated' more of the mRNA than the ribosome to the left. The anti-codon at the base of each tRNA must make a perfect complementary match with the codon on the mRNA before the amino acid is released. Once released, the amino acid is added to the growing polypeptide chain by enzymes.

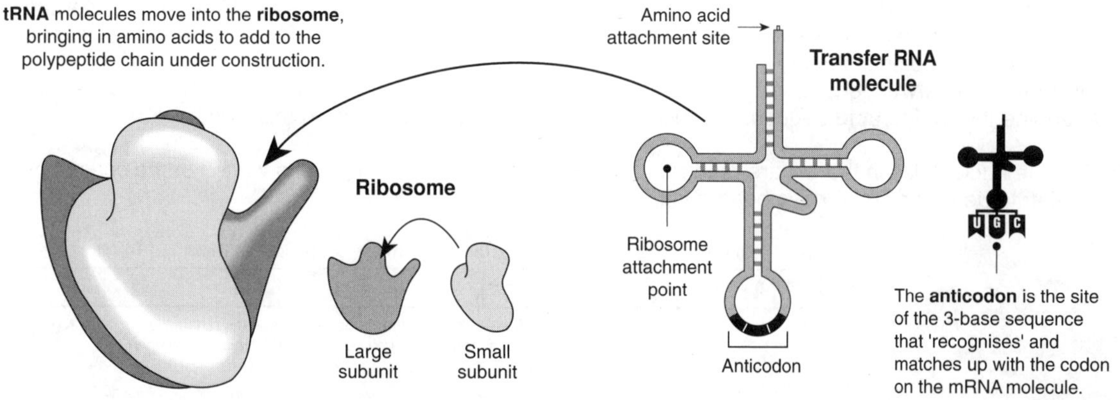

Ribosomes are made up of a complex of ribosomal RNA (rRNA) and proteins. They exist as two separate sub-units (above) until they are attracted to a binding site on the mRNA molecule, when they join together. Ribosomes have binding sites that attract transfer RNA (**tRNA**) molecules loaded with amino acids. The tRNA molecules are about 80 nucleotides in length and are made under the direction of genes in the chromosomes. There is a different tRNA molecule for each of the different possible anticodons (see the diagram below) and, because of the degeneracy of the genetic code, there may be up to six different tRNAs carrying the same amino acid.

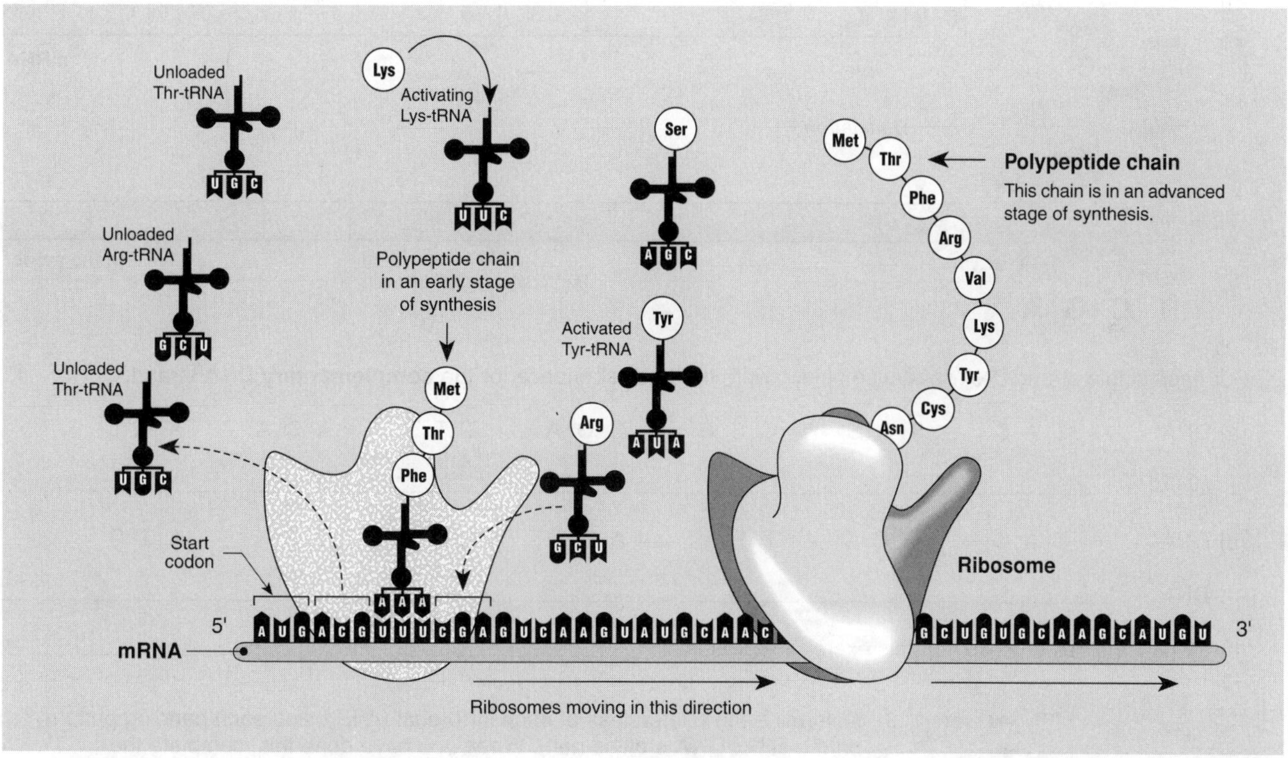

1. For the following codons on the mRNA, determine the **anti-codons** for each tRNA that would deliver the amino acids:

   Codons on the mRNA: U A C U A G C C G C G A U U U

   Anti-codons on the tRNAs: ______________________________

2. There are many different types of tRNA molecules, each with a different anti-codon (HINT: use the mRNA table).

   (a) State how many different tRNA types there are, each with a unique anticodon: ______________________

   (b) Explain your answer: ______________________________

   ____

   ____

Cellular Control

Analysing a DNA Sample

The nucleotide sequence of a section of DNA can be determined using DNA sequencing techniques (see the topic *Genomes and Gene Technology* later in this workbook for a description of this technology). The base sequence determines the amino acid sequence of the resulting protein therefore the DNA tells us what type of protein that gene encodes. This exercise reviews the areas of DNA replication, transcription, and translation using an analysis of a gel electrophoresis column. **Attempt it after you have completed the rest of this topic**. Remember that the gel pattern represents the sequence in the synthesised strand.

1. Determine the amino acid sequence of a protein from the nucleotide sequence of its DNA, with the following steps:
   (a) Determine the sequence of **synthesised DNA** in the gel
   (b) Convert it to the complementary sequence of the **sample DNA**
   (c) Complete the **mRNA** sequence
   (d) Determine the **amino acid** sequence by using the 'mRNA amino acid table' in this workbook.

   NOTE: The nucleotides in the gel are read from bottom to top and the sequence is written in the spaces provided from left to right (the first 4 have been done for you).

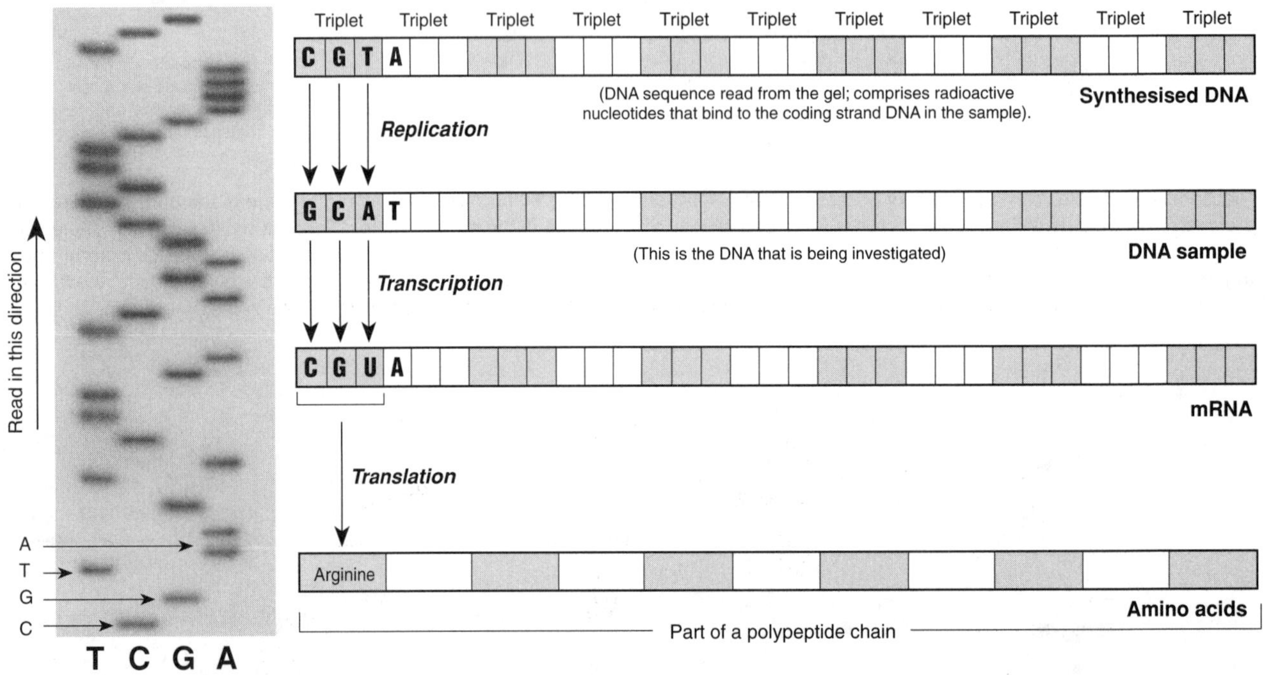

2. For each single strand DNA sequence below, write the base sequence for the **complementary DNA** strand:

   (a) DNA: T A C T A G C C G C G A T T T A C A A T T

   DNA: ____________________

   (b) DNA: T A C G C C T T A A A G G G C C G A A T C

   DNA: ____________________

   (c) Identify the cell process that this exercise represents: ____________________

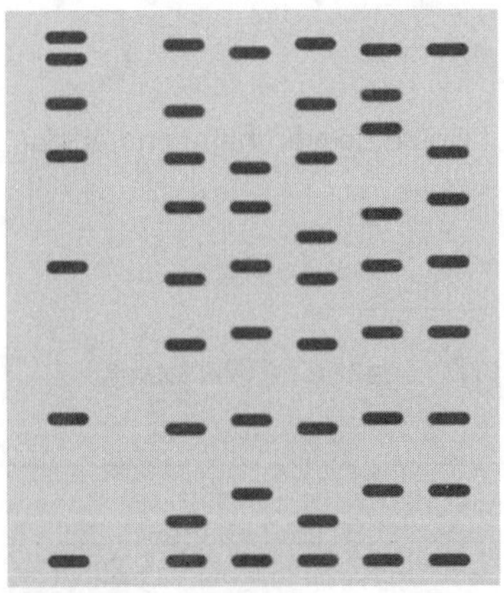

3. Determine the relatedness of each individual (A-E) using each banding pattern on the set of DNA profiles (left). When you have done this, complete the dendrogram by adding the letter of each individual.

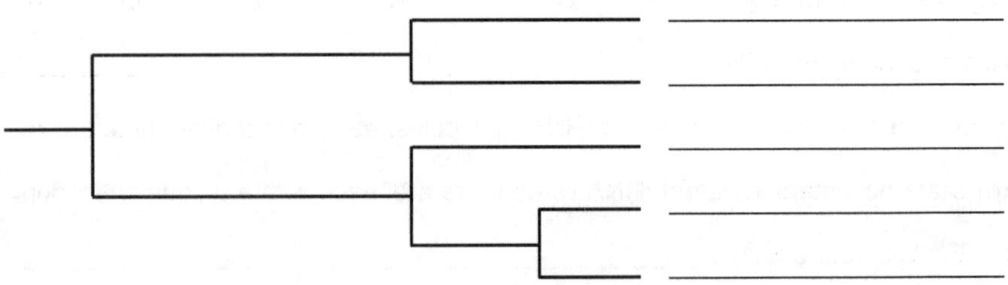

Related activities: Automated DNA Sequencing, The Genetic Code, Gel Electrophoresis

Protein Synthesis Summary

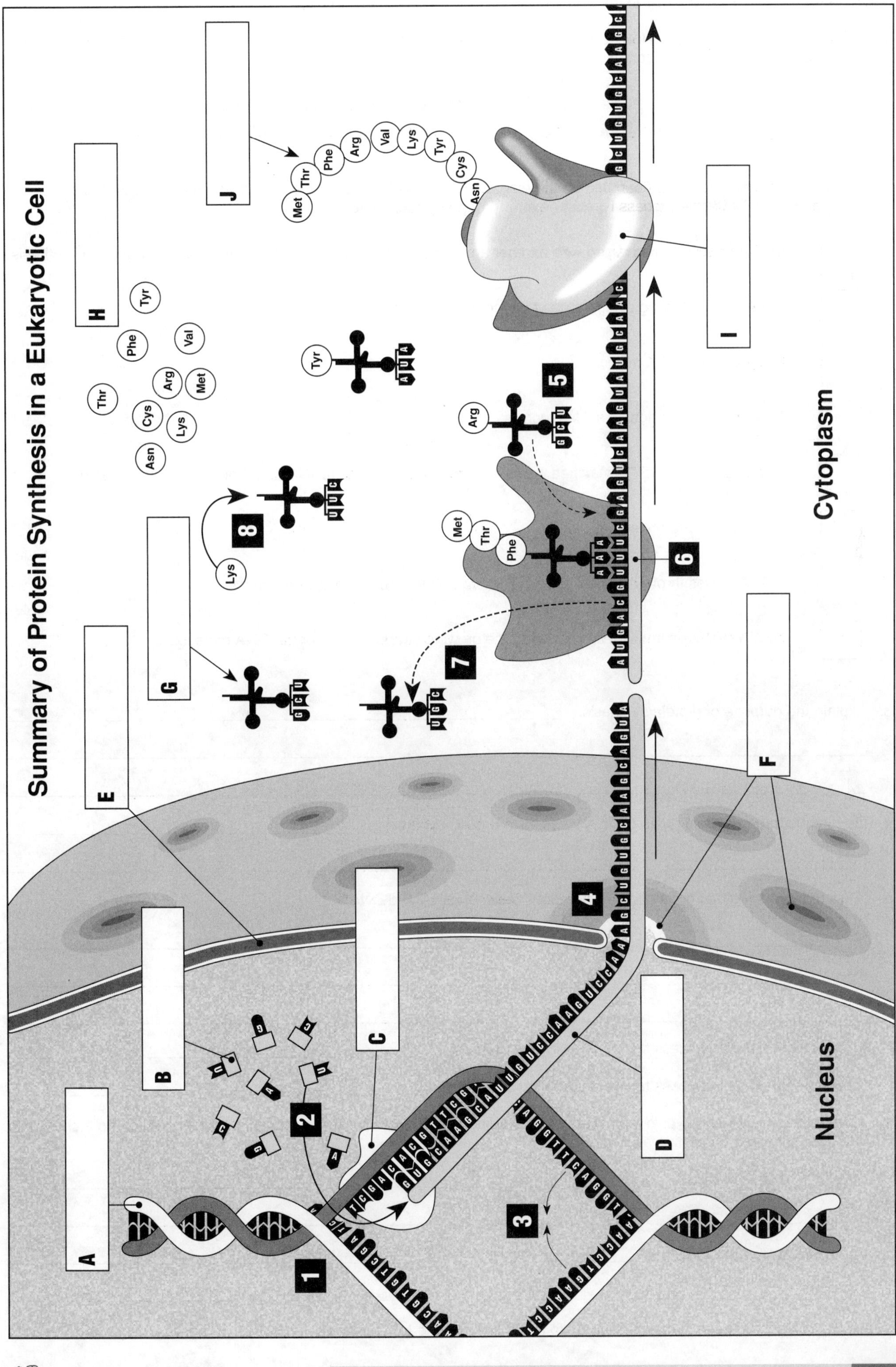

The diagram opposite shows an overview of the process of protein synthesis. Each of the structures involved is labelled with letters (**A-J**), while the major steps in the process are identified with numbers (**1-8**).

1. Using the word list provided below, identify each of the structures marked with a letter. Write the name of that structure in the spaces provided on the diagram.

DNA, nuclear pore, free nucleotides, tRNA, RNA polymerase enzyme, amino acids, mRNA, ribosome, nuclear membrane, polypeptide chain

2. Match each of the processes (identified on the diagram with numbers 1-8) to the correct summary of the process provided below. Write the process number next to the appropriate sentence.

☐ tRNA molecule is recharged with another amino acid of the same type, ready to take part in protein synthesis

☐ tRNA molecule brings in the correct amino acid to the ribosome

☐ Unwinding the DNA molecule

☐ DNA rewinds into double helix structure

☐ Anti-codon on the tRNA matches with the correct codon on the mRNA and drops off the amino acid

☐ tRNA leaves the ribosome

☐ mRNA moves through nuclear pore in nuclear membrane to the cytoplasm

☐ mRNA synthesis: nucleotides added to the growing strand of messenger RNA molecule

3. Explain the purpose of protein synthesis: ______________________________

____

____

4. Identify the three different types of RNA involved in protein synthesis: ______________________________

____

5. Outline three structural or functional differences between RNA and DNA:

(a) ______________________________

(b) ______________________________

(c) ______________________________

6. (a) Name the general process taking place in the **nucleus**: ______________________________

(b) Name the general process taking place in the **cytoplasm**: ______________________________

7. Consult the *mRNA-amino acid table* earlier in this workbook. Explain the result of a point mutation involving a change to the third base in a nucleotide as follows:

(a) UUU changes to UUC: ______________________________

____

(b) UUU changes to UUA: ______________________________

____

(c) State which of these mutations is likely to result in a change to the protein produced: ______________________________

Nature of Mutation

A **mutation** is a change in the genetic sequence of a genome. Mutations may occur spontaneously, as a result of errors occurring during meiosis or DNA replication, or they may be induced. The rate of spontaneous or natural mutation forms the background mutation rate, and it provides a means by which scientists can determine the divergence of taxa during evolution. Induced mutations are the result of agents called **mutagens**, which increase the natural mutation rate. These agents include ionising radiation, some viruses, and chemicals such as formaldehyde, asbestos, coal tar, and tobacco smoke. While changes to DNA are likely to be harmful, there are many documented cases of mutations conferring a survival advantage. These beneficial mutations occur most frequently in organisms with short generation times, such as viruses, bacteria, and insects. Mutations that cause no change in the amino acid sequence are called **silent**. Until recently, it was supposed that these could be carried without effect until subjected to selection pressure at a later time. However, recent research indicates that even these silent mutations can influence function in unpredictable ways by altering mRNA stability and the accuracy of protein synthesis.

Harmful Mutations

There are many well-documented examples of mutations that cause harmful effects. Examples are the mutations giving rise to cystic fibrosis (CF) and sickle cell disease. The sickle cell mutation involves a change to only one base in the DNA sequence, whereas the CF mutation involves the loss of a single triplet (three nucleotides). The malformed proteins that result from these mutations cannot carry out their normal biological functions (although interestingly, the CF mutation, which disrupts chloride transport, makes carriers less susceptible to cholera). Albinism is caused by a mutation in the gene that produces an enzyme in the metabolic pathway to produce melanin. It is common in most vertebrate taxa. Albinos are more visible to predators, and are also more susceptible to the damaging effects of ultraviolet radiation because they lack protective pigmentation.

Beneficial Mutations

it:Utente:Cits

In the small village of Limone, Italy, about 40 villagers have extraordinarily high levels of blood cholesterol, with no apparent harmful effects on their coronary arteries. The villagers possess a mutation that alters the protein produced by just one amino acid. This improved protein is ten times more effective at mopping up excess cholesterol. No matter how much excess cholesterol is ingested, it is always disposed of. All carriers of the mutation are related and descended from one couple who arrived in Limone in 1636. The village (above) has a population of 980 and was, until recently, largely isolated from the rest of the world by its geography. Generally, the people of Limone live longer and show a high resistance to heart disease.

Are Silent Mutations Really Silent?

So-called **silent** or **synonymous mutations** are those that result in no change in the sequence of amino acids making up a protein; the redundancy of the genetic code provides a buffer against the effect of DNA changes that affect the third base. Such mutations have routinely been assumed to be neutral, meaning that, at that time, they have no effect on the phenotype or fitness of the individual carrying the mutation.

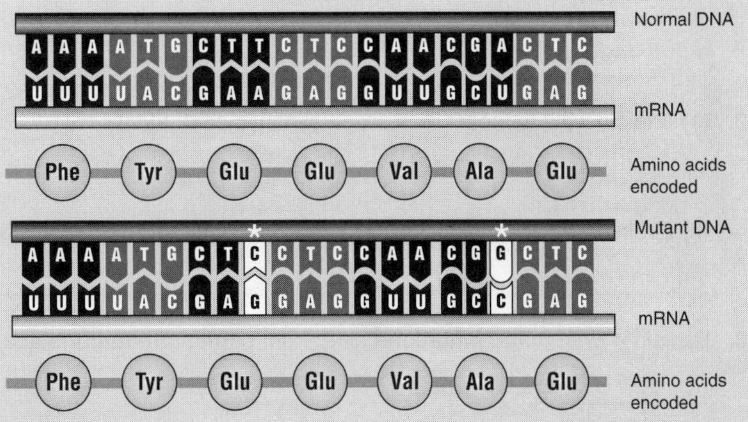

Right: A change to the third base of a codon may not change the amino acid encoded, but it does change the exonic sequence.

However, so-called silent changes still affect transcription, splicing, and mRNA stability, even though they do not change the codon information. Disruptions to RNA splicing sequences can cause exon skipping and lead to RNA not being processed properly. Synonymous variations have been associated with a number of diseases including cystic fibrosis and mental disorders. For example, one silent mutation causes the dopamine receptor D2 gene to be less stable and degrade faster, under-expressing the gene. Experimental evidence with the CFTR gene also shows that synonymous mutations cause exon skipping, yielding a short CFTR protein.

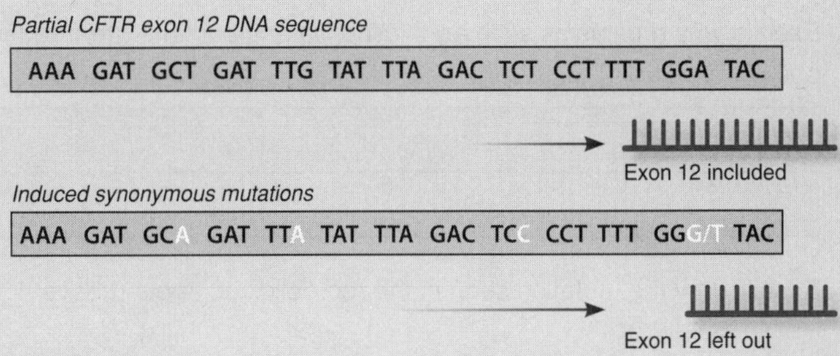

Periodicals: What is a mutation? The price of silent mutations

Related activities: Gene Mutations
Web links: Radiation and DNA, Evolution in E.coli

Only mutations taking place in the cells that produce gametes are inherited. If they occur in a body cell after the organism has begun to develop beyond the zygote stage, then they may give rise to a **chimaera** (an organism with a mix of genetically different cells). In some cases, mutations trigger the onset of **cancer** through the disruption of the normal controls regulating cell division.

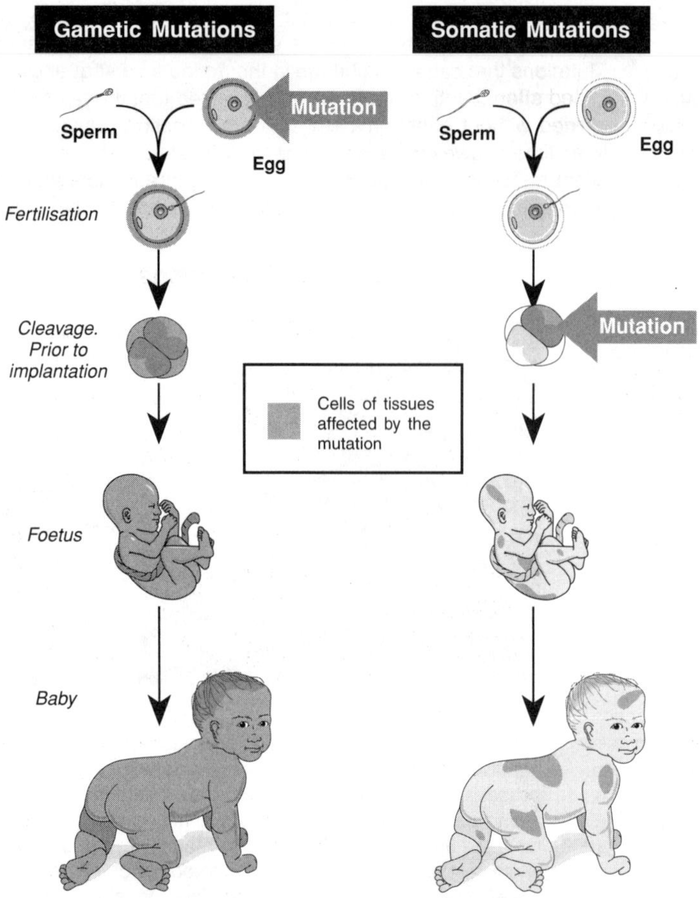

Gametic mutations are *inherited* and occur in the testes of males and the ovaries of females.

Somatic mutations occur in body cells. They are *not inherited* but may affect the person during their lifetime.

The Effect of Mutagens on DNA

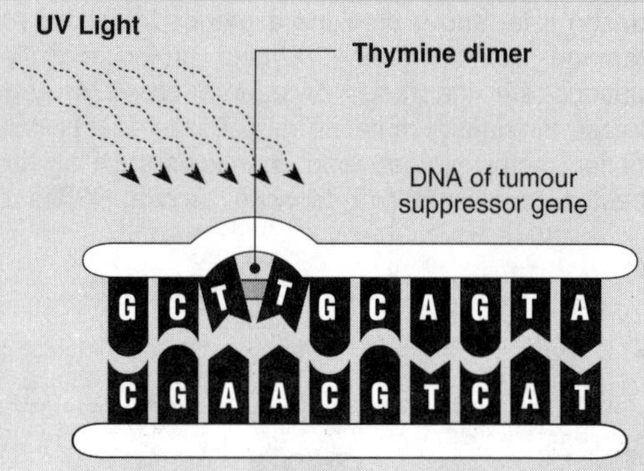

An example of how mutagens cause damage to the genes controlling the normal cell cycle is shown above. After exposure to UV light (a potent mutagen), adjacent thymine bases in DNA become cross-linked to form a 'thymine dimer'. This disrupts the normal base pairing and throws the controlling gene's instructions into chaos.

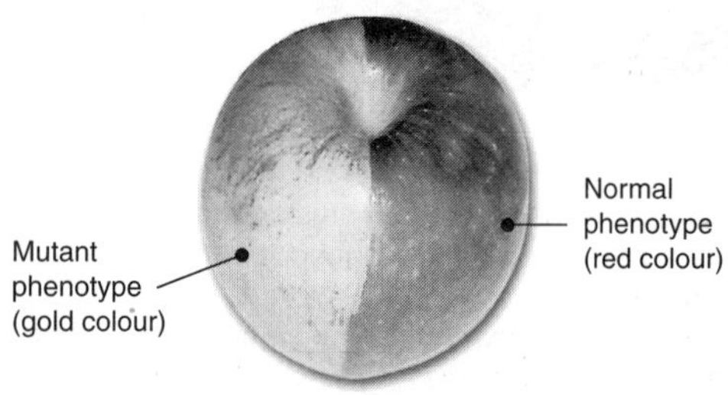

The photo above shows an example of a somatic mutation in a red delicious apple. A mutation occurred in the part of the flower that eventually developed into the fleshy part of the apple. The seeds would not be mutant.

1. Explain the difference between beneficial and harmful mutations: ______

2. (a) Explain what is meant by a silent (synonymous) mutation: ______

   (b) Explain why silent mutations are now no longer seen as always being neutral in their effect: ______

3. Explain how **somatic mutations** differ from **gametic mutations** and comment on the significance of the difference:

4. Explain why organisms such as *Drosophila* and bacteria are frequently used in the study of mutations:

5. Explain why the mutation seen in the red delicious apple (above right) will not be inherited: ______

Gene Mutations

Gene mutations are small, localised changes in the structure of a DNA strand. These mutations may involve change in a single nucleotide (often called **point mutations**), or they may involve changes to a triplet (e.g. deletion or triplet repeat). If one amino acid in a protein is wrong, the biological function of the entire protein can be disrupted. Not all mutations may result in altered proteins. Because of the degeneracy of the genetic code, a substitution of the 3rd base in a codon may code for the same amino acid. The diagrams below and opposite show how various point mutations can occur. These alterations in the DNA are at the **nucleotide** level where individual **codons** are affected. Alteration of the precise nucleotide sequence of a coded gene in turn alters the mRNA transcribed from the mutated DNA and may affect the polypeptide chain that it normally creates.

Base Mismatching – Tautomerism

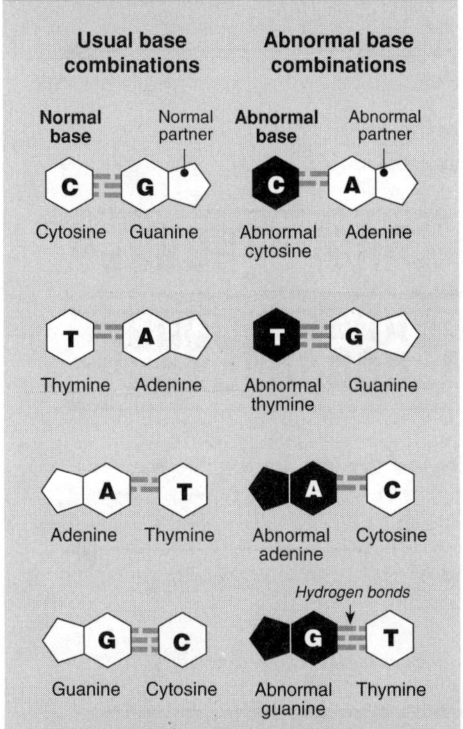

Base Mismatching

Watson and Crick proposed a theory of how base mismatching could occur. The diagram on the left shows suggested changes in bases and the resulting mismatch of complementary bases. On rare occasions some bases may have altered hydrogen-bond positions. As a result, during DNA replication, such abnormal bases pair with incorrect complementary bases. This gives rise to mutations in DNA molecules, which in turn are expressed as altered forms of mRNA and often altered proteins. NOTE: The abnormal bases on the right hand side of the diagram have a different arrangement of hydrogen bonds than normal.

A normal sequence without mutations

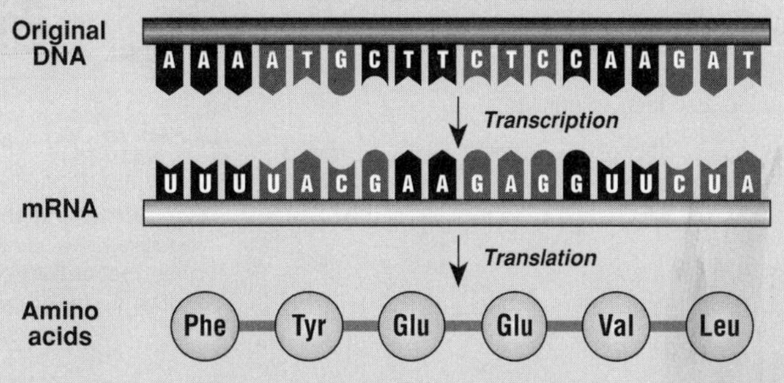

Amino acid sequence forms a normal polypeptide chain

Missense substitution

A single base is substituted for another base which may result in a codon that codes for a different amino acid. Some substitutions, however, may still code for the same amino acid, because of the high degree of degeneracy in the genetic code (i.e. many amino acids have 4 or 6 codons coding for them). In the illustrated example, placing a T where a C should have been, results in the amino acid **lysine** appearing where **glutamic** acid should be. This could affect how this protein functions.

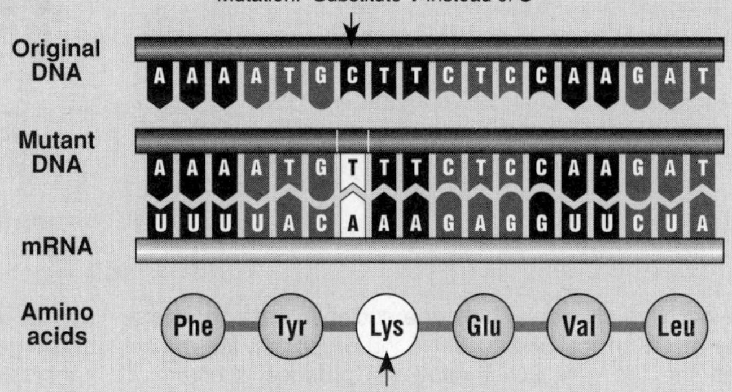

Polypeptide chain with wrong amino acid

Nonsense substitution

Some amino acids can be coded for by 4 or 6 different codons and are therefore less affected by substitutions. In the example illustrated, a single base substitution in the first nucleotide of the third codon has a dramatic effect on the nature of the polypeptide chain it is coding for. The codon no longer codes for an amino acid, but instead is an instruction for the termination of the translation process of protein synthesis. This results in a very short polypeptide chain that is likely to have little or no function since the **STOP** codon is introduced near the **START** codon.

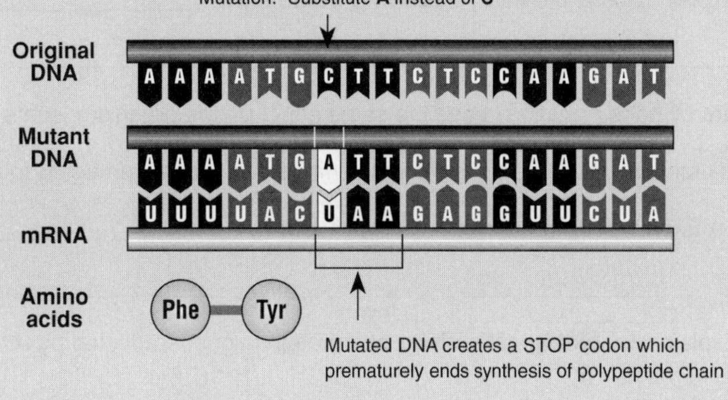

Mutated DNA creates a STOP codon which prematurely ends synthesis of polypeptide chain

Cellular Control

Periodicals:
The DNA damage response

***Related activities:** Sickle Cell Mutation, Cystic Fibrosis Mutation*
***Web links:** Mutation Exercise*

Reading frame shift by insertion

A major upset can occur when a single extra base is inserted into the DNA sequence. This has the effect of displacing all the other bases along one position and thereby creating a whole new sequence of codons. Such mutations are almost always likely to lead to a non-functional protein, but this does depend on the distance of the insertion or deletion from the START codon (i.e. the closer the insertion is to the START codon, the more the protein will be affected).

NOTE: could also lead to nonsense

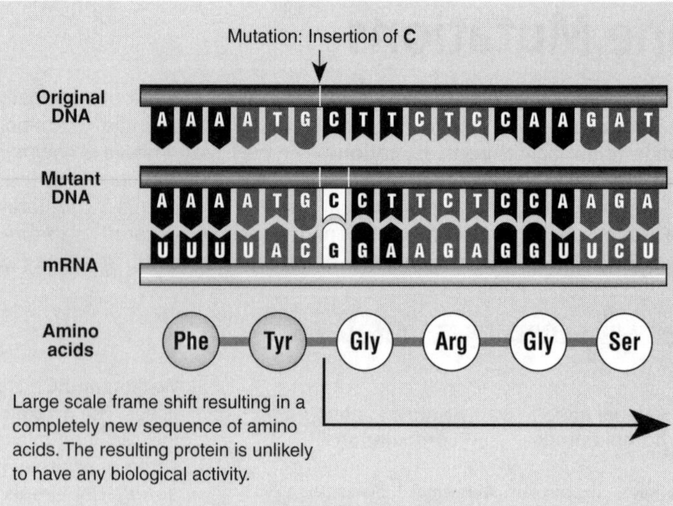

Reading frame shift by deletion

In the same way that an insertion of an extra base into the DNA sequence has a large scale damaging effect, a deletion may also cause a frame shift. Again the result is usually a polypeptide chain of doubtful biological activity.

NOTE: could also lead to nonsense

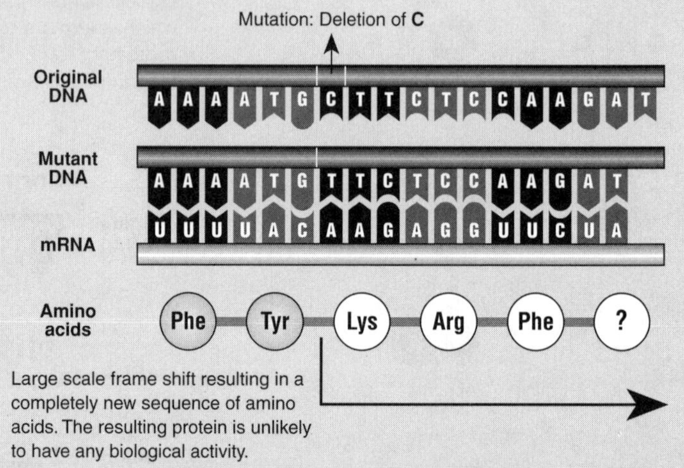

Partial reading frame shift

Both an insertion and a deletion of bases within a gene can cause a frame shift effect where each codon no longer has the correct triplet of three bases. In this example, three codons have been affected, along with the amino acids they code for. The error is limited to the codons including and between the insertion and deletion. There is no biological activity if the amino acids altered are important to the functioning of the resulting protein.

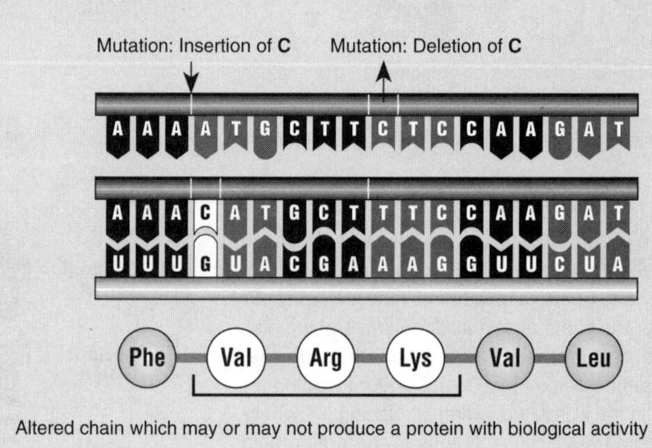

Mutations involving change in only one nucleotide may have no observable effect on the phenotype of the organism; the subtle changes in the DNA sequence may still produce a chain of identical amino acids in the protein, or at least produce a protein that is unaffected by the change. Because of the degeneracy of the genetic code, many mutations of this type are unlikely to cause any change in the biological activity of the protein (there are exceptions, e.g. sickle cell disease).

1. Explain what is meant by a **reading frame shift**: ____________________

2. Not all gene mutations have the same effect on the organism, some are more disruptive than others.

   (a) Identify which type of gene mutations are the most damaging to an organism: ____________________

   (b) Explain why they are the most disruptive: ____________________

3. Explain why **biological activity** of a protein might be affected by a reading frame shift: ____________________

Inherited Metabolic Disorders

Humans have more than 6000 physiological diseases attributed to mutations in single genes and over one hundred syndromes known to be caused by chromosomal abnormality. The number of genetic disorders identified increases every year. Rapid progress of the Human Genome Project is enabling the identification of the genetic basis of these disorders. This will facilitate the development of new drug therapies and gene therapies. Four genetic disorders are summarised below.

Sickle Cell Disease	β-Thalassaemia	Cystic Fibrosis	Huntington Disease
Synonym: Sickle cell anaemia	**Synonyms**: Cooley anaemia, Mediterranean anaemia	**Synonyms**: Mucoviscidosis, CF	**Synonyms**: Huntington's chorea, HD (abbreviated)
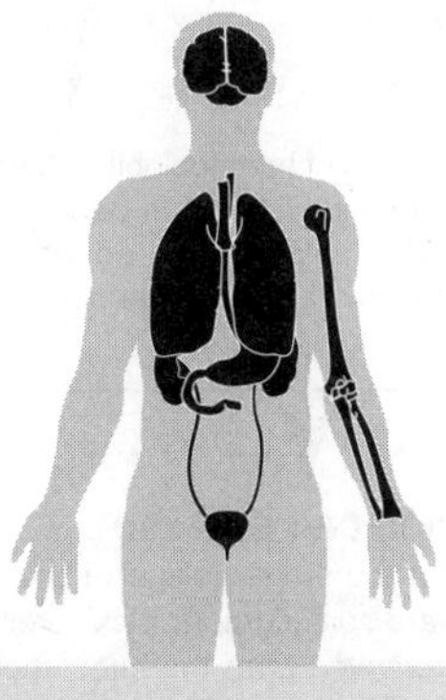	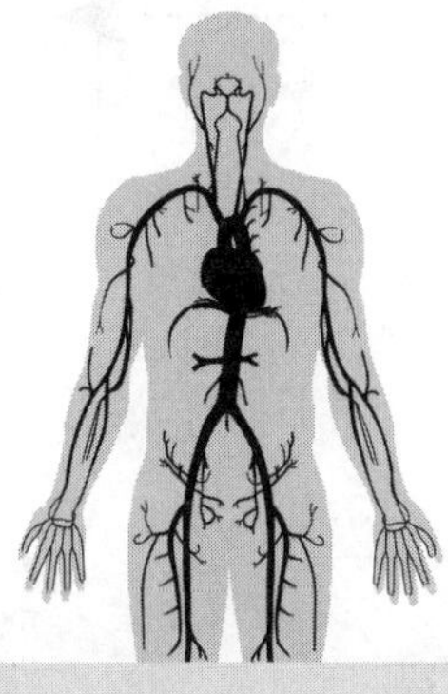	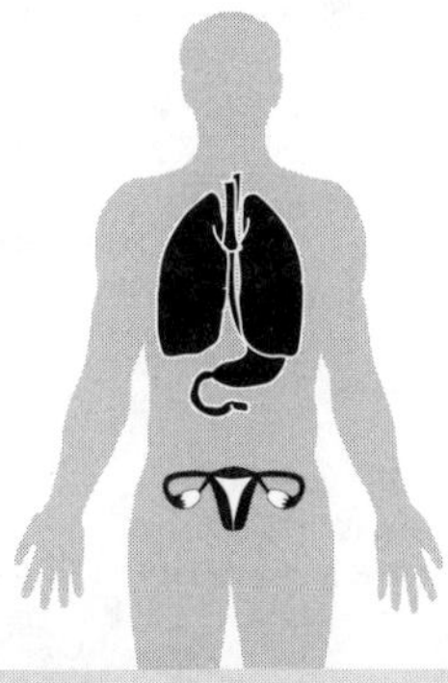	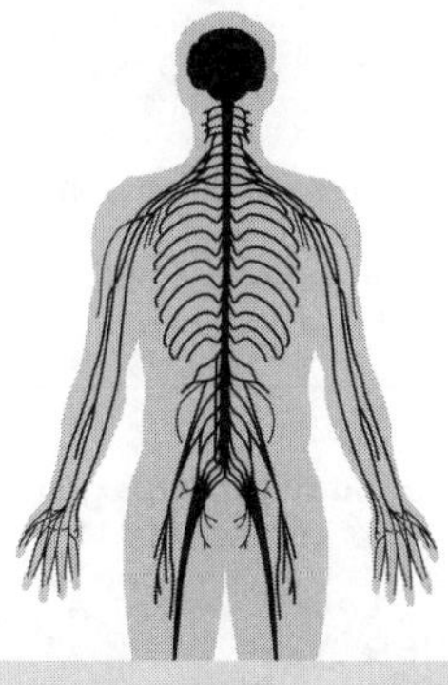
Incidence: Most common in people of African, Mediterranean, Middle Eastern, and Indian descent.	**Incidence**: More common in people from Mediterranean and Middle Eastern descent.	**Incidence**: 1:25 people in the UK carry the CF gene. About 8 000 people in the UK have CF.	**Incidence**: An uncommon disease present in 1 in 20 000.An estimated 6 500 - 8 000 people in the UK have Huntington disease.
Gene type: Autosomal mutation which results in the substitution of a single nucleotide in the HBB gene that codes for the beta haemoglobin chain. The allele is codominant.	**Gene type**: Autosomal recessive mutation of the HBB gene coding for the haemoglobin beta chain. It may arise through a gene deletion or a nucleotide deletion or insertion.	**Gene type**: Autosomal recessive. Over 500 different recessive mutations (deletions, missense, nonsense, terminator codon) of the CFTR gene have been identified.	**Gene type**: An autosomal dominant mutation of the HD gene (IT15) caused by an increase in the length (36-125) of a CAG repeat region (normal range is 11-30 repeats).
Gene location: Chromosome 11	**Gene location**: Chromosome 11	**Gene location**: Chromosome 7	**Gene location**: Chromosome 4
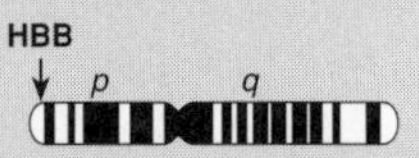 HBB, *p*, *q*	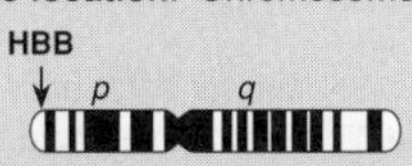 HBB, *p*, *q*	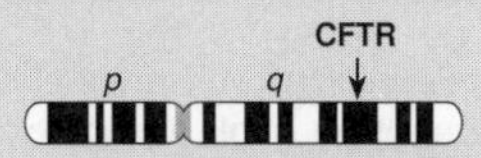 *p*, *q*, CFTR	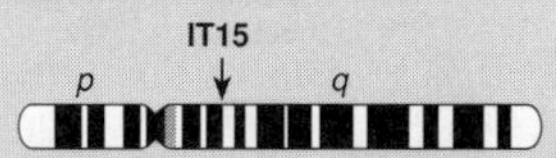 *p*, IT15, *q*
Symptoms: Include: anaemia; mild to severe pain in the chest, joints, back, or abdomen; jaundice; kidney failure; repeated infections, in particular pneumonia or meningitis; eye problems including blindness; swollen hands and feet; gallstones (at an early age); strokes.	**Symptoms**: The result of haemoglobin with few or no beta chains, causes a severe anaemia during the first few years of life. People with this condition are tired and pale because not enough oxygen reaches the cells.	**Symptoms**: Disruption of glands: the *pancreas, intestinal glands, biliary tree* (biliary cirrhosis), *bronchial glands* (chronic lung infections), and *sweat glands* (high salt content of which becomes depleted in a hot environment). *Infertility* occurs in males/females.	**Symptoms**: Mutant gene forms defective protein: **huntingtin**. Progressive, selective *nerve cell death* associated with chorea (jerky, involuntary movements), *psychiatric disorders,* and *dementia* (memory loss, disorientation, impaired ability to reason, and personality changes).
Treatment and outlook: Patients are given folic acid. Acute episodes may require oxygen therapy, intravenous infusions of fluid, and antibiotic drugs. Experimental therapies include bone marrow transplants and gene therapy.	**Treatment and outlook**: Patients require frequent blood transfusions. This causes iron build-up in the organs, which is treated with drugs. Bone marrow transplants and gene therapy hold promise and are probable future treatments.	**Treatment and outlook**: Conventional: chest physiotherapy, a modified diet, and the use of TOBI antibiotic to control lung infections. Outlook: Gene transfer therapy inserting normal CFTR gene using adenovirus vectors and liposomes.	**Treatment and outlook**: Surgical treatment may be possible. Research is underway to discover drugs that interfere with *huntingtin* protein. Genetic counselling coupled with genetic screening of embryos may be developed in the future.

1. For each of the genetic disorder below, indicate the following:

   (a) Sickle cell disease: Gene name: HBB Chromosome: 11 Mutation type: Substitution

   (b) β-thalassaemia: Gene name: ________ Chromosome: ____ Mutation type: ________________

   (c) Cystic fibrosis: Gene name: ________ Chromosome: ____ Mutation type: ________________

   (d) Huntington disease: Gene name: ________ Chromosome: ____ Mutation type: ________________

2. Explain the cause of the symptoms for people suffering from β-thalassaemia: ________________

   ____

3. Suggest a reason for the differences in the country-specific incidence rates for some genetic disorders:

   ____

   ____

Cellular Control

Related activities: Sickle Cell Mutation, Cystic Fibrosis Mutation

Sickle Cell Mutation

Sickle cell disease (formerly called sickle cell anaemia) is an inherited disorder caused by a gene mutation which codes for a faulty beta (β) chain haemoglobin (Hb) protein. This in turn causes the red blood cells to deform causing a whole range of medical problems. The DNA sequence below is the beginning of the transcribing sequence for the **normal** β-chain Hb molecule.

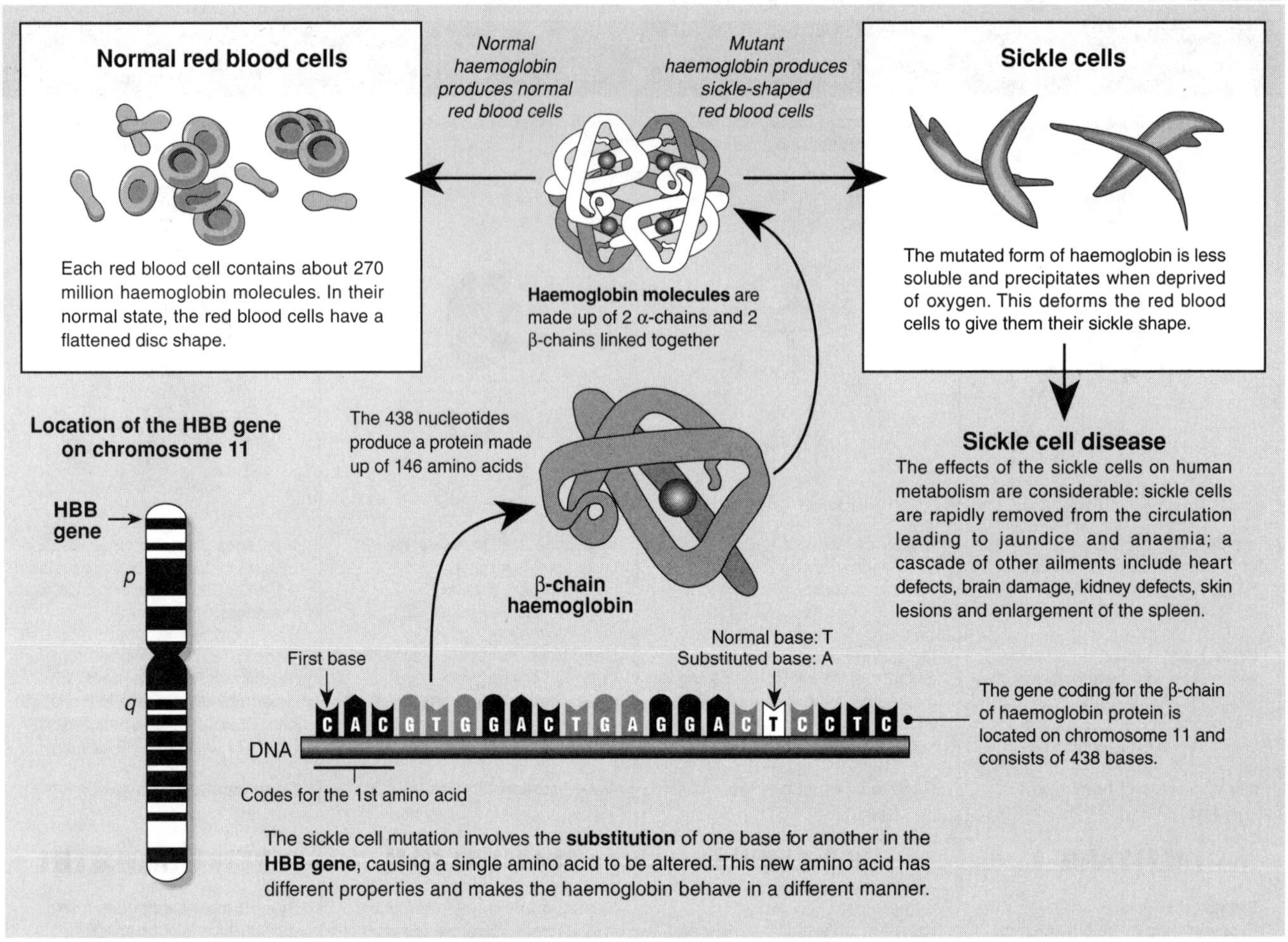

1. Identify how many of the following are exhibited or coded for in the DNA sequence above:

   (a) Bases: ______________ (b) Triplets: ________________ (c) Amino acids coded for: ________________

2. Write the mRNA sequence for the transcribing DNA strand above:

   ____

3. Determine the amino acid sequence coded by the mRNA (in question 2 above) for the fragment of the **normal** protein we are studying here. Use the mRNA-amino acid table in this workbook (consult the index):

   Amino acids: ____

4. Rewrite the transcribing DNA sequence above with the 17th nucleotide (base) changed from a **T** to **A.** This is the mutation that causes sickle cell disease.

   Mutant DNA: ____________________________________ Type of mutation: ________________

5. Write the mRNA sequence for the **mutant** DNA strand above:

   ____

6. Determine the amino acid sequence coded by the mRNA (in question 5 above) for the fragment of the **mutant** protein we are studying here. Use the mRNA-amino acid table in this workbook (consult the index):

   ____

7. Explain how the sickle cell mutation results in the symptoms of the disease: ________________________

   ____

   ____

Cystic Fibrosis Mutation

Cystic fibrosis an inherited disorder caused by a mutation of the **CF gene**. It is one of the most common lethal autosomal recessive conditions affecting caucasians, with an incidence of 1 in 2500 live births and a **carrier frequency** of 4%. It is uncommon in Asians and Africans. The CF gene's protein product, **CFTR**, is a membrane-based protein with a role in regulating chloride transport. A faulty gene in turn codes for a faulty CFTR. More than 500 mutations of the CF gene have been described, giving rise to disease symptoms of varying severity. One mutation is particularly common and accounts for more than 70% of all defective CF genes. This mutation, called δF508, leads to the absence of CFTR from its proper position in the membrane (below). Another CF mutation, R117H, which is also relatively common, produces a partly functional CFTR protein. The DNA sequence below is part of the transcribing sequence for the **normal** CF gene.

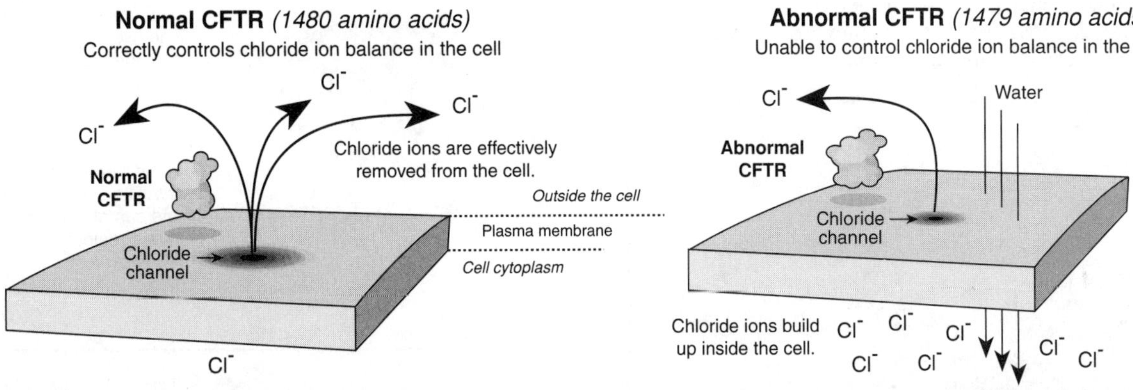

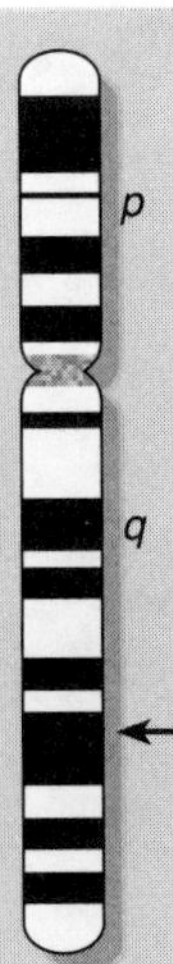

The CF gene on chromosome 7

The CF gene is located on chromosome 7. The δF508 mutation of the CF gene describes a deletion of the 508th triplet, which in turn causes the loss of a single **amino acid** from the gene's protein product, the cystic fibrosis transmembrane conductance regulator (CFTR). This protein normally regulates the chloride channels in cell membranes, but the mutant form fails to achieve this. The portion of the DNA containing the mutation site is shown below:

The CFTR protein consists of 1480 amino acids

CFTR protein

The δF508 mutant form of CFTR fails to take up its position in the membrane. Its absence results in defective chloride transport and leads to a net increase in water absorption by the cell. This accounts for the symptoms of cystic fibrosis, where mucus-secreting glands, particularly in the lungs and pancreas, become fibrous and produce abnormally thick mucus. The widespread presence of CFTR throughout the body also explains why CF is a multisystem condition affecting many organs.

1. (a) Write the mRNA sequence for the transcribing DNA strand above: ____________________

   ____

   (b) Use the mRNA-amino acid table earlier in this workbook to determine the amino acid sequence coded by the mRNA for the fragment of the normal protein we are studying here:

   ____

2. (a) Rewrite the mRNA sequence for the mutant DNA strand: ____________________

   ____

   (b) State what kind of mutation δF508 is: ____________________

   (c) Determine the amino acid sequence coded by the mRNA for the fragment of the δF508 mutant protein:

   ____

   (d) Identify the amino acid that has been removed from the protein by this mutation: ____________________

3. Suggest why cystic fibrosis is a disease with varying degrees of severity: ____________________

   ____

   ____

Cellular Control

Related activities: *Nature of Mutation, Inherited Metabolic Disorders*

Protein Activation by Cyclic AMP

Cyclic AMP (cAMP) is a second messenger which targets specific intracellular enzymes to induce a cellular response. Its actions allow hormones that cannot cross the plasma membrane to still initiate an effect within a target cell. cAMP does not act directly on its target, but acts via other enzymes to initiate a response. **Protein kinases** (right) are an important family of target enzymes for cAMP. Kinase activation modifies the function of other proteins by adding phosphate groups to them. These changes to function include altering enzymatic activity, cellular location, or protein association. Approximately 30% of human proteins can be modified by kinase activity, so its activation is very important in controlling many pathways involved in metabolism and gene induction (below).

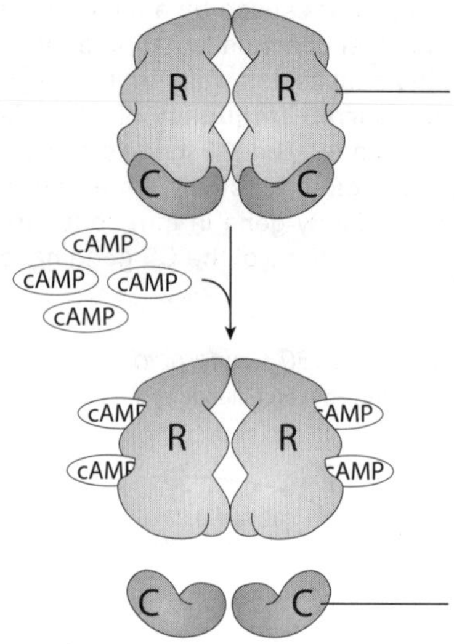

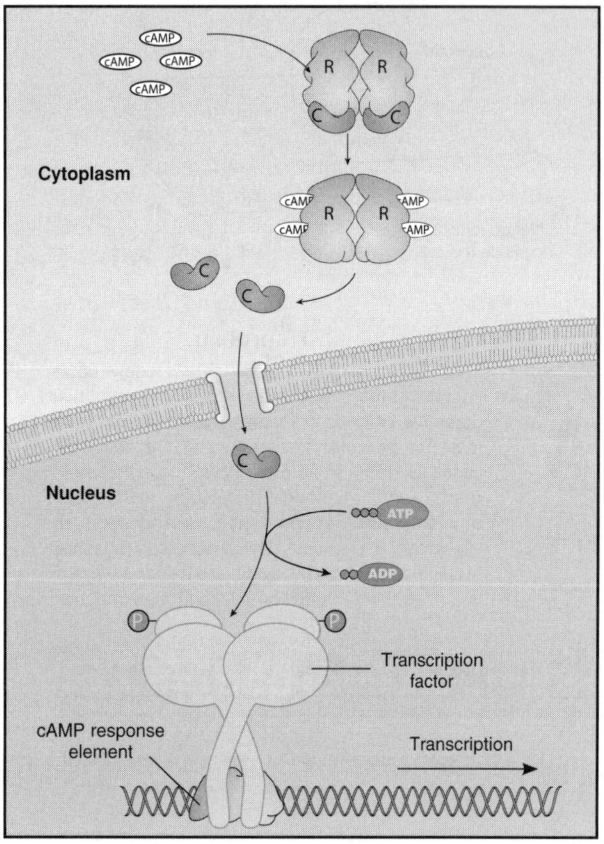

Protein kinase A is involved in controlling the transcription of many genes. In the example above, cAMP activation of protein kinase results in a catalytic subunit crossing the nuclear membrane. It then binds to, and then activates, a protein transcription factor resulting in the expression of the gene.

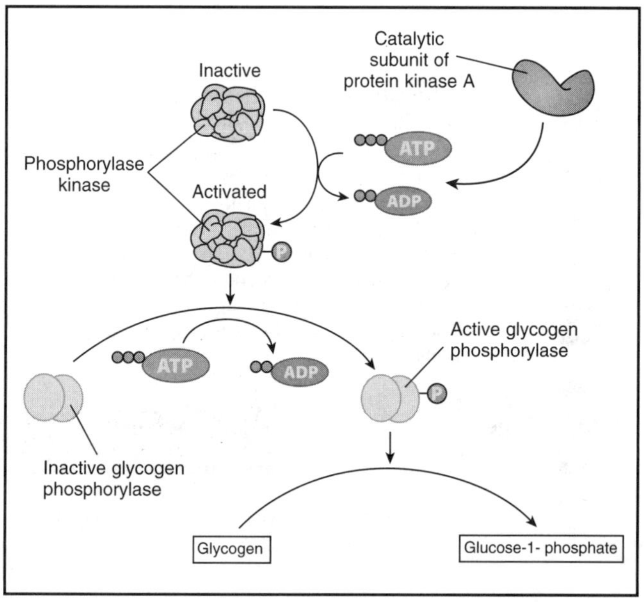

Protein kinase A has an important role in regulating glycogen metabolism. It adds a phosphate group to the enzyme phosphorylase kinase to activate it. Phosphorylase kinase in turn phosphorylates and activates glycogen phosphorylase, catalysing the breakdown of glycogen to glucose-1-phosphate.

1. Describe the structure of inactivated protein kinase A: ______________________________

____

2. Explain how protein kinase A becomes active once cAMP is bound to it: ______________________

____

____

____

3. Describe in general terms how protein kinase A can regulate other proteins: ___________________

____

____

____

Gene Control in Prokaryotes

The **operon** mechanism was proposed by **Jacob** and **Monod** to account for the regulation of gene activity in response to the needs of the cell. Their work was carried out with the bacterium *Escherichia coli* and the model is not applicable to eukaryotic cells where the genes are not found as operons. An operon consists of a group of closely linked genes that act together and code for the enzymes that control a particular **metabolic pathway**. These may be for the metabolism of an energy source (e.g. lactose) or the synthesis of a molecule such as an amino acid. The structural genes contain the information for the production of the enzymes themselves and they are transcribed as a single **transcription unit**. These structural genes are controlled by a **promoter**, which initiates the formation of the mRNA, and a region of the DNA in front of the structural genes called the **operator**. A gene outside the operon, called the **regulator gene**, produces a **repressor** molecule that can bind to the operator, and block the transcription of the structural genes. It is the repressor that switches the structural genes on or off and controls the metabolic pathway. Two mechanisms operate in the operon model: gene induction and gene repression. **Gene induction** occurs when genes are switched on by an inducer binding to the repressor molecule and deactivating it. In the ***Lac* operon model** based on *E.coli*, lactose acts as the **inducer**, binding to the repressor and permitting transcription of the structural genes for the utilisation of lactose (an infrequently encountered substrate). **Gene repression** occurs when genes that are normally switched on (e.g. genes for synthesis of an amino acid) are switched off by activation of the repressor.

Control of Gene Expression Through Induction: the *Lac* Operon

Structure of the operon

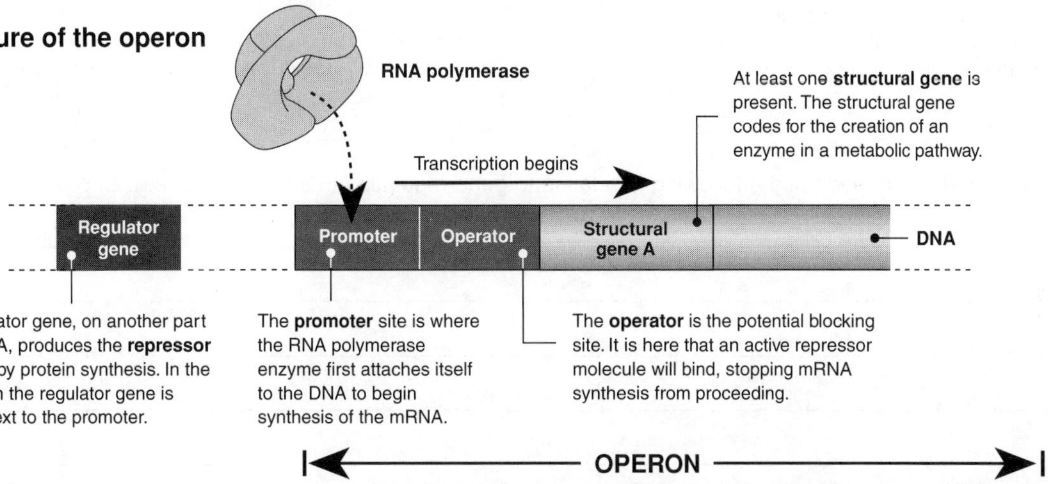

The operon consists of the structural genes and the promoter and operator sites

Structural genes switched off

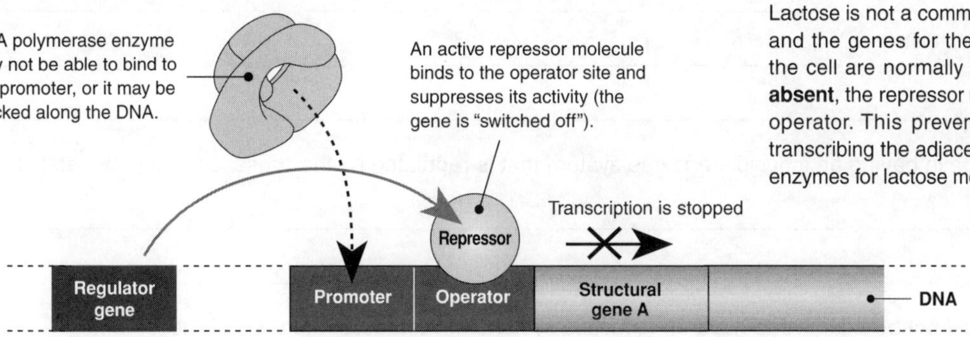

Lactose is not a common energy source for *E. coli* and the genes for the metabolism of lactose by the cell are normally switched off. With **lactose absent**, the repressor molecule binds tightly to the operator. This prevents RNA polymerase from transcribing the adjacent structural genes and the enzymes for lactose metabolism are not produced.

Gene induction

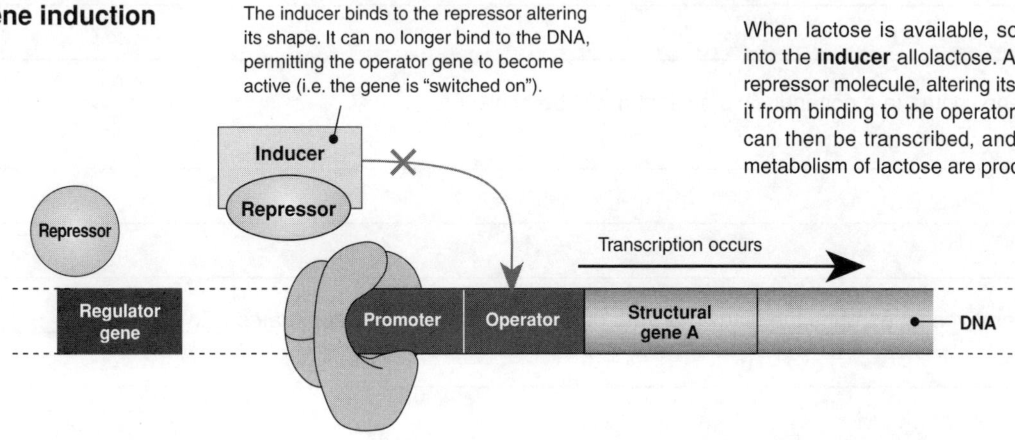

When lactose is available, some of it is converted into the **inducer** allolactose. Allolactose binds to the repressor molecule, altering its shape and preventing it from binding to the operator. The structural genes can then be transcribed, and the enzymes for the metabolism of lactose are produced.

Diauxie in *E.coli*

Diauxie means two growth phases. **Diauxic growth** describes how microbes grown on a mixed sugar source in batch culture will preferentially metabolise one sugar source before moving on to the second. This sequential metabolism results in two distinct growth phases (right).

In the example right, *E.coli* is grown on a mixed substrate of glucose and lactose. Diauxie occurs because the presence of glucose in excess suppresses the *Lac* operon so that only the enzymes required for glucose metabolism are produced. As the glucose supply diminishes, the *Lac* operon becomes activated, and *E.coli* begins to metabolise lactose.

The lag period represents the time taken for the *Lac* operon to become active and the synthesis of the enzymes required for lactose metabolism to begin. This mechanism allows *E.coli* to preferentially metabolise the substrate it can grow fastest on, before moving to the second substrate.

The diauxic growth curve of *E.coli* when grown on glucose and lactose

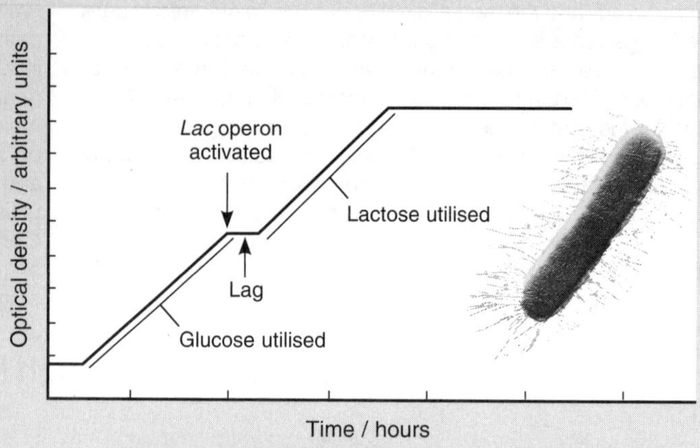

Jacques Monod discovered diauxic growth in 1941 prior to the discovery of the lac operon, which explained the phenomenon at the genetic level.

1. Explain the functional role of each of the following in relation to gene regulation in a prokaryote, e.g. *E. coli*:

   (a) Operon: ______________________________

   (b) Regulator gene: ______________________________

   (c) Operator: ______________________________

   (d) Promoter: ______________________________

   (e) Structural genes: ______________________________

2. (a) Explain the advantage in having an inducible enzyme system that is regulated by the presence of a substrate:

   ____

   (b) Suggest when it would not be adaptive to have an inducible system for metabolism of a substrate: ______________________________

   (c) Suggest how gene control in a non-inducible system might be achieved:

   ____

3. Explain how the operon model explains the diauxic growth of bacteria on two sugar substrates: ______________________________

Genes and the Control of Development

The study of development is providing scientists with new insights into the mechanisms underlying changes in body form and function. Scientists now know that a class of highly conserved **homeobox genes** directs development in organisms as diverse as fungi, plants, and animals. A homeobox is about 180 base pairs long and encodes transcription factors responsible for switching on gene expression. The ***Hox* genes** are a particular group of homeobox genes in animals. They are found in clusters and determine where particular body segments and limbs grow. Very disparate organisms share this same tool kit of genes, but regulate them differently. This means that large changes in morphology or function are attributable to changes in gene regulation, rather than the evolution of new genes, and natural selection associated with gene switches plays a major role in evolution.

The Role of *Hox* Genes

Hox genes control the development of back and front parts of the body.The same genes (or homologous ones) are present in essentially all animals, including humans.

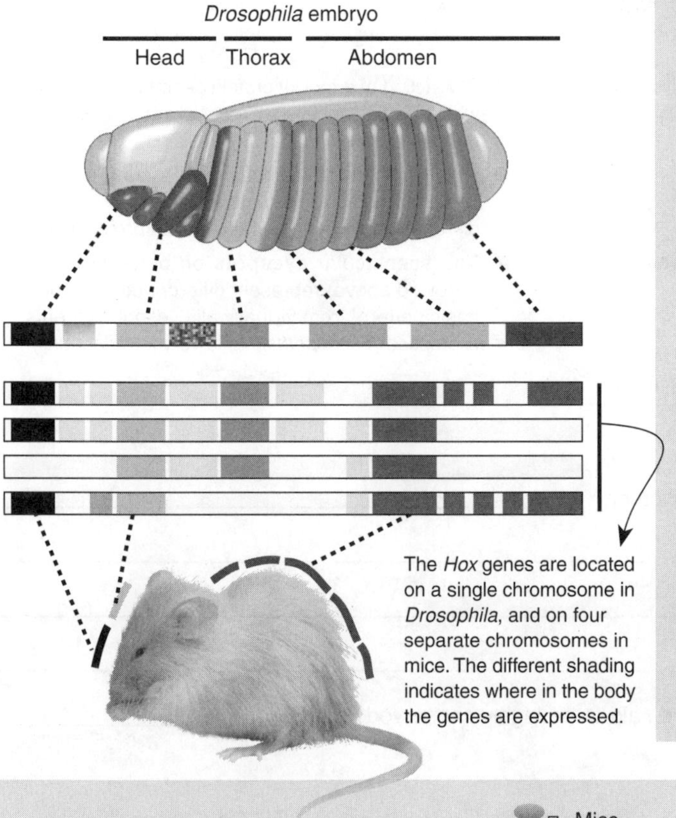

The *Hox* genes are located on a single chromosome in *Drosophila*, and on four separate chromosomes in mice. The different shading indicates where in the body the genes are expressed.

The Evolution of Novel Forms

Even very small changes (mutations) in the *Hox* genes can have a profound effect on morphology. Such changes to the genes controlling development have almost certainly been important in the evolution of novel structures and body plans. Four principles underly the role of developmental genes in the evolution of novel forms:

- **Evolution works with what is already present**: New structures are modifications of pre-existing structures.
- **Multifunctionality** and **redundancy**: Functional redundancy in any part of a multifunctional structure allows for specialisation and division of labour through the development of two separate structures.

  Example: the diversity of appendages (including mouthparts) in arthropods.
- **Modularity**: Modular architecture in animals (arthropods, vertebrates) allows for the modification and specialisation of individual body parts. Genetic switches allow changes in one part of a structure, independent of other parts.

Shifting *Hox* Expression

Huge diversity in morphology in organisms within and across phyla could have arisen through small changes in the genes controlling development.

Differences in neck length in vertebrates provides a good example of how changes in gene expression can bring about changes in morphology. Different vertebrates have different numbers of neck vertebrae.The boundary between neck and trunk vertebrae is marked by expression of the ***Hox c6* gene** (c6 denotes the sixth cervical or neck vertebra) in all cases, but the position varies in each animal relative to the overall body. The forelimb (arrow) arises at this boundary in all four-legged vertebrates. In snakes, the boundary is shifted forward to the base of the skull and no limbs develop. As a result of these differences in expression, mice have a short neck, geese a long neck, and snakes, no neck at all.

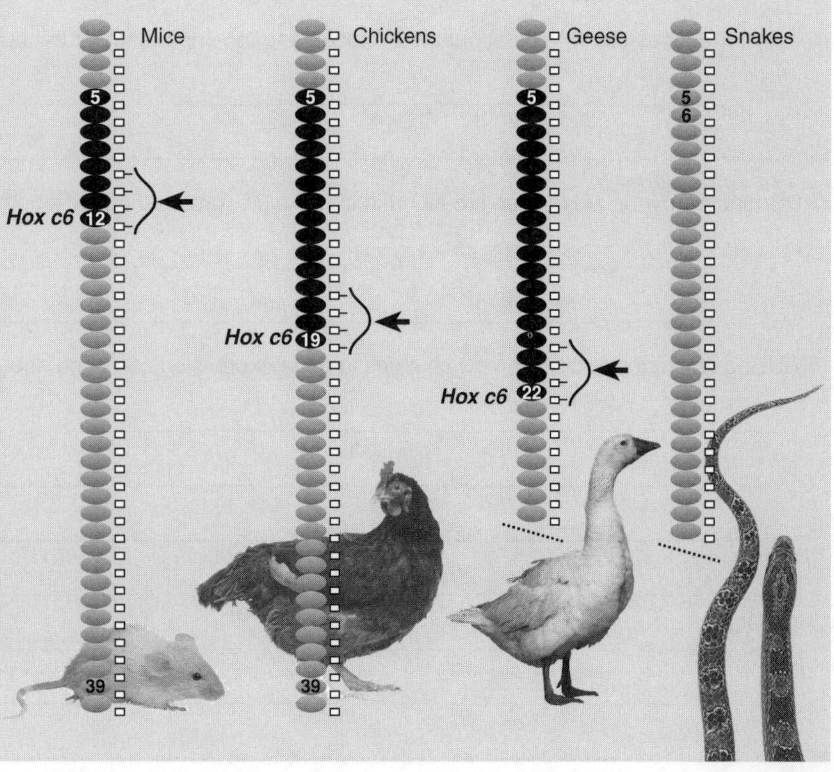

Genetic Switches in Evolution

The *Hox* genes are just part of the collection of genes that make up the genetic tool kit for animal development. The genes in the tool kit act as switches, shaping development by affecting how other genes are turned on or off. The distribution of genes in the tool kit indicates that it is ancient and was in place before the evolution of most types of animals. Differences in form arise through changes in genetic switches. One example is the evolution of eyespots in butterflies:

- The ***Distal-less*** gene is one of the important **master body-building genes** in the genetic tool kit. Switches in the *Distal-less* gene control expression in the embryo (E), larval legs (L), and wing (W) in flies and butterflies, but butterflies have also evolved an extra switch (S) to control eyespot development.
- Once *Distal-less* spots evolved, changes in *Distal-less* expression (through changes in the switch) produced more or fewer spots.

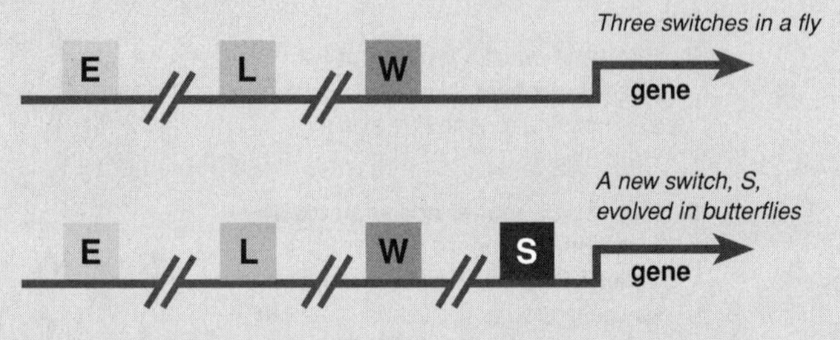

Changes in *Distal-less* regulation were probably achieved by changing specific sequences of the *Distal-less* gene eyespot switch. The result? Changes in eyespot size and number.

Same Gene, New Tricks

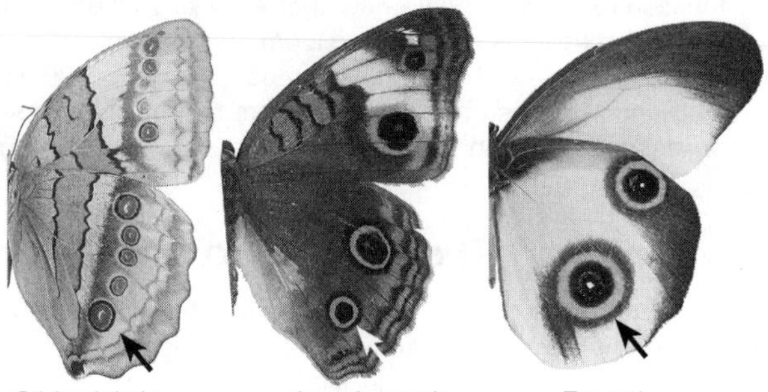

Stichophthalma camadeva — *Junonia coenia (buckeye)* — *Taenaris macrops*

- The action of a tool kit protein depends on context: where particular cells are located at the time when the gene is switched on.
- Changes in the DNA sequence of a genetic switch can change the zone of gene expression without disrupting the function of the tool kit protein itself.
- The spectacular **eyespots** on butterfly wings (arrowed above) represent different degrees of a basic pattern, from virtually all eyespot elements expressed (*Stichophthalma*) to very few (*Taenaris*).

1. Briefly describe the role of homeobox genes in development: ______________________

____

____

____

2. (a) What does it mean when the homeobox genes are said to be highly conserved? ______________________

____

(b) What does this tell you about the evolution and the importance of the homeobox sequences? ______________________

____

____

3. Suggest why the *Hox* genes are found in clusters (i.e. grouped tightly together): ______________________

____

____

4. Using an example, discuss how changes in gene expression can bring about changes in morphology:

____

____

____

____

____

____

____

Apoptosis: Programmed Cell Death

Apoptosis or programmed cell death (PCD) is a normal and necessary mechanism in multicellular organisms to trigger the death of a cell. Apoptosis has a number of crucial roles in the body, including the maintenance of adult cell numbers, and defence against damaged or dangerous cells, such as virus-infected cells and cells with DNA damage. Apoptosis also has a role in "sculpting" embryonic tissue during its development, e.g. in the formation of fingers and toes in a developing human embryo. Programmed cell death involves an orderly series of biochemical events that result in set changes in cell morphology and end in cell death. The process is carried out in such a way as to safely dispose of cell remains and fragments. This is in contrast to another type of cell death, called **necrosis**, in which traumatic damage to the cell results in spillage of cell contents. Apoptosis is tightly regulated by a balance between the factors that promote cell survival and those that trigger cell death. An imbalance between these regulating factors leads to defective apoptotic processes and is implicated in an extensive variety of diseases. For example, low rates of apoptosis result in uncontrolled proliferation of cells and cancers.

Stages in Apoptosis

Apoptosis is a normal cell suicide process in response to particular cell signals. It characterised by an overall compaction (shrinking) of the cell and its nucleus, and the orderly dissection of chromatin by endonucleases. Death is finalised by a rapid engulfment of the dying cell by phagocytosis. The cell contents remain membrane-bound and there is no inflammation.

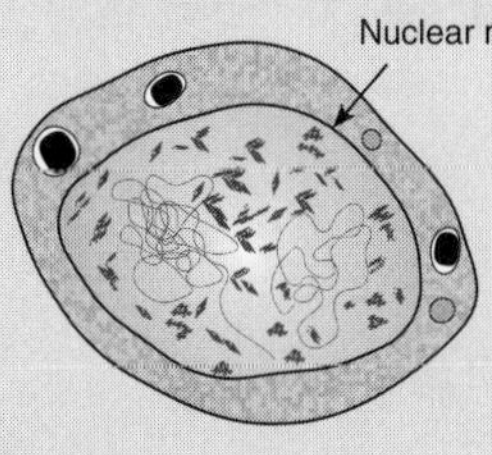

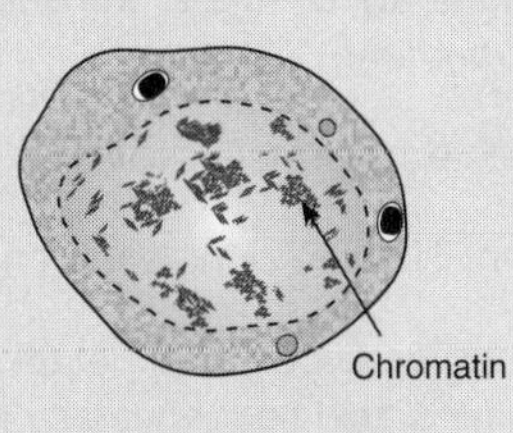

1. The cell shrinks and loses contact with neighbouring cells. The chromatin condenses and begins to degrade.

2. The nuclear membrane degrades. The cell loses volume. The chromatin clumps into **chromatin bodies**.

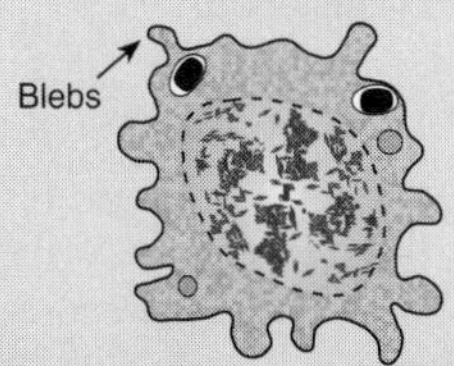

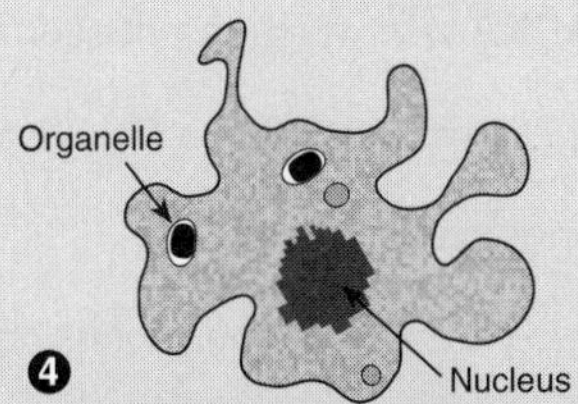

3. **Zeiosis**: The plasma membrane forms bubble like **blebs** on its surface.

4. The nucleus collapses, but many membrane-bound organelles are unaffected.

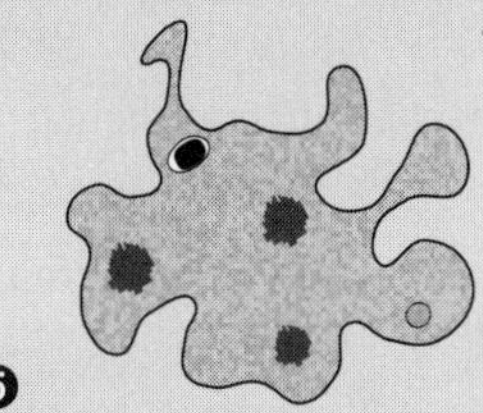

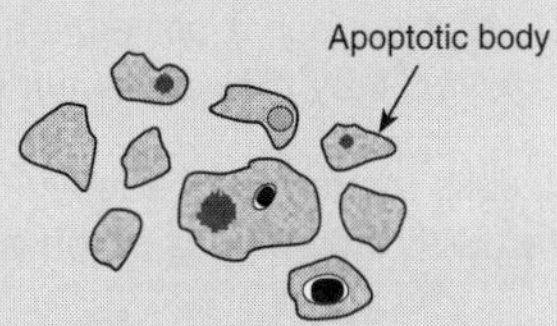

5. The nucleus breaks up into spheres and the DNA breaks up into small fragments.

6. The cell breaks into numerous **apoptotic bodies**, which are quickly resorbed by phagocytosis.

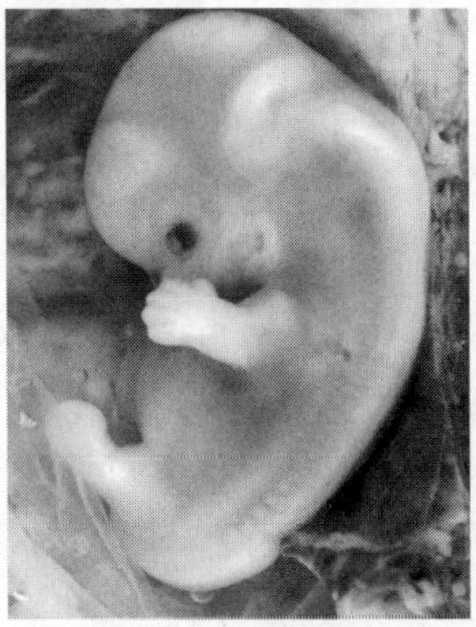

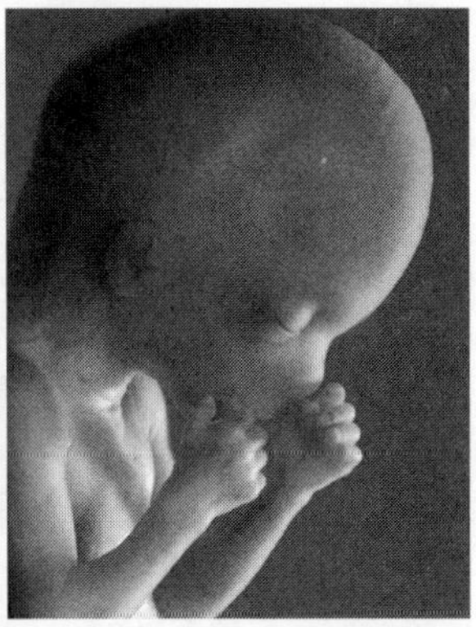

Ed Uthman

In humans, the mesoderm initially formed between the fingers and toes is removed by apoptosis. 41 days after fertilisation (top left), the digits of the hands and feet are webbed, making them look like small paddles. Apoptosis selectively destroys this superfluous webbing and, later in development, each of the digits can be individually seen (right).

Regulating Apoptosis

Apoptosis is a complicated and tightly controlled process, distinct from cell necrosis (uncontrolled cell death), when the cell contents are spilled. Apoptosis is regulated through both:

Positive signals, which prevent apoptosis and allow a cell to function normally. They include:

- interleukin-2
- bcl-2 protein and growth factors

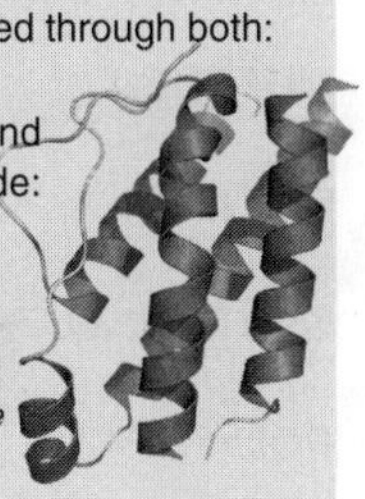

Interleukin-2 is a positive signal for cell survival. Like other signalling molecules, it binds to surface receptors on the cell to regulate metabolism.

Negative signals (death activators), which trigger the changes leading to cell death. They include:

- inducer signals generated from within the cell itself in response to stress, e.g. DNA damage or cell starvation.
- signalling proteins and peptides such as lymphotoxin.

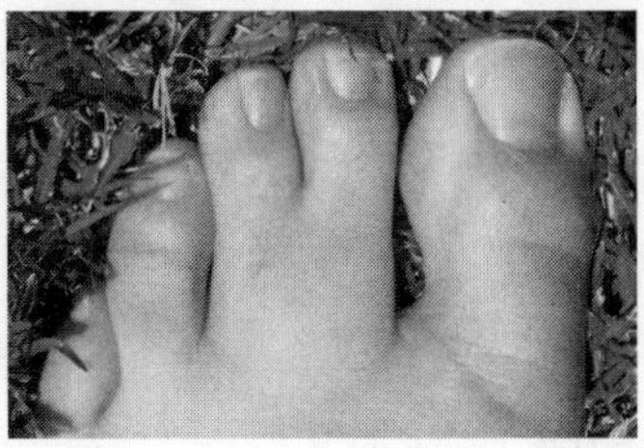

1. The photograph (right) depicts a condition called syndactyly. Explain what might have happened during development to result in this condition:

____

____

2. Describe one difference between apoptosis and necrosis: _______________

____

3. Describe two situations, other than digit formation in development, in which apoptosis plays a crucial role:

(a) _______________

____

(b) _______________

____

Cellular Control

KEY TERMS: Mix and Match

INSTRUCTIONS: Test your vocabulary by matching each term to its definition, as identified by its preceding letter code.

ANTICODONS

APOPTOSIS

BENEFICIAL MUTATION

CODING STRAND

CODON

CYCLIC AMP

EXON

GENE EXPRESSION

GENE INDUCTION

GENETIC CODE

HARMFUL MUTATION

HOMEOBOX SEQUENCE

INTRON

LAC OPERON

MESSENGER RNA (mRNA)

MUTAGEN

MUTATION

NEUTRAL MUTATION

POLYPEPTIDE

REDUNDANCY

RIBOSOME

RNA POLYMERASE

SECOND MESSENGER

SILENT (SYNONYMOUS) MUTATION

START CODON

STOP CODON

TEMPLATE STRAND

TRANSCRIPTION

TRANSFER RNA (tRNA)

TRANSLATION

A The strand of DNA that has the nucleotide sequence complementary to the template strand.

B Protein coding segments of DNA that alternate with non-protein coding segments.

C Cluster of genes in *E. coli* that regulates the metabolism of lactose.

D A type of RNA that carries amino acids to the ribosome during protein synthesis.

E A process of genetically programmed cell death by which multicellular organisms trigger cell death as part of normal growth and development, and cellular regulation.

F The genetic code in which a sequence of three nucleotides code for the synthesis of a specific amino acid.

G Mutation that confers some kind of advantage to the survival and reproduction of an organism in the prevailing environment.

H A molecule that acts as a template for protein synthesis.

I Three nucleotide sequence in mRNA that signals the end point of translation.

J The set of rules by which information encoded in genetic material (DNA or RNA sequences) is translated into amino acid sequences by living cells.

K A mutation that is not currently subjected to selection pressure.

L Three nucleotide sequence in mRNA with which the ribosome starts translation.

M Enzyme capable of constructing RNA chains from a DNA template.

N An important second messenger derived from ATP.

O A highly conserved gene sequence involved in the regulation of anatomical development.

P The entire process of transferring of information encoded in a gene into a gene product.

Q Activation of an inactive gene to carry out transcription.

R Mutations that do not result in a change in a protein's amino acid sequence, even though there is a codon change. However, they may be detrimental, causing RNA instability.

S A small structure found in all cells made of ribosomal RNA and protein. They may be free in the cytoplasm or associated with the surface of the endoplasmic reticulum.

T A group of three consecutive bases in tRNA complementary to a codon on mRNA.

U The DNA strand that stores the information that is transcribed into mRNA.

V A change to the DNA sequence of an organism.

W Mutations that confer a disadvantage to the survival or reproduction of an organism.

X The process by which some amino acids are encoded for by more than one codon.

Y The process by which mRNA is decoded to produce a specific polypeptide.

Z A non-protein-coding DNA segment that is removed before a gene is translated.

AA A chain of amino acids joined together by peptide bonds.

BB Any chemical, influence, or object that is able to increase the mutation rate of an organism. This may be radiation, industrial or environmental chemicals, or viral infection.

CC A molecule that relays signals from receptors on the cell surface to a target molecule inside the cell.

DD The process by which the code contained in the DNA molecule is transcribed into a mRNA molecule.

UNIT F215

5.1.2

Meiosis and Variation

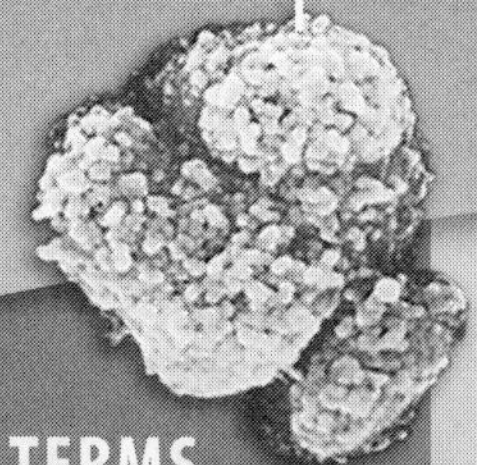

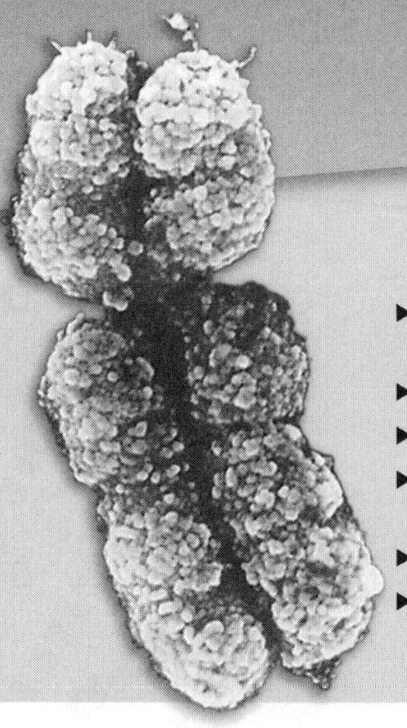

KEY TERMS

allele
centrioles
chi squared test
codominant
continuous variation
crossing over
discontinuous variation
dominant
epistasis
epistatic gene
genotype
heterozygous
homologous chromosome
homozygous
independent assortment
linkage
locus (pl. loci)
meiosis
nuclear envelope
phenotype
polygenes (=multiple genes)
probabliity
Punnett square
qualitative inheritance
quantitative inheritance
recessive
recombination
sex linkage

Periodicals:
Listings for this chapter are on page 341

Weblinks:
www.biozone.co.uk/weblink/OCR-A2-2832.html

KEY CONCEPTS

- Crossing over and independent assortment during meiosis contribute to genetic variation in the offspring.
- Linked genes tend to be inherited together.
- Codominant alleles are equally and independently expressed.
- The characters encoded by sex linked genes are usually seen only in the heterogametic sex.
- Genes at different loci can interact to determine phenotype.
- Polygenic inheritance and environment contribute to quantitative characters exhibiting continuous variation.

OBJECTIVES

☐ 1. Use the **KEY TERMS** to help you understand and complete these objectives.

Events in meiosis — pages 129-136

☐ 2. Describe the behaviour of homologous chromosomes during meiosis, including:
- the associated behaviour of the nuclear envelope, plasma membrane, and centrioles (centrioles are absent from fungal and higher plant cells).
- the **independent assortment** of maternal and paternal chromosomes.
- the **recombination** of segments of homologous chromosomes in **crossing over**.

☐ 3. Explain how meiosis and fertilisation produce genetic variation in the offspring.

☐ 4. With respect to inheritance, explain what is meant by the term **linkage**. Explain the consequences of linkage to the inheritance of alleles.

☐ 5. Recall that recombination refers to the exchange of alleles between homologous chromosomes as a result of crossing over. Explain the consequences of recombination to the inheritance of alleles.

Inheritance — pages 128, 137-156

☐ 6. Explain the terms **allele** and **locus** and distinguish between **dominant**, **recessive**, and **codominant** alleles. Use the terms homozygous and heterozygous appropriately.

☐ 7. Distinguish between **genotype** and **phenotype** and use these terms appropriately when discussing the outcomes of genetic crosses.

☐ 8. REVIEW: Recall monohybrid and dihybrid inheritance. Understand commonly used terms in inheritance studies: test-cross, back-cross, F_1 generation.

☐ 9. Describe codominance and solve problems involving the inheritance of phenotypic traits governed by codominant alleles. Explain how you would recognise codominance in genetic crosses.

☐ 10. Explain what is meant by **sex linkage**. Solve problems involving sex linked genes (e.g. inheritance of red-green colour-blindness and haemophilia).

☐ 11. Describe epistatic interactions between genes at different loci. Solve problems involving the inheritance of phenotypic traits involving **epistasis**.

☐ 12. Demonstrate an ability to use the **chi-squared test** to test the significance of differences between the observed and expected results of genetic crosses.

☐ 13. Using examples, distinguish between **continuous** and **discontinuous variation**.

☐ 14. Explain the basis of continuous and discontinuous variation with reference to the number of genes involved in determining a phenotypic character. Describe the distribution pattern of phenotypic variation produced by polygenic inheritance. Describe examples illustrating this type of **quantitative inheritance** pattern.

☐ 15. Explain how both genotype and environment contribute to phenotypic variation.

Alleles

Sexually reproducing organisms in nearly all cases have paired sets of chromosomes, one set coming from each parent. The equivalent chromosomes that form a pair are termed **homologues**. They contain equivalent sets of genes on them. But there is the potential for different versions of a gene to exist in a population and these are termed **alleles**.

Homologous Chromosomes

In sexually reproducing organisms, most cells have a homologous pair of chromosomes (one coming from each parent). This diagram shows the position of three different genes on the same chromosome that control three different traits (A, B and C).

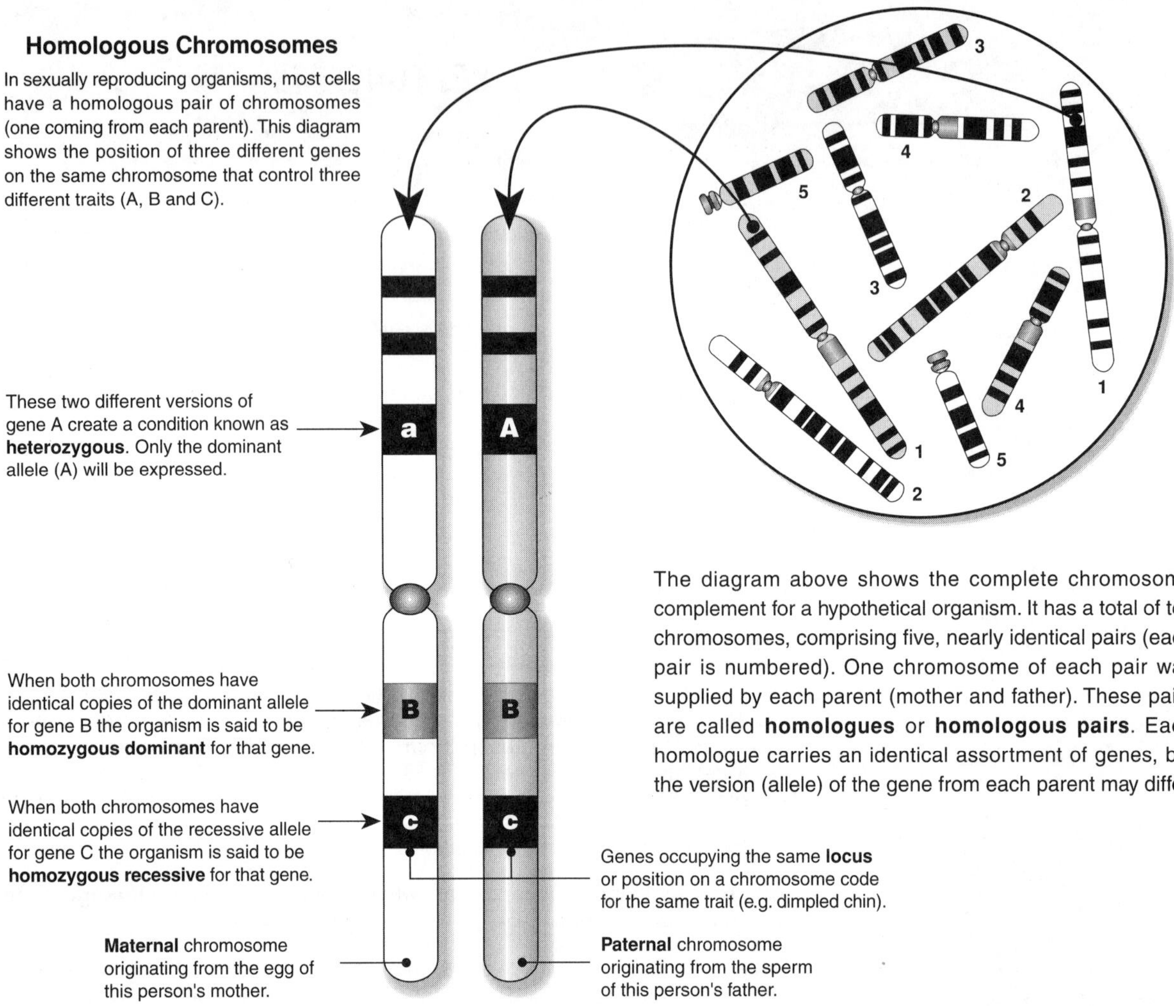

The diagram above shows the complete chromosome complement for a hypothetical organism. It has a total of ten chromosomes, comprising five, nearly identical pairs (each pair is numbered). One chromosome of each pair was supplied by each parent (mother and father). These pairs are called **homologues** or **homologous pairs**. Each homologue carries an identical assortment of genes, but the version (allele) of the gene from each parent may differ.

1. Define the following terms used to describe the allele combinations in the genotype for a given gene:

   (a) Heterozygous: ____________________

   (b) Homozygous dominant: ____________________

   (c) Homozygous recessive: ____________________

2. For a gene given the symbol '**A**', name the alleles present in an organism that is identified as:

   (a) Heterozygous: __________ (b) Homozygous dominant: __________ (c) Homozygous recessive: __________

3. Explain what a homologous pair of chromosomes is: ____________________

4. Discuss the significance of genes existing as **alleles**: ____________________

Sources of Variation

Variation refers to the diversity of genetic and phenotypic traits within and between species. Variation is a feature of sexually reproducing populations and the essential raw material for selection. Variation gives species greater opportunity to adapt to and survive in a dynamic environment. Populations of highly variable species will include individuals with different **fitness** in the prevailing environment. It is this variability that offers the chance of reproductive advantage if environments change. Species with low variability (such as populations of parthenogenetic clones) can be highly successful in stable conditions, but reproduce sexually when environments become unfavourable for just this reason. Phenotype is influenced by both genotype and the environment. Even organisms of fixed genotype may differ in the degree to which they can alter their phenotype in response to environmental change; a phenomenon known as **phenotypic plasticity**. Phenotypic plasticity allows organisms a greater chance of survival in ever-changing surroundings and it is particularly well developed in immobile species, such as plants.

Mutations

gene mutations; chromosome mutations

Mutations are the source of all **new** alleles. Existing genes are modified by base substitutions and deletions, causing the formation of new alleles. Silent mutations may escape selection pressure until conditions change.

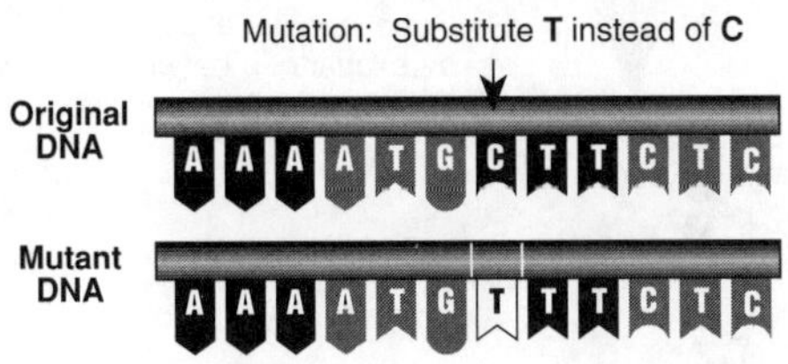

Sexual Reproduction

independent assortment; crossing over and recombination; mate selection

Sexual reproduction rearranges and reshuffles the genetic material into new combinations.

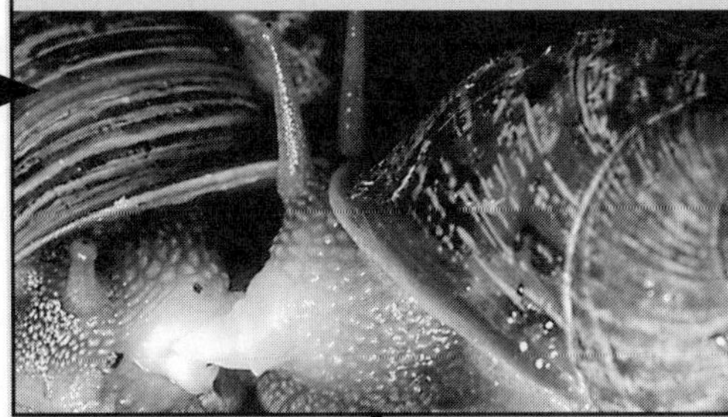

Genotype

Determines the **genetic potential** of an individual

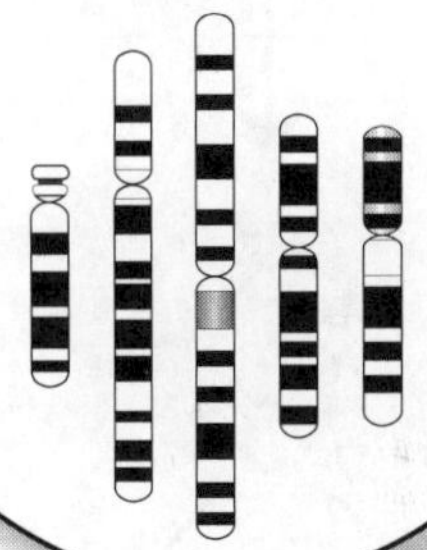

Dominant, recessive, codominant and multiple allele systems, as well as interactions between genes and epigenetic inheritance, combine in their effects.

Phenotype

An individual's phenotype is the result of the ineraction of genetic and environmental factors during its lifetime (including during development). The genetic instructions for creating the individual may be modified by the internal and external environment both during and after development. Phenotypic plasticity in response to environment can be adaptive if it increases fitness.

Some snail populations show phenotypic plasticity with respect to shell thickness; individuals can develop thicker shells when subjected to heavy predation.

Environmental Factors

The external and internal environments can influence the expression of the genotype. The external environment may include physical factors such as temperature or light intensity, or biotic factors such as competition. The internal environment, e.g presence or absence of hormones or growth factors during development, may also affect genotypic expression.

1. Using examples, explain how the environment of a particular genotype can affect the phenotype:

____

____

____

2. Discuss the significance of variation in selection: _______________

____

____

____

Related activities: *Meiosis, Nature of Mutation*

Mitosis vs Meiosis

Cell division is fundamental to all life, as cells arise only by the division of existing cells. All types of cell division begin with replication of the cell's DNA. In eukaryotes, this is followed by division of the nucleus. There are two forms of nuclear division: **mitosis** and **meiosis**, and they have quite different purposes and outcomes. Mitosis is the simpler of the two and produces two identical daughter cells from each parent cell. Mitosis is responsible for growth and repair processes in multicellular organisms and reproduction in single-celled and asexual eukaryotes. Meiosis involves a **reduction division** in which haploid gametes are produced for the purposes of sexual reproduction. Fusion of haploid gametes in fertilisation restores the diploid cell number in the **zygote**. These two fundamentally different types of cell division are compared below.

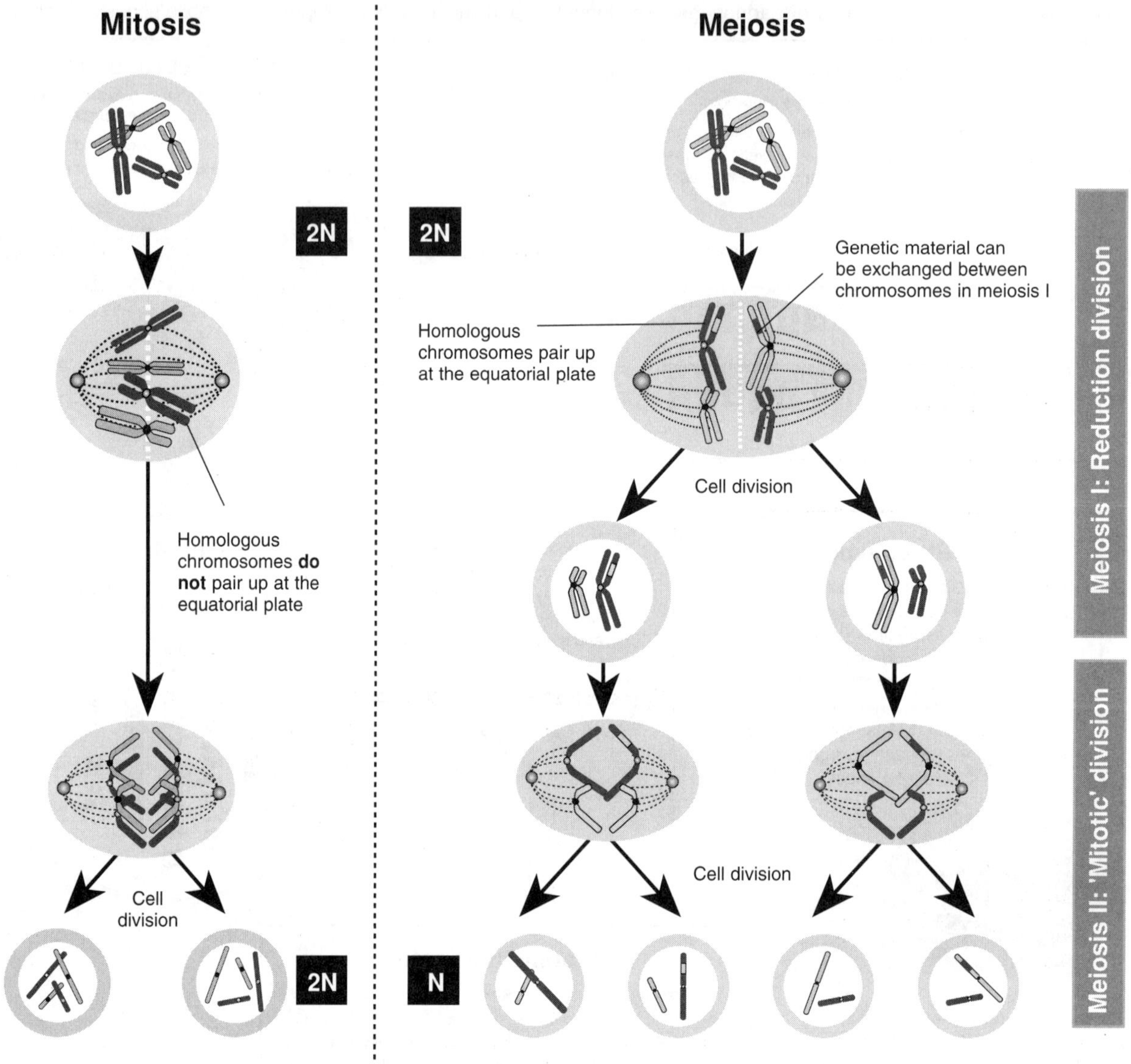

1. Describe the fundamental differences between mitosis and meiosis: ____________________

2. Explain why meiosis introduces genetic variability but why mitosis does not: ____________________

3. Explain why meiosis II is sometimes referred to as a 'mitotic division': ____________________

Meiosis

Meiosis is a special type of cell division concerned with producing sex cells (gametes) for the purpose of sexual reproduction. It involves a single chromosomal duplication followed by two successive nuclear divisions, and results in a halving of the diploid chromosome number. Meiosis occurs in the sex organs of plants and animals. If genetic mistakes (**gene** and **chromosome mutations**) occur here, they will be passed on to the offspring (they will be inherited).

Meiosis I

(Reduction division)

The first division separates the homologous chromosomes into two intermediate cells.

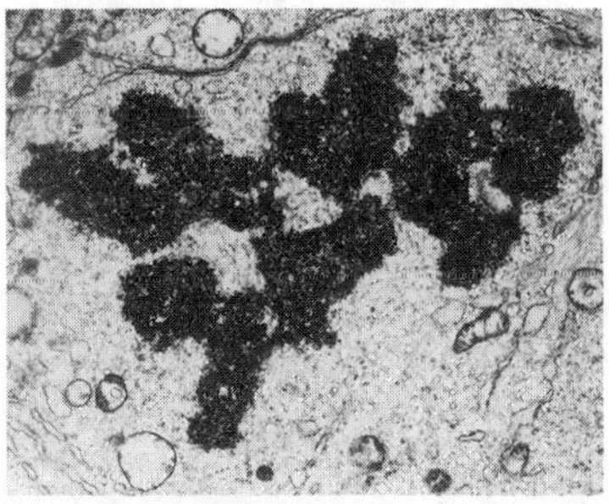

Chromosomes in anaphase of meiosis I

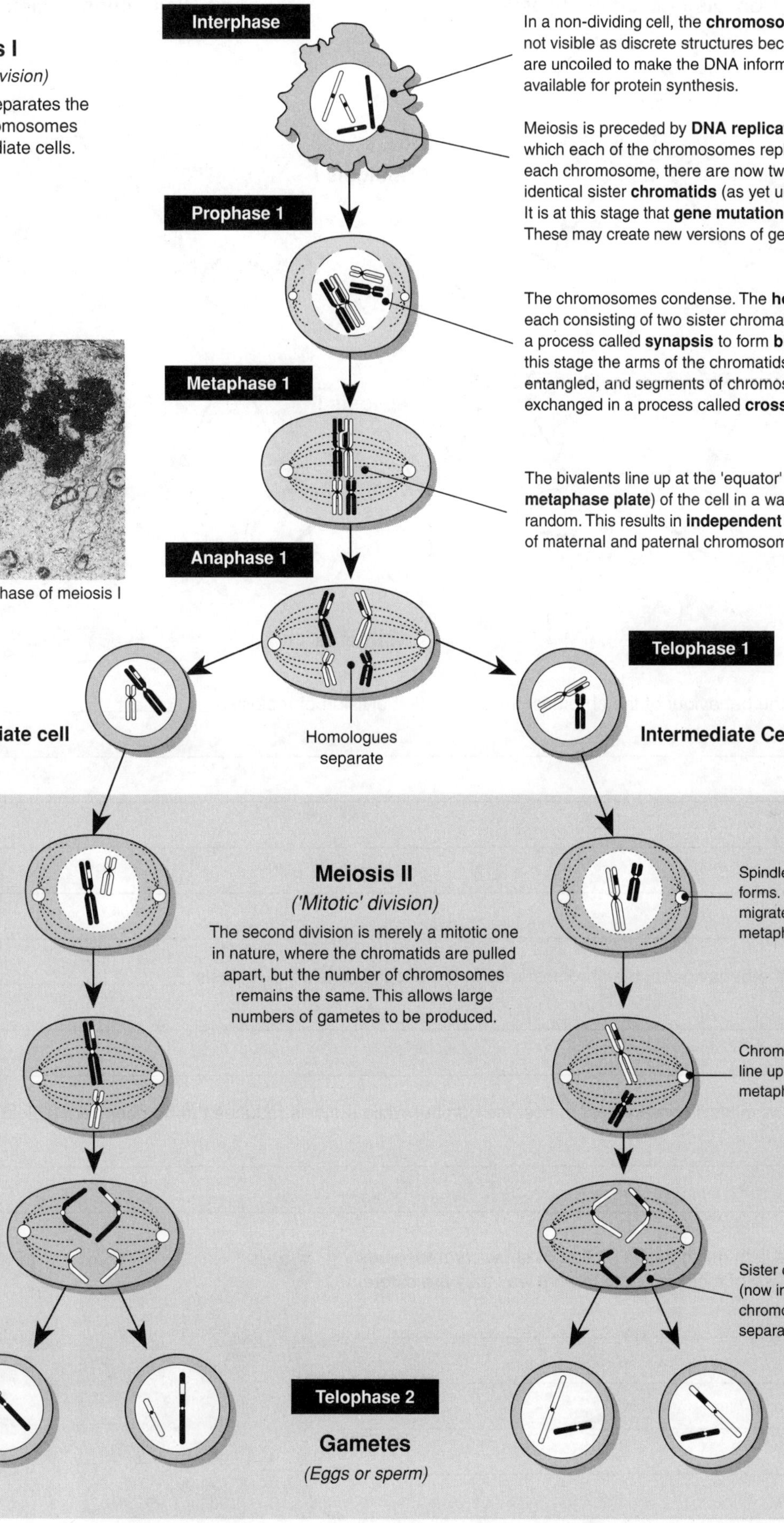

In a non-dividing cell, the **chromosomes** are not visible as discrete structures because they are uncoiled to make the DNA information available for protein synthesis.

Meiosis is preceded by **DNA replication**, during which each of the chromosomes replicates. For each chromosome, there are now two genetically identical sister **chromatids** (as yet unseparated). It is at this stage that **gene mutations** may occur. These may create new versions of genes (alleles).

The chromosomes condense. The **homologues**, each consisting of two sister chromatids, pair up in a process called **synapsis** to form **bivalents**. At this stage the arms of the chromatids can become entangled, and segments of chromosome can be exchanged in a process called **crossing over**.

The bivalents line up at the 'equator' (the **metaphase plate**) of the cell in a way that is random. This results in **independent assortment** of maternal and paternal chromosomes.

Meiosis II

('Mitotic' division)

The second division is merely a mitotic one in nature, where the chromatids are pulled apart, but the number of chromosomes remains the same. This allows large numbers of gametes to be produced.

Spindle apparatus forms. Chromosomes migrate towards the metaphase plate.

Chromosomes line up on the metaphase plate.

Sister chromatids (now individual chromosomes), separate.

Gametes

(Eggs or sperm)

The meiotic spindle normally distributes chromosomes to daughter cells without error. However, mistakes can occur in which the homologous chromosomes fail to separate properly at anaphase during meiosis I, or sister chromatids fail to separate during meiosis II. In these cases, one gamete receives two of the same type of chromosome and the other gamete receives no copy. This mishap, called **non-disjunction**, results in abnormal numbers of chromosomes passing to the gametes. If either of the aberrant gametes unites with a normal one at fertilisation, the offspring will have an abnormal chromosome number, known as an **aneuploidy**.

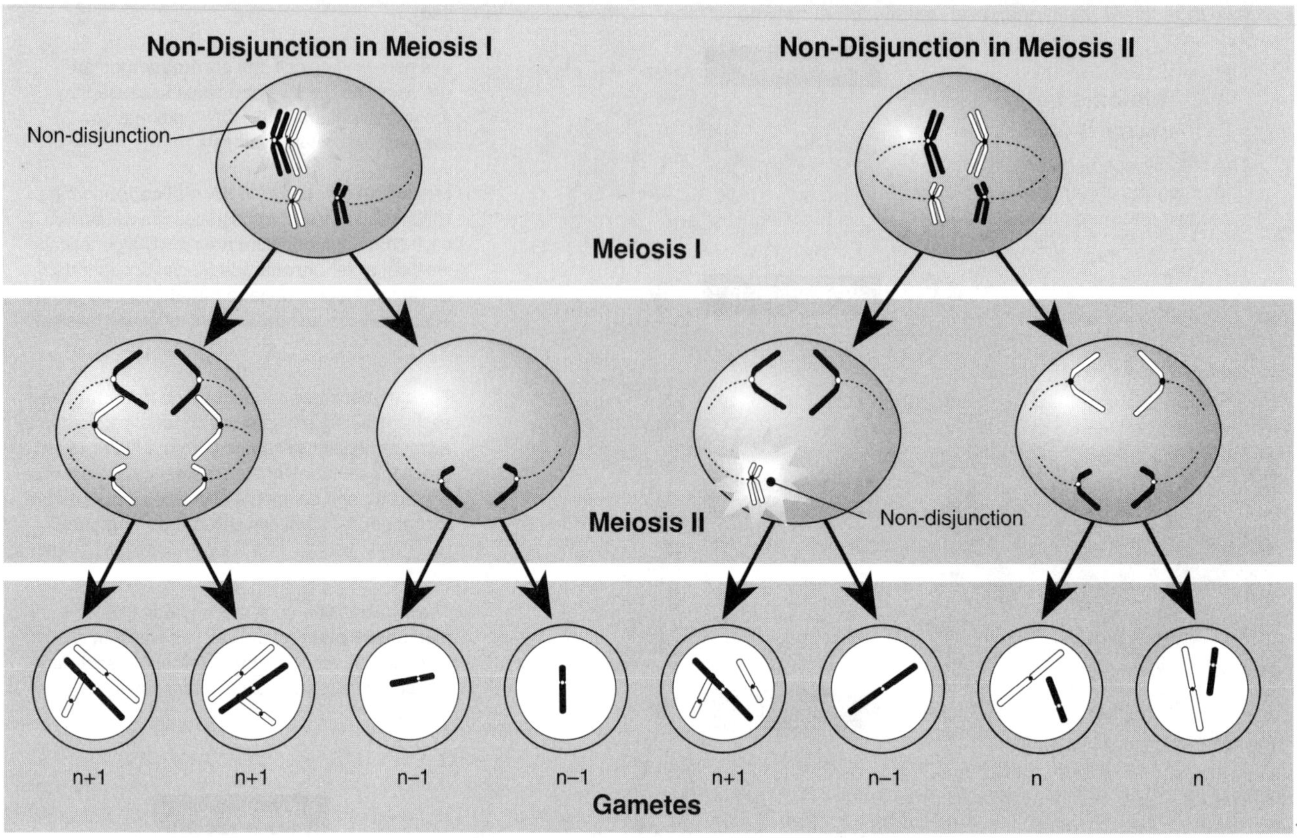

1. Describe the behaviour of the chromosomes in the first division of meiosis: ______

2. Describe the behaviour of the chromosomes in the second division of meiosis: ______

3. Explain how mitosis conserves chromosome number while meiosis reduces the number from diploid to haploid: ______

4. Both these light micrographs (A and B) show chromosomes in metaphase of meiosis. State in what way they are different: ______

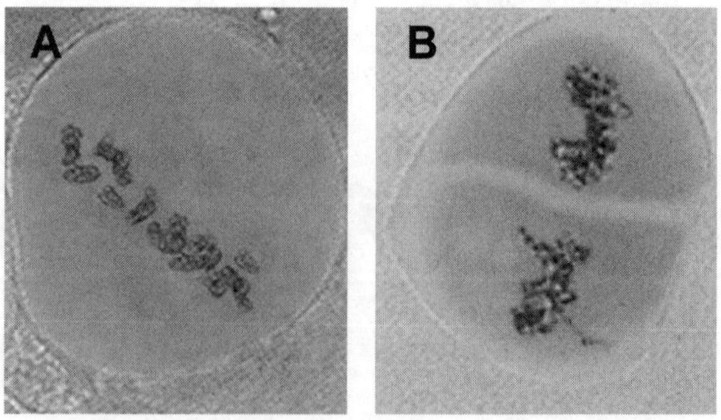

Crossing Over

Crossing over refers to the mutual exchange of pieces of chromosome and involves the swapping of whole groups of genes between the **homologous** chromosomes. This process can occur only during the first division of **meiosis**. Errors in crossing over can result in **chromosome mutations** which can be very damaging to development. Crossing over can upset expected frequencies of offspring in dihybrid crosses. The frequency of crossing over (COV) for different genes (as followed by inherited, observable traits) can be used to determine the relative positions of genes on a chromosome and provide a **genetic map**. There has been a recent suggestion that crossing over may be necessary to ensure accurate cell division.

Pairing of Homologous Chromosomes

Every somatic cell contains a pair of each type of chromosome, one from each parent. These are called **homologous pairs** or **homologues**. In prophase of meiosis I, the homologues pair up to form **bivalents**. This process is called **synapsis** and it brings the chromatids of the homologues into close contact.

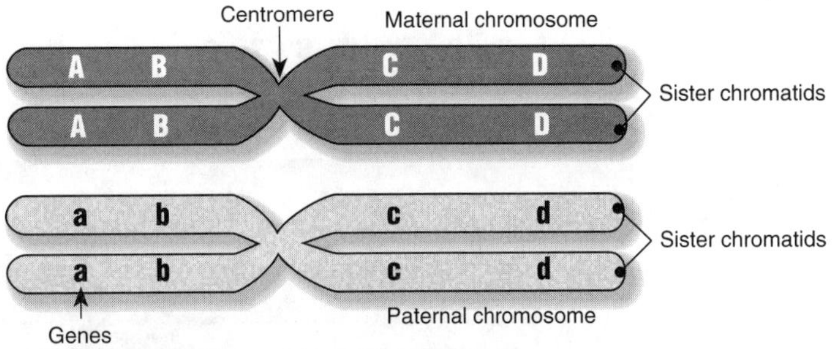

Chiasma Formation and Crossing Over

Synapsis allows the homologous, non-sister chromatids to become entangled and the chromosomes exchange segments. This exchange occurs at regions called **chiasmata** (sing. chiasma). In the diagram (centre), a chiasma is forming and the exchange of pieces of chromosome has not yet taken place. Numerous chiasmata may develop between homologues.

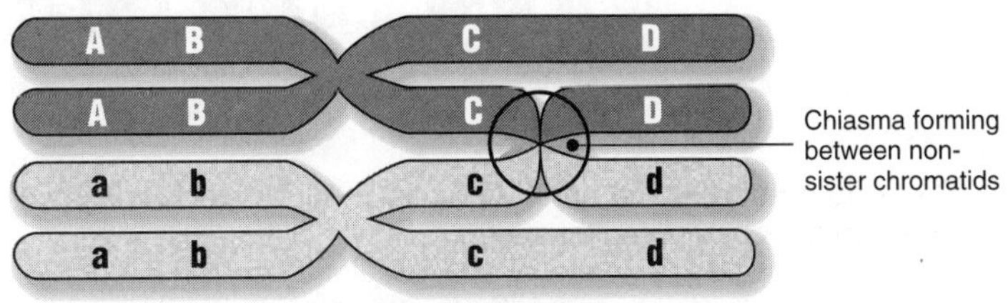

Separation

Crossing over produces new allele combinations, a phenomenon known as **recombination**. When the homologues separate in anaphase of meiosis I, each of the chromosomes pictured will have new mix of alleles that will be passed into the gametes soon to be formed. Recombination is an important source of variation in population gene pools.

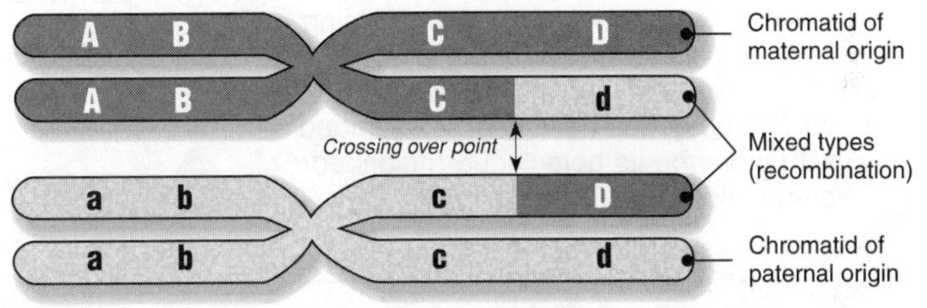

Gamete Formation

Once the final division of meiosis is complete, the two chromatids that made up each replicated chromosome become separated and are now referred to as chromosomes. As a result of the crossing over, **four** genetically different chromosomes are produced. If no crossing over had occurred, there would have been only two parental types (two copies of each).

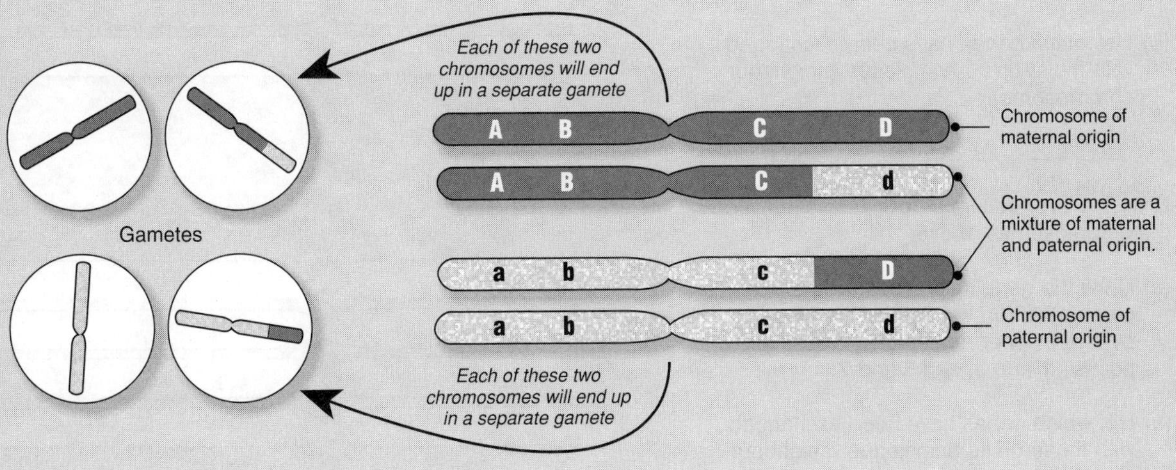

1. Explain how the process of crossing over is going to alter the genotype of gametes: ____________________

2. Describe the evolutionary significance of crossing over: ____________________

Related activities: *Crossing Over Problems*
Web links: *Crossing Over Animation*

Crossing Over Problems

The diagram below shows a pair of homologous chromosomes about to undergo chiasma formation during the first division of meiosis. There are known crossover points along the length of the chromatids (same on all four chromatids shown in the diagram). In the prepared spaces below, draw the gene sequences after crossing over has occurred on three unrelated and separate occasions (it would be useful to use different coloured pens to represent the genes from the two different chromosomes). See the diagrams on the previous page as a guide.

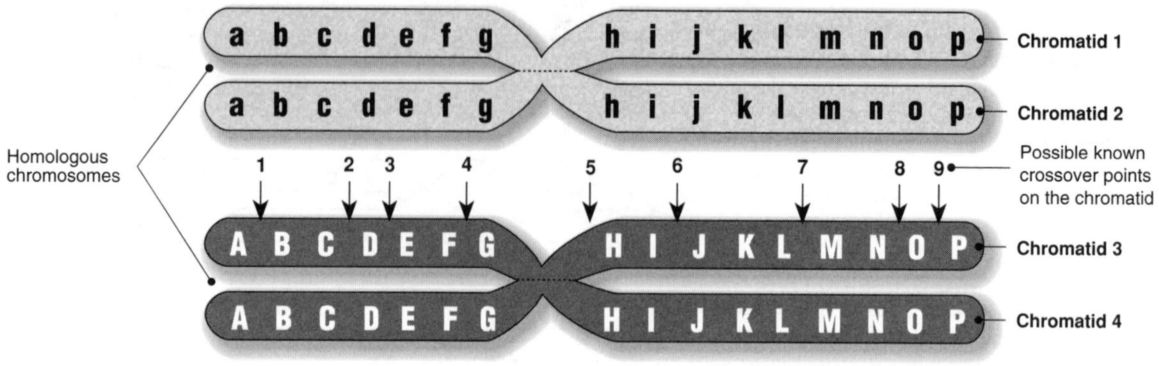

1. Crossing over occurs at a **single** point between the chromosomes above.

   (a) Draw the gene sequences for the four chromatids (on the right), after crossing over has occurred at crossover point: **2**

   (b) List which genes have been exchanged with those on its homologue (neighbour chromosome):

   ____

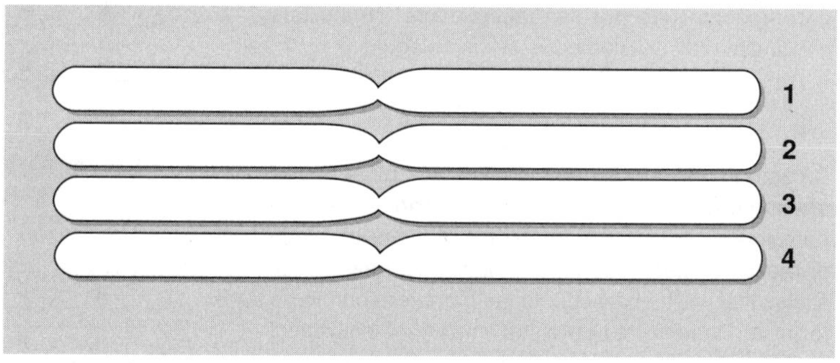

2. Crossing over occurs at **two** points between the chromosomes above.

   (a) Draw the gene sequences for the four chromatids (on the right), after crossing over has occurred between crossover points: **6** and **7**.

   (b) List which genes have been exchanged with those on its homologue (neighbour chromosome):

   ____

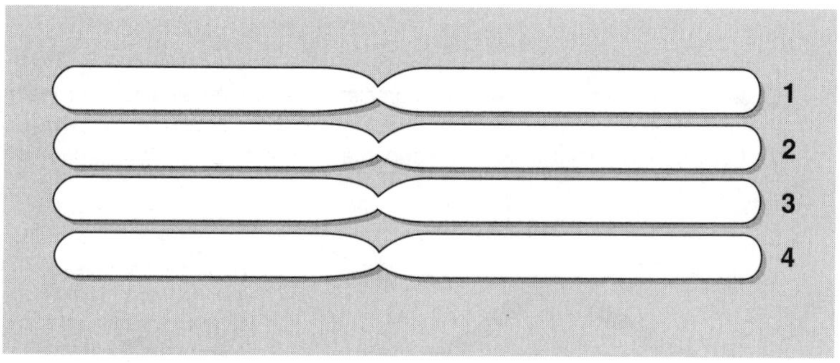

3. Crossing over occurs at **four** points between the chromosomes above.

   (a) Draw the gene sequences for the four chromatids (on the right), after crossing over has occurred between crossover points: **1** and **3**, and **5** and **7**.

   (b) List which genes have been exchanged with those on its homologue (neighbour chromosome):

   ____

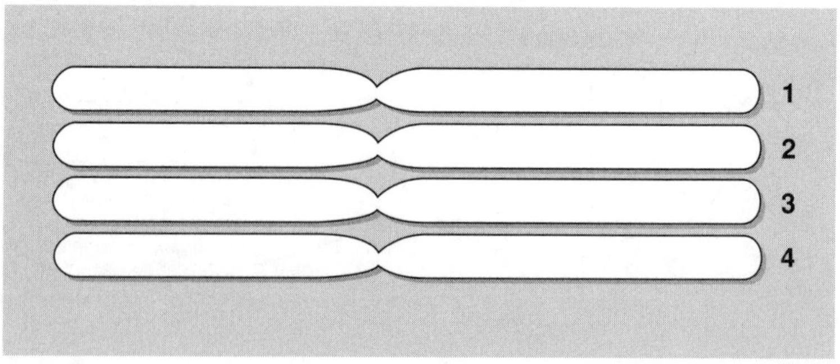

4. Explain the genetic significance of **crossing over**: ___________________________

____

____

____

Linkage

Linkage refers to genes that are located on the same chromosome. Linked genes tend to be inherited together and fewer genetic combinations of their alleles are possible. Linkage reduces the variety of offspring that can be produced (contrast this with recombination). In genetic crosses, linkage is indicated when a greater proportion of the progeny resulting from a cross are of the parental type (than would be expected if the alleles were assorting independently). If the genes in question had been on separate chromosomes, there would have been more genetic variation in the gametes and therefore in the offspring. Note that in the example below, wild type alleles are dominant and are denoted by an upper case symbol of the mutant phenotype (Cu or Eb). This symbology used for *Drosophila* departs from the convention of using the dominant gene to provide the symbol. This is necessary because there are many mutant alternative phenotypes to the wild type (e.g. curled and vestigial wings). Alternatively, the wild type is sometimes denoted with a raised plus sign e.g. cu^+cu^+ and all symbols are in lower case.

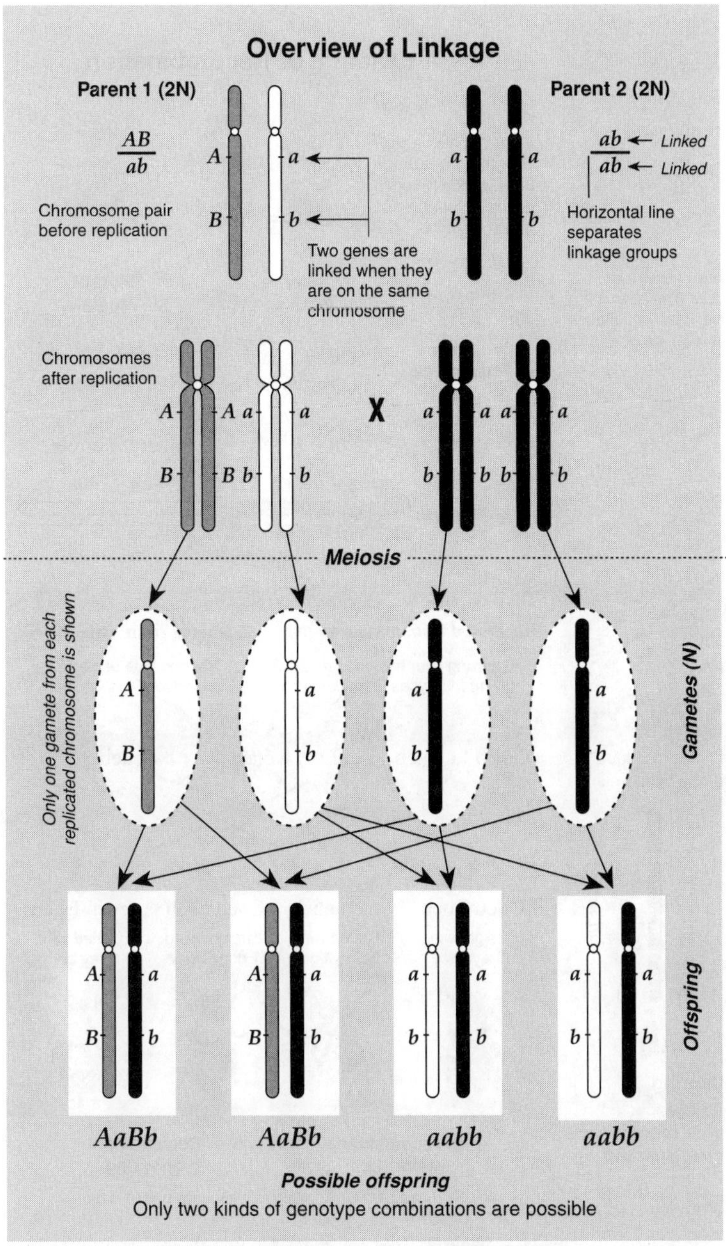

An Example of Linked Genes in *Drosophila*

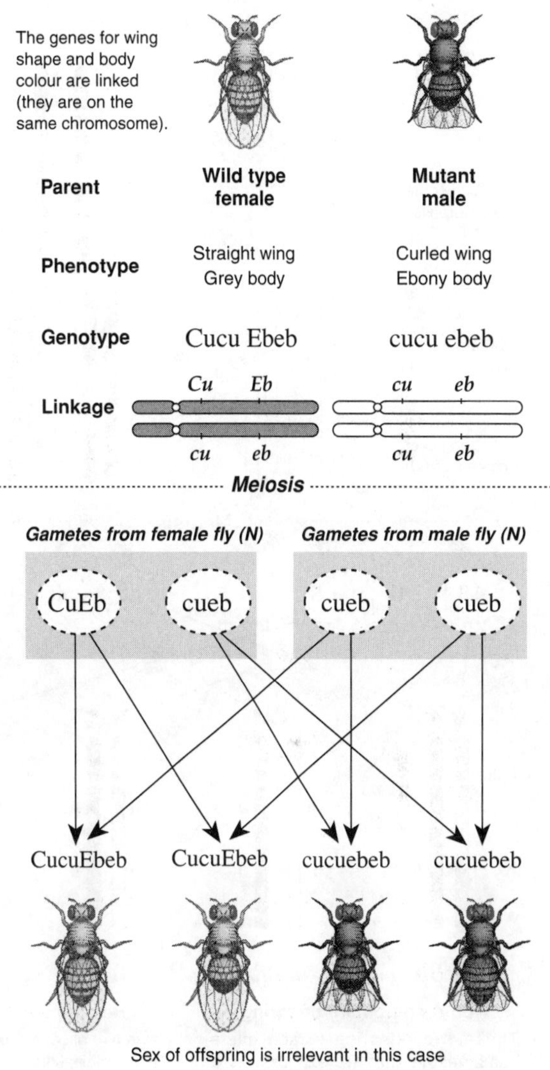

Contact **Newbyte Educational Software** for details of their superb *Drosophila Genetics* software package which includes coverage of linkage and recombination. *Drosophila* images © Newbyte Educational Software.

1. Describe the effect of **linkage** on the inheritance of genes: ______________________________

____

2. (a) List the possible genotypes in the offspring (above, left) if genes A and B had been on **separate chromosomes**:

____

(b) If the female *Drosophila* had been homozygous for the dominant wild type alleles (CuCu EbEb), state:

The genotype(s) of the F_1: ______________ The phenotype(s) of the F_1: ______________

3. Explain how linkage decreases the amount of genetic variation in the offspring: ______________________________

____

Recombination

Genetic recombination refers to the exchange of alleles between homologous chromosomes as a result of **crossing over**. The alleles of parental linkage groups separate and new associations of alleles are formed in the gametes. Offspring formed from these gametes show new combinations of characteristics and are known as **recombinants** (offspring with genotypes unlike either parent). The proportion of recombinants in the offspring can be used to calculate the frequency of recombination (crossover value). These values are fairly constant for any given pair of alleles and can be used to produce gene maps indicating the relative positions of genes on a chromosome. In contrast to linkage, recombination increases genetic variation. Recombination between the alleles of parental linkage groups is indicated by the appearance of recombinants in the offspring, although not in the numbers that would be expected had the alleles been on separate chromosomes (independent assortment). The example below uses the same genotypes as the previous activity, *Linkage*, but in this case crossing over occurs between the alleles in a linkage group in one parent. The notation is the same for both activities.

Overview of Recombination

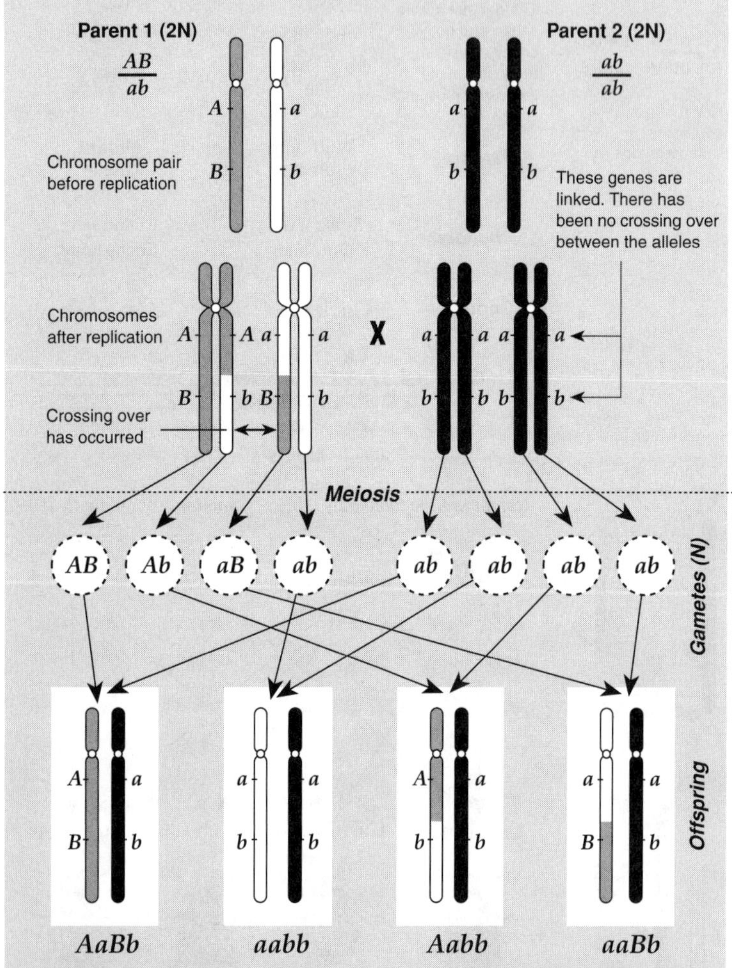

Non-recombinant offspring

These two offspring exhibit allele combinations that are expected as a result of independent assortment during meiosis. Also called parental types.

Recombinant offspring

These two offspring exhibit unexpected allele combinations. They can only arise if one of the parent's chromosomes has undergone crossing over.

Possible offspring

Offspring with **four** kinds of genotype combinations are produced instead of the two kinds expected (*AaBb* and *aabb*) if no crossing over had occurred.

An Example of Recombination

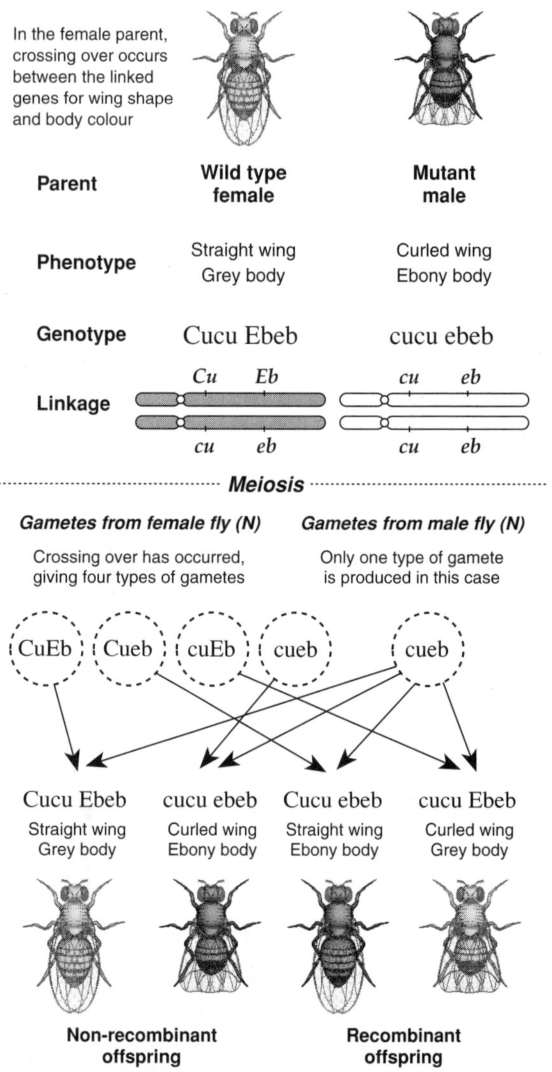

The sex of the offspring is irrelevant in this case

Contact **Newbyte Educational Software** for details of their superb *Drosophila Genetics* software package which includes coverage of linkage and recombination. *Drosophila* images © Newbyte Educational Software.

1. Describe the effect of **recombination** on the inheritance of genes: ____________________

2. Explain how recombination increases the amount of genetic variation in offspring: ____________________

3. Explain why it is not possible to have a recombination frequency of greater than 50% (half recombinant progeny):

Basic Genetic Crosses

For revision purposes, examine the diagrams below on monohybrid crosses and complete the exercises for dihybrid (two gene) inheritance. A **back cross** (not shown) refers to any cross between an offspring and one of its parents (or an individual genetically identical to one of its parents).

Monohybrid Cross F_1

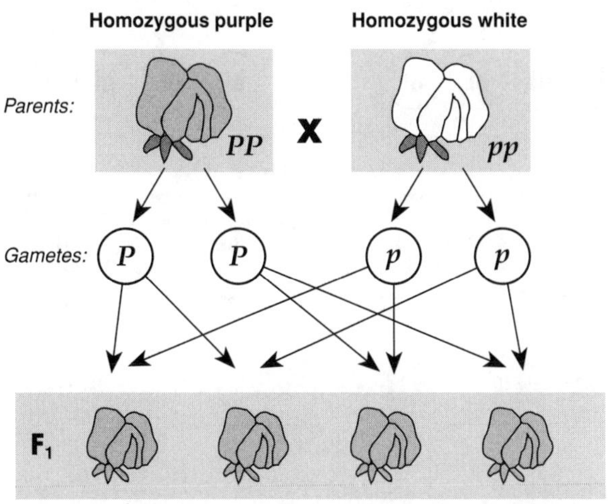

Genotypes: All *Pp* **Phenotypes:** All purple

The F_1 offspring of a cross between two **true breeding** parent plants are all purple (*Pp*).

Monohybrid Cross F_2

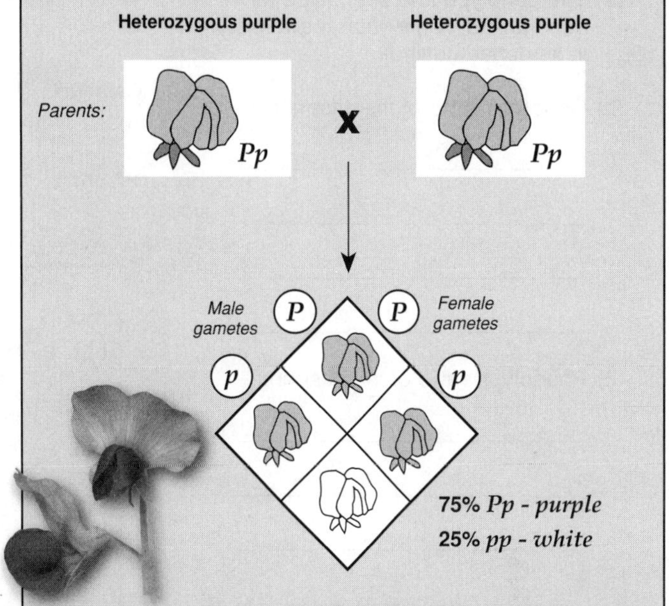

A cross between the F_1 offspring (*Pp* x *Pp*) would yield a 3:1 ratio in the F_2 of purple (*PP*, *Pp*, *Pp*) to white (*pp*).

Dihybrid Cross

In pea seeds, yellow colour (*Y*) is dominant to green (*y*) and round shape (*R*) is dominant to wrinkled (*r*). Each **true breeding** parental plant has matching alleles for each of these characters (*YYRR* or *yyrr*). F_1 offspring will all have the same genotype and phenotype (yellow-round: *YyRr*).

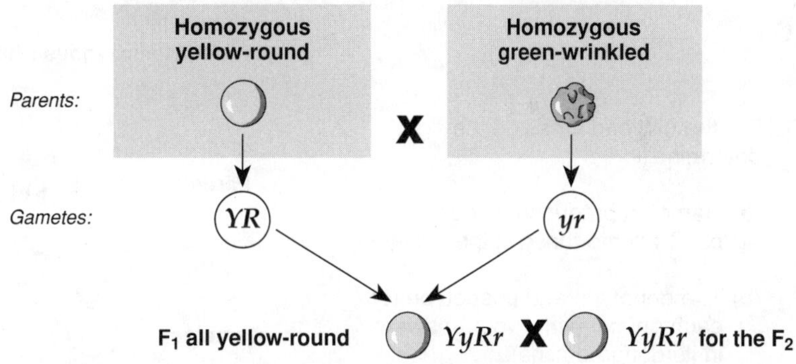

1. Fill in the Punnett square (below right) to show the genotypes of the F_2 generation.

2. In the boxes below, use fractions to indicate the numbers of each phenotype produced from this cross.

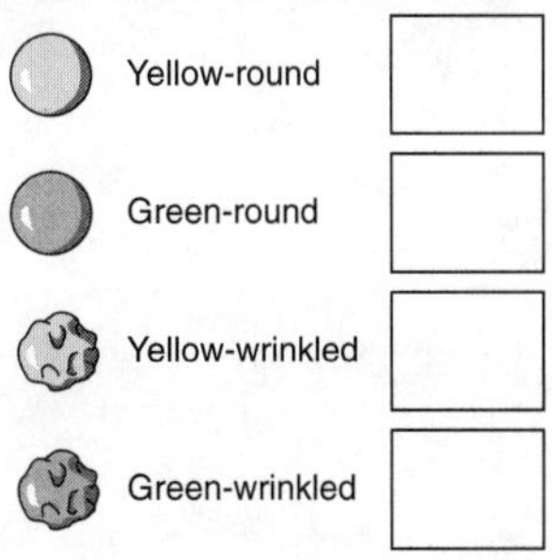

3. Express these numbers as a ratio:

____

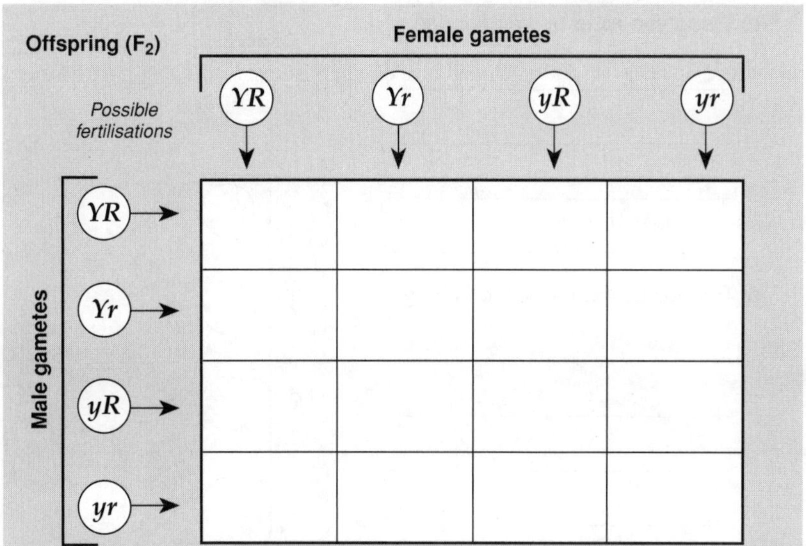

4. The dihybrid cross on the right has been partly worked out for you. You must determine:

   (a) The genotype and phenotype for each animal (write your answers in its dotted outline).

   (b) Genotype **ratio** of the offspring:

   ___

   (c) Phenotype **ratio** of the offspring:

   ___

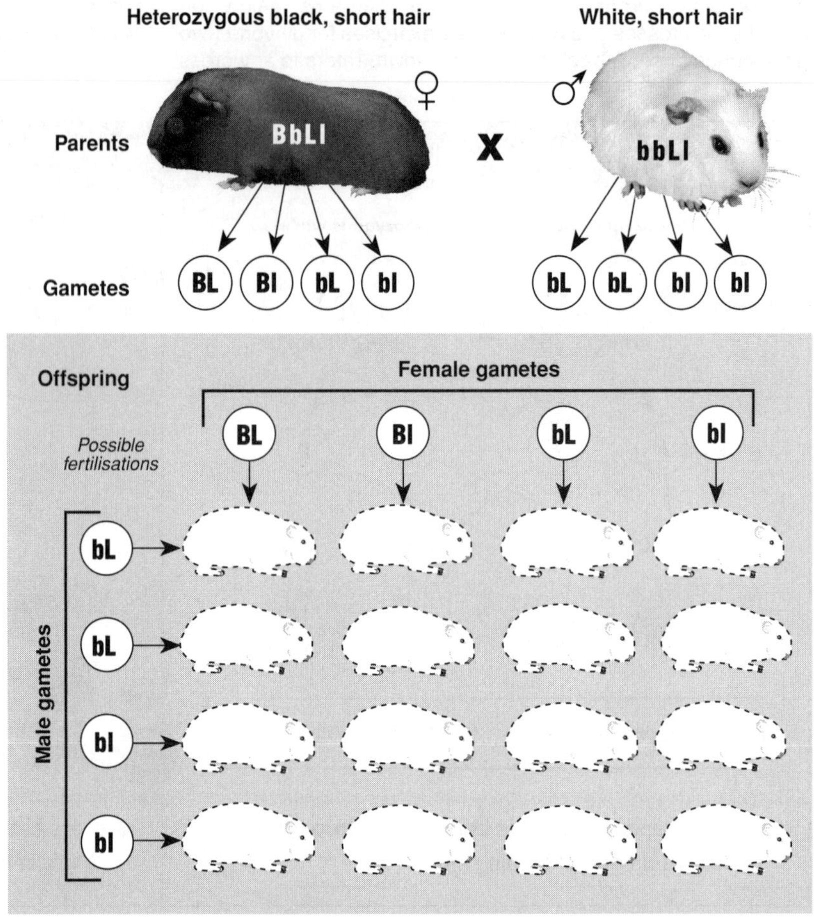

5. For the dihybrid cross on the right, determine:

   (a) Gametes produced by each parent (write these in the circles).

   (b) The genotype and phenotype for each animal (write your answers in its dotted outline).

   (c) Genotype **ratio** of the offspring:

   ___

   (d) Phenotype **ratio** of the offspring:

   ___

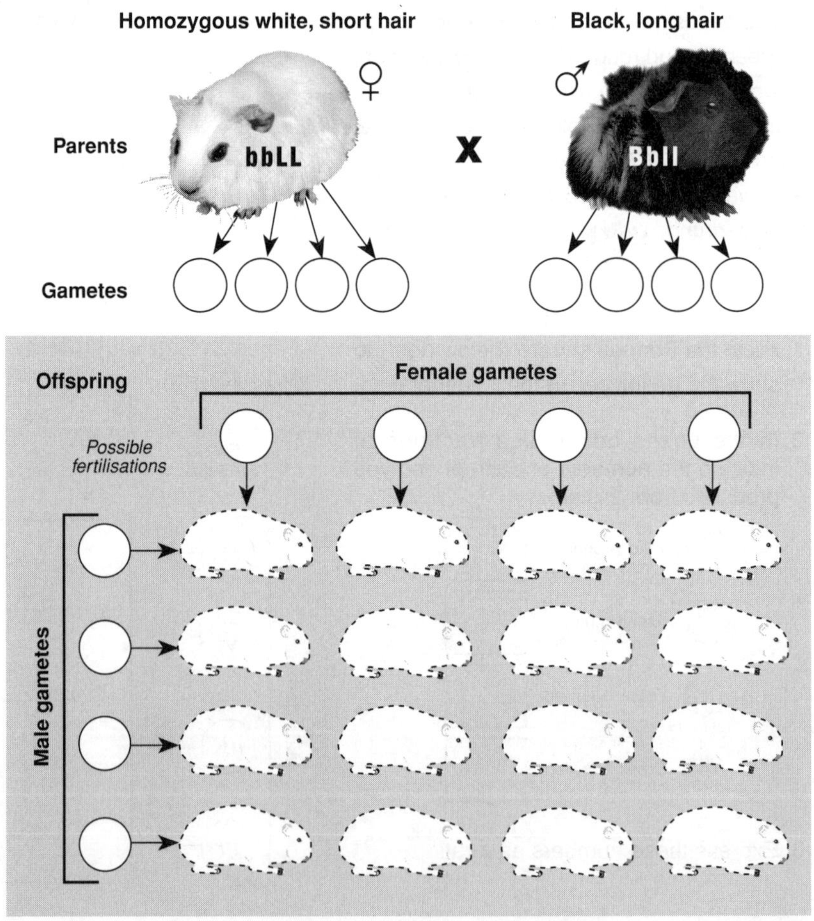

The Test Cross

It is not always possible to determine an organism's genotype by its appearance because the expression of genes is complicated by patterns of dominance and by gene interactions. The **test cross** was developed by Gregor Mendel as a way to establish the genotype of an organism with the dominant phenotype for a particular trait. The principle of the test cross is simple. The individual with the unknown genotype is bred with a homozygous recessive individual for the trait(s) of interest. The homozygous recessive can produce only one type of allele (recessive), so the phenotypes of the resulting offspring will reveal the genotype of the unknown parent. For example, if the unknown individual is homozygous for the trait, all of the offspring will display the dominant phenotype. However, if the offspring display both dominant and recessive phenotypes, then the unknown must be heterozygous for that trait. The test cross can be used to determine the genotype of single genes or multiple genes.

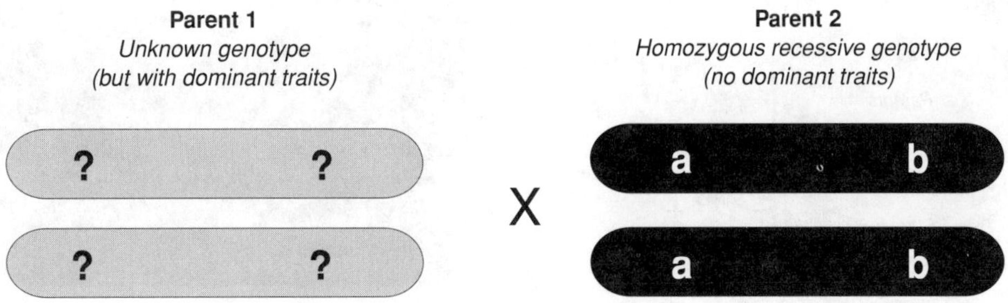

The common fruit fly (*Drosophila melanogaster*) is often used to illustrate basic principles of inheritance because it has several genetic markers whose phenotypes are easily identified . Once such phenotype is body colour. Wild type (normal) *Drosophila* have yellow-brown bodies. The allele for yellow-brown body colour (E) is dominant. The allele for an ebony coloured body (e) is recessive. The test crosses below show the possible outcomes for an individual with homozygous and heterozygous alleles for ebony body colour.

A. A homozygous recessive female (ee) with an ebony body is crossed with a homozyogous dominant male (EE).

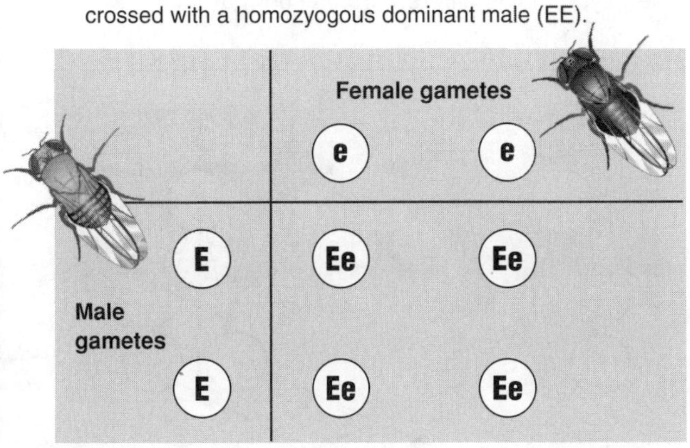

Cross A:

(a) Genotype frequency: 100% Ee

(b) Phenotype frequency: 100% yellow-brown

B. A homozygous recessive female (ee) with an ebony body is crossed with a heterozygous male (Ee).

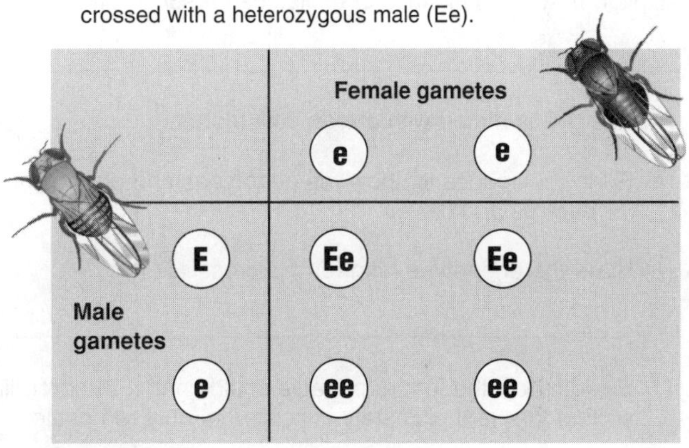

Cross B:

(a) Genotype frequency: 50% Ee, 50% ee

(b) Phenotype frequency: 50% yellow-brown, 50% ebony

1. In *Drosophila*, the allele for brown eyes (b) is recessive, while the red eye allele (B) is dominant. Explain how you would set up a **two gene test cross** to determine the genotype of a male who has a normal body colour and red eyes:

2. List all of the **possible genotypes** for the male *Drosophila*:

3. 50% of the resulting progeny are yellow-brown bodies with red eyes, and 50% have ebony bodies with red eyes.

   (a) State the genotype of the male *Drosophila*:

   (b) Explain how you came to this conclusion:

Codominance

Codominance refers to an inheritance pattern in which both alleles in a heterozygote contribute to the phenotype. Both alleles are **independently** and **equally expressed**. One example includes the human blood group AB which is the result of two alleles: A and B, both being equally expressed. Other examples include certain coat colours in horses and cattle. Reddish coat colour is equally dominant with white. Animals that have both alleles have coats that are roan-coloured (coats with a mix of red and white hairs). The red hairs and white hairs are expressed equally and independently (not blended to produce pink).

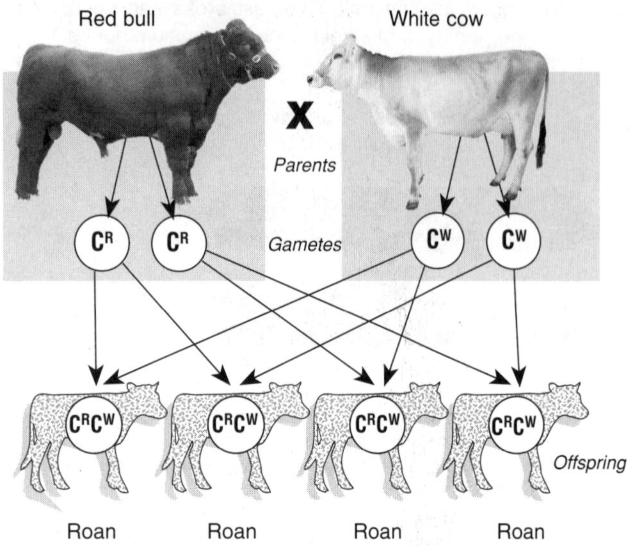

In the shorthorn cattle breed, coat colour is inherited. White shorthorn parents always produce calves with white coats. Red parents always produce red calves. However, when a red parent mates with a white one, the calves have a coat colour that is different from either parent; a mixture of red and white hairs, called roan. Use the example (left) to help you to solve the problems below.

1. Explain how codominance of alleles can result in offspring with a phenotype that is different from either parent:

2. A white bull is mated with a roan cow (right):

   (a) Fill in the spaces to show the genotypes and phenotypes for parents and calves:

   (b) State the phenotype ratio for this cross:

   (c) Explain how the farmer of cattle could control the breeding so that the herd ultimately consisted of only red cattle:

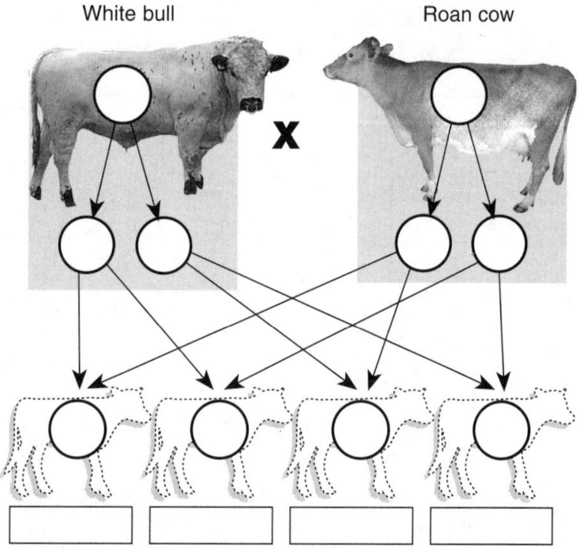

3. A farmer has only roan cattle on his farm. He suspects that one of the neighbours' bulls may have jumped the fence to mate with his cows earlier in the year because half the calves born were red and half were roan. One neighbour has a red bull, the other has a roan.

   (a) Fill in the spaces (right) to show the genotype and phenotype for parents and calves.

   (b) Which bull serviced the cows? **red** or **roan** (*delete one*)

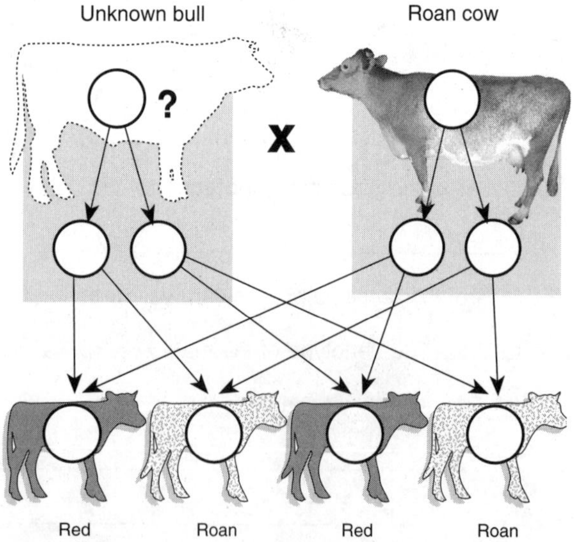

4. Describe the classical phenotypic ratio for a codominant gene resulting from the cross of two heterozygous parents (e.g. a cross between two roan cattle):

Related activities: *Codominance in Multiple Allele Systems*
Web links: *Drag and Drop Genetics*

Codominance in Multiple Allele Systems

The four common blood groups of the human 'ABO blood group system' are determined by three alleles: ***A***, ***B***, and ***O*** (also represented in some textbooks as: $\mathbf{I^A}$, $\mathbf{I^B}$, and $\mathbf{i^O}$ or just **i**). This is an example of a **multiple allele** system for a gene. The ABO antigens consist of sugars attached to the surface of red blood cells. The alleles code for enzymes (proteins) that join these sugars together. The allele ***O*** produces a non-functioning enzyme that is unable to make any changes to the basic antigen (sugar) molecule. The other two alleles *(**A**, **B**)* are **codominant** and are expressed equally. They each produce a different functional enzyme that adds a different, specific sugar to the basic sugar molecule. The blood group A and B antigens are able to react with antibodies present in the blood from other people and must be matched for transfusion.

Recessive allele:	***O***	produces a non-functioning protein
Dominant allele:	***A***	produces an enzyme which forms **A antigen**
Dominant allele:	***B***	produces an enzyme which forms **B antigen**

Blood group (phenotype)	Possible genotypes	Frequency in NZ
O	OO	49%
A	AA AO	40%
B		9%
AB		2%

If a person has the ***AO*** allele combination then their blood group will be group **A**. The presence of the recessive allele has no effect on the blood group in the presence of a dominant allele. Another possible allele combination that can create the same blood group is ***AA***.

1. Use the information above to complete the table for the possible genotypes for blood group B and group AB.

2. Below are six crosses possible between couples of various blood group types. The first example has been completed for you. Complete the genotype and phenotype for the other five crosses below:

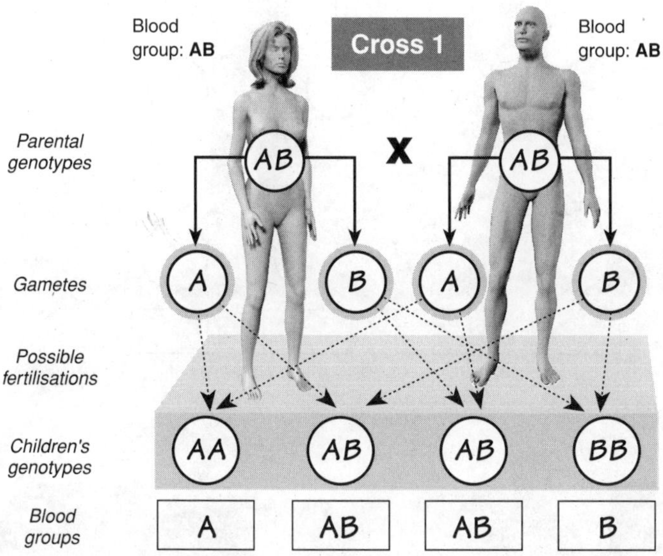

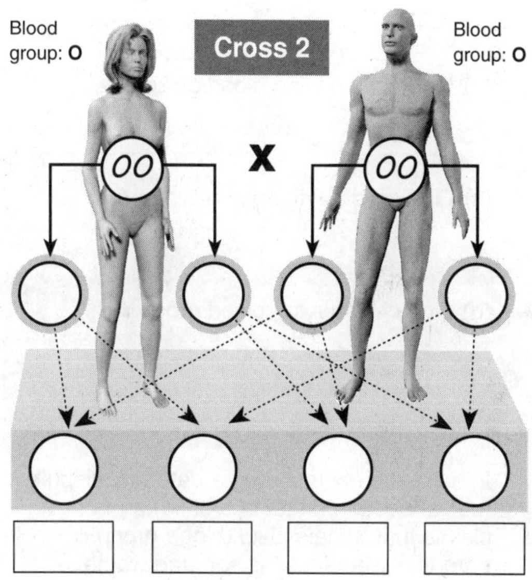

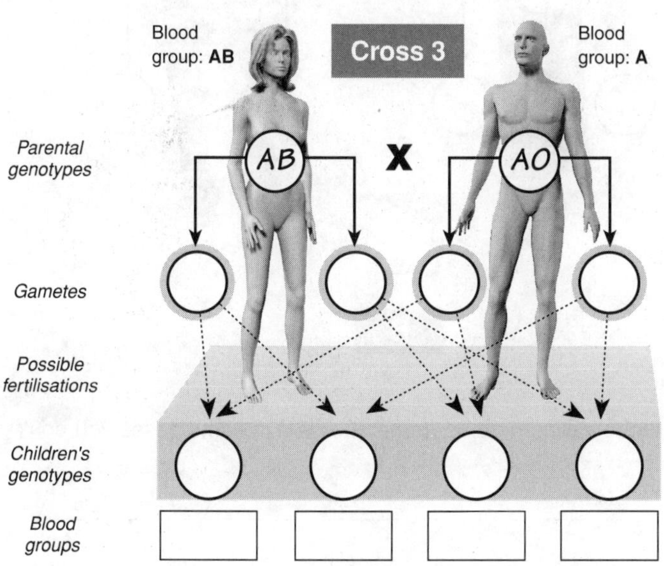

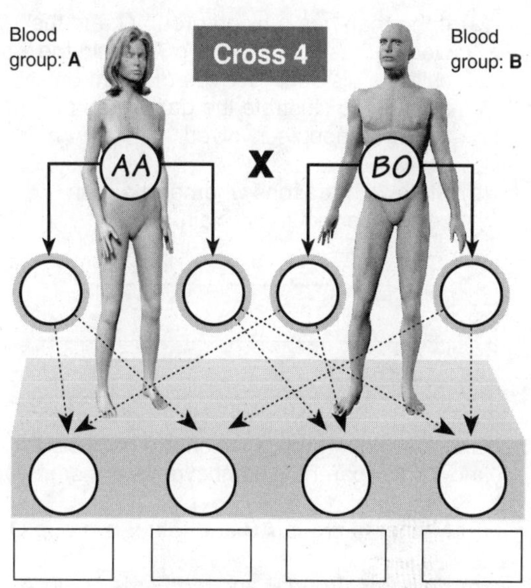

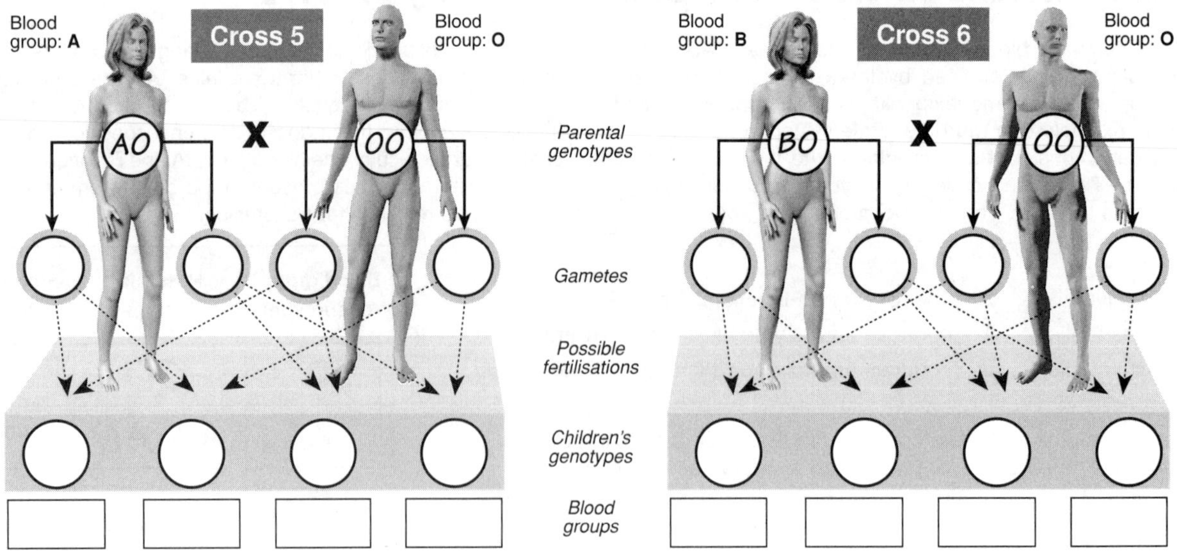

3. A wife is heterozygous for blood group **A** and the husband has blood group **O**.

   (a) Give the genotypes of each parent (fill in spaces on the diagram on the right).

   Determine the probability of:

   (b) One child having blood group **O**: ______________________

   (c) One child having blood group **A**: ______________________

   (d) One child having blood group **AB**: ______________________

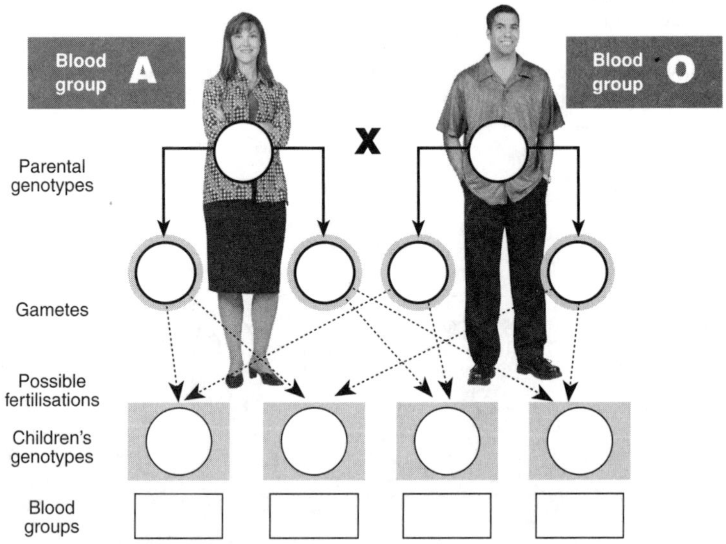

4. In a court case involving a paternity dispute (i.e. who is the father of a child) a man claims that a male child (blood group **B**) born to a woman is his son and wants custody. The woman claims that he is not the father.

   (a) If the man has a blood group **O** and the woman has a blood group **A**, could the child be his son? Use the diagram on the right to illustrate the genotypes of the three people involved.

   (b) State with reasons whether the man can be correct in his claim:

   ____

   ____

   ____

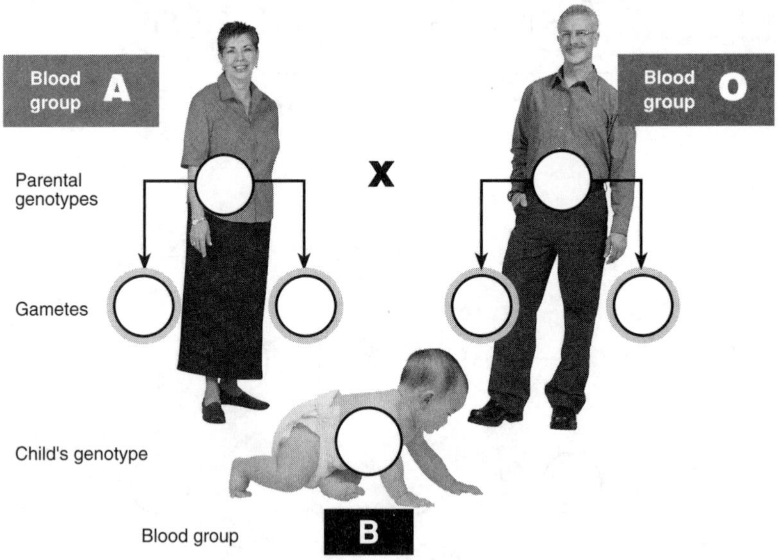

5. Give the blood groups which are possible for children of the following parents (remember that in some cases you don't know if the parent is homozygous or heterozygous).

   (a) Mother is group **AB** and father is group **O**: ______________________

   (b) Father is group **B** and mother is group **A**: ______________________

Sex Linkage

Sex linkage is a special case of linkage occurring when a gene is located on a sex chromosome (usually the X). The result of this is that the character encoded by the gene is usually seen only in one sex (the heterogametic sex) and occurs rarely in the homogametic sex. In humans, recessive sex linked genes are responsible for a number of heritable disorders in males, e.g. haemophilia. Women who have the recessive alleles on their chromosomes are said to be **carriers**. One of the gene loci controlling coat colour in cats is sex-linked. The two alleles, red and non-red (or black), are found only on the X-chromosome.

Allele types

X_o = Non-red (=black)
X_O = Red

Genotypes | **Phenotypes**

X_oX_o, X_oY = Black coated female, male
X_OX_O, X_OY = Orange coated female, male
X_OX_o = Tortoiseshell (intermingled black and orange in fur) in female cats only

1. An owner of a cat is thinking of mating her black female cat with an orange male cat. Before she does this, she would like to know what possible coat colours could result from such a cross. Use the symbols above to fill in the diagram on the right. Summarise the possible genotypes and phenotypes of the kittens in the tables below.

	Genotypes	Phenotypes
Male kittens		

	Genotypes	Phenotypes
Female kittens		

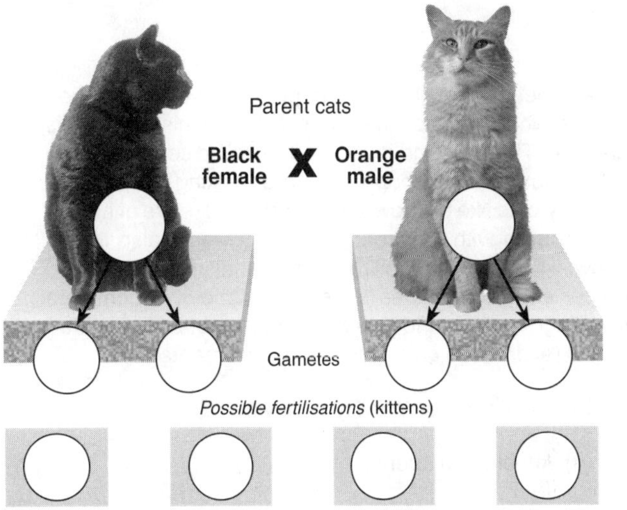

2. A female tortoiseshell cat mated with an unknown male cat in the neighbourhood and has given birth to a litter of six kittens. The owner of this female cat wants to know what the appearance and the genotype of the father was of these kittens. Use the symbols above to fill in the diagram on the right. Also show the possible fertilisations by placing appropriate arrows.

   Describe the father cat's:

   (a) Genotype: ______________________________

   (b) Phenotype: ______________________________

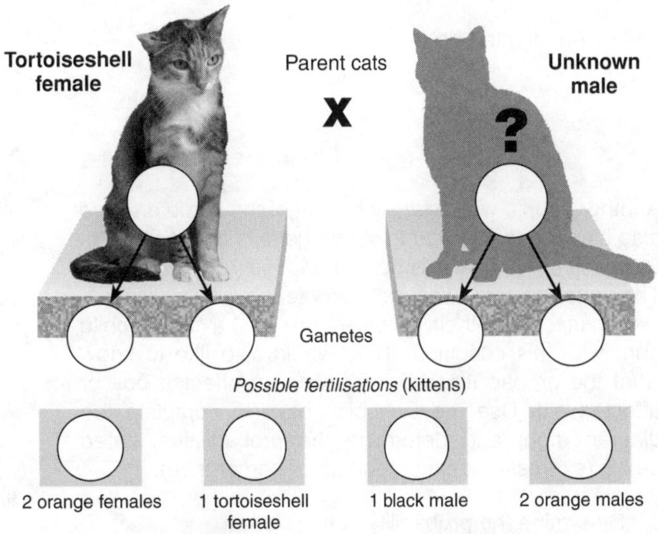

3. The owner of another cat, a black female, also wants to know which cat fathered her two tortoiseshell female and two black male kittens. Use the symbols above to fill in the diagram on the right. Show the possible fertilisations by placing appropriate arrows.

   Describe the father cat's:

   (a) Genotype: ______________________________

   (b) Phenotype: ______________________________

   (c) Was it the same male cat that fathered both this litter and the one above?
   YES / NO *(delete one)*

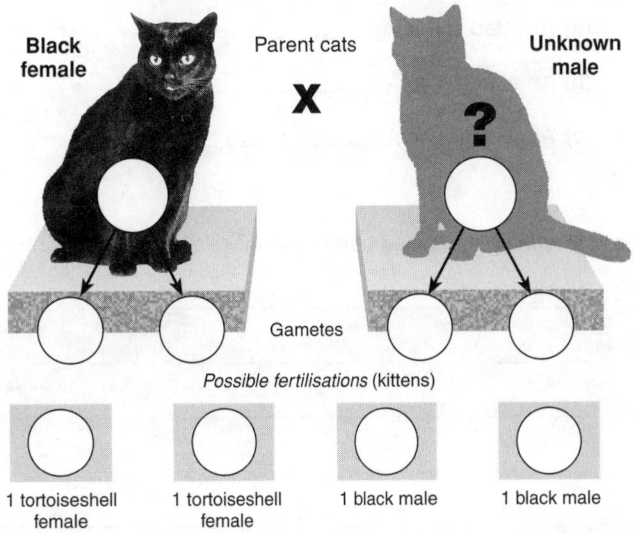

Dominant allele in humans

A rare form of rickets in humans is determined by a **dominant** allele of a gene on the **X chromosome** (it is not found on the Y chromosome). This condition is not successfully treated with vitamin D therapy. The allele types, genotypes, and phenotypes are as follows:

Allele types		Genotypes		Phenotypes
X_R = affected by rickets		X_RX_R, X_RX	=	Affected female
X = normal		X_RY	=	Affected male
		XX, XY	=	Normal female, male

As a genetic counsellor you are presented with a married couple where one of them has a family history of this disease. The husband is affected by this disease and the wife is normal. The couple, who are thinking of starting a family, would like to know what their chances are of having a child born with this condition. They would also like to know what the probabilities are of having an affected boy or affected girl. Use the symbols above to complete the diagram right and determine the probabilities stated below (expressed as a proportion or percentage).

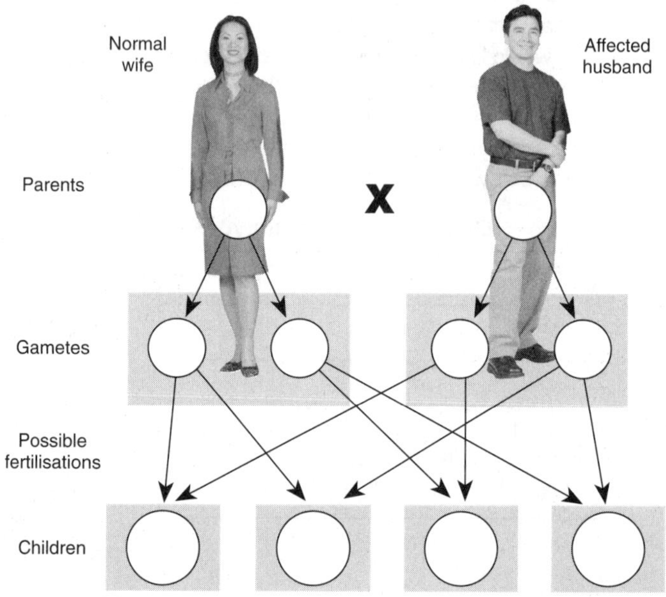

4. Determine the probability of having:

   (a) Affected children: ________________

   (b) An affected girl: ________________

   (c) An affected boy: ________________

Another couple with a family history of the same disease also come in to see you to obtain genetic counselling. In this case the husband is normal and the wife is affected. The wife's father was not affected by this disease. Determine what their chances are of having a child born with this condition. They would also like to know what the probabilities are of having an affected boy or affected girl. Use the symbols above to complete the diagram right and determine the probabilities stated below (expressed as a proportion or percentage).

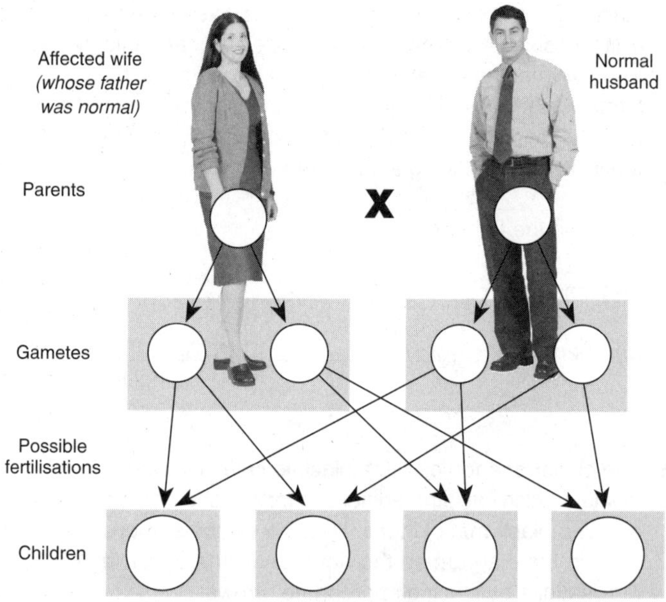

5. Determine the probability of having:

   (a) Affected children: ________________

   (b) An affected girl: ________________

   (c) An affected boy: ________________

6. Describing examples other than those above, discuss the role of **sex linkage** in the inheritance of genetic disorders:

____

____

____

____

____

Inheritance Patterns

Complete the following monohybrid crosses for different types of inheritance patterns in humans: autosomal recessive, autosomal dominant, sex linked recessive, and sex linked dominant inheritance.

1. **Inheritance of autosomal recessive traits**
   Example: *Albinism*

   Albinism (lack of pigment in hair, eyes and skin) is inherited as an autosomal recessive allele (not sex-linked).

   Using the codes: **PP** (normal)
   Pp (carrier)
   pp (albino)

   (a) Enter the parent phenotypes and complete the Punnett square for a cross between two carrier genotypes.

   (b) Give the ratios for the phenotypes from this cross.

   Phenotype ratios: ______________________________

   ____

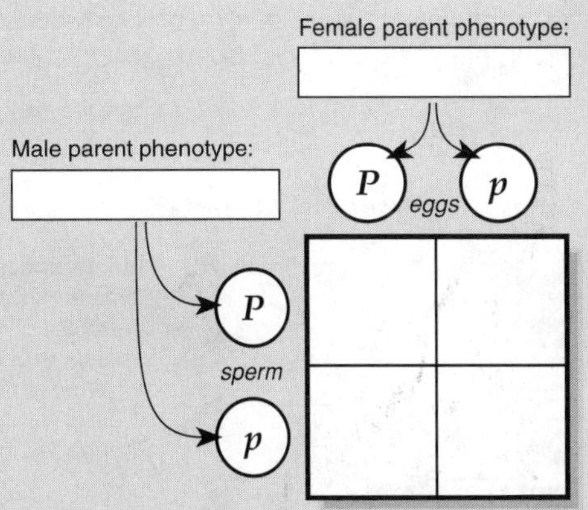

2. **Inheritance of autosomal dominant traits**
   Example: *Woolly hair*

   Woolly hair is inherited as an autosomal dominant allele. Each affected individual will have at least one affected parent.

   Using the codes: **WW** (woolly hair)
   Ww (woolly hair, heterozygous)
   ww (normal hair)

   (a) Enter the parent phenotypes and complete the Punnett square for a cross between two heterozygous individuals.

   (b) Give the ratios for the phenotypes from this cross.

   Phenotype ratios: ______________________________

   ____

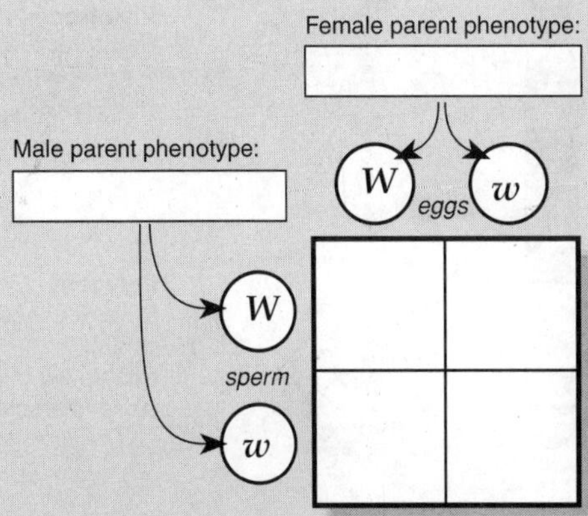

3. **Inheritance of sex linked recessive traits**
   Example: *Haemophilia*

   Inheritance of haemophilia is sex linked. Males with the recessive (haemophilia) allele, are affected. Females can be carriers.

   Using the codes: **XX** (normal female)
   XX_h (carrier female)
   X_hX_h (haemophiliac female)
   XY (normal male)
   X_hY (haemophiliac male)

   (a) Enter the parent phenotypes and complete the Punnett square for a cross between a normal male and a carrier female.

   (b) Give the ratios for the phenotypes from this cross.

   Phenotype ratios: ______________________________

   ____

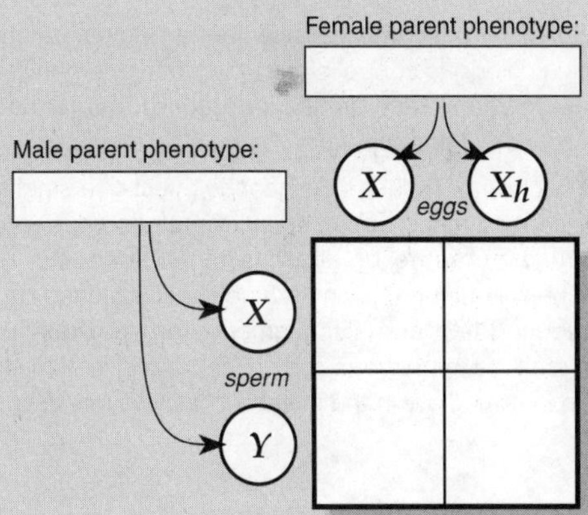

4. **Inheritance of sex linked dominant traits**
   Example: *Sex linked form of rickets*

   A rare form of rickets is inherited on the X chromosome.

   Using the codes: **XX** (normal female); **XY** (normal male)
   X_RX (affected heterozygote female)
   X_RX_R (affected female)
   X_RY (affected male)

   (a) Enter the parent phenotypes and complete the Punnett square for a cross between an affected male and heterozygous female.

   (b) Give the ratios for the phenotypes from this cross.

   Phenotype ratios: ______________________________

   ____

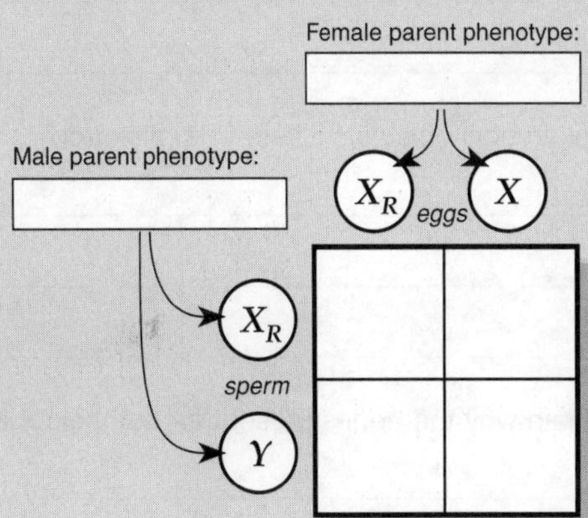

Gene Interactions

It is not always the case the that one gene product produces a single phenotypic character without the influence of other genes. Instead, genes frequently interact to produce the phenotype we finally see. Several genes may control the expression of a single character, or one gene, because of its protein product may have wide ranging phenotypic effects. Some genes, called **epistatic genes**, can even override the expression of other genes, regardless of their dominance status. The gene or genes that are overridden are termed hypostatic. For some of these gene interactions (e.g. epistasis in albinos and pleiotropy in sickle cell disease), the phenotypic effect is the end result of the absence or defectiveness of the functional gene product.

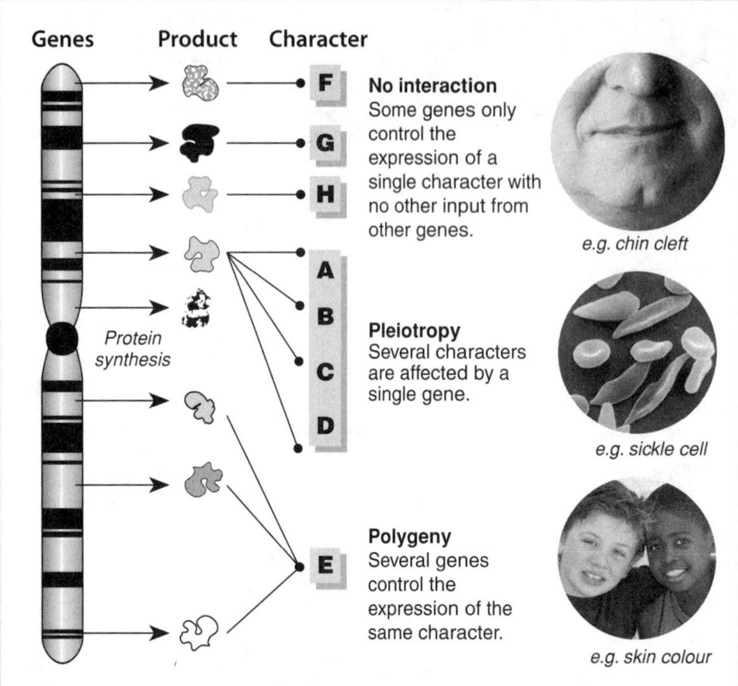

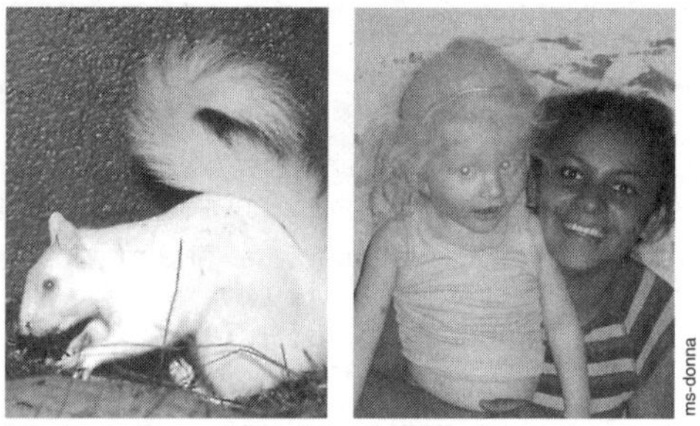

The homozygous condition for the albino allele (cc) overrides any other genes present for hair colour.

A hairline widow's peak, which is a dominant trait (as seen on Jude Law, left) is not evident if the epistatic gene for male pattern baldness is present (right).

Polygeny and Pleiotropy

- Polygeny describes cases where a single phenotypic characteristic (such as skin colour) is controlled by more than one gene. This phenomenon is known as polygeny (polygenic inheritance) and leads to continuous phenotypic variation in the population.
- Pleiotropy describes the genetic effect of a single gene on multiple traits. As a consequence of pleiotropy, a mutation in a gene may have a phenotypic effect on some or all traits simultaneously. The human disease, PKU (phenylketonuria) is one example. This disease causes mental retardation and reduced hair and skin pigmentation, and results from any of a number of mutations in the gene coding for the conversion of phenylalanine to tyrosine, an intermediate in the metabolic pathway leading to melanin production.

Epistasis: One Gene Overrides Others

Epistasis involves two non-allelic genes (at different loci), where the action of one gene masks or otherwise alters the expression of other genes. A common example is **albinism**, which appears in rodents that are homozygous recessive for the 'albino' allele (a mutation) even if they have the alleles for agouti or black fur.

Albinism is widespread in animal phyla. In every case, the presence two albino alleles (cc) overrides pigment expression. Another epistatic gene is that encoding male pattern baldness.

1. Explain the differences between **polygeny** and **pleiotropy**, giving examples to illustrate your answer:

2. Explain how epistasis differs from pleiotropy:

3. Explain why the genes present for hair colour are irrelevant if an animal is homozygous recessive for the albino gene:

***Related activities**: Sickle Cell Mutation, Epistasis, Polygenes*

Epistasis

In its narrowest definition, **epistatic genes** are those that mask the effect of other genes. Typically there are **three possible phenotypes** for a dihybrid cross involving this type of gene interaction. One example is in the genes controlling coat colour in rodents and other mammals. Skin and hair colour is the result of melanin, a pigment which may be either black/brown (**eumelanin**) or reddish/yellow (**phaeomelanin**). Melanin itself is synthesised via several biochemical steps from the amino acid tyrosine. The control of coat colour and patterning in mammals is complex and involves at least five major interacting genes. One of these genes (gene C), controls the production of the pigment melanin, while another gene (gene B), is responsible for whether the colour is black or brown (this interaction is illustrated for mice, below). Epistasis literally means "standing upon". In albinism, the homozygous recessive condition, cc, "stands upon" the other coat colour genes, blocking their expression.

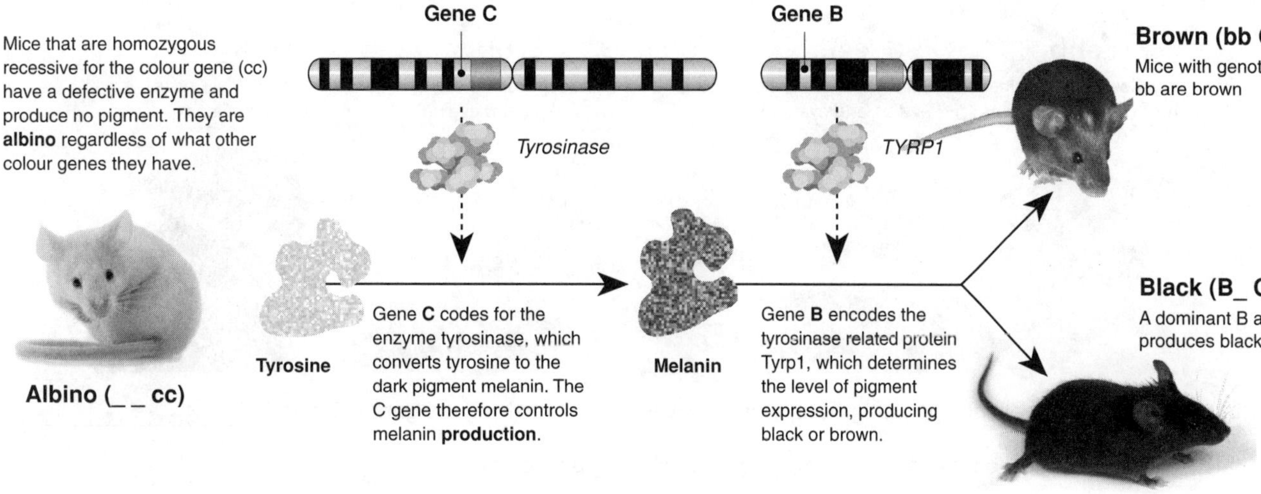

1. State how many phenotypes are possible for a dihybrid cross involving this gene interaction:

   ____

2. State which alleles must be present/absent for the following phenotypes:

   Black: ______________________________

   Brown: ______________________________

   Albino: ______________________________

3. Complete the Punnett square for the F2 (right) by entering the **genotype** and **phenotype** for each possible offspring from BbCc x BbCc. Determine the **ratio** of the phenotypes in this type of cross:

   ____

   ____

   ____

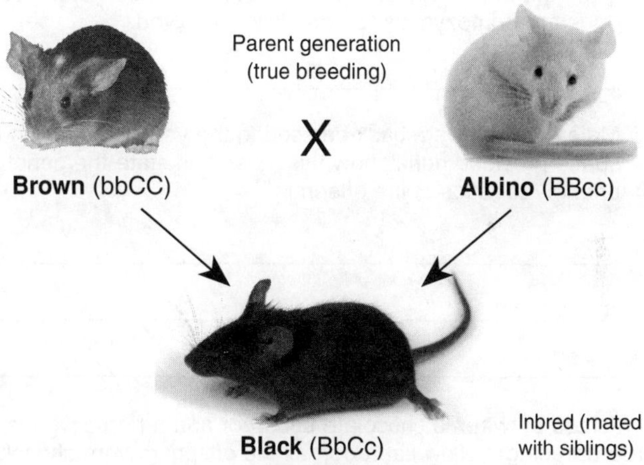

Sperm

Eggs	BC	Bc	bC	bc
BC				
Bc				
bC				
bc				

For the following crosses between parent rats (all homozygous for the genes involved), determine the **phenotypes** and possible **genotypes** of the offspring:

4. A mating of albino with black:

   ____

   ____

5. A mating of brown with black:

   ____

   ____

   ____

Related activities: *Dihybrid Cross*

Allele Combinations and Coat Colour

Epistatic interactions also regulate coat colour in Labrador retrievers. The basic coat colours (yellow, chocolate, and black) are controlled by the interaction of two genes, each with two alleles. The epistatic E gene determines if pigment will be present in the coat, and the B gene determines the pigment density (depth of colour). Dogs with genotype ee will always be yellow, but the presence of bb modifies the effect of any dark pigment. In Labradors, coat colour variation also depends on the influence of the C gene, which always produces phaeomelanin no matter what the E or B genes are producing (in dark coats, it is not visible). As a result, four main coat colour variations are possible in Labradors, with a further three variations possible in the yellow coated dog from dark yellow to very pale (CC, Cc, and cc, but do not confuse the yellow coated variations with the albino gene).

ee
No dark pigment in coat

eebb
yellow coat, brown nose, lips, and eye rims

eeB_
yellow coat, black nose, lips, and eye rims

E_
Dark pigment in coat

E_bb
brown coat, brown nose, lips, and eye rims

E_B_
black coat, black nose, lips, and eye rims

6. State how many main phenotypes are possible for a dihybrid cross involving the genes E and B: ______________

7. State which alleles must be present and absent for the following phenotypes:

Black: ______________________ Brown: ______________________

Yellow with black nose: ______________________ Yellow with brown nose: ______________________

8. (a) State the phenotype and genotype of the F1 in a cross between a male black and a female yellow Labrador. Both dogs are homozygous for the alleles involved:

____

(b) Male F1 dogs were back-crossed to the yellow parent. In the working space provided right, show this cross and state the genotype and phenotype ratios of the offspring:

____

____

____

Working space

9. In a cross between a chocolate Labrador and a homozygous recessive (true-breeding) yellow Labrador, all the offspring were chocolate. Determine the genotype of the chocolate parent:

____

10. In a cross between a black Labrador and a true-breeding chocolate Labrador, 50% of the offspring were chocolate.

(a) Determine the possible genotypes of the black parent:

____

(b) Determine the phenotype(s) of the remaining offspring:

____

11. Explain how epistasis differs from dominance and how this relates to the phenotype in the individual:

____

____

____

Polygenes

Some phenotypes (e.g. kernel colour in maize and skin colour in humans) are determined by more than one gene and show **continuous variation** in a population. The production of the skin pigment melanin in humans is controlled by at least three genes. The amount of melanin produced is directly proportional to the number of dominant alleles for either gene (from 0 to 6).

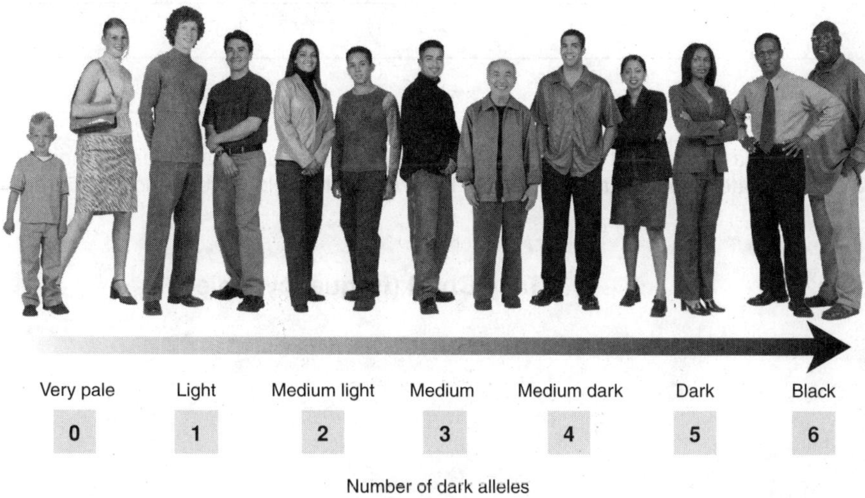

A light-skinned person

A dark-skinned person

There are seven shades skin colour ranging from very dark to very pale, with most individual being somewhat intermediate in skin colour. No dominant allele results in a lack of dark pigment (aabbcc). Full pigmentation (black) requires six dominant alleles (AABBCC).

1. Complete the Punnett square for the F_2 generation (below) by entering the genotypes and the number of dark alleles resulting from a cross between two individuals of intermediate skin colour. Colour-code the offspring appropriately for easy reference.

   (a) State how many of the 64 possible offspring of this cross will have darker skin than their parents:

   ____

   (b) State how many genotypes are possible for this type of gene interaction:

   ____

2. Explain why in reality we see many more than seven shades of skin colour:

   ____

   ____

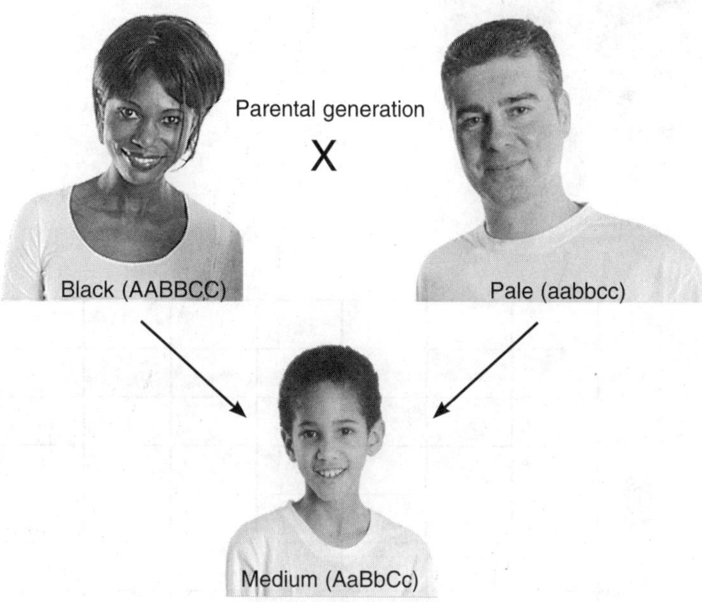

F2 generation (AaBbCc X AaBbCc)

GAMETES	ABC	ABc	AbC	Abc	aBC	aBc	abC	abc
ABC								
ABc								
AbC								
Abc								
aBC								
aBc								
abC								
abc								

3. Discuss the differences between **continuous** and **discontinuous** variation, giving examples to illustrate your answer:

4 From a sample of no less than 30 adults, collect data (by request or measurement) for one continuous variable (e.g. height, weight, shoe size, or hand span). Record and tabulate your results in the space below, and then plot a frequency histogram of the data on the grid below:

Raw data

Tally Chart (frequency table)

Variable: ....

Frequency

(a) Calculate each of the following for your data. See *Descriptive Statistics* if you need help and attach your working:

Mean: ______ **Mode**: ______ **Median**: ______

Standard deviation: ______

(b) Describe the pattern of distribution shown by the graph, giving a reason for your answer: ______

(c) Explain the genetic basis of this distribution: ______

(d) Explain the importance of a large sample size when gathering data relating to a continuous variable:

Problems in Mendelian Genetics

The following problems involve Mendelian crosses through to the F_2 generation. The problems describe genetic crosses involving dominant and recessive alleles, sex linkage, and gene interactions.

1. A recessive allele, a, is responsible for albinism, an ability to produce or deposit melanin in tissues. Humans and a variety of other animals can exhibit this phenotype. In each of the following cases, determine the possible genotypes of the mother and father, and of their children:

   (a) Both parents have normal phenotypes; some of their children are albino and others are unaffected:

   (b) Both parents are albino and have only albino children:

   (c) The woman is unaffected, the man is albino, and they have one albino child and three unaffected children:

2. Male domestic cats may be black or orange. Females may be black, tortoise-shell pattern or orange.

   (a) If these colours are sex-linked, explain these results:

   (b) Using appropriate symbols, determine the phenotypes expected in the offspring from the mating of an orange female to a black male:

   (c) In breeding experiments, a reciprocal cross is a breeding experiment designed to test the role of parental sex on a given inheritance pattern. The parents must be true-breeding. In one cross, a female expressing the trait of interest will be crossed with a male not expressing the trait. In the other (reciprocal) cross, a male expressing the trait is crossed with a female that is not expressing the trait. Determine the phenotypes expected in a **reciprocal cross** of (b):

   (d) A certain kind of mating produces females, half of which are black and half of which are tortoiseshell; half the males are black and half are orange. Determine the phenotypes of the parents in such crosses:

   (e) Another kind of mating produces offspring, 1/4 of which are orange males, 1/4 orange females, 1/4 black males, and 1/4 tortoise-shell females. Determine the phenotypes of the parents in such crosses:

3. Coat colours of Labrador dogs depend on the action of at least two genes. One gene is involved in melanin production; allele B (black) of this gene is dominant to allele b (brown). Another gene influences the deposition of melanin pigment in individual hairs; allele E of this gene promotes deposition, and dogs that are homozygous recessive for this gene (ee) are always yellow. Chocolate Labradors are brown because they have at least one dominant E allele.

   (a) Using the symbols above, indicate the genotype of each Labrador (black, golden, or chocolate) below its photograph.

(b) Determine the outcome (genotype and phenotype) of a cross between a homozygous black Labrador and a homozygous yellow Labrador (the F_1):

Genotype: ____________________ Phenotype: ____________________

(c) Use the Punnett square to show the outcome of a cross between the F_1 (the F_2):

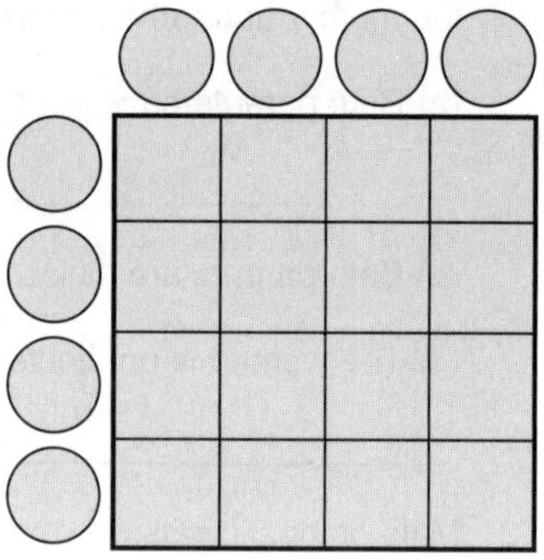

(d) Using ratios, state the genotypes and phenotypes of the F_2 generation:

____

____

____

____

____

(e) Identify this type of gene interaction: ____________________

4. Two mothers give birth to sons at a busy hospital. The son of the first couple has haemophilia, which is a recessive, X-linked disease (see the activity *Inheritance Patterns* in the workbook). Neither parent from couple #1 has the disease. The second couple has a normal (unaffected) son, despite the fact that the father has haemophilia. The two couples challenge the hospital in court, claiming their babies must have been swapped at birth. Your job is to provide expertise to advise whether or not the sons could have been swapped. Explain what would you tell the jury:

____

____

____

____

____

____

5. The sex of fishes is determined by the same XY system as in humans. An allele of one locus on the Y-chromosome for *Lebistes* (guppy) causes a pigmented spot to occur on the dorsal fin. A 'spotted' male fish mates with a female fish that has an unspotted dorsal fin. Describe the phenotypes of the F_1 and F_2 generations from this cross:

____

____

____

____

6. The expression of an allele called 'frizzle' in chickens causes abnormalities of the feathers, and consequently the animal's body temperature is lowered, adversely affecting the functions of many internal organs.

(a) Describe this gene interaction: ____________________

____

(b) Describe another example of the same phenomenon: ____________________

____

____

The Chi-Squared Test in Genetics

The **chi-squared test**, χ^2, is frequently used for testing the outcome of dihybrid crosses against an expected (predicted) Mendelian ratio, and it is appropriate for use in this way. When using the chi-squared test for this purpose, the null hypothesis predicts the ratio of offspring of different phenotypes according to the expected Mendelian ratio for the cross, assuming independent assortment of alleles (no linkage). Significant departures from the predicted Mendelian ratio indicate linkage of the alleles in question. Raw counts should be used and a large sample size is required for the test to be valid.

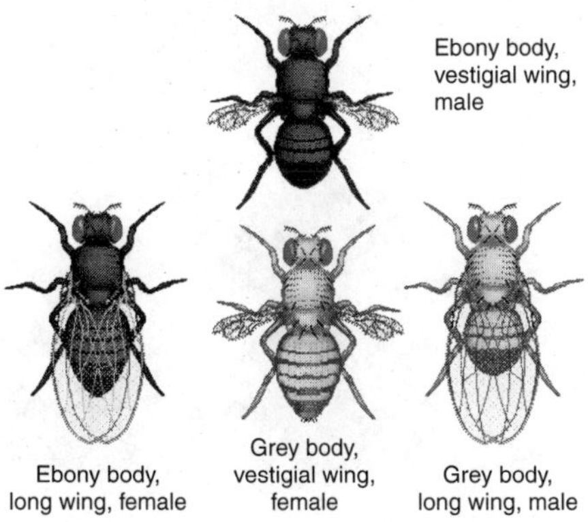

Images of *Drosophila* courtesy of **Newbyte Educational Software**: *Drosophila* Genetics Lab (**www.newbyte.com**)

Using χ^2 in Mendelian Genetics

In a *Drosophila* genetics experiment, two individuals were crossed (the details of the cross are not relevant here). The predicted Mendelian ratios for the offspring of this cross were 1:1:1:1 for each of the four following phenotypes: grey body-long wing, grey body-vestigial wing, ebony body-long wing, ebony body-vestigial wing.The observed results of the cross were not exactly as predicted. The following numbers for each phenotype were observed in the offspring of the cross:

Observed results of the example *Drosophila* cross

Grey body, long wing	**98**	Ebony body, long wing	**102**
Grey body, vestigial wing	**88**	Ebony body, vestigial wing	**112**

Using χ^2, the probability of this result being consistent with a 1:1:1:1 ratio could be tested. Worked example as follows:

Step 1: Calculate the expected value (E)

In this case, this is the sum of the observed values divided by the number of categories (see note below) $\frac{400}{4} = 100$

Step 2: Calculate O – E

The difference between the observed and expected values is calculated as a measure of the deviation from a predicted result. Since some deviations are negative, they are all squared to give positive values. This step is usually performed as part of a tabulation (right, darker grey column).

Step 3: Calculate the value of χ^2

$$\chi^2 = \sum \frac{(O - E)^2}{E}$$

Where: O = the observed result; E = the expected result; $\sum$ = sum of

The calculated χ^2 value is given at the bottom right of the last column in the tabulation.

Step 4: Calculating degrees of freedom

The probability that any particular χ^2 value could be exceeded by chance depends on the number of degrees of freedom. This is simply ***one less than the total number of categories*** (this is the number that could vary independently without affecting the last value). ***In this case: 4–1 = 3.***

Category	O	E	O – E	$(O - E)^2$	$\frac{(O-E)^2}{E}$
Grey, long wing	98	100	–2	4	0.04
Grey, vestigial wing	88	100	–12	144	1.44
Ebony, long wing	102	100	2	4	0.04
Ebony, vestigial wing	112	100	12	144	1.44
	Total = 400				χ^2 → Σ = 2.96

Step 5a: Using the χ^2 table

On the χ^2 table (part reproduced in Table 1 below) with 3 degrees of freedom, the calculated value for χ^2 of 2.96 corresponds to a probability of between 0.2 and 0.5 (see arrow). *This means that by chance alone a χ^2 value of 2.96 could be expected between 20% and 50% of the time.*

Step 5b: Using the χ^2 table

The probability of between 0.2 and 0.5 is higher than the 0.05 value which is generally regarded as significant. The null hypothesis cannot be rejected and we have no reason to believe that the observed results differ significantly from the expected (at $P = 0.05$).

Footnote: Many Mendelian crosses involve ratios other than 1:1. For these, calculation of the expected values is not simply a division of the total by the number of categories. Instead, the total must be apportioned according to the ratio. For example, for a total of 400 as above, in a predicted 9:3:3:1 ratio, the total count must be divided by 16 (9+3+3+1) and the expected values will be 225: 75: 75: 25 in each category.

Table 1: Critical values of χ^2 at different levels of probability. By convention, the critical probability for rejecting the null hypothesis (H_0) is 5%. If the test statistic is less than the tabulated critical value for $P = 0.05$ we cannot reject H_0 and the result is not significant. If the test statistic is greater than the tabulated value for $P = 0.05$ we reject H_0 in favor of the alternative hypothesis.

Degrees of freedom	Level of probability (*P*)									
	0.98	0.95	0.80	0.50	0.20	0.10	0.05	0.02	0.01	0.001
1	0.001	0.004	0.064	0.455	1.64	2.71	3.84	5.41	6.64	10.83
2	0.040	0.103	0.466	1.386	3.22	4.61	5.99	7.82	9.21	13.82
3	0.185	0.352	1.005	2.366	4.64	6.25	7.82	9.84	11.35	16.27
4	0.429	0.711	1.649	3.357	5.99	7.78	9.49	11.67	13.28	18.47
5	0.752	0.145	2.343	4.351	7.29	9.24	11.07	13.39	15.09	20.52

← *Do not reject H_0* | *Reject H_0* →

Using Chi-Squared in Genetics

The following problems examine the use of the chi-squared (χ^2) test in genetics. A worked example of the use of the chi-squared test for a genetic cross is provided on the previous page. Use the table of critical values provided at the bottom of the page.

1. In a tomato plant experiment, two heterozygous individuals were crossed (the details of the cross are not relevant here). The predicted Mendelian ratios for the offspring of this cross were **9:3:3:1** for each of the **four following phenotypes**: purple stem-jagged leaf edge, purple stem-smooth leaf edge, green stem-jagged leaf edge, green stem-smooth leaf edge.

   The observed results of the cross were not exactly as predicted.
   The numbers of offspring with each phenotype are provided below:

Observed results of the tomato plant cross

Purple stem-jagged leaf edge	**12**	Green stem-jagged leaf edge	**8**
Purple stem-smooth leaf edge	**9**	Green stem-smooth leaf edge	**0**

(a) State your null hypothesis for this investigation (Ho): ______________________

(b) State the alternative hypothesis (HA): ______________________

2. Use the chi-squared (χ^2) test to determine if the differences observed between the phenotypes are significant. The table of critical values of χ^2 at different *P* values is provided on the previous page.

   (a) Enter the observed values (number of individuals) and complete the table to calculate the χ^2 value:

Category	O	E	O — E	(O — E)^2	$\frac{(O-E)^2}{E}$
Purple stem, jagged leaf					
Purple stem, smooth leaf					
Green stem, jagged leaf					
Green stem, smooth leaf					
	Σ				Σ

   (b) Calculate χ^2 value using the equation:

$$\chi^2 = \sum \frac{(O-E)^2}{E}$$

   χ^2 = ________

   (c) Calculate the degrees of freedom: ________

   (d) Using the χ^2 table, state the *P* value corresponding to your calculated χ^2 value:

   ____

   (e) State your decision: reject Ho / do not reject Ho

   (circle one)

3. Students carried out a pea plant experiment, where two heterozygous individuals were crossed. The predicted Mendelian ratios for the offspring were **9:3:3:1** for each of the **four following phenotypes**: round-yellow seed, round-green seed, wrinkled-yellow seed, wrinkled-green seed.

   The observed results were as follows:

Round-yellow seed	**441**	Wrinkled-yellow seed	**143**
Round-green seed	**159**	Wrinkled-green seed	**57**

   Use a separate piece of paper to complete the following:

   (a) State the null and alternative hypotheses (Ho and HA).

   (b) Calculate the χ^2 value.

   (c) Calculate the degrees of freedom and state the *P* value corresponding to your calculated χ^2 value.

   (d) State whether or not you reject your null hypothesis: reject Ho / do not reject Ho (circle one)

4. Comment on the whether the χ^2 values obtained above are similar. Suggest a reason for any difference:

____

____

***Related activities:** Chi-Squared test in Genetics*

Gene-Environment Interactions

External environmental factors can modify the phenotype encoded by genes. This can occur both during development and later in life. Even identical twins have minor differences in their appearance due to environmental factors such as diet and intrauterine environment before birth. Environmental factors that affect the phenotype of plants and animals include nutrients or diet, temperature, altitude or latitude, and the presence of other organisms.

Sources of Variation in Organisms

Sources of genetic variation

Dominant alleles
Recessive alleles
Mutations
Crossing over
Independent assortment
Gene interactions

Sources of environmentally induced variation

Climate and altitude
Water availability
Acidity (pH)
Soil type
Light
Predation
Competition

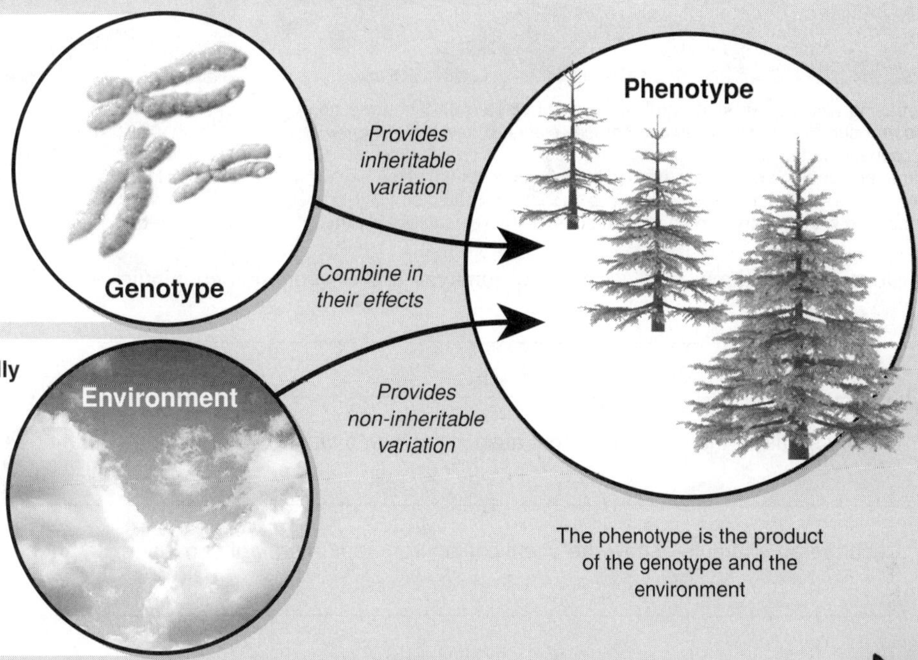

The phenotype is the product of the genotype and the environment

The Effect of Temperature

The sex of some animals is determined by the temperature at which they were incubated during their embryonic development. Examples include turtles, crocodiles, and the American alligator. In some species, high incubation temperatures produce males and low temperatures produce females. In other species, the opposite is true. Temperature regulated sex determination may be advantageous by preventing inbreeding (since all siblings will tend to be of the same sex).

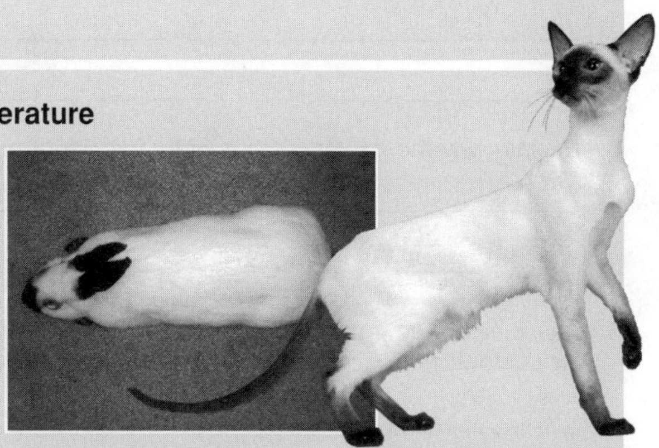

Colour-pointing in breeds of cats and rabbits (e.g. Siamese, Himalyan) is a result of a temperature sensitive mutation in one of the enzymes in the metabolic pathway from tyrosine to melanin. The dark pigment is only produced in the cooler areas of the body (face, ears, feet, and tail), while the rest of the body is a paler version of the same colour, or white.

The Effect of Other Organisms

The presence of other individuals of the same species may control sex determination for some animals. Some fish species, including some in the wrasse family (e.g. *Coris sandageri,* above), show this phenomenon. The fish live in groups consisting of a single male with attendant females and juveniles. In the presence of a male, all juvenile fish of this species grow into females. When the male dies, the dominant female will undergo physiological changes to become a male. The male has distinctive bands, whereas the female is pale in colour and has very faint markings.

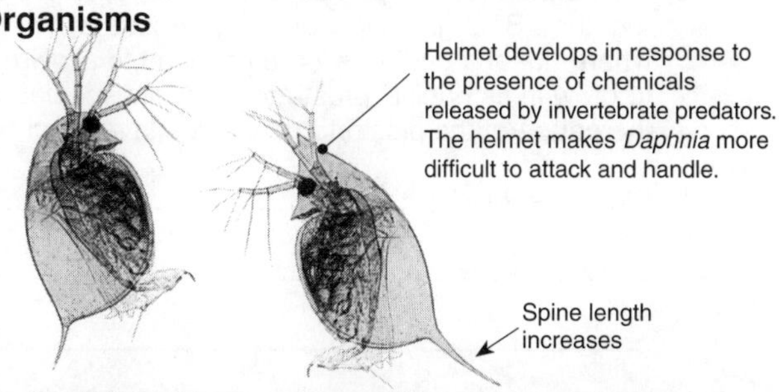

Non-helmeted form **Helmeted form with long tail spine**

Some organisms respond to the presence of other, potentially harmful, organisms by changing their morphology or body shape. Invertebrates such as *Daphnia* will grow a large helmet when a predatory midge larva is present. Such responses are usually mediated through chemicals produced by the predator (or competitor), and are common in plants as well as animals.

The Effect of Altitude

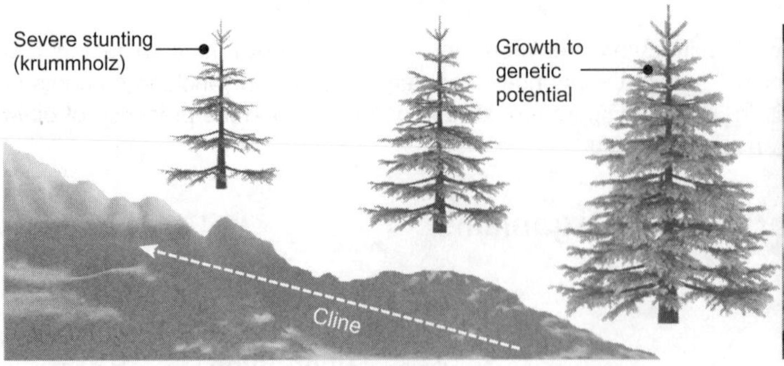

Increasing altitude can stunt the phenotype of plants with the same genotype. In some conifers, e.g. Engelmann spruce, plants at low altitude grow to their full genetic potential, but become progressively more stunted as elevation increases, forming krummholz (gnarled bushy growth forms) at the highest, most severe sites. A continuous gradation in a phenotypic character within a species, associated with a change in an environmental variable, is called a cline.

The Effect of Chemical Environment

The chemical environment can influence the expressed phenotype in both plants and animals. In hydrangeas, flower colour varies according to soil pH. Flowers are blue in more acid soils (pH 5.0-5.5), but pink in more alkaline soils (pH 6.0-6.5). The blue colour is due to the presence of aluminium compounds in the flowers and aluminium is more readily available when the soil pH is low.

1. Describe an example to illustrate how genotype and environment contribute to phenotype: ______

2. Identify some of the physical factors associated with altitude that could affect plant phenotype: ______

3. Describe an example of how the chemical environment of a plant can influence phenotype: ______

4. Explain why the darker patches of fur in colour-pointed cats and rabbits are found only on the face, paws and tail: ______

5. There has been much amusement over the size of record-breaking vegetables, such as enormous pumpkins, produced for competitions. Explain how you could improve the chance that a vegetable would reach its maximum genetic potential: ______

6. (a) Explain what is meant by a **cline**: ______

   (b) On a windswept portion of a coast, two different species of plant (species A and species B) were found growing together. Both had a low growing (prostrate) phenotype. One of each plant type was transferred to a greenhouse where "ideal" conditions were provided to allow maximum growth. In this controlled environment, species B continued to grow in its original prostrate form, but species A changed its growing pattern and became erect in form. Identify the **cause** of the prostrate phenotype in each of the coastal grown plant species and explain your answer:

   Plant species A: ______

   Plant species B: ______

   (c) Identify which of these species (A or B) would be most likely to exhibit clinal variation: ______

KEY TERMS: Flash Card Game

The cards below have a keyword or term printed on one side and its definition printed on the opposite side. The aim is to win as many cards as possible from the table. To play the game.....

1) Cut out the cards and lay them definition side down on the desk. You will need one set of cards between two students.
2) Taking turns, choose a card and, BEFORE you pick it up, state your own best definition of the keyword to your opponent.
3) Check the definition on the opposite side of the card. If both you and your opponent agree that your stated definition matches, then keep the card. If your definition does not match then return the card to the desk.
4) Once your turn is over, your opponent may choose a card.

Allele	Homozygous	Meiosis
Dominant	Phenotype	Discontinuous variation
Heterozygous	Recessive	Codominant
Continuous variation	Epistasis	Recombination
Genotype	Crossing over	Chi squared test
Homologous chromosome	Locus (pl. loci)	Independent assortment

When you've finished the game keep these cutouts and use them as flash cards!

The process of double nuclear division (reduction division) to produce four nuclei, each containing half the original number of chromosomes (haploid).	Possessing two identical alleles of a particular gene (e.g AA), one inherited from each parent.	One of a number of alternative versions of a gene that can occupy a given genetic locus on a chromosome.
Variation between individuals of a population in which differences are marked and phenotypes are discrete.	Observable characteristics in an organism.	Allele that expresses its trait irrespective of the other allele.
Inheritance in which both alleles in a heterozygous organism are equally and independently expressed in the phenotype.	Allele that will only express its trait in the absence of the dominant allele. (i.e. when both recessive alleles are present).	Possessing two different alleles for a particular gene (e.g. Aa), one inherited from each parent.
The exchange of alleles between homologous chromosomes as a result of crossing over.	Gene interaction where one gene masks or otherwise alters the expression of another gene.	Variation between individuals of a population in which differences are the result of polygenic interactions and the phenotypic variation exhibits a normal distribution.
Statistical test for determining the significance of departures of observed data from an expected result.	Event during meiosis where two homologous chromosomes exchange genetic material.	The allele combination of an organism. The genotype determines the genetic potential of the individual (e.g. potential to grow to a certain height).
The random allocation of chromosomes to newly forming gametes.	The position of a gene on a chromosome.	Chromosome pairs, one paternal and one maternal, of the same length, centromere position, and staining pattern, with genes for the same characteristics at corresponding loci.

UNIT F215

5.1.2 Variation and Evolution

KEY CONCEPTS

- Variation provides the raw material for natural selection.
- Natural selection and genetic drift contribute to change in allele frequencies in populations over time.
- Natural selection operates in the prevailing environment and may be stabilising or a force of change.
- Selection and isolation are important in speciation.
- Biological and phylogenetic species are determined using different criteria.
- Artificial selection has produced modern livestock breeds and crop varieties.

KEY TERMS

allele frequency
artificial selection (=selective breeding)
balanced polymorphism
balancing selection
biological species concept (BSC)
deme
directional selection
disruptive selection
ecological isolating mechanism
founder effect
gene flow
gene pool
genetic bottleneck
genetic equilibrium
Hardy-Weinberg equation
isolating mechanism
natural selection
phylogenetic species concept (PSC)
reproductive isolating mechanism
stabilising selection
temporal isolating mechanism

Periodicals:
Listings for this chapter are on page 341

Weblinks:
www.biozone.co.uk/weblink/OCR-A2-2832.html

Teacher Resource CD-ROM:
Darwin's Theory

OBJECTIVES

☐ 1. Use the **KEY TERMS** to help you understand and complete these objectives.

Variation and selection — page 129

☐ 2. Recall the sources of **variation** in populations and explain how variation provides the raw material on which selection can act.

Processes in gene pools — pages 160-176

☐ 3. BACKGROUND: Explain the terms **gene pool** and **allele frequency**. Recognise that populations may be of various sizes and geographical extent. Explain how allele frequencies are expressed for a population

☐ 4. State the (Hardy-Weinberg) principle of **genetic equilibrium**. State the conditions required for **genetic equilibrium** in a population and explain the consequences of these conditions rarely, if ever, being satisfied.

☐ 5. Use the **Hardy-Weinberg equation** to calculate allele frequencies.

☐ 6. Explain how the environment in which selection acts can be a stabilising influence or promote evolutionary change. Describe examples of **stabilising**, **directional**, **balancing**, and **disruptive selection** and relate these to the prevailing environment. Examples could include:
- Human skin colour as a result of opposing selective forces.
- Directional selection resulting in transient polymorphism as shown by industrial melanism in peppered moths during the Industrial Revolution.
- The sickle cell trait as the basis for balanced polymorphism in malarial regions.

☐ 7. UNDERSTANDING: Use diagrams to demonstrate natural selection, genetic drift, gene flow, and mutation in a gene pool. Identify which of these increase genetic variation in populations and which decrease it.

☐ 8. Explain genetic drift and how it may lead to loss or fixation of alleles. Describe the conditions under which genetic drift is important, e.g. in populations subjected to the **founder effect** or **genetic bottlenecks**.

Selection and speciation — pages 177-183

☐ 9. Explain the role of natural selection and isolating mechanisms in **speciation**. Describe examples of isolating mechanisms with reference to **ecological**, seasonal (**temporal**), and **reproductive isolating mechanisms**.

☐ 10. Explain the significance of the various concepts of a species, with reference to the **biological species concept** and the **phylogenetic species concept**.

☐ 11. Define the term **artificial selection** (**selective breeding**) and explain its genetic basis. Compare and contrast artificial selection and natural selection.

☐ 12. Describe how artificial selection has produced modern crop varieties and livestock breeds, as illustrated by modern bread wheat and dairy cattle.

Small Flies and Giant Buttercups

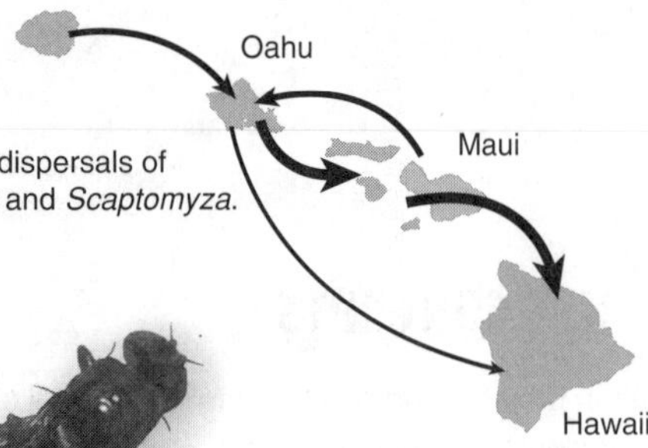

The major dispersals of *Drosophila* and *Scaptomyza.*

Drosophila setosimentum, a picture winged fly.

Photo: Karl Magnacca

Drosophilidae (commonly known as fruit flies) are a group of small flies found almost everywhere in the world. Two genera, *Drosophila* and *Scaptomyza* are found in the Hawaiian islands and between them there are more than 800 species present on a land area of just 16,500 km^2; it is one of the densest concentrations of related species found anywhere. The flies range from 1.5 mm to 20 mm in length and display a startling range of wing forms and patterns, body shapes and colours, and head and leg shapes. This diverse array of species and characteristics has made these flies the subject of much evolutionary and genetics research. Genetic analyses show that they are all related to a single species that may have arrived on the islands around 8 million years ago and diversified to exploit a range of unoccupied niches. Older species appear on the older islands and more recent species appear as one moves from the oldest to the newest islands. Such evidence points to numerous colonisation events as new islands emerged from the sea. The volcanic nature of the islands means that newly isolated environments are a frequent occurrence. For example, forested areas may become divided by lava flows, so that flies in one region diverge rapidly from flies in another just tens of metres away. One such species is *D. silvestris.* Males have a series of hairs on their forelegs, which they brush against females during courtship. Males in the northeastern part of the island have many more of these hairs than the males on the southwestern side of the island. While still the same species, the two demes are already displaying structural and behavioural isolation. Behavioural isolation is clearly an important phenomenon in drosophilid speciation. A second species, *D. heteroneura*, is closely related to *D. silvestris* and the two species live sympatrically. Although hybrid offspring are fully viable, hybridisation rarely occurs because male courtship displays are very different.

New Zealand alpine buttercups (*Ranunculus*) are some of the largest in the world and are also the product of repeated speciation events. There are 14 species of *Ranunculus* in New Zealand; more than in the whole of North and South America combined. They occupy five distinct habitats ranging from snowfields and scree slopes to bogs. Genetic studies have shown that this diversity is the result of numerous isolation events following the growth and recession of glaciers. As the glaciers retreat, alpine habitat becomes restricted and populations are isolated at the tops of mountains. This restricts gene flow and provides the environment for species divergence. When the glaciers expand again, the extent of the alpine habitat increases, allowing isolated populations to come in contact and closely related species to hybridise.

1. Explain why so many drosophilidae are present in Hawaii: ____________________

2. Explain why these flies are of interest: ____________________

3. Describe the relationship between the age of the islands and the age of the fly species: ____________________

4. Explain why New Zealand has so many alpine buttercups: ____________________

Gene Pools and Evolution

The diagram below illustrates the dynamic nature of **gene pools**. It portrays two imaginary populations of one beetle species. Each beetle is a 'carrier' of genetic information, represented here by the alleles (A and a) for a single **codominant gene** that controls the beetle's colour. Normally, there are three versions of the phenotype: black, dark, and pale. Mutations may create other versions of the phenotype. Some of the **microevolutionary processes** that can affect the genetic composition (**allele frequencies**) of the gene pool are illustrated below. Some are discussed in more detail in subsequent activities.

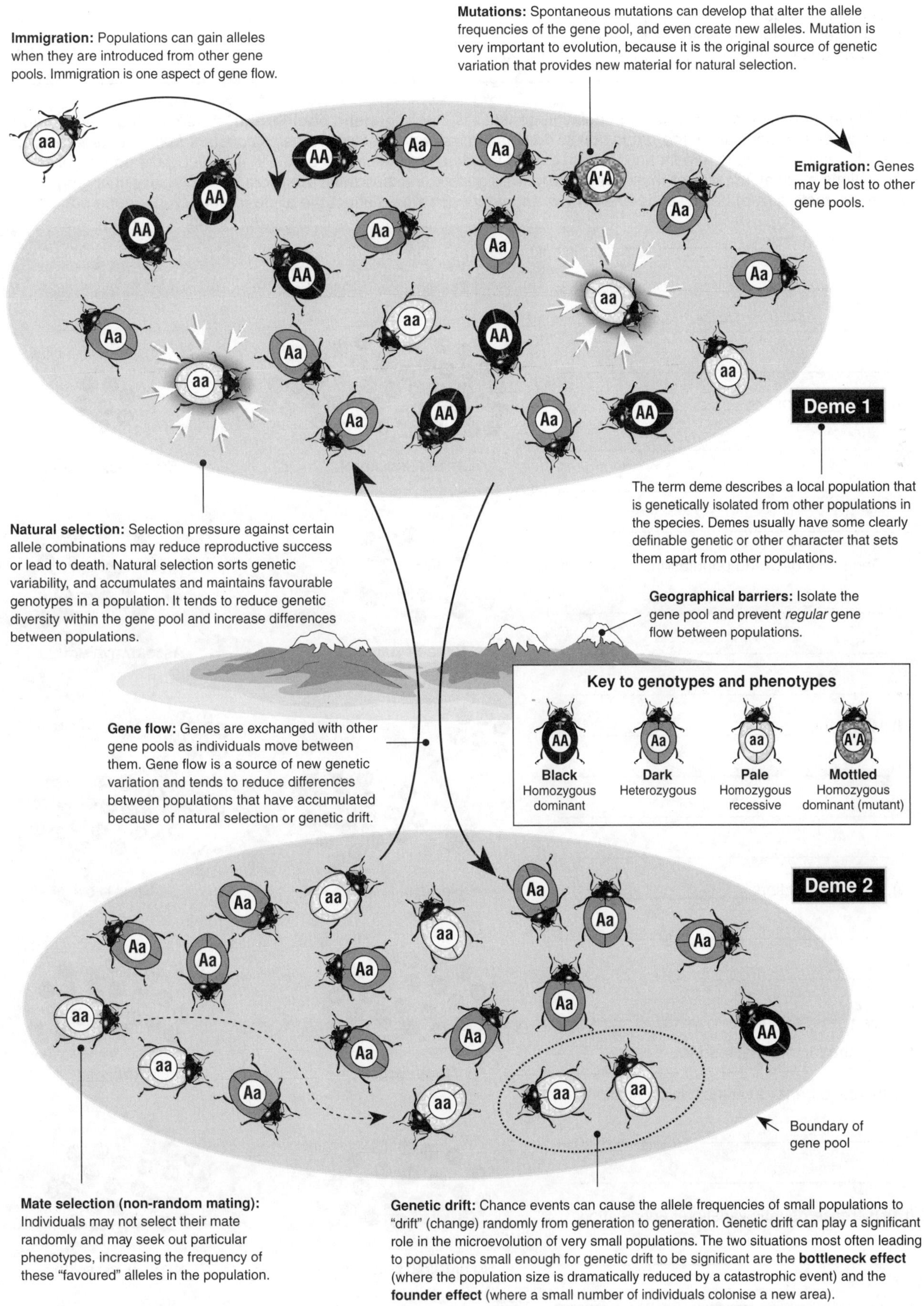

Related activities: *Natural Selection, Sexual Selection, Genetic Drift*
Web links: *Mechanisms of Evolution, Speciation, Changes in a Gene Pool*

1. For each of the two demes shown on the previous page (treating the mutant in deme 1 as AA):

   (a) Count up the numbers of **allele types** (**A** and **a**).

   (b) Count up the numbers of **allele combinations** (**AA, Aa, aa**).

2. Calculate the frequencies as percentages (%) for the allele types and combinations:

Deme 1		Number counted	%
Allele types	**A**		
	a		
Allele combinations	**AA**		
	Aa		
	aa		

Deme 2		Number counted	%
Allele types	**A**		
	a		
Allele combinations	**AA**		
	Aa		
	aa		

3. One of the fundamental concepts for population genetics is that of **genetic equilibrium**, stated as: *"For a very large, randomly mating population, the proportion of dominant to recessive alleles remains constant from one generation to the next"*. If a gene pool is to remain unchanged, it must satisfy all of the criteria below that favour gene pool stability. Few populations meet all (or any) of these criteria and their genetic makeup must therefore be continually changing. For each of the five factors (a-e) below, state briefly **how** and **why** each would affect the allele frequency in a gene pool:

   (a) Population size: ______________________

   ____

   ____

   ____

   (b) Mate selection: ______________________

   ____

   ____

   ____

   (c) Gene flow between populations:

   ____

   ____

   ____

   (d) Mutations: ______________________

   ____

   ____

   ____

   (e) Natural selection: ______________________

   ____

   ____

   ____

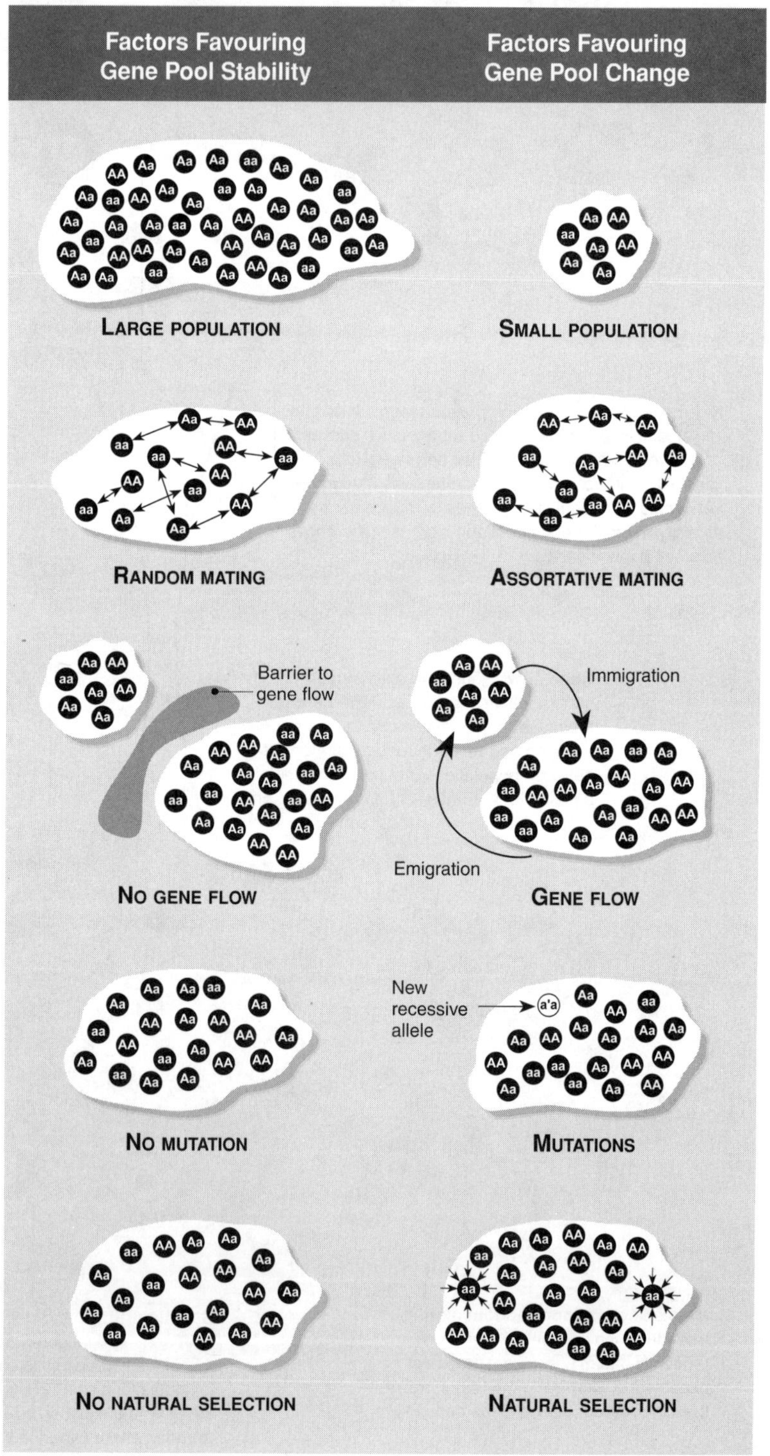

4. Identify the factors that tend to:

   (a) Increase genetic variation in populations:

   ____

   ____

   (b) Decrease genetic variation in populations:

   ____

   ____

Hardy-Weinberg Calculations

The **Hardy-Weinberg equation** provides a simple mathematical model of genetic equilibrium in a gene pool, but its main application in population genetics is in calculating allele and genotype frequencies in populations, particularly as a means of studying changes and measuring their rate. The use of the Hardy-Weinberg equation is described below.

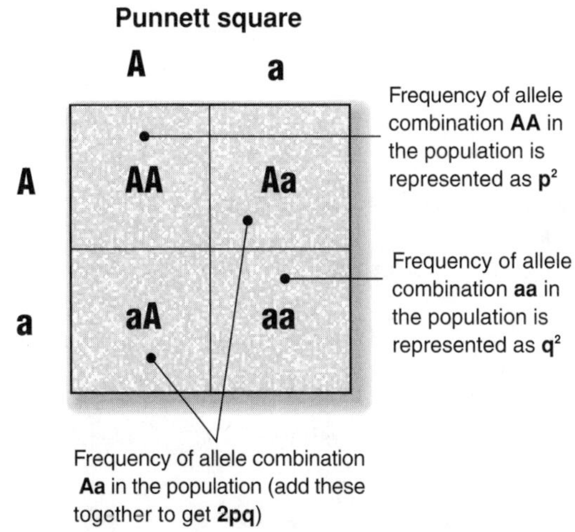

$$(p + q)^2 = p^2 + 2pq + q^2 = 1$$

Frequency of allele types	Frequency of allele combinations
p = Frequency of allele A	p^2 = Frequency of AA (homozygous dominant)
q = Frequency of allele a	2pq = Frequency of Aa (heterozygous)
	q^2 = Frequency of aa (homozygous recessive)

The Hardy-Weinberg equation is applied to populations with a simple genetic situation: dominant and recessive alleles controlling a single trait. The frequency of all of the dominant (A) and recessive alleles (a) equals the total genetic complement, and adds up to 1 or 100% of the alleles present.

How To Solve Hardy-Weinberg Problems

In most populations, the frequency of two alleles of interest is calculated from the proportion of homozygous recessives (q^2), as this is the only genotype identifiable directly from its phenotype. If only the dominant phenotype is known, q^2 may be calculated (1 – the frequency of the dominant phenotype). The following steps outline the procedure for solving a Hardy-Weinberg problem:

Remember that all calculations must be carried out using proportions, NOT PERCENTAGES!

1. Examine the question to determine what piece of information you have been given about the population. In most cases, this is the percentage or frequency of the homozygous recessive phenotype q^2, or the dominant phenotype $p^2 + 2pq$ (see note above).
2. The first objective is to find out the value of p or q, If this is achieved, then every other value in the equation can be determined by simple calculation.
3. Take the square root of q^2 to find q.
4. Determine p by subtracting q from 1 (i.e. p = 1 – q).
5. Determine p^2 by multiplying p by itself (i.e. $p^2 = p \times p$).
6. Determine 2pq by multiplying p times q times 2.
7. Check that your calculations are correct by adding up the values for $p^2 + q^2 + 2pq$ (the sum should equal 1 or 100%).

Worked example

In the American white population approximately 70% of people can taste the chemical phenylthiocarbamide (PTC) (the dominant phenotype), while 30% are non-tasters (the recessive phenotype).

Determine the frequency of:	***Answers***
(a) Homozygous recessive phenotype(**q^2**).	30% - provided
(b) The dominant allele (**p**).	45.2%
(c) Homozygous tasters (**p^2**).	20.5%
(d) Heterozygous tasters (**2pq**).	49.5%

Data: The frequency of the dominant phenotype (70% tasters) and recessive phenotype (30% non-tasters) are provided.

Working:
Recessive phenotype: **q^2** = 30%
use 0.30 for calculation
therefore: **q** = 0.5477
square root of 0.30
therefore: **p** = 0.4523
1 – q = p
1 – 0.5477 = 0.4523

Use p and q in the equation (top) to solve any unknown:
Homozygous dominant **p^2** = 0.2046
(p x p = 0.4523 x 0.4523)
Heterozygous: **2pq** = 0.4953

1. A population of hamsters has a gene consisting of 90% M alleles (black) and 10% m alleles (grey). Mating is random.
Data: Frequency of recessive allele (10% m) and dominant allele (90% M).

Determine the proportion of offspring that will be black and the proportion that will be grey (show your working):

____

____

Recessive allele:	q	=	
Dominant allele:	p	=	
Recessive phenotype:	q^2	=	
Homozygous dominant:	p^2	=	
Heterozygous:	2pq	=	

2. You are working with pea plants and found 36 plants out of 400 were dwarf.
Data: Frequency of recessive phenotype (36 out of 400 = 9%)

(a) Calculate the frequency of the tall gene: ____________________

(b) Determine the number of heterozygous pea plants:

____

____

Recessive allele:	q	=	
Dominant allele:	p	=	
Recessive phenotype:	q^2	=	
Homozygous dominant:	p^2	=	
Heterozygous:	$2pq$	=	

3. In humans, the ability to taste the chemical phenylthiocarbamide (PTC) is inherited as a simple dominant characteristic. Suppose you found out that 360 out of 1000 college students could not taste the chemical.
Data: Frequency of recessive phenotype (360 out of 1000).

(a) State the frequency of the gene for tasting PTC:

____

(b) Determine the number of heterozygous students in this population:

____

Recessive allele:	q	=	
Dominant allele:	p	=	
Recessive phenotype:	q^2	=	
Homozygous dominant:	p^2	=	
Heterozygous:	$2pq$	=	

4. A type of deformity appears in 4% of a large herd of cattle. Assume the deformity was caused by a recessive gene.
Data: Frequency of recessive phenotype (4% deformity).

(a) Calculate the percentage of the herd that are carriers of the gene:

____

(b) Determine the frequency of the dominant gene in this case:

____

Recessive allele:	q	=	
Dominant allele:	p	=	
Recessive phenotype:	q^2	=	
Homozygous dominant:	p^2	=	
Heterozygous:	$2pq$	=	

5. Assume you placed 50 pure bred black guinea pigs (dominant allele) with 50 albino guinea pigs (recessive allele) and allowed the population to attain genetic equilibrium (several generations have passed).
Data: Frequency of recessive allele (50%) and dominant allele (50%).

Determine the proportion (%) of the population that becomes white:

____

Recessive allele:	q	=	
Dominant allele:	p	=	
Recessive phenotype:	q^2	=	
Homozygous dominant:	p^2	=	
Heterozygous:	$2pq$	=	

6. It is known that 64% of a large population exhibit the recessive trait of a characteristic controlled by two alleles (one is dominant over the other).
Data: Frequency of recessive phenotype (64%). Determine the following:

(a) The frequency of the recessive allele: ____________________

(b) The percentage that are heterozygous for this trait: ____________________

(c) The percentage that exhibit the dominant trait: ____________________

(d) The percentage that are homozygous for the dominant trait: ____________________

(e) The percentage that has one or more recessive alleles: ____________________

7. Albinism is recessive to normal pigmentation in humans. The frequency of the albino allele was 10% in a population.
Data: Frequency of recessive allele (10% albino allele).

Determine the proportion of people that you would expect to be albino:

____

____

____

Recessive allele:	q	=	
Dominant allele:	p	=	
Recessive phenotype:	q^2	=	
Homozygous dominant:	p^2	=	
Heterozygous:	$2pq$	=	

Analysis of a Squirrel Gene Pool

In Olney, Illinois, in the United States, there is a unique population of albino (white) and grey squirrels. Between 1977 and 1990, students at Olney Central College carried out a study of this population. They recorded the frequency of grey and albino squirrels. The albinos displayed a mutant allele expressed as an albino phenotype only in the homozygous recessive condition. The data they collected are provided in the table below. Using the **Hardy-Weinberg equation** for calculating genotype frequencies, it was possible to estimate the frequency of the normal 'wild' allele (G) providing grey fur colouring, and the frequency of the mutant albino allele (g) producing white squirrels. This study provided real, first hand, data that students could use to see how genotype frequencies can change in a real population.

Thanks to **Dr. John Stencel**, Olney Central College, Olney, Illinois, US, for providing the data for this exercise.

Grey squirrel, usual colour form

Albino form of grey squirrel

Population of grey and white squirrels in Olney, Illinois (1977-1990)

Year	Grey	White	Total	GG	Gg	gg	Freq. of g	Freq. of G
1977	602	182	784	26.85	49.93	23.21	48.18	51.82
1978	511	172	683	24.82	50.00	25.18	50.18	49.82
1979	482	134	616	28.47	49.77	21.75	46.64	53.36
1980	489	133	622	28.90	49.72	21.38	46.24	53.76
1981	536	163	699	26.74	49.94	23.32	48.29	51.71
1982	618	151	769	31.01	49.35	19.64	44.31	55.69
1983	419	141	560	24.82	50.00	25.18	50.18	49.82
1984	378	106	484	28.30	49.79	21.90	46.80	53.20
1985	448	125	573	28.40	49.78	21.82	46.71	53.29
1986	536	155	691	27.71	49.86	22.43	47.36	52.64
1987	*No data collected this year*							
1988	652	122	774	36.36	47.88	15.76	39.70	60.30
1989	552	146	698	29.45	49.64	20.92	45.74	54.26
1990	603	111	714	36.69	47.76	15.55	39.43	60.57

1. **Graph population changes**: Use the data in the first three columns of the table above to plot a line graph. This will show changes in the phenotypes: numbers of grey and white (albino) squirrels, as well as changes in the total population. Plot: **grey**, **white**, and **total** for each year:

   (a) By how much have total population numbers fluctuated over the sampling period (as a %):

   ____

   (b) Describe the overall trend in total population numbers and any pattern that may exist:

   ____

   ____

   ____

   ____

   ____

   ____

   ____

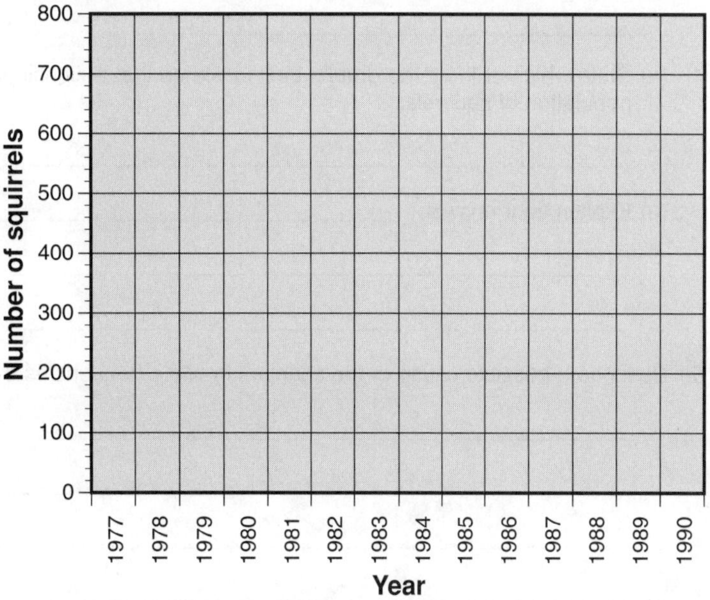

2. **Graph genotype changes**: Use the data in the genotype columns of the table on the previous page to plot a line graph. This will show changes in the allele combinations (**GG**, **Gg**, **gg**). Plot: **GG**, **Gg**, and **gg** for each year:

Describe the overall trend in the frequency of:

(a) Homozygous dominant (**GG**) genotype:

(b) Heterozygous (**Gg**) genotype:

(c) Homozygous recessive (**gg**) genotype:

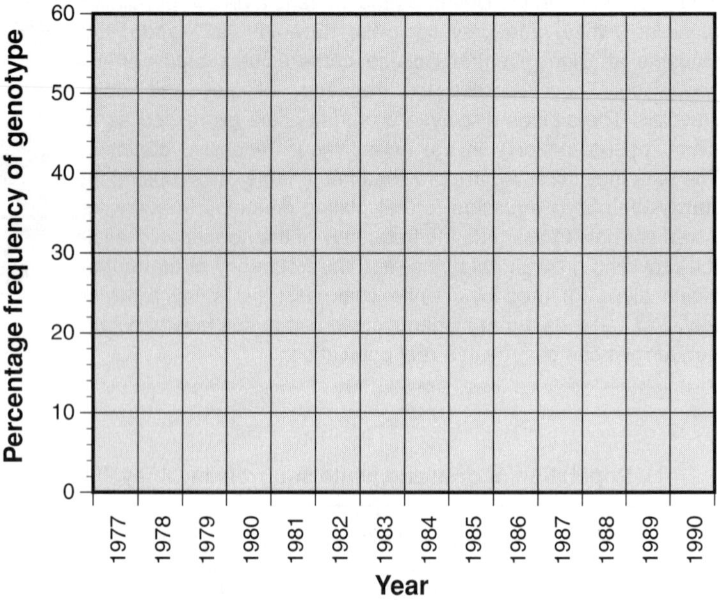

3. **Graph allele changes**: Use the data in the last two columns of the table on the previous page to plot a line graph. This will show changes in the *allele frequencies* for each of the dominant (**G**) and recessive (**g**) alleles. **Plot**: the frequency of **G** and the frequency of **g**:

(a) Describe the overall trend in the frequency of the dominant allele (**G**):

(b) Describe the overall trend in the frequency of the recessive allele (**g**):

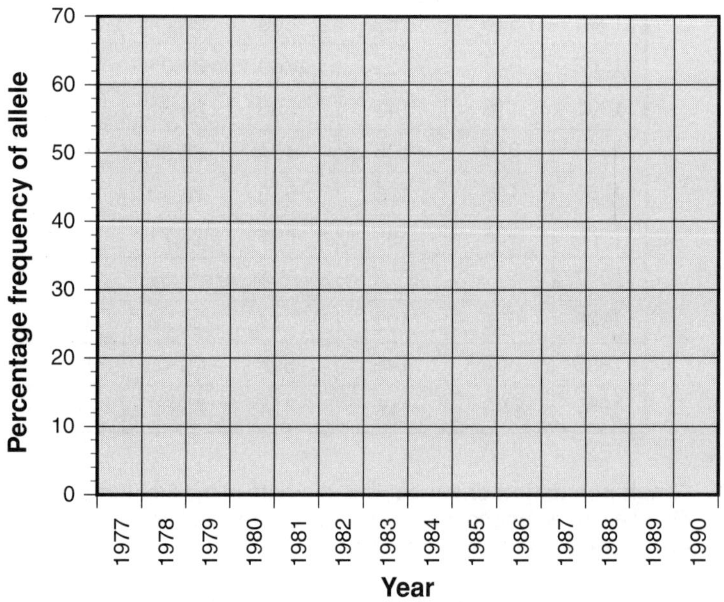

4. (a) State which of the three graphs best indicates that a significant change may be taking place in the gene pool of this population of squirrels:

(b) Explain your answer:

5. Describe a possible cause of the changes in allele frequencies over the sampling period:

Natural Selection

Natural selection operates on the phenotypes of individuals, produced by their particular combinations of alleles. The differential survival of some genotypes over others is called **natural selection** and, as a result of it, organisms with phenotypes most suited to the prevailing environment are more likely to survive and breed than those with less suited phenotypes. Favourable phenotypes become more numerous while unfavourable phenotypes become less common or may disappear altogether. Natural selection is not a static phenomenon; it is always linked to phenotypic suitability in the prevailing environment. It may favour existing phenotypes or shift the phenotypic median one way or another, as is shown in the diagrams below. The top row of diagrams represents the population phenotypic spread before selection, and the bottom row the spread afterwards. Note that balancing selection is similar to disruptive selection, but the polymorphism that results is not associated with phenotypic extremes.

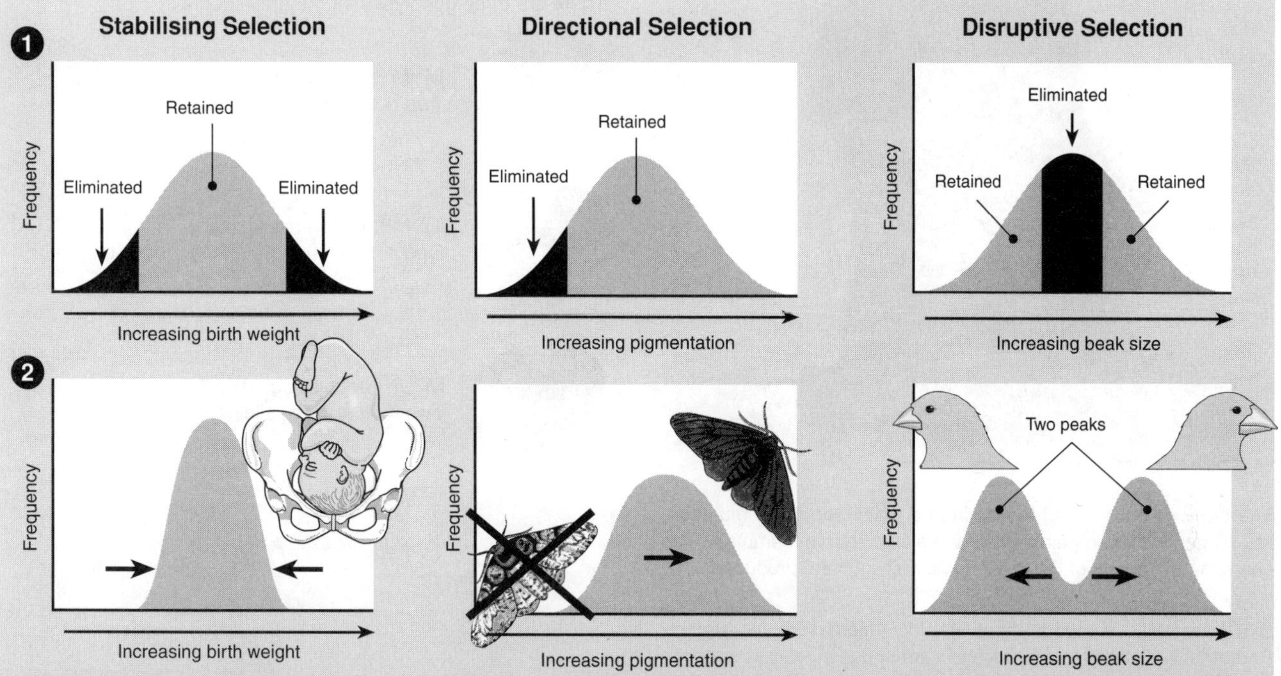

Extreme variations are selected against and the middle range (most common) phenotypes are retained in greater numbers. Stabilising selection results in decreased variation for the phenotypic character involved. This type of selection operates most of the time in most populations and acts to prevent divergence of form and function, e.g. birth weight of human infants.

The adaptive phenotype is shifted in one direction and one phenotype is favoured over another. Directional selection was observed in peppered moths in England during the Industrial Revolution. In England's current environment, the selection pressures on the moths are more typically balanced, and the proportions of each morph vary in different regions of the country.

Disruptive selection favors two phenotypic extremes at the expense of intermediate forms. During a prolonged drought on Santa Cruz Island in the Galapagos, it resulted in a population of ground finches that was bimodal for beak size. Competition for the usual seed sources was so intense that birds able to exploit either small or large seeds were favoured, although intermediate phenotypes remained in low numbers.

1. Explain why fluctuating (as opposed to stable) environments favour disruptive (diversifying) selection:

2. Disruptive selection can be important in the formation of new species:

   (a) Describe the evidence from the ground finches on Santa Cruz Island that provides support for this statement:

   (b) The ground finches on Santa Cruz Island are one interbreeding population with a strongly bimodal distribution for the phenotypic character beak size. Suggest what conditions could lead to the two phenotypic extremes diverging further:

   (c) Predict the consequences of the end of the drought and an increased abundance of medium size seeds as food:

Black is the New Grey

The North American grey squirrel (*Sciurus carolinensis*) was introduced into the UK in the 19th century. By 1958 it had spread to most of England and Wales, displacing the smaller native red squirrel (*Sciurus vulgaris*). Now, a black variation of the grey squirrel is beginning to displace the original grey variety, and is common in four areas of Britain (below right). Observations suggest the black form is more aggressive than the grey. This behaviour may give them a competitive advantage and may provide a characteristic for selection. This would help explain why the numbers of black squirrels are increasing locally.

Photo: D. Gordon E. Robertson

Most gene mutations are recessive, but the mutation for black coat colour shows incomplete dominance. This allows the black variant to spread more rapidly through the population. There are three genotypes for the grey squirrel:

M^GM^G: Grey coat
Two normal grey alleles

M^GM^B: Brown-black coat
One normal grey allele, one mutant black allele

M^BM^B: Jet black coat
Two mutant black alleles

The black colour (above) results from a major sequence mutation in the MC1R gene which regulates hair and skin colour in mammals. The gene controls the amount of the black eumelanin pigment produced.

Black squirrel numbers have rapidly increased in Hertfordshire, Bedfordshire, Huntingdonshire and Cambridgeshire. It is proposed that the genetic development of black coat colour affords the black squirrels a competitive advantage over grey variants. Although none have yet been proven, likely advantages include higher levels of aggression than the grey varieties, and the possibility that the females find the black coat more attractive when selecting mates. A Canadian study has shown that black squirrels have a lower basal metabolic rate and lose heat more slowly than grey squirrels. This would benefit the black variant in cold conditions.

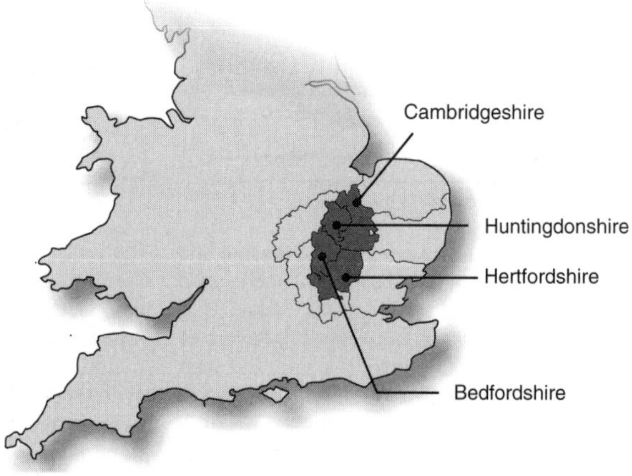

The Punnett square (right) shows the offspring produced when a grey squirrel (M^GM^G) is mated with brown-black squirrel (M^GM^B). Use it to help you answer the following questions.

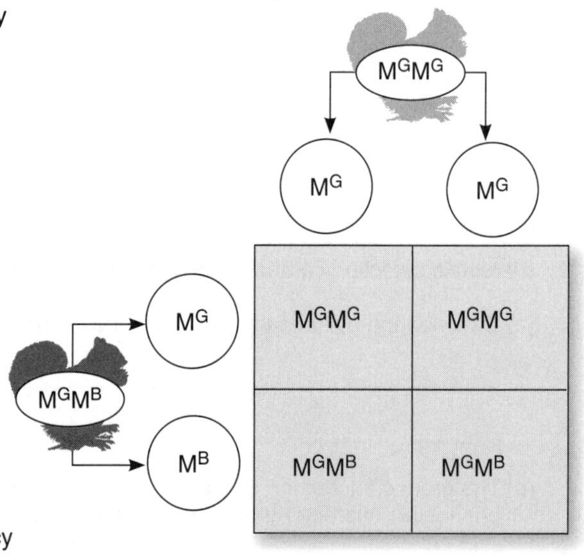

1. (a) Explain why the frequency of the black squirrel is increasing relative to the grey variety:

(b) Explain what would happen to the rate of increase in frequency of black squirrels if the mutation for black colour was recessive:

Selection for Skin Colour in Humans

Pigmented skin of varying tones is a feature of humans that evolved after early hominins lost the majority of their body hair. However, the distribution of skin colour globally is not random; people native to equatorial regions have darker skin tones than people from higher latitudes. For many years, biologists postulated that this was because darker skins had evolved to protect against skin cancer. The problem with this explanation was that skin cancer is not tied to evolutionary fitness because it affects post-reproductive individuals and cannot therefore provide a mechanism for selection. More complex analyses of the physiological and epidemiological evidence has shown a more complex picture in which selection pressures on skin colour are finely balanced to produce a skin tone that regulates the effects of the sun's ultraviolet radiation on the nutrients vitamin D and folate, both of which are crucial to successful human reproduction, and therefore evolutionary fitness.

Skin Colour in Humans: A Product of Natural Selection

Human skin colour is the result of two opposing selection pressures. Skin pigmentation has evolved to protect against destruction of folate from ultraviolet light, but the skin must also be light enough to receive the light required to synthesise vitamin D. Vitamin D synthesis is a process that begins in the skin and is inhibited by dark pigment. Folate is needed for healthy neural development in humans and a deficiency is associated with fatal neural tube defects. Vitamin D is required for the absorption of calcium from the diet and therefore normal skeletal development. Women also have a high requirement for calcium during pregnancy and lactation. Populations that live in the tropics receive enough ultraviolet (UV) radiation to synthesise vitamin D all year long. Those that live in northern or southern latitudes do not. In temperate zones, people lack sufficient UV light to make vitamin D for one month of the year. Those nearer the poles lack enough UV light for vitamin D synthesis most of the year (above). Their lighter skins reflect their need to maximise UV absorption (the photos show skin colour in people from different latitudes).

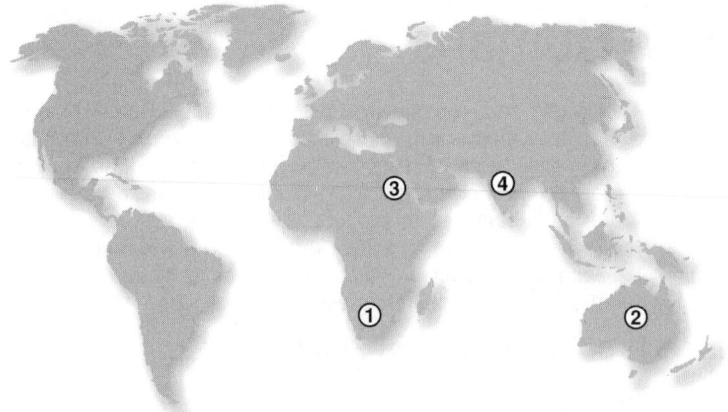

Long-term resident **Recent immigrant**

① **Southern Africa: ~20-30°S**

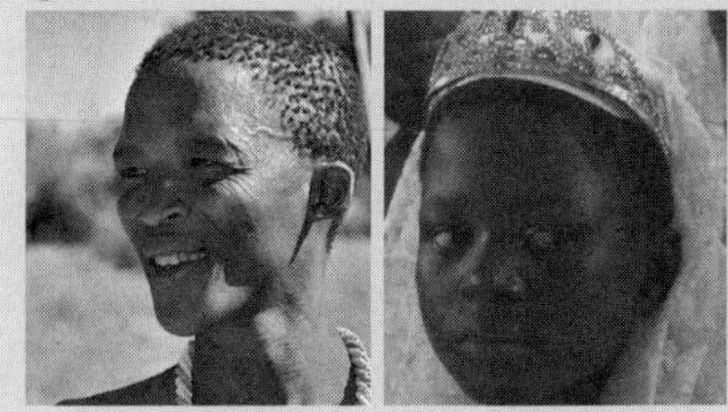

Khoisan-Namibia *Zulu: 1000 years ago*

② **Australia: ~10-35°S**

Aborigine *European: 300 years ago*

③ **Banks of the Red Sea: ~15-30°N**

Nuba-Sudan *Arab: 2000 years ago*

④ **India: ~10-30°S**

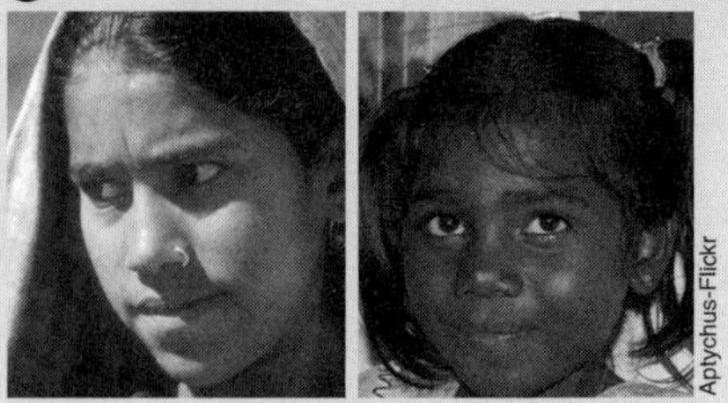

West Bengal *Tamil: ~100 years ago*

The skin of people who have inhabited particular regions for millennia has adapted to allow sufficient vitamin D production while still protecting folate stores. In the photos above, some of these original inhabitants are illustrated to the left of each pair and compared with the skin tones of more recent immigrants (to the right of each pair, with the number of years since immigration). The numbered locations are on the map.

1. (a) Describe the role of folate in human physiology: ______

   (b) Describe the role of vitamin D in human physiology: ______

2. (a) Early hypotheses to explain skin colour linked pigmentation level only to the degree of protection it gave from UV-induced skin cancer. Explain why this hypothesis was inadequate in accounting for how skin colour evolved:

   ______

   ______

   (b) Explain how the new hypothesis for the evolution of skin colour overcomes these deficiencies: ______

   ______

   ______

   ______

3. Explain why, in any given geographical region, women tend to have lighter skins (by 3-4% on average) than men:

   ______

   ______

4. The Inuit people of Alaska and northern Canada have a diet rich in vitamin D and their skin colour is darker than predicted on the basis of UV intensity at their latitude. Explain this observation:

   ______

   ______

5. (a) Describe the health problems that could be expected for people of African origin now living in northern UK:

   ______

   ______

   (b) Explain how these people could avoid these problems in their new higher latitude environment: ______

   ______

   ______

Industrial Melanism

Natural selection may act on the frequencies of phenotypes (and hence genotypes) in populations in one of three different ways (through stabilising, directional, or disruptive selection). Over time, natural selection may lead to a permanent change in the genetic makeup of a population. The increased prevalence of melanic forms of the peppered moth, *Biston betularia*, during the Industrial Revolution, is one of the best known examples of directional selection following a change in environmental conditions. Although the protocols used in the central experiments on *Biston*, and the conclusions drawn from them, have been queried, it remains one of the clearest documented examples of phenotypic change in a polymorphic population.

Industrial melanism in peppered moths, *Biston betularia*

The **peppered moth**, *Biston betularia*, occurs in two forms (morphs): the grey mottled form, and a dark melanic form. Changes in the relative abundance of these two forms was hypothesised to be the result of selective predation by birds, with pale forms suffering higher mortality in industrial areas because they are more visible. The results of experiments by H.D. Kettlewell supported this hypothesis but did not confirm it, since selective predation by birds was observed but not quantified. Other research indicates that predation by birds is not the only factor determining the relative abundance of the different colour morphs.

Grey or mottled morph: vulnerable to predation in industrial areas where the trees are dark.

Melanic or carbonaria morph: dark colour makes it less vulnerable to predation in industrial areas.

Museum collections of the peppered moth made over the last 150 years show a marked change in the frequency of the melanic form. Moths collected in 1850 (above left), prior to the major onset of the industrial revolution in England. Fifty years later (above right) the frequency of the darker melanic forms had greatly increased. Even as late as the mid 20th century, coal-based industries predominated in some centres, and the melanic form occurred in greater frequency in these areas (see map, right).

Frequency of peppered moth forms in 1950

This map shows the relative frequencies of the two forms of peppered moth in the UK in 1950; a time when coal-based industries still predominated in some major centres.

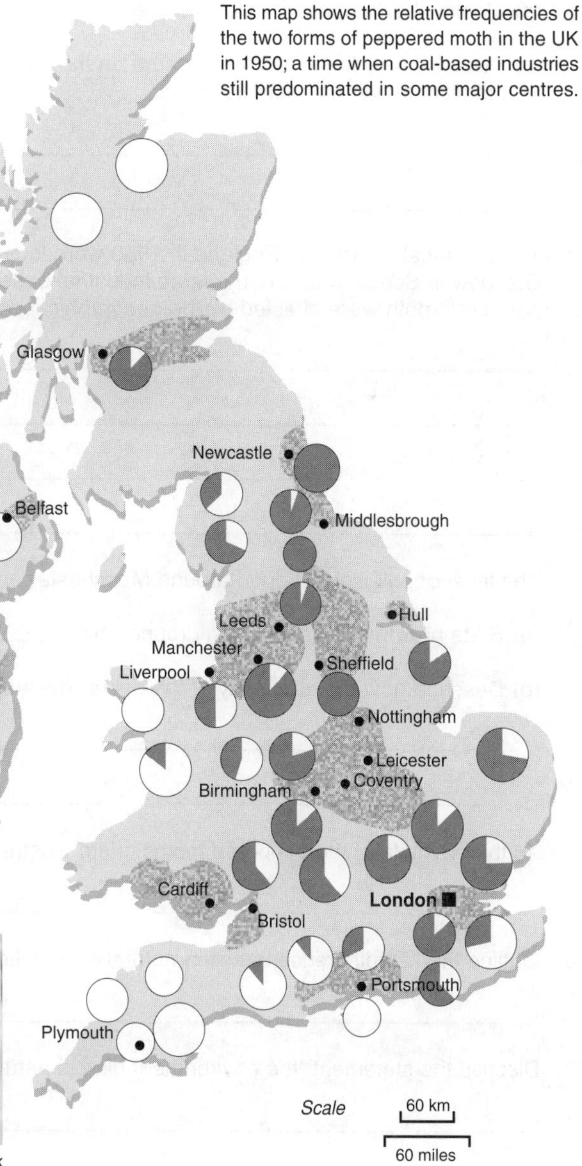

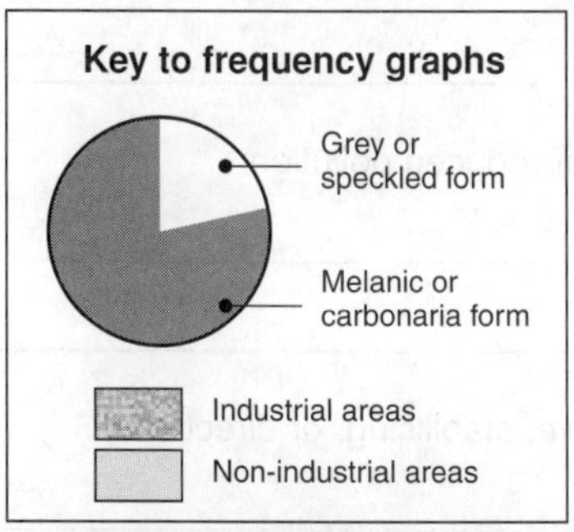

A grey (mottled) form of *Biston*, camouflaged against a lichen covered bark surface. In the absence of soot pollution, mottled forms appear to have the selective advantage.

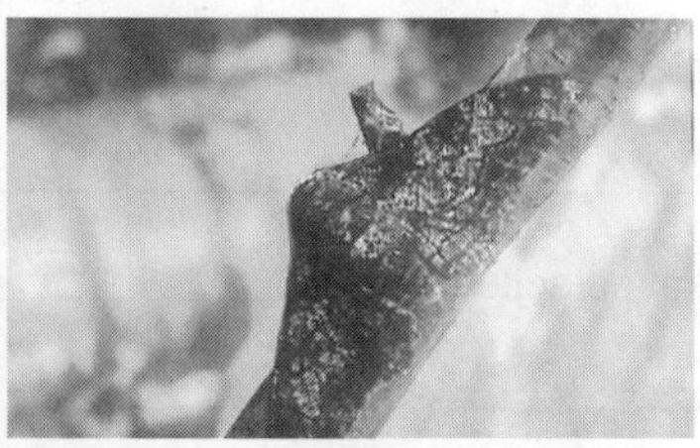

A melanic form of *Biston*, resting on a dark branch, so that it appears as part of the branch. Note that the background has been faded out so that the moth can be seen.

Changes in frequency of melanic peppered moths

In the 1940s and 1950s, coal burning was still at intense levels around the industrial centres of Manchester and Liverpool. During this time, the melanic form of the moth was still very dominant. In the rural areas further south and west of these industrial centres, the grey or speckled forms increased dramatically. With the decline of coal burning factories and the Clean Air Acts in cities, the air quality improved between 1960 and 1980. Sulfur dioxide and smoke levels dropped to a fraction of their previous levels. This coincided with a sharp fall in the relative numbers of melanic moths.

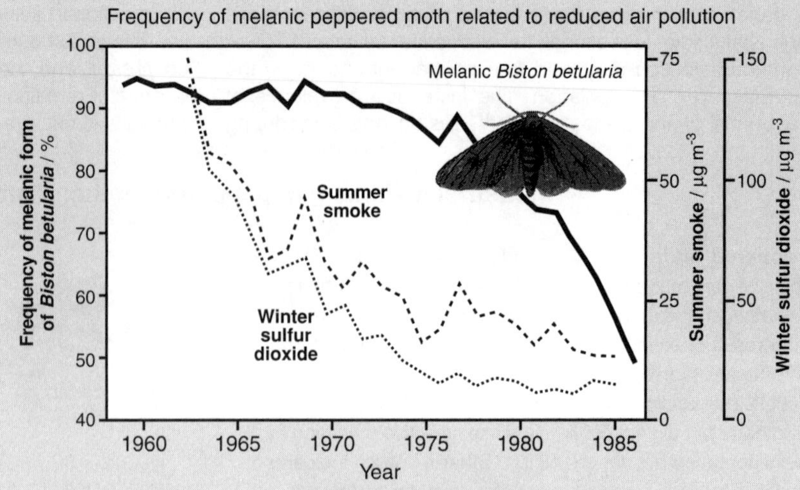

1. The populations of peppered moth in England have undergone changes in the frequency of an obvious phenotypic character over the last 150 years. Describe the phenotypic character that changed in its frequency:

2. (a) Identify the (proposed) selective agent for phenotypic change in *Biston*:

   (b) Describe how the selection pressure on the light coloured morph has changed with changing environmental conditions over the last 150 years:

3. The industrial centres for England in 1950 were located around London, Birmingham, Liverpool, Manchester, and Leeds. Glasgow in Scotland also had a large industrial base. Comment on how the relative frequencies of the two forms of peppered moth were affected by the geographic location of industrial regions:

4. The level of pollution dropped around Manchester and Liverpool between 1960 and 1985.

   (a) State how much the pollution dropped by:

   (b) Describe how the frequency of the darker melanic form changed during the period of reduced pollution:

5. In the example of the peppered moths, state whether the selection pressure is disruptive, stabilising, or directional:

6. Outline the key difference between natural and artificial selection:

7. Discuss the statement "the environment directs natural selection":

Heterozygous Advantage

There are two mechanisms by which natural selection can affect allele frequencies. Firstly, there may be selection against one of the homozygotes. When one homozygous type (for example, aa), has a lower fitness than the other two genotypes (in this case, Aa or AA), the frequency of the deleterious allele will tend to decrease until it is completely eliminated. In some situations, both homozygous conditions (aa and AA) have lower fitness than the heterozygote; a situation that leads to **heterozygous advantage** and may result in the stable coexistence of both alleles in the population (**balanced polymorphism**). There are remarkably few well-documented examples in which the evidence for heterozygous advantage is conclusive. The maintenance of the sickle cell mutation (a codominant allele) in malaria-prone regions is one such example.

The Sickle Cell Allele (Hb^S)

Sickle cell disease is caused by a mutation to a gene that directs the production of the human blood protein called haemoglobin. The mutant allele is known as **Hb^S** and produces a form of haemoglobin that differs from the normal form by just one amino acid in the β-chain. This minute change however causes a cascade of physiological problems in people with the allele. Some of the red blood cells containing mutated haemoglobin alter their shape to become irregular and spiky; the so-called **sickle cells**.

Sickle cells have a tendency to clump together and work less efficiently. In people with just one sickle cell allele plus a normal allele (the heterozygote condition **Hb^SHb**), there is a mixture of both red blood cell types and they are said to have the sickle cell trait. They are generally unaffected by the disease except in low oxygen environments (e.g. climbing at altitude). People with two Hb^S genes (**Hb^SHb^S**) suffer severe illness and even death. For this reason Hb^S is considered **a lethal gene**.

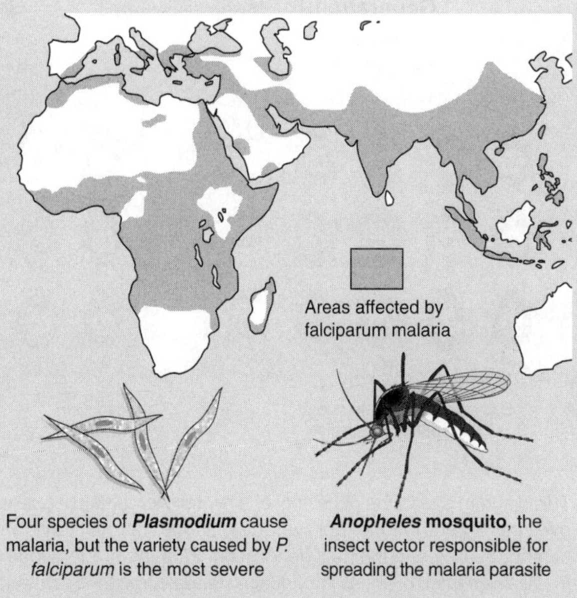

Four species of ***Plasmodium*** cause malaria, but the variety caused by *P. falciparum* is the most severe

Anopheles **mosquito**, the insect vector responsible for spreading the malaria parasite

Fig. 1: Incidence of falciparum malaria

Heterozygous Advantage in Malarial Regions

Falciparum malaria is widely distributed throughout central Africa, the Mediterranean, Middle East, and tropical and semi-tropical Asia (Fig. 1). It is transmitted by the *Anopheles* mosquito, which spreads the protozoan *Plasmodium falciparum* from person to person as it feeds on blood.

SYMPTOMS: These appear 1-2 weeks after being bitten, and include headache, shaking, chills, and fever. Falciparum malaria is more severe than other forms of malaria, with high fever, convulsions, and coma. It can be fatal within days of the first symptoms appearing.

THE PARADOX: The Hb^S allele offers considerable protection against malaria. Sickle cells have low potassium levels, which causes plasmodium parasites inside these cells to die. Those with a normal phenotype are very susceptible to malaria, but heterozygotes (**Hb^SHb**) are much less so. This situation, called **heterozygous advantage**, has resulted in the Hb^S allele being present in moderately high frequencies in parts of Africa and Asia despite its harmful effects (Fig. 2). This is a special case of balanced polymorphism, called a **balanced lethal system** because neither of the homozygotes produces a phenotype that survives, but the heterozygote is viable.

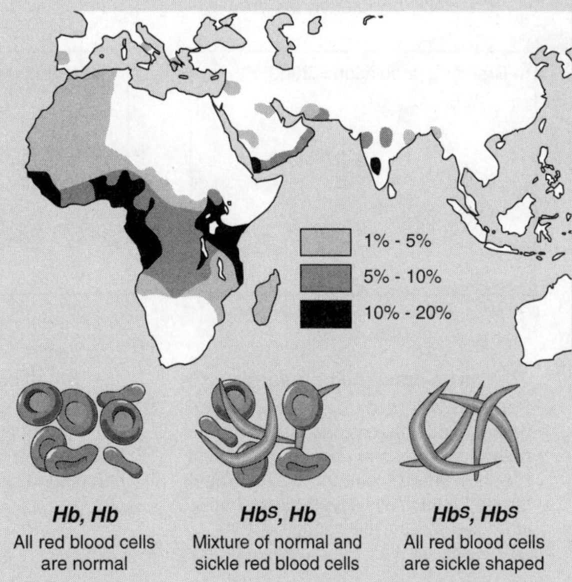

Hb, Hb All red blood cells are normal

Hb^S, Hb Mixture of normal and sickle red blood cells

Hb^S, Hb^S All red blood cells are sickle shaped

Fig. 2: Frequency of the sickle cell allele

1. With respect to the sickle cell allele, explain how **heterozygous advantage** can lead to **balanced polymorphism**:

Genetic Drift

Not all individuals, for various reasons, will be able to contribute their genes to the next generation. **Genetic drift** (also known as the Sewell-Wright Effect) refers to the *random changes in allele frequency* that occur in all populations, but are much more pronounced in small populations. In a small population, the effect of a few individuals not contributing their alleles to the next generation can have a great effect on allele frequencies. Alleles may even become **lost** from the gene pool altogether (frequency becomes 0%) or **fixed** as the only allele for the gene present (frequency becomes 100%).

The genetic makeup (allele frequencies) of the population changes randomly over a period of time

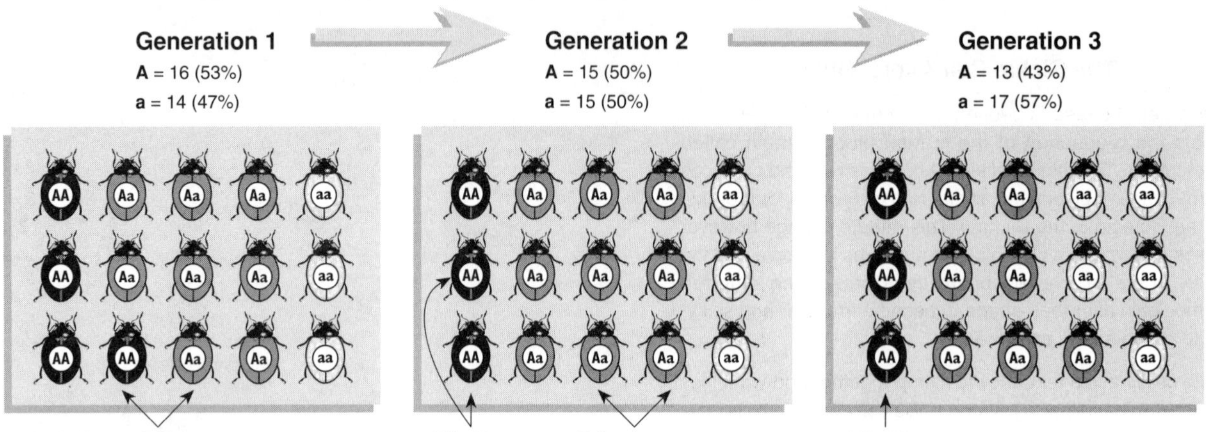

This diagram shows the gene pool of a hypothetical small population over three generations. For various reasons, not all individuals contribute alleles to the next generation. With the random loss of the alleles carried by these individuals, the allele frequency changes from one generation to the next. The change in frequency is directionless as there is no selecting force. The allele combinations for each successive generation are determined by how many alleles of each type are passed on from the preceding one.

Computer Simulation of Genetic Drift

Below are displayed the change in allele frequencies in a computer simulation showing random genetic drift. The breeding population progressively gets smaller from left to right. Each simulation was run for 140 generations.

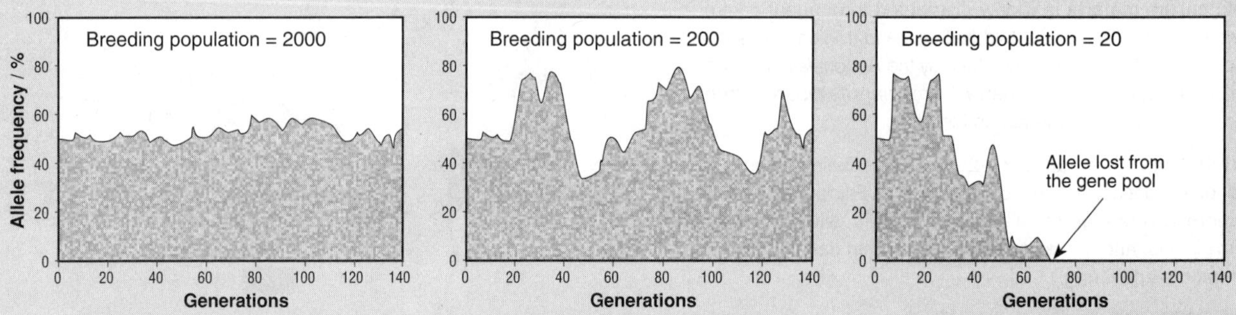

Large breeding population
Fluctuations are minimal in large breeding populations because the large numbers buffer the population against random loss of alleles. On average, losses for each allele type will be similar in frequency and little change occurs.

Small breeding population
Fluctuations are more severe in smaller breeding populations because random changes in a few alleles cause a greater percentage change in allele frequencies.

Very small breeding population
Fluctuations in very small breeding populations are so extreme that the allele can become fixed (frequency of 100%) or lost from the gene pool altogether (frequency of 0%).

1. Explain what is meant by **genetic drift**: ______________________________

____

2. Describe how genetic drift affects the amount of genetic variation within very small populations: ______________________________

____

____

____

3. Identify a small breeding population of animals or plants in Britain or Europe in which genetic drift could be occurring:

____

The Founder Effect

Occasionally, a small number of individuals from a large population may migrate away, or become isolated from, their original population. If this colonising or 'founder' population is made up of only a few individuals, it will probably have a non-representative sample of alleles from the parent population's gene pool. As a consequence of this **founder effect**, the colonising population may evolve differently from that of the parent population, particularly since the environmental conditions for the isolated population may be different. In some cases, it may be possible for certain alleles to be missing altogether from the individuals in the isolated population. Future generations of this population will not have this allele.

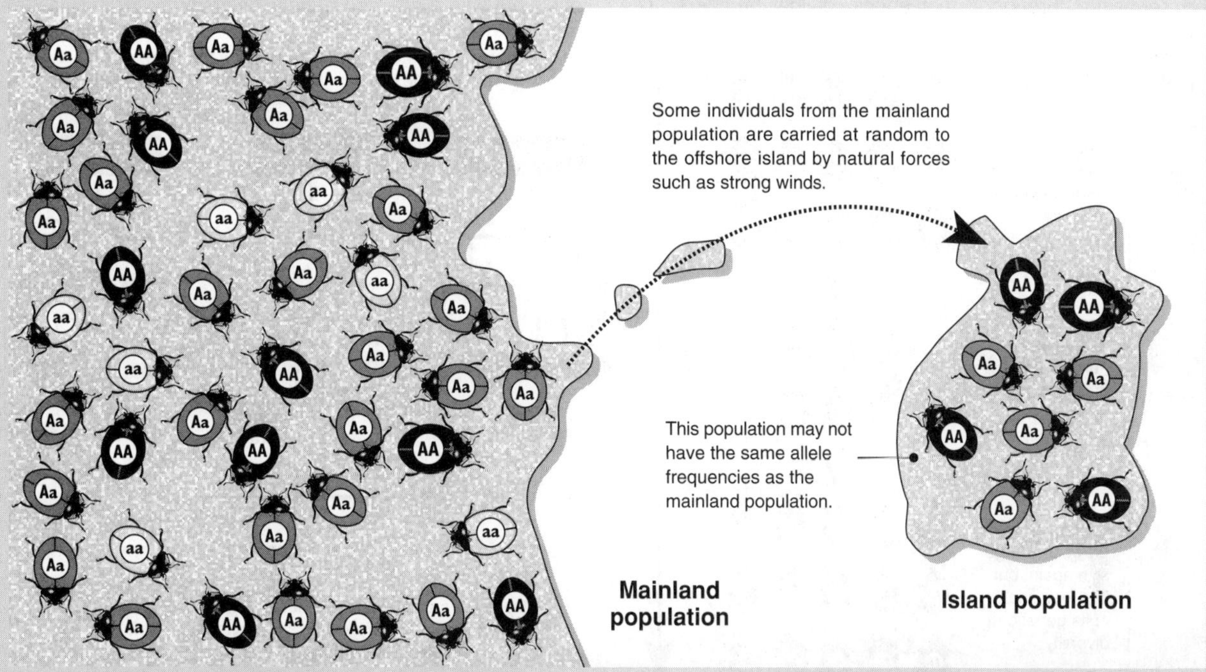

Mainland Population

	Allele frequencies	
	Actual numbers	Calculate %
Allele A		
Allele a		
Total		

Phenotype frequencies		
Black	Dark	Pale

Colonising Island Population

	Allele frequencies	
	Actual numbers	Calculate %
Allele A		
Allele a		
Total		

Phenotype frequencies		
Black	Dark	Pale

1. Compare the mainland population to the population which ended up on the island (use the spaces in the tables above):
   (a) Count the **phenotype** numbers for the two populations (i.e. the number of black, dark and pale beetles).
   (b) Count the **allele** numbers for the two populations: the number of dominant alleles (A) and recessive alleles (a). Calculate these as a percentage of the total number of alleles for each population.

2. Describe how the allele frequencies of the two populations are different: ______________________

____

3. Describe some possible ways in which various types of organism can be carried to an offshore island:

   (a) Plants: ______________________

   (b) Land animals: ______________________

   (c) Non-marine birds: ______________________

4. Since founder populations are often very small, describe another process that may further alter the allele frequencies:

____

____

Population Bottlenecks

Populations may sometimes be reduced to low numbers by predation, disease, or periods of climatic change. A population crash may not be 'selective': it may affect all phenotypes equally. Large scale catastrophic events, such as fire or volcanic eruption, are examples of such non-selective events. Humans may severely (and selectively) reduce the numbers of some species through hunting and/or habitat destruction. These populations may recover, having squeezed through a 'bottleneck' of low numbers. The diagram below illustrates how population numbers may be reduced as a result of a catastrophic event. Following such an event, the small number of individuals contributing to the gene pool may not have a representative sample of the genes in the pre-catastrophe population, i.e. the allele frequencies in the remnant population may be severely altered. Genetic drift may cause further changes to allele frequencies. The small population may return to previous levels but with a reduced genetic diversity.

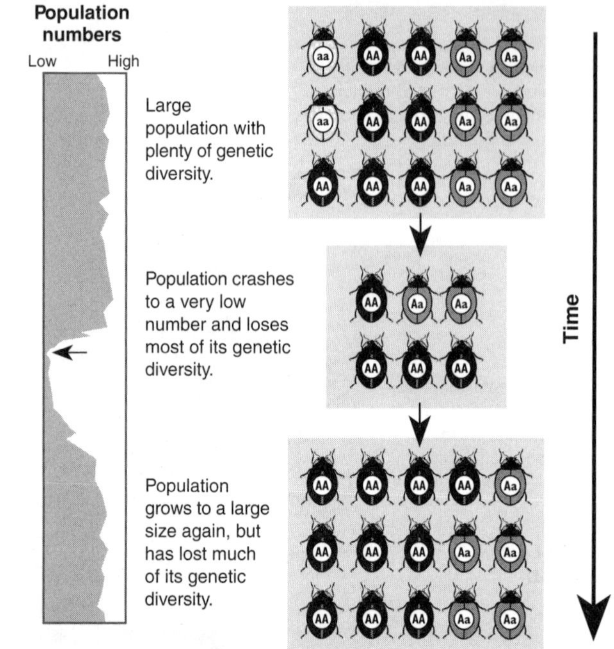

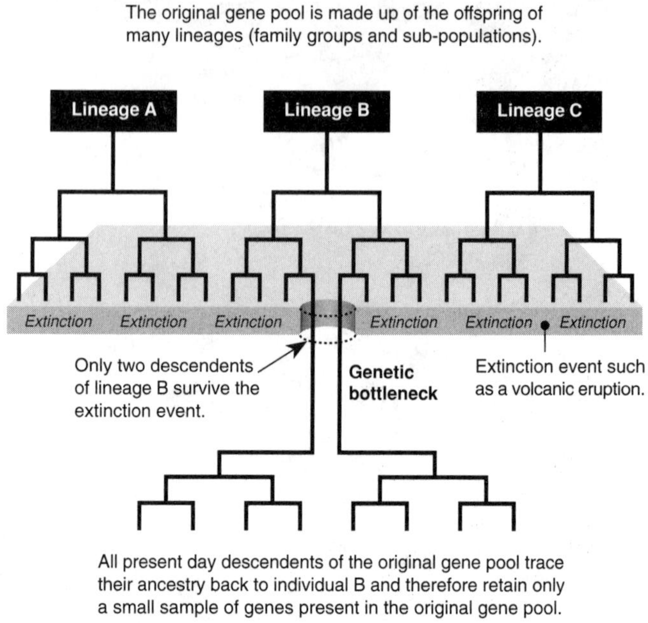

Modern Examples of Population Bottlenecks

Cheetahs: The world population of cheetahs currently stands at fewer than 20 000. Recent genetic analysis has found that the entire population enhibits very little genetic diversity. It appears that cheetahs may have narrowly escaped extinction at the end of the last ice age, about 10-20 000 years ago. If all modern cheetahs arose from a very limited genetic stock, this would explain their present lack of genetic diversity. The lack of genetic variation has resulted in a number of problems that threaten cheetah survival, including sperm abnormalities, decreased fecundity, high cub mortality, and sensitivity to disease.

Illinois prairie chicken: When Europeans first arrived in North America, there were millions of prairie chickens. As a result of hunting and habitat loss, the Illinois population of prairie chickens fell from about 100 million in 1900 to fewer than 50 in the 1990s. A comparison of the DNA from birds collected in the mid-twentieth century and DNA from the surviving population indicated that most of the genetic diversity has been lost.

Photo: Dept. of Natural Resources, Illinois

1. Endangered species are often subjected to population bottlenecks. Explain how population bottlenecks affect the ability of a population of an endangered species to recover from its plight:

2. Explain why the lack of genetic diversity in cheetahs has increased their sensitivity to disease:

3. Describe the effect of a population bottleneck on the potential of a species to adapt to changes (i.e. its ability to evolve):

The Biological Species Concept

The **species** is the basic unit of taxonomy. A **biological species** is defined as a group of organisms capable of interbreeding to produce fertile offspring. However, there are some difficulties in applying the biological species concept (BSC) in practice. Morphologically identical but reproductively isolated cryptic species and closely related species that interbreed to produce fertile hybrids (e.g. *Canis* species), indicate that the boundaries of a species gene pool can be unclear. The BSC is also more successfully applied to animals than to plants. Plants hybridise easily and can reproduce vegetatively. For some, e.g. cotton and rice, F_1 hybrids are fertile but hybrid breakdown in subsequent generations stops hybrids proliferating and maintains the parental types in the wild. In addition, the BSC cannot be applied to asexually reproducing or extinct organisms. Increasingly, biologists are using DNA analyses to clarify relationships between the related populations that we regard as one species.

Geographical distribution of selected *Canis* species

The global distribution of most of the species of *Canis* (dogs and wolves) is shown on the map, right. The grey wolf inhabits the forests of North America, northern Europe, and Siberia. The red wolf and Mexican wolf (original distributions shown) were once distributed more widely, but are now extinct in the wild except for reintroduction efforts. In contrast, the coyote has expanded its original range and is now found throughout North and Central America. The range of the three jackal species overlap in the open savannah of eastern Africa. The dingo is distributed throughout the Australian continent. Distribution of the domesticated dog is global as a result of the spread of human culture. The dog has been able to interbreed with all other members of the genus listed here to form fertile hybrids. Contrast this with members of the horse family, in which hybrid offspring are viable but sterile.

Interbreeding between *Canis* species

The *Canis* species illustrate problems with the traditional species concept. The domesticated dog is able to breed with other members of the same genus to produce fertile hybrids. Red wolves, grey wolves, Mexican wolves, and coyotes are all capable of interbreeding to produce fertile hybrids. Red wolves are very rare, and it is possible that hybridisation with coyotes has been a factor in their decline. By contrast, the ranges of the three distinct species of jackal overlap in the Serengeti of eastern Africa. These animals are highly territorial, but simply ignore members of the other jackal species and no interbreeding takes place.

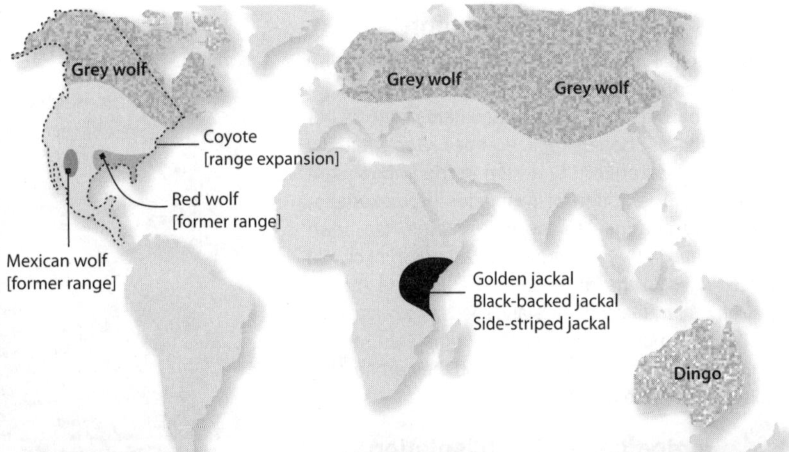

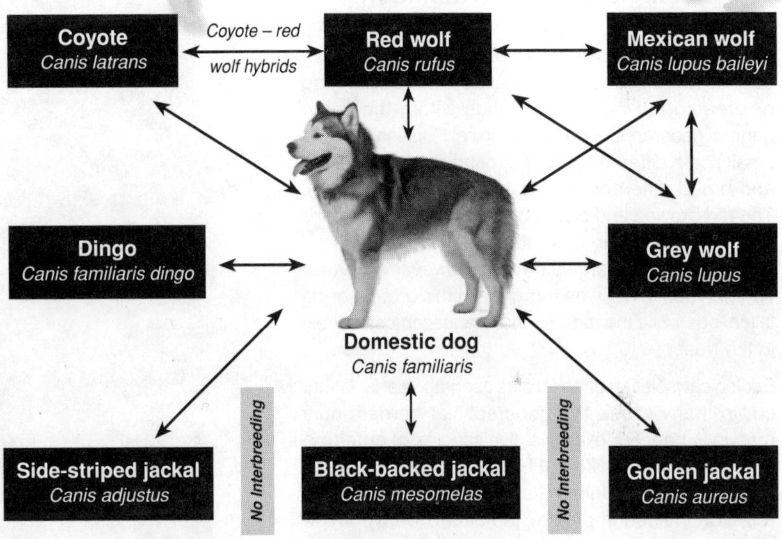

1. Describe the type of barrier that prevents the three species of jackal from interbreeding: ____________

____

2. Describe the factor that has prevented the dingo from interbreeding with other *Canis* species (apart from the dog):

____

3. Describe a possible contributing factor to the occurrence of interbreeding between the coyote and red wolf:

____

4. The grey wolf is a widely distributed species. Explain why the North American population is considered to be part of the same species as the northern European and Siberian populations:

____

____

5. Explain some of the limitations of using the biological species concept to assign species: ____________

____

____

Isolating Mechanisms

Isolating mechanisms are barriers to successful interbreeding between species. Reproductive isolation is fundamental to the **biological species concept**, which defines a species by its inability to breed with other species to produce fertile offspring. Prezygotic isolating mechanisms act before fertilisation occurs, preventing species ever mating, whereas postzygotic barriers take effect after fertilisation. **Geographical barriers** are not regarded as reproductive isolating mechanisms because they are not part of the species' biology, although they are often a necessary precursor to reproductive isolation in sexually reproducing populations. Ecological isolating mechanisms are those that isolate gene pools on the basis of ecological preferences, e.g. habitat selection. Although ecological and geographical isolation are sometimes confused, they are quite distinct, as ecological isolation involves a component of the species biology. In a similar way, the **temporal isolation** of species, through differences in the timing of important life cycle events, effectively prevents potentially interbreeding species from successfully reproducing.

Geographical Isolation

Geographical isolation describes the isolation of a species population (gene pool) by some kind of physical barrier, for example, mountain range, water body, isthmus, desert, or ice sheet. Geographical isolation is a frequent first step in the subsequent reproductive isolation of a species. For example, geological changes to the lake basins has been instrumental in the subsequent proliferation of cichlid fish species in the rift lakes of East Africa (right). Similarly, many Galapagos Island species (e.g. iguanas, finches) are now quite distinct from the Central and South American species from which they arose after isolation from the mainland.

Ecological (Habitat) Isolation

Ecological isolation describes the existence of a **prezygotic reproductive barrier** between two species (or sub-species) as a result of them occupying or breeding in different habitats within the same general geographical area. Ecological isolation includes small scale differences (e.g. ground or tree dwelling) and broad differences (e.g. desert vs grasslands). The red-browed and brown **treecreepers** (*Climacteris* spp.) are sympatric in south-eastern Australia and both species feed largely on ants. However the brown spends most of its time foraging on the ground or on fallen logs while the red-browed forages almost entirely in the trees.

Ecological isolation often follows geographical isolation, but in many cases the geographical barriers may remain in part. For example, five species of **antelope squirrels** occupy different habitat ranges throughout the southwestern United States and northern Mexico, a region divided in part by the Grand Canyon. The white tailed antelope squirrel is widely distributed in desert areas to the north and south of the canyon, while the smaller, more specialised Harris' antelope squirrel has a much more limited range only to the south in southern Arizona.The Grand Canyon still functions as a barrier to dispersal but the species are now ecologically isolated as well.

Geographical and Ecological Isolation of Species

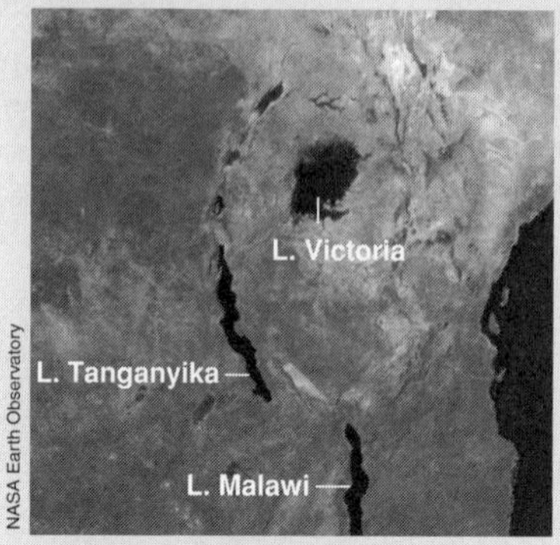

Red-browed treecreeper

Brown treecreeper

White-tailed antelope squirrel

The Grand Canyon - a massive rift in the Colorado Plateau

Harris' antelope squirrel

1. Describe the role of isolating mechanisms in maintaining the integrity of a species: ______________________

2. (a) Explain why geographical isolation is not regarded as a reproductive isolating mechanism: ______________________

(b) Explain why, despite this, it often precedes reproductive isolation: ______________________

3. Distinguish between geographical and ecological isolation: ______________________

Reproductive Isolation

Reproductive isolation prevents interbreeding (and therefore gene flow) between species. Any factor that impedes two species from producing viable, fertile hybrids contributes to reproductive isolation. Single barriers may not completely stop gene flow, so most species commonly have more than one type of barrier. Single barriers to reproduction (including geographical barriers) often precede the development of a suite of reproductive isolating mechanisms (RIMs). Most operate before fertilisation (prezygotic RIMs) with postzyotic RIMs being important in preventing offspring between closely related species.

Temporal Isolation

Individuals from different species do not mate because they are active during different times of the day, or in different seasons. Plants flower at different times of the year or even at different times of the day to avoid hybridisation (e.g. the orchid genus *Dendrobium*, which occupy the same location and flower on different days). Closely related animal species may have quite different breeding seasons or periods of emergence. **Periodical cicadas** of the genus *Magicicada* are so named because members of each species in a particular region are developmentally synchronised, despite very long life cycles. Once their underground period of development (13 or 17 years depending on the species) is over, the entire population emerges at much the same time to breed.

Gamete Isolation

The gametes from different species are often incompatible, so even if they meet they do not survive. For animals where fertilisation is internal, the sperm may not survive in the reproductive tract of another species. If the sperm does survive and reach the ovum, chemical differences in the gametes prevent fertilisation. Gamete isolation is particularly important in aquatic environments where the gametes are released into the water and fertilised externally, such as in reproduction in frogs. Chemical recognition is also used by flowering plants to recognise pollen from the same species.

Behavioural (ethological) Isolation

Behavioural isolation operates through differences in species courtship behaviours. Courtship is a necessary prelude to mating in many species and courtship behaviours are species specific. Mates of the same species are attracted with distinctive, usually ritualised, dances, vocalisations, and body language. Because they are not easily misinterpreted, the courtship behaviours of one species will be unrecognised and ignored by individuals of another species. Birds exhibit a remarkable range of courtship displays. The use of song is widespread but ritualised movements, including nest building, are also common. For example, the elaborate courtship bowers of bowerbirds are well known, and Galapagos frigatebirds have an elaborate display in which they inflate a bright red gular pouch (right). Amongst insects, empid flies have some of the most elaborate of courtship displays. They are aggressive hunters so ritualised behaviour involving presentation of a prey item facilitates mating. The sexual organs of the flies are also like a lock-and-key, providing mechanical reproductive isolation as well (see below).

Mechanical (morphological) Isolation

Structural differences (incompatibility) in the anatomy of reproductive organs prevents sperm transfer between individuals of different species. This is an important isolating mechanism preventing breeding between closely related species of arthropods. Many flowering plants have coevolved with their animal pollinators and have flowers structures to allow only that insect access. Structural differences in the flowers and pollen of different plant species prevents cross breeding because pollen transfer is restricted to specific pollinators and the pollen itself must be species compatible.

Prezygotic Isolating Mechanisms

Bruce Marlin

Lorax

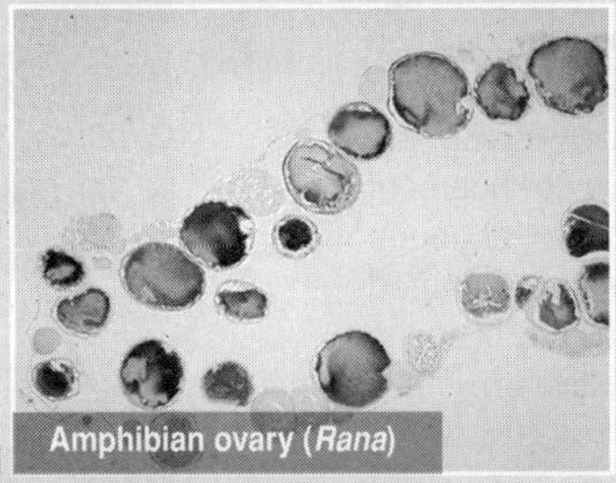

Amphibian ovary (*Rana*)

Ell

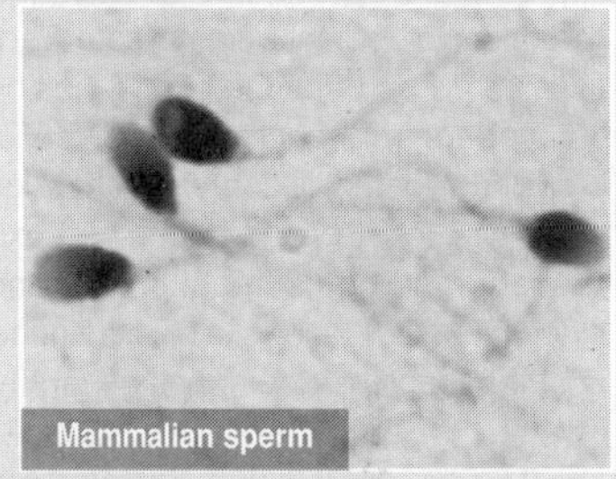

Mammalian sperm

RCN

Empid flies mating

Onno Zweers

Male frigatebird courtship display

CA

Male tree frog calling

CA

Wing beating in male sage grouse

CA

Damselflies mating

CA

Complex flowers in orchids

istock

Postzygotic Isolating Mechanisms

Hybrid sterility

Even if two species mate and produce hybrid offspring that are vigorous, the species are still reproductively isolated if the hybrids are sterile (genes cannot flow from one species' gene pool to the other). Such cases are common among the horse family (such as the zebra and donkey shown on the right). One cause of this sterility is the failure of meiosis to produce normal gametes in the hybrid. This can occur if the chromosomes of the two parents are different in number or structure (see the **"zebronkey"** karyotype on the right). The **mule**, a cross between a donkey stallion and a horse mare, is also an example of **hybrid vigour** (they are robust) as well as **hybrid sterility**. Female mules sometimes produce viable eggs but males are infertile.

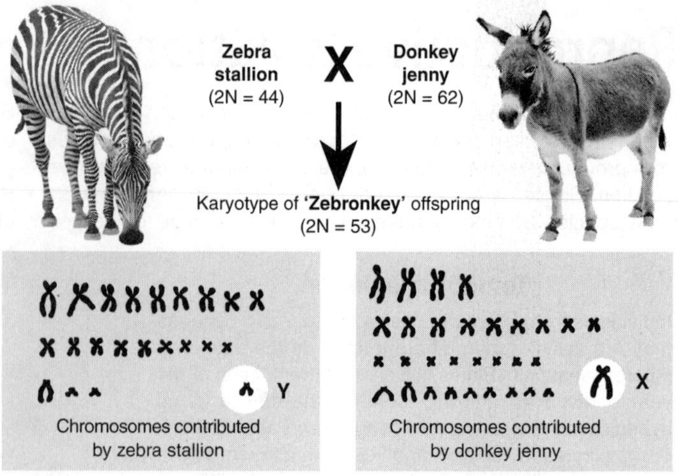

Hybrid inviability

Mating between individuals of two species may produce a zygote, but genetic incompatibility may stop development of the zygote. Fertilised eggs often fail to divide because of mis-matched chromosome numbers from each gamete. Very occasionally, the hybrid zygote will complete embryonic development but will not survive for long. For example, although sheep and goats seem similar and can be mated together, they belong to different genera. Any offspring of a sheep-goat pairing is generally stillborn.

Sheep (*Ovis*) 54 chromosomes

Goat (*Capra*) 60 chromosomes

Hybrid breakdown

Hybrid breakdown is common feature of some plant hybrids. The first generation (F_1) may be fertile, but the second generation (F_2) are infertile or inviable. Examples include hybrids between cotton species (near right), species within the genus *Populus*, and strains of the cultivated rice *Oryza* (far right)

1. In the following examples, classify the reproductive isolating mechanism as either **prezygotic** or **postzygotic** and describe the mechanisms by which the isolation is achieved (e.g. structrual isolation, hybrid sterility etc.):

   (a) Some different cotton species can produce fertile hybrids, but breakdown of the hybrid occurs in the next generation when the offspring of the hybrid die in their seeds or grow into defective plants:

   Prezygotic / postzygotic (delete one) Mechanism of isolation: ______________

   (b) Many plants have unique arrangements of their floral parts that stops transfer of pollen between plants:

   Prezygotic / postzygotic (delete one) Mechanism of isolation: ______________

   (c) Two skunk species do not mate despite having habitats that overlap because the mate at different times of the year:

   Prezygotic / postzygotic (delete one) Mechanism of isolation: ______________

   (d) Several species of the frog genus *Rana*, live in the same regions and habitats, where they may occasionally hybridise. The hybrids generally do not complete development, and those that do are weak and do not survive long:

   Prezygotic / postzygotic (delete one) Mechanism of isolation: ______________

2. Postzygotic isolating mechanisms are said to reinforce prezygotic ones. Explain why this is the case:

____

____

____

____

The Phylogenetic Species Concept

Although the biological species concept is useful, there are many situations in which it is difficult to apply, e.g. for asexual populations, (including bacteria) or extinct organisms. In such situations, the phylogenetic species concept (PSC) can be more useful. It not reliant on the criterion of successful interbreeding and can be applied to asexually or sexually reproducing organisms, and to extinct organisms. Phylogenetic species are defined on the basis of their shared evolutionary ancestry, which is determined on the basis of **shared derived characteristics**, which may be morphological, especially for higher taxonomic ranks, or biochemical (e.g. DNA differences). The PSC defines a species as the smallest group that all share a derived character state. It is widely applicable in palaeontology because biologists can compare both living and extinct organisms. While the phylogenetic species concept solves some difficulties, it creates others. It does not apply well to morphologically different species that are connected by gene flow. Similarly, the ability to distinguish genetically distinct but morphologically identical cryptic species on the basis of DNA analyses can lead to a proliferation of extant species that is not helpful in establishing a phylogeny.

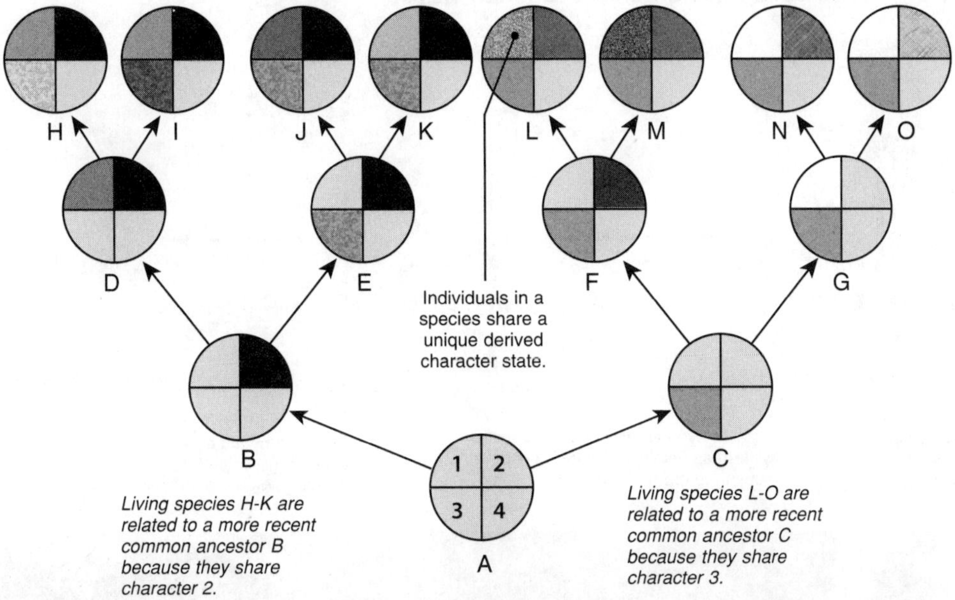

This simplified phylogenetic tree traces four characters among 15 species (8 present and 7 ancestral). The 8 modern species (species H-O) share a character (4) derived from a distant common ancestor (A). Although the primitive character unites all 8 species, the branching of the tree is based on characters derived from the ancestral ones. Classification on the basis of shared derived characters defines the species as the smallest group diagnosable by a unique combination of characters. If large numbers of characters are included in the analysis, it is easy to see how this method results in a proliferation of species that may or may not be meaningful. Under the PSC model, there are no subspecies; either a population is a phylogenetic species or it is not taxonomically distinguishable.

Tree sparrows (*P. montanus*) are ~10% smaller than the similar house sparrow but the two species hybridise freely.

House sparrows (*P. domesticus*) are widespread with many intermediate "subspecies" of unknown status.

Mallards are infamous for their ability to hybridise freely with a large number of other duck "species".

True sparrows all belong to the genus *Passer*. There are a large number of species distinguished on the basis of song, plumage, and size. A vestigial dorsal outer primary feather and an extra bone in the tongue are ancestral characters. Many populations are not good biological species in that they hybridise freely to produce fertile off-spring. A similar situation exists within the genus *Anas* of dabbling ducks (which includes the mallards). Many birds are best described using the PSC rather than the BSC.

1. (a) Explain the basis by which species are assigned under the PSC: ______________________________

____

____

(b) Describe one problem with the use of the PSC: ______________________________

____

(c) Describe situations where the use of the PSC might be more appropriate than the BSC: ______________________________

____

____

2. Suggest how genetic techniques could be used to elucidate the phylogeny of a cluster of related phylogenetic species:

____

____

Breeding Modern Wheat

Wheat has been cultivated for more than 9000 years and has undergone many genetic changes during its domestication. The evolution of modern bread wheat from its wild ancestors (below) involved two natural hybridisation events, accompanied by polyploidy. Once wheat became domesticated, artificial selection under cultivation emphasised characteristics such as high protein (gluten) content, high yield, and pest resistance to pests and disease. Hybrid vigour in wheat cultivars is produced by crossing inbred lines and selecting for desirable traits in the progeny, which can now be identified using genetic techniques such as marker assisted selection. This is an indirect selection process where a trait of interest is selected on the basis of a marker linked to it. Increasingly, research is focused on enhancing the genetic diversity of wheat to provide for future crop development. With this in mind, there is renewed interest in some of the lower yielding, ancient wheat varieties, such as wild emmer, Kamut®, and spelt, which pre-date common wheat. Not only do these older varieties offer a broader spectrum of nutrients than common and durum wheat, but they contain alleles no longer present in modern inbred varieties.

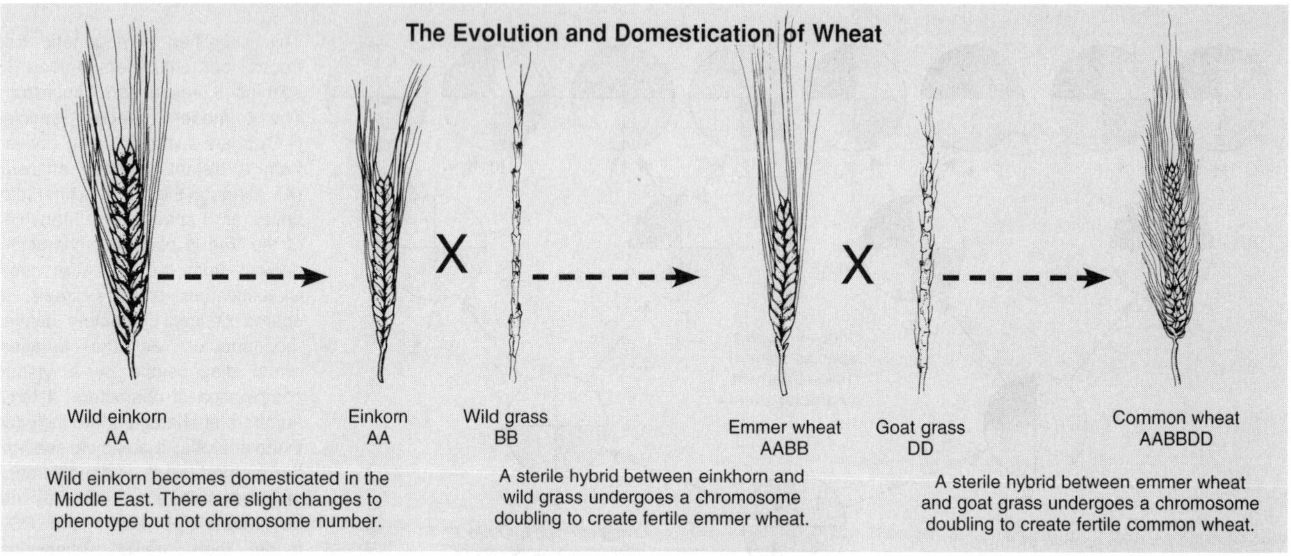

Ancient cereal grasses had heads which shattered easily so that the seeds were widely scattered. In this more primitive morphology, the wheat ear breaks into spikelets when threshed, and milling or pounding is needed to remove the hulls and obtain the grain. Cultivation and repeated harvesting and sowing of the grains of wild grasses led to domestic strains with larger seeds and sturdier heads. Modern selection methods incorporate genetic techniques to identify and isolate beneficial genes, e.g. the RHt dwarfing gene, which gave rise to shorter stemmed modern wheat varieties.

Modern bread wheat has been selected for its non-shattering heads, high yield, and high gluten (protein) content. The grains are larger and the seeds (spikelets) remain attached to the ear by a toughened rachis during harvesting. On threshing, the chaff breaks up, releasing the grains. Selection for these traits by farmers might not necessarily have been deliberate, but occurred because these traits made it easier to gather the seeds. Such 'incidental' selection was an important part of crop domestication. Hybrid vigour in cultivars is generated by crossing inbred lines.

Durum wheat is a modern variety developed by artificial selection of the domesticated emmer wheat strains. Durum (also called hard wheat) has large firm kernels with a high protein content. These properties make it suitable for pasta production. As with all new wheat varieties, new cultivars are produced by crossing two lines using hand pollination, then selfing or inbreeding the progeny that combine the desirable traits of both parents. Progeny are evaluated for several years for the traits of interest, until they can be released as established varieties or cultivars.

1. Describe three phenotypic characteristics that would be desirable in a wheat plant:

   (a) ______________________

   (b) ______________________

   (c) ______________________

2. Explain how both natural events and artificial selection have contributed to the high yielding modern wheat varieties:

____

____

Designer Herds

Most of the economically important traits in dairy cattle are quantitative traits, i.e. they are traits that are affected by many genes, as well as environment. The most important traits (below right) are expressed only in females, but the main opportunity for selection is in males. Intense selection of the best bulls, combined with their worldwide use through **artificial insemination** and frozen semen has seen a rapid genetic gain in dairy cattle since the 1970s. Bulls are assigned statistically-determined and unbiased **breeding values** based on the performance of their daughters and granddaughters. In this way, the bulls and cows with the best genetics can be selected to produce the next generation. More recent genetic techniques include **marker selected selection**, in which a genetic marker is used screen for particular alleles associated with traits of interest. Such techniques have enabled farmers to improve the accuracy of their herd records and the certainty with which they select their breeding stock.

Selective Breeding and Genetic Gain in Cattle

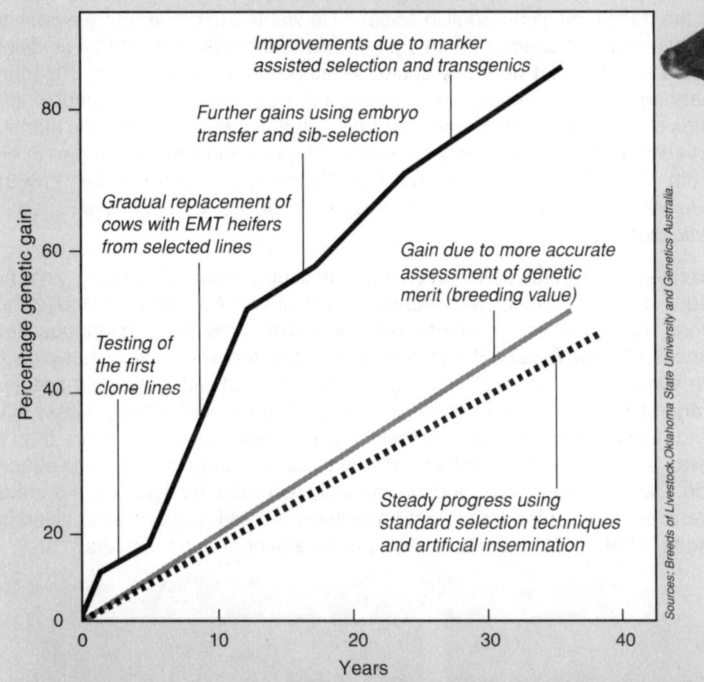

Cattle are selected on the basis of particular desirable traits (e.g. milk solids or muscle mass). Most of the genetic improvement in dairy cattle has relied on selection of high quality progeny from proven stock and extensive use of superior sires through artificial insemination (AI). Improved breeding techniques accelerate the **genetic gain**, i.e. the gain toward the desirable phenotype of a breed. The graph (above) shows the predicted gains based on artificial insemination and standard selection techniques (based on criteria such as production or temperament). These are compared with the predicted gains using breeding values (the value of the genes to the progeny) and reproductive technologies such as embryo multiplication and transfer (EMT) of standard and transgenic stock, marker assisted selection, and sib-selection (selecting bulls on the basis of their sisters' performance).

The Perfect Dairy Cow

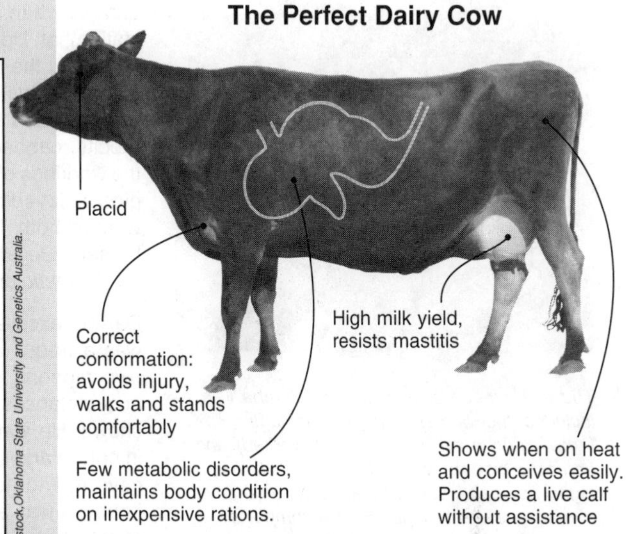

Breeding programmes select not only for milk production, but also for fertility, udder characteristics, and good health. In addition, artificial selection can be based on milk composition, e.g. high butterfat content (a feature of the Jersey breed, above).

A2 milk, which contains the A2 form of the beta casein protein, has recently received worldwide attention for claims that its consumption lowers the risk of childhood diabetes and coronary heart disease. Selection for the A2 variant in **Holstein cattle** has increased the proportion of A2 milk produced in some regions. A2 milk commands a higher price than A1 milk, so there is a commercial incentive to farmers to produce it.

1. Explain why artificial selection can effect changes in phenotype much more rapidly than can natural selection:

2. Suggest why selective breeding has proceeded particularly rapidly in dairy cattle:

3. Explain how molecular genetics has enhanced modern artificial selection techniques in the diary cow:

Darwin: Pigeon Fancier?

The rock pigeon: a versatile progenitor

The rock pigeon or rock dove (Columba livia) includes the domestic pigeon (including the fancy pigeons on which Darwin worked) and domestic pigeons which become feral. It is a highly adaptable species and shows a range of phenotypes. Feral pigeons for example show many different plumage colorations.

Pigeon Fanciers and Selective Breeding

"*... from so simple a beginning endless forms most beautiful and most wonderful have been, and are being evolved.*" This quotation closes Charles Darwin's most famous work "*The Origin of Species by Means of Natural Selection*". Most students of biology know of Darwin's voyage aboard *The Beagle*" and his precise and careful documenting of the variety of species he encountered on his travels, to the Galapagos in particular. But the naturalist's careful attention to biological detail extended to his work at home in England. Darwin began to formulate his theory of evolution during his five year voyage aboard *The Beagle*, but this work continued in earnest when he returned home to England and established a home (and research station) at Down House. Darwin delayed publishing his greatest work, fearing ridicule in the deeply religious English society. He wanted to gather more evidence to support his idea that species could change. He found this evidence by studying domesticated species that he knew could be shaped through breeding. Pigeons, rabbits, cabbages, gooseberries; these organisms would become his window into the workings of selection. Thus Darwin became a pigeon fancier. Indeed, the humble pigeon, loved by generations of English people, played a most important part in his work on both 'The Origin of Species' (1859) and 'Variation in Domestication' (1868). He said "*Believing that it is always best to study some special group, I have . . . taken up domestic pigeons.*"

Darwin excelled in careful observation and meticulous record keeping and he was a frequent correspondent with like-minded thinkers. As well as breeding his own pigeons, he managed to secure skins and skeletons from colleagues and acquaintances all over Britain. But Darwin was interested in evolution, not pigeon shows. He wanted a sense of how much variation existed within a single species in nature and saw selective breeding as a "speeded up version" of the process that gave rise to new species in nature. Darwin's pigeon work was much more than a hobby; it was a way to get his point across and to demonstrate the dramatic effects of selection. Darwin skeletonised and meticulously recorded the details of hundreds of specimens and concluded that if artificial selection could produce such diversity over decades, what might natural selection produce over millions of years?

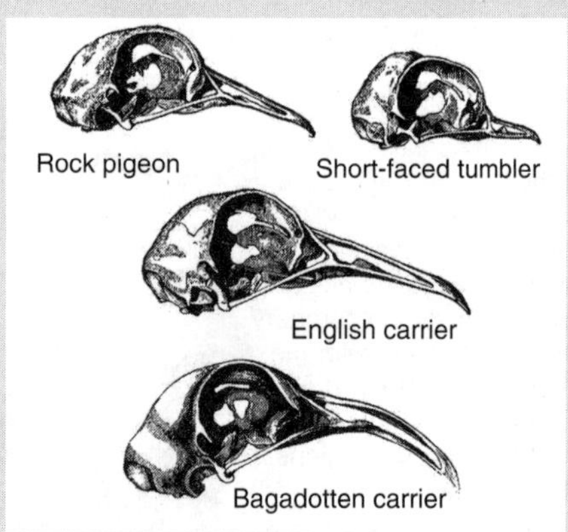

Skulls of various pigeon breeds as drawn by Darwin. Relative sizes accurate. Darwin noted that difference in breed appearance extended even to the skeletal features.
(Charles Darwin/Frances Darwin - out of copyright)

Pouters: This group includes breeds developed for the ability to inflate their crops. The pygmy pouter's bizarre appearance has made it one of the least popular breeds, except in shows.

The fantail is characterised by a fan-shaped tail composed of 30 to 40 feathers; more than most members of the pigeon family, which usually have only 12 to 14 feathers. A feather mutation called silky produces yet another variety.

1. Explain why Darwin sought support for his evolutionary theory from his pigeon breeding work: ______________________

2. Explain why his findings supported his ideas that species could change over time: ______________________

UNIT F215 5.2.1

Cloning in Plants and Animals

KEY TERMS

blastocyst
clone
corm
cutting
embryo splitting
embryonic stem cells (ESCs)
grafting
micropropagation
non-reproductive cloning (=therapeutic cloning)
reproductive cloning
rhizomes
rootstock
somatic cell nuclear transfer (SCNT)
suckers
tissue culture
tuber

Periodicals:
Listings for this chapter are on page 342

Weblinks:
www.biozone.co.uk/weblink/OCR-A2-2832.html

KEY CONCEPTS

- Clones are individuals that are genetically identical.
- Reproductive cloning and therapeutic cloning have different aims and present different ethical issues.
- Many plants are able to reproduce vegetatively because their tissues contain meristematic cells.
- Micropropagation is widely used to propagate and maintain superior plant genotypes.
- Animal cloning is technically more difficult than cloning plants and has still not been widely adopted.

OBJECTIVES

☐ 1. Use the **KEY TERMS** to help you understand and complete these objectives.

What is cloning? — page 186

☐ 2. Distinguish between **reproductive cloning** and **non-reproductive cloning** (also called therapeutic cloning), outlining the differences in both the techniques and outcomes.

Cloning in plants — pages 187-190

☐ 3. Distinguish between natural **vegetative propagation** and **artificial propagation** of plants.

☐ 4. Describe the variety of natural vegetative structures in plants, including **corms**, **tubers**, **bulbs**, and **rhizomes**. Using the example of **suckering** in elm trees, describe the production of **natural clones** in plants.

☐ 5. Describe how humans take advantage of the ability of plants to propagate vegetatively, e.g. through **grafting** and **cuttings**. Such techniques are enhancements of natural processes. Note that plants arising from cuttings will be **clones**, but grafting is often not a complete cloning method because sexual seedlings are often used as **rootstocks**. In these cases, only the top of the plant is clonal.

☐ 6. Describe how artificial clones of plants are produced using **micropropagation** techniques (plant **tissue culture**).

☐ 7. Discuss the benefits and disadvantages of plant cloning in agriculture.

Cloning in animals — pages 191-193

☐ 8. Describe how artificial clones of animals can be produced. In particular, describe techniques involved in **somatic cell nuclear transfer** (SCNT) and contrast these with cloning by **embryo splitting**.

☐ 9. Discuss the benefits and disadvantages of cloning animals, including the ethical and welfare issues associated with nuclear transfer techniques and with cloning in general.

☐ 10. EXTENSION: Describe the current and potential uses of cloning technology, including the cloning of transgenic organisms.

What is Cloning?

Cloning produces individuals that are genetically identical. It can occur naturally as a result of asexual reproduction or splitting of an embryo very early in development (twinning), or artificially, as the result of cloning technologies. The techniques for producing clones artificially fall into two categories: reproductive and non-reproductive cloning. **Reproductive cloning** is performed with the intent of creating another organism, genetically identical to the organism from which it was cloned (e.g. Dolly the sheep). **Non-reproductive** (therapeutic) **cloning** produces genetically identical embryos for the express purpose of harvesting embryonic stem cells (ESCs). Until recently, this has involved destroying the embryo.

Reproductive Cloning

Reproductive cloning technology is used to create an organism with the same DNA as an existing donor organism. Reproductive cloning is commonly performed using a technique called Somatic Cell Nuclear Transfer (SCNT). In this technique, an egg containing the transplanted genetic material is transferred into the uterus of a surrogate mother, where it will complete its development. Strictly speaking, the clone may not be identical to its donor because of mutations in the nuclear DNA and the genetic material acquired from the mitochondrial DNA.

There are many potential uses for reproductive cloning, including the cloning of endangered species. Some institutions, such as the San Diego Zoo, have cryogenic facilities where tissue samples of critically endangered species are stored. There is also the potential to clone extinct species if viable tissue samples are available.
Although there are many ethical and religious objections to reproductive cloning, the main biological concerns relate to the possible long term biological effects of SCNT. Although these are still largely unknown, they are likely to include defects, higher susceptibility to disease, and shortened life span.

A number of species have been cloned using reproductive cloning technology, including livestock breeds (e.g. the rare Enderby Island cattle) and Snuppy (left), an afghan hound cloned in South Korea in 2005.

Non-Reproductive Cloning

Non-reproductive cloning is also sometimes referred to as **therapeutic cloning**. Initially the process begins in the same way as reproductive cloning. However, the goal is not to create a cloned organism, but to produce embryos (or more specifically, embryonic stem cells) for use in research. ESCs are taken from **blastocysts** (right) which are five day old embryos containing 50-150 cells. In general, ESCs come from embryos which have been fertilised *in vitro* at fertilisation clinics and then have been donated for research.

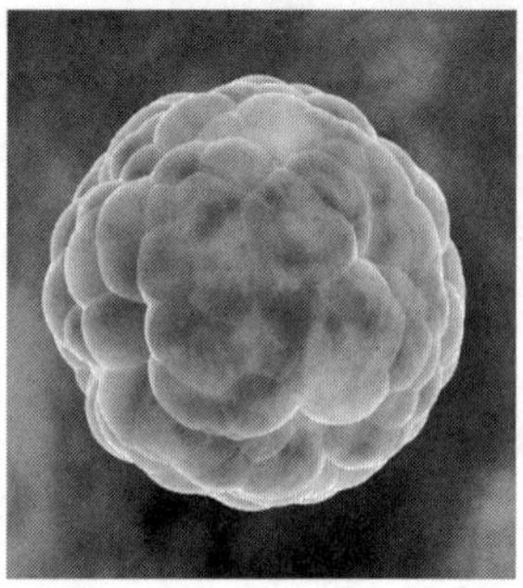

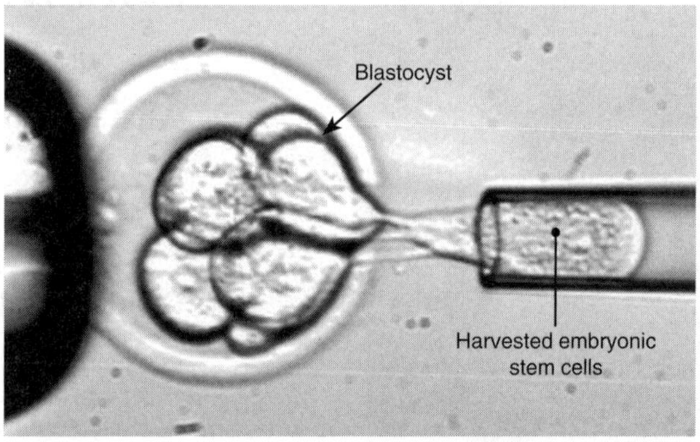

In the past, harvesting ESC from blastocysts (above) has destroyed the embryo, raising ethical issues about its use. However, recently stem cells have been harvested from embryos at the eight cell stage, and the embryos have developed to the 10 cell stage at the same rate as untouched IVF embryos. This advance may allow non-reproductive cloning research to progress more quickly in the future as it bypasses some of the ethical objections against its use.

1. Describe the differences between **reproductive cloning** and **non-reproductive cloning** techniques:

2. Discuss how recent advances in embryo survival after ESC have been removed may advance non-reproductive cloning:

3. Explain why a reproductively cloned organism may not be genetically identical to the donor organism:

Vegetative Propagation

Meristematic cells that are capable of differentiating are present in many plant tissues, and virtually all types of shoots and roots in flowering plants are capable of reproducing asexually by **vegetative propagation.** Humans exploit this ability and today many successful crop varieties are rarely grown from seed. Plants can spread quickly by vegetative means when conditions are favourable. By doing this, they do not need to produce flowers, pollen or seeds, structures which carry a high energy cost to the plant. Vegetative propagation by artificial means, such as cuttings and micropropagation, produces genetically identical plants (clones) year after year so that successful varieties are maintained. New varieties can be developed by grafting, which combines the favourable characteristics of two existing varieties.

Natural Vegetative Structures in Plants

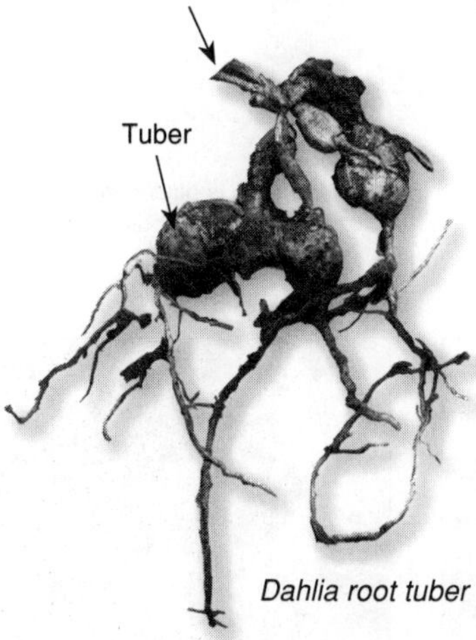

Dahlia root tuber

Root tubers, e.g. dahlias (above), lack terminal and lateral buds. Both stem and root tubers can give rise to new individuals.

Tubers are the swollen part of an underground stem or root, usually modified for storing food. The potato (below) is a **stem tuber**, as indicated by the presence of terminal and lateral buds.

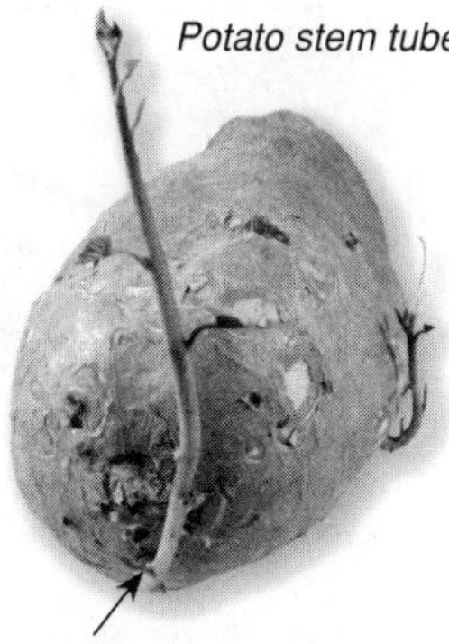

Potato stem tuber

Bulbs

A true bulb is really just a typical shoot compressed into a shortened form. Fleshy storage leaves are attached to a stem plate and form concentric circles around the growing tip. New roots form from the lower part of the stem.

Growth in crocus, a typical corm

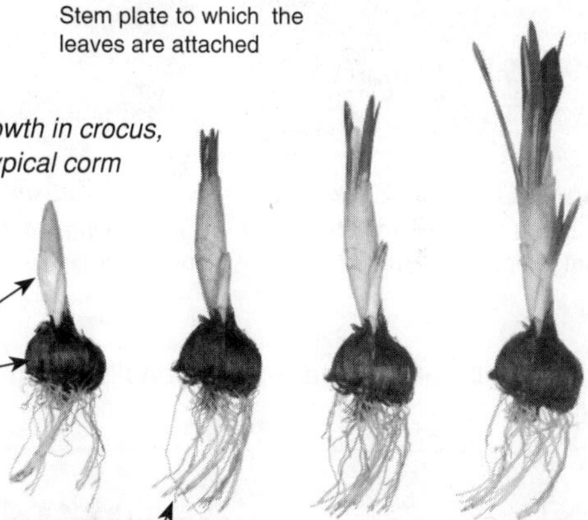

In a **corm**, food is stored in stem tissue. Corms look like bulbs, but if you cut a corm in half you see a mass of homogenous tissue rather than concentric rings of fleshy leaves as in a bulb. Cyclamen, gladiolus, and crocus (above) are corms.

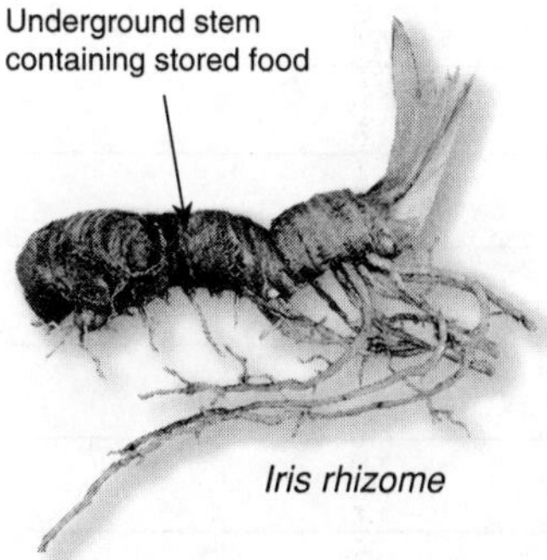

Iris rhizome

In **rhizomes**, as in corms, food is stored in the horizontal, underground stem. Rhizomes tend to be thick, fleshy or woody, and bear nodes with scale or foliage leaves and buds. Growth occurs at the buds on the ends of the rhizome or nearby nodes. Ginger, irises and lily-of-the-valley are rhizomes.

Vegetative Propagation in Elm

Elm trees (*Ulmus* spp.) reproduce vegetatively by sending up a series of **basal shoots** which grow from a bud on an existing root. This form of budding is also called **suckering**. Basal shoots can emerge at the base of the parent tree or some distance away. Much of the tree's energy is diverted into the shoots rather than into the growth of the parent plant.

Elm trees are valued for their timber quality and aesthetic appeal, but their numbers have been greatly reduced over the last century by dutch elm disease. Clones obtained by vegetative propagation of natural elm populations have been used by scientists to establish field gene banks of elms in an attempt to conserve the species.

Photo: Basal shoots on wych elm

1. Explain the term **vegetative propagation**: ____________________

2. Describe one major advantage (to the plant) of having a stem, tuber, or bulb filled with stored food:

Related activities: *Natural Vegetative Propagation, Artificial Vegetative Propagation*

Grafting

Grafting involves joining structures from two or more plants. Typically a twig section (scion) from one plant is joined to the shoot of another (root stock). Grafting is used for many fruit and landscape trees (see photo series below).

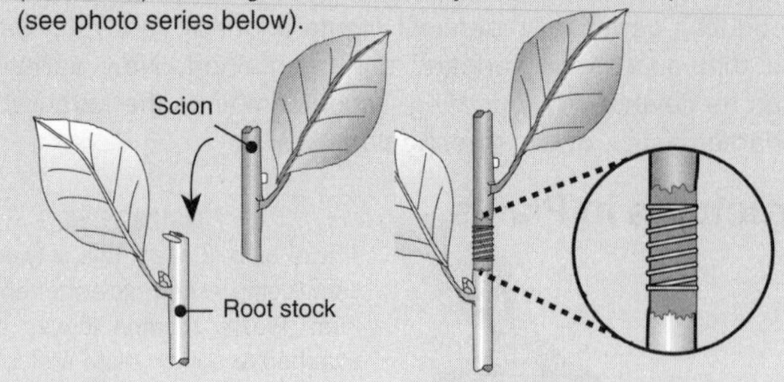

1. A **scion** is prepared by taking a cutting. The scion is then grafted to another plant (root stock).
2. The graft is covered in wax to prevent infection and held together with twine or raffia.

Cutting

Cuttings are sections of a parent plant, which are removed and grown as new individuals. Cuttings are used to propagate herbaceous plants, but can be used on woody plants with the use of hormones to promote root growth.

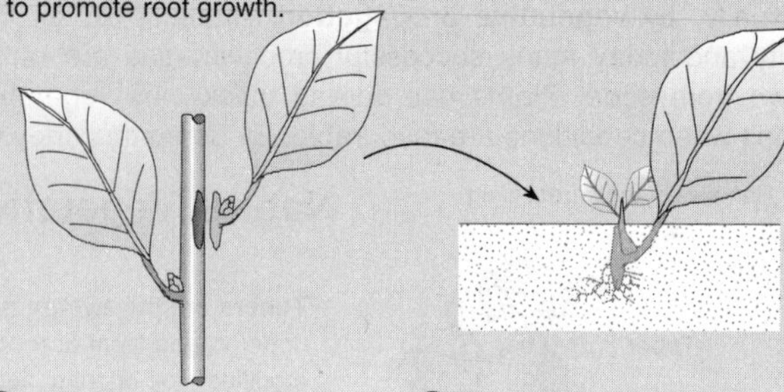

1. A leaf and accompanying axial bud is cut from the parent stock.
2. The cutting is placed in a growth medium containing rooting hormones.

A scion is removed from the parent plant prior to grafting.

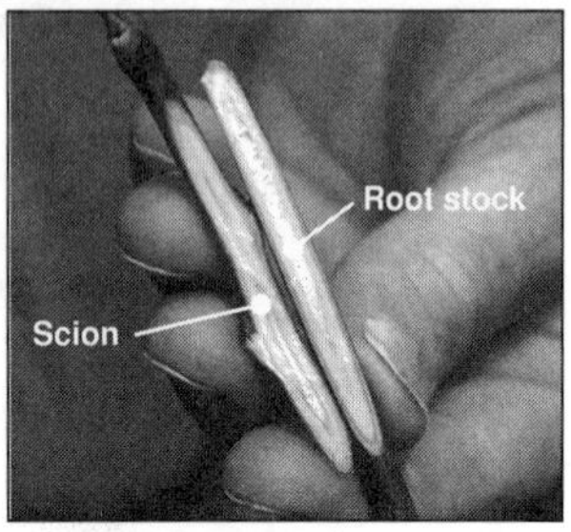

Scion being grafted onto the stem of the root stock.

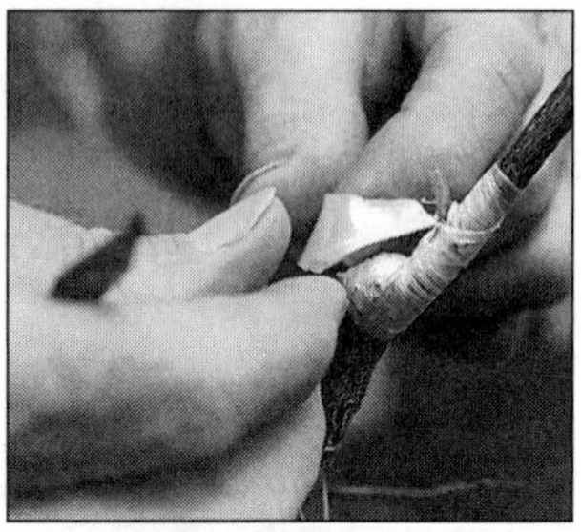

The graft is sealed and covered to prevent water loss and infection.

The graft is then labelled for future reference and monitoring.

3. Describe how humans have benefited from the vegetative propagation of plants: ______________________

4. Describe how plants benefit by reproducing vegetatively: ______________________

5. (a) Explain how vegetative propagation of plant material can be used as a strategy in species conservation:

(b) Suggest why stocks of rare plants could be reproduced this way, rather than using seed: ______________________

(c) Describe a potential disadvantage of vegetative propagation plants, such as elm, that are endangered by disease:

6. Distinguish between cutting and grafting, including reference their modern applications: ______________________

Plant Tissue Culture

The Issue

- Individuals vary in characteristics, even within specific varieties of the same species.
- Plants that are uniform are easier to manage, but are difficult to produce in large numbers from naturally pollinated stock.
- It is advantageous for crop management, quality control, and dissemination of transgenics to be able to produce large numbers of genetically uniform plants. The technology can also be applied in the recovery of endangered species.

Concept 1

Plants can be cut into many pieces, almost all of which have the potential to grow into new plants.

Concept 2

Plants propagated from the same tissues will all have the same genetic make up. They will all be clones.

Concept 3

Different **growth hormones** in plants cause the development of different parts of the plant, e.g. the shoots or roots.

Concept 4

If desirable plants are used for the original tissue then all the plants propagated from them will also be desirable.

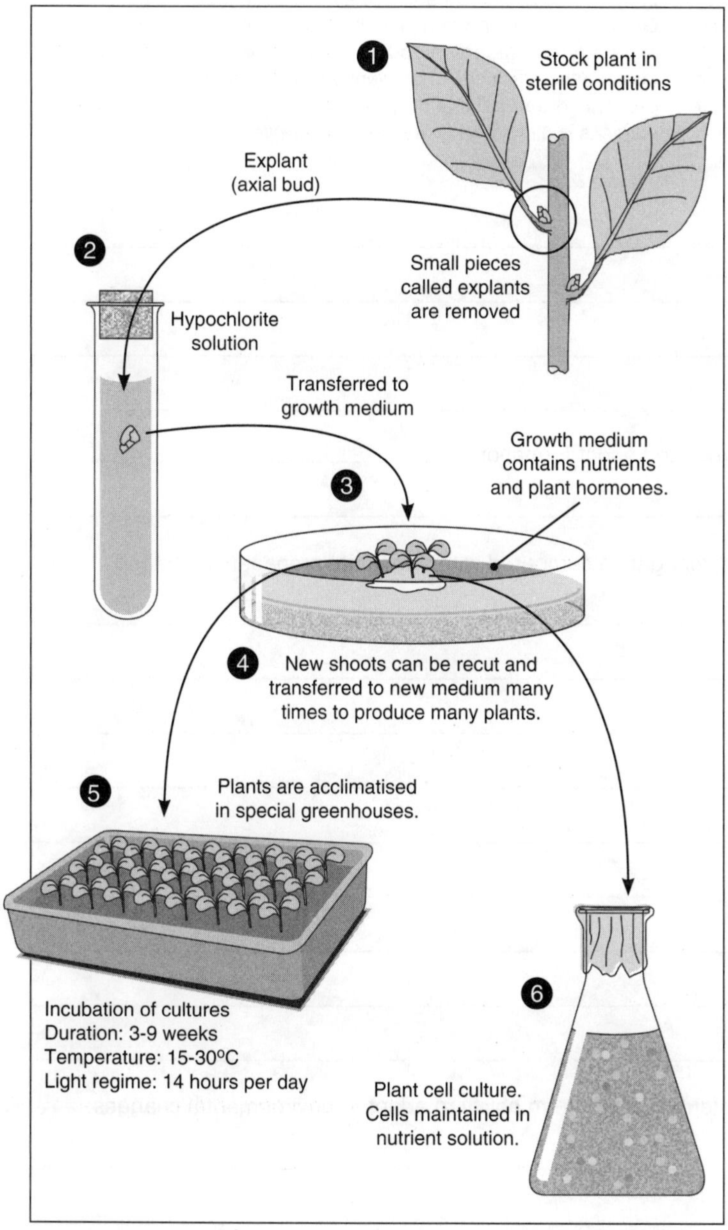

Techniques

Pest free stock plants have small pieces cut (**excised**) from them. These pieces, called **explants**, may be stem tissue, nodes, flower buds, leaves or sections of shoot tip meristem.

The surface of the explants are sterilised using a solution of **sodium hypochlorite**.

The explants are transferred to a **culture vessel** under sterile conditions.

Growth hormones are added. By changing the concentrations of different hormones, the explants can be made to grow shoots, roots, stems, or an undifferentiated cell mass (callus).

Plants induced to grow shoots and roots are transferred to growing containers under controlled greenhouse conditions to be acclimatised before planting outside.

Calluses are mechanically broken up into separate cells and placed into a growth medium where they can be maintained indefinitely.

Outcomes

Plants propagated in this way may be genetically unstable or infertile, with chromosomes structurally altered or in unusual numbers. The success of tissue culture is affected by factors such as selection of **explant** material, the composition of the culturing media, plant hormone levels, lighting, and temperature. New genetic stock may be introduced into cloned lines periodically to prevent reduction in genetic diversity.

Further Applications

Plant tissue culture is extensively used in **forestry** to produce trees of uniform height and diameter. It has a number of advantages, including the ability to generate large numbers of plants from one explant and rapid propagation of species that have a long generation times or low seed production.

Micropropagation of the Tasmanian blackwood tree *(Acacia melanoxylon)*

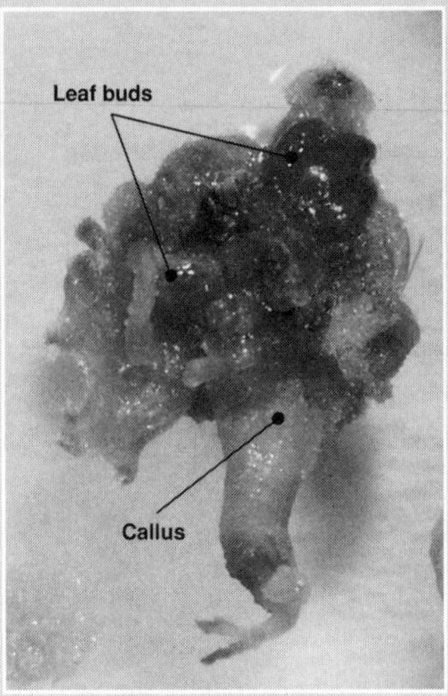

Greening and formation of leaf buds on a callus growing on culturing medium.

Normal shoots with juvenile leaves growing from a callus on media. They appear identical to those produced directly from seeds.

Seedling with juvenile foliage 6 months after transfer to greenhouse.

Micropropagation is increasingly used in conjunction with genetic engineering to propagate transgenic plants. Genetic engineering and micropropagation achieve similar results to conventional selective breeding but more precisely, quickly, and independently of growing season. The **Tasmanian blackwood** (above) is well suited to this type of manipulation. It is a versatile hardwood tree now being extensively trialled in some countries as a replacement for tropical hardwoods. The timber is of high quality, but genetic variations between individual trees lead to differences in timber quality and colour. Tissue culture allows the multiple propagation of trees with desirable traits (e.g. uniform timber colour). Tissue culture could also help to find solutions to problems that cannot be easily solved by forestry management. When combined with genetic engineering (introduction of new genes into the plant) problems of pest and herbicide susceptibility may be resolved. Genetic engineering may also be used to introduce a gene for male sterility, thereby stopping pollen production. This would improve the efficiency of conventional breeding programmes by preventing self-pollination of flowers (the manual removal of stamens is difficult and very labour intensive).

Information courtesy of Raewyn Poole, University of Waikato (Unpublished Msc. thesis).

1. Explain the general purpose of tissue culturing plants:

2. (a) Explain what a **callus** is:

   (b) Explain how a callus may be stimulated to initiate root and shoot formation:

3. Discuss the **advantages** and **disadvantages** of micropropagation compared with traditional propagation methods:

4. Describe a potential problem with micropropagation in terms of long term ability to adapt to environmental changes:

Cloning by Nuclear Transfer

PHOTO: Courtesy Roslin Institute ©

The Issue

- Individuals vary in characteristics, even within specific breeds of animal, such as sheep.
- Clones remove the variability and produce livestock that would develop in a predictable way or produce a consistent quality of product such as wool or milk.
- Clones produced using traditional embryo-splitting are derived from an embryo whose physical characteristics are not completely known. Scientists wanted to speed up the process and produce clones from a proven phenotype.

Concept 1

Somatic cells can be made to return to a dormant or embryonic state so that their genes will not be expressed.

Concept 2

The nucleus of a cell can be removed and replaced with the nucleus of an unrelated cell. Cells can be made to fuse together.

Concept 3

Fertilised egg cells produce embryos. Egg cells that contain the nucleus of a donor cell will produce embryos with DNA identical to the donor cell.

Concept 4

Embryos can be implanted into surrogate mothers and develop to full term with seemingly no ill effects.

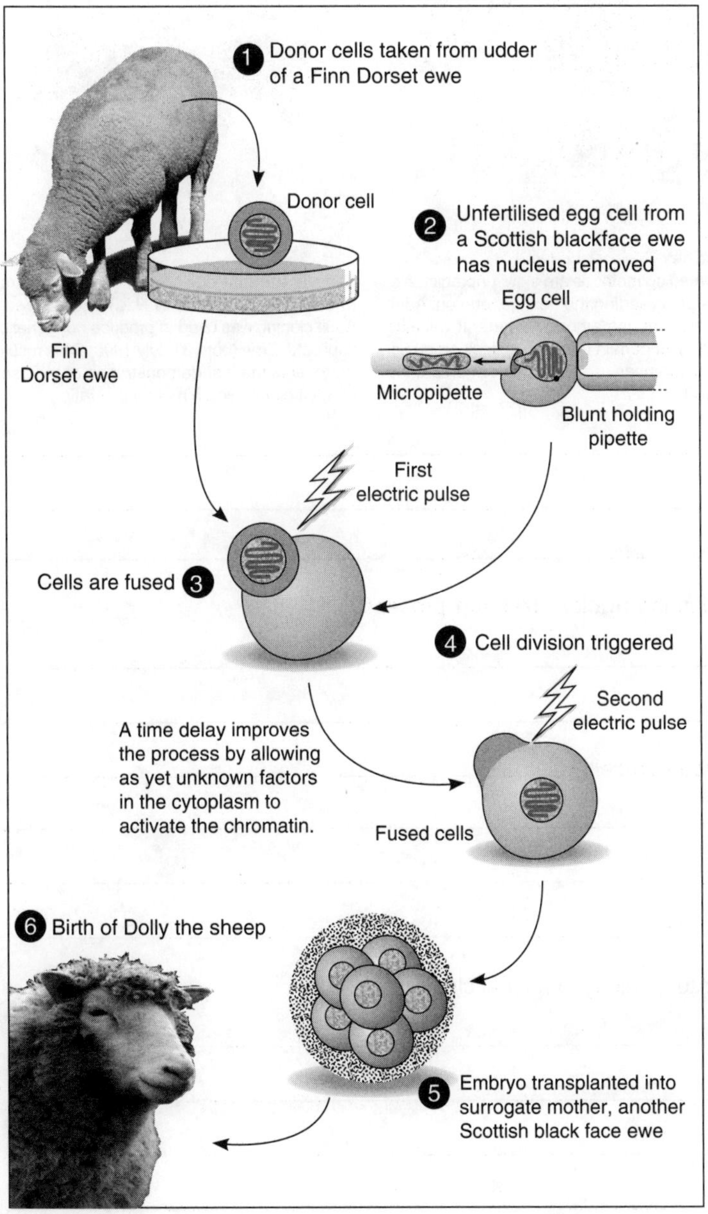

PHOTO: Courtesy Roslin Institute ©

Techniques

Donor cells from the udder of a Finn Dorset ewe are taken and cultured in a low nutrient media for a week. The nutrient deprived cells stop dividing and become **dormant**.

An **unfertilised egg** from a Scottish blackface ewe has the nucleus removed using a micropipette. The rest of the cell contents are left intact.

The dormant udder cell and the recipient denucleated egg cell are fused using a mild electric pulse.

A second electric pulse triggers cellular activity and cell division, jump starting the cell into development. This can also be triggered by chemical means.

After six days the embryo is transplanted into a surrogate mother, another Scottish blackface ewe.

After a 148 day gestation 'Dolly' is born. DNA profiling shows she is genetically identical to the original Finn Dorset cell donor.

Outcomes

Dolly, a Finn Dorset lamb, was born at the Roslin Institute (near Edinburgh) in July 1996. She was the first mammal to be cloned from **non-embryonic** cells, i.e. cells that had already differentiated into their final form. Dolly's birth showed that the process leading to cell specialisation is not irreversible and that cells can be 'reprogrammed' into an embryonic state. Although cloning seems relatively easy there are many problems that occur. Of the hundreds of eggs that were reconstructed only 29 formed embryos and only Dolly survived to birth.

Further Applications

In animal reproductive technology, cloning has facilitated the rapid production of genetically superior stock. These animals may then be dispersed among commercial herds. The **primary focus** of the new cloning technologies is to provide an economically viable way to rapidly produce transgenic animals with very precise genetic modifications.

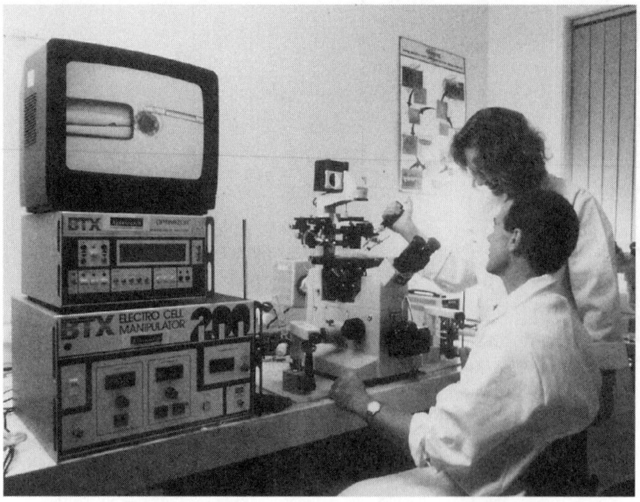

Dr David Wells and Pavla Misica in the embryo micromanipulation laboratory at AgResearch in Hamilton, New Zealand (monitor's image is enlarged on the right).

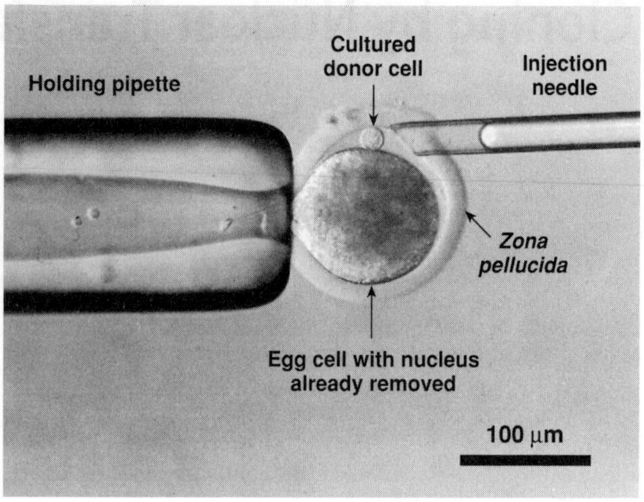

A single cultured cell is injected underneath the *zona pellucida* (the outer membrane) and positioned next to the egg cell (step 3 of diagram on the left).

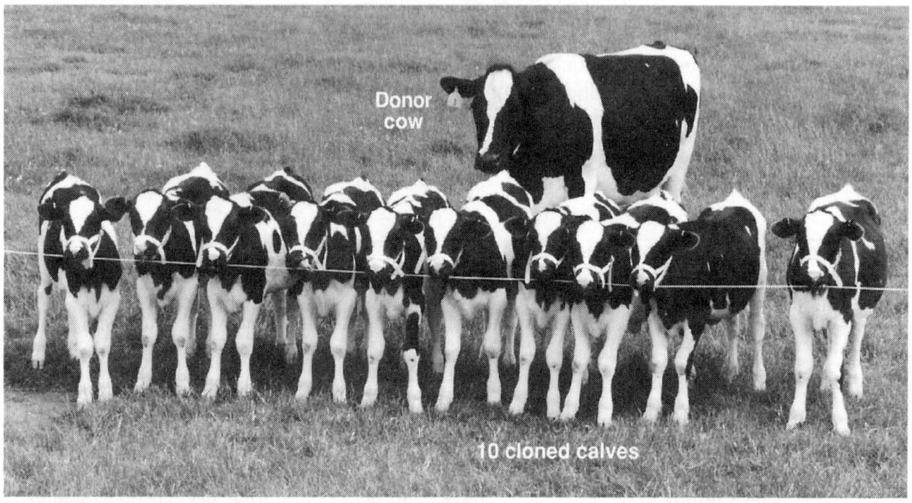

Adult cloning heralds a new chapter in the breeding of livestock. Traditional breeding methods are slow, unpredictable, and suffer from a time delay in waiting to see what the phenotype is like before breeding the next generation. Adult cloning methods now allow a rapid spread of valuable livestock into commercial use among farmers. It will also allow the livestock industry to respond rapidly to market changes in the demand for certain traits in livestock products. In New Zealand, 10 healthy clones were produced from a single cow (the differences in coat colour patterns arise from the random migration of pigment cells in early embryonic development).

Lady is the last surviving cow of the rare Enderby Island (south of N.Z.) cattle breed. Adult cloning was used to produce her genetic duplicate, Elsie (born 31 July 1998). This result represents the first demonstration of the use of adult cloning in animal conservation.

1. Explain the significance of the production of Dolly: ______________________

2. Explain how each of the following events is controlled in the **nuclear transfer** process:

   (a) The switching off of all genes in the donor cell: ______________________

   (b) The fusion (combining) of donor cell with enucleated egg cell: ______________________

   (c) The activation of the cloned cell into producing an embryo: ______________________

3. Describe two potential applications of nuclear transfer technology in animal cloning:

   (a) ______________________

   (b) ______________________

Cloning by Embryo Splitting

Livestock breeds frequently produce only one individual per pregnancy and all individuals in a herd will have different traits. Cloning (by embryo splitting or other means) makes it possible to produce high value herds with identical traits more quickly. **Embryo splitting**, or artificial twinning, was developed in the 1980s and quickly adopted by livestock breeders. It is the simplest way in which to create a clone because it simply replicates the natural twinning process. A fertilised egg is grown into eight cells before being split into four individual embryos, each consisting of just two cells. The four genetically identical embryos are then implanted into surrogate mothers. While this technique produces multiple clones, the clones are derived from an embryo whose physical characteristics are not completely known. This represents a serious limitation for practical applications when the purpose of the procedure is to produce high value livestock. In 2000, a rhesus macaque was cloned in this manner, with the goal of producing identical individuals that could be used to perfect new therapies for human disease. Cloning technology can also be used to produce early embryos from which undifferentiated stem cells can be isolated for use in tissue and cell engineering.

Livestock are selected for cloning on the basis of desirable qualities such as wool, meat, or milk productivity.

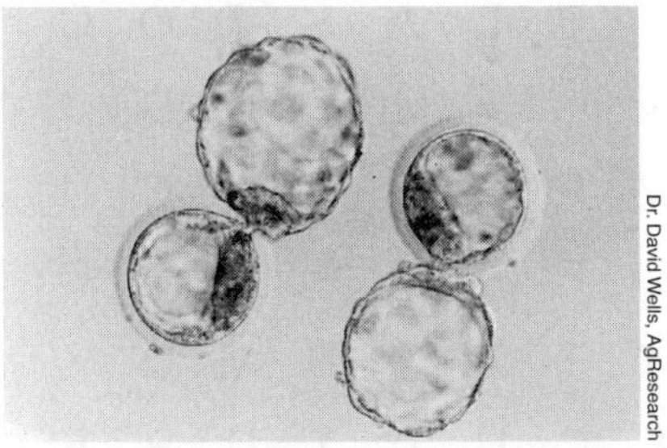

Cloned embryos immediately prior to implantation into a surrogate. These are at the blastocyst stage (a mass of cells that have begun to differentiate).

The individuals produced by embryo splitting have the same characteristics as the parents.

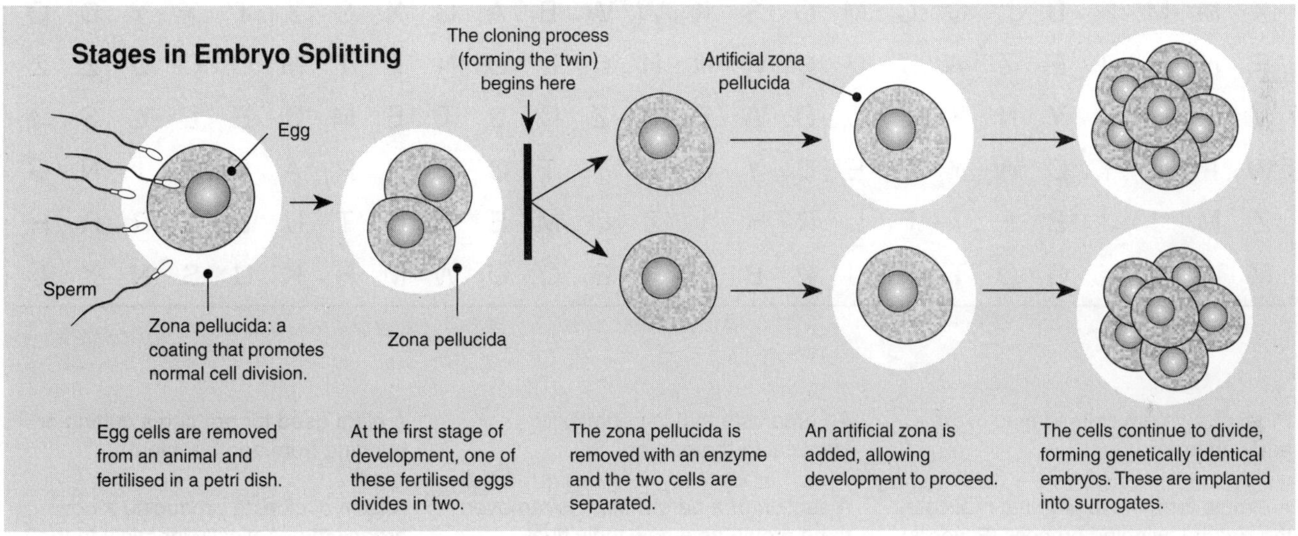

1. (a) Explain how embryo splitting differs from nuclear transfer as a means by which to clone animals:

(b) Describe one potential disadvantage of cloning using embryo splitting as opposed to producing clones by SCNT:

2. Describe the potential medical benefits to be gained from producing cloned early-stage embryos:

3. Explain why it would be undesirable to produce all livestock using cloning methodologies:

Periodicals: *History of cloning*

Related activities: *Cloning by Nuclear Transfer, What is Cloning?*
Web links: *What is Cloning?*

KEY TERMS: Word Find

Use the clues below to find the relevant key terms in the WORD FIND grid

L	L	C	T	H	E	R	A	P	E	U	T	I	C	C	L	O	N	I	N	G	I	T	N	A
R	D	S	Z	A	Y	B	R	O	O	T	S	T	O	C	K	U	C	H	Z	R	K	W	V	C
I	D	E	M	B	R	Y	O	S	P	L	I	T	T	I	N	G	L	T	Q	Q	C	I	H	H
P	U	Q	R	E	P	R	O	D	U	C	T	I	V	E	C	L	O	N	I	N	G	A	D	E
C	S	C	N	T	X	J	T	F	B	L	A	S	T	O	C	Y	S	T	K	E	K	V	B	M
W	Y	W	C	U	T	T	I	N	G	I	J	F	N	D	J	V	E	N	Z	M	S	L	E	C
O	U	D	A	R	O	I	F	M	P	S	P	Z	X	S	U	C	K	E	R	B	V	T	I	P
R	M	I	C	R	O	P	R	O	P	A	G	A	T	I	O	N	H	A	H	R	P	A	U	N
P	R	I	C	Y	G	F	F	K	T	Z	Y	B	M	Q	X	W	L	O	Y	Y	K	U	X	U
G	X	K	T	I	S	S	U	E	C	U	L	T	U	R	E	I	O	I	K	O	Y	X	U	U
P	P	E	D	C	E	E	Z	Q	G	D	Y	I	S	R	O	F	K	L	Z	N	I	X	Q	P
X	M	M	F	B	L	C	O	M	O	S	K	W	W	B	A	G	X	C	X	I	X	Y	D	O
F	H	U	J	E	Z	W	T	U	U	W	H	H	C	L	O	N	E	T	M	C	O	U	Z	Z
V	W	H	U	Y	N	K	S	L	D	W	B	J	Z	C	S	T	E	M	C	E	L	L	S	J
W	P	C	Y	C	W	Y	P	E	C	Y	H	E	I	T	O	H	G	R	A	F	T	I	N	G
Z	M	J	J	B	F	T	F	L	R	H	I	Z	O	M	E	R	U	T	U	B	E	R	R	H
M	W	R	K	G	O	T	H	U	P	B	M	H	B	Q	O	W	M	H	K	U	S	N	X	L

Pluripotent stem cells formed in the early embryo.

A simple form of cloning that replicates the natural twinning process (2 words).

A method of cloning plants using explant tissue which is grown in sterile conditions in a culture vessel.

These are unspecialised cells that may differentiate into one of many kinds of cell (2 words).

The growth of tissue or cells in a medium separate from the donor organism (2 words).

The production of cloned embryonic stem cells for purposes of repairing damaged organs (2 words).

A type of vegetative propagation which involves joining structures from two or more plants.

An organism that is genetically identical to the parent.

A section of a parent plant is removed to be grown as a new individual.

Name given to a five day old embryo. It contains 50-150 cells.

The transfer of the nucleus from a somatic cell into an egg from which the nucleus has been removed (Acronym).

A shoot produced by the root a plant, can give rise to a new plant.

A vertical, swollen underground plant stem that stores food.

A horizontal, underground stem used to store food.

The swollen part of an underground stem or root, usually modified for storing food.

A plant used for grafting a cutting or budding from another plant.

A form of cloning producing a new organism genetically identical to the organism from which it was cloned (2 words).

UNIT F215

5.2.2

Biotechnology

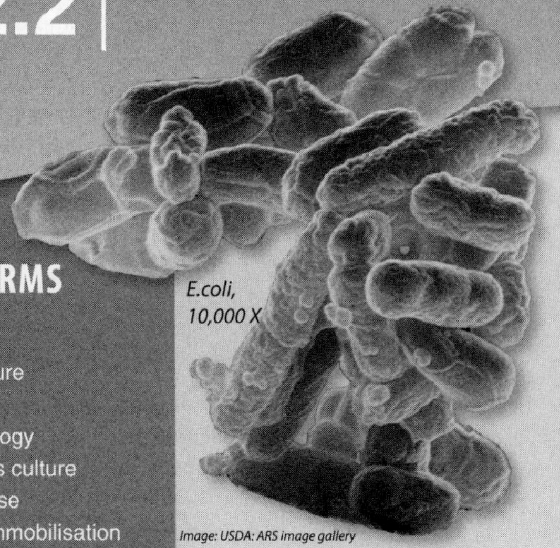
E.coli, 10,000 X

Image: USDA: ARS image gallery

KEY TERMS

asepsis
batch culture
bioreactor
biotechnology
continuous culture
death phase
enzyme immobilisation
enzyme isolation
exponential phase
fermentation
lag phase
microorganism
primary metabolite
secondary metabolite
stationary phase
yield

KEY CONCEPTS

- Biotechnology describes the industrial use of living organisms to produce useful commodities.
- Microbial cultures must be controlled to optimise the growth conditions for maximising product yield.
- Batch cultures and continuous cultures operate under different principles for different purposes.
- Primary metabolites are directly involved in normal growth; secondary metabolites are not.
- Enzymes are immobilised to maximise efficiency and reduce costs in industrial processes.

OBJECTIVES

☐ 1. Use the **KEY TERMS** to help you understand and complete these objectives.

What is biotechnology? page 196

☐ 2. Define the term biotechnology. Identify areas traditionally associated with biotechnology and the areas now encompassed by the term. Appreciate the role of biotechnology in providing employment and trade, and in improving productivity and quality of life in today's world.

Microorganisms and biotechnology? pages 197-202

☐ 3. Explain why microorganisms are often used in biotechnological processes and describe examples, e.g. soy sauce production or extraction of metals.

☐ 4. Use a diagram to describe the standard growth curve of a microorganism (e.g. bacterium or fungus) in closed culture. Identify the **lag phase**, the phase of rapid (sometimes **exponential**) **growth**, the **stationary phase**, and the **death phase**. Suggest how microbial cultures might be maintained in the rapid phase of growth.

☐ 5. Explain the difference between **primary metabolites** and **secondary metabolites** and describe examples.

☐ 6. With reference to specific examples, compare and contrast the processes of **batch culture** and **continuous culture**. Illustrative examples could include production of secondary metabolites (e.g. penicillin) by batch culture, and enzymes (e.g. protease) or biomass (e.g. mycoprotein) in continuous culture.

☐ 7. Describe features of the large scale industrial culture of microorganisms in **bioreactors** (also called biofermenters). Describe the problems and advantages associated with these large scale **fermentations**. Explain the importance of manipulating the growing conditions in the culture vessel to maximise the **yield** of product.

☐ 8. Explain the importance of **asepsis** in the manipulation of microorganisms and microbial cultures.

Enzyme technology pages 203-206

☐ 9. BACKGROUND: Describe the properties necessary in the enzymes used in industry (e.g. thermostability) and describe the basic procedure for producing enzymes from microorganisms.

☐ 10. Describe how enzymes can be **immobilised**.

☐ 11. Explain the advantages of **enzyme isolation** and immobilisation in large-scale industrial processes.

Periodicals:
Listings for this chapter are on page 342

Weblinks:
www.biozone.co.uk/weblink/OCR-A2-2832.html

Teacher Resource CD-ROM:
Case Studies in Biotech

What is Biotechnology?

Biotechnology (also called **biotech**) is a term describing any technological application using living things (or components of living things) to produce products or processes for a specific use. Medicine, agriculture, aquaculture, food processing, non-food industrial processes, and the environment all benefit from the applications of biotechnology. Biotechnology uses the techniques and principles from many areas of biological science including genetics, molecular biology, biochemistry, embryology, immunology, and cell biology. It may also draw upon other scientific disciplines such as chemical engineering and information technology. Humans have used traditional biotechnology for thousands of years to improve crop and livestock characteristics and alter the properties of foods using microorganisms (e.g. cheese production and brewing). Modern biotechnology practices are much more recent, with many significant breakthroughs occurring only in the last 60 years (e.g. the discovery of the structure of DNA, and the discovery of the first restriction enzyme).

BIOTECHNOLOGY

Medicine

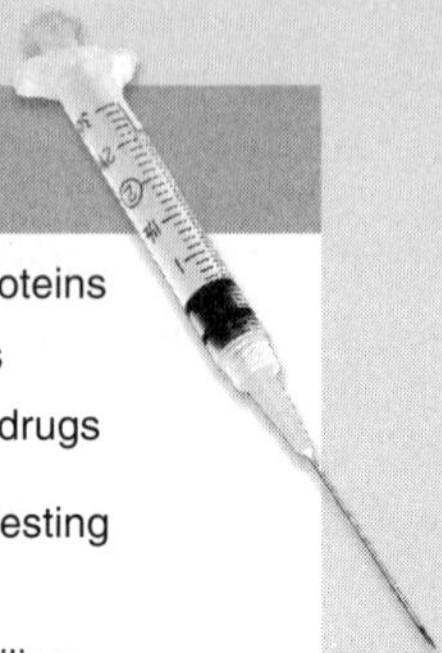

- **Pharmaceutical production**
  - Human proteins
  - Antibiotics
  - Synthetic drugs
- **Diagnostic testing**
  - Antibody testing
  - Imaging
  - Gene profiling
- **Vaccine development**
  - Traditional vaccines
  - Recombinant vaccines
- **Gene therapy**
  - Vectors for gene therapy
  - Gene delivery systems
- **Organ transplants**
  - Organ transplant
  - Xenotransplantion
  - Stem cell technology

Food Production & Processing

- **Agriculture & aquaculture**
  - Increased disease resistance
  - Herbicide/insecticide resistance
  - Increased nutritional value
  - Improved stress tolerance
  - Increased production rate
- **Food processing**
  - Fermentation technology
  - Enzymatic modification (includes recombinant enzymes)
  - Improved process control and efficiency
  - Enhanced characteristics (e.g. flavour, nutritional value, shelf life)
  - Diagnostic food testing

Environment

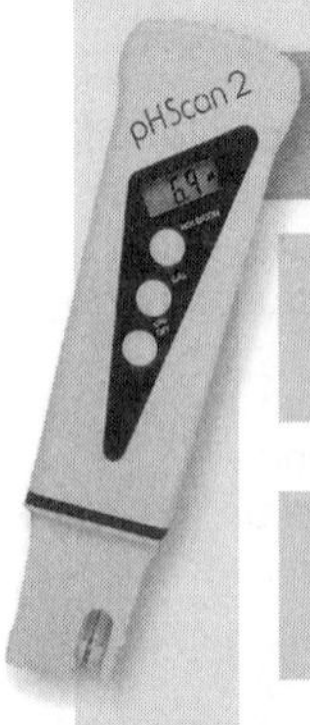

- **Bioremediation**
  - Organic spills (petroleum)
  - Metal contamination
  - Radioactive material
- **Biosensors**
  - Chemical monitoring
  - Pathogen monitoring
- **Water treatment**
  - Waste water
  - Sewage
- **Pest control**
  - Weed control
  - Control of feral animals

Industry

- **Biofuels**
  - Production of fuels using alternatives to fossil fuels (e.g. sugar cane, maize)
- **Biocatalysts**
  - Synthesis of chemicals
  - Brewing industry
  - Pharmaceutical production
- **Green plastics**
  - Production of plastics using petroleum alternatives (e.g. sugar cane)
- **Mining**
  - Ore leaching
  - Metal extraction
  - Coal cleaning

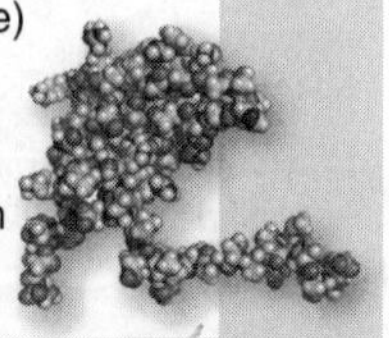

Periodicals:
Growth industry

Microbes and Biotechnology

Industrial production of microbial products involves large scale culture of fungi and bacteria to produce commercially valuable substances. Many pharmaceuticals and food ingredients (flavourings, thickeners, stabilisers, and enzymes) are produced using these microbial fermentations. The microbes are first **isolated** and then cultured in an appropriate environment. The desired product is then extracted from the cells themselves (e.g. enzymes) or from the culture medium (e.g. antibiotics). While it is relatively easy to grow microbes on a small scale, **scaling up** these procedures for use on an industrial scale creates problems. **Bioreactors**, designed for either **batch culture** or **continuous culture**, optimise the conditions for microbial growth and production of the desired product. This requires constant monitoring and adjustment of growth conditions. Many of the microbes used in industry produce valuable commodities as by-products of their normal metabolism. Others are natural mutants with faulty metabolic pathways, and some are genetically engineered to express a particular gene as its protein product.

Industrial Fermenter (Bioreactor) Technology

The photograph above shows an industrial scale bioreactor used for the production of diphtheria and pertussis vaccine. The microorganisms that are well suited to use in industry show certain properties: they have simple nutritional requirements, temperature and pH optima for maximum growth, amenability to culture in large scale fermenters, and a high growth rate (therefore high productivity).

During production it is important to keep the process as free as possible of undesirable contaminants. The absence of undesirable microorganisms within a biotechnology process is termed **asepsis**. Many biotech processes rely on the presence and action of specific microbes to work, but the presence of an undesirable microbe within the process can be catastrophic. Problems include:

- Product contamination and spoilage
- Undesirable product characteristics
- Loss of production time (and profit)
- Low product yield
- Increased costs associated with machinery cleanup

Asepsis should not be confused with **sterilisation** which is the complete removal of all microorganisms.

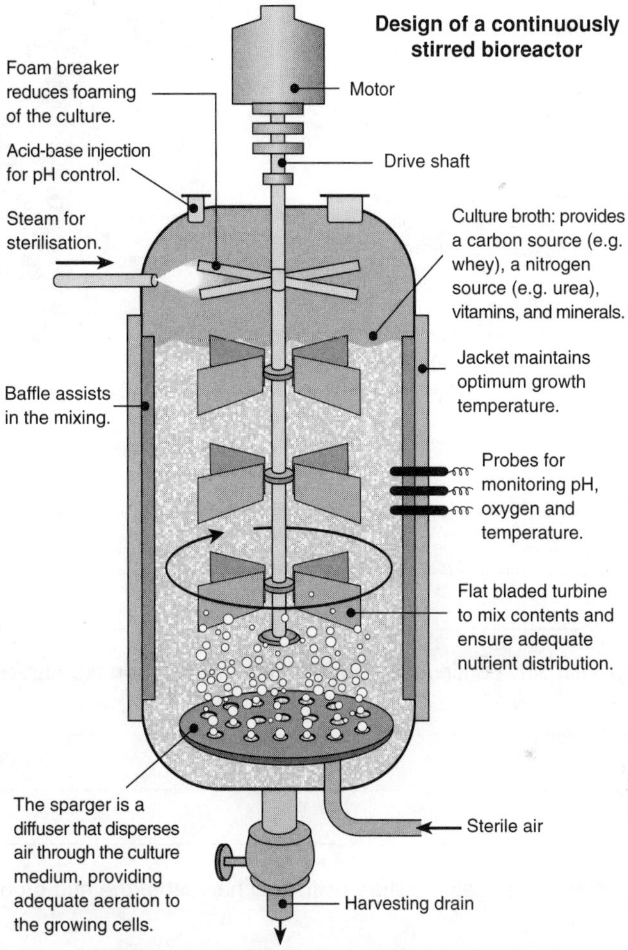

The Problems Associated With Scaling Up

Effective scaling up of relatively simple laboratory procedures to full sized industrial biofermenters requires microbiologists and bioengineers to solve a number of problems:

- All undesirable organisms must be prevented from entering the fermenter. There can be no risk of contamination.
- Cultures of aerobic microbes must be given an adequate supply of oxygen. This can be difficult in large volume cultures.
- Powerful motors are needed to mix the culture which has a porridge like consistency.
- Nutrient levels need to be maintained at optimum levels throughout the life of the culture.
- The heat generated by microbial activity needs to dissipated. The entire culture must be keep at a constant temperature.
- Waste products need to be constantly removed.
- The build up of foam due to the production of carbon dioxide must be monitored and controlled.
- Rigorous testing using scale models (*left*) must be carried out to ensure that the problems associated with scaling up have been eliminated.

Continuous Culture

Continuous culturing involves a constant flow of fresh culture medium into the bioreactor, and removal of material out of the bioreactor. The desired components are harvested from the material removed from the bioreactor. Nutrient addition and product removal occurs at an equal rate to maintain a constant volume. Continuous culturing is often used when a young culture of actively producing cells is required (e.g. some antibiotics are only produced during active growth).

Advantages
- Continuous growth over long periods.
- Population can be maintained in exponential growth for extended periods.
- Equipment is in constant use, so there is less down time.
- Nutrients are added and inhibitory metabolites are constantly removed to maintain optimum growth.

Disadvantages
- Difficulty in maintaining optimum culture conditions.
- Contamination is more likely to occur.
- Product consistency can be difficult to control.

Batch Culture

Batch culturing involves adding cells to a fixed volume of culture medium. The culture medium is harvested as a batch at the end of the process. The process is halted when all of the nutrients are used, or a threshold level of toxic metabolites is reached and further growth of the culture is inhibited. Most large scale production is carried out by batch cultures.

Advantages
- Bioreactor conditions are easier to manipulate.
- There is less risk of contamination.
- Product quality is easier to control.

Disadvantages
- More down time as equipment must be cleaned between each batch.
- Product output is determined by the limited nutrient supply, and build up of inhibitory metabolites.

1. Describe the primary difference between a continuous and batch culture system: ______

2. Explain why continuous culture is often used when the harvested product is biomass (cells) or a primary metabolite:

3. Explain when batch culture (with final harvest of the end-product) would be used in preference to continuous culture:

4. Explain the importance of asepsis in industrial processes involving microbial cultures: ______

5. Outline how industrial biofermenters overcome the following problems associated with scaling up:

(a) Heat generated by microbial activity: ______

(b) Microbial demand for oxygen: ______

(c) Nutrient demand: ______

Microbial Growth and Metabolites

Microbial growth follows a well established pattern comprising several phases (below). During their growth, microbes produce intermediate and end products as part of their normal metabolism. Such products are termed **metabolites** and fall into two categories. **Primary metabolites** are compounds that are essential for the continuation of the microbes metabolic activity. They are usually produced in small quantities and may be utilised by the organism. **Secondary metabolites** are not required for microbial metabolism, but may be useful for the microbe (e.g. in inhibiting competitors). They frequently accumulate in large quantities during the stationary phase of growth. Examples of secondary metabolites that are produced commercially for human use include penicillin, quinine, and codeine. Bioreactor conditions can be manipulated to promote the production of specific metabolites, although it is generally more difficult to control the production and harvest of primary (as opposed to secondary) metabolites.

Microbial Growth in a Closed Culture

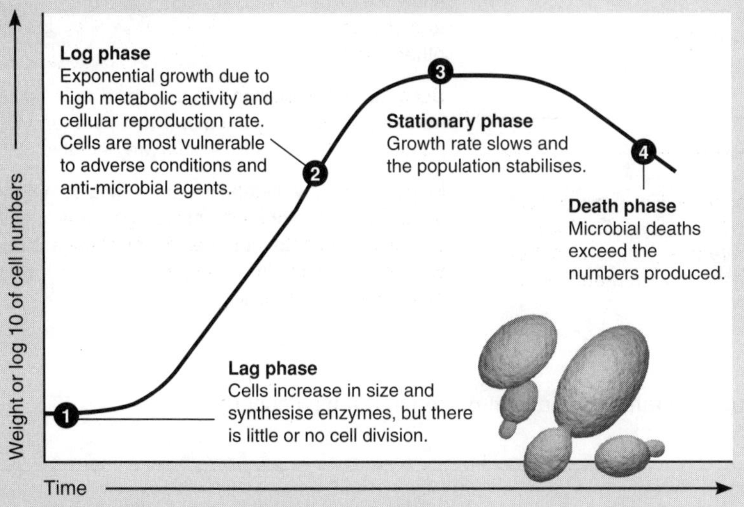

The graph above illustrates the growth curve for a yeast culture grown within a closed culture system. Bacteria show a similar growth curve. Growth curves of microbial cell numbers against time typically show these four phases.

1. **Lag phase:** Cell numbers are relatively constant as the organisms adjust to the conditions and prepare for growth.

2. **Log phase:** The phase of **exponential growth**. In conditions optimal for microbial growth, the cells begin multiplying at an exponential rate, quickly increasing cell numbers. For yeast, the generation time is approximately 1 hour, but the doubling time of some bacteria can be as little as 15 minutes.

3. **Stationary phase:** In a closed culture system no new nutrients are added and waste products are not removed. Microbial growth slows as the nutrients become depleted and waste products build up. The growth rate equals the death rate, so there is no net growth in the microbial population, and numbers stabilise.

4. **Death phase:** Microbial numbers decrease as the death rate exceeds growth rate; a result of a lack of nutrients and build of toxic metabolites.

Production of Primary Metabolites

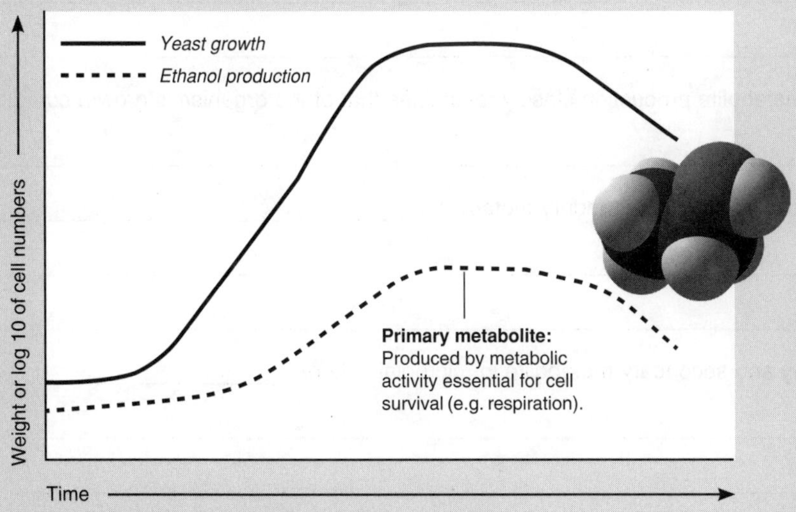

Amino acids, nucleotides, proteins, carbohydrates, lipids, and vitamins are primary metabolites needed for culture growth. Acetone, ethanol, butanol, and organic acids are required for deriving energy. The quantity of some of these metabolites exceeds the requirements of the producers and accumulates in the culture.

During the log phase of microbial growth (in culture), many intermediate metabolic products are produced, which are further required for growth or for energy-yielding catabolism. These **primary metabolites** are produced in excess of requirements and accumulate in the culture, from which they can be extracted and purified.

Primary metabolites form at the same time as the cells grow, so their production curves are very similar to the organism's growth curve. Microbial production of primary metabolites contributes significantly in modern biotechnology. Through fermentation, microorganisms growing on inexpensive carbon sources can produce valuable products such as amino acids, nucleotides, organic acids, and vitamins.

The graph (left) compares the production curve of the primary metabolite ethanol, with the growth curve for yeast.

Production of Secondary Metabolites

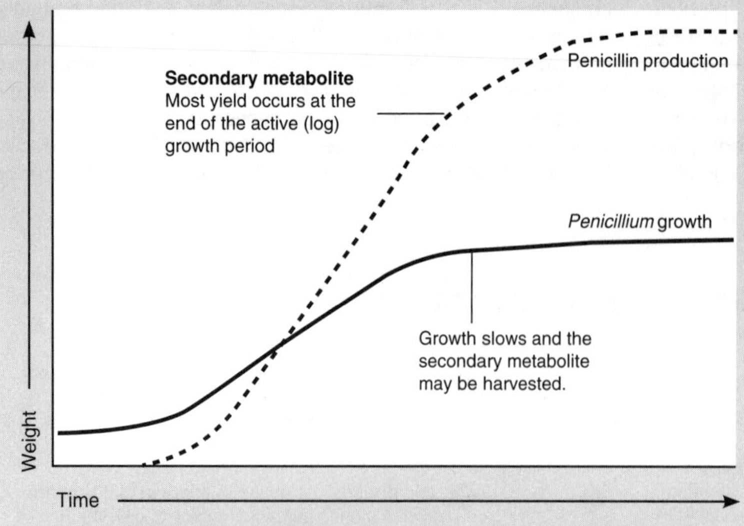

The graph (above) illustrates the production of penicillin, a secondary metabolite produced by species of the fungus, Penicillium. Penicillin is produced once the microbe has largely completed its growth and has entered the stationary phase. Many important antibiotics are produced as secondary metabolites by bacteria and fungi.

Secondary metabolites are organic compounds which are not immediately essential to microbial survival or reproduction. Secondary metabolites are often produced as defence mechanisms or to allow the organism to compete against other species.

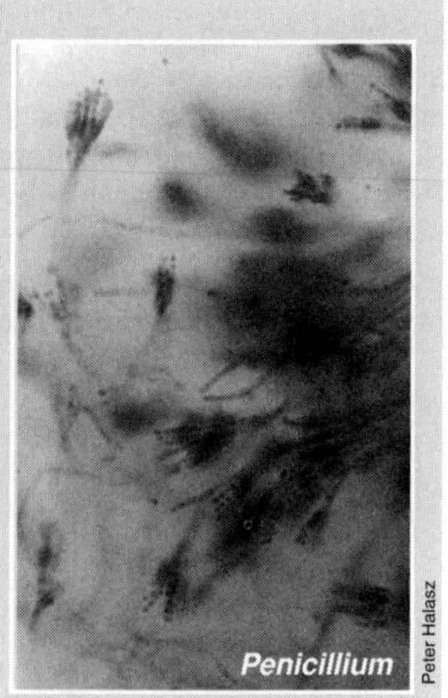

Secondary metabolites are produced by a limited number of microorganisms, when one or more nutrients in the culture medium are depleted.

Many secondary metabolites (including some from genetically engineered microorganisms) have beneficial uses to humans as pharmaceuticals. Examples include atropine, erythromycin, morphine, and penicillin.

1. (a) Explain why there is an initial lag in the growth of a microorganism placed into a new culture:

   (b) Suggest how this time lag could be reduced when starting new culture:

2. Describe the effect on the microbial growth curve of adding fresh nutrients and removing toxic by-products:

3. (a) Explain why the curve for a primary metabolite production closely resembles that of the organism's growth curve:

   (b) Explain why this is not the case for production of a secondary metabolite:

4. Explain the differences between a primary and secondary metabolite in microbial culture:

5. Explain why a secondary metabolite might be produced after a microbe had completed most of its growth phase:

Soy Sauce Production

Soy sauce manufacture originated in China 2500 years ago. The traditional fermentation process takes months to complete, and conditions during fermentation are carefully monitored to ensure the final product has the correct flavour characteristics. There are three main steps in the traditional **soy sauce fermentation** process: **Koji-making**, **brine fermentation**, and **refinement**. During Koji-making, a soy and wheat mixture is cooked, cooled, and inoculated with a fungus, usually ***Aspergillus oryzae*** or ***Aspergillus sojae***. Enzymes produced by the mould break down the starch and proteins to simple sugars and peptides. These are used as fuel by the microorganisms in the brine fermentation stage. In this stage, which can take up to 11 months, lactic acid bacteria ferment the sugars to lactic acid which lowers the pH. Yeasts also produce alcohols, which contribute to the flavour of soy sauce. Salt provides flavour and establishes a favourable chemical environment for the lactic acid bacteria and yeast. Salt also helps to protect the finished product from spoilage. The final stage of refinement involves separating the liquid from the more solid by-product, and pasteurisation to kill microorganisms. Some modern manufacturing techniques use a **chemical hydrolysis method** (rather than fermentation) to produce soy sauce in a matter of days rather than months. Soy sauce produced by these chemical methods are considered inferior to the traditional fermented product and may contain potentially harmful residues.

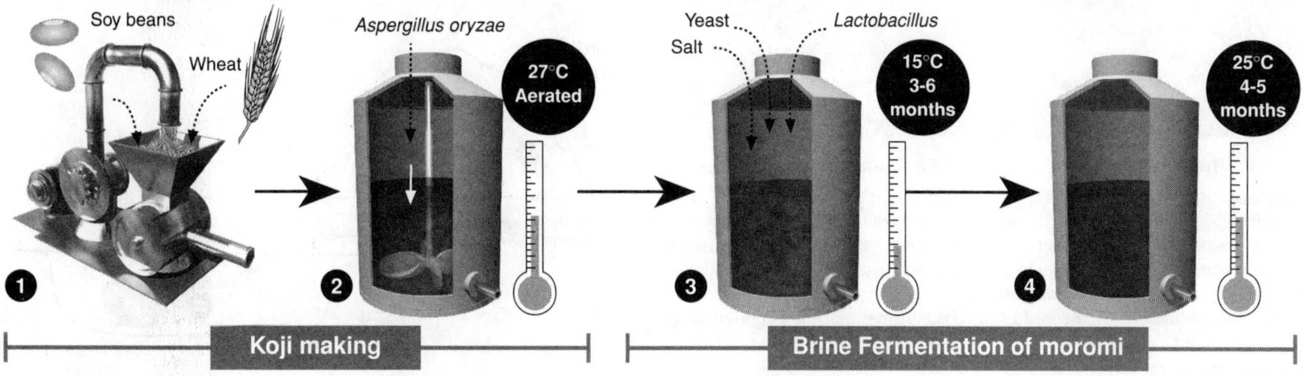

1. In the first stage of the koji-making process, soy beans and wheat are crushed and mixed together with water to produce a mash.

2. The mash is cooked, cooled to 27°C, **inoculated** with the fungi ***Aspergillus*** and matured in large aerated vats for three days. The mash is now called **koji**.

3. The koji is fermented with salt in deep tanks. ***Lactobacillus*** and **yeast** enhance fermentation. The mixture is now called **moromi**. This fermentation takes 3-6 months at 15°C.

4. A second fermentation at 25°C for 4-5 months ages the soy sauce. Brine fermentation utilises the sugars and peptides produced during the koji making stage.

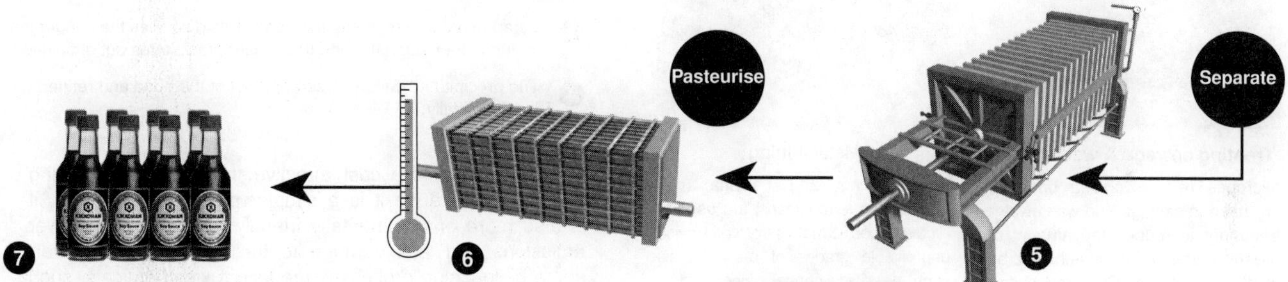

Refinement

5. The mixture is now a thick paste. The liquid soy sauce is **separated** from solid material using a filter press. A hydraulic press pushes the liquid through layers of cloth filters.

6. The liquid is pasteurised to kill any microorganisms and enhance the flavour profile of the soy sauce.

7. The pasteurised soy sauce may be filtered a second time to improve clarity. Alcohol, sodium benzoate or benzoic acid may be added as preservatives before the soy is bottled.

1. How would crushing the soy beans and wheat before inoculation enhance the Koji-making process:

____

2. Explain the contribution of each of the following microorganisms to the production of fermented soy sauce:

   (a) Fungus (*Aspergillus* spp.) ______________________________

   (b) Lactic acid bacteria: ______________________________

   (c) Yeasts: ______________________________

3. (a) Suggest why the soy sauce produced using chemical hydrolysis is regarded as inferior to the fermented product:

   ____

   ____

   (b) Suggest why commercial producers might choose to use this method anyway: ______________________________

   ____

Environmental Biotechnology

Environmental biotechnology utilises microorganisms for a wide variety of environmental applications. Examples include the clean up and treatment of waste water, as biosensors to detect chemical or microbial contaminants, and in bioremediation to clean up oil spills. The mining industry uses microbes to extract metals from low grade ores in a process termed bioleaching. Many metals, including copper, a commercially important metal, are extracted in this way (see below).

Uses of Microorganisms in the Environment

Bioremediation

Bacteria (e.g. *Pseudomonas* spp.) metabolise the hydrocarbons in oil spills, breaking down the oil into its basic constituents. The extremophilic bacterium *Deinococcus radiodurans* has been genetically engineered to digest ionic mercury produced from radioactive nuclear waste.

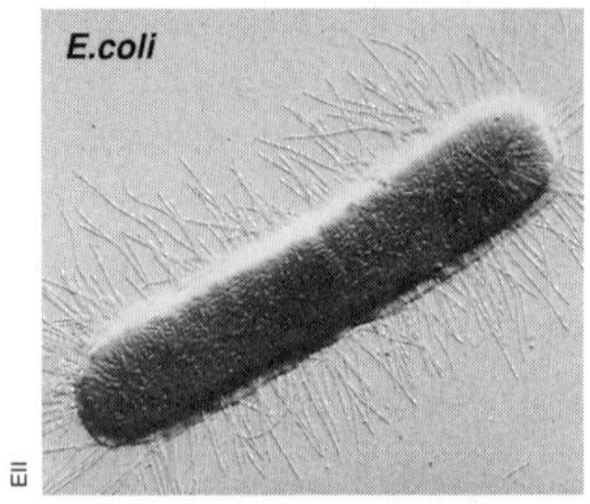

Environmental biosensors

Bacteria (e.g. Lactococcus, *E.coli, Vibrio fischeri, Photobacterium*) can be genetically engineered to detect specific chemical or pathogenic pollutants in the environment. The pollutant may activate a light-emitting compound in the bacterium, which is easily detected.

Treating sewage & wastewater

Microbes (e.g. *Zoogloea* bacteria) are used in sewage and wastewater treatment to reduce the amount of organic material. This is achieved by oxidising waste to CO_2 and water. Treatment can be anaerobic or aerobic, depending on the treatment phase and type of bacteria used.

Metal mining

Various fungi and bacteria (e.g. *Thiobacillus ferrooxidans*) are used to recover specific metals from otherwise unprofitable grades of ores. Metals such as gold, copper, zinc, nickel, uranium and cobalt can be extracted using microbial action. The process is referred to as bioleaching or biomining.

Microorganisms and Bioleaching

Microbes play an important role in the mining industry where they are used to recover metals from low grade ores which would be unprofitable to mine by conventional methods. A common example is the use of the bacterium *Thiobacillus ferrooxidans* to extract copper. The process is outlined below.

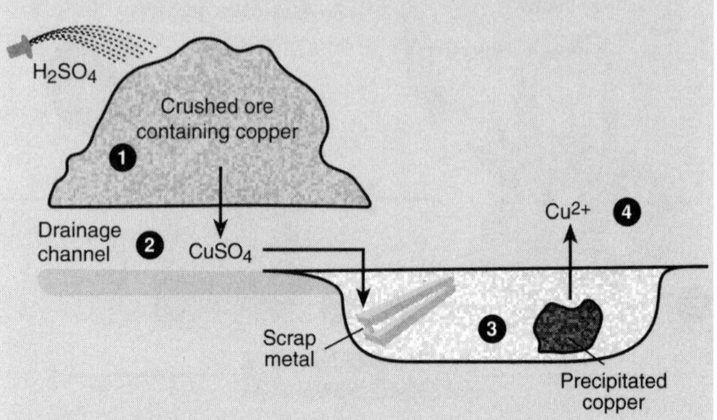

1. Crushed ore is acidified with sulphuric acid to encourage microbial growth. Microbes oxidise the ore releasing Fe (III), which reacts with the copper compound releasing copper ions.
2. The copper ions then form copper sulphate, which is removed from the ore along a drainage channel and into a shallow pond.
3. Scrap metal is placed into the pond. This displaces the copper ion in the copper sulphate, and the copper precipitates out of solution.
4. The precipitated copper is scraped out of the pond and refined electrolytically.

Bioleaching is more cost effective than traditional mining techniques because it is a simpler process. In general, it is also more environmentally friendly as it results in fewer emissions and less damage to the landscape. However, some bioleaching processes produce toxic chemicals, such as sulphuric acid, which could contaminate ground water. Bioleaching takes up a lot of space and is a slower process than smelting. This may also be seen as a disadvantage.

1. Describe two examples of how microorganisms are used in environmental monitoring and clean up:

   (a) ____

   ____

   ____

   (b) ____

   ____

   ____

2. Discuss the advantages of using biomining over traditional metal mining techniques: ______________________

   ____

   ____

   ____

Industrial Production of Enzymes

Enzymes have been used in the production of food for many thousands of years, but the use of specific enzymes for industrial processes in comparatively new. Many industries now rely on the large scale use of enzymes for the manufacture of products that would otherwise require high temperatures or pressures. Industrial enzymes need to be relatively robust against denaturation and capable of working over a large range of conditions. Most enzymes for industry are microbial in origin and are produced in large scale fermentation vats using both solid and liquid growth media. Note that the word **fermentation** when used in industry applies to both aerobic and anaerobic microbial growth in **bioreactors**. The generalised plans for the production of both intracellular and extracellular enzymes is illustrated below.

1 Microbial growth
Microorganisms (bacteria or fungi) are grown under optimised conditions until the desired product is ready for harvesting.

2 Separation
Drum filtration separates the components of the fermenter vat. At this point, production methods diverge:

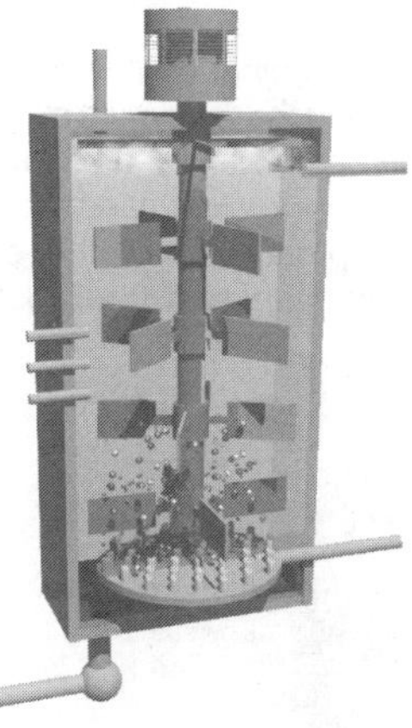

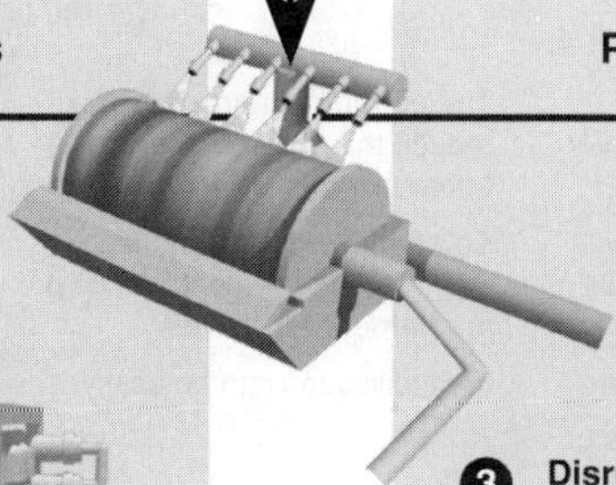

Producing Extracellular Enzymes

Culture medium and secreted (extracellular) enzymes

3 Concentration
The enzyme solution is concentrated by reducing its water content, e.g. by **reverse osmosis**.

Preservation
Antibacterial agents are added to prevent contamination.

3a: Crude product

4 Purification and processing
The crude enzyme product may be dried to produce a powder, or further purified by precipitation, crystallisation or adsorption (e.g. on to clays).

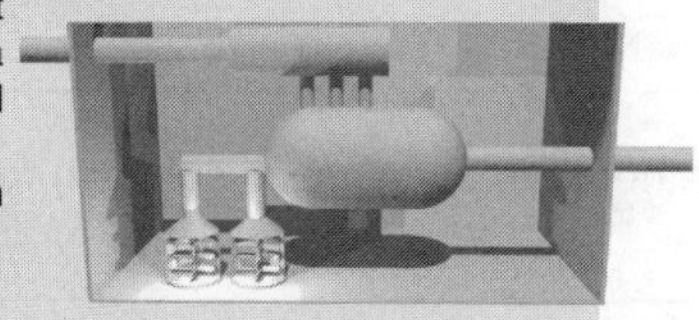

Producing Intracellular Enzymes

Microbial cells and the enzymes contained within them

3 Disruption
Once the cells have been separated from the culture medium, they must be disrupted (using ultrasound) to release the enzymes within the cells.

4 Centrifugation
The cellular debris remaining after disruption is removed by centrifugation or filtration.

5 Purification and processing
Initial purification involves precipitation with ammonium sulfate or organic solvents. Further purification occurs by ion exchange chromatography or gel electrophoresis.

1. Giving an example, describe the benefits of using microbial enzymes in industrial processes:

2. Compare the processes for producing intracellular and extracellular enzymes, above:

   (a) Explain the main way in which the two production methods differ:

   (b) Suggest the reason for this difference:

3. Describe one benefit of packaging and using crude enzyme extracts (3a):

Putting Enzymes to Use

Depending on the way in which the desired end-product is produced, enzymes may be used as crude whole cell preparations or as cell-free enzyme extracts. Whole cell preparations are cost effective, and appropriate when the processes involved in production of the end product are complex, as in waste treatment and the production of semi-synthetic antibiotics. Cell free enzyme extracts are more expensive to produce, but can be a more efficient option overall. To reduce costs and improve the efficiency of product production, enzymes are sometimes immobilised within a matrix of some kind and the reactants are passed over them. The various methods by which enzymes are put to work are compared in the diagram below.

Industrial enzymes

	Advantages	Disadvantages
Cell free enzyme extract Enzyme is used in solution	There is generally a high level of enzyme activity when the enzymes are free in solution.	The enzyme may be washed away after use. The end-product is not enzyme free and may require purification.
Immobilised enzyme Enzyme is held in an inert material	The enzymes can be used repeatedly and recovered easily (this reduces costs). The enzyme-free end-product is easily harvested. The enzymes are more stable due to the protection of a matrix. The life of some enzymes, e.g. proteases, is extended by immobilisation.	The entrapment process may reduce the enzyme activity (more enzyme will be needed). Some methods offering high stability (e.g. covalent bonding) are harder to achieve. Immobilisation can be costly.
Whole cell preparation Whole cells may be immobilised	Useful for enzymes that are unstable or inactivated when outside the cell. Useful for complex processes utilising more than one intracellular enzyme.	Less expensive and more rapid than first producing a pure enzyme extract. Some of the substrate is used for microbial growth, so the process is less efficient overall.

Methods of Enzyme Immobilisation

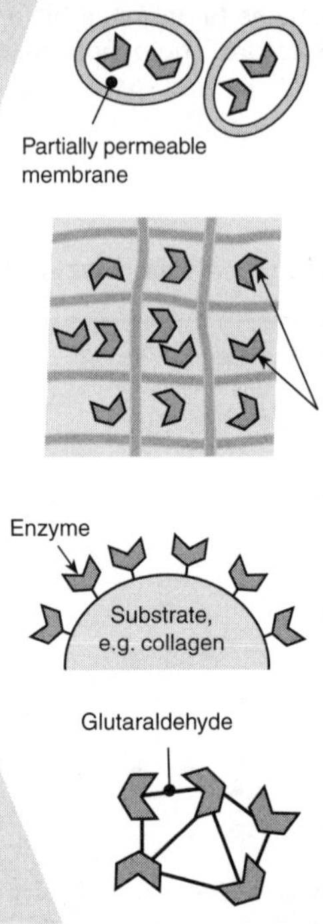

Micro-encapsulation The enzyme is held within a membrane, or within alginate or polyacrylamide capsules.

Lattice entrapment Enzyme is trapped in a gel lattice, e.g. silica gel. The substrate and reaction products diffuse in and out of the matrix.

Covalent attachment Enzyme is covalently bonded to a solid surface e.g. collagen or a synthetic polymer.

Direct cross-linking Glutaraldehyde is used to cross-link the enzymes. They then precipitate out and are immobilised without support.

1. (a) Explain one benefit of using a cell free enzyme extract to produce a high-value end-product:

   (b) Identify one factor that might be important when deciding *not* to use a cell free extract:

2. (a) Describe two benefits of using immobilised enzymes (rather than enzymes in solution) for industrial processes:

   (b) Describe a disadvantage associated with the use of immobilised enzymes:

   (c) Describe a factor that would affect the rate of end-product harvest from immobilised enzymes:

3. The useful life of protease enzymes is extended when they are immobilised (as opposed to being in solution). Using what you know of enzyme structure, explain why immobilisation has this effect in this case:

4. Suggest why immobilisation would reduce the activity of certain enzymes:

Applications of Enzymes

Microbes are ideal organisms for the industrial production of enzymes because of their high productivity, ease of culture in industrial fermenters, and the ease with which they can be genetically modified to produce particular products. In addition, because there is an enormous diversity in microbial metabolism, the variety of enzymes available for exploitation is very large. Some of the microorganisms involved in industrial fermentations, and their enzymes and their applications are described below.

Enzymes are used in various stages of **cheese production**, e.g. chymosin from GE microbes now replaces the rennin previously obtained from calves.

In **beer brewing**, **proteases** (from bacteria) are added to prevent cloudiness. Amyloglucosidases are used to produce low calorie beers.

Citric acid is used in **jam production** and is synthesized by a mutant strain of the fungus ***Aspergillus niger***, which produces the enzyme citrate synthase.

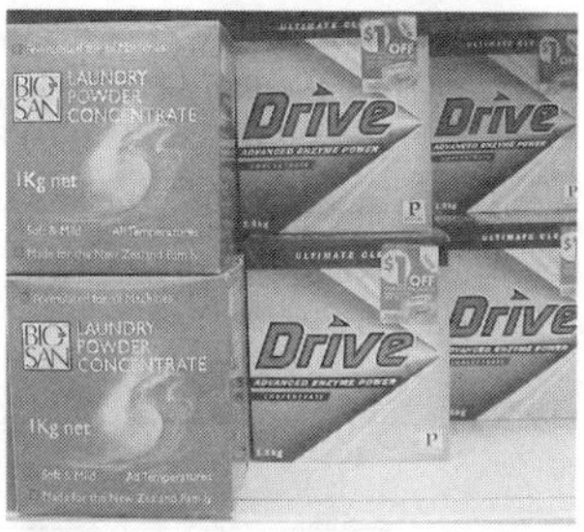

Biological detergents use **proteases**, **lipases**, and **amylases** extracted from fungi and thermophilic bacteria to break down organic material in stains.

Fungal ligninases are used in **pulp and paper industries** to remove lignin from wood pulp and treat wood waste.

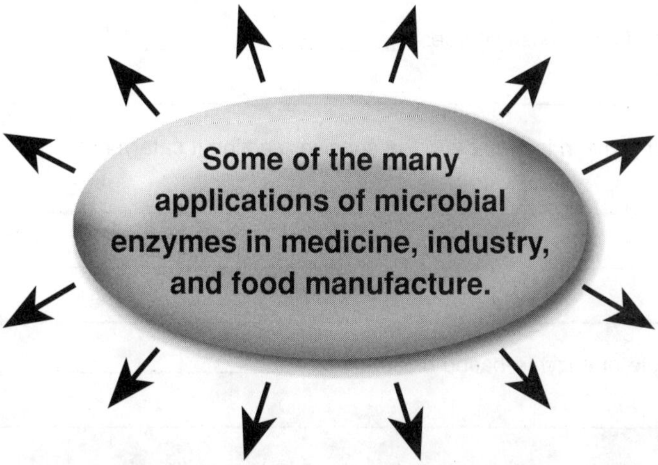

In **soft centered chocolates**, **invertase** from yeast breaks down the solid filling to produce the soft center.

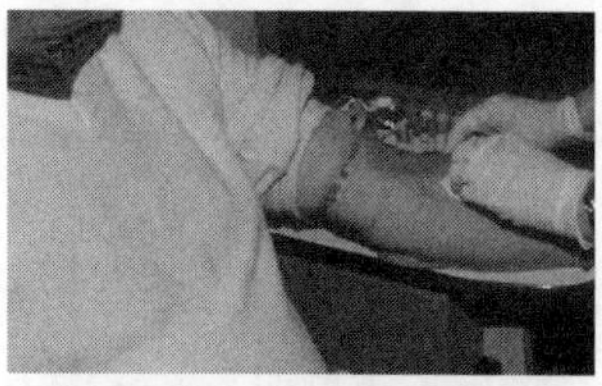

Medical treatment of blood clots employs protease enzymes such as streptokinase from *Streptomyces* spp.

Bacterial proteases are used to break down the wheat protein (gluten) in flour, to produce low gluten breads.

Cellulases and pectinases are used in the manufacture of packaged (as opposed to fresh) fruit juices to speed juice extraction and prevent cloudiness.

The silver residues from old photographs can be reclaimed for reuse when proteases are employed to digest the gelatin of old films.

The lactase from bacteria is used to convert lactose to glucose and galactose in the production of low-lactose and lactose free milk products.

Tanning industries now use proteases from *Bacillus subtilis* instead of toxic chemicals, such as sulfide pastes, to remove hairs and soften hides.

The enzyme, **glucose oxidase**, from *Aspergillus niger*, is immobilized in a semi-conducting silicon chip. It catalyzes the conversion of glucose (from the blood sample) to gluconic acid.

Hydrogen ions from the gluconic acid cause a movement of electrons in the silicon, which is detected by a transducer. The strength of the electric current is directly proportional to the blood glucose concentration.

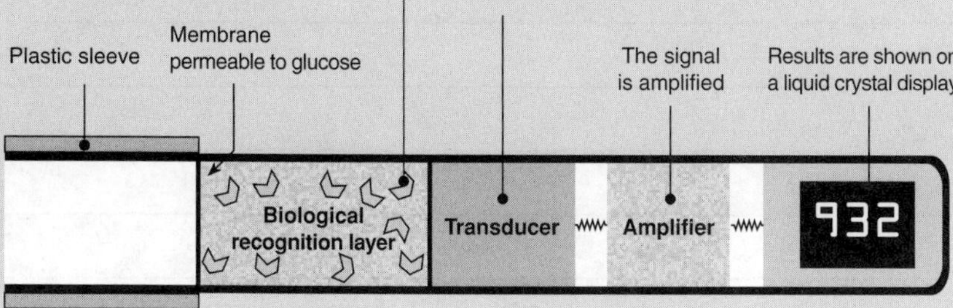

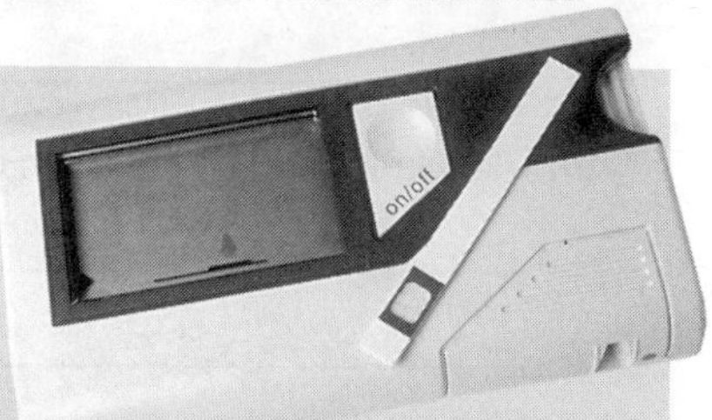

Biosensors are electronic monitoring devices that use biological material to detect the presence or concentration of a particular substance. Enzymes are ideally suited for use in biosensors because of their specificity and sensitivity. This example illustrates how **glucose oxidase** from the fungus *Aspergillus niger* is used in a biosensor to measure blood glucose level in diabetics.

Periodicals:
Enzymes from fungi

Related activities: *Putting Enzymes to Use*

1. Identify two probable consequences of the absence of enzymes from a chemical reaction that normally uses them:

(a) ___

(b) ___

2. Identify three properties of microbial enzymes that make them highly suitable as industrial catalysts. For each, explain why the property is important:

(a) ___

(b) ___

(c) ___

3. Choose one example from those described on the previous page and, in more detail, identify:

(a) The enzyme and its specific microbial source: ___

(b) The application of the enzyme in industry and the specific reaction it catalyses: ___

4. (a) Outline the basic principle of enzyme-based biosensors: ___

(b) Suggest how a biosensor could be used to monitor blood alcohol level: ___

5. For each of the examples described below, suggest how the use of microbial enzymes has improved the efficiency, cost effectiveness, and/or safety of processing compared with traditional methods:

(a) Use of microbial proteases to treat hides in the tanning industry: ___

(b) Use of microbial chymosin in cheese production: ___

(c) Use of fungal ligninases to treat wood waste: ___

UNIT F215

5.2.3

Genomes and Gene Technologies

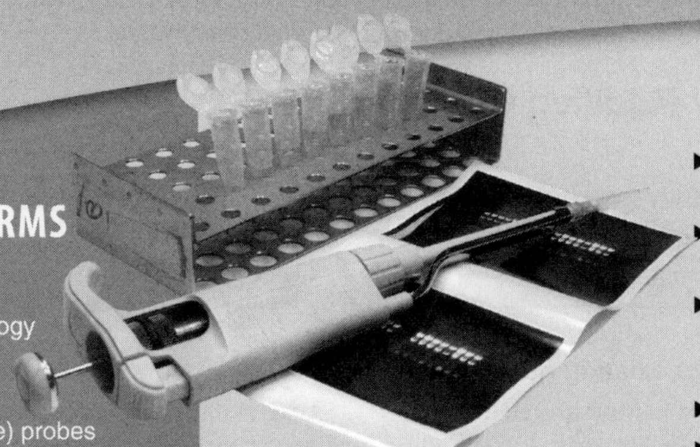

KEY CONCEPTS

- Genome sequencing has enabled researchers to locate genes and know their composition.
- PCR is a method used to amplify DNA and is an essential technique in modern gene technologies.
- DNA fragments can be produced by restriction digestion, separated by gel electrophoresis, and identified by DNA probes.
- Ligation is used to produce plasmid vectors.
- Genetic engineering has a wide range of applications in medicine, agriculture, and industry.

KEY TERMS

annealing
biotechnology
blunt end
cloning
DNA (gene) probes
DNA (genetic) profiling
DNA chip (microarray)
DNA ligase
DNA ligation
DNA polymerase
DNA sequencing
forensics
gel electrophoresis
gene technology
gene therapy
genetic modification
genome sequencing
germ line cell gene therapy
GMO
marker genes
microsatellite
molecular clone
plasmid
polymerase chain reaction
primer
recognition site
recombinant DNA technology
restriction digestion
restriction enzyme
reverse transcription
somatic cell gene therapy
sticky end
transformation
transgenesis
vector
xenotransplant

OBJECTIVES

- ☐ 1. Use the **KEY TERMS** to help you understand and complete these objectives.
- ☐ 2. Appreciate that several basic techniques (restriction digestion, ligation, PCR, and gel electrophoresis) are used in a range of different processes.

DNA sequencing and genome analysis

pages 215-226, 246

- ☐ 3. Outline how **genome sequencing** provides information about the location of genes and enables genome-wide comparisons between individuals or species.
- ☐ 4. Outline the steps involved in genome sequencing. Appreciate the role of automated sequencing in the feasibility of large-scale genome analyses.

Genetic engineering

pages 209-214, 227-245, 247-250

- ☐ 5. Outline the principles of **genetic engineering** (recombinant DNA technology).
- ☐ 6. Explain the use of **restriction enzymes** in genetic engineering.
- ☐ 7. Explain how DNA fragments are separated by **gel electrophoresis**.
- ☐ 8. Describe the applications of **DNA probes** in gene technology, explaining how they are used to identify specific DNA sequences. Applications include the use of probes in DNA chips and in the earlier methods of DNA profiling.
- ☐ 9. Explain the essential role of the **polymerase chain reaction** (PCR) in gene technology and describe the basic technique.
- ☐ 10. Describe **DNA ligation**, including the role of **DNA ligase**. Explain how DNA ligation is used to incorporate DNA fragments into **plasmids** and other **vectors**.
- ☐ 11. Outline the techniques involved in making a **transgenic organism**, including the role of vectors in integrating foreign DNA into another genome. Explain how recombinant plasmid vectors may be taken up by microbial cells to produce a transgenic organism that can express a valuable gene product.
- ☐ 12. Explain why the ability to take up **plasmid DNA** from the environment would be advantageous to a microorganism.
- ☐ 13. Explain the role of **genetic markers** in identifying **transformed cells**. Describe different types of genetic markers, e.g. genes for antibiotic resistance or genes for enzymes that produce fluorescent substances.
- ☐ 14. Describe how human insulin is produced from genetically engineered bacteria.
- ☐ 15. Describe the process by which carotenoid-rich golden rice is produced.
- ☐ 16. Describe the role of genetic engineering in **xenotransplant** technology.
- ☐ 17. Explain what is meant by **gene therapy** and distinguish between **somatic cell gene therapy** and **germ line cell gene therapy**, both in technique and in the long term consequences of the therapy.
- ☐ 18. Discuss (in a balanced way) the relevant ethical, social, and economic issues associated with the use of **genetically modified organisms**.

Periodicals:
Listings for this chapter are on page 342

Weblinks:
www.biozone.co.uk/weblink/OCR-A2-2832.html

Teacher Resource CD-ROM: *Solving Gene Technology Problems*

What is Genetic Modification?

The genetic modification of organisms is a vast industry, and the applications of the technology are exciting and far reaching. It brings new hope for medical cures, promises to increase yields in agriculture, and has the potential to help solve the world's pollution and resource crises. Organisms with artificially altered DNA are referred to as **genetically modified organisms** or **GMOs**. They may be modified in one of three ways (outlined below). Some of the current and proposed applications of gene technology raise complex ethical and safety issues, where the benefits of their use must be carefully weighed against the risks to human health, as well as the health and well-being of other organisms and the environment as a whole.

Producing Genetically Modified Organisms (GMOs)

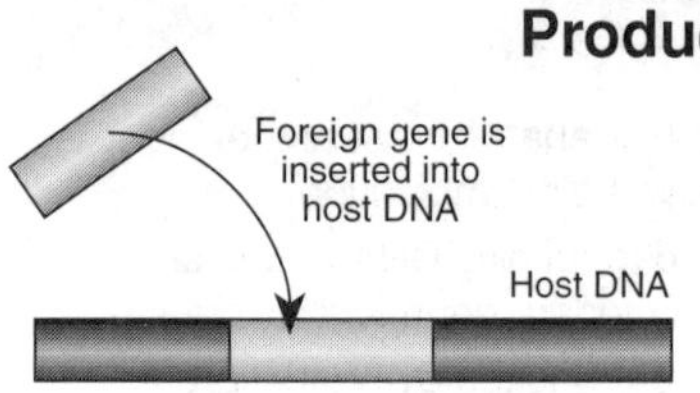

Add a foreign gene

A novel (foreign) gene is inserted from another species. This will enable the GMO to express the trait coded by the new gene. Organisms genetically altered in this way are referred to as **transgenic**.

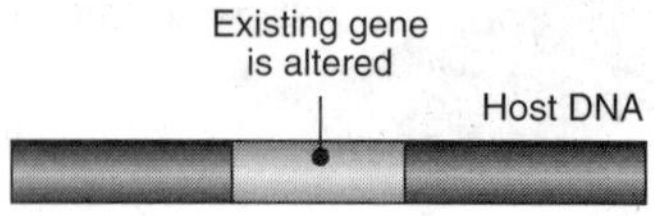

Alter an existing gene

An existing gene may be altered to make it express at a higher level (e.g. growth hormone) or in a different way (in tissue that would not normally express it). This method is also used for gene therapy.

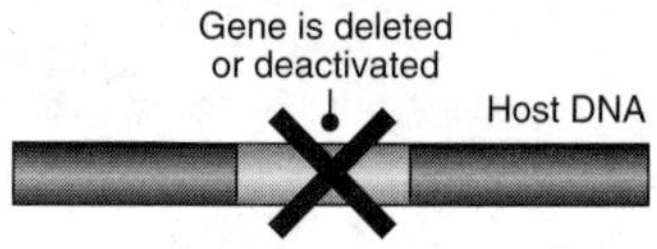

Delete or 'turn off' a gene

An existing gene may be deleted or deactivated (switched off) to prevent the expression of a trait (e.g. the deactivation of the ripening gene in tomatoes produced the Flavr-Savr tomato).

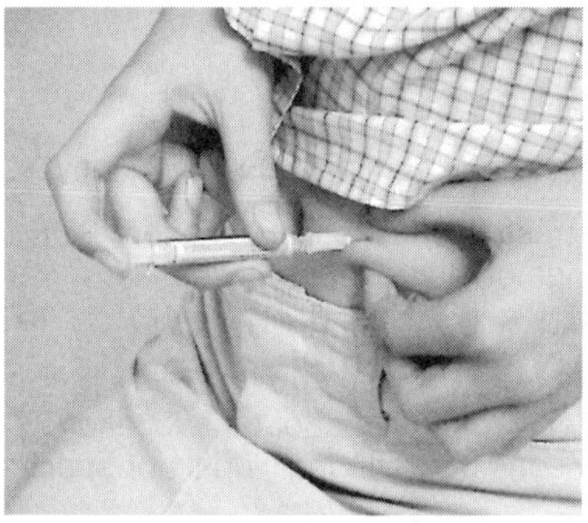

Human insulin, used to treat diabetic patients, is now produced using transgenic bacteria.

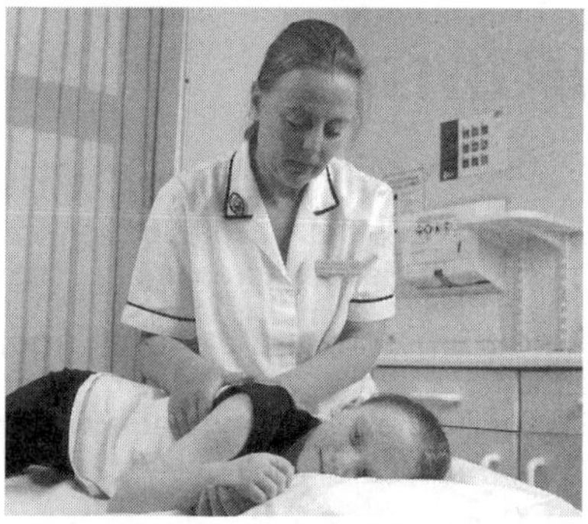

Gene therapy could be used treat genetic disrorders, such as cystic fibrosis.

Manipulating gene action is one way in which to control processes such as ripening in fruit.

1. Using examples, discuss the ways in which an organism may be genetically modified (to produce a GMO):

2. Explain how human needs or desires have provided a stimulus for the development of the following biotechnologies:

(a) Gene therapy:

(b) The production and use of transgenic organisms:

(c) Plant micropropagation (tissue culture):

Restriction Enzymes

One of the essential tools of genetic engineering is a group of special **restriction enzymes** (also known as restriction endonucleases). These have the ability to cut DNA molecules at very precise sequences of 4 to 8 base pairs called **recognition sites**. These enzymes are the "molecular scalpels" that allow genetic engineers to cut up DNA in a controlled way. Although first isolated in 1970, these enzymes were discovered earlier in many bacteria (see panel opposite). The purified forms of these bacterial restriction enzymes are used today as tools to cut DNA (see table on the facing page for examples). Enzymes are named according to the bacterial species from which they were first isolated. By using a 'tool kit' of over 400 restriction enzymes recognising about 100 recognition sites, genetic engineers can isolate, sequence, and manipulate individual genes derived from any type of organism. The sites at which the fragments of DNA are cut may result in overhanging "sticky ends" or non-overhanging "blunt ends". Pieces may later be joined together using an enzyme called **DNA ligase** in a process called **ligation**.

Sticky End Restriction Enzymes

1. A **restriction enzyme** cuts the double-stranded DNA molecule at its specific **recognition site** (see the table opposite for a representative list of restriction enzymes and their recognition sites).

2. The cuts produce a DNA fragment with two **sticky ends** (ends with exposed nucleotide bases at each end). The piece it is removed from is also left with sticky ends.

Restriction enzymes may cut DNA leaving an overhang or sticky end, without its complementary sequence opposite. DNA cut in such a way is able to be joined to other exposed end fragments of DNA with matching sticky ends. Such joins are specific to their recognition sites.

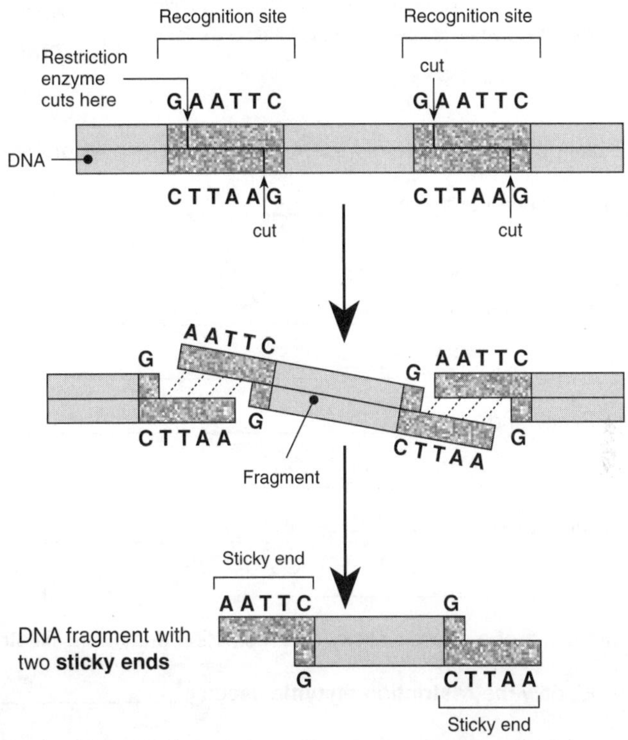

Blunt End Restriction Enzymes

1. A **restriction enzyme** cuts the double-stranded DNA molecule at its specific **recognition site** (see the table opposite for a representative list of restriction enzymes and their recognition sites).

2. The cuts produce a DNA fragment with two **blunt ends** (ends with no exposed nucleotide bases at each end). The piece it is removed from is also left with blunt ends.

It is possible to use restriction enzymes that cut leaving no overhang. DNA cut in such a way is able to be joined to any other blunt end fragment, but tends to be nonspecific because there are no sticky ends as recognition sites.

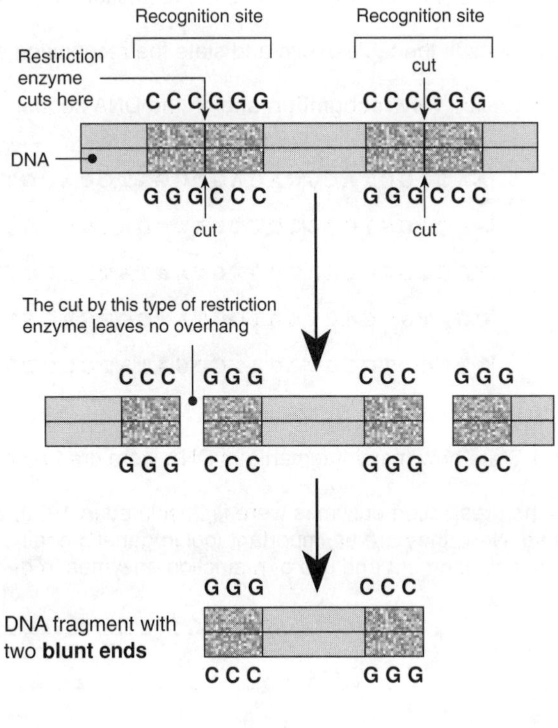

Origin of Restriction Enzymes

Restriction enzymes have been isolated from many bacteria. It was observed that certain *bacteriophages* (viruses that infect bacteria) could not infect bacteria other than their usual hosts. The reason was found to be that other potential hosts could destroy almost all of the phage DNA using *restriction enzymes* present naturally in their cells; a defence mechanism against the entry of foreign DNA. Restriction enzymes are named according to the species they were first isolated from, followed by a number to distinguish different enzymes isolated from the same organism.

Recognition sites for selected restriction enzymes

Enzyme	Source	Recognition sites
***Eco*RI**	*Escherichia coli* RY13	GAATTC
***Bam*HI**	*Bacillus amyloliquefaciens* H	GGATCC
***Hae*III**	*Haemophilus aegyptius*	GGCC
***Hind*III**	*Haemophilus influenzae* Rd	AAGCTT
***Hpa*I**	*Haemophilus parainfluenzae*	GTTAAC
***Hpa*II**	*Haemophilus parainfluenzae*	CCGG
***Mbo*I**	*Moraxella bovis*	GATC
***Not*I**	*Norcardia otitidis-caviarum*	GCGGCCGC
***Taq*I**	*Thermus aquaticus*	TCGA

1. Explain the following terms, identifying their role in recombinant DNA technology:

   (a) Restriction enzyme: ______________________________

   (b) Recognition site: ______________________________

   (c) Sticky end: ______________________________

   (d) Blunt end: ______________________________

2. The action of a specific sticky end restriction enzyme is illustrated on the previous page (top). Use the table above to:

   (a) Identify the **restriction enzyme** used: ______________________________

   (b) Name the organism from which it was first isolated: ______________________________

   (c) State the **base sequence** for this restriction enzyme's recognition site: ______________________________

3. A genetic engineer wants to use the restriction enzyme ***Bam*HI** to cut the DNA sequence below:

   (a) Consult the table above and state the recognition site for this enzyme: ______________________________

   (b) Circle every **recognition site** on the DNA sequence below that could be cut by the enzyme ***Bam*HI**:

```
          10         20         30         40         50         60
|AATGGGTACG|CACAGTGGAT|CCACGTAGTA|TGCGATGCGT|AGTGTTTATG|GAGAGAAGAA|
          70         80         90        100        110        120
|AACGCGTCGC|CTTTTATCGA|TGCTGTACGG|ATGCGGAAGT|GGCGATGAGG|ATCCATGCAA|
         130        140        150        160        170        180
|TCGCGGCCGA|TCGXGTAATA|TATCGTGGCT|GCGTTTATTA|TCGTGACTAG|TAGCAGTATG|
         190        200        210        220        230        240
|CGATGTGACT|GATGCTATGC|TGACTATGCT|ATGTTTTTAT|GCTGGATCCA|GCGTAAGCAT|
         250        260        270        280        290        300
|TTCGCTGCGT|GGATCCCATA|TCCTTATATG|CATATATTCT|TATACGGATC|GCGCACGTTT|
```

   (c) State how many fragments of DNA were created by this action: ______________________________

4. When restriction enzymes were first isolated in 1970, there were not many applications to which they could be put to use. Now, they are an important tool in genetic engineering. Describe the human needs and demands that have driven the development and use of restriction enzymes in genetic engineering:

   ____

Ligation

DNA fragments produced using restriction enzymes may be reassembled by a process called **ligation**. Pieces are joined together using an enzyme called **DNA ligase**. DNA of different origins produced in this way is called **recombinant DNA** (because it is DNA that has been recombined from different sources). The combined techniques of using restriction enzymes and ligation are the basic tools of genetic engineering (also known as recombinant DNA technology). The DNA is inserted into vectors which carry the DNA to other organisms. Common vectors include certain viruses, liposomes and naked DNA.

Creating a Recombinant DNA Plasmid

1. If two pieces of DNA are cut by the same restriction enzyme, they will produce fragments with matching **sticky ends** (ends with exposed nucleotide bases at each end).

2. When two such matching sticky ends come together, they can join by base-pairing. This process is called **annealing**. This can allow DNA fragments from a different source, perhaps a **plasmid**, to be joined to the DNA fragment.

3. The joined fragments will usually form either a linear molecule or a circular one, as shown here for a **plasmid**. However, other combinations of fragments can occur.

4. The fragments of DNA are joined together by the enzyme **DNA ligase**, producing a molecule of **recombinant DNA**.

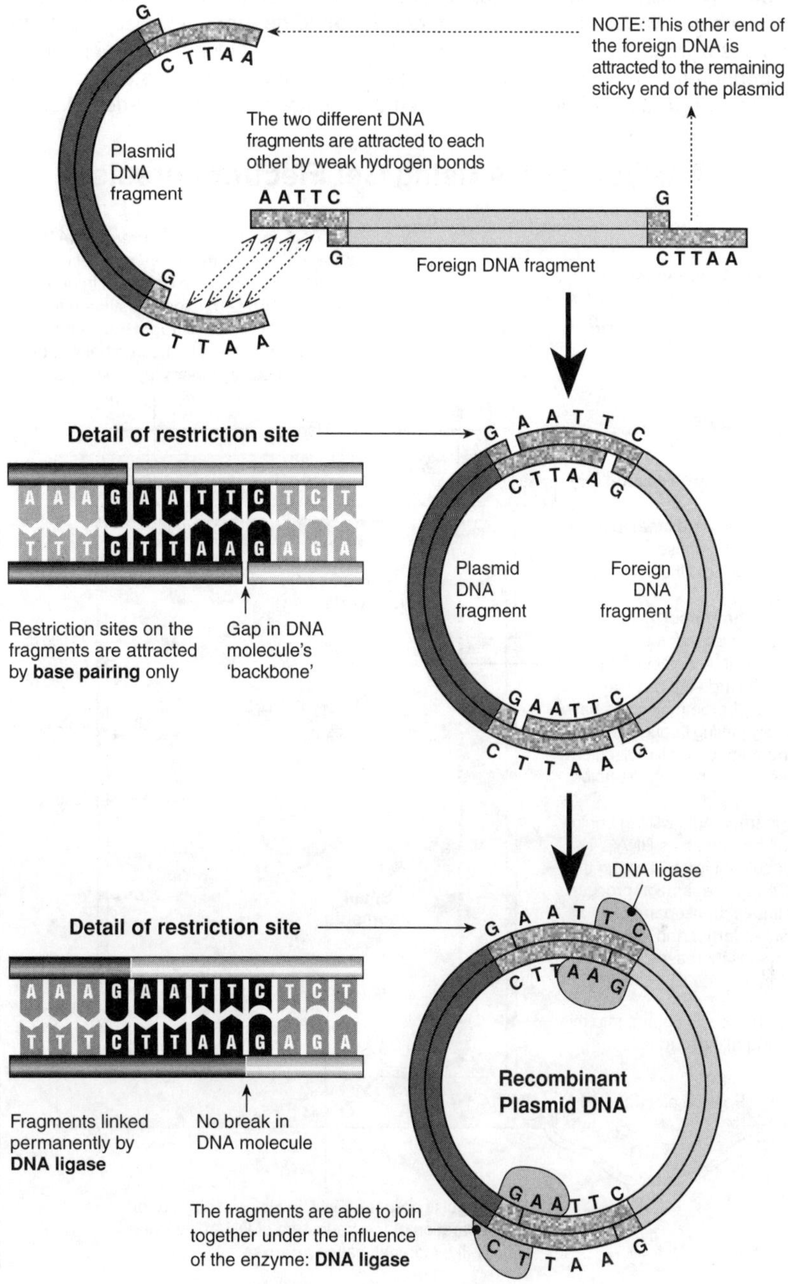

1. Explain in your own words the two main steps in the process of joining two DNA fragments together:

   (a) Annealing: ______________________________

   (b) DNA ligase: ______________________________

2. Describe the usual role of DNA ligase in a cell: ______________________________

3. Explain why **ligation** can be considered the reverse of the **restriction enzyme** process: ______________________________

Gel Electrophoresis

Gel electrophoresis is a method that separates large molecules (including nucleic acids or proteins) on the basis of size, electric charge, and other physical properties. Such molecules possess a slight electric charge (see DNA below). To prepare DNA for gel electrophoresis the DNA is often cut up into smaller pieces. This is done by mixing DNA with restriction enzymes in controlled conditions for about an hour. Called **restriction digestion**, it produces a range of DNA fragments of different lengths. During electrophoresis, molecules are forced to move through the pores of a **gel** (a jelly-like material), when the electrical current is applied. Active electrodes at each end of the gel provide the driving force. The electrical current from one electrode repels the molecules while the other electrode simultaneously attracts the molecules. The frictional force of the gel resists the flow of the molecules, separating them by size. Their rate of migration through the gel depends on the strength of the electric field, size and shape of the molecules, and on the ionic strength and temperature of the buffer in which the molecules are moving. After staining, the separated molecules in each lane can be seen as a series of bands spread from one end of the gel to the other.

Analysing DNA using Gel Electrophoresis

DNA solutions: Mixtures of different sizes of DNA fragments are loaded in each well in the gel.

DNA markers, a mixture of DNA molecules with known molecular weights (size) are often run in one lane. They are used to estimate the sizes of the DNA fragments in the sample lanes. The figures below are hypothetical markers (bp = base pairs).

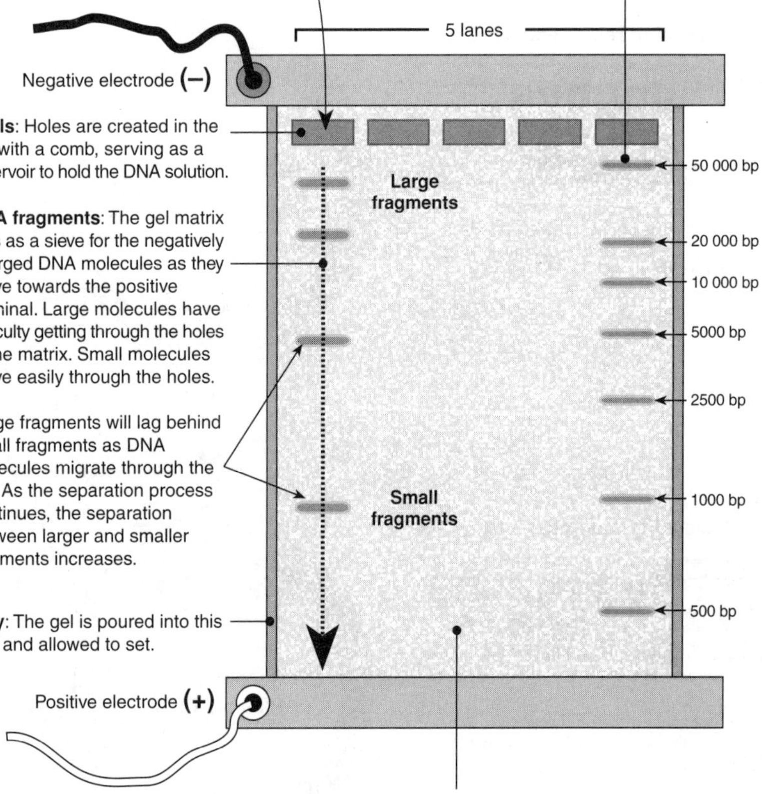

Wells: Holes are created in the gel with a comb, serving as a reservoir to hold the DNA solution.

DNA fragments: The gel matrix acts as a sieve for the negatively charged DNA molecules as they move towards the positive terminal. Large molecules have difficulty getting through the holes in the matrix. Small molecules move easily through the holes.

Large fragments will lag behind small fragments as DNA molecules migrate through the gel. As the separation process continues, the separation between larger and smaller fragments increases.

Tray: The gel is poured into this tray and allowed to set.

Gel: A gel is prepared, which will act as a support for separation of the fragments of DNA. The gel is a jelly-like material, called **agarose**.

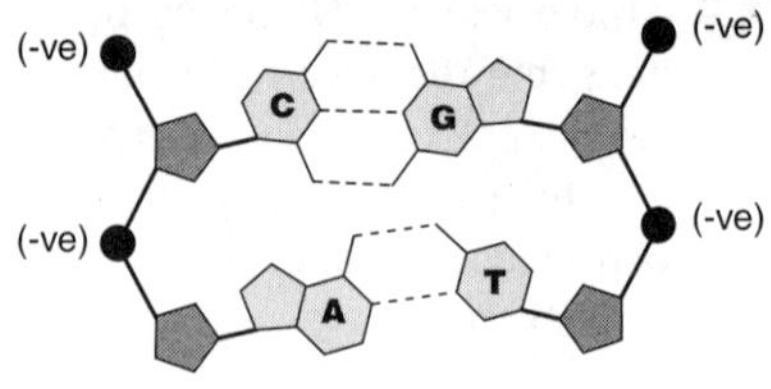

DNA is negatively charged because the phosphates (black) that form part of the backbone of a DNA molecule have a negative charge.

Steps in the process of gel electrophoresis of DNA

1. A tray is prepared to hold the gel matrix.
2. A gel comb is used to create holes in the gel. The gel comb is placed in the tray.
3. Agarose gel powder is mixed with a buffer solution (the liquid used to carry the DNA in a stable form). The solution is heated until dissolved and poured into the tray and allowed to cool.
4. The gel tray is placed in an electrophoresis chamber and the chamber is filled with buffer, covering the gel. This allows the electric current from electrodes at either end of the gel to flow through the gel.
5. DNA samples are mixed with a "loading dye" to make the DNA sample visible. The dye also contains glycerol or sucrose to make the DNA sample heavy so that it will sink to the bottom of the well.
6. A safety cover is placed over the gel, electrodes are attached to a power supply and turned on.
7. When the dye marker has moved through the gel, the current is turned off and the gel is removed from the tray.
8. DNA molecules are made visible by staining the gel with **methylene blue** or ethidium bromide (which binds to DNA and fluoresces in UV light).

1. Explain the purpose of gel electrophoresis: ______________________

____

____

2. Describe the two forces that control the speed at which fragments pass through the gel:

(a) ______________________

(b) ______________________

3. Explain why the smallest fragments travel through the gel the fastest: ______________________

____

____

Polymerase Chain Reaction

Many procedures in DNA technology (such as DNA sequencing and DNA profiling) require substantial amounts of DNA to work with. Some samples, such as those from a crime scene or fragments of DNA from a long extinct organism, may be difficult to get in any quantity. The diagram below describes the laboratory process called **polymerase chain reaction** (**PCR**). Using this technique, vast quantities of DNA identical to trace samples can be created. This process is often termed **DNA amplification**. Although only one cycle of replication is shown below, following cycles replicate DNA at an exponential rate. PCR can be used to make billions of copies in only a few hours.

A Single Cycle of the Polymerase Chain Reaction

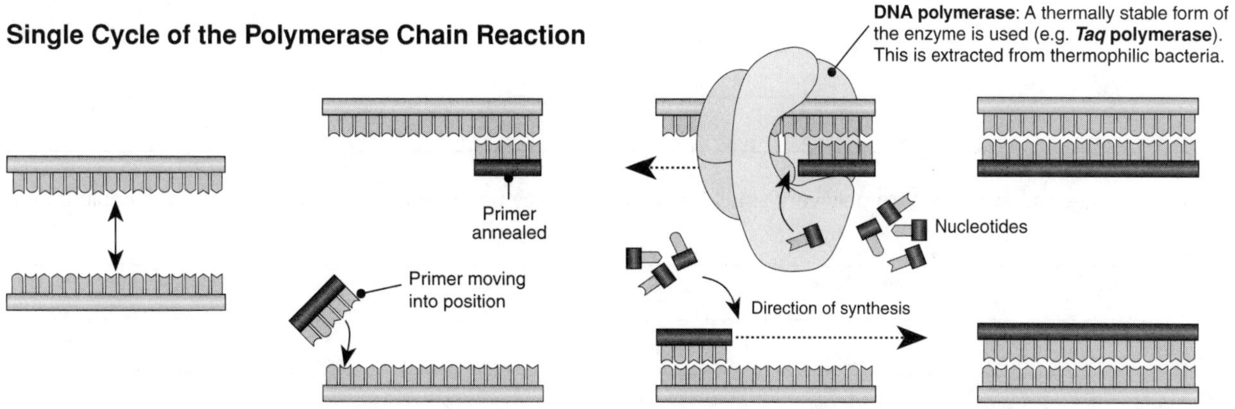

1. A DNA sample (called target DNA) is obtained. It is **denatured** (DNA strands are separated) by heating at 98°C for 5 minutes.
2. The sample is cooled to 60°C. Primers are **annealed** (bonded) to each DNA strand. In PCR, the primers are short strands of DNA; they provide the starting sequence for DNA extension.
3. Free nucleotides and the enzyme DNA polymerase are added. DNA polymerase binds to the primers and, using the free nucleotides, synthesises complementary strands of DNA.
4. After one cycle, there are now two copies of the original DNA.

Repeat for about 25 cycles

Repeat cycle of heating and cooling until enough copies of the target DNA have been produced

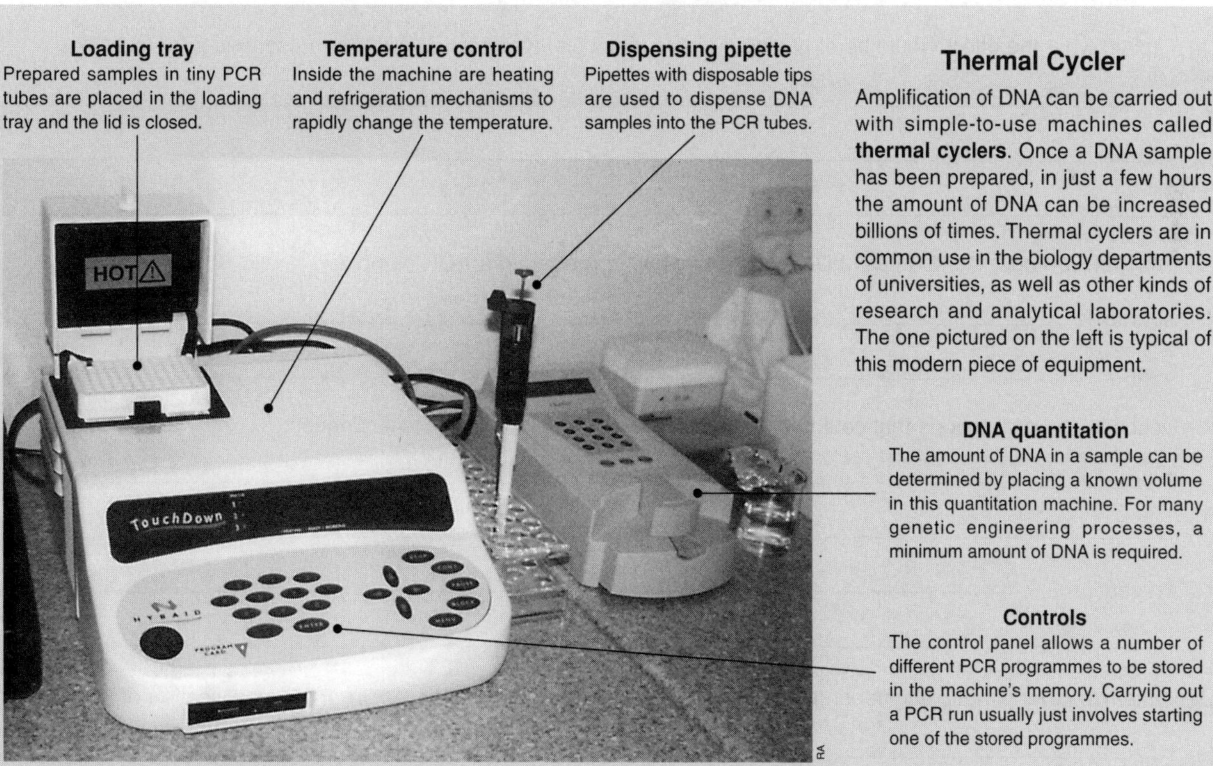

Thermal Cycler

Amplification of DNA can be carried out with simple-to-use machines called **thermal cyclers**. Once a DNA sample has been prepared, in just a few hours the amount of DNA can be increased billions of times. Thermal cyclers are in common use in the biology departments of universities, as well as other kinds of research and analytical laboratories. The one pictured on the left is typical of this modern piece of equipment.

1. Explain the purpose of PCR: ______________________________

____

____

____

Periodicals:
DNA polymerase

Related activities: *Preparing a Gene for Cloning*

2. Briefly describe how the **polymerase chain reaction** works: ______

3. Describe three situations where only very small DNA samples may be available for sampling and PCR could be used:

(a) ______

(b) ______

(c) ______

4. After only two cycles of replication, four copies of the double-stranded DNA exist. Calculate how much a DNA sample will have increased after:

(a) 10 cycles: ______ (b) 25 cycles: ______

5. The risk of contamination in the preparation for PCR is considerable.

(a) Explain what the effect would be of having a single molecule of unwanted DNA in the sample prior to PCR:

(b) Describe two possible sources of DNA contamination in preparing a PCR sample:

Source 1: ______

Source 2: ______

(c) Describe two precautions that could be taken to reduce the risk of DNA contamination:

Precaution 1: ______

Precaution 2: ______

6. Describe two other genetic engineering/genetic manipulation procedures that require PCR amplification of DNA:

(a) ______

(b) ______

Manual DNA Sequencing

DNA sequencing techniques are used to determine the nucleotide (base) sequence of DNA. Two manual methods are in current use: the **Maxim-Gilbert** procedure and the most common method, the **Sanger** procedure (illustrated below). Both methods use a procedure called **electrophoresis**. The Sanger method is based on the premature termination of DNA synthesis resulting from the inclusion of specially modified nucleotides. DNA synthesis is initiated from a **primer** which is **radio-labelled** (contains a radioactive isotope that will appear on a photographic film called an **autoradiograph**). Four separate reactions are run, each containing a modified nucleotide mixed with its normal counterpart, as well as the three other normal nucleotides. When a modified nucleotide is added to the growing complementary DNA, synthesis stops. Each reaction yields a series of different sized fragments extending from the radioactive primer. The fragments from the four reactions are separated by electrophoresis and analysed by autoradiography to determine the DNA sequence.

The Sanger Method for DNA Sequencing

Four sequencing reactions

Using the same DNA sample to be sequenced (example used: **A C T G G T C T A G**), a separate sequencing reaction is carried out for each of the 4 bases: T, C, G, and A. In addition to the DNA sample, each reaction has normal (unaltered) copies of nucleotides: **T**, **C**, **G**, and **A**, plus a small quantity of one of the modified nucleotides:

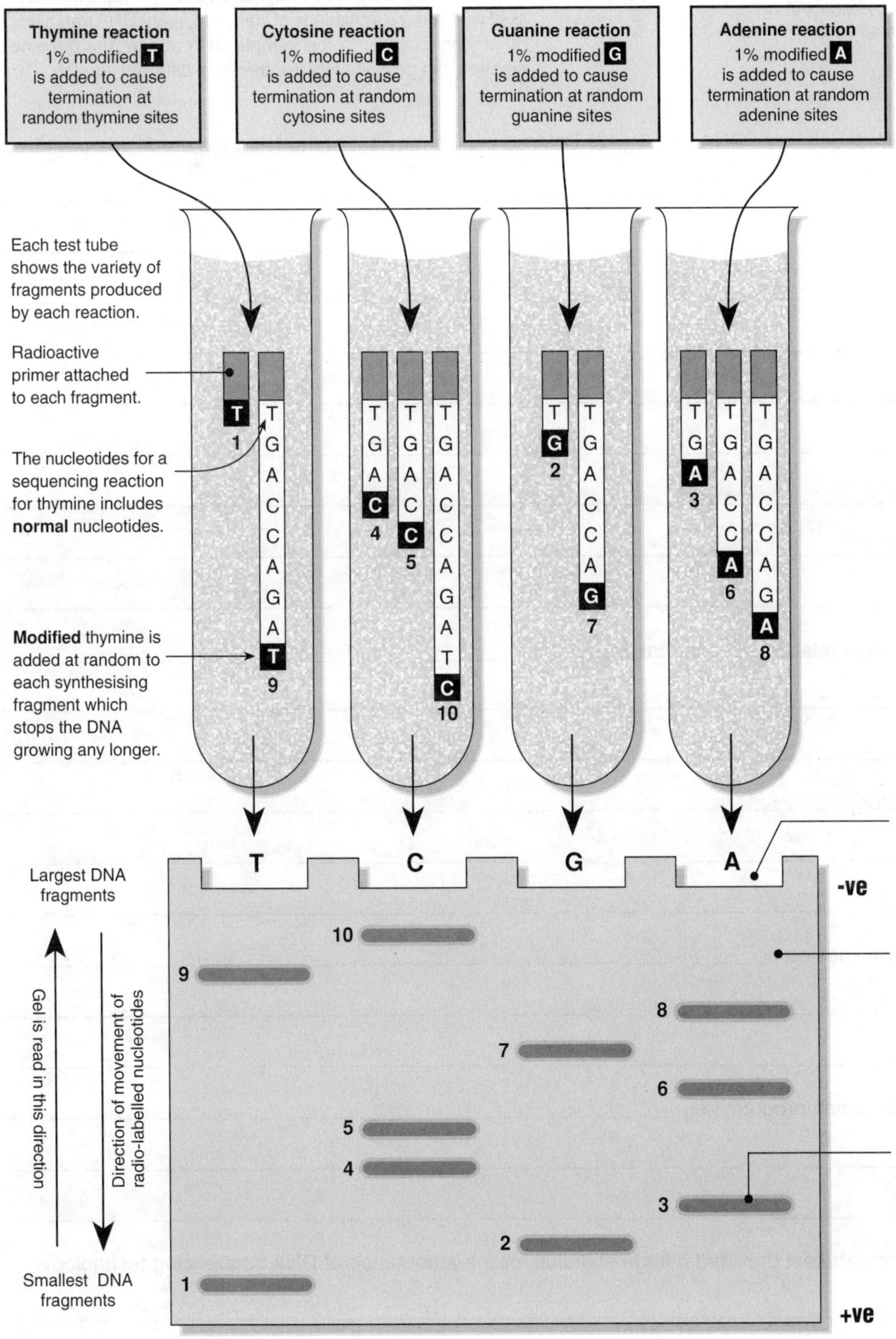

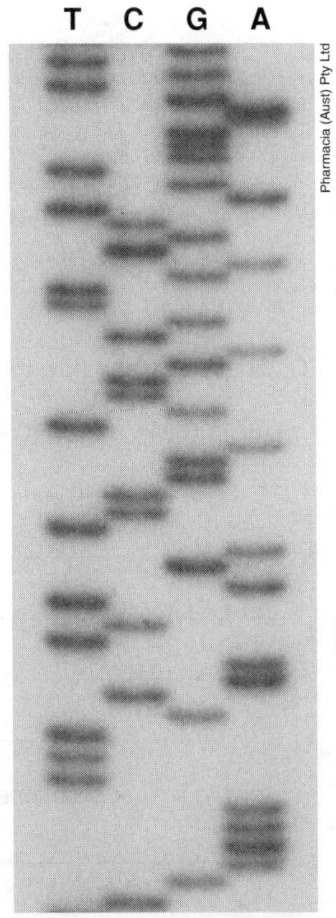

A typical **autoradiograph** showing a DNA sequence. The unexposed film is laid in contact with the gel after it has run. Radioactivity from the clustered DNA fragments create the dark shadows (blobs). Each blob contains millions of fragments.

How Fragments Are Formed

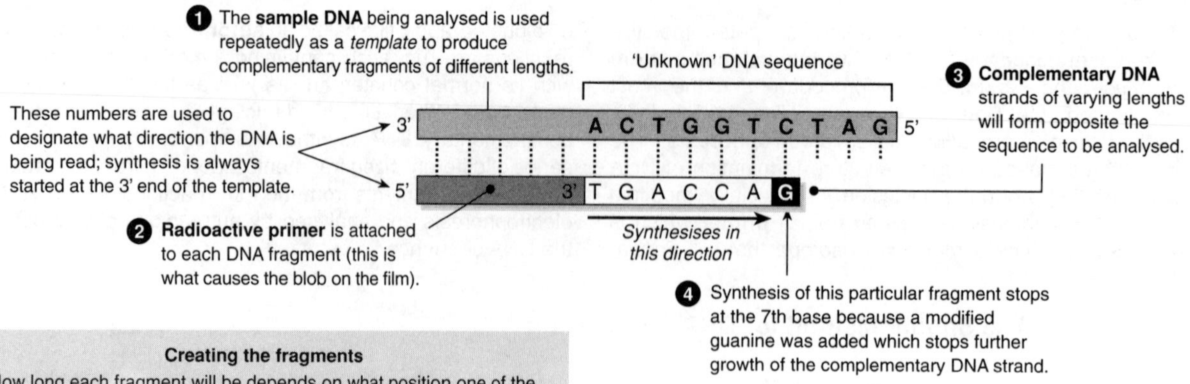

Creating the fragments

How long each fragment will be depends on what position one of the *chemically altered nucleotides* is incorporated into the sequence:

- **T** Thymine
- **C** Cytosine
- **G** Guanine
- **A** Adenine

} Chemically altered so that they prevent further synthesis of the complementary DNA

What must be realised is that the DNA sample being analysed consists of many millions of individual molecules, each being used as a template to make fragments. Each template molecule itself will produce thousands of complementary DNA fragments of varying lengths. In the sample DNA above, the guanine reaction can produce two fragments of different lengths.

1. Briefly describe how PCR, DNA sequencing, DNA profiling, or DNA screening may assist the following areas of study:

 (a) Forensic science: ______________________________

 ____

 ____

 (b) Legal disputes: ______________________________

 ____

 ____

 (c) Medical applications: ______________________________

 ____

 ____

 (d) Investigations into evolutionary relationships and taxonomy: ______________________________

 ____

 ____

 (e) Archaeology and anthropology: ______________________________

 ____

 ____

 (f) Conservation of endangered species: ______________________________

 ____

 ____

 (g) Management of livestock breeding programmes: ______________________________

 ____

 ____

2. Explain why the Human Genome Project provided a large stimulus for the automation of DNA sequencing technology:

 ____

 ____

Automated DNA Sequencing

The process of DNA sequencing can be automated using **gel electrophoresis** machines that can sequence up to 600 bases at a time. Automation improves the speed at which samples can be sequenced and has made large scale sequencing projects possible. Instead of using radio-labelled fragments, automated sequencing uses nucleotides labelled with **fluorescent dyes**. Another advantage is that the entire base sequence for a sample can be determined from a single lane on the gel (not four lanes as with manual sequencing). Computer software automatically interprets the data from the gel and produces a base sequence. Also see the weblink pdf download, which covers manual sequencing and provides questions relevant to both activities.

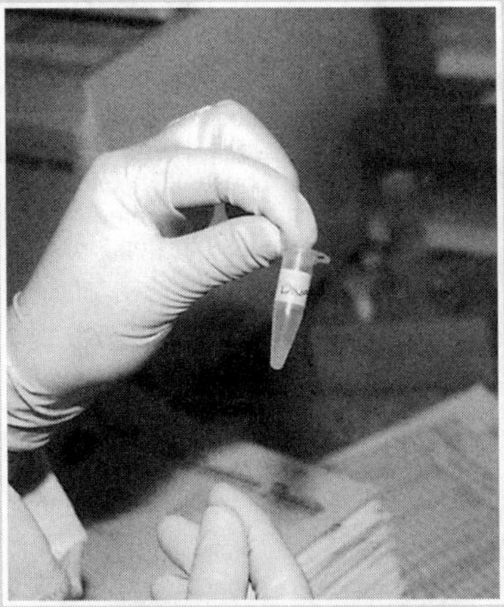

1. DNA sample arrives

Purified DNA samples may contain linear DNA or plasmids. The sample should contain about 1×10^{11} DNA molecules. The sample is checked to ensure that there is enough DNA present in the sample to work with.

2. Primer and reaction mix added

A **DNA primer** is added to the sample which provides a starting sequence for synthesis. Also added is the **sequencing reaction mix** containing the *polymerase enzyme* and free nucleotides, some which are labelled with dye.

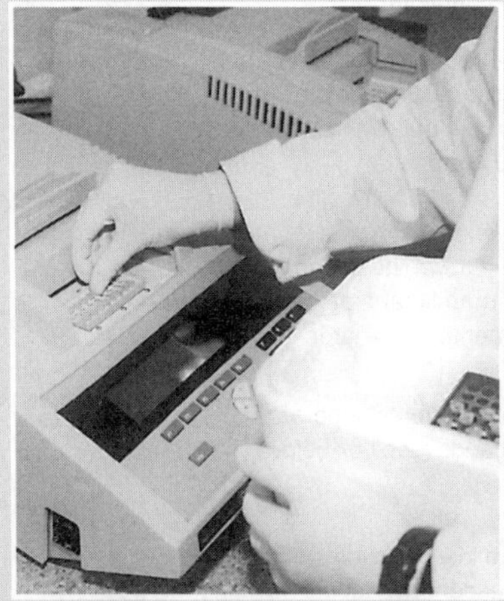

All photos are RA (unless indicated otherwise)

3. Create dye-labelled fragments

A **PCR** machine creates fragments of DNA complementary to the original template DNA. Each fragment is tagged with a fluorescent dye-labelled nucleotide. Running for 25 cycles, it creates 25×10^{11} single-stranded DNA molecules.

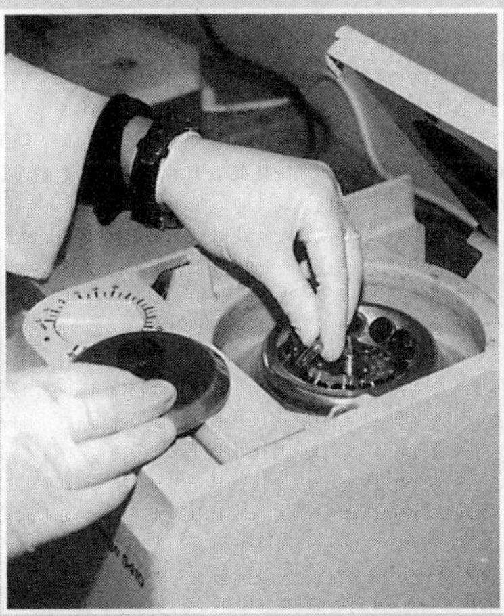

4. Centrifuge to create DNA pellet

The sample is chemically precipitated and centrifuged to settle the DNA fragments as a solid pellet at the bottom of the tube. Unused nucleotides, still in the liquid, are discarded.

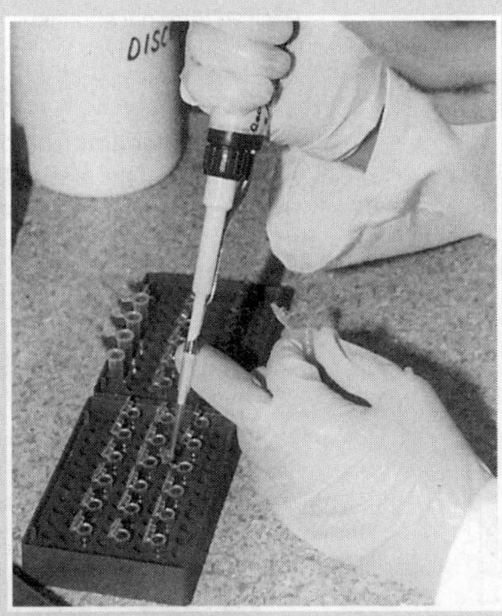

5. DNA pellet washed, buffer added

The pellet is washed with ethanol, dried, and a gel loading buffer is added. All that remains now is single stranded DNA with one dye-labelled nucleotide at the end of each molecule.

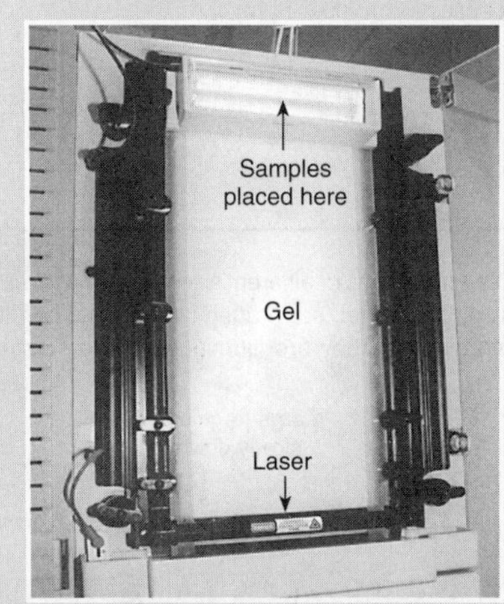

6. Acrylamide gel is loaded

The DNA sequencer is prepared by placing the gel (sandwiched between two sheets of glass) into position. A 36 channel 'comb' for receiving the samples is placed at the top of the gel.

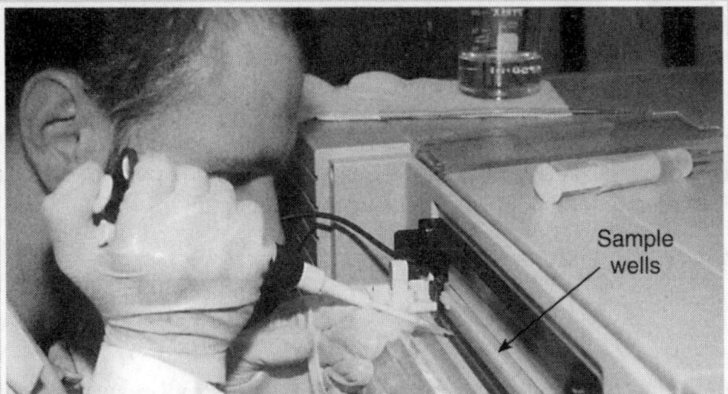

BOB

7. Loading DNA samples onto gel

Different samples can be placed in each of the 36 wells (funnel shaped receptacles) above the gel. A control DNA sample of known sequence is applied to the first lane of the sequencer. If there are problems with the control sequence then results for all other lanes are considered invalid.

8. Running the DNA sequencer

Powerful computer software controls the activity of the DNA sequencer. The gel is left to run for up to 10 hours. During this time an argon laser is constantly scanning across the bottom of the gel to detect the passing of dye-labelled nucleotides attached to DNA fragments.

Related activities: *Polymerase Chain Reaction, The Human Genome Project, Genome Projects*
Web links: *Manual DNA Sequencing*

How a DNA Sequencer Operates

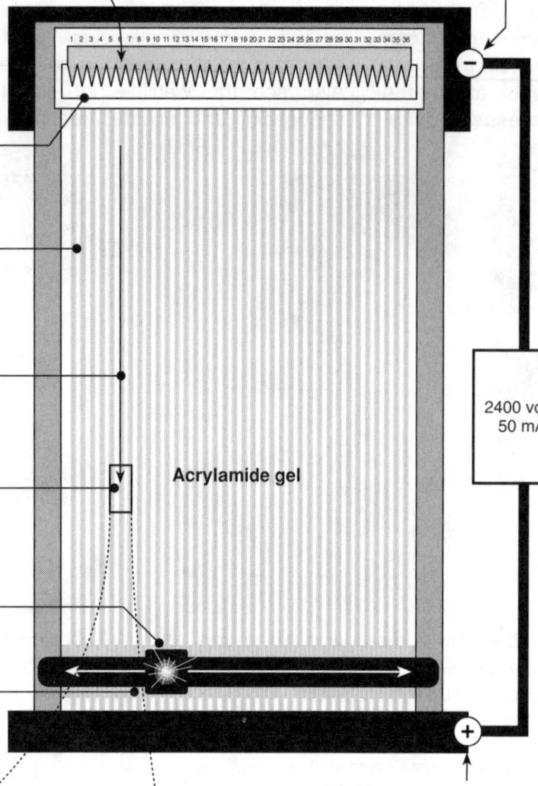

Creating the dye labelled fragments for gel electrophoresis is outlined in step 3. Key ingredients are:

(a) Original DNA template (the sample)

A C C G T A T G A T T C

(b) Many normal unlabelled nucleotides:

A T G C

(c) Terminal nucleotides labelled with fluorescent dye (a different colour for each of the 4 bases). The structure of the nucleotides is altered so they act as terminators to stop further synthesis of the strand:

A T G C

Two examples of synthesised DNA fragments are shown below. One is relatively short, the other is longer:

Normal nucleotides — Terminal nucleotide labelled with dye

T G G
A C C G T A T G A T T C

T G G C A T A C T
A C C G T A T G A T T C

DNA fragments of different sizes are drawn down through the gel, separating into distinct bands of colour as they are illuminated by the laser:

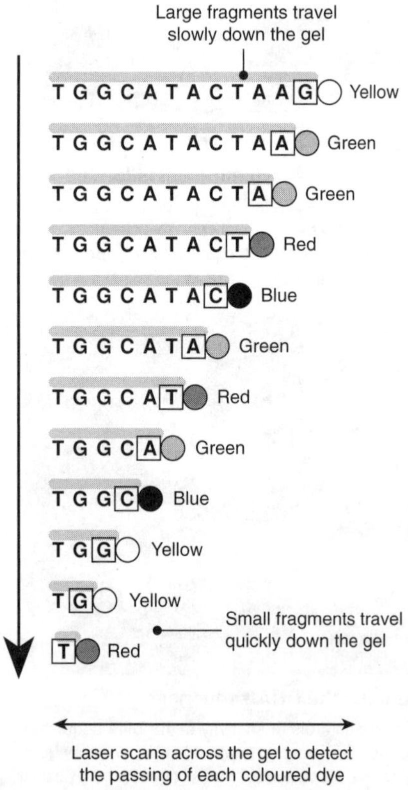

Data collection: The data from the digital camera are collected by computer software. The first of 23 samples is highlighted below in lane 1 with base sequences appearing on the far left.

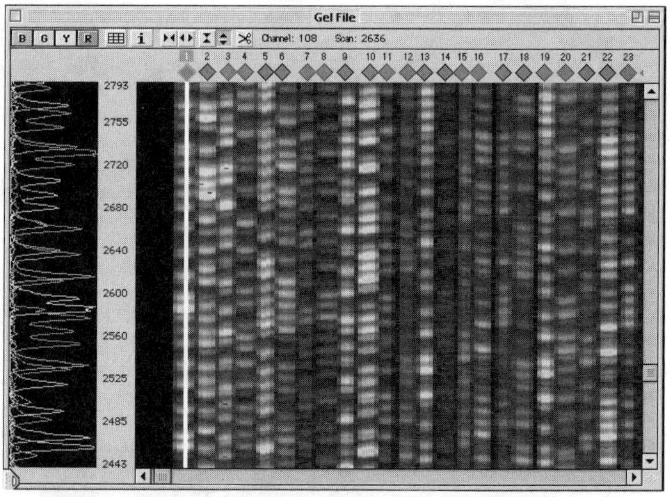

Data analysis: The data can be saved as a file for analysis by other computer software. Such software can provide a printout of the base sequence and perform comparisons with other DNA sequences (e.g. when looking for mutations).

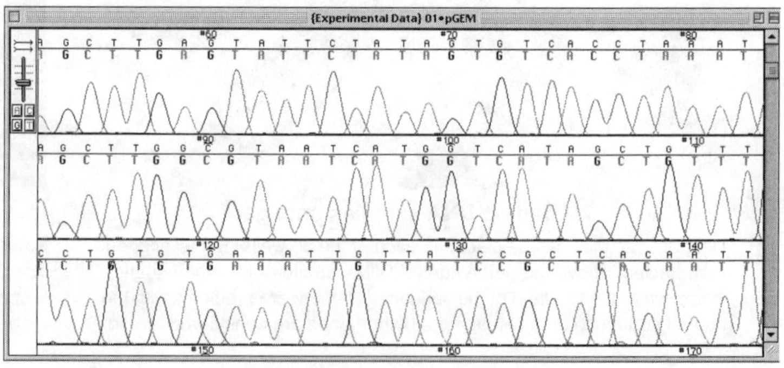

Genome Analysis

Genome analysis involves determining the exact order of all of the millions of bases making up the DNA of an organism's **genome**. Genome analysis must also identify all the genes present, their correct and exact location in the base sequence, and the regions of DNA that control the activity of the genes. Chromosomes range in size from 50 million to 250 million bases; too large to handle for high resolution mapping and sequencing. They must be broken down into much shorter pieces, cloned, and sequenced. It is important to be able to assemble all of the sequenced fragments into a complete, continuous sequence for each chromosome. This is achieved by mapping known **genetic markers** at regular intervals along each chromosome. When DNA fragments are sequenced, the presence of DNA markers enables them to be correctly positioned in the overall sequence. A wide variety of applications are currently or potentially available for genome analysis, from the treatment and diagnosis of disease to ecological studies of diversity and phylogeny. Note that a small proportion of an organism's DNA occurs outside the nucleus, in the mitochondria, and is called the **mitochondrial genome** (mtDNA). Mitochondrial DNA is often targeted in studies of phylogeny because it is highly **conserved** (it codes for vital functions and changes very little over evolutionary time).

Mapping and Sequencing the Genome

1 Chromosome cut into large fragments:

A human chromosome, consisting of 50-280 million base-pairs, is cut randomly into large fragments with **restriction enzymes**. Each fragment is 150 000 - 1 million base pairs long.

2 Create a clone library:

Each large fragment is inserted into a separate vector (yeast or bacterial plasmid) using DNA **ligation**. The plasmids are then cloned in cells to produce many copies of the fragments; known as a **clone library** (each type of DNA fragment resides in a separate culture).

3 Map fragment with DNA markers:

Each of the fragments are then mapped using **PCR** and **gel electrophoresis** to determine the position of **DNA markers** on each fragment.

4 Create a low resolution map of a chromosome:

Overlaps between the large fragments can be determined and a low resolution map of the chromosome can be built up. In reality, there would be many hundreds of large fragments created by the cutting up of a single chromosome (only four are shown here).

5 Each large fragment is cut into smaller pieces:

A large fragment is cut into smaller pieces (1500 - 5000 base pairs) with **restriction enzymes**. These smaller fragments are inserted into vectors using DNA **ligation** techniques. These vectors are then cloned to make copies; a **sub-clone library**.

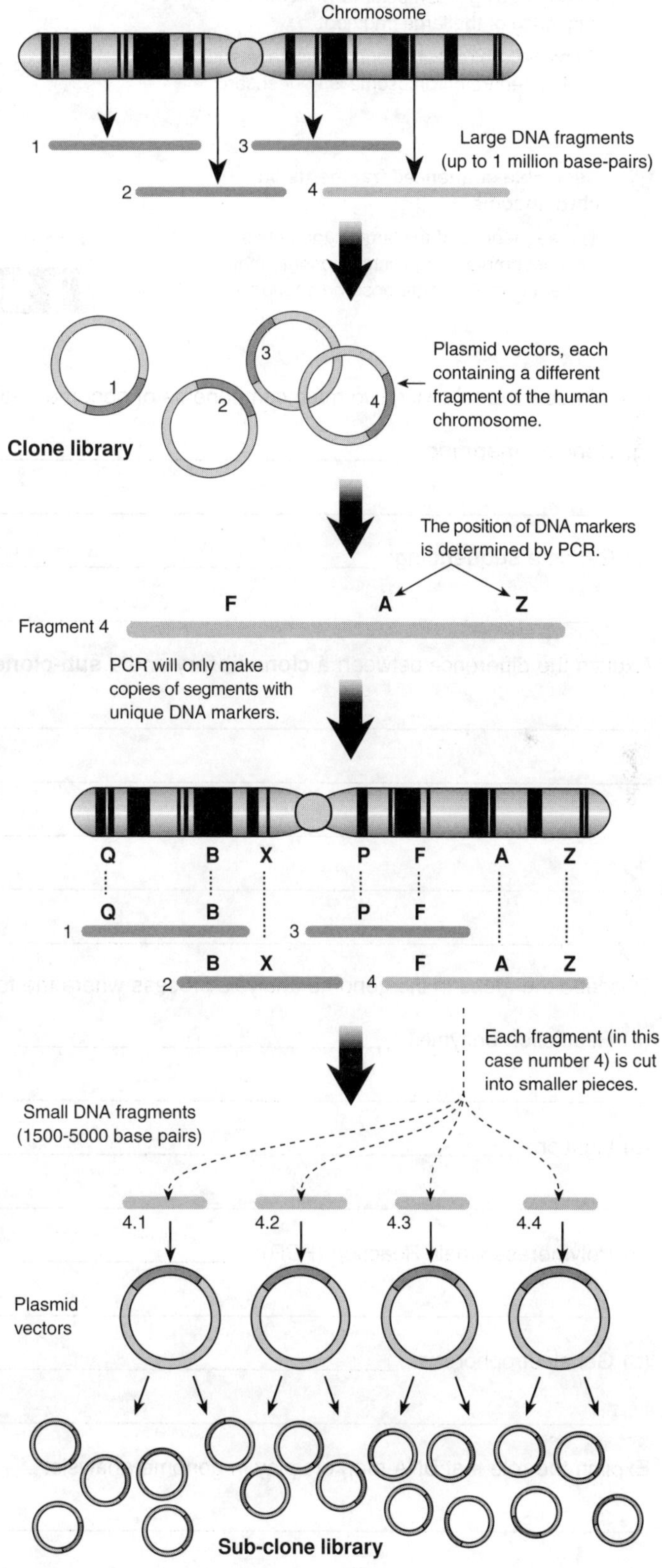

6 Sequence fragments:

The small fragments are then sequenced using **gel electrophoresis** to find the exact order of the bases. Note: the examples on the right show only 15 base-pairs in each small fragment. In reality, they would be 1500 to 5000 base pairs in length.

7 Overlapping sequences are assembled:

Overlapping sequences are assembled together using a computer to work out the sequence of the large fragment.

Steps 5-7 are repeated for all large fragments until the entire chromosome is sequenced.

8 Assemble sequenced fragments on chromosome:

The sequences of the large fragments are then assembled on the chromosome map to make a complete chromosome sequence.

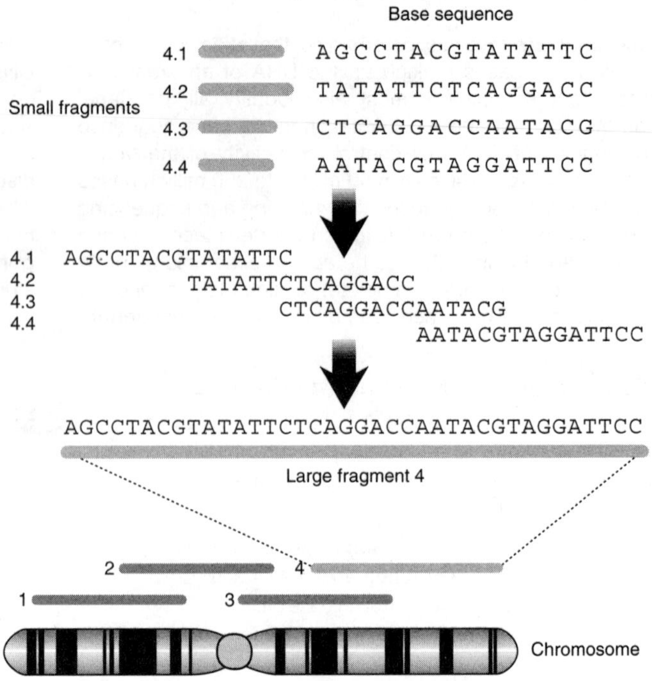

1. Explain how the following two main components of genome analysis contribute to the overall process:

   (a) Genome **mapping**: __________

   (b) Genome **sequencing**: __________

2. Explain the difference between a **clone library** and a **sub-clone library**, identifying their role in genome analysis:

3. Describe the steps in the genome analysis process where the following techniques are used:

   (a) Restriction enzymes: __________

   (b) Ligation: __________

   (c) Polymerase Chain Reaction (PCR): __________

   (d) Gel electrophoresis: __________

4. Explain the role that DNA markers play in genome analysis: __________

Investigating Genetic Diversity

PCR and **DNA sequencing** can be used in the assessment of **genetic biodiversity**. From a conservation point of view, large amounts of genetic variation within a species may be indicative of a greater ability to adapt to environmental change (e.g. changes in climate). The amount of variation between populations of a species is of particular interest. Sometimes the genetic variation found between populations is enough to warrant separating them into two or more '**morphologically cryptic**' species (containing populations that are identical in appearance, but different genetically). **Springtails** are abundant arthropods, closely related to insects, which live in soil throughout the world. One particular species, *Gomphiocephalus hodgsoni*, is the largest year-round inhabitant of the Antarctic continent. It is being studied in an area of Antarctica known as the Dry Valleys, particularly in Taylor Valley. This region is largely ice-free, and the springtails survive in moist habitats such as at the edges of lakes and glacial streams. Springtails collected throughout Taylor Valley appear to be morphologically identical. However, after DNA analysis of a gene from springtail **mitochondrial DNA**, significant genetic biodiversity has been found between populations. This may indicate the presence of more than one species. As climate change and the presence of humans affect the habitat of Taylor Valley over time, it is important to understand and monitor the genetic structure of the springtail populations in order to ensure that biodiversity is conserved.

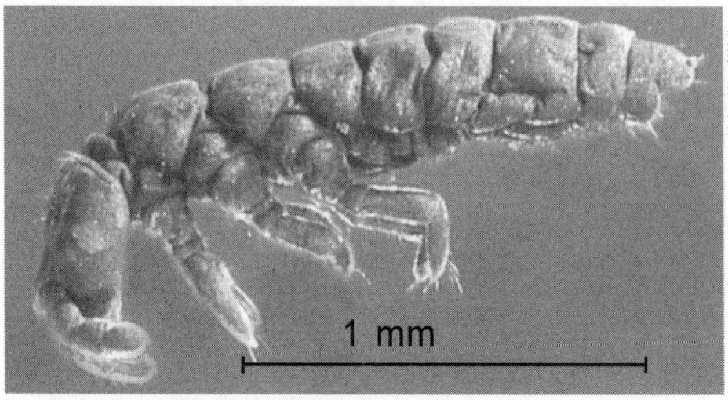

The **springtail** *Gomphiocephalus hodgsoni* (above) is a small arthropod, just over 1 mm long. Liam Nolan investigated the genetic relatedness of populations in and around Taylor Valley in Antarctica.

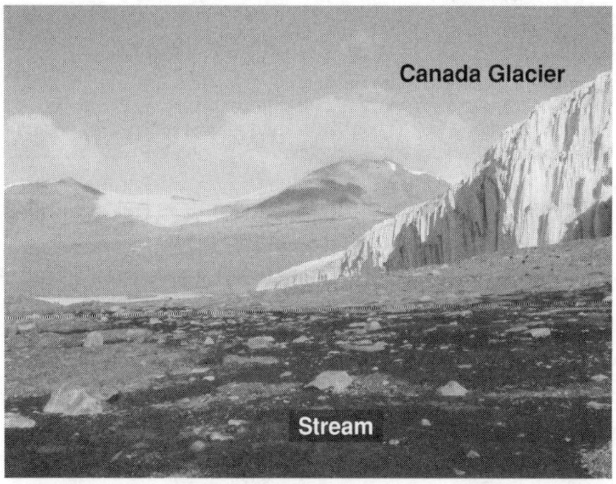

Taylor Valley, one of the Dry Valleys in Antarctica, is clear of snow much of the year. The ephemeral stream is ideal springtail habitat.

The Process of DNA Analysis of Two Springtails (A and B) is illustrated below:

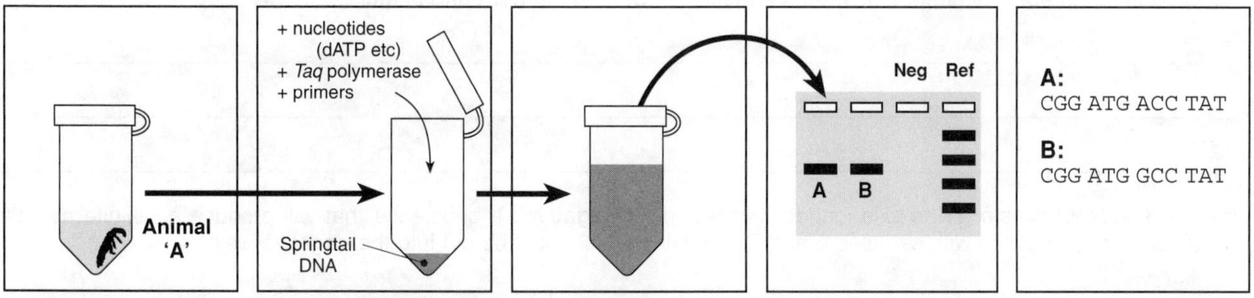

Extraction of DNA
Proteinase enzyme dissolves the tissues of the springtail to release DNA

PCR Mixture
Primers anneal to the start and end of the gene in the mitochondrial DNA

PCR
DNA amplification
92°C, 45°C, 72°C
45 cycles

Gel Electrophoresis
of PCR product for both animal 'A' and 'B'

Sequencing of PCR product

Source: Many thanks to Liam Nolan, teacher at Tauranga Girls' College, for supplying the information for these pages. Liam studied with the **Centre for Biodiversity and Ecology Research** (University of Waikato, Hamilton, New Zealand), whilst the recipient of a study award from the NZ Ministry of Education.

Conditions in Antarctica are harsh, even at the best of times. Members of the research group shared a tent at their camp in Taylor Valley, set aside as a field laboratory. Despite overnight temperatures well below freezing, the tent often became very hot during the day as the mid-summer sun heated it for most of the 24 hour cycle.

Related activities: *Gel Electrophoresis, Polymerase Chain Reaction, Automated DNA Sequencing*

Leo Sanchez

Leo Sanchez

Scientific expeditions into the field in Antarctica are fraught with logistical problems. Apart from making sure that sophisticated scientific equipment functions properly in freezing temperatures, just getting the equipment from Scott Base to the field station is difficult, requiring the use of helicopters.

Scott Base is the centre for research by New Zealand scientists. They work mostly during the summer months, when there is perpetual daylight. There are facilities for carrying out some lab work, as well as recreational facilities for the expedition members.

1. Explain why a **proteinase** enzyme is helpful in the extraction of DNA from springtails:

2. (a) Describe the function of *Taq* polymerase in **PCR**:

   (b) Explain why nucleotides are added to the PCR mixture:

   (c) Explain the effect of different temperatures (used in PCR) on the DNA and primers:

3. (a) The **electrophoresis gel** is also loaded with a known '**negative**'; a substance that will produce a definite negative result, for comparison with samples A and B. Describe what would be put into the negative well:

   (b) A **reference**, which contains a mixture of DNA segments of known length, is also loaded onto the gel. Explain why such fragments are added into the reference well:

4. (a) The given DNA sequences (on the previous page) are taken from two different individuals. Describe the kind of mutation observed:

   (b) Mutations are most frequently found at the third base of a codon. Discuss the significance of this mutation in the springtails' DNA sequence:

The Human Genome Project

The **Human Genome Project** (HGP) is a publicly funded venture involving many different organisations throughout the world. In 1998, Celera Genomics in the USA began a competing project, as a commercial venture, in a race to be the first to determine the human genome sequence. In 2000, both organisations reached the first draft stage, and the entire genome is now available as a high quality (golden standard) sequence. In addition to determining the order of bases in the human genome, genes are being identified, sequenced, and mapped (their specific chromosomal location identified). The next challenge is to assign functions to the identified genes. By identifying and studying the protein products of genes (a field known as **proteomics**), scientists can develop a better understanding of genetic disorders. Long term benefits of the HGP are both medical and non-medical (see next page). Many biotechnology companies have taken out patents on gene sequences. This practice is controversial because it restricts the use of the sequence information to the patent holders. Other genome sequencing projects have arisen as a result of the initiative to sequence the human one. In 2002 the International HapMap Project was started with the aim of developing a haplotype map (HapMap) of the human genome. Initially data was gathered from four populations with African, Asian and European ancestry and additional populations may be included as analysis of human genetic variation continues.

Gene Mapping

This process involves determining the precise position of a gene on a chromosome. Once the position is known, it can be shown on a diagram.

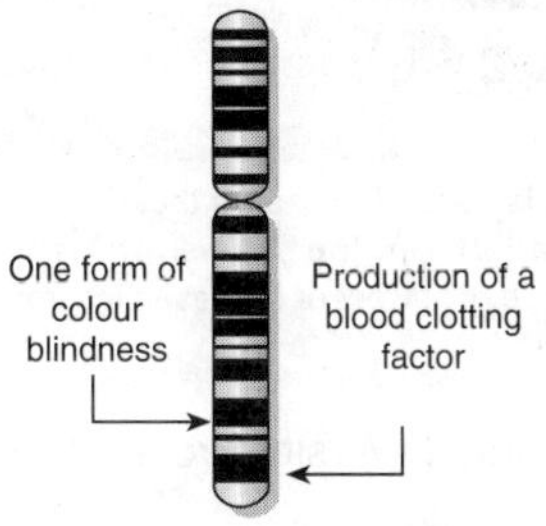

X chromosome

Equipment used for DNA Sequencing

Banks of PCR machines prepare DNA for the sequencing gel stage. The DNA is amplified and chemically tagged (to make the DNA fluoresce and enable visualisation on a gel).

Banks of DNA sequencing gels and powerful computers are used to determine the base order in DNA.

Count of Mapped Genes

The length and number of mapped genes to date for each chromosome are tabulated below. The entire human genome contains approximately 20 000-25 000 genes.

Chromosome	Length (Mb)	No. of Mapped Genes
1	263	1873
2	255	1113
3	214	965
4	203	614
5	194	782
6	183	1217
7	171	995
8	155	591
9	145	804
10	144	872
11	144	1162
12	143	894
13	114	290
14	109	1013
15	106	510
16	98	658
17	92	1034
18	85	302
19	67	1129
20	72	599
21	50	386
22	56	501
X	164	1021
Y	59	122
	Total:	19 447

Data to March 2008 from gdb.org (now offline)

Composition of the Genome

About 97% of the genome does not code for protein and its function was largely unknown. Recent genomic analyses have revealed that some this DNA (the intronic DNA) codes for functional RNA molecules with important regulatory roles. Some of it is repeat sequence DNA, which means the same section (the repeating unit) of DNA sequence is present many times, often in close proximity. The length of a repeating unit varies from two to many hundred bases and may be present hundreds of times. Some repeat DNA can be difficult, or impossible, to sequence; a consequence of technical difficulties of working with sections of DNA with unusual chemistry. As a result of this, 8-10% of the human genome will probably remain unsequenced.

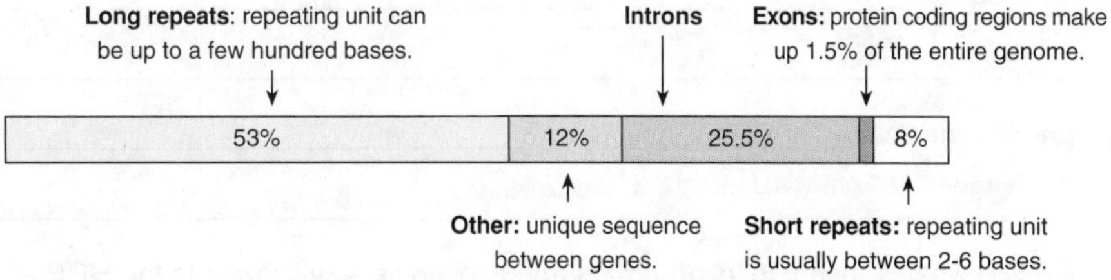

Qualities of DNA Sequence Data

The aim of the HGP was to produce a continuous block of sequence information for each chromosome. Initially the sequence information was obtained to draft quality, with an error rate of 1 in 1000 bases. The **Gold Standard sequence**, with an error rate of <1 per 100 000 bases, was completed in October 2004. Key results of the research are:

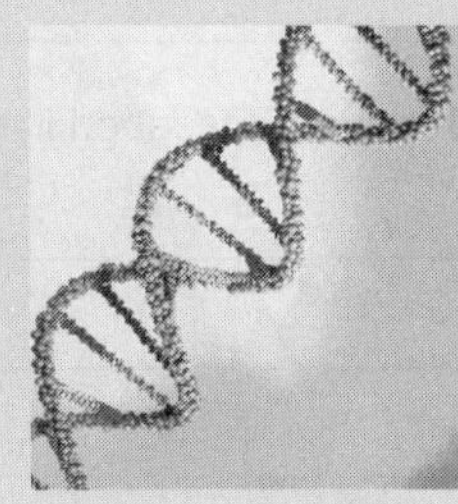

- The analysis suggests that there are perhaps only 20 000-25 000 protein-coding genes in our human genome.
- The number of gaps has been reduced 400-fold to only 341
- It covers 99% of the gene containing parts of the genome and is 99.999% accurate.
- The new sequence correctly identifies almost all known genes (99.74%).
- Its accuracy and completeness allows systematic searches for causes of disease.

Periodicals:
Revolution postponed

Related activities: *Genome Analysis, Genome Projects*

Benefits and ethical issues arising from the Human Genome Project

Medical benefits

- Improved **diagnosis** of disease and predisposition to disease by genetic testing.
- Better identification of disease carriers, through genetic testing.
- Better **drugs** can be designed using knowledge of protein structure (from gene sequence information) rather than by trial and error.
- Greater possibility of successfully using **gene therapy** to correct genetic disorders.

Couples can already have a limited range of genetic tests to determine the risk of having offspring with some disease-causing mutations.

Non-medical benefits

- Greater knowledge of **family relationships** through genetic testing, e.g. paternity testing in family courts.
- Advances **forensic science** through analysis of DNA at crime scenes.
- Improved knowledge of the evolutionary relationships between humans and other organisms, which will help to develop better, more accurate classification systems.

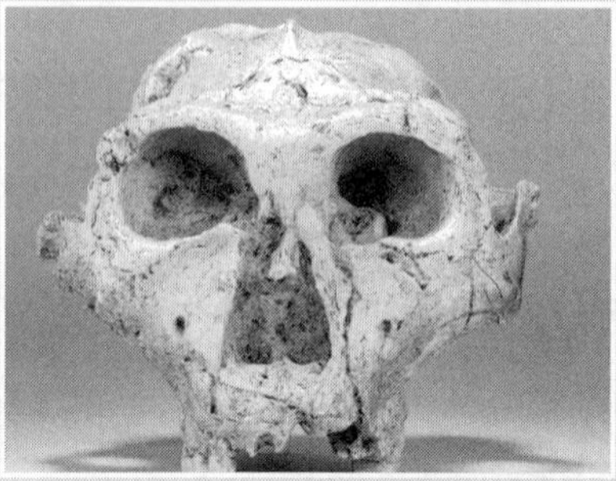

When DNA sequences are available for humans and their ancestors, comparative analysis may provide clues about human evolution.

Possible ethical issues

- It is unclear whether third parties, e.g. health insurers, have rights to genetic test results.
- If treatment is unavailable for a disease, genetic knowledge about it may have no use.
- Genetic tests are costly, and there is no easy answer as to who should pay for them.
- Genetic information is hereditary so knowledge of an individual's own genome has implications for members of their family.

Legislation is needed to ensure that there is no discrimination on the basis of genetic information, e.g. at work or for health insurance.

1. Briefly describe the objectives of the Human Genome Project (HGP) and the Human Genome Diversity Project (HGDP):

   HGP: ______________________________

   ____

   HGDP: ______________________________

2. Suggest a reason why indigenous peoples around the world are reluctant to provide DNA samples for the HGDP:

   ____

   ____

3. Describe two possible **benefits** of Human Genome Project (HGP):

   (a) Medical: ______________________________

   ____

   (b) Non-medical: ______________________________

   ____

4. Explain what is meant by **proteomics** and explain its significance to the HGP and the ongoing benefits arising from it:

   ____

   ____

   ____

   ____

5. Suggest two possible points of view for one of the **ethical issues** described in the list above:

   (a) ______________________________

   ____

   (b) ______________________________

   ____

Genome Projects

There are many genome projects underway around the world, including the Human Genome Project. The aim of most genome projects is to determine the DNA sequence of the organism's entire genome. Over one hundred bacterial and viral genomes, as well as a number of larger genomes (including honeybee, nematode worm, African clawed frog, pufferfish, zebra fish, rice, cow, dog, and rat) have already been sequenced. Genomes that are, for a variety of reasons, high priority for DNA sequencing include the sea urchin, kangaroo, pig, cat, baboon, silkworm, rhesus monkey, turkey and banana. Genome sequencing is costly, so candidates are carefully chosen. Important factors in this choice include the value of the knowledge to practical applications, the degree of technical difficulty involved, and the size of the genome (very large genomes are generally avoided). Genome sizes and the number of genes per genome vary, and are not necessarily correlated with the size and structural complexity of the organism itself. Once completed, genome sequences are analysed by computer to identify genes.

Yeast (*Saccharomyces cerevisiae*)

Status: Completed in 1996

Number of genes: 6000

Genome size: 13 Mb

The first eukaryotic genome to be completely sequenced. Yeast is used as a model organism to study human cancer.

Bacteria (*Escherichia coli*)

Status: Completed in 1997

Number of genes: 4403

Genome size: 4.6 Mb

E. coli has been used as a laboratory organism for over 70 years. Various strains of *E. coli* are responsible for several human diseases.

Mouse (*Mus musculus*)

Status: Completed in 2002

Number of genes: 30 000

Genome size: 2500 Mb

New drugs destined for human use are often tested on mice because more than 90% of their proteins show similarities to human proteins.

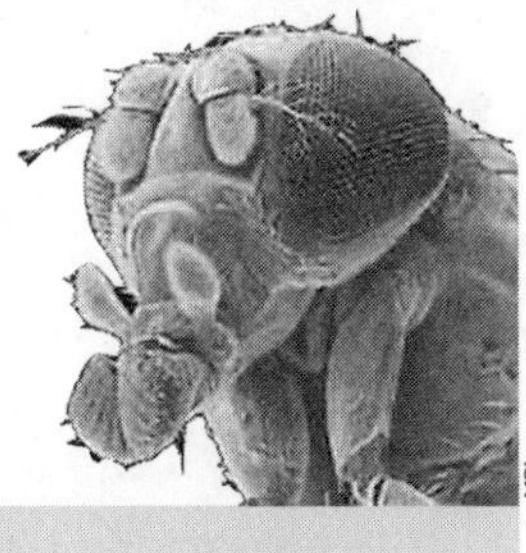

MPI

Fruit fly (*Drosophila melanogaster*)

Status: Completed in 2000

Number of genes: 14 000

Genome size: 150 Mb

Drosophila has been used extensively for genetic studies for many years. About 50% of all fly proteins show similarities to mammalian proteins.

Chimpanzee (*Pan troglodytes*)

Status: Draft, Dec. 2003, Completed, Sept. 2005

Genome size: 3000 Mb

Chimp and human genomes differ by <2%. Identifying differences could provide clues to the genetics of diseases such as cancer, to which chimps are less prone.

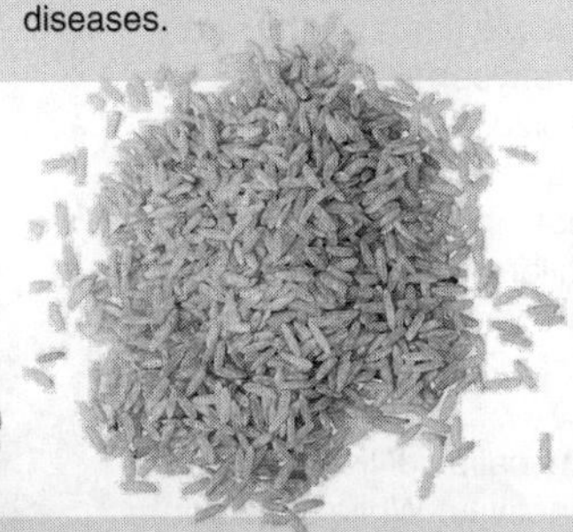

Rice (*Oryza sativa*)

Status: Completed 2002 for two varieties (*indica* and *japonica*)

Genome size: 466 and 420 Mb

A food staple for much of the world's population. An international consortium is currently working on a third rice genome sequence, which will be the Gold Standard.

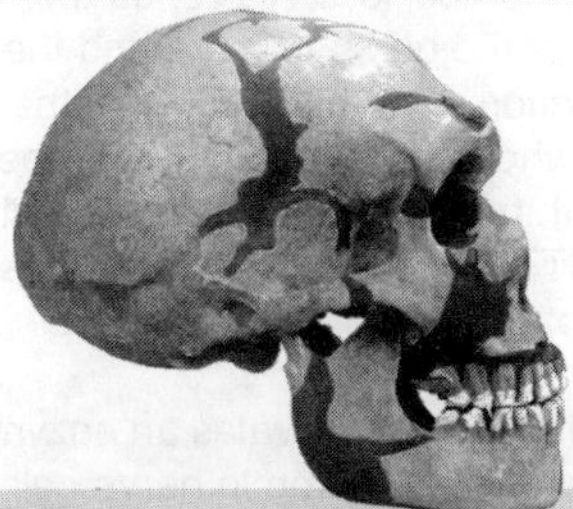

Neanderthal (*H. neanderthalensis*)

Status: Draft completed May 2010

Genome size: 3000 Mb

Completion of this draft enables the first genome-wide comparison of the human and Neanderthal genomes. Researchers may now be able to identify the genetic variations that gave rise to humans.

Chicken (*Gallus gallus*)

Status: Completed in Feb. 2004

Genome size: 1200 Mb

Various human viruses were first found in chickens making this species important for the study of human disease and cross-species transfers. It was the first bird genome to be sequenced.

1. Calculate the number of genes per Mb of DNA for the organisms above:

   (a) Yeast: ______________ (b) *E. coli*: ______________ (c) Fruit fly: ______________ (d) Mouse: ______________

2. Suggest why the number of genes per Mb of DNA varies between organisms (hint: consider relative sizes of introns):

3. Suggest why researchers want to sequence the genomes of plants such as wheat, rice, and maize:

4. Explain the rationale for sequencing the Neanderthal genome even though Neanderthals are extinct:

A Gene That Can Tell Your Future

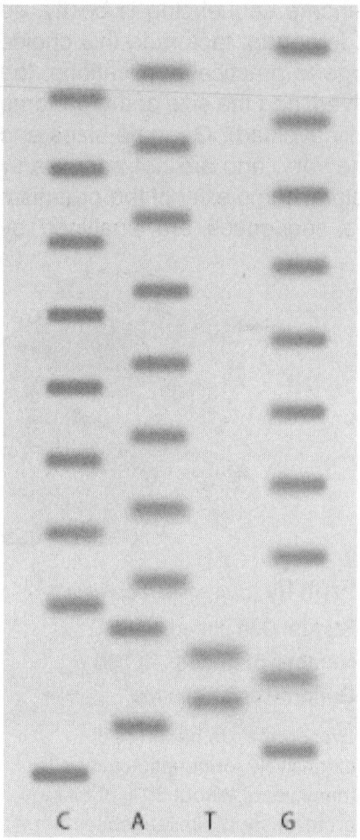

Huntington's disease (HD) is a genetic neuro-degenerative disease that normally does not affect people until about the age of 40. Its symptoms usually appear first as a shaking of the hands and an awkward gait. Later manifestations of the disease include serious loss of muscle control and mental function, often ending in dementia and ultimately death.

All humans have the huntingtin (**HTT**) gene, which in its normal state produces a protein with roles in gene transcription, synaptic transmission, and brain cell survival. The mutant gene (**mHTT**) causes changes to and death of the cells of the cerebrum, the hippocampus, and cerebellum, resulting in the atrophy (reduction) of brain matter. The gene was discovered by Nancy Wexler in 1983 after ten years of research working with cell samples and family histories of more than 10,000 people from the town of San Luis in Venezuela, where around 1% of the population have the disease (compared to about 0.01% in the rest of the world). Ten years later the exact location of the gene on the chromosome 4 was discovered.

The identification of the HD gene began by looking for a gene probe that would bind to the DNA of people who had HD, and not to those who didn't. Eventually a marker for HD, called **G8**, was found. The next step was to find which chromosome carried the marker and where on the chromosome it was. The researchers hybridised human cells with those of mice so that each cell contained only one human chromosome, a different chromosome in each cell. The hybrid cell with chromosome 4 was the one with the G8 marker. They then found a marker that overlapped G8 and then another marker that overlapped that marker. By repeating this many times, they produced a map of the genes on chromosome 4. The researchers then sequenced the genes and found people who had HD had one gene that was considerably longer than people who did not have HD. Moreover the increase in length was caused by the repetition of the base sequence CAG.

The HD mutation (mHTT) is called a trinucleotide repeat expansion. In the case of mHTT, the base sequence CAG is repeated multiple times on the short arm of chromosome 4. The normal number of CAG repeats is between 6 and 30. The mHTT gene causes the repeat number to be 35 or more and the size of the repeat often increases from generation to generation, with the severity of the disease increasing with the number of repeats. Individuals who have 27 to 35 CAG repeats in the HTT gene do not develop Huntington disease, but they are at risk of having children who will develop the disorder. The mutant allele, mHTT, is also dominant, so those who are homozygous or heterozygous for the allele are both at risk of developing HD.

New research has shown that the mHTT gene activates an enzyme called JNK3, which is expressed only in the neurones and causes a drop in nerve cell activity. While a person is young and still growing, the neurones can compensate for the accumulation of JNK3. However, when people get older and neurone growth stops, the effects of JNK3 become greater and the physical signs of HD become apparent. Because of mHTT's dominance, an affected person has a 50% chance of having offspring who are also affected. Genetic testing for the disease is relatively easy now that the genetic cause of the disease is known. While locating and counting the CAG repeats does not give a date for the occurrence of HD, it does provide some understanding of the chances of passing on the disease.

NYWTS

American singer-songwriter and folk musician Woody Guthrie died from complications of HD

1. Describe the physical effects of Huntington's disease: ______________________

____

2. Describe how the mHTT gene was discovered: ______________________

____

____

____

3. Discuss the cause of Huntington's disease and its pattern of increasing severity with each generation: __________

____

____

____

____

____

DNA Chips

Microarrays (DNA chips or gene chips) are relatively recent tools in gene research. Their development a decade ago built on earlier DNA probe technology and provided a tool to quickly compare the (known) DNA on a chip with (unknown) DNA to determine which genes were present in a sample or to determine the code of an unsequenced string of DNA. Microarrays have also provided a tool which, increasingly, is being used to investigate the activity level (the expression) of those genes. Microarrays rely on **nucleic acid hybridisation**, in which a known DNA fragment is used as a **probe** to find complementary sequences. In a microarray, DNA fragments, corresponding to known genes, are fixed to a solid support in an orderly pattern, usually as a series of dots. The fragments are tested for hybridisation with samples of labelled cDNA molecules. Computer analysis then reveals which genes are active in different tissues, in different stages of development, or in tissues in different states of health.

What is a DNA Chip?

A **microarray** (DNA chip) consists of DNA probes fixed to a small solid support such as a glass slide or a nylon filter. Each spot on the microarray has thousands to millions of copies of a different **DNA probe**. The probes are single stranded DNA molecules, each representing a gene.

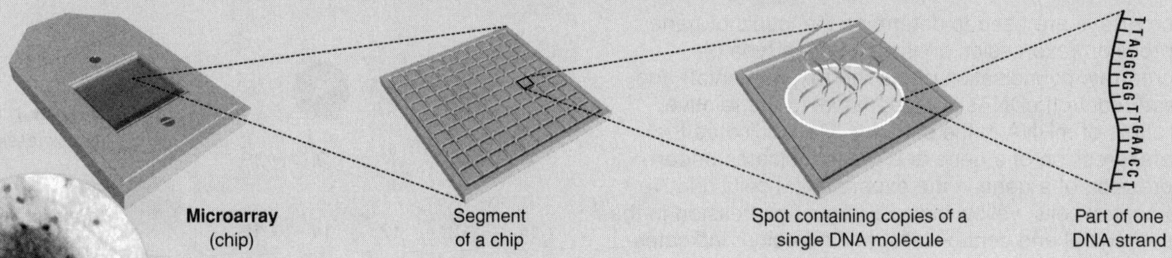

How DNA Chips Work

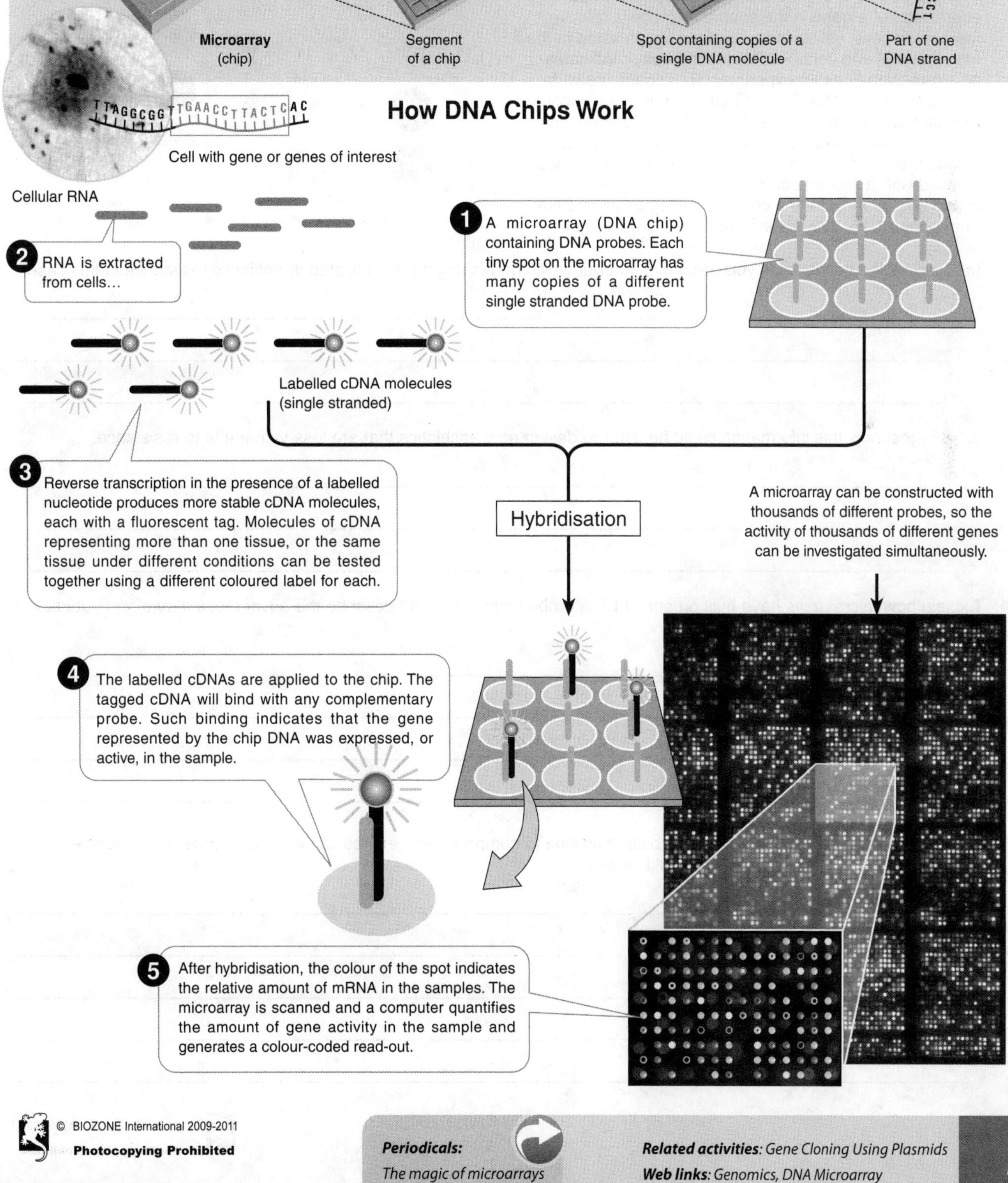

1. Describe one purpose of microarrays: ______________________________

2. (a) Identify the basic principle by which microarrays work: ______________________________

(b) Identify the role of reverse transcription in microarray technology: ______________________________

3. Microarrays are used to determine the levels of gene expression (expression analysis). In one type of microarray, hybridisation of the red (experimental) and green (control) cDNAs is proportional to the relative amounts of mRNA in the samples. Red indicates the overexpression of a gene and green indicates under-expression of a gene in the experimental cells relative the control cells, yellow indicates equal expression in the experimental and control cells, and no colour indicates no expression in either experimental or control cells. In an experiment, cDNA derived from a strain of antibiotic resistant bacteria (experimental cells) was labelled with a red fluorescent tag and cDNA derived from a a non-resistant strain of the same bacterium (control cells) was labelled with a green fluorescent tag. The cDNAs were mixed and hybridised to a chip containing spots of DNA from genes 1-25. The results are shown on the right.

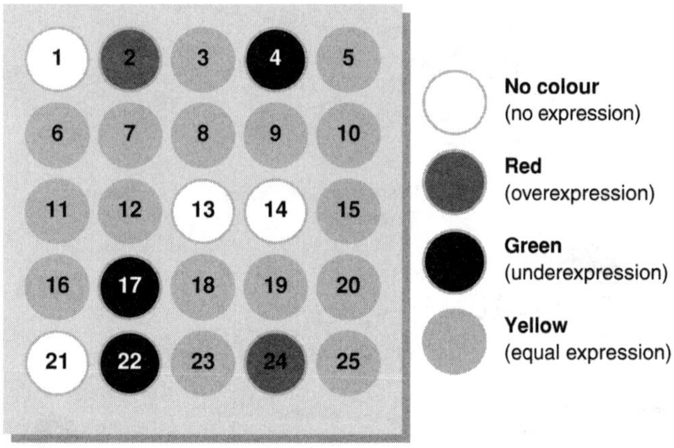

(a) Discuss the conclusions you could make about which genes might be implicated in antibiotic resistance in this case:

(b) Suggest how this information could be used to design new antibiotics that are less vulnerable to resistance:

4. Explain how microarrays have built on earlier DNA probe technology and describe the advantages they offer in studies of gene expression:

5. Microarrays are frequently used in diagnostic medicine to compare gene expression in cancerous and non-cancerous tissue. Suggest how this information could be used:

DNA Profiling Using Probes

Although DNA profiling using PCR is becoming increasingly the dominant procedure, the older technology of using DNA probes is still in use. This method uses another type of repeat sequence to that used in profiling with PCR. The repeat sequences are called **minisatellites** or **variable number tandem repeats** (VNTRs), and comprise longer repeating units (a few tens of nucleotides long). Equivalent sequences in different people have the same core sequence of 10-15 bases (to which a DNA **probe** is attached), but thereafter the patterns vary considerably in length from one person to another. This phenomenon has been used to develop a DNA profiling procedure called the Southern blot (illustrated below). In humans, the chance that two people will have an identical DNA profile is less than one in a billion, making DNA profiling a useful tool for forensic investigations.

Southern Blotting Method

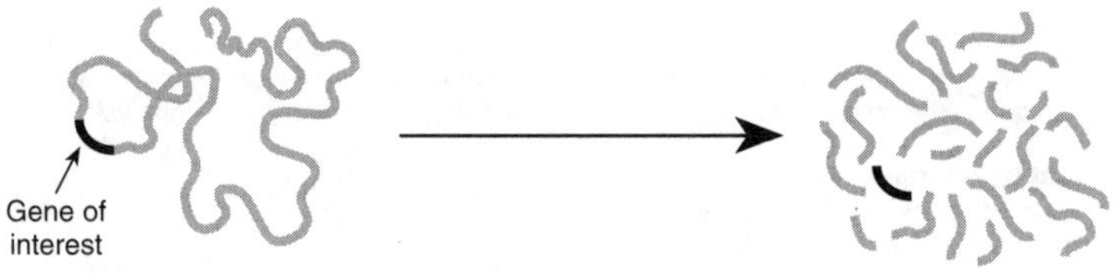

1 Extract DNA from sample

A sample of tissue from a living or dead organism is treated with chemicals and enzymes to extract the DNA, which is separated and purified.

2 Cut up DNA

Using **restriction enzymes**, the DNA is cut up into thousands of fragments of all different sizes.

3 Separate fragments

The fragments are separated by length, using **gel electrophoresis**. DNA, which is negatively charged, moves toward the positive terminal. The shorter fragments travel faster and further than longer ones.

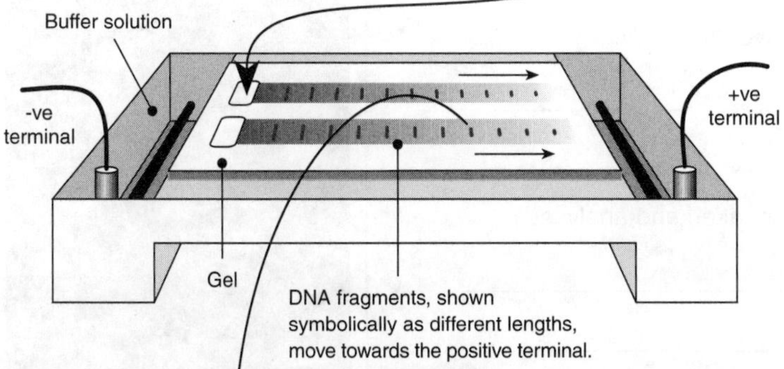

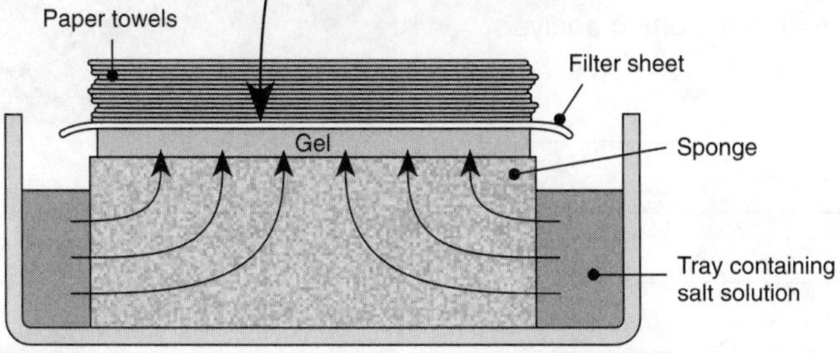

4 Transfer DNA fragments to filter sheet

DNA molecules are split into single strands using alkaline chemicals. The DNA is transferred onto a nitrocellulose filter sheet by pressing it against the gel. The salt solution passes through the gel, carrying the DNA fragments onto the surface of the filter sheet. This is the blot.

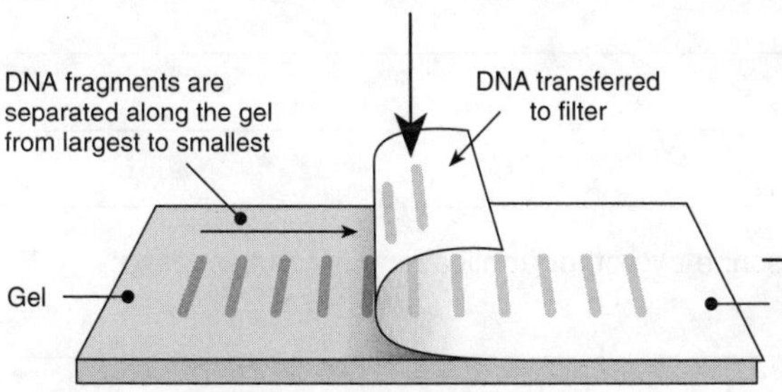

5 Remove filter sheet

The gel with filter sheet still attached is removed and separated. The DNA fragments that have now moved to the filter sheet are in exactly the same position as on the gel.

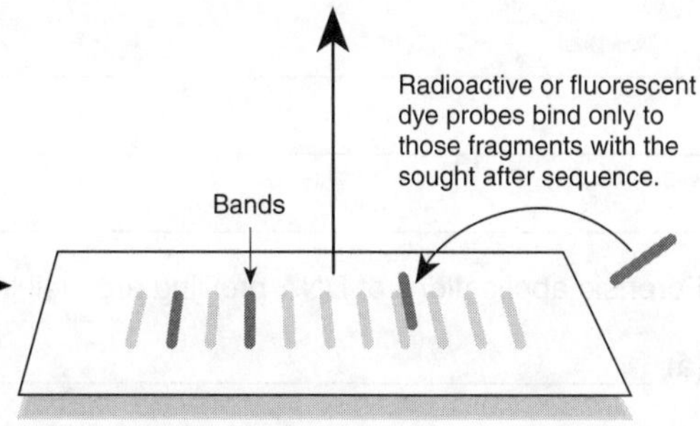

6 Attach radioactively labelled probes

The filter sheet is immersed in a bath with **radioactive probes** (synthetic complementary DNA). Many thousands of these segments bind to the sample DNA fragments where they are localised as bands.

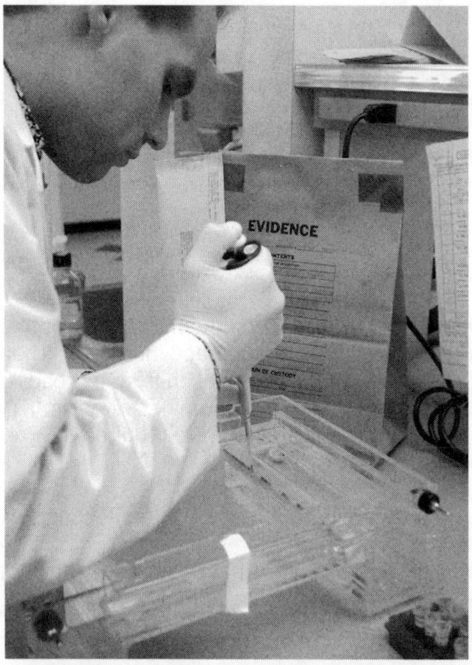

A technician carrying out a DNA profiling test of samples taken from the scene of a crime. Such tests are admissible in a court of law as forensic evidence.

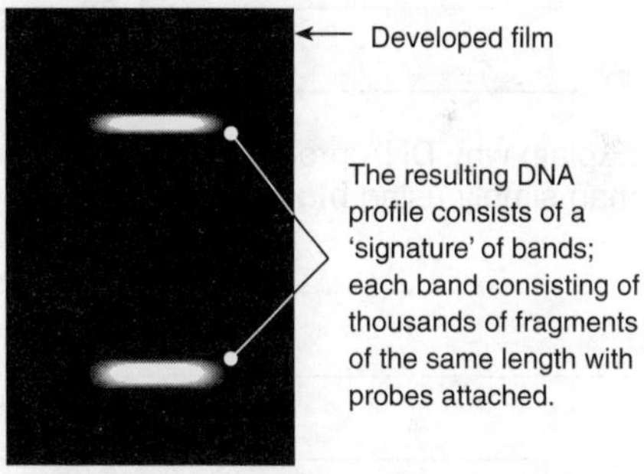

7 Create autoradiograph

When using radioactive probes, the filter sheet is exposed to X-ray film. The radioactive probes attached to the sorted fragments show up as dark bands on the film. The spacing of these bands is the **DNA profile**, which is used as evidence.

How DNA probes may be used

Artificially constructed DNA probes work by binding to a specific sequence on DNA that is of interest to the investigator. Gene probes may be used to search for:

- The presence of a specific allele of a gene (e.g. cystic fibrosis gene).
- The approximate location of a gene on a chromosome (i.e. which chromosome and what position on its *p* or *q* arm it binds to).
- The 'genetic fingerprint' of a person to tell them apart from others (e.g. paternity testing, forensic identification of suspects).

How a DNA probe works

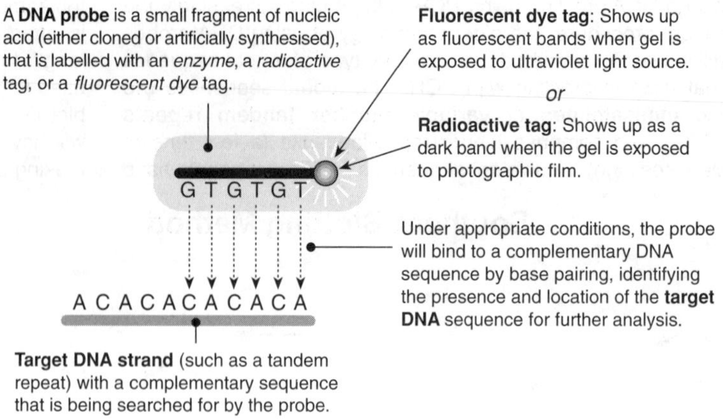

1. The DNA profile on the right is a hypothetical example of a forensic result where the victim was raped and murdered. There were three suspects in the case. A semen sample was taken from the body of the victim and this was used as the evidence (see arrow on the X-ray film). Two probes were used in this investigation. The three suspects were required to give blood samples and a sample was also taken from the victim.

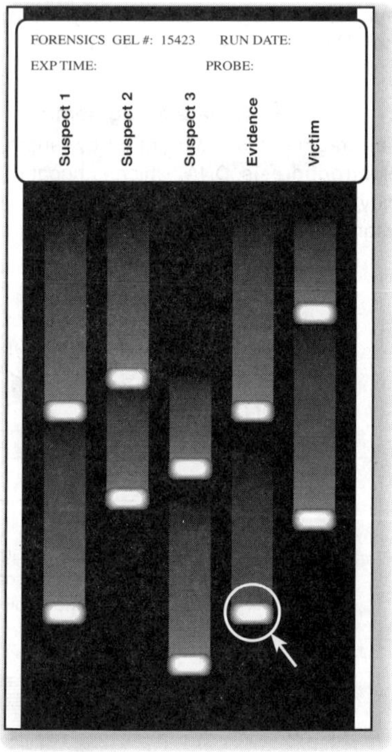

   (a) Identify which of the three suspects was probably the killer: ______________

   (b) Explain with what degree of certainty do you give this verdict:

   (c) Explain why a sample from the **victim** was also taken and analysed:

2. Explain why DNA profiling is a more useful diagnostic tool for **forensic** analysis than simply using **blood types**:

3. In some well-known criminal trials in recent years (e.g. the trial of 'O.J. Simpson' for the murder of his wife, USA, 1995) the prosecution cases relied heavily on DNA evidence. Despite providing a DNA profile of the accused that clearly implicated them in the crime, the evidence was successfully challenged by defence counsel on technical grounds (concerning what is called the '**chain of evidence**'). Explain why such DNA evidence has failed to gain a prosecution:

4. Forensic applications of DNA profiling are well known. Briefly describe two other applications of DNA profiling:

   (a) ______________

   (b) ______________

Forensic Applications of DNA Profiling

The use of DNA as a tool for solving crimes such as homicide is well known, but it can also be used to as a solution to many other problems. DNA evidence has been used to identify body parts, solve cases of industrial sabotage and contamination, for paternity testing, and even in identifying animal products illegally made from endangered species.

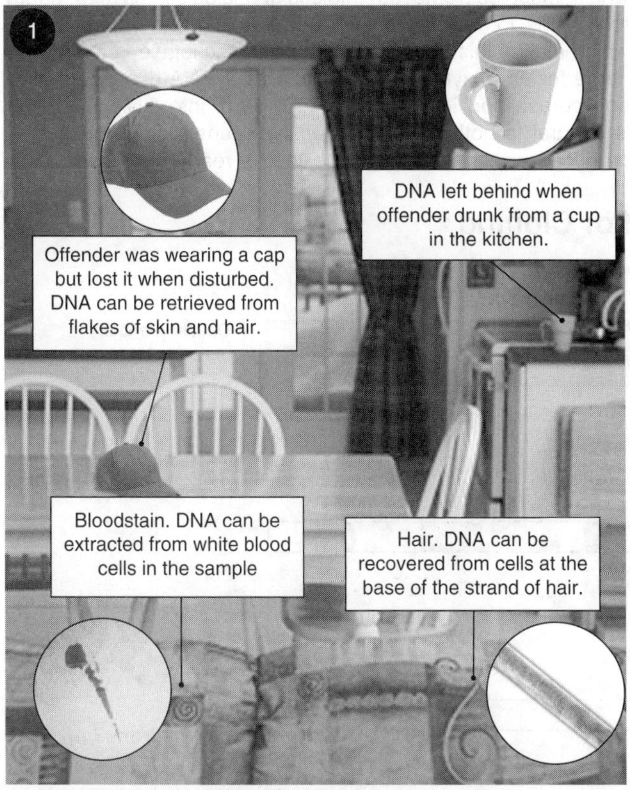

During the initial investigation, samples of material that may contain DNA are taken for analysis. At a crime scene, this may include blood and body fluids as well as samples of clothing or objects that the offender might have touched. Samples from the victim are also taken to eliminate them as a possible source of contamination.

2 DNA is isolated and profiles are made from all samples and compared to known DNA profiles such as that of the victim.

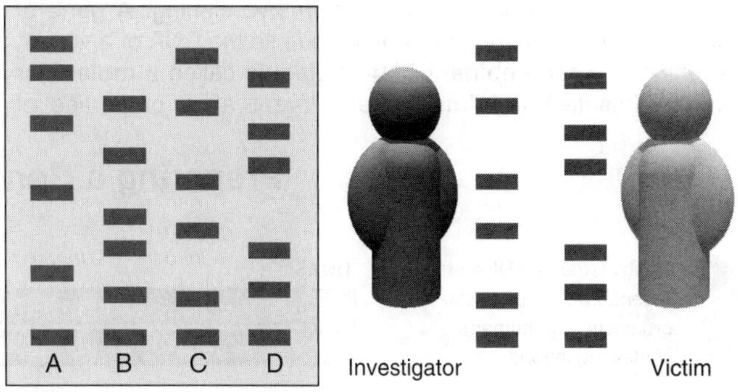

Profiles from collected DNA

3 Unknown DNA samples are compared to DNA databases of convicted offenders and to the DNA of the alleged offender.

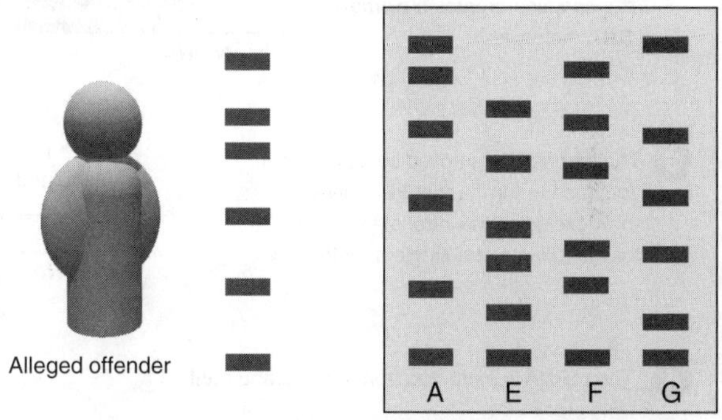

Profiles from DNA database

4 Although it does not make a complete case, DNA profiling, in conjunction with other evidence, is one of the most powerful tools in identifying offenders or unknown tissues.

1. In the above case two sets of DNA profiles are shown. Describe the purpose of lane A in each set of profiles:

____

____

2. Explain why DNA profiles are obtained for both the victim and investigator:

____

____

3. Use the evidence to decide if the alleged offender is innocent or guilty and explain your decision:

____

____

____

4. Explain how DNA profiling could be used to refute official claims of the number of whales being captured and sold in fish markets:

____

____

____

Whale DNA: Tracking Illegal Slaughter

Under International Whaling Commission regulations, some species of whales can be captured for scientific research and their meat sold legally. Most, including humpback and blue whales, are fully protected and to capture or kill them for any purpose is illegal. Between 1999 and 2003 Scott Baker and associates from Oregon State University's Marine Mammal Institute investigated whale meat sold in markets in Japan and South Korea. Using DNA profiling techniques, they found around 10% of the samples tested were from fully protected whales including western gray whales and humpbacks. They also found that many more whales were being killed than were being officially reported.

Preparing a Gene for Cloning

Gene cloning is the process of making large quantities of a piece of DNA once it has been isolated. Its purpose is to yield large quantities of an individual gene or its protein product when the gene is expressed. Genes can be cloned *in vitro* in an automated process called PCR, which amplifies the DNA. Genes can also be cloned when they are part of an organism, in a technique called *in vivo* cloning. A gene of interest (e.g. a human gene) is inserted into the DNA of a vector, resulting in a **recombinant DNA molecule** called a **molecular clone**. This technique uses the self-replicating properties of the vector to make copies of the gene. The genes of interest are rarely ready for cloning in their native form because they include pieces of non-protein coding DNA, called **introns**, which must be removed. Molecular biologists have a handy tool in the form of an enzyme, called **reverse transcriptase**, which makes this possible. Reverse transcriptase is a common name for an enzyme that functions as a RNA-dependent DNA polymerase and it is used to copy RNA into DNA. This task is integral to both *in vitro* and *in vivo* gene cloning because it produces a reconstructed gene that is ready for amplification.

Preparing a Gene For Cloning

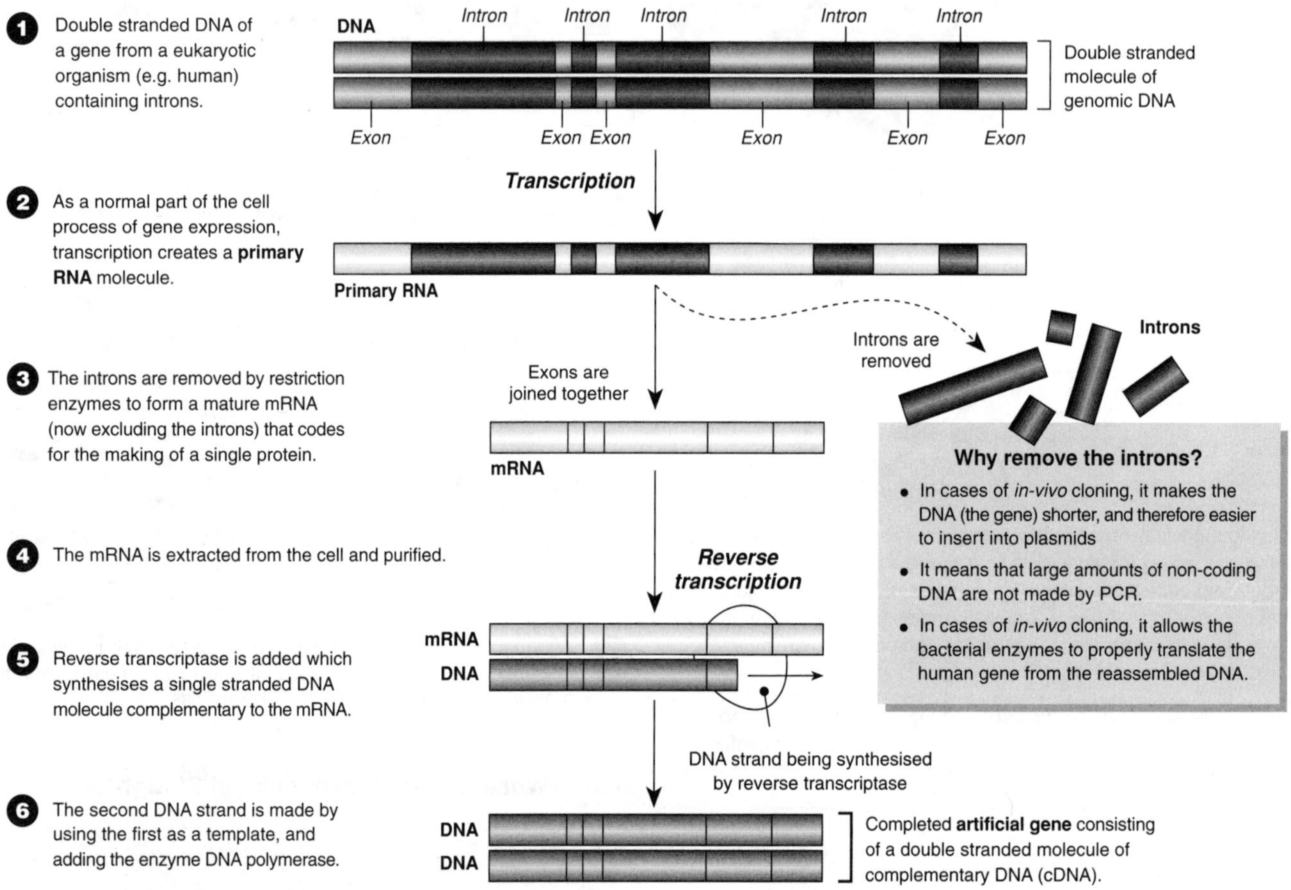

1. Explain the role of restriction enzymes in preparing a clone: ______________________________

____

____

2. (a) Explain why introns are removed before cloning a gene: ______________________________

____

____

(b) Describe the role of reverse transcriptase in this process: ______________________________

____

____

3. Describe the normal role of reverse transcriptase: ______________________________

____

____

Related activities: *In Vivo Gene Cloning, Polymerase Chain Reaction*

In Vivo Gene Cloning

It is possible to use the internal replication machinery of a cell to clone a gene, or even many genes, at once. By using cells to copy desired genes, it is also possible to produce any protein product the genes may code for. Recombinant DNA techniques (restriction digestion and ligation) are used to insert a gene of interest into the DNA of a vector (e.g. plasmid or viral DNA). This produces a **recombinant DNA molecule** that can used to transmit the gene of interest to another organism. To be useful, all vectors must be able to replicate inside their host organism, they must have one or more sites at which a restriction enzyme can cut, and they must have some kind of **genetic marker** that allows them to be easily identified. Viruses, and organisms such as bacteria and yeasts have DNA that behaves in this way. Bacterial plasmids are commonly used because they are easy to manipulate, their restriction sites are well known, and they are readily taken up by cells in culture. Once the recombinant plasmid vector (containing the desired gene) has been taken up by bacterial cells, and those cells are identified, the gene can be replicated many times as the bacteria grow and divide.

Cloning a Human Gene

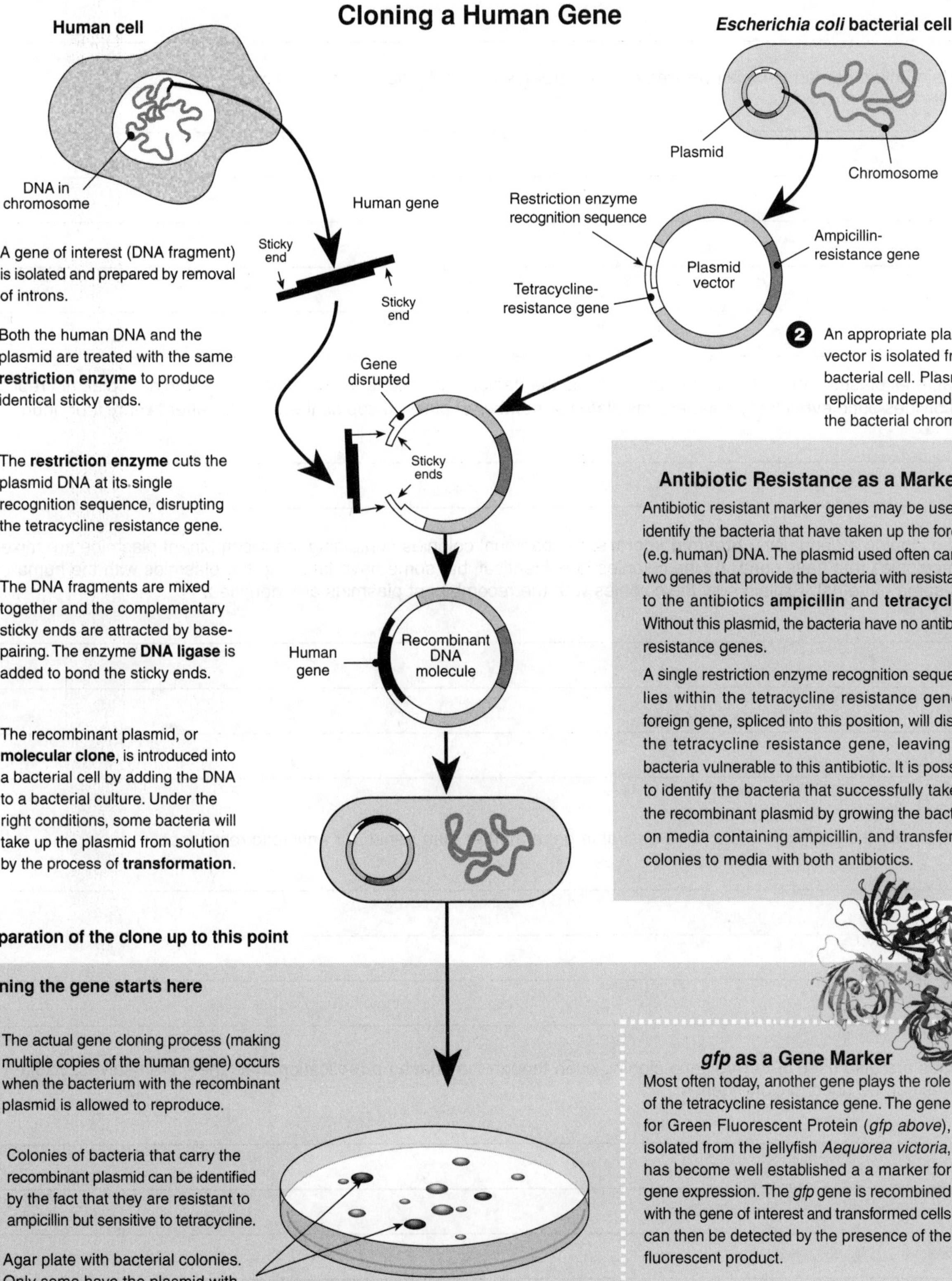

1. A gene of interest (DNA fragment) is isolated and prepared by removal of introns.

2. An appropriate plasmid vector is isolated from a bacterial cell. Plasmids replicate independently of the bacterial chromosome.

3. Both the human DNA and the plasmid are treated with the same **restriction enzyme** to produce identical sticky ends.

4. The **restriction enzyme** cuts the plasmid DNA at its single recognition sequence, disrupting the tetracycline resistance gene.

5. The DNA fragments are mixed together and the complementary sticky ends are attracted by base-pairing. The enzyme **DNA ligase** is added to bond the sticky ends.

6. The recombinant plasmid, or **molecular clone**, is introduced into a bacterial cell by adding the DNA to a bacterial culture. Under the right conditions, some bacteria will take up the plasmid from solution by the process of **transformation**.

Preparation of the clone up to this point

Cloning the gene starts here

7. The actual gene cloning process (making multiple copies of the human gene) occurs when the bacterium with the recombinant plasmid is allowed to reproduce.

8. Colonies of bacteria that carry the recombinant plasmid can be identified by the fact that they are resistant to ampicillin but sensitive to tetracycline.

Agar plate with bacterial colonies. Only some have the plasmid with the human gene.

Antibiotic Resistance as a Marker

Antibiotic resistant marker genes may be used to identify the bacteria that have taken up the foreign (e.g. human) DNA. The plasmid used often carries two genes that provide the bacteria with resistance to the antibiotics **ampicillin** and **tetracycline**. Without this plasmid, the bacteria have no antibiotic resistance genes.

A single restriction enzyme recognition sequence lies within the tetracycline resistance gene. A foreign gene, spliced into this position, will disrupt the tetracycline resistance gene, leaving the bacteria vulnerable to this antibiotic. It is possible to identify the bacteria that successfully take up the recombinant plasmid by growing the bacteria on media containing ampicillin, and transferring colonies to media with both antibiotics.

gfp as a Gene Marker

Most often today, another gene plays the role of the tetracycline resistance gene. The gene for Green Fluorescent Protein (*gfp above*), isolated from the jellyfish *Aequorea victoria*, has become well established a a marker for gene expression. The *gfp* gene is recombined with the gene of interest and transformed cells can then be detected by the presence of the fluorescent product.

1. Explain why it might be desirable to use *in vivo* methods to clone genes rather than PCR: ______

2. Explain when it may not be desirable to use bacteria to clone genes: ______

3. Explain how a human gene is removed from a chromosome and placed into a plasmid. ______

4. A bacterial plasmid replicates at the same rate as the bacteria. If a bacteria containing a recombinant plasmid replicates and divides once every thirty minutes, calculate the number of plasmid copies there will be after twenty four hours:

5. When cloning a gene using **plasmid vectors**, the bacterial colonies containing the recombinant plasmids are mixed up with colonies that have none. All the colonies look identical, but some have taken up the plasmids with the human gene, and some have not. Explain how the colonies with the recombinant plasmids are identified:

6. Explain why the *gfp* marker is a more desirable gene marker than genes for antibiotic resistance:

7. Viruses are also used in *in vivo* gene cloning even though they have no replication machinery themselves. Explain how viruses can be used to clone genes:

Vectors in Transgenesis

Transgenesis is concerned with the movement of genes from one species to another. An organism developing from a cell into which foreign DNA has been inserted is called a **transgenic organism**. Transgenic techniques have been applied to plants, animals, and bacteria. They allow direct modification of a genome and enable traits to be introduced that are not even naturally present in a species. The applications of this technology are various, e.g. improvement of crop yields, production of herbicide resistant plants, enhancement of desirable features in livestock, production of human proteins, and the treatment of genetic defects through **gene therapy**. Cloning technology can be used to propagate transgenic organisms so that introduced genes quickly become part of the germ line (and are inherited). Some methods involved in transgenesis are shown below:

Liposomes

Liposomes are small spherical vesicles made of a single membrane. They can be made commercially to precise specifications and, when coated with specific surface molecules, they are attracted to target cell types. DNA carried within the liposome can enter the cell by endocytosis or fusion. They can be used to deliver genes to these cells to correct defective or missing genes, providing gene therapy.

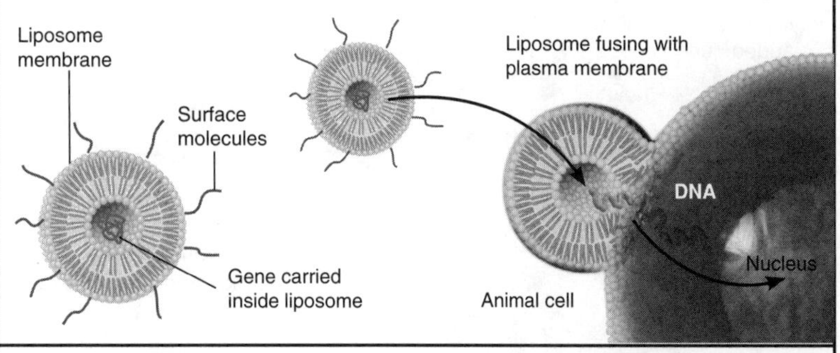

Plasmid Vectors

Plasmids are naturally occurring accessory chromosomes found in bacteria. Plasmids are usually transferred between related bacteria by cell-to-cell contact (conjugation). Simple chemical treatments can make mammalian cells, yeast cells and some bacterial cells that do not naturally transfer DNA, take up external, naked DNA. The Ti plasmid of the bacterium *Agrobacterium tumefaciens* can transfer DNA directly into plant cells.

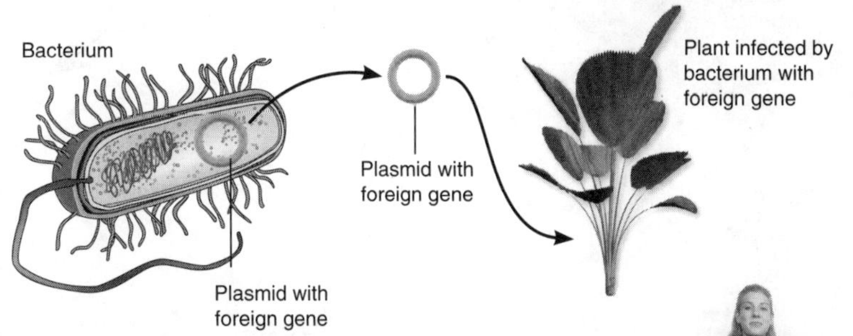

Viral Vectors

Viruses are well suited as vectors for gene transfer. They can accommodate up to 7500 bases of inserted DNA in their protein capsule and when they infect target cells, they are able to replicate and spread the recombinant DNA. Retroviruses even integrate the DNA into the host's chromosome. Viral vectors are already used in gene therapy trials, although there are problems with disruption of useful genes and host immune reaction to the viral infection.

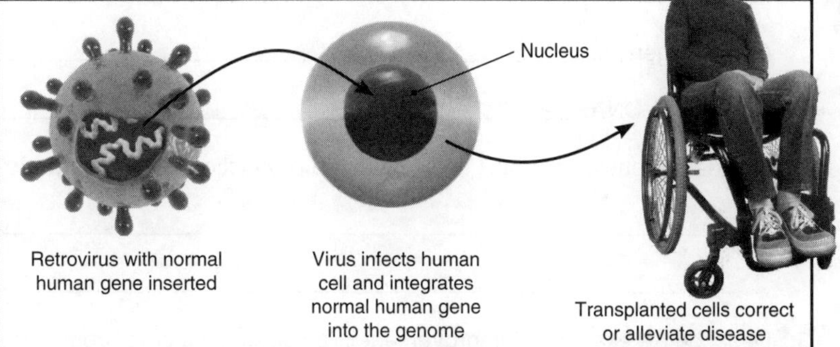

Ballistic DNA Injection

This remarkable way of introducing foreign DNA into living tissue literally shoots it directly into the organism using a "gene gun" (e.g. Helios gene gun made by Bi-Rad). Microscopic particles of gold or tungsten are coated with DNA. They are propelled by a burst of helium into the skin and organs of animals (e.g. rabbit, mouse, pig, fish) and tissues of intact plants. Some of the cells express the introduced DNA as if it were their own.

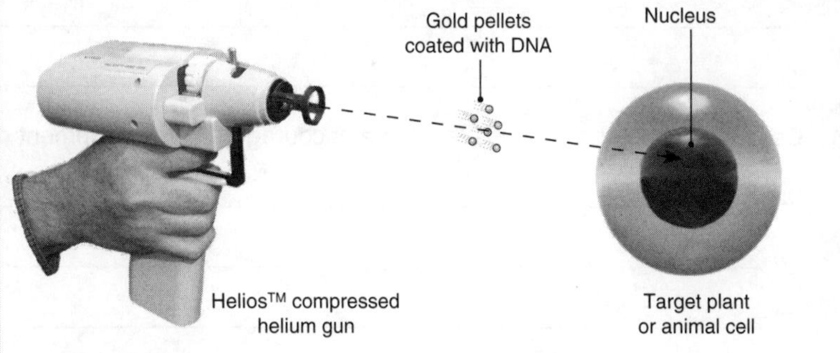

Protoplast Fusion

This process requires the cell walls of plants to be removed by enzymatic digestion. The resulting protoplasts (cells that have lost their cell walls) are then treated with polyethylene glycol, which increases their frequency of fusion. In the new hybrid cell, the DNA derived from the two "parent" cells may undergo natural recombination (they may merge).

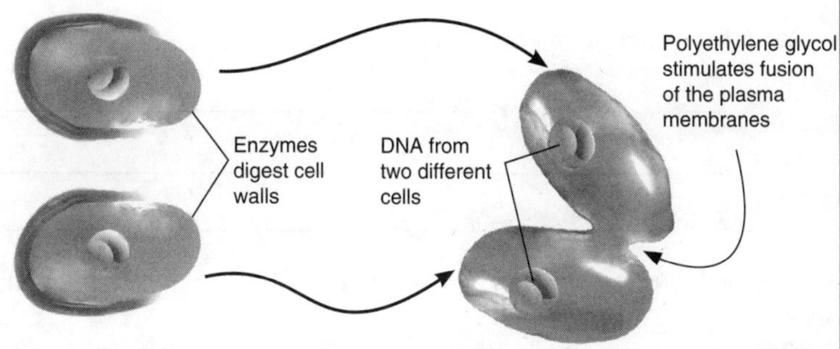

Genomes and Gene Technologies

Pronuclear Injection

DNA can be introduced directly into an animal cell by microinjection. Multiple copies of the desired transgene are injected via a glass micropipette into a recently fertilised egg cell, which is then transferred to a surrogate mother. Transgenic mice and livestock are produced in this way, but the process is inefficient: only 2-3% of eggs give rise to transgenic animals and only a proportion of these animals express the added gene adequately.

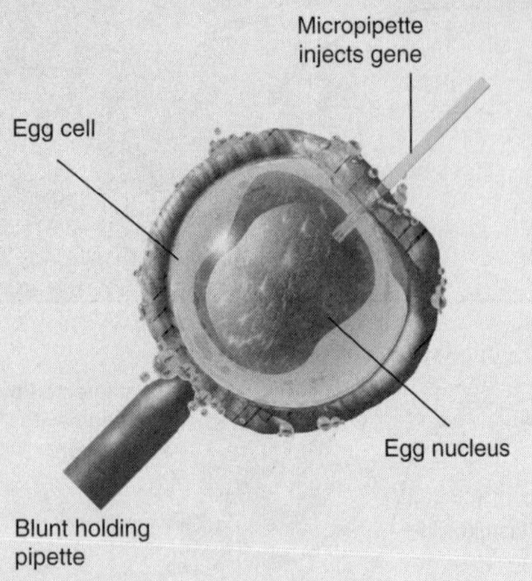

Creating Transgenic Mice Using Pronuclear Injection

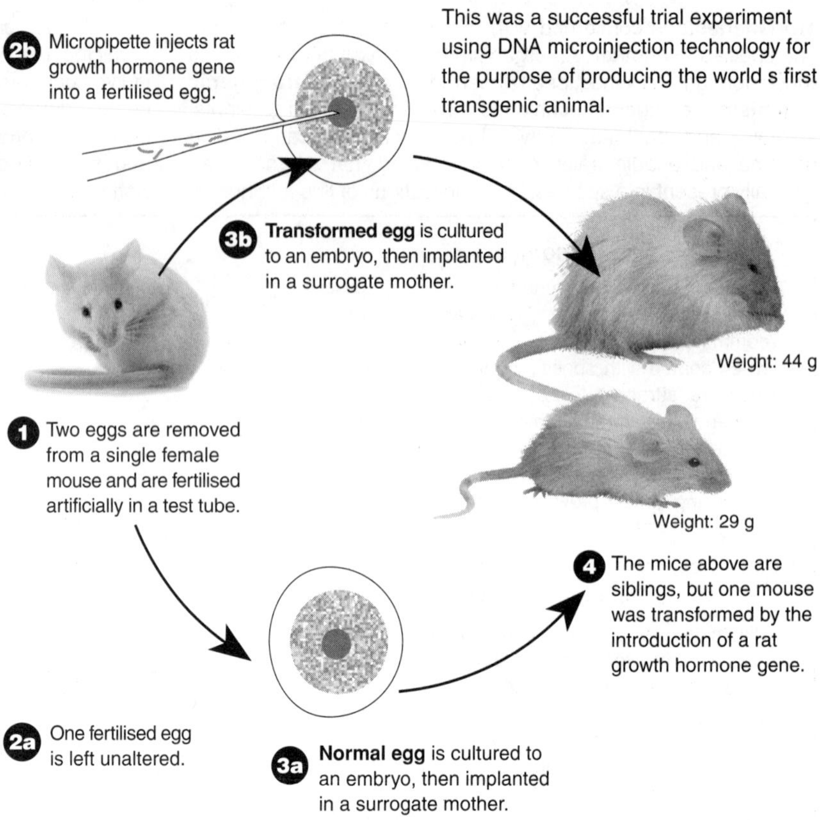

1. In the context of recombinant DNA technology, define the terms:

   (a) Transgenesis: ______

   (b) Foreign DNA: ______

2. Outline the basic principles involved in the production of a **transgenic organism**: ______

3. Describe an example of improvement in a commercial crop brought about by the application of transgenic techniques:

4. Describe three human needs that have encouraged the development of transgenic techniques:

   (a) ______

   (b) ______

   (c) ______

5. Describe two advantages and one disadvantage of using viruses as vectors for gene delivery:

   (a) Advantages: ______

   (b) Disadvantage: ______

6. Explain the purpose behind the transgenic mice experiment (above): ______

Production of Human Insulin

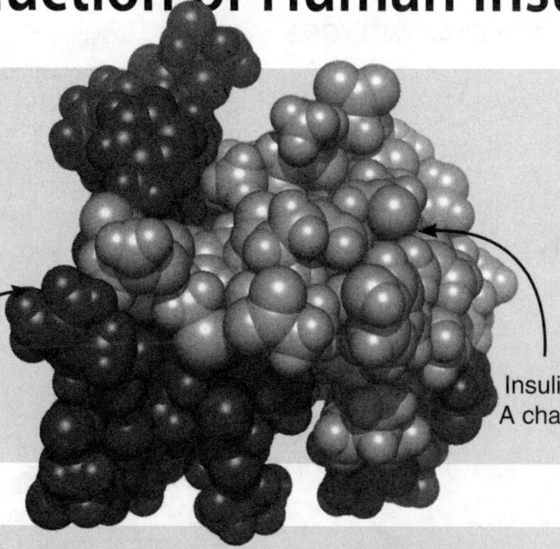

The Issue

- **Type 1 diabetes mellitus** is a metabolic disease caused by a lack of **insulin**. Around 25 people in every 100,000 suffer from type 1 diabetes.
- It is treatable only with injections of insulin.
- In the past, insulin was taken from the pancreases of cows and pigs and purified for human use. The method was expensive and some patients had severe allergic reactions to the foreign insulin or its contaminants.

Concept 1

DNA can be cut at specific sites using **restriction enzymes** and joined together using **DNA ligase**. New genes can be inserted into self-replicating bacterial **plasmids** at the point where the cuts are made.

Concept 2

Plasmids are circular pieces of DNA found in some bacteria. They usually carry genes useful to the bacterium. In the bacterium *E. coli*, the gene controlling gene transcription is carried on a plasmid.

Concept 3

Under certain conditions, Bacteria are able to lose or pick up plasmids from their environment. Bacteria can be readily grown in vat cultures at little expense.

Concept 4

The DNA sequences coding for the production of the two polypeptide chains (A and B) that form human insulin can be isolated from the human genome.

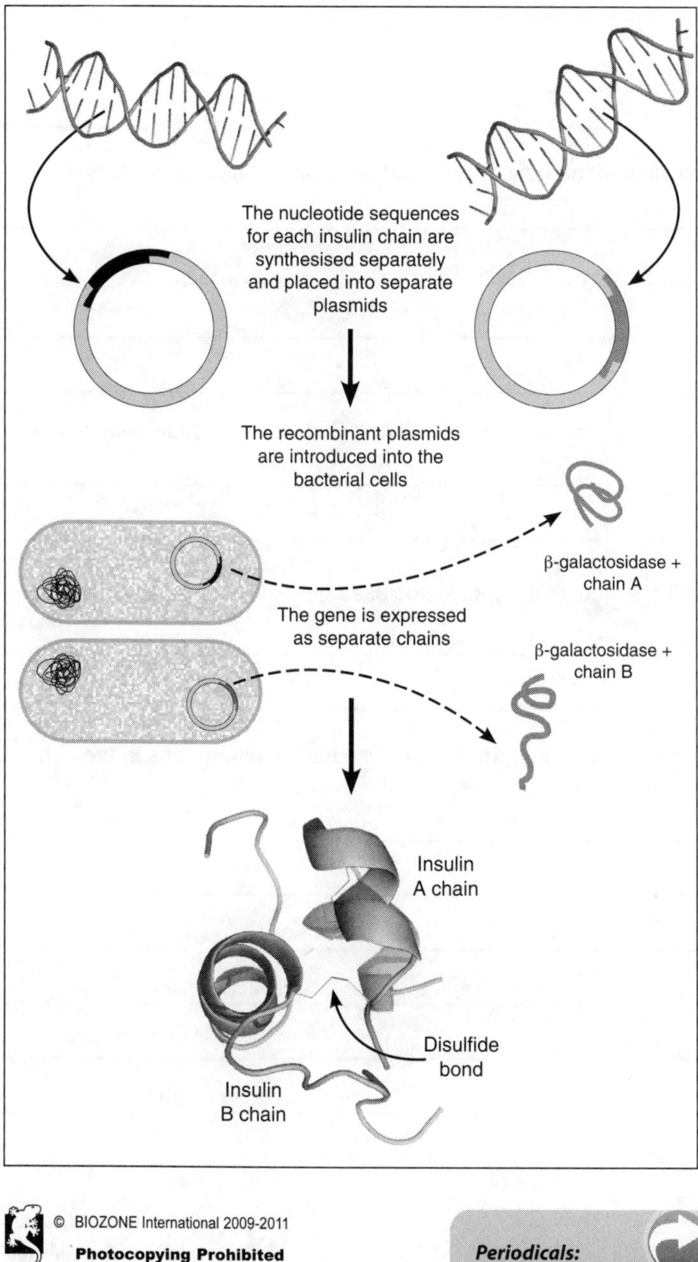

Techniques

The **gene** is **chemically synthesised** as two nucleotide sequences, one for the **insulin A chain** and one for the **insulin B chain**. The two sequences are small enough to be inserted into a plasmid.

Plasmids are extracted from *Escherichia coli*. The gene for the bacterial enzyme **β-galactosidase**, which controls the transcription of genes, is located on the plasmid. To make the bacteria produce insulin, the insulin gene must be linked to the **β-galactosidase** gene.

Restriction enzymes are used to cut plasmids at the appropriate site and the A and B insulin sequences are inserted. The sequences are joined with the plasmid DNA using **DNA ligase**.

The **recombinant plasmids** are inserted back into the bacteria by placing them together in a culture that favours plasmid uptake by bacteria.

The bacteria are then grown and multiplied in vats under carefully controlled growth conditions.

Outcomes

The product consists partly of β-galactosidase, joined with either the A or B chain of insulin. The chains are extracted, purified, and mixed together. The A and B insulin chains connect via **disulfide cross linkages** to form the functional insulin protein. The insulin can then be made ready for injection in various formulations.

Further Applications

The techniques involved in producing human insulin from genetically modified bacteria can be applied to a range human proteins and hormones. Proteins currently being produced include human growth hormone, interferon, and factor VIII.

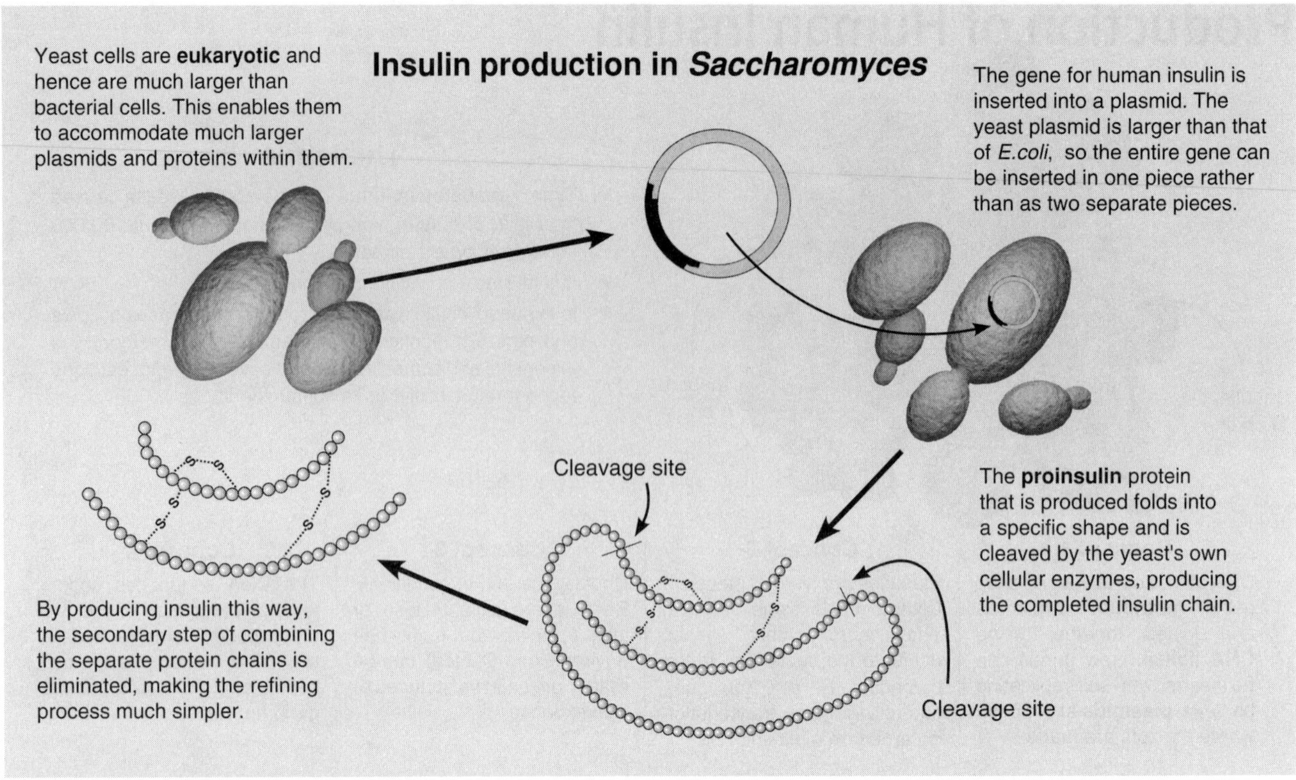

1. Describe the three major problems associated with the traditional method of obtaining insulin to treat diabetes:

   (a) ____

   (b) ____

   (c) ____

2. Explain the reasoning behind using *E. coli* to produce insulin and the benefits that GM technology has brought to diabetics:

3. Explain why, when using *E. coli*, the insulin gene is synthesised as two separate A and B chain nucleotide sequences:

4. Explain why the synthetic nucleotide sequences ('genes') are 'tied' to the β-galactosidase gene:

5. Yeast (*Saccharomyces cerevisiae*) is also used in the production of human insulin. Discuss the differences in the production of insulin using yeast and *E. coli* with respect to:

   (a) Insertion of the gene into the plasmid:

   (b) Secretion and purification of the protein product:

Golden Rice

The Issue

- **Beta-carotene** (β-carotene) is a precursor to **vitamin A** which is involved in many functions including vision, immunity, foetal development, and skin health.
- Vitamin A deficiency is common in developing countries where up to 500,000 children suffer from night blindness, and death rates due to infections are high due to a lowered immune response.
- Providing enough food containing useful quantities of β-carotene is difficult and expensive in many countries.

Concept 1

Rice is a staple food in many developing countries. It is grown in large quantities and is available to most of the population, but it lacks many of the essential nutrients required by the human body for healthy development. It is low in β-carotene.

Concept 2

Rice plants produce β-carotene but not in the edible rice **endosperm**. Engineering a new biosynthetic pathway would allow β-carotene to be produced in the endosperm. Genes expressing enzymes for carotene synthesis can be inserted into the rice genome.

Concept 3

The enzyme **carotene desaturase (CRT1)** in the soil bacterium *Erwinia uredovora,* catalyses multiple steps in carotenoid biosynthesis. **Phytoene synthase (PSY)** overexpresses a colourless carotene in the daffodil plant *Narcissus pseudonarcissus*.

Concept 4

DNA can be inserted into an organism's genome using a suitable **vector**. ***Agrobacterium tumefaciens*** is a tumour-forming bacterial plant pathogen that is commonly used to insert novel DNA into plants.

The Development of Golden Rice

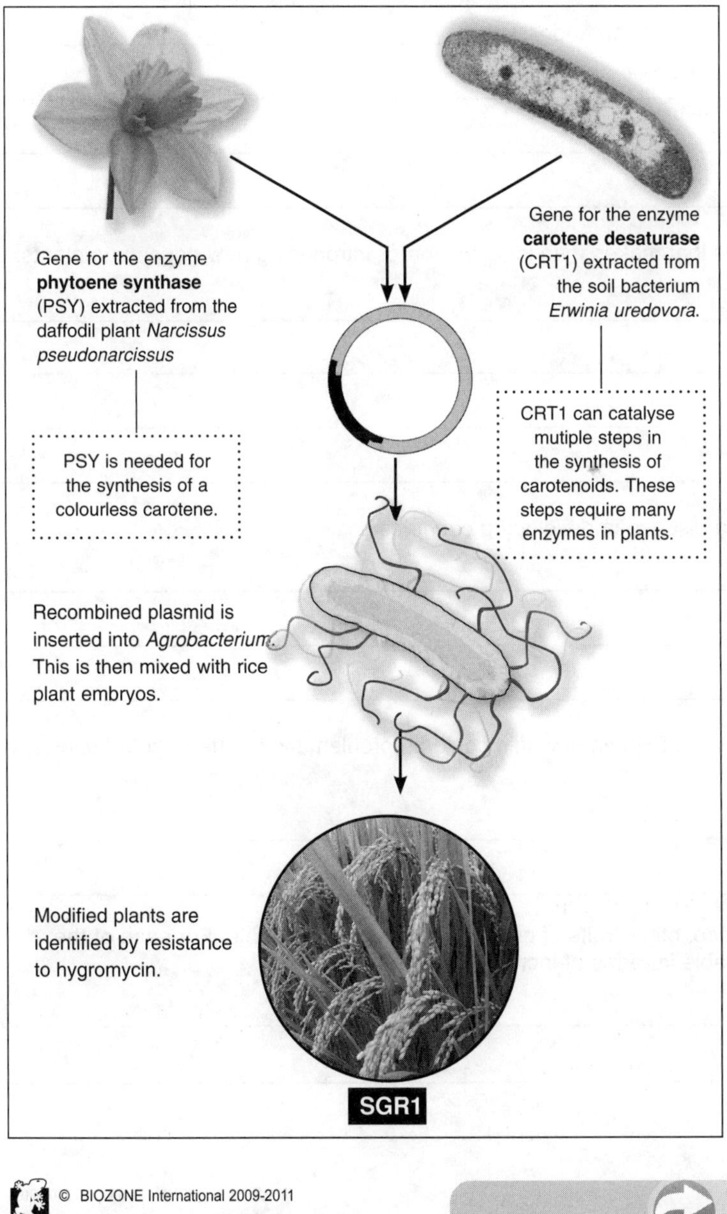

Techniques

The **PSY** gene from daffodils and the **CRT1** gene from *Erwinia uredovora* are sequenced.

DNA sequences are synthesised into packages containing the CRT1 or PSY gene, terminator sequences, and **endosperm specific promoters** (these ensure expression of the gene only in the edible portion of the rice).

The ***Ti* plasmid** from *Agrobacterium* is modified using restriction enzymes and DNA ligase to delete the tumour-forming gene and insert the synthesised DNA packages. A gene for resistance to the antibiotic **hygromycin** is also inserted so that transformed plants can be identified later. The parts of the *Ti* plasmid required for plant transformation are retained.

Modified *Ti* plasmid is inserted into the bacterium.

Agrobacterium is incubated with rice plant embryo. Transformed embryos are identified by their resistance to hygromycin.

Outcomes

The rice produced had endosperm with a distinctive yellow colour. Under greenhouse conditions golden rice (**SGR1**) contained 1.6 µg per g of carotenoids. Levels up to five time higher were produced in the field, probably due to improved growing conditions.

Further Applications

Further research on the action of the PSY gene identified more efficient methods for the production of β-carotene. The second generation of golden rice now contains up to 37 µg per g of carotenoids. Golden rice was the first instance where a complete biosynthetic pathway was engineered. The procedures could be applied to other food plants to increase their nutrient levels.

Periodicals:
Rice, risk, and regulations, The engineering of crop plants

Related activities: *Restriction Enzymes, Ligation, In Vivo Gene Cloning*

All photos USDA

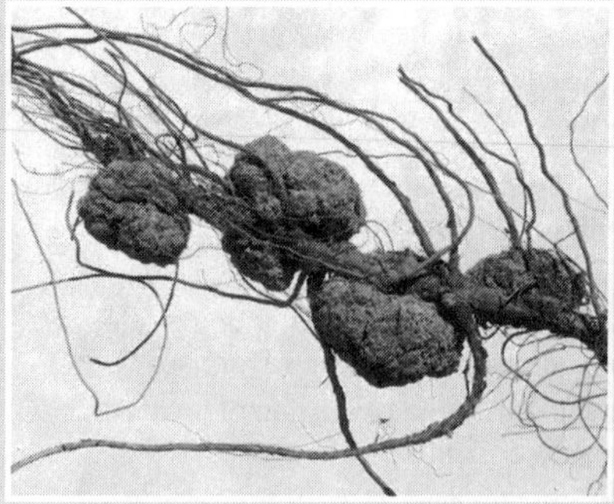

The ability of *Agrobacterium* to transfer genes to plants is exploited for crop improvement. The tumour-inducing *Ti* plasmid is modified to delete the tumour-forming gene and insert a gene coding for a desirable trait. The parts of the *Ti* plasmid required for plant transformation are retained.

Soybeans are one of the many food crops that have been genetically modified for broad spectrum herbicide resistance. The first GM soybeans were planted in the US in 1996. By 2007, nearly 60% of the global soybean crop was genetically modified; the highest of any other crop plant.

GM cotton was produced by inserting the gene for the BT toxin into its genome. The bacterium *Bacillus thuringiensis* naturally produces BT toxin, which is harmful to a range of insects, including the larvae that eat cotton. The BT gene causes cotton to produce this insecticide in its tissues.

1. Describe the basic methodology used to create golden rice: ______

2. Explain how scientists ensured β-carotene was produced in the endosperm: ______

3. Describe the property of *Agrobacterium tumefaciens* that makes it an ideal vector for introducing new genes into plants:

4. (a) Explain how this new variety of rice could reduce disease in developing countries:

   (b) Absorption of vitamin A requires sufficient dietary fat. Explain how this could be problematic for the targeted use of golden rice in developing countries:

5. As well as increasing nutrient content as in golden rice, other traits of crop plants are also desirable. For each of the following traits, suggest features that could be desirable in terms of increasing yield:

   (a) Grain size or number: ______

   (b) Maturation rate: ______

   (c) Pest resistance: ______

Xenotransplantation

Xenotransplantation is the transplantation of living cells, tissues, or organs from one species into another. The procedure is most commonly used to treat patients with organ failure, where organs from the donor species (usually pigs), are transplanted into the human patient. Xenotransplants can be used to save lives while waiting for a suitable human transplant to become available. Future applications may include cell therapies such as bone marrow treatments, or the transfer of pancreatic islet cells to treat type 1 diabetes. Clinical trials are underway for treating the neurological disorder Parkinson's disease, and patients suffering from Huntington's disease may also benefit from this technology in the future. Cross-species organ transplants have not been very successful to date because organ rejection and differences in organ size and shape make the procedure difficult. **Genetic engineering** may hold the key to making xenotransplants successful. By altering the genes that code for cell surface proteins it may be possible to produce immunocompatible tissues and avoid immune rejection in the transplant recipient.

Genetically engineered Pigs for Xenotransplantation

Immune rejection, in which the immune system reacts against foreign material, is a major problem for xenotransplant recipients. The main rejection response to pig tissue is triggered by the α-1,3-galactosyltransferase (GT) enzyme present on the surface of pig cells. Humans have natural pre-formed antibodies to this antigen and have an immediate (acute) rejection response against pig tissue as a result.The rejection response can be reduced by genetic modification of the donors to make them immuno-compatible. Pig cells have been genetically modified in this way. The GE pig cells either express human proteins on their surface (so they are not recognised as foreign) or they fail to express the GT antigen (below).

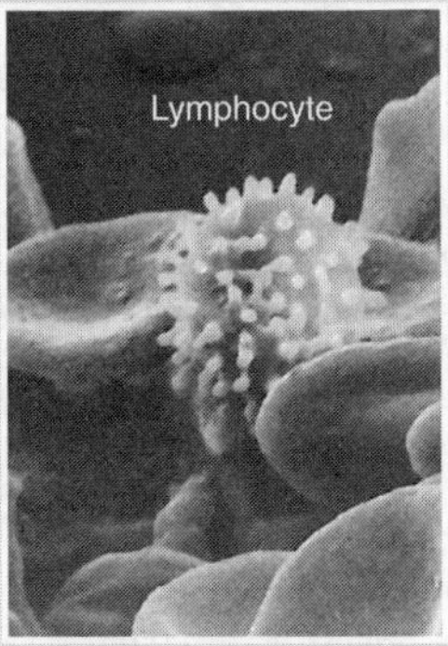

EII

T lymphocytes will recognise and attack transplanted cells with surface GT antigens.

An important development in the field of xenotransplantation came with the production of GT-KO pigs genetically engineered to lack the GT enzyme. Although this means the immune rejection of transplanted tissue is not immediate, other immune responses to do with blood clotting have still to be overcome before clinical trials can proceed. Of particular importance is a strain of miniature pig that lacks a viable Porcine Endogenous Retrovirus (PERV), meaning the chance of cross species infection by a new pathogen is reduced.

Right: Swine Influenza Virus. This virus has crossed the species barrier with the incorporation of some of its genome into a new strain of H1N1 flu.

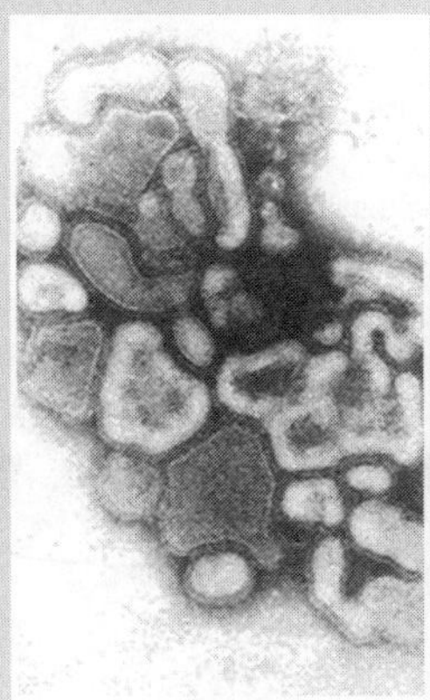

CDC

At present pigs are considered to be the most appropriate non-human source of donor organs and tissues. They produce large litters that develop quickly and the size of their organs are comparable to human organs. They are also suitable for genetic engineering and, because they are already bred on farms for market, the techniques for raising large numbers of genetically engineered pigs are already available.

EII

Xenotransplantation raises ethical, cultural and religious issues. Animal rights groups oppose breeding and killing animals so their cells and organs can be harvested for human use. Some individuals within Jewish or Muslim cultures, where eating pork is prohibited, may not wish to receive porcine tissue (e.g. pig heart valve).

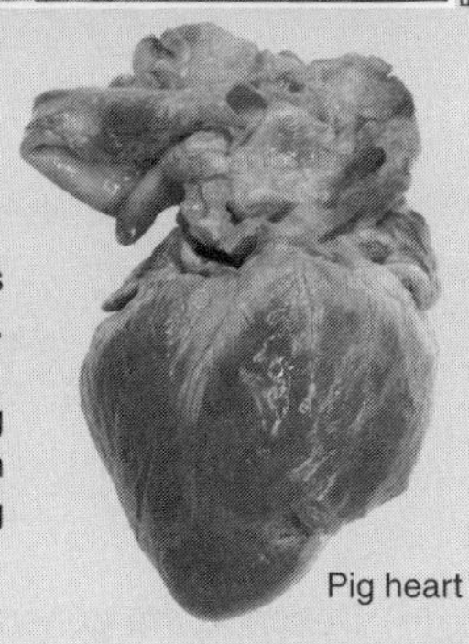

Pig heart

1. (a) Explain why xenotransplants have not been particularly successful to date:

   (b) Explain the potential role of genetic engineering in overcoming problems with xenotransplant technology:

2. Explain why pigs are considered to be the most appropriate "donors" for xenotransplants of organs:

3. Explain how the immediate rejection of pig tissues by the immune system has been overcome:

Gene Therapy

Gene therapy refers to the application of gene technology to treat disease by correcting or replacing faulty genes. It was first envisioned as a treatment, or even a cure, for genetic disorders, but it could also be used to treat a wide range of diseases, including those that resist conventional treatments. Although varying in detail, all gene therapies are based around the same technique. Normal (non-faulty) DNA containing the correct gene is inserted into a vector, which is able to transfer the DNA into the patient's cells in a process called **transfection**. The vector may be a virus, liposome, or any one of a variety of other molecular transporters. The vector is introduced into a sample of the patient's cells and these are cultured to amplify the correct gene. The cultured cells are then transferred back to the patient. The use of altered stem cells instead of mature somatic cells has so far achieved longer lasting results in many patients. The treatment of somatic cells or stem cells may be **therapeutic** but the changes are not inherited. **Germline therapy** would enable genetic changes to be passed on. To date there have been limited successes with gene therapy because transfection of targeted cells is inefficient and side effects can be severe or even fatal. However there have been a small number of successes, including the treatment of one form of SCID, a genetic disease affecting the immune system.

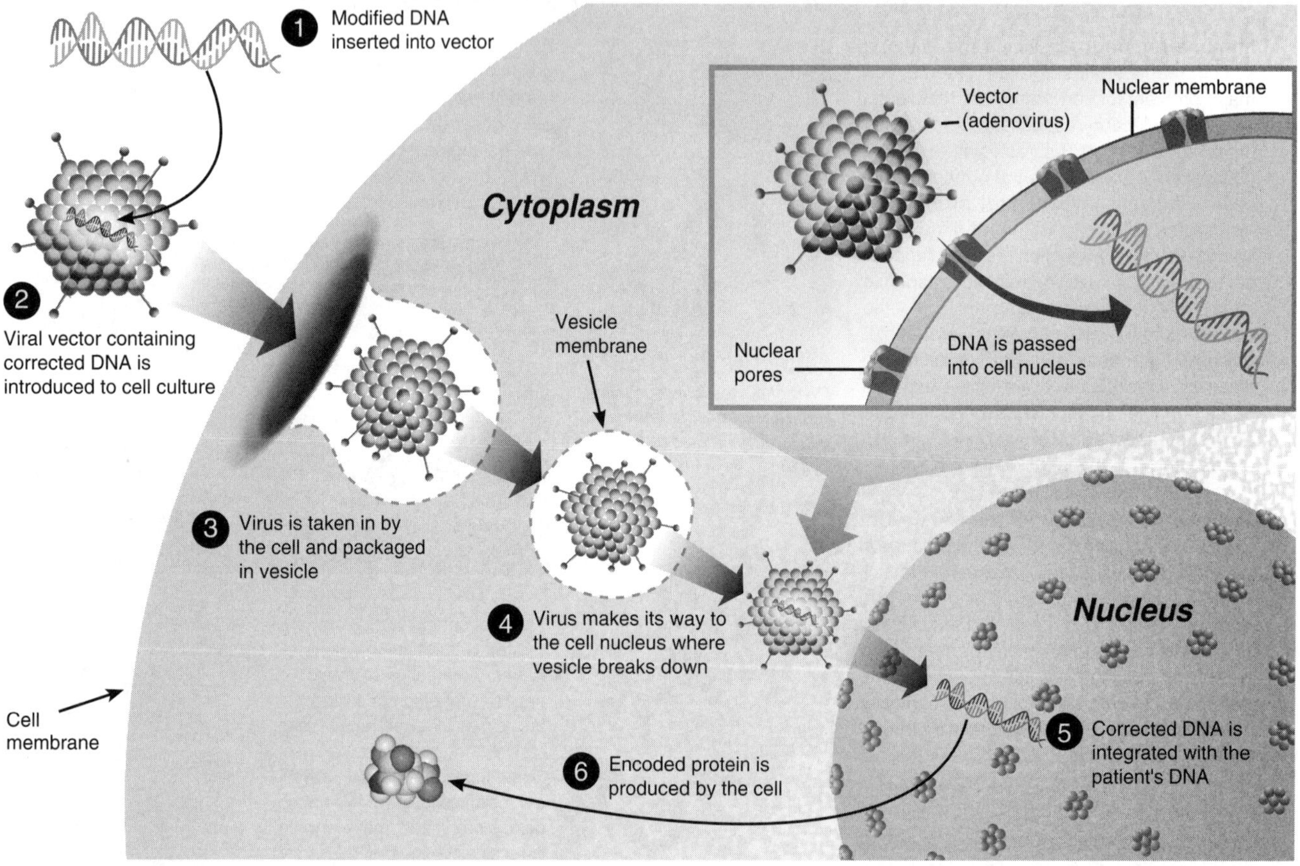

1. (a) Describe the general principle of gene therapy: ___

   (b) Describe the medical areas where gene therapy might be used: ___

2. Explain the significance of transfecting **germline cells** rather than **somatic cells**: ___

3. Describe the purpose of **gene amplification** in gene therapy: ___

4. Explain why genetically modified stem cells offer greater potential in gene therapy treatments than GM somatic cells:

Gene Delivery Systems

The mapping of the human genome has improved the feasibility of gene therapy as a option for treating an increasingly wide range of diseases, but it remains technically difficult to deliver genes successfully to a patient. Even after a gene has been identified, cloned, and transferred to a patient, it must be expressed normally. To date, the success of gene therapy has been generally poor, and improvements have been short-lived or counteracted by adverse side effects. Inserted genes may reach only about 1% of target cells and those that reach their destination may work inefficiently and produce too little protein, too slowly to be of benefit. In addition, many patients react immunologically to the vectors used in gene transfer. Much of the current research is focussed on improving the efficiency of gene transfer and expression. One of the first gene therapy trials was for **cystic fibrosis** (CF). CF was an obvious candidate for gene therapy because, in most cases, the disease is caused by a single, known gene mutation. However, despite its early promise, gene therapy for this disease has been disappointing (below right). Another candidate for gene therapy, again because the disease is caused by single, known mutations, is Severe Combined Immune Deficiency (SCID) (below left). Gene therapies developing for this disease have so far proved promising.

Treating SCID using Gene Therapy

The most common form of **SCID** (Severe Combined Immune Deficiency) is **X-linked SCID**, which results from mutations to a gene on the X chromosome encoding the **common gamma chain**, a protein forming part of a receptor complex for numerous types of leukocytes. A less common form of the disease, (**ADA-SCID**) is caused by a defective gene that codes for the enzyme adenosine deaminase (ADA).

Both of these types of SCID lead to immune system failure. A common treatment for SCID is bone marrow transplant, but this is not always successful and runs the risks of infection from unscreened viruses. **Gene therapy** appears to hold the best chances of producing a cure for SCID because the mutation affects only one gene whose location is known. DNA containing the corrected gene is placed into a **gutted retrovirus** and introduced to a sample of the patient's **bone marrow.** The treated cells are then returned to the patient.

In some patients with ADA-SCID, treatment was so successful that supplementation with purified ADA was no longer required. The treatment carries risks though. In early trials, two of ten treated patients developed leukemia when the corrected gene was inserted next to a gene regulating cell growth.

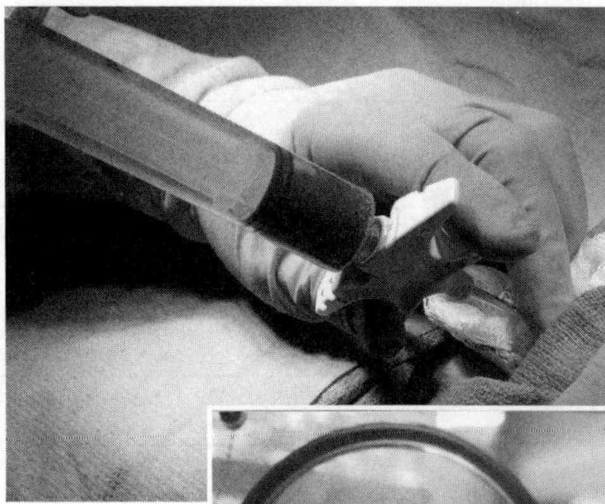
Georgetown University Hospital

Samples of bone marrow being extracted prior to treatment with gene therapy.

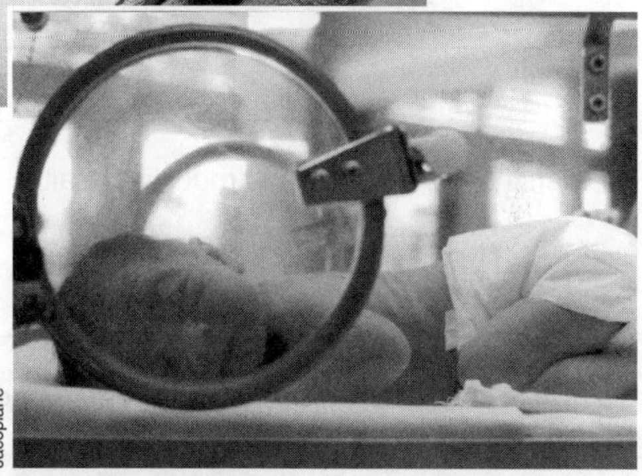
Jacoplane

Detection of SCID is difficult for the first months of an infant's life due to the mother's antibodies being present in the blood. Suspected SCID patients must be kept in sterile conditions at all times to avoid infection.

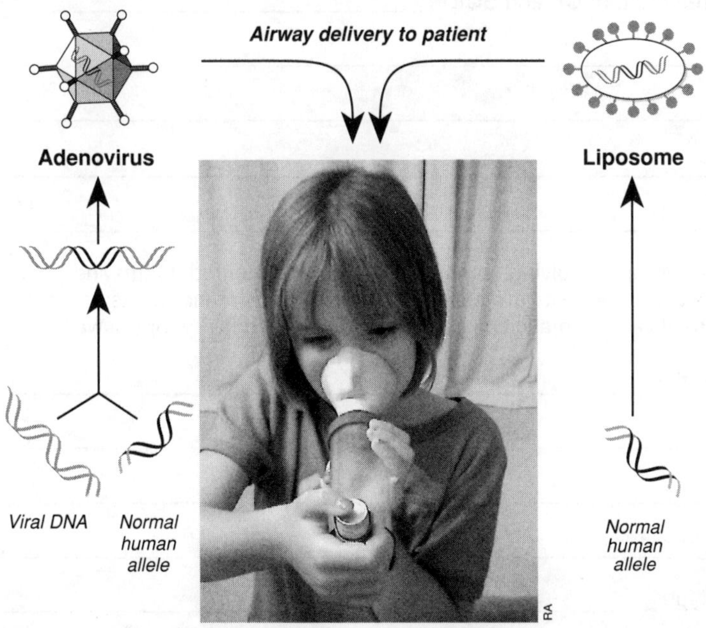

An **adenovirus** that normally causes colds is genetically modified to make it safe and to carry the normal (unmutated) CFTR ('cystic fibrosis') gene.

Liposomes are tiny fat globules. Normal CF genes are enclosed in liposomes, which fuse with plasma membranes and deliver the genes into the cells.

Gene Therapy - Potential Treatment for Cystic Fibrosis?

Cystic fibrosis (CF) is caused by a mutation to the gene coding for a chloride ion channel important in creating sweat, digestive juices, and mucus. The dysfunction results in abnormally thick, sticky mucus that accumulates in the lungs and intestines. The identification and isolation of the CF gene in 1989 meant that scientists could look for ways in which to correct the genetic defect rather than just treating the symptoms using traditional therapies.

The main target of CF gene therapy is the lung, because the progressive lung damage associated with the disease is eventually lethal.

In trials, normal genes were isolated and inserted into patients using vectors such as **adenoviruses** and **liposomes**, delivered via the airways (left). The results of trials were disappointing: on average, there was only a 25% correction, the effects were short lived, and the benefits were quickly reversed. Alarmingly, the adenovirus used in one of the trials led to the death of one patient.

Source: Cystic Fibrosis Trust, UK.

1. A great deal of current research is being devoted to discovering a gene therapy solution to treat **cystic fibrosis** (CF):

   (a) Describe the symptoms of CF: ______________________________

   (b) Explain why this genetic disease has been so eagerly targeted by gene therapy researchers: ______________________________

   (c) Outline some of the problems so far encountered with gene therapy for CF: ______________________________

2. Identify two vectors for introducing healthy CFTR genes into CF patients.

   (a) Vector 1: ______________________________

   (b) Vector 2: ______________________________

3. (a) Describe the difference between X-linked SCID and ADA-SCID: ______________________________

   (b) Identify the vector used in the treatment of SCID: ______________________________

4. Briefly outline the differences in the gene therapy treatment of CF and SCID: ______________________________

5. Changes made to chromosomes as a result of gene therapy involving somatic cells are not inherited. Germ-line gene therapy has the potential to cure disease, but the risks and benefits are still not clear. For each of the points outlined below, evaluate the risk of germ-line gene therapy relative to somatic cell gene therapy and explain your answer:

   (a) Chance of interfering with an essential gene function: ______________________________

   (b) Misuse of the therapy to selectively alter phenotype: ______________________________

Vectors for Gene Therapy

Gene therapy usually requires a **vector** (carrier) to introduce the DNA. The majority of approved clinical gene therapy protocols (63%) employ **retroviral vectors** to deliver the selected gene to the target cells, although there is considerable risk in using these vectors (below). Other widely used vectors include adenoviral vectors (16%), and liposomes (13%). The remaining 8% employ a variety of vector systems, the majority of which include injection of naked plasmid DNA.

	Vectors That Can Be Used For Gene Therapy			
		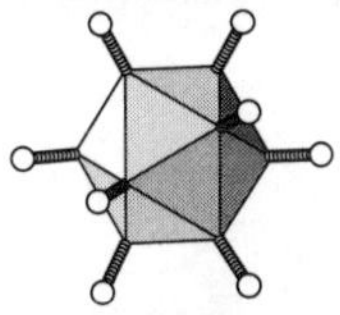	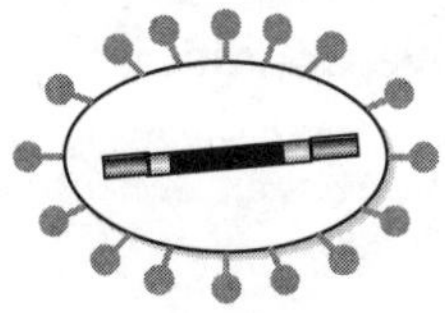	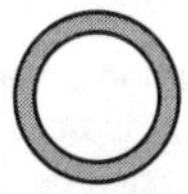
	Retrovirus	**Adenovirus**	**Liposome**	**Naked DNA**
Insert size:	8000 bases	8000 bases	>20 000 bases	>20 000 bases
Integration:	Yes	No	No	No
***In vivo* delivery:**	Poor	High	Variable	Poor
Advantages	• Integrate genes into the chromosomes of the human host cell. • Offers chance for long-term stability.	• Modified for gene therapy, they infect human cells and express the normal gene. • Most do not cause disease. • Have a large capacity to carry foreign genes.	• Liposomes seek out target cells using sugars in their membranes that are recognised by cell receptors. • Have no viral genes that may cause disease.	• Have no viral genes that may cause disease. • Expected to be useful for vaccination.
Disadvantages	• Many infect only cells that are dividing. • Genes integrate randomly into chromosomes, so might disrupt useful genes in the host cell.	• Viruses may have poor survival due to attack by the host's immune system. • Genes may function only sporadically because they are not integrated into host cell's chromosome.	• Less efficient than viruses at transferring genes into cells, but recent work on using sugars to aid targeting have improved success rate.	• Unstable in most tissues of the body. • Inefficient at gene transfer.

In the table above, the following terms are defined as follows: **Naked DNA**: the genes are applied by ballistic injection (firing using a gene gun) or by regular hypodermic injection of plasmid DNA. **Insert size**: size of gene that can be inserted into the vector. **Integration**: whether or not the gene is integrated into the host DNA (chromosomes). ***In vivo* delivery**: ability to transfer a gene directly into a patient.

1. (a) Describe the features of viruses that make them well suited as **vectors** for gene therapy: ______________________

____

____

(b) Identify two problems with using viral vectors for gene therapy: ______________________

____

____

2. (a) Suggest why it may be beneficial for a (therapeutic) gene to integrate into the patient's chromosome:

____

____

(b) Explain why this has the potential to cause problems for the patient: ______________________

____

3. (a) Suggest why naked DNA is likely to be unstable within a patient's tissues: ______________________

____

(b) Suggest why enclosing the DNA within liposomes might provide greater stability: ______________________

____

Genetic Counselling

Genetic counselling is an analysis of the risk of producing offspring with known gene defects within a family. Counsellors identify families at risk, investigate the problem present in the family, interpret information about the disorder, analyse inheritance patterns and risks of recurrence, and review available options with the family. Increasingly, there are DNA tests for the identification of specific defective genes. People usually consider genetic counselling if they have a family history of a genetic disorder, or if a routine prenatal screening test yields an unexpected result. While screening for many genetic disorders is now recommended, the use of presymptomatic tests for adult-onset disorders, such as Alzheimer's, is still controversial.

Autosomal Recessive Conditions

Common inherited disorders caused by recessive alleles on autosomes. Recessive conditions are evident only in homozygous recessive genotypes.

Cystic fibrosis: Malfunction of the pancreas and other glands; thick mucus leads to pneumonia and emphysema. Death usually occurs in childhood. CF is the most frequent lethal genetic disorder in childhood (about 1 case in 3700 live births).

Maple syrup urine disease: Mental and physical retardation produced by a block in amino acid metabolism. Isoleucine in the urine produces the characteristic odour.

Tay-Sachs disease: A lipid storage disease which causes progressive developmental paralysis, mental deterioration, and blindness. Death usually occurs by three years of age.

Autosomal Dominant Conditions

Inherited disorders caused by dominant alleles on autosomes. Dominant conditions are evident both in heterozygotes and in homozygous dominant individuals.

Huntington disease: Involuntary movements of the face and limbs with later general mental deterioration. The beginning of symptoms is highly variable, but occurs usually between 30 to 40 years of age.

Genetic testing may involve biochemical tests for gene products such as enzymes and other proteins, microscopic examination of stained or fluorescent chromosomes, or examination of the DNA molecule itself. Various types of genetic tests are performed for various reasons, including:

Carrier Screening
Identifying unaffected individuals who carry one copy of a gene for a disease that requires two copies for the disease to be expressed.

Preimplantation Genetic Diagnosis
Screens for genetic flaws in embryos used for *in vitro* fertilisation. The results of the analysis are used to select mutation-free embryos.

Prenatal Diagnostic Testing
Tests for chromosomal abnormalities such as Down syndrome.

Newborn Screening
Newborn babies are screened for a variety of enzyme-based disorders.

Presymptomatic Testing
Testing before symptoms are apparent is important for estimating the risk of developing adult-onset disorders, including Huntington's, cancers, and Alzheimer's disease.

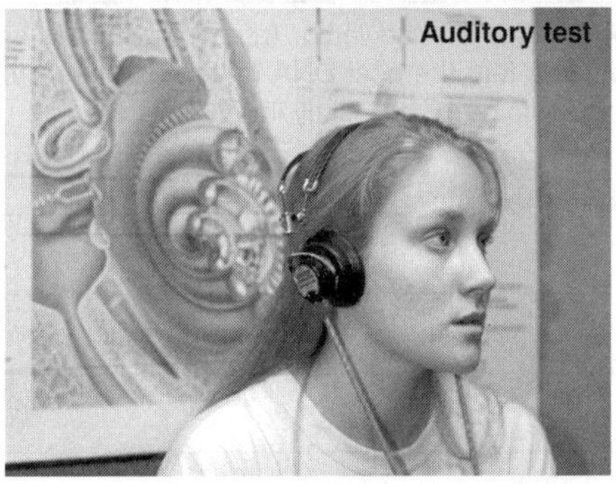

About half of the cases of childhood deafness are the result of an autosomal recessive disorder. Early identification of the problem prepares families and allows early appropriate treatment.

Genetic counselling provides information to families who have members with birth defects or genetic disorders, and to families who may be at risk for a variety of inherited conditions.

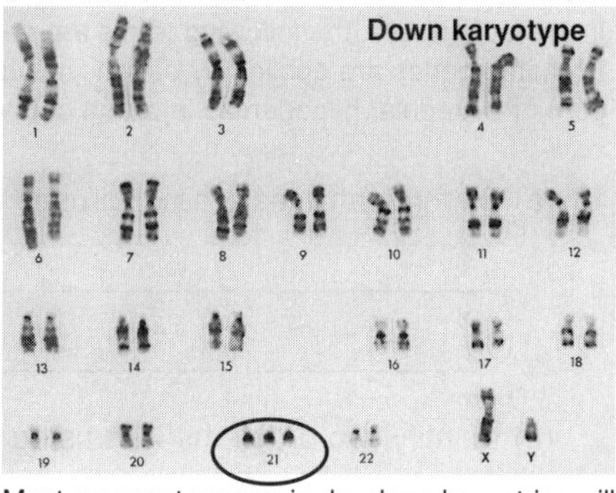

Cytogenetics Dept., Waikato Hospital

Most pregnant women in developed countries will have a prenatal test to detect chromosomal abnormalities such as Down syndrome and developmental anomalies such as neural defects.

1. Outline the benefits of **carrier screening** to a couple with a family history of a genetic disorder:

___

___

2. (a) Suggest why Huntington disease persists in the human population when it is caused by a lethal, dominant allele:

___

___

(b) Explain how presymptomatic genetic testing could change this: ___

___

___

Food for the Masses

It is estimated that by 2050 the world population will reach between 9 and 10 billion people. Currently **1 billion people** (one sixth of the world's population) are **undernourished**. If trends continue, 1.5 billion people will be living under the threat of starvation by 2050, and by 2100 (if global warming is taken into account) nearly half the world's population could be threatened with food shortages. The solution to the problem of food production is complicated. Most of the Earth's arable land has already been developed and currently uses 37% of the Earth's land area, leaving little room to grow more crops or farm more animals. Development of new fast growing and high yield crops appears to be a major part of the solution, but many crops can only be grown under a narrow range of conditions or are susceptible to disease. Moreover, the farming and irrigation of some areas is difficult, costly, and damaging to the environment because vast amounts of water are diverted from their natural courses. **Genetic modification** of plants may help to solve some of these looming problems by producing plants that will require less intensive culture or that will grow in areas previously considered not arable.

Useful Organisms

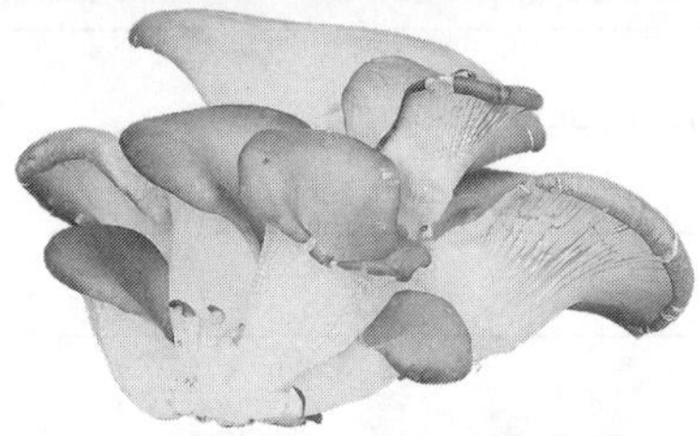

Fungus that is able to survive dry conditions using two enzymes WA-UT1 and Ter-UT2 to facilitate water uptake.

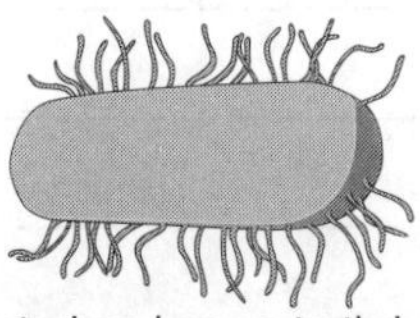

Bacterium known to thrive in dry conditions using a single enzyme DRI-X1 to catalyse multiple reactions.

Plant identified for modification

Enzymes

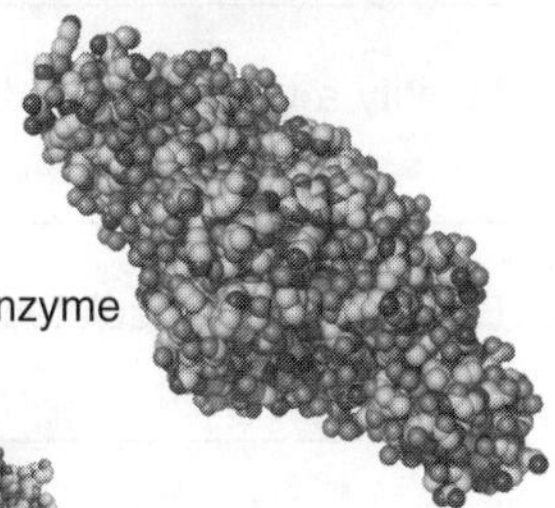

Restriction enzyme

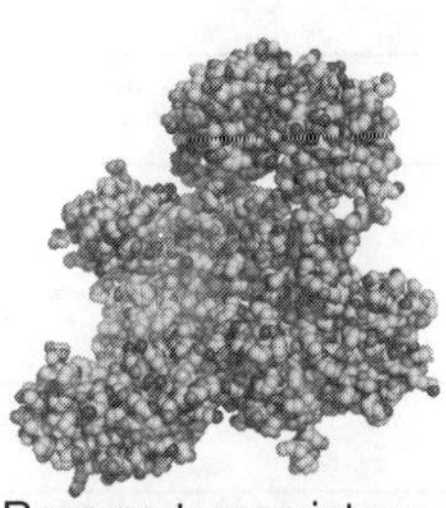

Reverse transcriptase

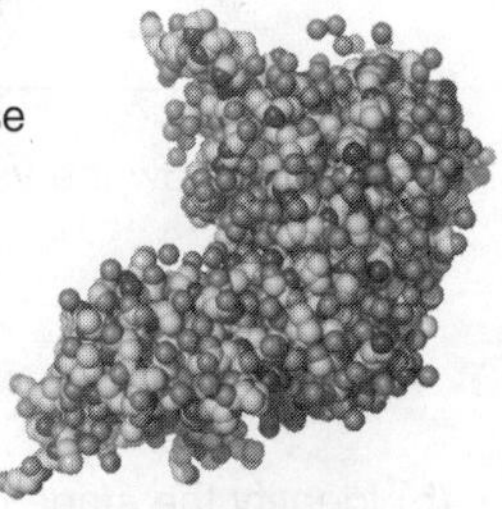

DNA ligase

Engineering Your Solution

A solution to the possible future food crisis is to genetically engineer food crops so that they can maximise their growth under adverse conditions. Standard selective breeding techniques could be used to do this, but in some plants this may not be possible or feasible and it may require more time than is available. A selection of genetic tools and organisms with useful characteristics are described. **Your task** is to use the items shown to devise a technique to successfully create a plant that could be successfully farmed in semi-desert environments such as sub-Saharan Africa. The following page will take you through the procedure. Not all the items will need to be used.

Equipment

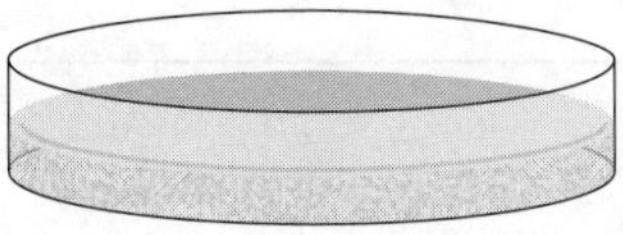

Petri dish

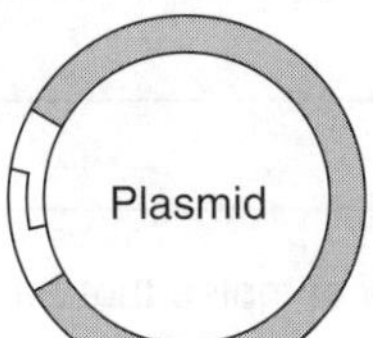

Plasmid

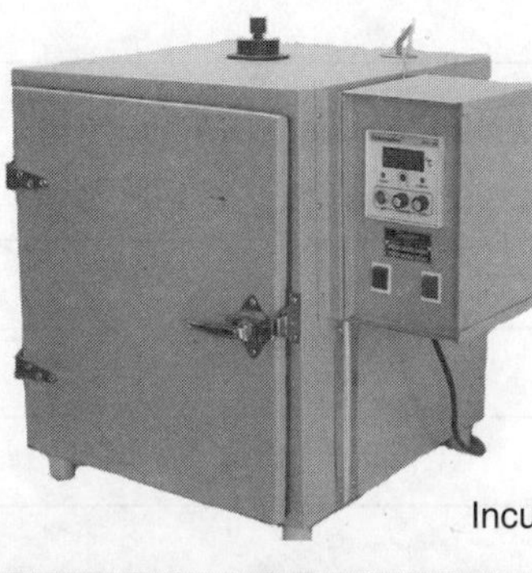

Incubator

Possible Vectors

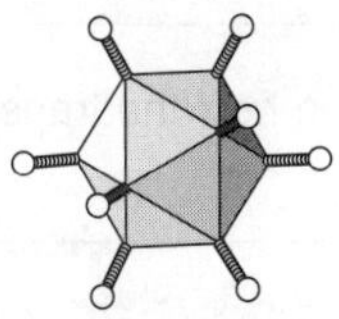

Adenovirus

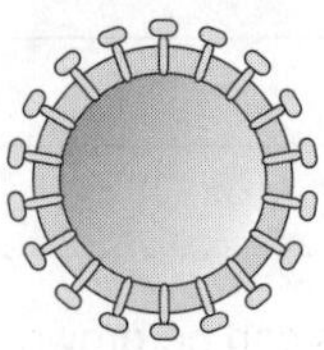

Retrovirus

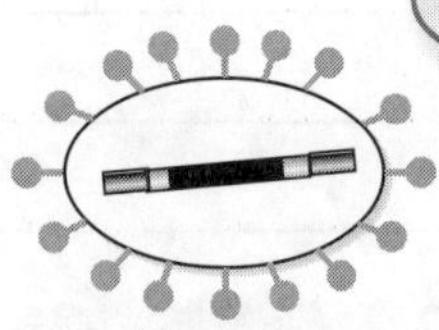

Liposome

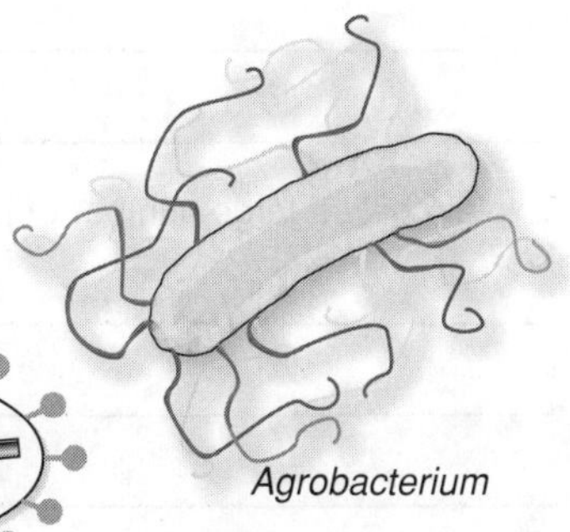

Agrobacterium

1. Identify the organism you would chose as a 'donor' of drought survival genes and explain your choice:

2. Describe a process to identify and isolate the required gene(s) and identify the tools to be used:

3. Identify a vector for the transfer of the isolated gene(s) into the crop plant and explain your decision:

4. Explain how the isolated gene(s) would be integrated into the vector's genome:

5. (a) Explain how the vector will transform the identified plant:

   (b) Identify the stage of development at which the plant would most easily be transformed. Explain your choice:

6. Explain how the transformed plants could be identified:

7. Explain how a large number of plants can be grown from the few samples that have taken up the new DNA:

The Ethics of GMO Technology

The risks associated with using **genetically modified organisms** (GMOs) have been the subject of much debate in recent times. Most experts agree that, provided GMOs are tested properly, the health risks to individuals should be minimal from plant products, although minor problems will occur. Health risks from animal GMOs are potentially more serious, especially when the animals are for human consumption. The potential benefits to be gained from the use of GMOs creates enormous pressure to apply the existing technology. However, there are many concerns, including the environmental and socio-economic effects, and problems of unregulated use. There is also concern about the environmental and economic costs of possible GMO accidents. GMO research is being driven by heavy investment on the part of biotechnology companies seeking new applications for GMOs. Currently a matter of great concern to consumers is the adequacy of government regulations for the labelling of food products with GMO content. This may have important trade implications for countries exporting and importing GMO produce.

Some important points about GMOs

1. The modified DNA is in every cell of the GMO.
2. The mRNA is only expressed in specific tissues.
3. The foreign protein is only expressed in particular tissues but it may circulate in the blood or lymph or be secreted (e.g. milk).
4. In animals, the transgene is only likely to be transmitted from parent to offspring. However, viral vectors may enable accidental transfer of the transgene between unrelated animals.
5. In plants, transmission of the transgene in GMOs is possible by pollen, cuttings, and seeds (even between species).
6. If we eat the animal or plant proper, we will also be eating DNA. The DNA will remain 'intact' if raw, but "degraded" if cooked.
7. Non-transgenic food products may be processed using genetically modified bacteria or yeast, and cells containing their DNA may be in the food product.
8. A transgenic product (e.g. a protein, polypeptide or a carbohydrate) may be in the GMO, but not in the portions sold to the consumer.

Potential effects of GMOs on the world

1. Increase in food production.
2. Decrease in use of pesticides, herbicides and animal remedies.
3. Improvement in the health of the human population and the medicines used to achieve it.
4. Possible development of transgenic products which may be harmful to some (e.g. new proteins causing allergies).
5. May have little real economic benefit to farmers (and the consumer) when increased production (as little as 10%) is weighed against cost, capital, and competition.
6. Possible (uncontrollable) spread of transgenes into other species: plants, indigenous species, animals, and humans.
7. Concerns that the release of GMOs into the environment may be irreversible.
8. Economic sanctions resulting from a consumer backlash against GMO foods and products.
9. Animal welfare and ethical issues: GM animals may suffer poor health and reduced life span.
10. GMOs may cause the emergence of pest, insect, or microbial resistance to traditional control methods.
11. May create a monopoly and dependence of developing countries on companies who are seeking to control the world's commercial seed supply.

© Greenpeace

GMO protestors are arrested

Issue: The accidental release of GMOs into the environment.

Problem: Recombinant DNA may be taken up by non-target organisms.Thes then may have the potential to become pests or cause disease.

Solution: Rigorous controls on the production and release of GMOs. GMOs could have specific genes deleted so that their growth requirements are met only in controlled environments.

CDC

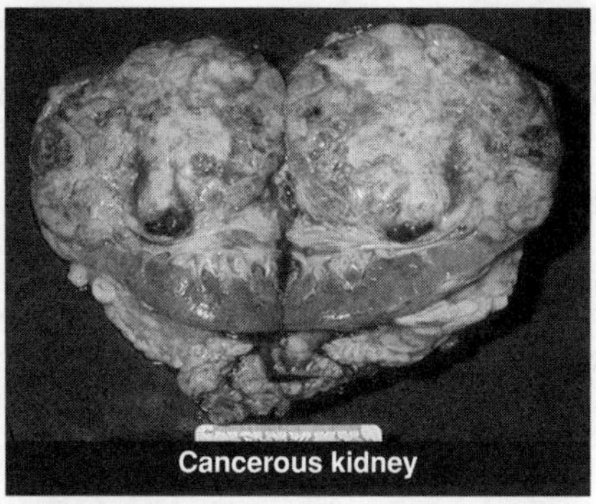

Cancerous kidney

Issue: A new gene or genes may disrupt normal gene function.

Problem: Gene disruption may trigger cancer. Successful expression of the desired gene is frequently very low.

Solution: A combination of genetic engineering, cloning, and genetic screening so that only those cells that have been successfully transformed are used to produce organisms.

© Greenpeace

Protest against GMOs in the environment

Issue: Targeted use of transgenic organisms in the environment.

Problem: Once their desired function, e.g. environmental clean-up, is completed, they may be undesirable invaders in the ecosystem.

Solution: GMOs can be engineered to contain "suicide genes" or metabolic deficiencies so that they do not survive for long in the new environment after completion of their task.

1. Suggest why genetically modified (GM) plants are thought to pose a greater environmental threat than GM animals:

2. Describe an advantage and a problem with the use of genetically engineered herbicide resistant crop plants:

(a) Advantage:

(b) Problem:

3. Describe an advantage and a problem with using tropical crops genetically engineered to grow in cold regions:

(a) Advantage:

(b) Problem:

4. Describe an advantage and a problem with using crops that are genetically engineered to grow in marginal habitats (for example, in very saline or poorly aerated soils):

(a) Advantage:

(b) Problem:

5. Describe two uses of transgenic animals within the livestock industry:

(a)

(b)

6. Some years ago, Britain banned the import of a GM, pest resistant corn variety containing marker genes for ampicillin antibiotic resistance. Suggest why the use of antibiotic-resistance genes as markers is no longer common practice:

7. Many agricultural applications of DNA technology make use of transgenic bacteria which infect plants and express a foreign gene. Explain one advantage of each of the following applications of genetic engineering to crop biology:

(a) Development of nitrogen-fixing *Rhizobium* bacteria that can colonise non-legumes such as corn and wheat:

(b) Addition of transgenic *Pseudomonas fluorescens* bacteria into seeds (bacterium produces a pathogen-killing toxin):

8. Some of the public's fears and concerns about genetically modified food stem from moral or religious convictions, while others have a biological basis and are related to the potential biological threat posed by GMOs.
(a) Conduct a class discussion or debate to identify these fears and concerns, and list them below:

(b) Identify which of those you have listed above pose a real biological threat:

KEY TERMS: Mix and Match

INSTRUCTIONS: Test your vocabulary by matching each term to its definition, as identified by its preceding letter code.

ANNEALING

BIOTECHNOLOGY

BLUNT END

DNA CHIP

DNA LIGATION

DNA LIGASE

DNA POLYMERASE

DNA SEQUENCING

FORENSICS

GEL ELECTROPHORESIS

GENE TECHNOLOGY

GMO

MARKER GENE

MICROSATELLITE

MOLECULAR CLONE

PCR

PLASMID

PRIMER

RECOGNITION SITE

RECOMBINANT DNA

RESTRICTION ENZYME

STICKY END

TRANSFORMATION

TRANSGENESIS

VECTOR

XENOTRANSPLANT

A An organism or artificial vehicle that is capable of transferring a DNA sequence of DNA to another organism.

B The attachment of a DNA primer to a length of DNA as a starter point for the process of replication by a polymerase enzyme.

C The process of transplanting living cells or organs from one species into another.

D A short length of DNA used to identify the starting sequence for PCR so that polymerase enzymes can begin amplification.

E An enzyme that is able to cut a length of DNA at a specific sequence or site.

F A branch of science associated with the application of living organisms and biological processes in industry, medicine, food technology and other related fields.

G Technique using a modified form of the polymerase chain reaction that allows the sequence of a sample of DNA to be identified.

H A reaction that is used to amplify fragments of DNA using cycles of heating and cooling (abbreviation).

I A small circular piece of DNA commonly found in bacteria.

J The application of scientific ideas and techniques in order to answer questions about material of interest.

K DNA that has had a new sequence added so that the original sequence has been changed.

L The acquisition of genetic material by the uptake of naked DNA by the recipient.

M A short (normally two base pairs) piece of DNA that repeats a variable number of times between people and so can be used to distinguish between individuals.

N An array of thousands of microscopic spots of DNA oligonucleotides that can be used to measure the level of gene expression or to search for novel genes.

O An enzyme that catalyses the polymerisation of deoxyribonucleotides into a DNA strand and is also used in PCR to amplify DNA.

P An organism that has had part of its DNA sequence altered either by the removal or insertion of a piece of DNA.

Q A process that is used to separate different lengths of DNA by placing them in a gel matrix placed in a buffered solution through which an electric current is passed.

R The manipulation of DNA and gene sequences in order to modify the characteristics of organisms.

S The site or sequence of DNA at which a restriction enzyme attaches and cuts the DNA.

T A cut in a length of DNA by a restriction enzyme that results in two strands of DNA being different lengths with one strand overhanging the other.

U A type of cut in a length of DNA caused by a restriction enzyme that results in both strands of DNA being the same length.

V The repairing or attaching of fragmented DNA by ligase enzymes.

W An enzyme that is capable of joining fragments of DNA together.

X A gene, with an identifiable effect, used to determine if a piece of DNA has been successfully inserted into the host organism.

Y One of multiple copies of an isolated defined sequence of (often recombinant) DNA.

Z The process of introducing an exogenous gene into a living organism so that the organism will exhibit a novel property.

UNIT F215

5.3.1

Ecosystems

KEY CONCEPTS

- Ecosystems are dynamic entities comprising the community and the physical environment.
- Producers, consumers, and decomposers are trophic groups; energy is transferred between them.
- Succession is a natural process of ecosystem change characterised by successive species replacements.
- The distribution and abundance of organisms can be quantified using transects and quadrats.
- Microorganisms play a central role in nitrogen cycling.

KEY TERMS

abiotic factor
abundance
belt transect
biotic factor
climax community
community
consumer
decomposer
decomposition
denitrification
detritivore
distribution
ecological pyramid
ecological succession
ecosystem
energy flow diagram
energy transfer
food chain
food web
line transect
microorganism
nitrification
Nitrobacter
nitrogen fixation
Nitrosomonas
primary consumer
primary succession
producer
quadrat
Rhizobium
secondary consumer
ten percent law
trophic level

Periodicals:
Listings for this chapter are on page 342

Weblinks:
www.biozone.co.uk/weblink/OCR-A2-2832.html

Teacher Resource CD-ROM:
The Darkest Depths

OBJECTIVES

☐ 1. Use the **KEY TERMS** to help you understand and complete these objectives.

Energy in ecosystems — pages 253-264

☐ 2. Define the term **ecosystem**. Recognise ecosystems as dynamic systems and describe their components, identifying them as **biotic** or **abiotic factors**.

☐ 3. Using examples, distinguish between **producers**, **consumers**, **detritivores**, and **decomposers**, identifying the relationship between them and the role of each of these groups in energy transfer and nutrient cycling. Describe how the energy flow in ecosystems is described using **trophic levels**.

☐ 4. Describe how energy is transferred between trophic levels in **food chains** and **food webs**. Explain how the energy transfers are measured.

☐ 5. Explain how the energy flow in an ecosystem can be described quantitatively using an **energy flow diagram**. Include reference to: trophic levels, direction of energy flow, processes in energy transfer, and energy sources and sinks.

☐ 6. Describe food chains quantitatively using **ecological pyramids**. Explain how these may be based on numbers, biomass, or energy at each trophic level. Interpret ecological pyramids for different communities.

☐ 7. Compare the amount of energy available to each trophic level. State the efficiency of energy transfer in food chains and explain the small biomass and low numbers of organisms at higher trophic levels.

☐ 8. Use examples to explain how human activities can manipulate the flow of energy through ecosystems.

Ecological succession — pages 265-266

☐ 9. Recognise **ecological succession** as a process of community change over time. Describe factors that might cause a successional change.

☐ 10. Describe an example of primary succession, e.g. the development of a **climax community** on a new island or after volcanic activity. Students should recognise that a climax community is itself subject to change and should not be regarded as a static, unchanging entity.

Measuring distribution and abundance — pages 267-274

☐ 11. Describe techniques to measure the **distribution** and **abundance** of organisms: frame and/or point **quadrats**, **belt transects**, and **line transects**.

Microbes and the nitrogen cycle — pages 275-276

☐ 12. Describe the role of decomposers in ecosystems.

☐ 13. Describe the cycling of nitrogen within ecosystems, including the role of microorganisms in the cycle: nitrifying bacteria (***Nitrosomonas***, ***Nitrobacter***), nitrogen-fixing bacteria (***Rhizobium***), and denitrifying bacteria.

Components of an Ecosystem

The concept of the ecosystem was developed to describe the way groups of organisms are predictably found together in their physical environment. A community comprises all the organisms within an ecosystem. Both physical (abiotic) and biotic factors affect the organisms in a community, influencing their distribution and their survival, growth, and reproduction.

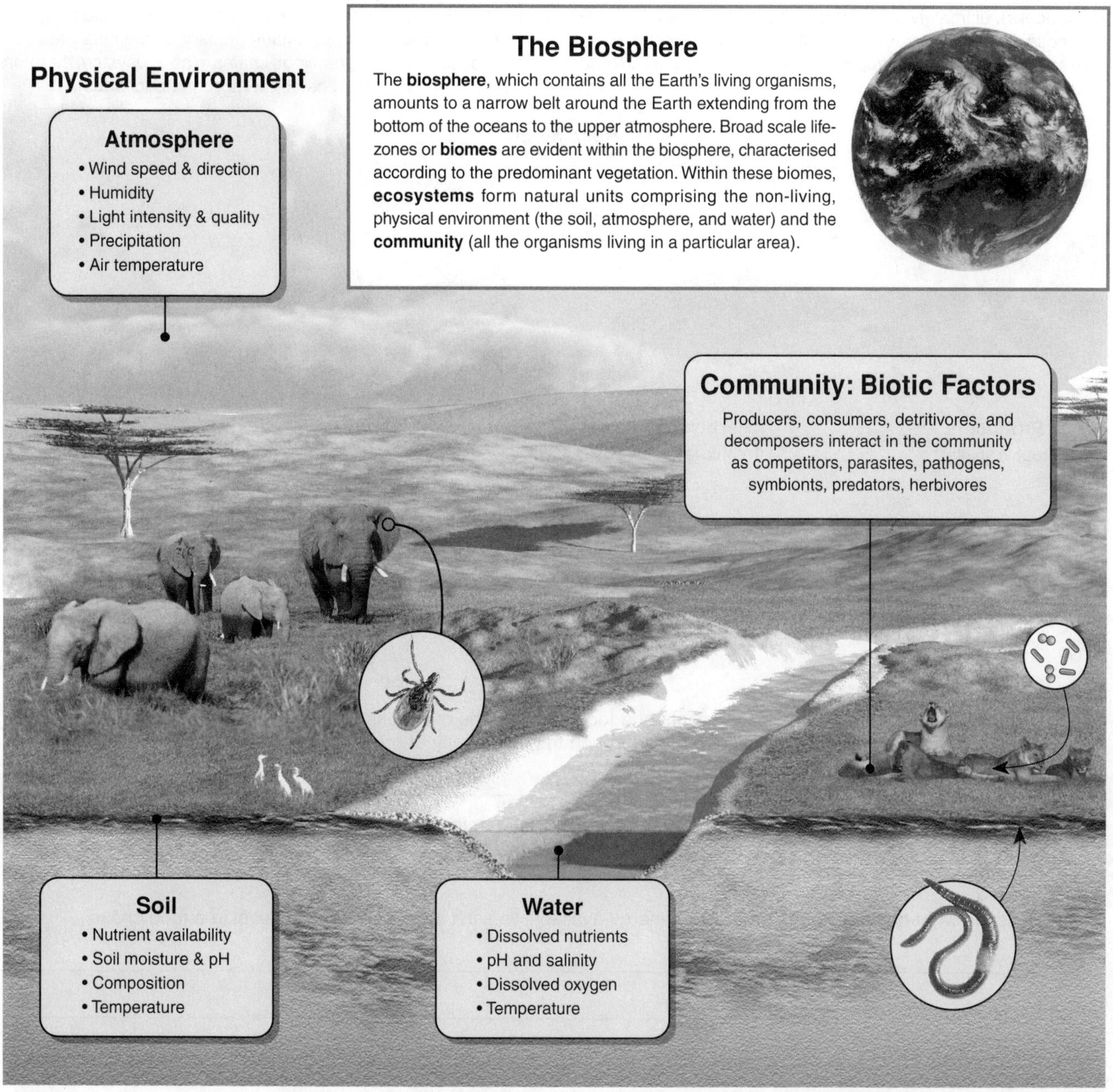

1. Distinguish clearly between a community and an ecosystem: ______________________

2. Distinguish between biotic and abiotic factors: ______________________

3. Use one or more of the following terms to describe each of the features of a rainforest listed below:
Terms: *population, community, ecosystem, physical factor.*

(a) All the green tree frogs present: ______________

(b) The entire forest: ______________

(c) All the organisms present: ______________

(d) The humidity: ______________

Food Chains

Every ecosystem has a **trophic structure**: a hierarchy of feeding relationships that determines the pathways for energy flow and nutrient cycling. Species are divided into trophic levels on the basis of their sources of nutrition. The first trophic level (**producers**), ultimately supports all other levels. The consumers are those that rely on producers for their energy. Consumers are ranked according to the trophic level they occupy (first order, second order, etc.). The sequence of organisms, each of which is a source of food for the next, is called a **food chain**. Food chains commonly have four links but seldom more than six. Those organisms whose food is obtained through the same number of links belong to the same trophic level. Note that some consumers (particularly "top" carnivores and omnivores) may feed at several different trophic levels, and many primary consumers eat many plant species. The different food chains in an ecosystem therefore tend to form complex webs of interactions (food webs).

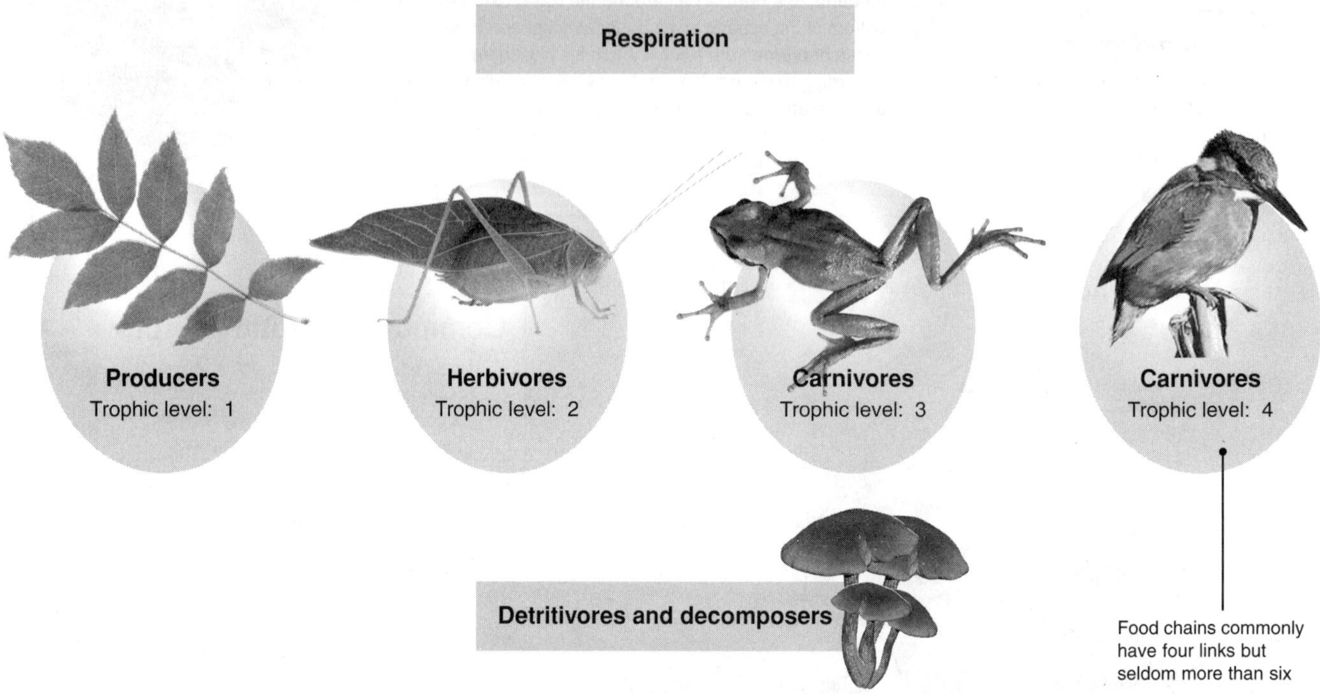

The diagram above represents the basic elements of a food chain. In the questions below, you are asked to add to the diagram the features that indicate the flow of energy through the community of organisms.

1. (a) State the original energy source for this food chain: ____________________

   (b) Draw arrows on the diagram to show how the energy flows from the original energy source to all the organisms.

   (c) Label each of the arrows with the process that carries out this transfer of energy.

   (d) Draw arrows on the diagram to show how the energy is lost by way of respiration.

2. (a) Describe what happens to the **amount** of energy available to each successive trophic level in a food chain:

   (b) Explain why this is the case:

3. Discuss the trophic structure of ecosystems, including reference to **food chains** and **trophic** levels:

4. Explain what you could infer about the tropic level(s) of the kingfisher, if it was found to eat both katydids and frogs:

Related activities: *Constructing a Food Web, Energy Inputs and Outputs, Energy Flow in an Ecosystem*

Periodicals: *Getting to grips with ecology*

Energy Inputs and Outputs

The way living things obtain their energy can be classified into two categories. The group upon which all others depend are called **producers** or **autotrophs**: organisms that are able to manufacture their food from simple inorganic substances. The **consumers** or **heterotrophs** (comprising the herbivores, carnivores, omnivores, decomposers, and detritivores), feed on the autotrophs or other heterotrophs to obtain their energy. The energy flow into and out of each trophic level in a food chain can be identified and represented diagrammatically using arrows of different sizes. The sizes of the arrows (see the diagrams below and on the next page) represent different amounts of energy lost from that particular trophic level.

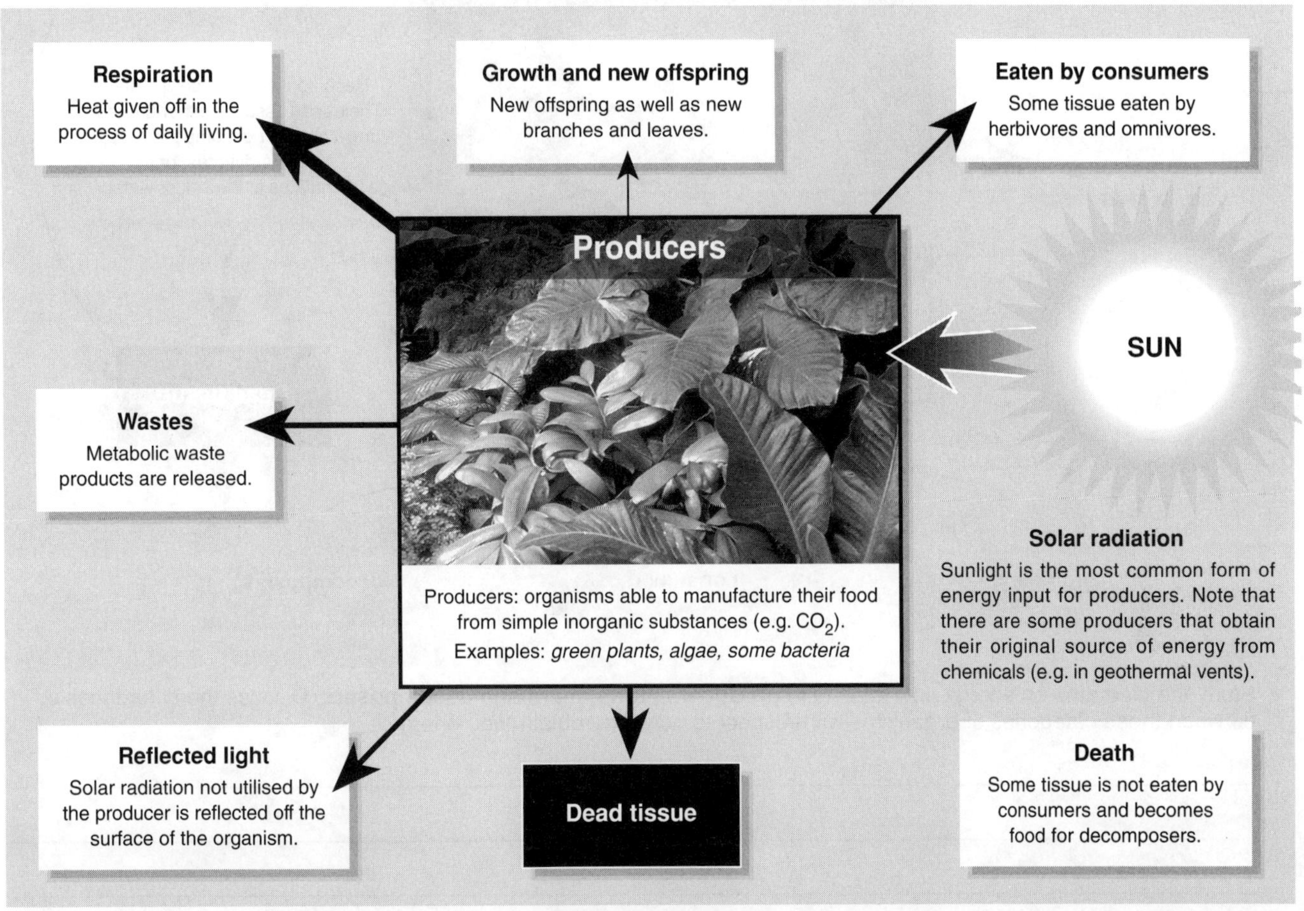

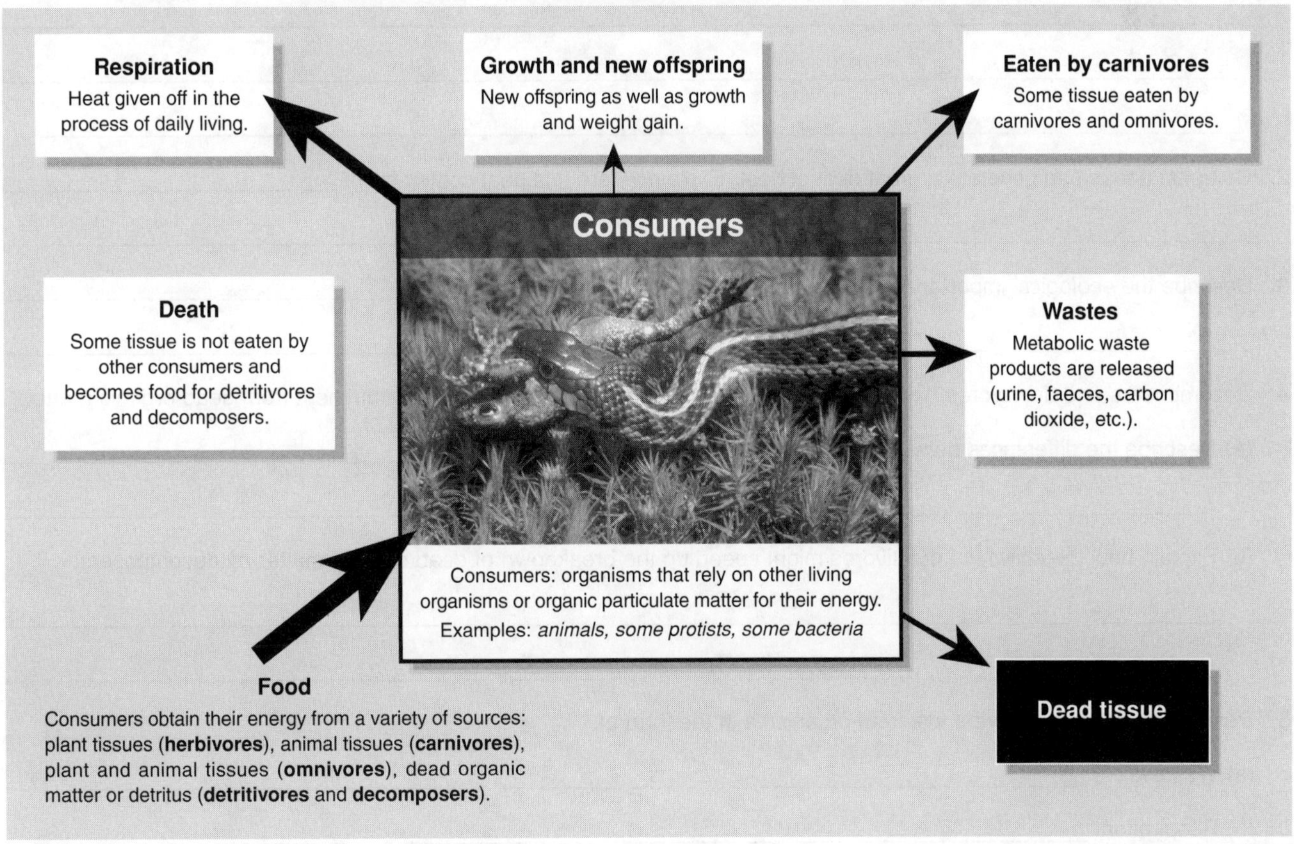

Ecosystems

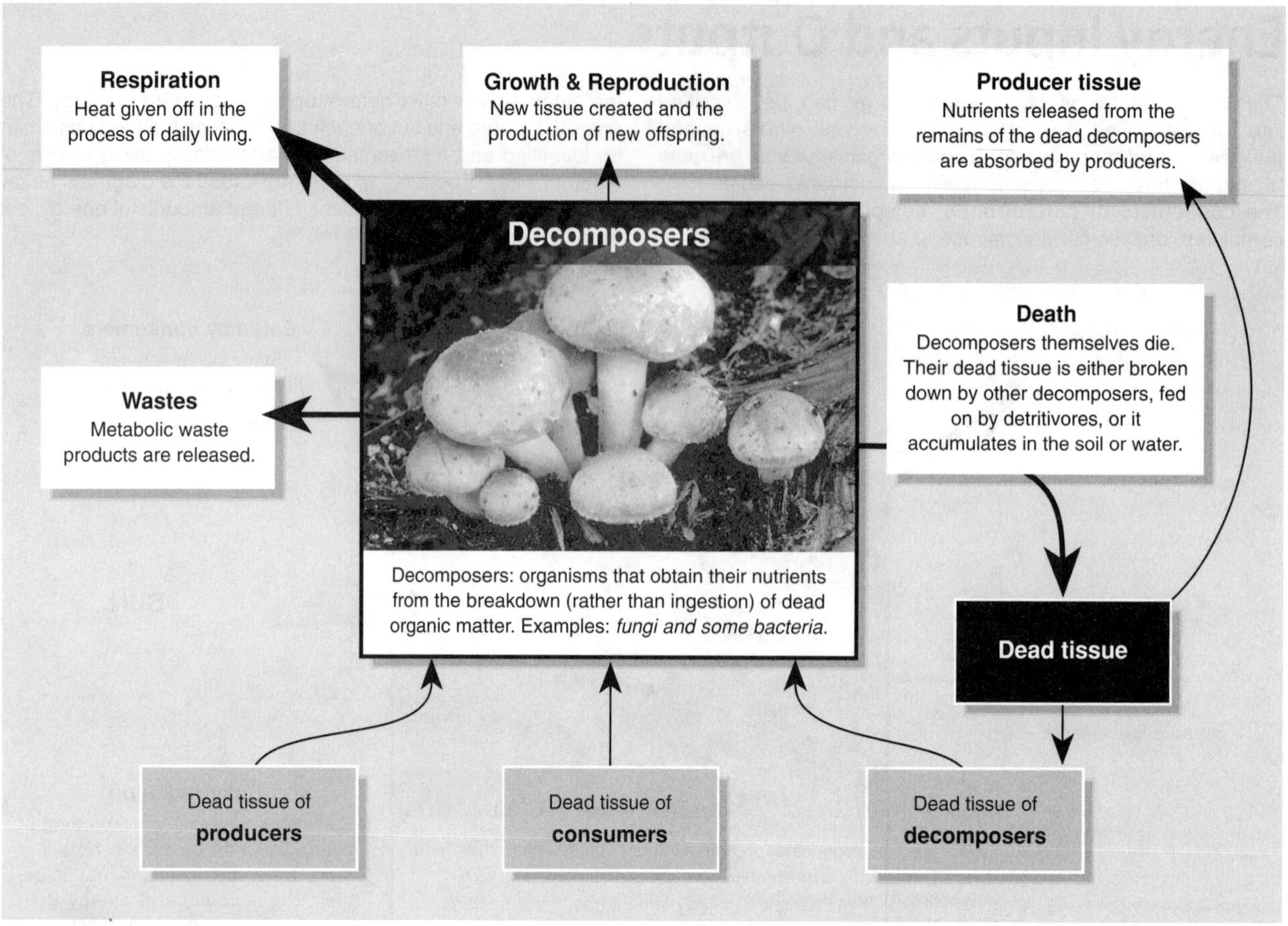

1. Study the diagrams on energy flow relating to **producers**, **consumers** and **decomposers**. Discuss the differences between these categories of organisms with respect to how they obtain their energy:

2. Compost heaps can generate a great deal of heat. Explain where this heat comes from:

3. Describe the ecological importance of decomposer organisms:

4. Decomposers and detritivores have similar ecological roles in that they both obtain nutriment from dead organic matter.

   (a) Describe the differences between decomposers and detritivores:

   (b) Explain how the activity of detritivores might speed up the breakdown of dead organic matter by decomposers:

5. Describe how energy may be lost from organisms in the form of:

   (a) Wastes:

   (b) Respiration:

Constructing a Food Web

The actual species inhabiting any particular lake may vary depending on locality, but certain types of organisms (as shown below) are typically represented. For the sake of simplicity, only fifteen organisms are represented here. Real lake communities may have hundreds of different species interacting together. The bulk of this species diversity is in the lower trophic levels (producers and invertebrate grazers). Your task is to assemble the organisms below into a food web, in a way that illustrates their trophic status and their relative trophic position(s). The food resource represented by **detritus** is not shown here. Detritus comprises the accumulated debris of dead organisms in varying stages of decay. This debris may arise from within the lake itself or it may be washed in from the surrounding lake margins and streams. The detritus settles through the water column and eventually forms a layer on the lake bottom. It provides a rich food source for any organism that can exploit it.

Feeding Requirements of Lake Organisms

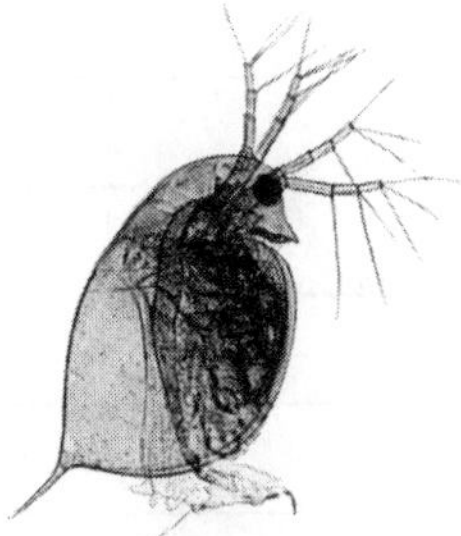

Daphnia
Small freshwater crustacean that forms part of the zooplankton. It feeds on planktonic algae by filtering them from the water with its limbs.

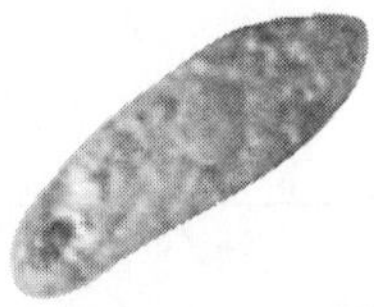

Autotrophic protoctists
e.g. Chlamydomonas, Euglena (pictured)
Two of genera that form the phytoplankton (commonly called **algae** or "plant plankton").

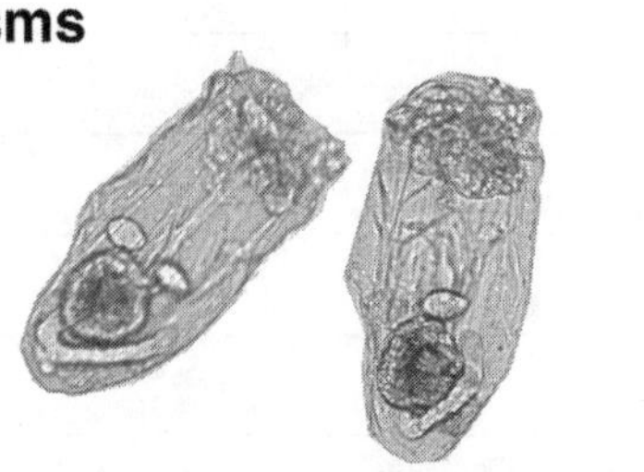

Asplanchna (planktonic rotifer)
A large, carnivorous rotifer that feeds on protozoa and young zooplankton (e.g. *Daphnia*). Note that most rotifers are small herbivores.

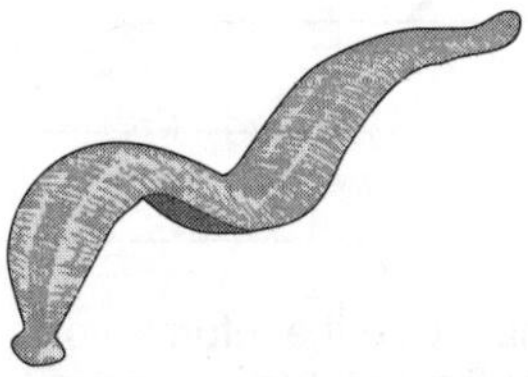

Leech (*Glossiphonia*)
Leeches are fluid feeding predators of smaller invertebrates, including rotifers, small pond snails and worms.

Macrophytes (various species)
A variety of flowering aquatic plants are adapted for being submerged, free-floating, or growing at the lake margin.

NYSDEC

Three-spined stickleback (*Gasterosteus*)
A common fish of freshwater ponds and lakes. It feeds mainly on small invertebrates such as *Daphnia* and insect larvae.

Diving beetle (*Dytiscus*)
Diving beetles feed on aquatic insect larvae and adult insects blown into the lake community. They will also eat organic detritus collected from the bottom mud.

Carp (*Cyprinus*)
A heavy bodied freshwater fish that feeds mainly on bottom living insect larvae and snails, but will also take some plant material (not algae).

Gina Mikel

Dragonfly larva
Large aquatic insect larvae that are voracious predators of small invertebrates including *Hydra*, *Daphnia*, other insect larvae, and leeches.

Great pond snail (*Limnaea*)
Omnivorous pond snail, eating both plant and animal material, living or dead, although the main diet is aquatic macrophytes.

Herbivorous water beetles (*e.g. Hydrophilus*)
Feed on water plants, although the young beetle larvae are carnivorous, feeding primarily on small pond snails.

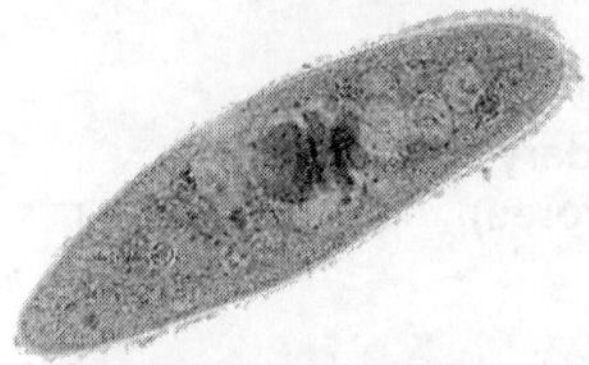

Protozan (*e.g. Paramecium*)
Ciliated protozoa such as *Paramecium* feed primarily on bacteria and microscopic green algae such as *Chlamydomonas*.

Pike (*Esox lucius*)
A top ambush predator of all smaller fish and amphibians, although they are also opportunistic predators of rodents and small birds.

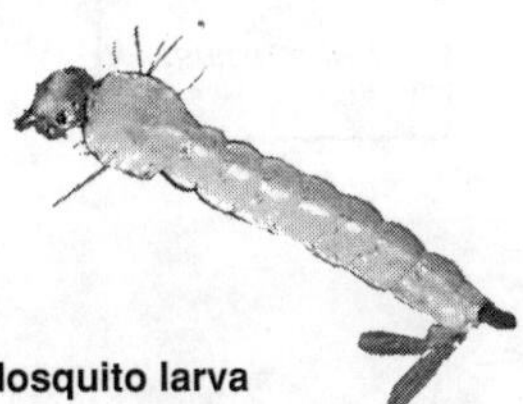

Mosquito larva
(*Culex* spp.)
The larvae of most mosquito species, e.g. *Culex*, feed on planktonic algae before passing through a pupal stage and undergoing metamorphosis into adult mosquitoes.

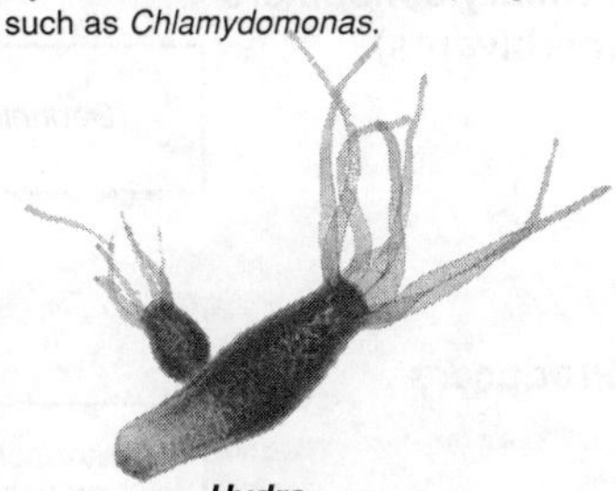

Hydra
A small carnivorous cnidarian that captures small prey items such as small *Daphnia* and insect larvae using its stinging cells on the tentacles.

Ecosystems

Periodicals:
The lake ecosystem

Related activities: *Food Chains, Energy Inputs and Outputs*
Web links: *Marine Food Webs, Cave Food Webs*

1. From the information provided for the lake food web components on the previous page, construct **ten** different **food chains** to show the feeding relationships between the organisms. Some food chains may be shorter than others and most species will appear in more than one food chain. An example has been completed for you.

Example 1:

(a) ______________________________

(b) ______________________________

(c) ______________________________

(d) ______________________________

(e) ______________________________

(f) ______________________________

(g) ______________________________

(h) ______________________________

(i) ______________________________

(j) ______________________________

2. (a) Use the food chains created above to help you to draw up a **food web** for this community. Use the information supplied to draw arrows showing the flow of **energy** between species (only energy **from** the detritus is required).

   (b) Label each species to indicate its position in the food web, i.e. its trophic level (**T1, T2, T3, T4, T5**). Where a species occupies more than one trophic level, indicate this, e.g. **T2/3**:

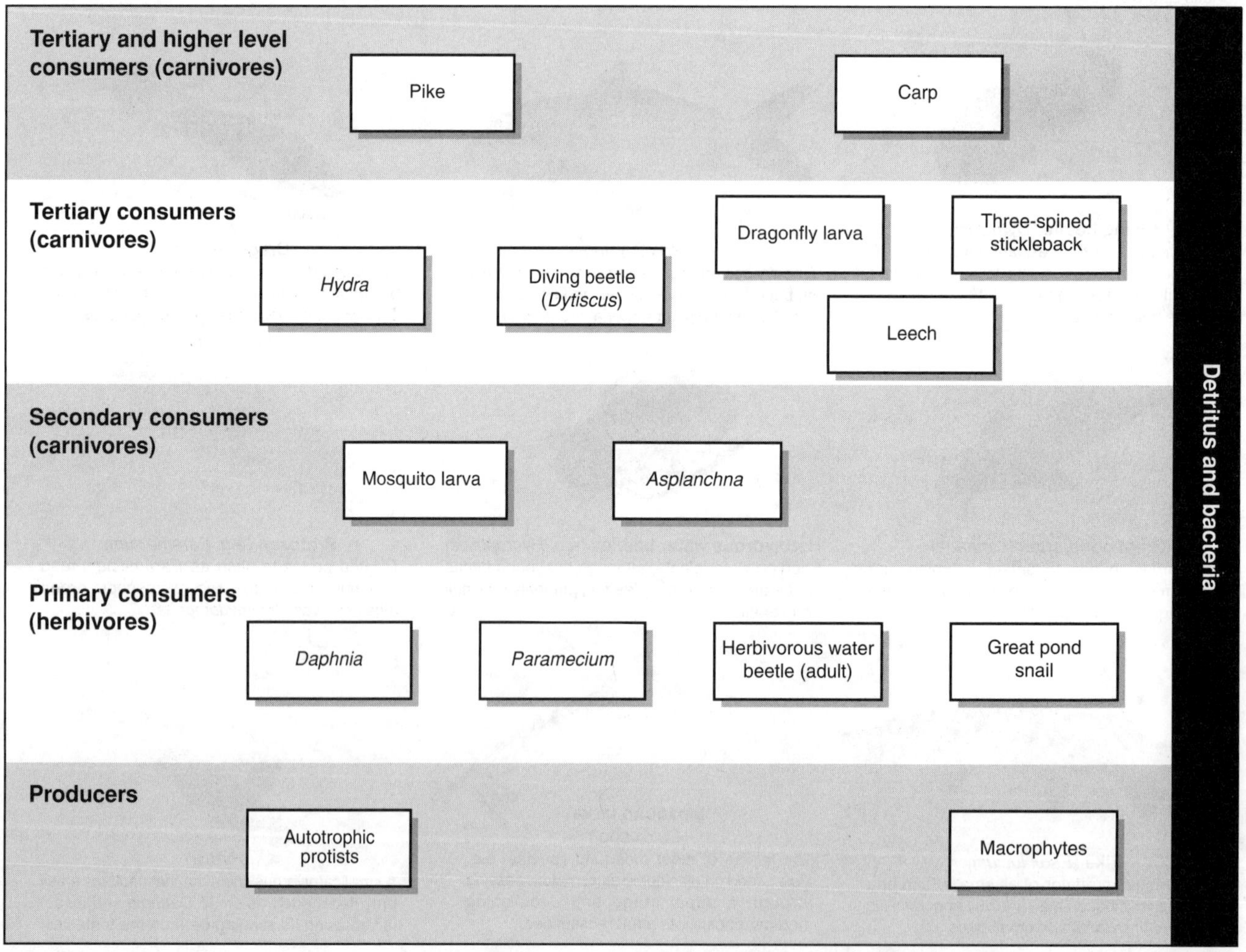

Energy Flow in an Ecosystem

The flow of energy through an ecosystem can be measured and analysed. It provides some idea as to the energy trapped and passed on at each trophic level. Each trophic level in a food chain or web contains a certain amount of biomass: the dry weight of all organic matter contained in its organisms. Energy stored in biomass is transferred from one trophic level to another (by eating, defaecation etc.), with some being lost as low-grade heat energy to the environment in each transfer. Three definitions are useful:

- **Gross primary production**: The total of organic material produced by plants (including that lost to respiration).
- **Net primary production**: The amount of biomass that is available to consumers at subsequent trophic levels.
- **Secondary production**: The amount of biomass at higher trophic levels (consumer production). Production figures are sometimes expressed as rates (productivity).

The percentage of energy transferred from one trophic level to the next varies between 5% and 20% and is called the **ecological efficiency** (efficiency of energy transfer). An average figure of 10% is often used. The path of energy flow in an ecosystem depends on its characteristics. In a tropical forest ecosystem, most of the primary production enters the detrital and decomposer food chains. However, in an ocean ecosystem or an intensively grazed pasture more than half the primary production may enter the grazing food chain.

Energy Flow Through an Ecosystem

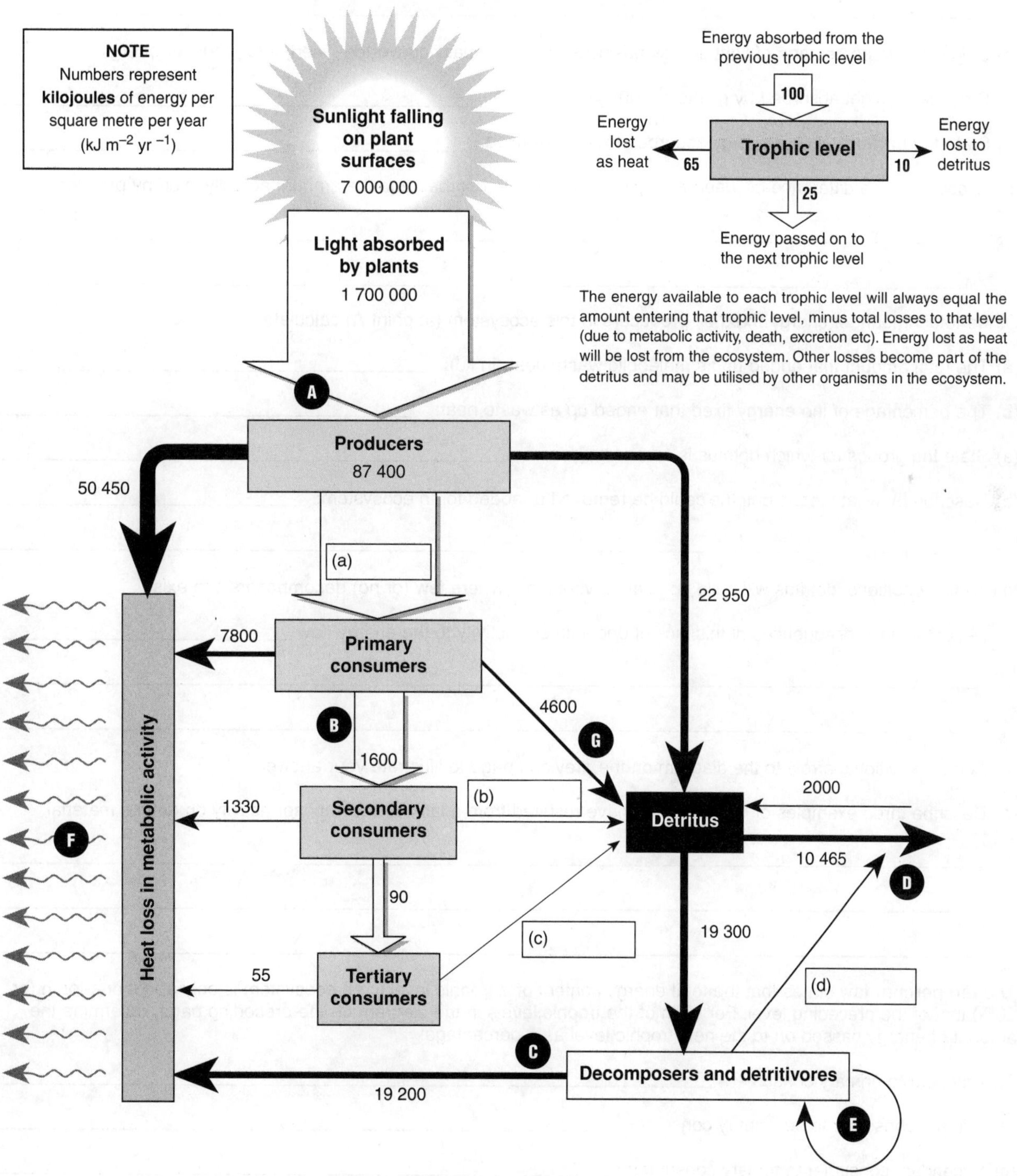

The energy available to each trophic level will always equal the amount entering that trophic level, minus total losses to that level (due to metabolic activity, death, excretion etc). Energy lost as heat will be lost from the ecosystem. Other losses become part of the detritus and may be utilised by other organisms in the ecosystem.

Ecosystems

1. Study the diagram on the previous page illustrating energy flow through a hypothetical ecosystem. Use the example at the top of the page as a guide to calculate the missing values (a)–(d) in the diagram. Note that the sum of the energy inputs always equals the sum of the energy outputs. Place your answers in the spaces provided on the diagram.

2. Describe the original source of energy that powers this ecosystem: ____________________

3. Identify the processes that are occurring at the points labelled **A – G** on the diagram on the previous page:

A. ____________________ E. ____________________

B. ____________________ F. ____________________

C. ____________________ G. ____________________

D. ____________________

4. (a) Calculate the percentage of light energy falling on the plants that is absorbed at point **A**:

Light absorbed by plants ÷ sunlight falling on plant surfaces x 100 = ____________________

(b) Describe what happens to the light energy that is not absorbed: ____________________

____

5. (a) Calculate the percentage of light energy absorbed that is actually converted (fixed) into producer energy:

Producers ÷ light absorbed by plants x 100 = ____________________

(b) State the **amount** of light energy absorbed that is **not** fixed: ____________________

(c) Account for the difference between the amount of energy absorbed and the amount actually fixed by producers:

____

____

6. Of the total amount of energy **fixed** by producers in this ecosystem (at point **A**) calculate:

(a) The total amount that ended up as metabolic waste heat (in kJ): ____________________

(b) The percentage of the energy fixed that ended up as waste heat: ____________________

7. (a) State the groups for which detritus is an energy source: ____________________

(b) Describe by what means detritus could be removed or added to an ecosystem: ____________________

____

8. In certain conditions, detritus will build up in an environment where few (or no) decomposers can exist.

(a) Describe the consequences of this lack of decomposer activity to the energy flow: ____________________

____

____

(b) Add an additional arrow to the diagram on the previous page to illustrate your answer.

(c) Describe three examples of materials that have resulted from a lack of decomposer activity on detrital material:

____

____

____

9. The **ten percent law** states that the total energy content of a trophic level in an ecosystem is only about one-tenth (or 10%) that of the preceding level. For each of the trophic levels in the diagram on the preceding page, determine the amount of energy passed on to the next trophic level as a percentage:

(a) Producer to primary consumer: ____________________

(b) Primary consumer to secondary consumer: ____________________

(c) Secondary consumer to tertiary consumer: ____________________

Production and Trophic Efficiency

The energy entering ecosystems is fixed by producers at a rate that is dependent on limiting factors such as temperature and the availability of light, water, and nutrients. The total energy fixed by a plant in photosynthesis is the **gross primary production** (**GPP**) and it is usually expressed as Jm^{-2} (or kJm^{-2}), or as gm^{-2}. However, a portion of this energy is required by the plant for respiration. Subtracting respiration from GPP gives the **net primary production**. The **rate** of biomass production, or **net primary productivity**, is the biomass produced per area per unit time. **Trophic efficiency** refers to the efficiency of energy transfer from one trophic level to the next. The trophic efficiencies of herbivores can vary widely, depending on how much of the producer biomass is consumed and assimilated. In some natural ecosystems this can be surprisingly high. Humans intervene in natural energy flows by simplifying the system and reducing the number of transfers occurring between trophic levels.

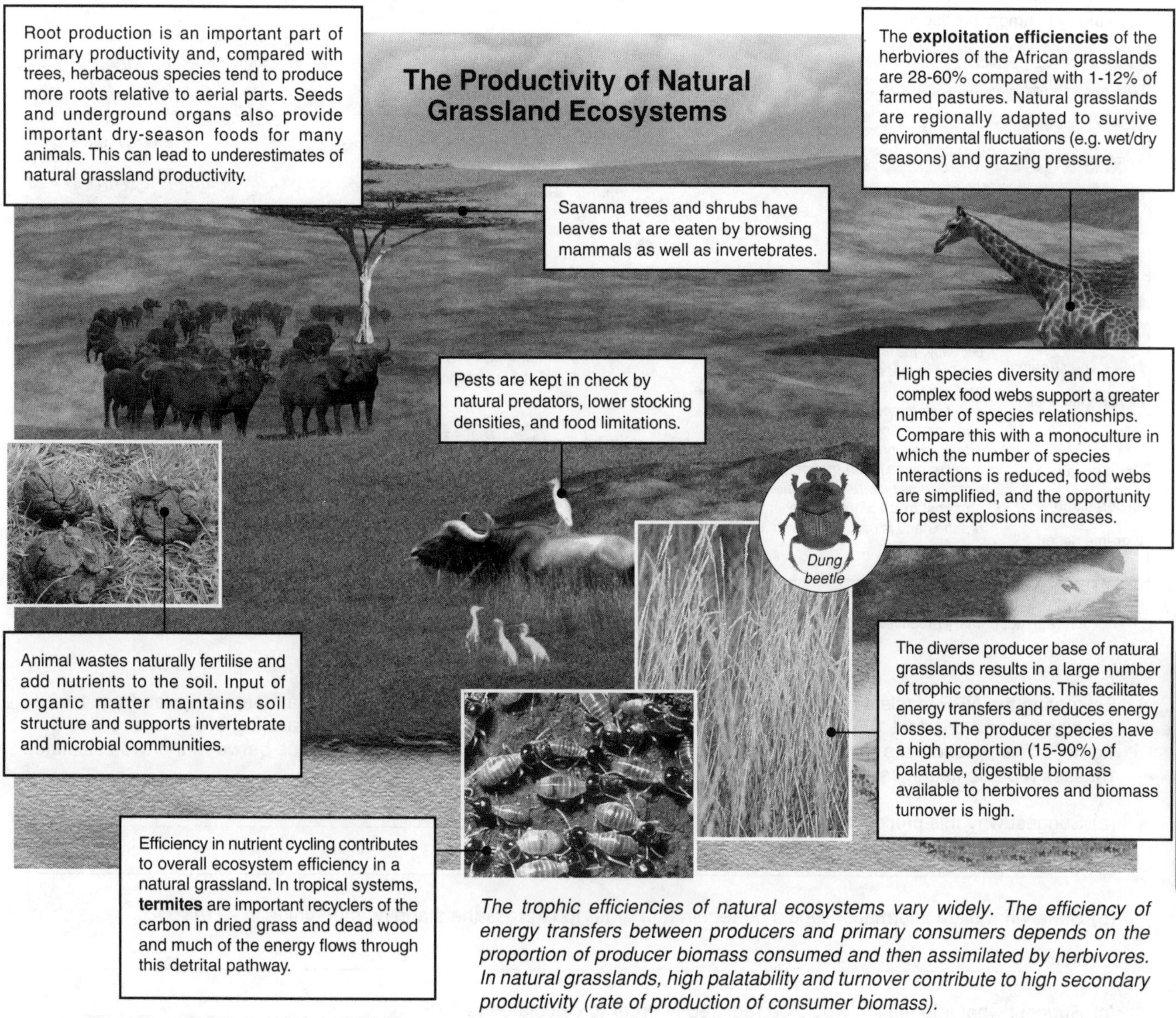

The trophic efficiencies of natural ecosystems vary widely. The efficiency of energy transfers between producers and primary consumers depends on the proportion of producer biomass consumed and then assimilated by herbivores. In natural grasslands, high palatability and turnover contribute to high secondary productivity (rate of production of consumer biomass).

1. Explain the difference between net primary production and net primary productivity: __________

2. Briefly describe three factors that may affect the primary productivity of an ecosystem:

(a)

(b)

(c)

3. Describe three reasons for the relatively high net primary productivity and high trophic efficiencies of savanna:

(a)

(b)

(c)

Measuring Productivity

The gross primary productivity of an ecosystem will depend on the capacity of the producers to capture and fix carbon in organic compounds. In most ecosystems, this is limited by constraints on photosynthesis (availability of light, nutrients, or water for example). The net primary productivity is then determined by how much of this goes into plant biomass per unit time, after respiratory needs are met. This will be the amount available to the next trophic level. It is difficult to measure productivity, but it is often estimated from the harvestable dry biomass or standing crop (the net primary production).

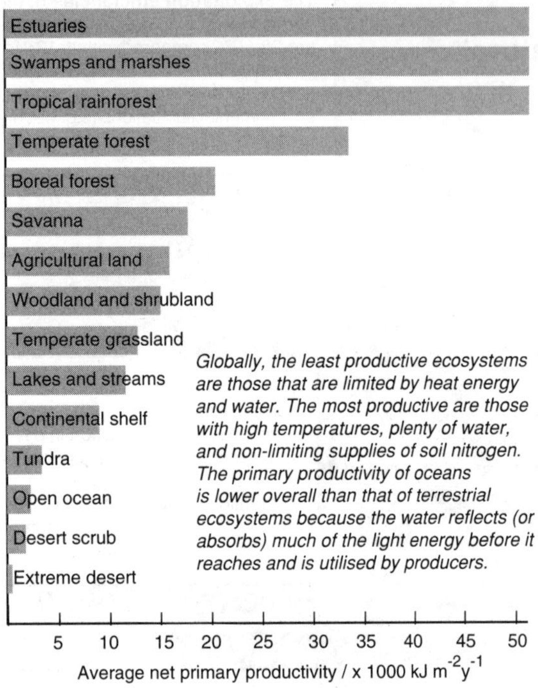

Globally, the least productive ecosystems are those that are limited by heat energy and water. The most productive are those with high temperatures, plenty of water, and non-limiting supplies of soil nitrogen. The primary productivity of oceans is lower overall than that of terrestrial ecosystems because the water reflects (or absorbs) much of the light energy before it reaches and is utilised by producers.

Agriculture and Productivity

Increasing net productivity in agriculture (increasing yield) is a matter of manipulating and maximising energy flow through a reduced number of trophic levels. On a farm, the simplest way to increase the net primary productivity is to produce a monoculture. Monocultures reduce competition between the desirable crop and weed species, allowing crops to put more energy into biomass. Other agricultural practices designed to increase productivity in crops include pest (herbivore) control and spraying to reduce disease. Higher productivity in feed-crops also allows greater secondary productivity (e.g. in livestock). Here, similar agricultural practices make sure the energy from feed-crops is efficiently assimilated by livestock.

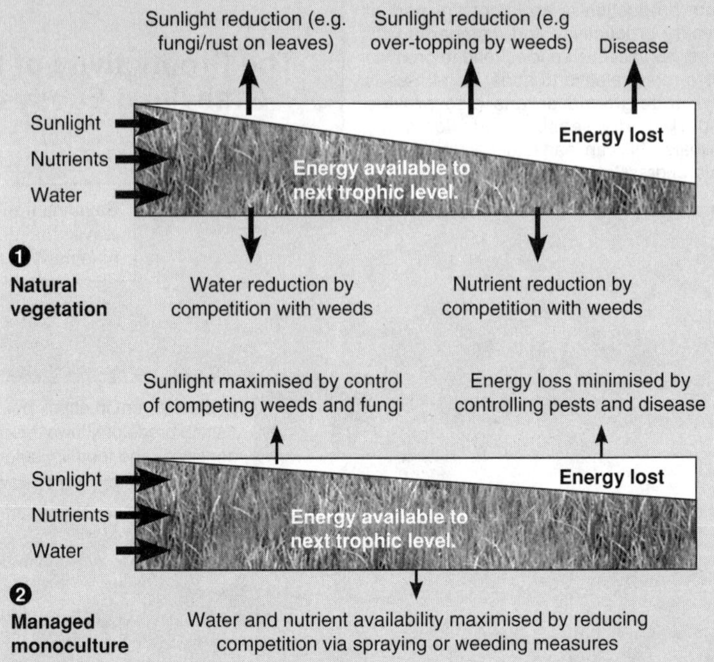

4. Estimating the NPP is relatively simple: all the plant material (including root material) from a measured area (e.g. 1 m^2) is collected and dried (at 105°C) until it reaches a constant mass. This mass, called the **standing crop**, is recorded (in kg m^{-2}). The procedure is repeated after some set time period (e.g. 1 month). The difference between the two calculated masses represents the estimated NPP:

   (a) Suggest why this procedure only provides an estimate of NPP: ______

   (b) State what extra information would be required in order to express the standing crop value in kJ m^{-2}: ______

   (c) Suggest what information would be required in order to calculate the GPP: ______

5. (a) Explain how a farmer is able to maximise the net primary productivity of a particular crop: ______

   (b) Suggest ways in which a farmer could maximise the productivity of their livestock: ______

6. Explain the contrasting net primary productivities of intensive horticultural land and desert: ______

Ecological Pyramids

The trophic levels of any ecosystem can be arranged in a pyramid shape. The first trophic level is placed at the bottom and subsequent trophic levels are stacked on top in their 'feeding sequence'. Ecological pyramids can illustrate changes in the numbers, biomass (weight), or energy content of organisms at each level. Each of these three kinds of pyramids tell us something different about the flow of energy and materials between one trophic level and the next. The type of pyramid you choose in order to express information about the ecosystem will depend on what particular features of the ecosystem you are interested in and, of course, the type of data you have collected.

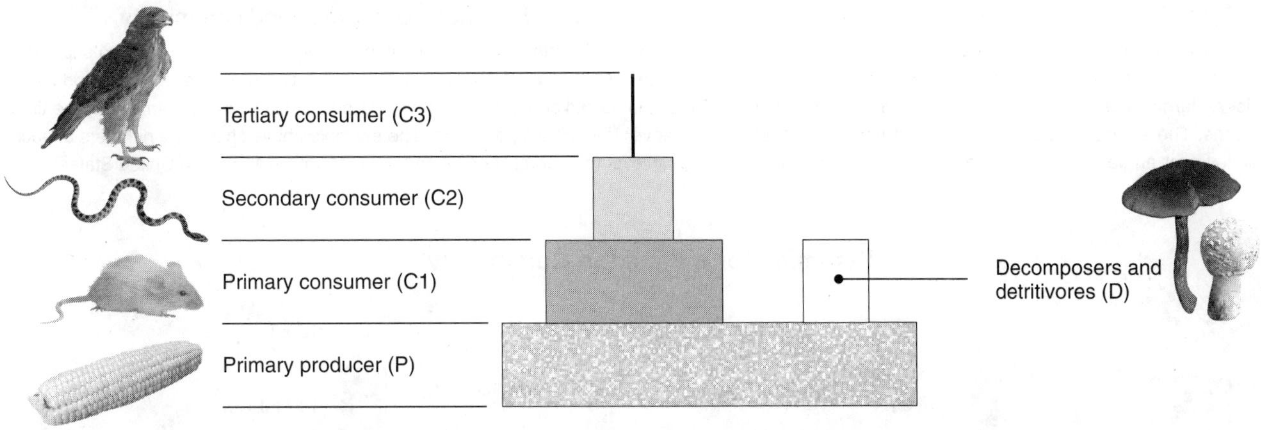

The generalised ecological pyramid pictured above shows a conventional pyramid shape, with a large number (or biomass) of producers forming the base for an increasingly small number (or biomass) of consumers. Decomposers are placed at the level of the primary consumers and off to the side. They may obtain energy from many different trophic levels and so do not fit into the conventional pyramid structure. For any particular ecosystem at any one time (e.g. the forest ecosystem below), the shape of this typical pyramid can vary greatly depending on whether the trophic relationships are expressed as numbers, biomass or energy.

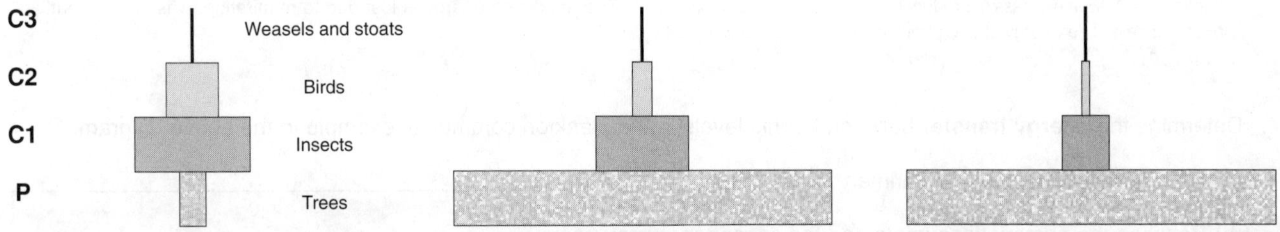

Numbers in a forest community

Pyramids of numbers display the number of individual organisms at each trophic level. The pyramid above has few producers, but they may be of a very large size (e.g. trees). This gives an 'inverted pyramid', although not all pyramids of numbers are like this.

Biomass in a forest community

Biomass pyramids measure the 'weight' of biological material at each trophic level. Water content of organisms varies, so 'dry weight' is often used. Organism size is taken into account, so meaningful comparisons of different trophic levels are possible.

Energy in a forest community

Pyramids of energy are often very similar to biomass pyramids. The energy content at each trophic level is generally comparable to the biomass (i.e. similar amounts of dry biomass tend to have about the same energy content).

1. Describe what the three types of ecological pyramids measure:

   (a) Number pyramid: ______________________________

   (b) Biomass pyramid: ______________________________

   (c) Energy pyramid: ______________________________

2. Explain the advantage of using a biomass or energy pyramid rather than a pyramid of numbers to express the relationship between different trophic levels:

   ____

   ____

   ____

3. Explain why it is possible for the forest ecosystem (on the next page) to have very few producers supporting a large number of consumers:

   ____

   ____

Related activities: *Food Chains, Energy Flow in an Ecosystem*

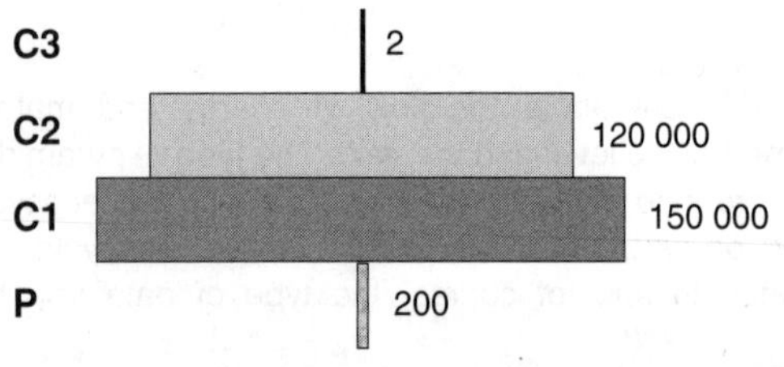

Pyramid of numbers: forest community

In a forest community a few producers may support a large number of consumers. This is due to the large size of the producers; large trees can support many individual consumer organisms. The example above shows the numbers at each trophic level for an oak forest in England, in an area of 10 m^2.

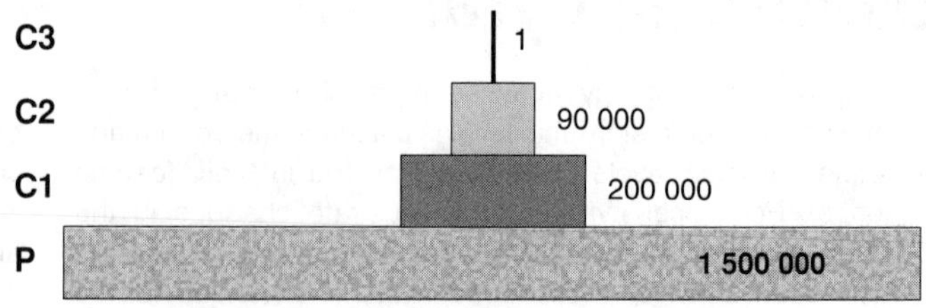

Pyramid of numbers: grassland community

In a grassland community a large number of producers are required to support a much smaller number of consumers. This is due to the small size of the producers. Grass plants can support only a few individual consumer organisms and take time to recover from grazing pressure. The example above shows the numbers at each trophic level for a derelict grassland area (10 m^2) in Michigan, United States.

Pyramids for a Plankton Community

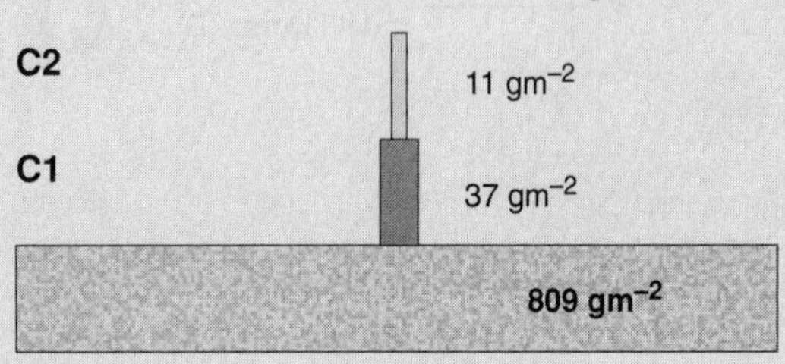

Biomass

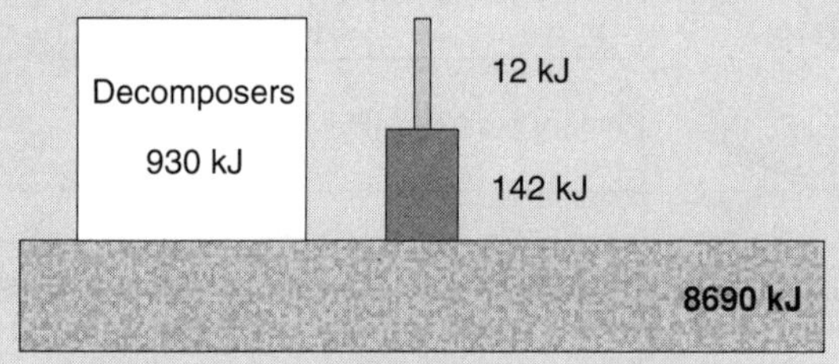

Energy

The pyramids of biomass and energy are virtually identical. The two pyramids illustrated here relate to the same hypothetical plankton community. A large biomass of producers supports a smaller biomass of consumers. The energy at each trophic level is reduced with each progressive stage in the food chain. As a general rule, a maximum of 10% of the energy is passed on to the next level in the food chain. The remaining energy is lost due to respiration, waste, and heat.

4. Determine the **energy transfer** between trophic levels in the plankton community example in the above diagram:

   (a) Between producers and the primary consumers: ____________________

   (b) Between the primary consumers and the secondary consumers: ____________________

   (c) Explain why the energy passed on from the producer to primary consumers is considerably less than the normally expected 10% occurring in most other communities (describe where the rest of the energy was lost to):

   ____

   ____

   (d) After the producers, which trophic group has the greatest energy content: ____________________

   (e) Give a likely explanation why this is the case: ____________________

   ____

   ____

An unusual biomass pyramid

The biomass pyramids of some ecosystems appear rather unusual with an inverted shape. The first trophic level has a lower biomass than the second level. What this pyramid does not show is the rate at which the producers (algae) are reproducing in order to support the larger biomass of consumers.

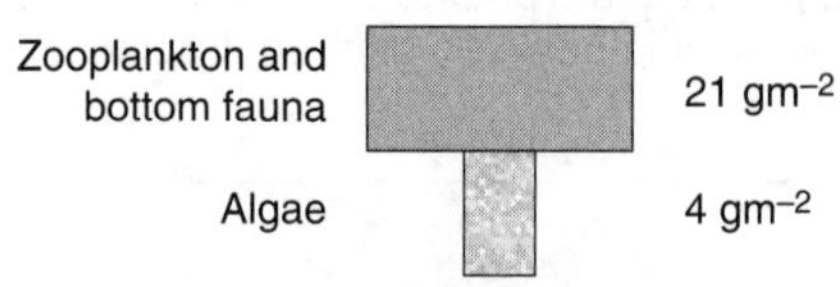

Biomass

5. Give a possible explanation of how a small biomass of producers (algae) can support a larger biomass of consumers (zooplankton):

   ____

   ____

   ____

Primary Succession

Ecological succession is the process by which communities in a particular area change over time. Succession takes place as a result of the complex interactions between biotic and abiotic factors. Early communities modify the physical environment causing it to change. This in turn alters the biotic community, which further alters the physical environment and so on. Each successive community makes the environment more favourable for the establishment of new species. An "idealised" succession (or sere) proceeds in seral stages, until the formation of a climax (old growth) community, which is generally stable until further disturbance. Early successional communities are characterised by a low species diversity, a simple structure, and broad niches. In contrast, climax communities are complex, with a large number of species interactions, narrow niches, and high species diversity.

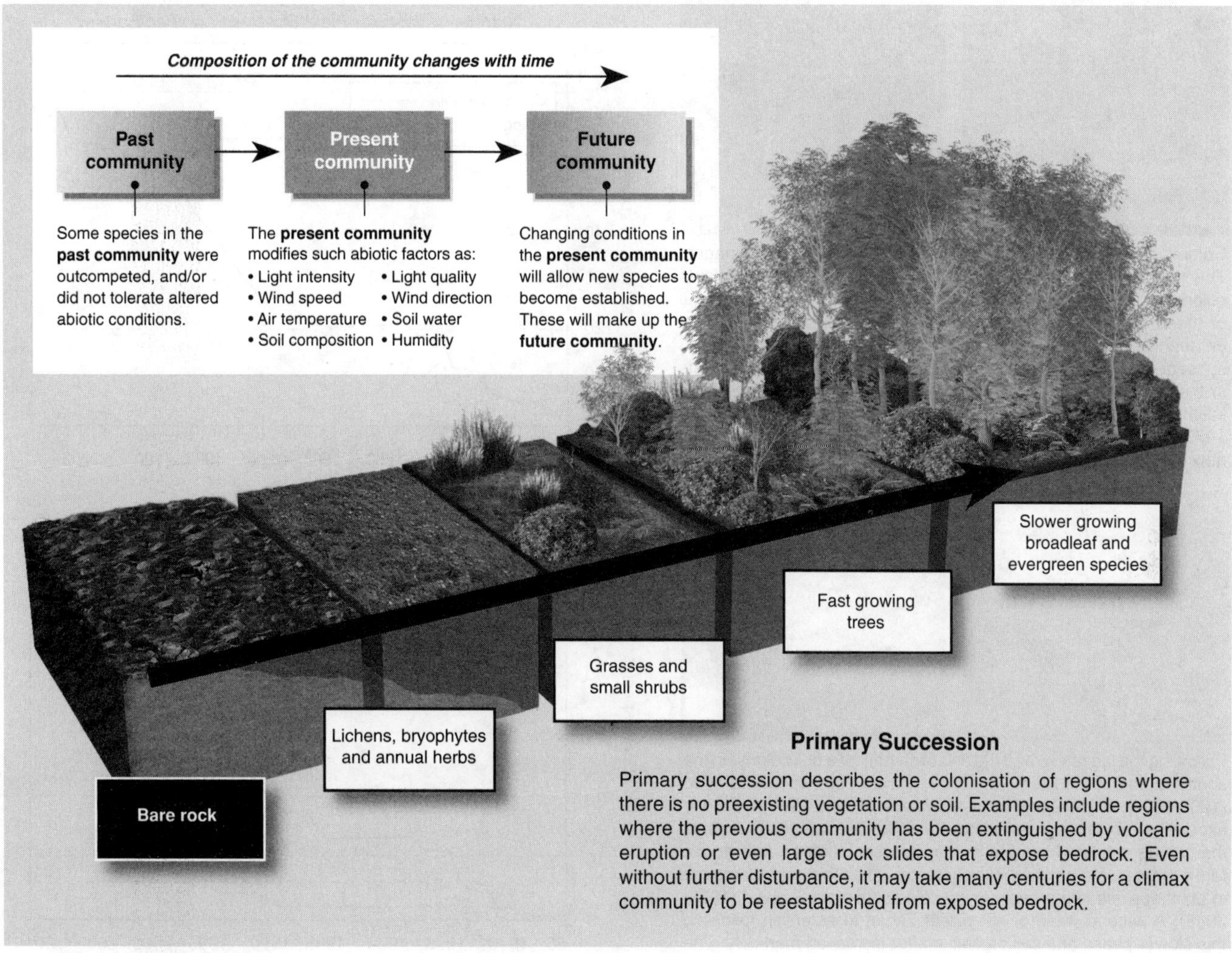

Primary Succession

Primary succession describes the colonisation of regions where there is no preexisting vegetation or soil. Examples include regions where the previous community has been extinguished by volcanic eruption or even large rock slides that expose bedrock. Even without further disturbance, it may take many centuries for a climax community to be reestablished from exposed bedrock.

1. Describe examples of where primary succession is likely to take place: ____________________

____

____

2. (a) Identify some early colonisers during the establishment phase of a community on bare rock: ____________________

____

(b) Describe two important roles of the species that are early colonisers of bare slopes: ____________________

____

____

3. Explain why climax communities are more stable and resistant to disturbance than early successional communities:

____

____

____

____

Succession on Surtsey Island

Surtsey Island is a volcanic island lying 33 km off the southern coast of Iceland. The island was formed over four years from 1963 to 1967 when a submarine volcano 130 m below the surface of the sea built up an island that initially reached 174 m above sea level and covered 2.7 km^2. Erosion has since reduced the island to around 150 m above sea level and 1.4 km^2. As an entirely new island, Surtsey was able to provide researchers with an ideal environment to study primary succession in detail. The colonisation of the island by plants and animals has been recorded since the island's formation. The first vascular plant there (sea rocket, *Cakile arctica*) was discovered in 1965, two years before the eruptions on the island ended. Since then, 69 plant species have colonised the island and there are a number of established seabird colonies.

Janke

Mikrolit

Colonisation of Surtsey by plants can be divided into four stages. The first stage (from 1965-1974) was dominated by shore plants colonising the northern shores of the island. The most successful of these colonisers was *Honckenya peploides* which established on tephra sand and gravel flats. It first set seed in 1971 and subsequently spread across the island. Carbon and nitrogen levels in the soil were recorded as being very low during this time. This initial colonisation by shore plants was followed by a lag phase (from 1975-1984). There was further establishment of shore plants but few new colonisers, which slowed the rate of succession.

Rasbak

Daderot

Following the lag phase and the establishment of a gull colony on the southern end of the island, a number of new plant species arrived (1985-1994). Populations of plants inside or near the gull colony expanded rapidly covering about 3 ha, while populations outside the colony remained low but stable. Grasses such as *Poa annua* formed extensive patches of vegetation. After this rapid increase in plant species, the arrival of new colonisers again slowed (1995-2008). A second wave of colonisers began to establish following this slower phase and soil organic matter increased markedly. The first bushy plants established in 1998, with the arrival of the willow *Salix phylicifolia*. The area of vegetation cover near the gull colony expanded to about 10 ha.

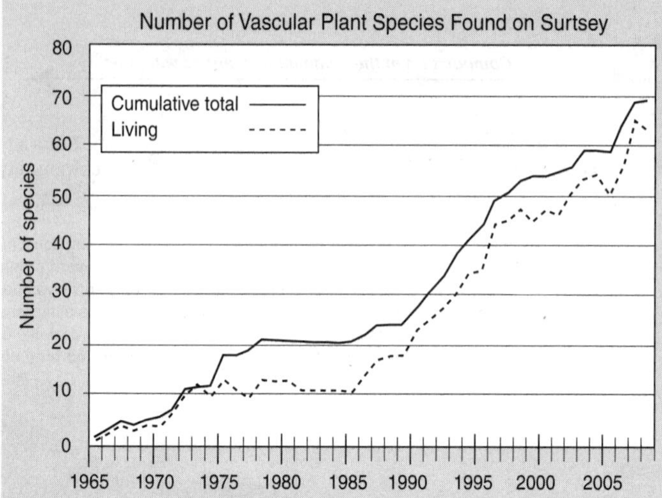

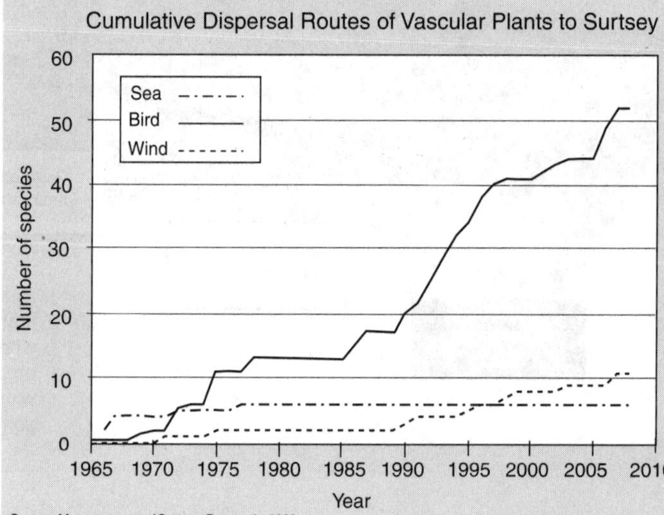

Source: Magnusson *et al* Surtsey Research, 2009

1. Explain why Surtsey provided ideal conditions for studying primary succession: ______________________

2. Explain why the first colonising plants established in the north of the island, while later colonisers established in the south.

3. Use the graphs to identify the following:

   (a) The year the gull colony established: ______________________

   (b) The most common method for new plant species to arrive on the island: ______________________

   (c) The year of the arrival of the second wave of plant colonisers. Suggest a reason for this second wave of colonisers:

Sampling Populations

In most ecological studies, it is not possible to measure or count all the members of a population. Instead, information is obtained through **sampling** in a manner that provides a fair (unbiased) representation of the organisms present and their distribution. This is usually achieved through **random sampling**, a technique in which every possible sample of a given size has the same chance of selection. Most practical exercises in community ecology involve the collection or census of living organisms, with a view to identifying the species and quantifying their abundance and other population features of interest. Sampling techniques must be appropriate to the community being studied and the information you wish to obtain. Any field study must also consider the time and equipment available, the organisms involved, and the impact of the sampling method on the environment. Often indicator species and **species diversity indices** are used as a way of quantifying biodiversity and ecosystem "health". Such indicators can be particularly useful when monitoring ecosystem change and looking for causative factors in species loss.

Quantifying the Diversity of Ecosystems

Reef community: high density, clumped distribution

The methods we use to sample communities and their constituent populations must be appropriate to the ecosystem being investigated. Communities in which the populations are at low density and have a random or clumped distribution will require a different sampling strategy to those where the populations are uniformly distributed and at higher density. There are many sampling options, each with advantages and drawbacks for particular communities. How would you assess aspects (e.g. species richness, abundance, or distribution) of the reef community above?

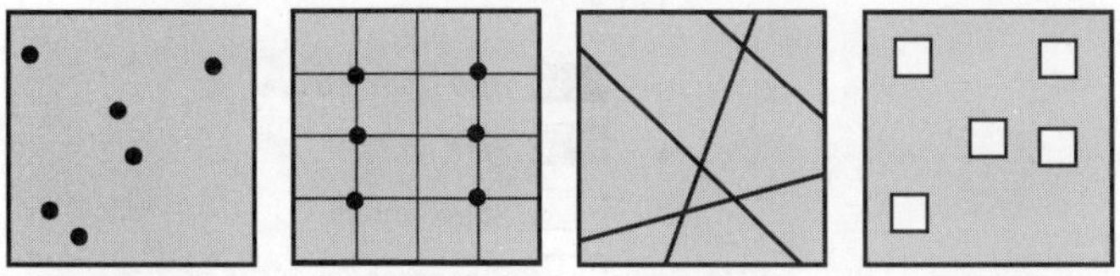

Random point sampling | *Point sampling: systematic grid* | *Line and belt transects* | *Random quadrats*

Photo: www.coastal planning.net

Marine ecologists use quadrat sampling to estimate biodiversity prior to works such as dredging.

RA

Line transects are appropriate to estimate biodiversity along an environmental gradient.

Tagging has been used for more than 30 years to follow the migration of monarch butterflies. The photograph here depicts an older tagging method, which has largely been replaced by a tag on the underside of the hindwing (inset). The newer method results in better survival and recapture rates and interferes less with flight.

Which Sampling Method?

Field biologists take a number of factors into consideration when deciding on a sampling method for a chosen population or community. The benefits and drawbacks of some common methods are outlined below:

Point sampling is time efficient and good for determining species abundance and community composition. However, organisms in low abundance may be missed.

Transects are well suited to determining changes in community composition along an environmental gradient but can be time consuming to do well.

Quadrats are also good for assessments of community diversity and composition but are largely restricted to plants and immobile animals. Quadrat size must also be appropriate for the organisms being sampled.

Mark and recapture is useful for highly mobile species which are otherwise difficult to record. However, it is time consuming to do well. **Radio-tracking** offers an alternative to mark and recapture and is now widely used in conservation to study the movements of both threatened species and pests.

Sensors and Measures

Various meters can be used to quantify aspects of the physical environment, including the pH, temperature, light levels, and turbidity. Meters that measure single factors have now largely been replaced by multi-purpose meters.

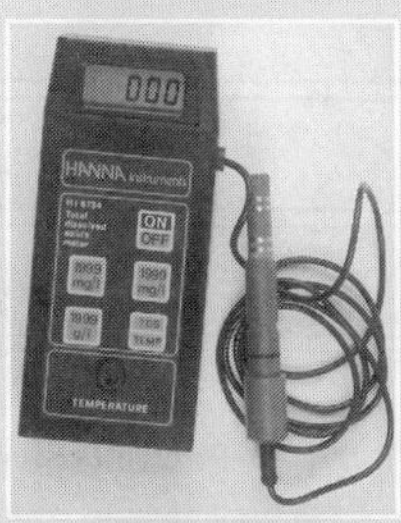

Total dissolved solids (TDS) meter: Measures the content of dissolved solids (as ions) in water in mgL^{-1} giving an indication of water quality. The probe measures the conductivity of the water to approximate the level of TDS. TDS can also be measured gravimetrically by evaporating a sample leaving the residue behind.

Quantum light meter: Measures light intensity levels but not light quality (wavelength). Light levels can change dramatically from a forest floor to its canopy. A light meter provides a quantitative measure of these changes, many of which are not detectable with our own visual systems.

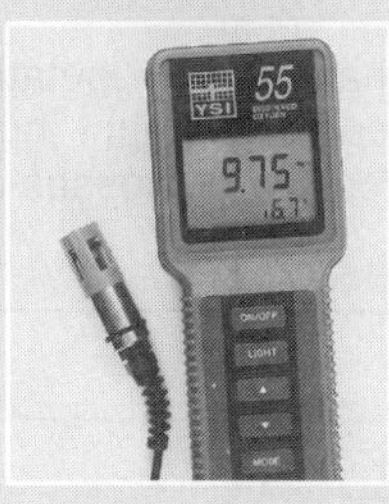

Dissolved oxygen meter: This measures the amount of oxygen dissolved in water (as mgL^{-1}), which gives and indication of water quality and suitability to support organisms such as fish. The **Winkler** method uses a titration of $MnSO_4$, KI, and $K_2S_2O_3$ to determine the concentration of O_2.

Ecosystems

Related activities: *Quadrat Sampling, Transect Sampling*

Using Dataloggers in Field Studies

Usually, when we collect information about populations in the field, we also collect information about the physical environment. This provides important information about the local habitat and can be useful in assessing habitat preference. With the advent of **dataloggers**, collecting this information is straightforward.

Dataloggers are electronic instruments that record measurements over time. They are equipped with a microprocessor, data storage facility, and sensor. Different sensors are used to measure a range of variables in water or air. The datalogger is connected to a computer, and software is used to set the limits of operation (e.g. the sampling interval) and initiate the logger. The logger is then disconnected and used remotely to record and store data. When reconnected to the computer, the data are downloaded, viewed, and plotted. Dataloggers make data collection quick and accurate, and they enable prompt data analysis.

Datalogger photos courtesy of PASCO

Dataloggers fitted with sensors are portable and easy to use in a wide range of aquatic (left) and terrestrial (right) environments. Different variables can be measured by changing the sensor attached to the logger.

1. Explain why we **sample** populations: ______________________________

2. Describe a sampling technique that would be appropriate for determining each of the following:

   (a) The percentage cover of a plant species in pasture: ______________________________

   (b) The density and age structure of a plankton population: ______________________________

   (c) Change in community composition from low to high altitude on a mountain: ______________________________

3. Explain why it is common practice to also collect information about the physical environment when sampling populations:

____

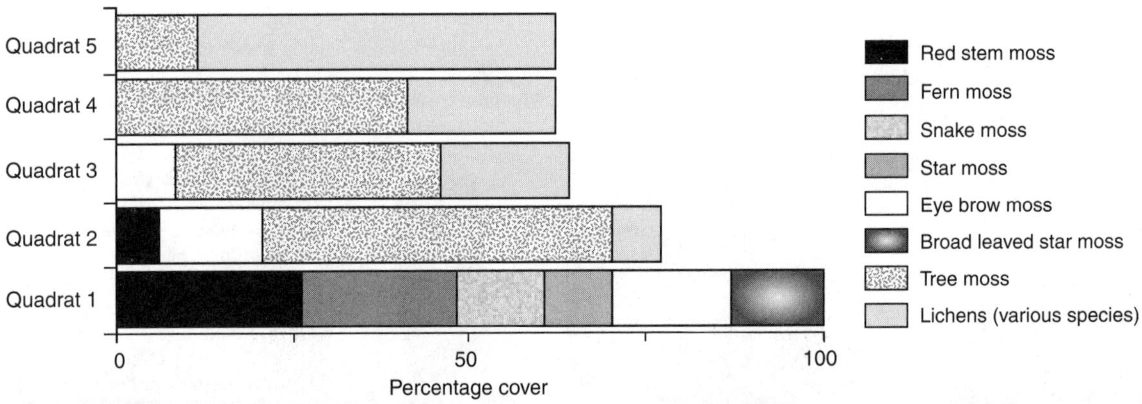

QUADRAT	1	2	3	4	5
Height / m	0.4	0.8	1.2	1.6	2.0
Light / arbitrary units	40	56	68	72	72
Humidity / percent	99	88	80	76	78
Temperature / °C	12.1	12.2	13	14.3	14.2

4. The figure (above) shows the changes in vegetation cover along a 2 m vertical transect up the trunk of an oak tree (*Quercus*). Changes in the physical factors light, humidity, and temperature along the same transect were also recorded. From what you know about the ecology of mosses and lichens, account for the observed vegetation distribution:

____

Quadrat Sampling

Quadrat sampling is a method by which organisms in a certain proportion (sample) of the habitat are counted directly. As with all sampling methods, it is used to estimate population parameters when the organisms present are too numerous to count in total. It can be used to estimate population **abundance** (number), **density**, **frequency of occurrence**, and **distribution**. Quadrats may be used without a transect when studying a relatively uniform habitat. In this case, the quadrat positions are chosen randomly using a random number table.

The general procedure is to count all the individuals (or estimate their percentage cover) in a number of quadrats of known size and to use this information to work out the abundance or percentage cover value for the whole area. The number of quadrats used and their size should be appropriate to the type of organism involved (e.g. grass vs tree).

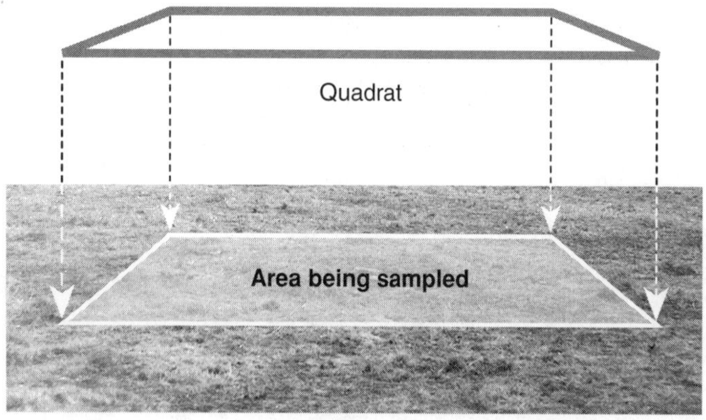

$$\text{Estimated average density} = \frac{\text{Total number of individuals counted}}{\text{Number of quadrats} \times \text{area of each quadrat}}$$

Guidelines for Quadrat Use:

1. The **area of each quadrat** must be known exactly and ideally quadrats should be the same shape. The quadrat does not have to be square (it may be rectangular, hexagonal etc.).
2. **Enough quadrat samples** must be taken to provide results that are representative of the total population.
3. The **population of each quadrat** must be known exactly. Species must be distinguishable from each other, even if they have to be identified at a later date. It has to be decided beforehand what the count procedure will be and how organisms over the quadrat boundary will be counted.
4. The size of the quadrat should be appropriate to the organisms and habitat, e.g. a large size quadrat for trees.
5. The quadrats must be **representative of the whole area**. This is usually achieved by **random sampling** (right).

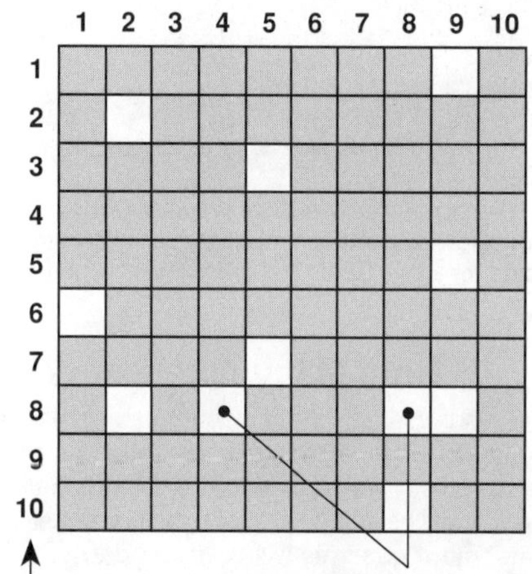

The area to be sampled is divided up into a grid pattern with indexed coordinates

Quadrats are applied to the predetermined grid on a random basis. This can be achieved by using a random number table.

Sampling a centipede population

A researcher by the name of Lloyd (1967) carried out a sampling of centipedes in Wytham Woods, near Oxford in England. A total of 37 hexagon–shaped quadrats were used, with a diameter of 30 cm (see diagram on right). These were arranged in a pattern so that they were all touching each other. Use the data in the diagram to answer the following questions.

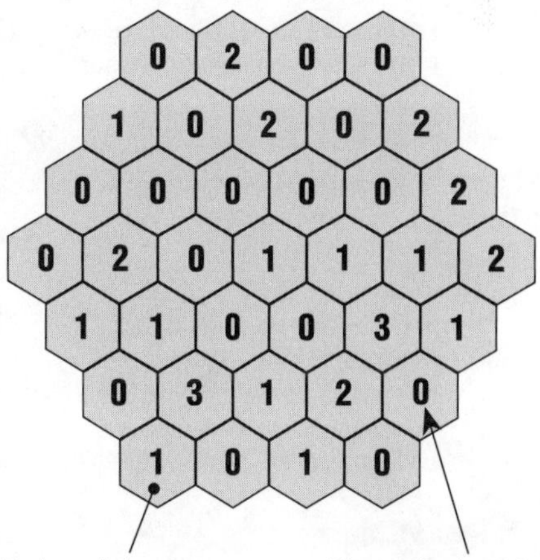

Each quadrat was a hexagon with a diameter of 30 cm and an area of 0.08 square metres.

The number in each hexagon indicates how many centipedes were caught in that quadrat.

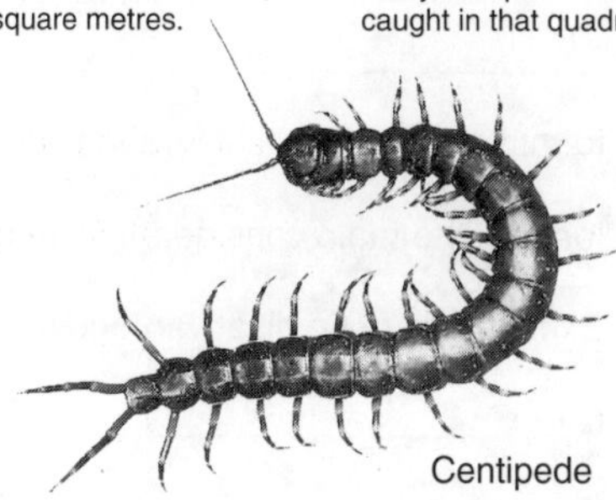

Centipede

1. Determine the average number of centipedes captured per quadrat:

 ____

2. Calculate the estimated average density of centipedes per square metre (remember that each quadrat is 0.08 square metres in area):

 ____

3. Looking at the data for individual quadrats, describe in general terms the distribution of the centipedes in the sample area:

 ____

 ____

4. Describe one factor that might account for the distribution pattern:

 ____

 ____

Quadrat-Based Estimates

The simplest description of a plant community in a habitat is a list of the species that are present. This qualitative assessment of the community has the limitation of not providing any information about the **relative abundance** of the species present. Quick estimates can be made using **abundance scales**, such as the ACFOR scale described below. Estimates of percentage cover provide similar information. These methods require the use of **quadrats**. Quadrats are used extensively in plant ecology. This activity outlines some of the common considerations when using quadrats to sample plant communities.

What Size Quadrat?

Quadrats are usually square, and cover 0.25 m^2 (0.5 m x 0.5 m) or 1 m^2, but they can be of any size or shape, even a single point. The quadrats used to sample plant communities are often 0.25 m^2. This size is ideal for low-growing vegetation, but quadrat size needs to be adjusted to habitat type. The quadrat must be large enough to be representative of the community, but not so large as to take a very long time to use.

A quadrat covering an area of 0.25 m^2 is suitable for most low growing plant communities, such as this alpine meadow, fields, and grasslands.

Larger quadrats (e.g. 1 m^2) are needed for communities with shrubs and trees. Quadrats as large as 4 m x 4 m may be needed in woodlands.

Small quadrats (0.01 m^2 or 100 mm x 100 mm) are appropriate for lichens and mosses on rock faces and tree trunks.

How Many Quadrats?

As well as deciding on a suitable quadrat size, the other consideration is how many quadrats to take (the sample size). In species-poor or very homogeneous habitats, a small number of quadrats will be sufficient. In species-rich or heterogeneous habitats, more quadrats will be needed to ensure that all species are represented adequately.

Determining the number of quadrats needed

- Plot the cumulative number of species recorded (on the *y* axis) against the number of quadrats already taken (on the *x* axis).
- The point at which the curve levels off indicates the suitable number of quadrats required.

Fewer quadrats are needed in species-poor or very uniform habitats, such as this bluebell woodland.

Describing Vegetation

Density (number of individuals per unit area) is a useful measure of abundance for animal populations, but can be problematic in plant communities where it can be difficult to determine where one plant ends and another begins. For this reason, plant abundance is often assessed using **percentage cover**. Here, the percentage of each quadrat covered by each species is recorded, either as a numerical value or using an abundance scale such as the ACFOR scale.

The ACFOR Abundance Scale

A = Abundant (30% +)
C = Common (20-29%)
F = Frequent (10-19%)
O = Occasional (5-9%)
R = Rare (1-4%)

The ACFOR scale could be used to assess the abundance of species in this wildflower meadow. Abundance scales are subjective, but it is not difficult to determine which abundance category each species falls into.

1. Describe one difference between the methods used to assess species abundance in plant and in animal communities:

2. Identify the main consideration when determining appropriate quadrat size:

3. Identify the main consideration when determining number of quadrats:

4. Explain two main disadvantages of using the ACFOR abundance scale to record information about a plant community:

   (a)

   (b)

Related activities: *Quadrat Sampling*
Web links: *Ecological Sampling Methods*

Sampling a Leaf Litter Population

The diagram on the next page represents an area of leaf litter from a forest floor with a resident population of organisms. The distribution of four animal species as well as the arrangement of leaf litter is illustrated. Leaf litter comprises leaves and debris that have dropped off trees to form a layer of detritus. This exercise is designed to practice the steps required in planning and carrying out a sampling of a natural population. It is desirable, but not essential, that students work in groups of 2–4.

1. **Decide on the sampling method**

   For the purpose of this exercise, it has been decided that the populations to be investigated are too large to be counted directly and a quadrat sampling method is to be used to estimate the average density of the four animal species as well as that of the leaf litter.

2. **Mark out a grid pattern**

   Use a ruler to mark out 3 cm intervals along each side of the sampling area (area of quadrat = 0.03 x 0.03 m). **Draw lines** between these marks to create a 6 x 6 grid pattern (total area = 0.18 x 0.18 m). This will provide a total of 36 quadrats that can be investigated.

3. **Number the axes of the grid**

   Only a small proportion of the possible quadrat positions are going to be sampled. It is necessary to select the quadrats in a random manner. It is not sufficient to simply guess or choose your own on a 'gut feeling'. The best way to choose the quadrats randomly is to create a numbering system for the grid pattern and then select the quadrats from a random number table. Starting at the *top left hand corner*, **number the columns** and **rows** from 1 to 6 on each axis.

4. **Choose quadrats randomly**

   To select the required number of quadrats randomly, use random numbers from a random number table. The random numbers are used as an index to the grid coordinates. Choose 6 quadrats from the total of 36 using table of random numbers provided for you at the bottom of the next page. Make a note of which column of random numbers you choose. Each member of your group should choose a different set of random numbers (i.e. different column: A–D) so that you can compare the effectiveness of the sampling method.

   Column of random numbers chosen: ______

   NOTE: Highlight the boundary of each selected quadrat with coloured pen/highlighter.

5. **Decide on the counting criteria**

   Before the counting of the individuals for each species is carried out, the criteria for counting need to be established.

   There may be some problems here. You must decide before sampling begins as to what to do about individuals that are only partly inside the quadrat. Possible answers include:

   (a) Only counting individuals if they are completely inside the quadrat.

   (b) Only counting individuals that have a clearly defined part of their body inside the quadrat (such as the head).

   (c) Allowing for 'half individuals' in the data (e.g. 3.5 snails).

   (d) Counting an individual that is inside the quadrat by half or more as one complete individual.

   Discuss the merits and problems of the suggestions above with other members of the class (or group). You may even have counting criteria of your own. Think about other factors that could cause problems with your counting.

6. **Carry out the sampling**

   Carefully examine each selected quadrat and **count the number of individuals** of each species present. Record your data in the spaces provided on the next page.

7. **Calculate the population density**

   Use the combined data TOTALS for the sampled quadrats to estimate the average density for each species by using the formula:

   $$\textbf{Density} = \frac{\textbf{Total number in all quadrats sampled}}{\textbf{Number of quadrats sampled} \times \textbf{area of a quadrat}}$$

   Remember that a total of 6 quadrats are sampled and each has an area of 0.0009 m^2. The density should be expressed as the number of individuals *per square metre (no.* m^{-2}*).*

   Woodlouse: [ ] False scorpion: [ ]

   Centipede: [ ] Leaf: [ ]

   Springtail: [ ]

8. (a) In this example the animals are not moving. Describe the problems associated with sampling moving organisms. Explain how you would cope with sampling these same animals if they were really alive and very active:

____

____

____

(b) Carry out a direct count of all four animal species and the leaf litter for the whole sample area (all 36 quadrats). Apply the data from your direct count to the equation given in (7) above to calculate the actual population density (remember that the number of quadrats in this case = 36):

Woodlouse: [ ] Centipede: [ ] False scorpion: [ ] Springtail: [ ] Leaf: [ ]

Compare your estimated population density to the actual population density for each species:

____

____

Ecosystems

Related activities: *Quadrat Sampling*

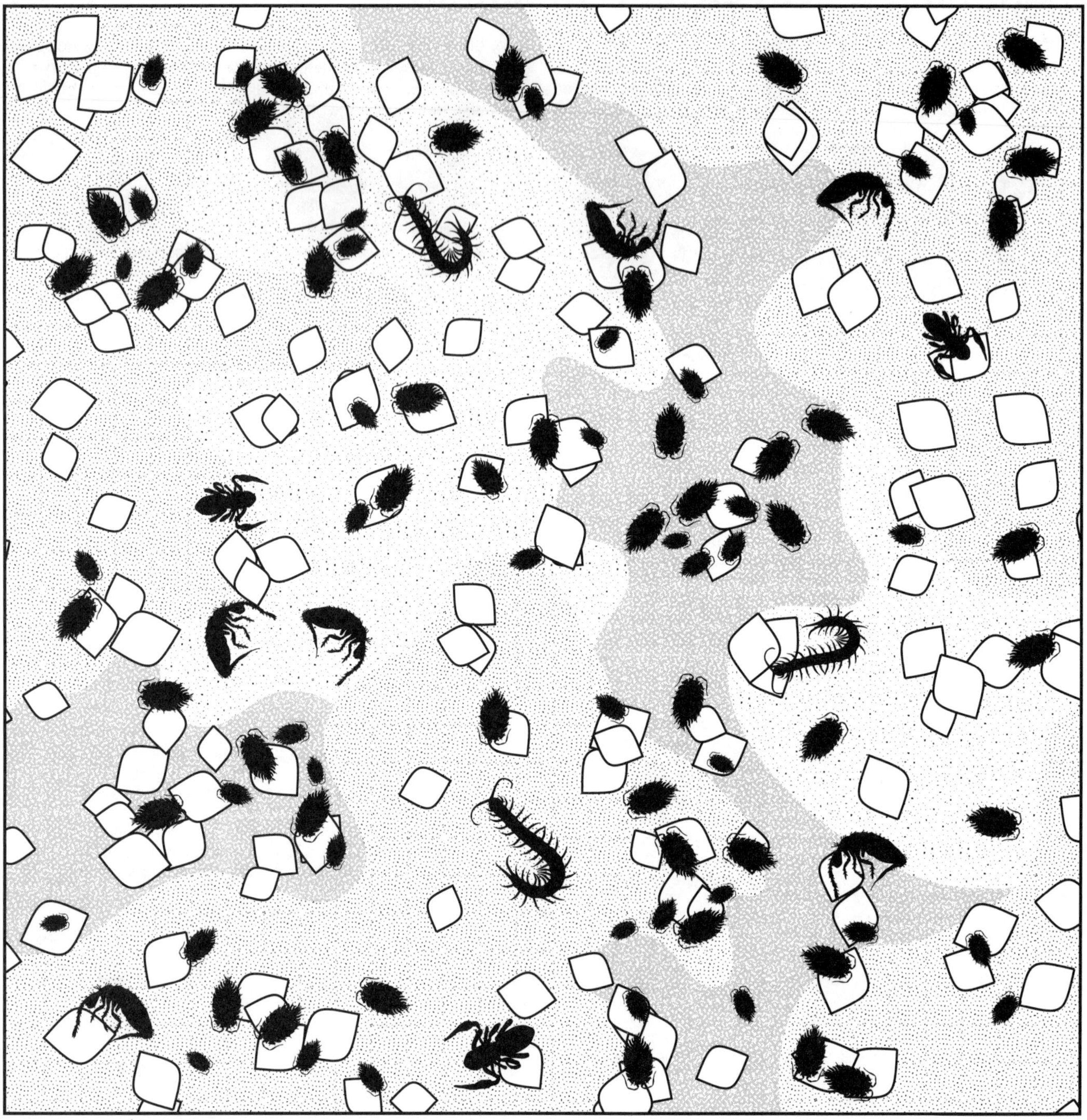

Coordinates for each quadrat	Woodlouse	Centipede	False scorpion	Springtail	Leaf
1:					
2:					
3:					
4:					
5:					
6:					
TOTAL					

Table of random numbers

A	B	C	D
2 2	3 1	6 2	2 2
3 2	1 5	6 3	4 3
3 1	5 6	3 6	6 4
4 6	3 6	1 3	4 5
4 3	4 2	4 5	3 5
5 6	1 4	3 1	1 4

The table above has been adapted from a table of random numbers from a statistics book. Use this table to select quadrats randomly from the grid above. Choose one of the columns (A to D) and use the numbers in that column as an index to the grid. The first digit refers to the row number and the second digit refers to the column number. To locate each of the 6 quadrats, find where the row and column intersect, as shown below:

Example: **5 2** refers to the 5th row and the 2nd column

Transect Sampling

A **transect** is a line placed across a community of organisms. Transects are usually carried out to provide information on the **distribution** of species in the community. This is of particular value in situations where environmental factors change over the sampled distance. This change is called an **environmental gradient** (e.g. up a mountain or across a seashore). The usual practice for small transects is to stretch a string between two markers. The string is marked off in measured distance intervals, and the species at each marked point are noted. The sampling points along the transect may also be used for the siting of quadrats, so that changes in density and community composition can be recorded. Belt transects are essentially a form of continuous quadrat sampling. They provide more information on community composition but can be difficult to carry out. Some transects provide information on the vertical, as well as horizontal, distribution of species (e.g. tree canopies in a forest).

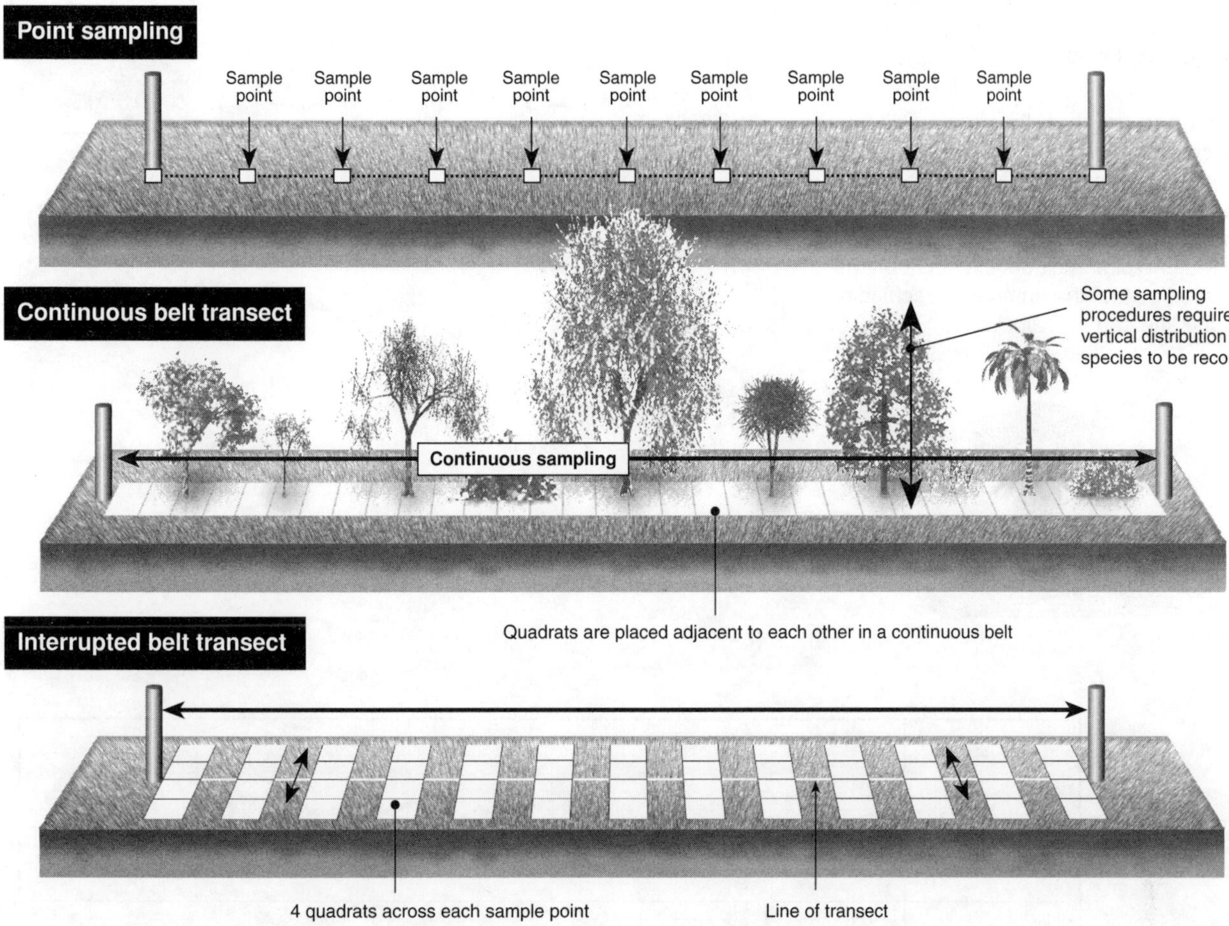

1. Belt transect sampling uses quadrats placed along a line at marked intervals. In contrast, point sampling transects record only the species that are touched or covered by the line at the marked points.

   (a) Describe one disadvantage of belt transects: ____________________

   (b) Explain why line transects may give an unrealistic sample of the community in question: ____________________

   (c) Explain how belt transects overcome this problem: ____________________

   (d) Describe a situation where the use of transects to sample the community would be inappropriate: ____________________

2. Explain how you could test whether or not a transect sampling interval was sufficient to accurately sample a community:

____

Ecosystems

Kite graphs are an ideal way in which to present distributional data from a belt transect (e.g. abundance or percentage cover along an environmental gradient. Usually, they involve plots for more than one species. This makes them good for highlighting probable differences in habitat preference between species. Kite graphs may also be used to show changes in distribution with time (e.g. with daily or seasonal cycles).

3. The data on the right were collected from a rocky shore field trip. Periwinkles from four common species of the genus *Littorina* were sampled in a continuous belt transect from the low water mark, to a height of 10 m above that level. The number of each of the four species in a 1 m^2 quadrat was recorded.

   Plot a **kite graph** of the data for all four species on the grid below. Be sure to choose a scale that takes account of the maximum number found at any one point and allows you to include all the species on the one plot. Include the scale on the diagram so that the number at each point on the kite can be calculated.

Field data notebook

Numbers of periwinkles (4 common species) showing vertical distribution on a rocky shore

Height above low water /m	Periwinkle species: *L. littorea*	*L. saxatalis*	*L. neritoides*	*L. littoralis*
0-1	0	0	0	0
1-2	1	0	0	3
2-3	3	0	0	17
3-4	9	3	0	12
4-5	15	12	0	1
5-6	5	24	0	0
6-7	2	9	2	0
7-8	0	2	11	0
8-9	0	0	47	0
9-10	0	0	59	0

Nutrient Cycles

Nutrient cycling is an important part of every ecosystem. Elements essential for the efficient operation of living systems move through the environment through the processes of uptake and deposition. Commonly, nutrients must be in an ionic (rather than elemental) form in order for plants and animals to have access to them. Some bacteria have the ability to convert elemental forms of nutrients, such as sulfur, into ionic forms and so play an important role in making nutrients available to plants and animals.

Essential Nutrients

Macronutrient	Common form	Function
Carbon (C)	CO_2	Organic molecules
Oxygen (O)	O_2	Respiration
Hydrogen (H)	H_2O	Cellular hydration
Nitrogen (N)	N_2, NO_3^-, NH_4^+	Proteins, nucleic acids
Potassium (K)	K^+	Principal ion in cells
Phosphorus (P)	$H_2PO_4^-$, HPO_4^{2-}	Nucleic acids, lipids
Calcium (Ca)	Ca^{2+}	Membrane permeability
Magnesium (Mg)	Mg^{2+}	Chlorophyll
Sulfur (S)	SO_4^{2-}	Proteins
Micronutrient	**Common form**	**Function**
Iron (Fe)	Fe^{2+}, Fe^{3+}	Chlorophyll, blood
Manganese (Mn)	Mn^{2+}	Enzyme activation
Molybdenum (Mo)	MoO_4^-	Nitrogen metabolism
Copper (Cu)	Cu^{2+}	Enzyme activation
Sodium (Na)	Na^+	Ion in cells
Silicon (Si)	$Si(OH)_4$	Support tissues

Tropical Rainforest

Temperate Woodland

The speed of nutrient cycling can vary markedly. Some nutrients are cycled slowly, others quickly. The environment and diversity of an ecosystem can also have a large effect on the speed at which nutrients are recycled.

The Role of Organisms in Nutrient Cycling

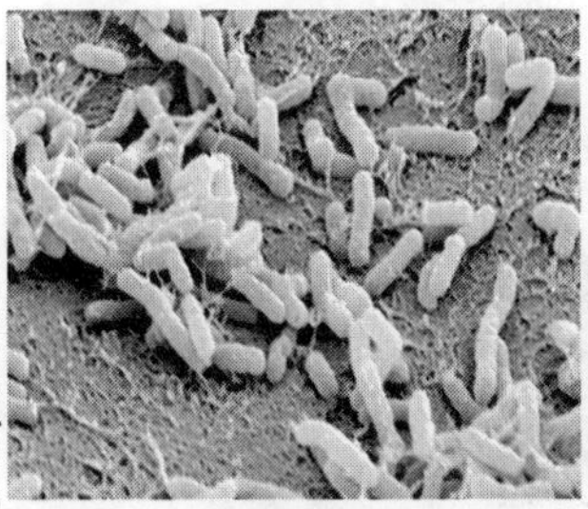

Shirley Owens MSU

Bacteria

Bacteria play an essential role in all nutrient cycles. They have the ability to act as saprophytes, decomposing material, but are also able to convert nutrients from inaccessible to accessible forms.

Fungi

Fungi are saprophytes and play a critical role in decomposing organic material, returning nutrients to the soil or converting them into forms accessible to plants and animals.

Plants

Plants have an important role in absorbing many nutrients from the soil and making them directly available to browsing animals. They also add their own decaying matter to soils.

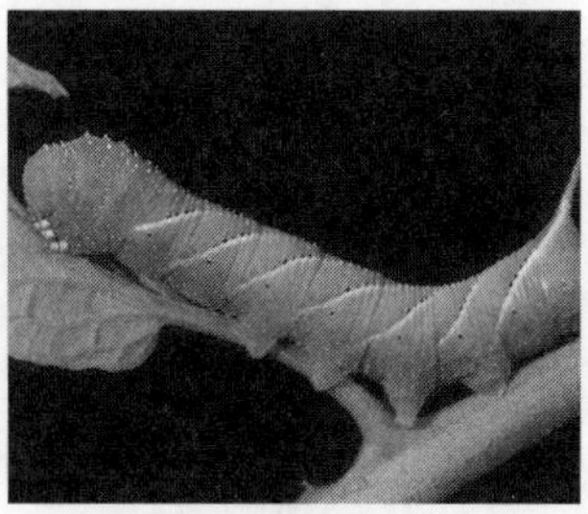

Animals

Animals utilise and break down materials from bacteria, plants and fungi and return the nutrients to soils and water via their wastes and when they die.

1. For each of the following briefly describe the role they play in nutrient cycling:

   (a) Bacteria: ______________________________

   (b) Fungi: ______________________________

   (c) Plants: ______________________________

   (d) Animals: ______________________________

2. Explain why soils in tropical rainforests are nutrient deficient in comparison to temperate woodlands: ______________________________

3. Distinguish between macronutrients and micronutrients: ______________________________

Ecosystems

Periodicals: *Microbes and nutrient cycling*

Related activities: *Energy Inputs and Outputs*

A 1

The Nitrogen Cycle

Nitrogen is a crucial element for all living things, forming an essential part of the structure of proteins and nucleic acids. The Earth's atmosphere is about 80% nitrogen gas (N_2), but molecular nitrogen is so stable that it is only rarely available directly to organisms and is often in short supply in biological systems. Bacteria play an important role in transferring nitrogen between the biotic and abiotic environments. Some bacteria are able to fix atmospheric nitrogen, while others convert ammonia to nitrate and thus make it available for incorporation into plant and animal tissues. Nitrogen-fixing bacteria are found living freely in the soil *(Azotobacter)* and living symbiotically with some plants in root nodules *(Rhizobium)*. Lightning discharges also cause the oxidation of nitrogen gas to nitrate which ends up in the soil. Denitrifying bacteria reverse this activity and return fixed nitrogen to the atmosphere. Humans intervene in the nitrogen cycle by producing, and applying to the land, large amounts of nitrogen fertiliser. Some applied fertiliser is from organic sources (e.g. green crops and manures) but much is inorganic, produced from atmospheric nitrogen using an energy-expensive industrial process. Overuse of nitrogen fertilisers may lead to pollution of water supplies, particularly where land clearance increases the amount of leaching and runoff into ground and surface waters.

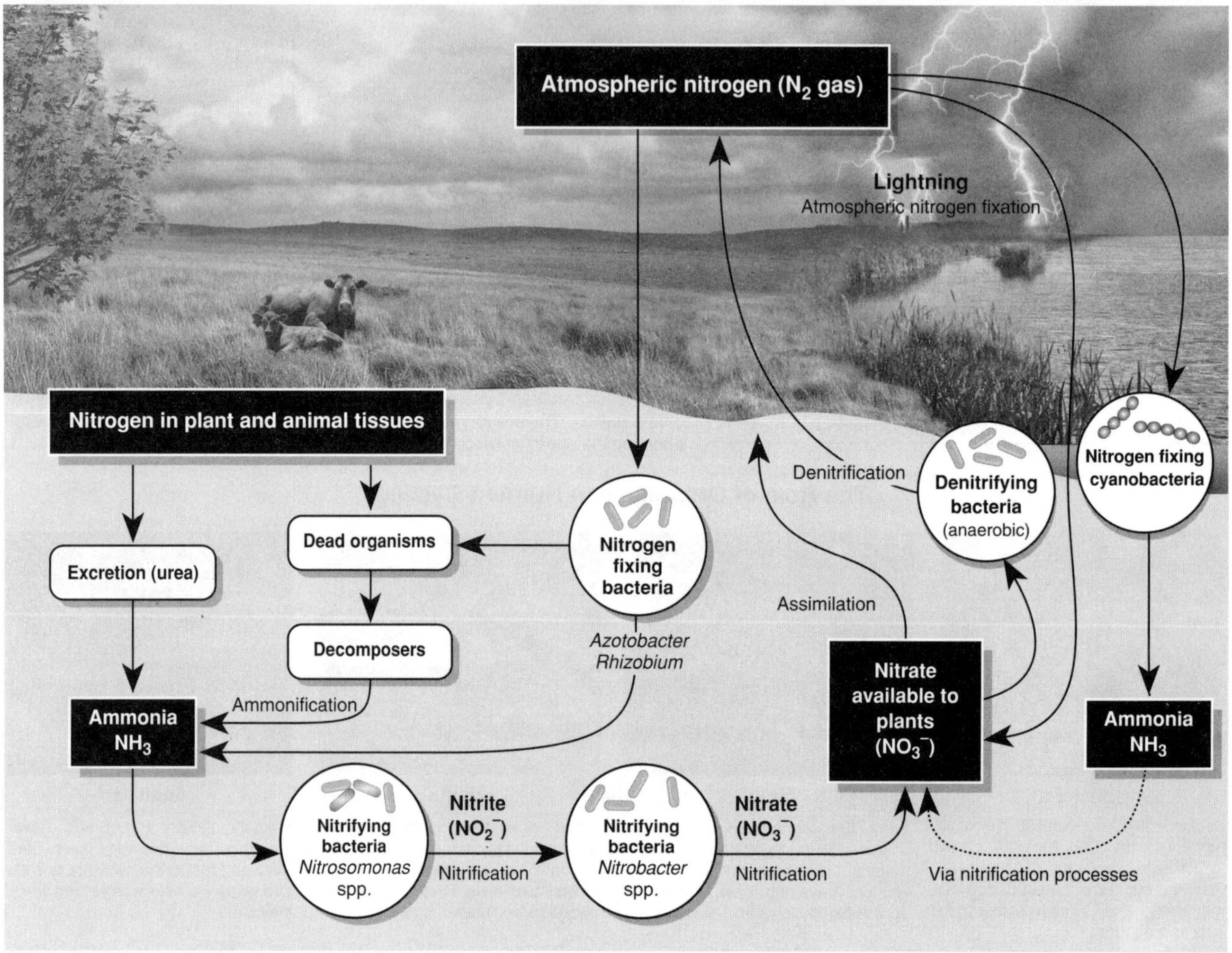

1. Describe five instances in the nitrogen cycle where **bacterial** action is important. Include the name of each of the processes and the changes to the form of nitrogen involved:

   (a) ______________________

   (b) ______________________

   (c) ______________________

   (d) ______________________

   (e) ______________________

2. Identify three processes that **fix** atmospheric nitrogen:

   (a) ____________ (b) ____________ (c) ____________

3. Identify the process that releases nitrogen gas into the atmosphere: ______________________

4. Identify the main geological reservoir that provides a source of nitrogen: ______________________

5. Identify the form in which nitrogen is available to most plants: ______________________

KEY TERMS: Mix and Match

INSTRUCTIONS: Test your vocabulary by matching each term to its definition, as identified by its preceding letter code.

ABIOTIC FACTOR

ABUNDANCE

BELT TRANSECT

BIOTIC FACTOR

CLIMAX COMMUNITY

COMMUNITY

CONSUMER

DECOMPOSER

DENITRIFICATION

DETRITIVORE

DISTRIBUTION

ECOLOGICAL PYRAMID

ECOLOGICAL SUCCESSION

ECOSYSTEM

ENERGY FLOW DIAGRAM

FOOD CHAIN

FOOD WEB

LINE TRANSECT

NITRIFICATION

NITROGEN FIXATION

PRIMARY CONSUMER

PRIMARY SUCCESSION

PRODUCER

QUADRAT

SECONDARY CONSUMER

TEN PERCENT LAW

TROPHIC LEVEL

A An organism that obtains its energy and carbon from the extracellular digestion and absorption of dead or decaying mater.

B A measured and marked region used to isolate a sample area for study.

C A succession sequence that occurs on land that has not had plants or soil in the past (usually bare rock) or on which the preexisting community has been completely obliterated.

D The removal of nitrogen compounds from the soil by bacteria.

E Factors including all living things within an environment, e.g consumers, producers.

F The arrangement or spread of individuals in a population in an area.

G The relative representation of a species within an ecosystem.

H Community of interacting organisms and the environment (both biotic and abiotic) in which they both live and interact.

I A naturally occurring group of different species living within the same environment and interacting together.

J The removal of nitrogen compounds from the soil by bacteria.

K The position an organism occupies on the food chain.

L An organism that obtains its carbon and energy from other organisms.

M A graphical representation of the biomass or productivity at each trophic level in an ecosystem.

N One of the non-living, chemical or physical components of an ecosystem.

O Diagram that shows how energy passes through an ecosystem from its source through the various trophic levels.

P An organism capable of manufacturing its own food.

Q A community that has reached an equilibrium with the environment and no longer appears to be changing in composition.

R The progression from initial colonisation of a newly cleared area to a climax community.

S The rule of thumb governing the maximum amount of energy that typically passes from one trophic level to another.

T A primary carnivore that consumes a primary consumer (herbivore).

U A sequence of steps describing how an organism derives energy from the ones before it.

V A line across a habitat along which organisms are sampled at set intervals to determine changes in community composition.

W A complex series of interactions showing the feeding relationships between organisms in an ecosystem.

X An organism at the second trophic level. A herbivore.

Y A form of continuous quadrat sampling along a line.

Z An organism that obtains energy by ingesting dead material mixed with inorganic material, e.g. earthworm.

AA The reduction of nitrogen gas and its incorporation into nitrogen compounds.

UNIT F215

5.3.2

Populations and Sustainability

KEY CONCEPTS

- Limiting factors determine final population size.
- The carrying capacity (K) is the maximum population size that an environment can sustain indefinitely.
- Natural predator-prey interactions may result in relatively stable cycles of population growth and decline.
- Competition constrains final population size.
- Conservation is an dynamic process.
- Sustainable management provides for the adequate future availability of resources.

KEY TERMS

carrying capacity
community
conservation
density-dependent
density-independent
ecotourism
exponential growth
interspecific competition
intraspecific competition
limiting factor
logistic growth
migration
mortality
natality
niche breadth
population
population density
population distribution
population growth
population size
predator
preservation
prey
reclamation
sustainability

OBJECTIVES

☐ 1. Use the **KEY TERMS** to help you understand and complete these objectives.

Factors affecting populations

pages 279-294

☐ 2. BACKGROUND: Explain the term **population**. Explain what is meant by **population density** and distinguish it from **population size**. Recognise the distribution patterns of organisms: uniform, random, and clumped distributions. Comment on the factors determining each type of distribution.

☐ 3. Recall that populations are dynamic entities and that population size is affected by **natality**, **mortality**, and **migration**. Explain the significance of **limiting factors** in determining population size.

☐ 4. Describe the factors that affect final population size, explaining clearly how they operate and providing examples where necessary. Include reference to:
- **Carrying capacity** of the environment (K).
- **Density dependent factors**, e.g. competition, predation.
- **Density independent factors**, e.g. climatic events.
- Limiting factors, e.g. a soil nutrient, nest sites.

☐ 5. EXTENSION: Describe how changes in population size can be shown in a population growth curve of numbers (Y axis) against time (X axis). Describe **exponential** and sigmoidal (**logistic**) growth. Recognise phases in logistic growth (lag phase, exponential phase, stationary phase) and identify the factors regulating population change at each stage.

☐ 6. Describe **predator-prey** relationships, including the possible effects of the interaction on the population size of both predator and prey populations.

☐ 7. Using examples, distinguish between **interspecific competition** and **intraspecific competition**. Describe the effects of each of these interactions on species distribution, population size, and/or niche breadth.

Conservation and sustainability

pages 295-298

☐ 8. Distinguish between **conservation** and **preservation** and discuss their applications. Describe conservation as a dynamic process involving management and **reclamation** of a resource or ecosystem.

☐ 9. Explain what is meant by **sustainability**, and explain the importance of managing ecosystems for the sustainable provision of resources. Use the example of timber production in a temperate country to illustrate the concept of sustainable ecosystem management.

☐ 10. Discuss the social, ethical, and economic reasons for conservation of biological resources.

☐ 11. Using examples (e.g. **ecotourism**), describe the effects of human activities on the plant and animal populations of the Galápagos Islands.

Periodicals:
Listings for this chapter are on page 342

Weblinks:
www.biozone.co.uk/weblink/OCR-A2-2832.html

Teacher Resource CD-ROM:
Human Demography

Features of Populations

Populations have a number of attributes that may be of interest. Usually, biologists wish to determine **population size** (the total number of organisms in the population). It is also useful to know the **population density** (the number of organisms per unit area). The density of a population is often a reflection of the **carrying capacity** of the environment, i.e. how many organisms a particular environment can support. Populations also have structure; particular ratios of different ages and sexes. These data enable us to determine whether the population is declining or increasing in size. We can also look at the **distribution** of organisms within their environment and so determine what particular aspects of the habitat are favoured over others. One way to retrieve information from populations is to **sample** them. Sampling involves collecting data about features of the population from samples of that population (since populations are usually too large to examine in total). Sampling can be done directly through a number of sampling methods or indirectly (e.g. monitoring calls, looking for droppings or other signs). Some of the population attributes that we can measure or calculate are illustrated on the diagram below.

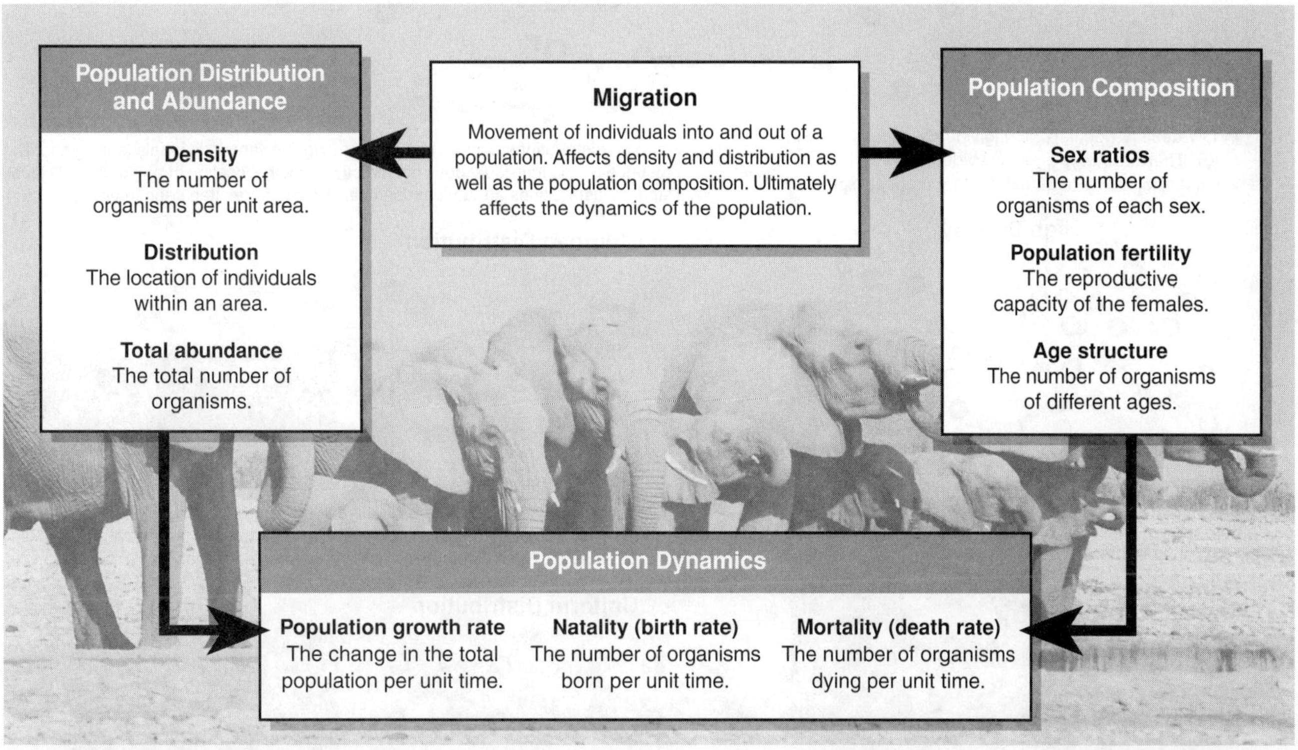

1. Describe one example of a population attribute that would be a good indicator of each of the following:

(a) Whether the population is increasing or decreasing: ______________________________

____

(b) The ability of the environment to support the population: ______________________________

____

2. (a) Identify the population attributes that can be measured directly from the population: ______________

____

(b) Identify the population attributes that must be calculated from the data collected: ______________

____

3. Describe the value of population sampling for each of the following situations:

(a) Conservation of a population of an endangered species: ______________________________

____

____

(b) Management of a fisheries resource: ______________________________

____

____

____

Populations and Sustainability

Related activities: *Density and Distribution*

Density and Distribution

Distribution and density are two interrelated properties of populations. Population density is the number of individuals per unit area (for land organisms) or volume (for aquatic organisms). Careful observation and precise mapping can determine the distribution patterns for a species. The three basic distribution patterns are: random, clumped and uniform. In the diagram below, the circles represent individuals of the same species. It can also represent populations of different species.

Low Density

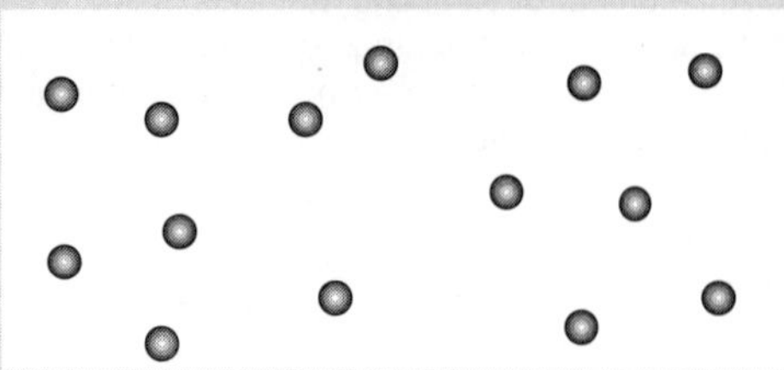

In low density populations, individuals are spaced well apart. There are only a few individuals per unit area or volume (e.g. highly territorial, solitary mammal species).

High Density

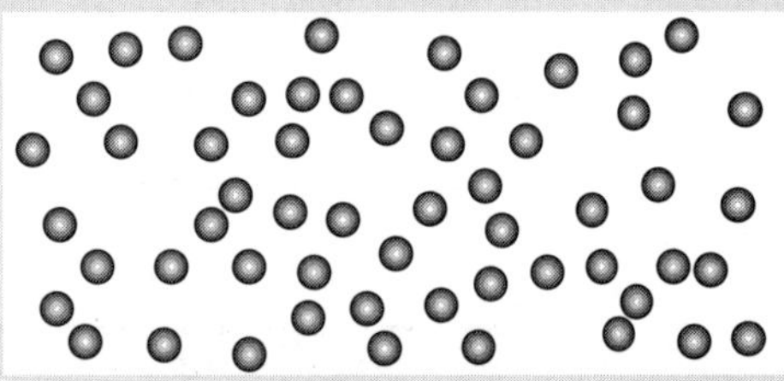

In high density populations, individuals are crowded together. There are many individuals per unit area or volume (e.g. colonial organisms, such as many corals).

Tigers are solitary animals, found at low densities.

Termites form well organised, high density colonies.

Random Distribution

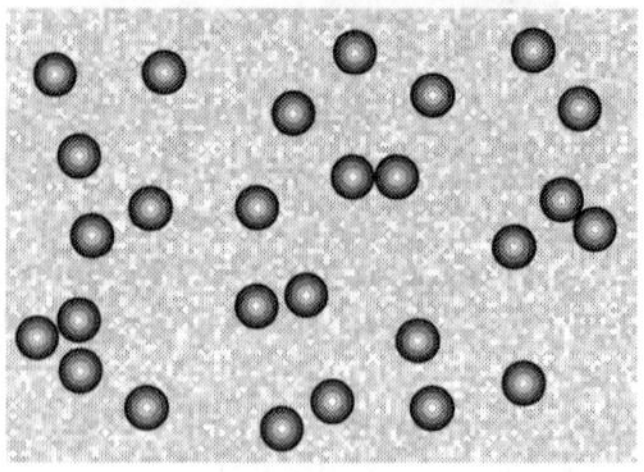

Random distributions occur when the spacing between individuals is irregular. The presence of one individual does not directly affect the location of any other individual. Random distributions are uncommon in animals but are often seen in plants.

Clumped Distribution

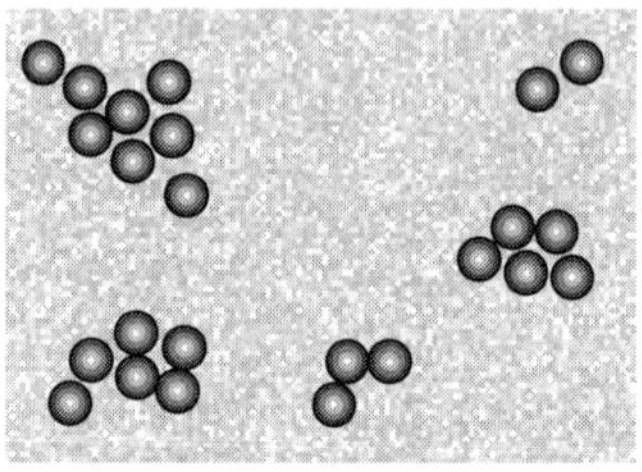

Clumped distributions occur when individuals are grouped in patches (sometimes around a resource). The presence of one individual increases the probability of finding another close by. Such distributions occur in herding and highly social species.

Uniform Distribution

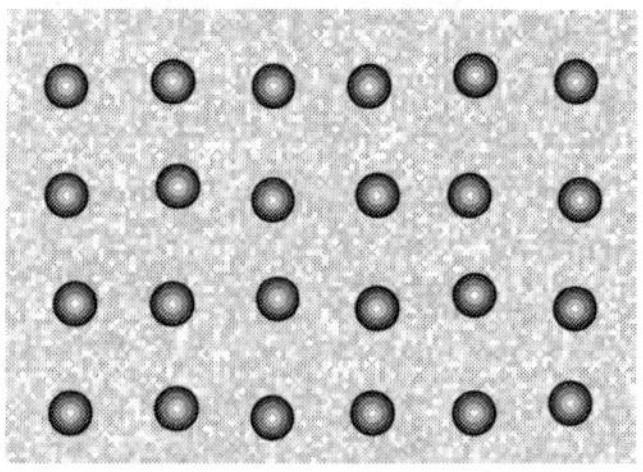

Regular distribution patterns occur when individuals are evenly spaced within the area. The presence of one individual decreases the probability of finding another individual very close by. The penguins illustrated above are also at a high density.

1. Explain why some organisms may exhibit a clumped distribution pattern because of:

   (a) Resources in the environment: ______________________________

   ____

   (b) A group social behaviour: ______________________________

   ____

2. Describe a social behaviour found in some animals that may encourage a uniform distribution: ______________________________

   ____

3. Describe the type of environment that would encourage uniform distribution: ______________________________

   ____

4. Describe an example of each of the following types of distribution pattern:

   (a) Clumped: ______________________________

   (b) Random (more or less): ______________________________

   (c) Uniform (more or less): ______________________________

Population Regulation

Very few species show continued exponential growth. Population size is regulated by factors that limit population growth. The diagram below illustrates how population size can be regulated by environmental factors. **Density independent factors** may affect all individuals in a population equally. Some, however, may be better able to adjust to them. **Density dependent factors** have a greater affect when the population density is higher. They become less important when the population density is low.

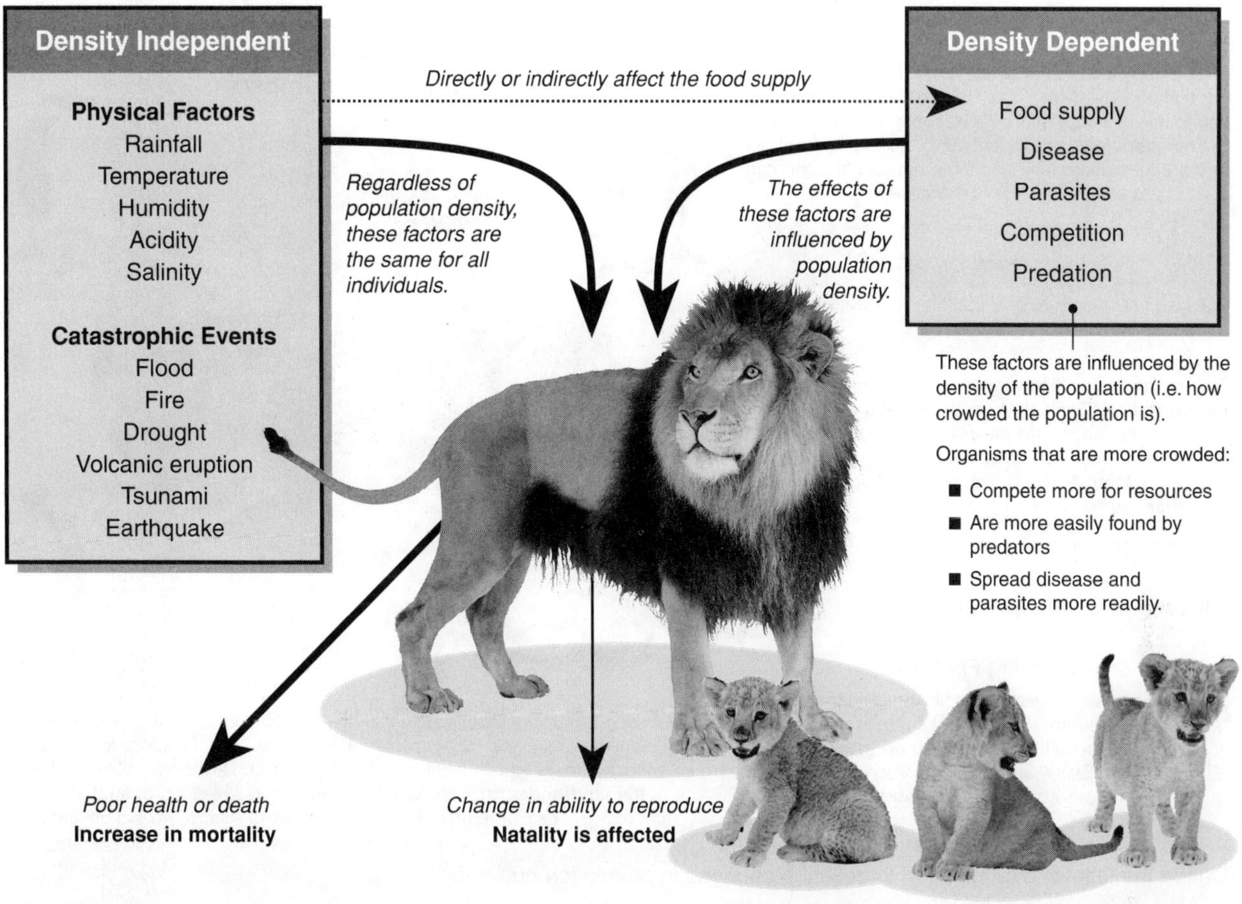

1. Discuss the role of **density dependent factors** and **density independent factors** in population regulation. In your discussion, make it clear that you understand the meaning of each of these terms:

2. Explain how an increase in population density allows disease to have a greater influence in regulating population size:

3. In cooler climates, aphids go through a huge population increase during the summer months. In autumn, population numbers decline steeply. Describe a density dependent and a density independent factor regulating the population:

   (a) Density dependent:

   (b) Density independent:

Population Growth

Organisms do not generally live alone. A **population** is a group of organisms of the same species living together in one geographical area. This area may be difficult to define as populations may comprise widely dispersed individuals that come together only infrequently (e.g. for mating). The number of individuals comprising a population may also fluctuate considerably over time. These changes make populations dynamic: populations gain individuals through births or immigration, and lose individuals through deaths and emigration. For a population in **equilibrium**, these factors balance out and there is no net change in the population abundance. When losses exceed gains, the population declines.

Births, deaths, immigrations (movements into the population) and emigrations (movements out of the population) are events that determine the numbers of individuals in a population. Population growth depends on the number of individuals added to the population from births and immigration, minus the number lost through deaths and emigration. This is expressed as:

Population growth =

Births – Deaths + Immigration – Emigration
(B) (D) (I) (E)

The difference between immigration and emigration gives **net migration**. Ecologists usually measure the **rate** of these events. These rates are influenced by environmental factors (see below) and by the characteristics of the organisms themselves. Rates in population studies are commonly expressed in one of two ways:

- Numbers per unit time, e.g. 20 150 live births per year.
- Per capita rate (number per head of population), e.g. 122 live births per 1000 individuals per year (12.2%).

Limiting Factors

Population size is also affected by **limiting factors**; factors or resources that control a process such as organism growth, or population growth or distribution. Examples include availability of food, predation pressure, or available habitat.

Calculating change in population numbers

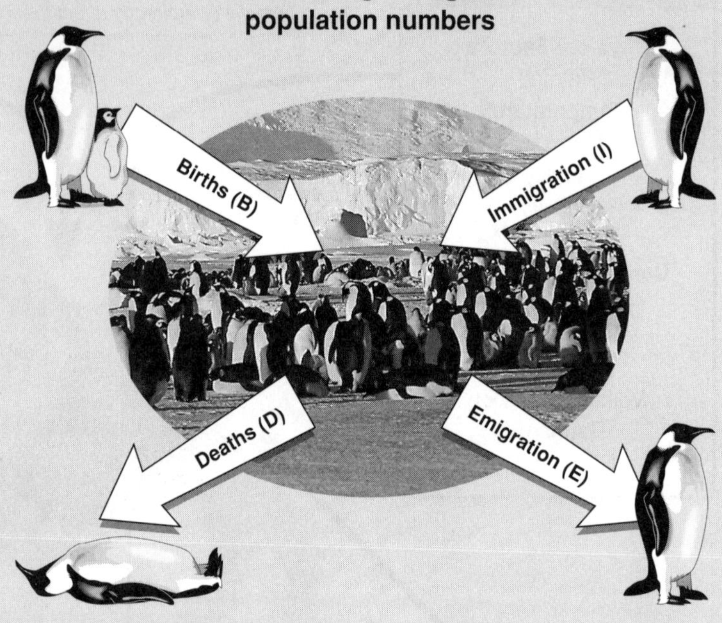

What might be the limiting factors for this penguin population? The breeding colony may be close enough to ocean food supplies sufficient to feed 1000 birds, but there may be nest sites for only 500. The availability of nest sites is the **limiting factor**. This is not uncommon in species that feed at sea but occupy nests or territories in specific areas of suitable habitat on shore.

1. Define the following terms used to describe changes in population numbers:

   (a) Death rate (mortality): ____________________

   (b) Birth rate (natality): ____________________

   (c) Net migration rate: ____________________

2. Explain how the concept of limiting factors applies to population biology: ____________________

3. Using the terms, B, D, I, and E (above), construct equations to express the following (the first is completed for you):

   (a) A population in equilibrium: B + I = D + E

   (b) A declining population: ____________________

   (c) An increasing population: ____________________

4. A population started with a total number of 100 individuals. Over the following year, population data were collected. Calculate birth rates, death rates, net migration rate, and rate of population change for the data below (as percentages):

   (a) Births = 14: Birth rate = __________ (b) Net migration = +2: Net migration rate = __________

   (c) Deaths = 20: Death rate = __________ (d) Rate of population change = __________

   (e) State whether the population is increasing or declining: __________

5. The human population is around 6.5 billion. Describe and explain two limiting factors for population growth in humans:

Population Growth Curves

Populations becoming established in a new area for the first time are often termed **colonising populations** (below, left). They may undergo a rapid **exponential** (logarithmic) increase in numbers as there are plenty of resources to allow a high birth rate, while the death rate is often low. Exponential growth produces a J-shaped growth curve that rises steeply as more and more individuals contribute to the population increase. If the resources of the new habitat were endless (inexhaustible) then the population would continue to increase at an **exponential** rate. However, this rarely happens in natural populations. Initially, growth may be exponential (or nearly so), but as the population grows, its increase will slow and it will stabilise at a level that can be supported by the environment (called the **carrying capacity** or **K**). This type of growth is called sigmoidal and produces the **logistic growth curve** (below, right). **Established populations** will fluctuate about K, often in a regular way (shaded area on the graph below, right). Some species will have populations that vary little from this stable condition, while others may oscillate wildly.

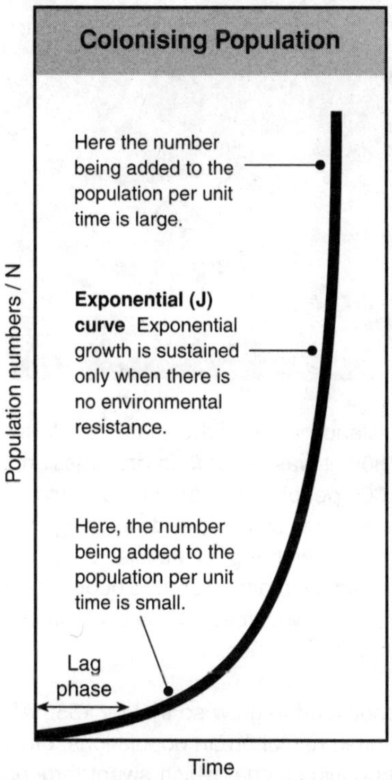

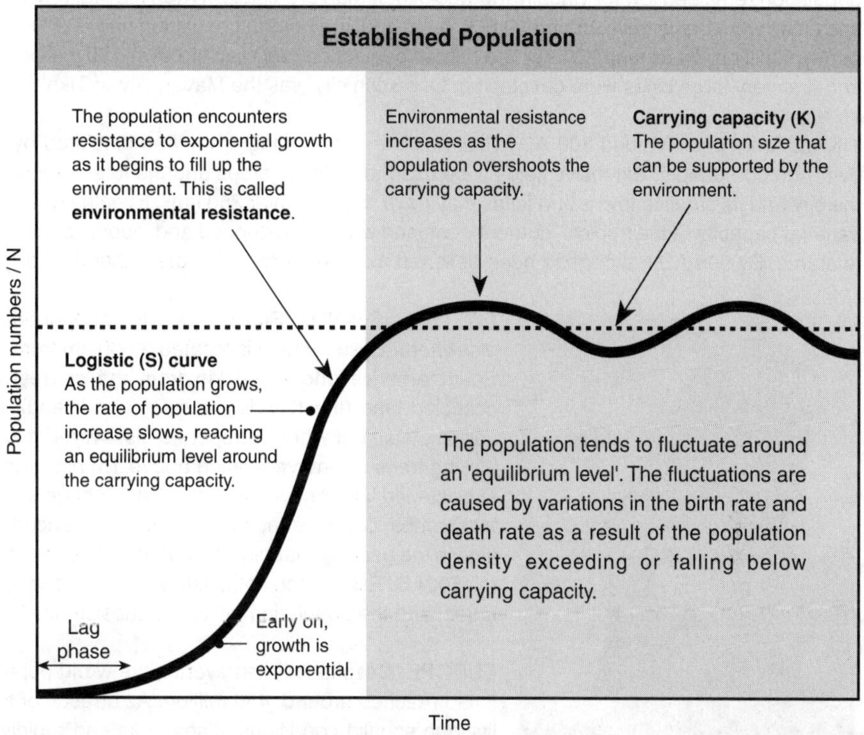

1. Explain why populations tend not to continue to increase exponentially in an environment: ______

2. Explain what is meant by environmental resistance: ______

3. (a) Explain what is meant by carrying capacity: ______

   (b) Explain the link between **carrying capacity** and **limiting factors**: ______

4. Species that expand into a new area, such as rabbits when originally introduced to Britain, typically show a period of rapid population growth followed by a slowing of population growth as density dependent factors become more important and the population settles around a level that can be supported by the carrying capacity of the environment.

   (a) Explain why a newly introduced consumer (e.g. rabbit) might initially exhibit a period of exponential population growth:

   ______

   (b) Describe a likely outcome for a rabbit population after the initial rapid increase had slowed: ______

5. Describe the effect that high rabbit numbers have had on the appearance and carrying capacity of British open lands:

______

Populations and Sustainability

The Rise and Fall of Human Populations

Human populations are subject to rises and collapses in the same way as natural animal populations. Throughout history there have been a number of peaks of human civilisation followed by collapse. These collapses have been triggered by various events but can generally be attributed either to the spread of disease or to the collapse of a food source (normally agriculture). Examples can be traced right back to the origins of humans.

Mitochondrial DNA analyses show that the human population may have been on the brink of extinction with only around 10,000 individuals alive 150,000 years ago. The population remained low for virtually the whole of human prehistory. When the first towns and cities were being built, around 10,000 years ago, the human population had reached barely 5 million. By around 700 AD, the human population had reached over 150 million, and first very large cities were developing. One such city was the Mayan city of Tikal.

TIKAL: At its peak around 800 AD, Tikal and the surrounding area, was inhabited by over 400,000 people. Extensive fields were used to cultivate crops and the total area of the city and its satellite towns and fields may have reached over 250 km^2. Eventually the carrying capacity of the tropical, nutrient-poor land was overextended and people began to starve. By 900 AD the city had been deserted and the surrounding area abandoned.

EASTER ISLAND: Similar events happened elsewhere. Easter Island is located 3,000 km from South America and 2,000 km from the nearest occupied land (the tiny, isolated Pitcairn Island). Easter Island has a mild climate and fertile volcanic soil, but when Europeans discovered it in the 1700s, it was covered in dry grassland, lacking trees or any vegetation above 1m high. Around 2,000 people survived on the island by subsistence farming, yet all around stood huge stone statues, some 30 m tall and weighing over 200 tonnes. Clearly a much larger more advanced society had been living on the island at some time in the past. Archaeological studies have found that populations reached 20,000 people prior to 1500AD. Exhaustion of the island's resources by the population was followed by war and civil unrest and the population fell to the subsistence levels found in the 1700s.

EUROPE: Despite isolated events, the world population continued to grow so that by 1350 AD it had reached around 450 million. As a result of the continued rise of urban populations, often living in squalid conditions, disease spread rapidly. The bubonic plague, which swept through Europe at this time, reduced its population almost by half, and reduced the world's population to 350 million. Despite further outbreaks of plague and the huge death tolls of various wars, the human population had reached 2.5 billion by 1950. By 1990 it was 5 billion and today it is around 6.5 billion. In slightly less than 60 years the human population has grown almost twice as much as it did in the whole of human history up until 1950. Much of this growth can be attributed to major advances in agriculture and medicine. However, signs are appearing that the human population are approaching maximum sustainable levels. Annual crop yields have ceased increasing and many common illnesses are becoming more difficult to treat. The rapid spread of modern pandemics, such as H1N1 swine flu, illustrates the vulnerability of modern human populations. Could it be, perhaps, that another great reduction in the human population is imminent?

1. Describe the general trend of human population growth over the last 100,000 years: ______________________

____

2. Explain why the human population has grown at such a increased rate in the last 60 years: ______________________

____

____

3. Discuss similarities between the events at Tikal and on the Easter Islands and how they can help us plan for the future:

____

____

____

____

____

Species Interactions

No organism exists in isolation. Each takes part in many interactions, both with other organisms and with the non-living components of the environment. Species interactions may involve only occasional or indirect contact (predation or competition) or they may involve close association or **symbiosis**. Symbiosis is a term that encompasses a variety of interactions involving close species contact. There are three types of symbiosis: **parasitism** (a form of exploitation), **mutualism**, and **commensalism**. Species interactions affect population densities and are important in determining community structure and composition. Some interactions, such as allelopathy, may even determine species presence or absence in an area.

Examples of Species Interactions

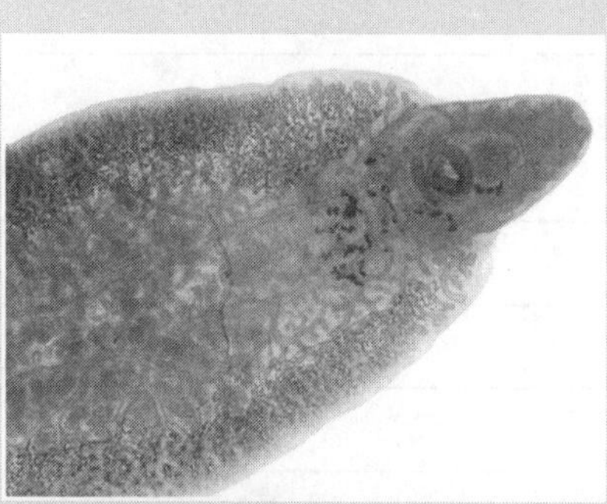

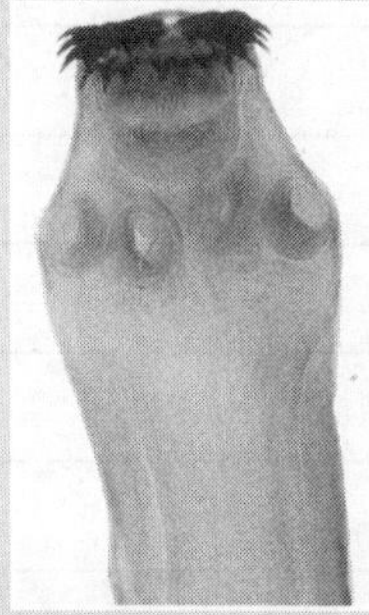

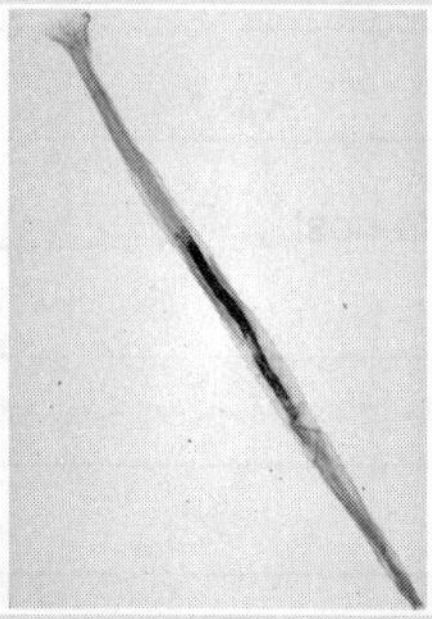

Parasitism is a common exploitative relationship in plants and animals. A parasite exploits the resources of its host (e.g. for food, shelter, warmth) to its own benefit. The host is harmed, but usually not killed. **Endoparasites**, such as liver flukes (left), tapeworms (centre) and nematodes (right)), are highly specialised to live inside their hosts, attached by hooks or suckers to the host's tissues.

Ectoparasites, such as ticks (above), mites, and fleas, live attached to the outside of the host, where they suck body fluids, cause irritation, and may act as vectors for disease causing microorganisms.

Mutualism involves an intimate association between two species that offers advantage to both. **Lichens** (above) are the result of a mutualism between a fungus and an alga (or cyanobacterium).

Termites have a mutualistic relationship with the cellulose digesting bacteria in their guts. A similar mutualistic relationship exists between ruminants and their gut microflora of bacteria and ciliates.

In **commensal** relationships, such as between this large grouper and a remora, two species form an association where one organism, the commensal, benefits and the other is neither harmed or helped.

Many species of decapod crustaceans, such as this anemone shrimp, are commensal with sea anemones. The shrimp gains by being protected from predators by the anemone's tentacles.

Interactions involving **competition** for the same food resources are dominated by the largest, most aggressive species. Here, hyaenas compete for a carcass with vultures and maribou storks.

Predation is an easily identified relationship, as one species kills and eats another (above). Herbivory is similar type of exploitation, except that the plant is usually not killed by the herbivore.

1. Discuss each of the following interspecific relationships, including reference to the species involved, their role in the interaction, and the specific characteristics of the relationship:

   (a) **Mutualism** between ruminant herbivores and their gut microflora: ______________________

   ____

   ____

   ____

   ____

(b) **Commensalism** between a shark and a remora: ____________________

____

____

____

(c) **Parasitism** between a tapeworm and its human host: ____________________

____

____

____

(d) **Parasitism** between a cat flea and its host: ____________________

____

____

____

2. Summarise your knowledge of species interactions by completing the following, entering a (+), (–), or (0) for species B, and writing a brief description of each term. Codes: (+): species benefits, (–): species is harmed, (0): species is unaffected.

Interaction	Species		Description of relationship
	A	B	
(a) Mutualism	+		
(b) Commensalism	+		
(c) Parasitism	–		
(d) Amensalism	0		
(e) Predation	–		
(f) Competition	–		
(g) Herbivory	+		
(h) Antibiosis	+ / 0		

3. For each of the interactions between two species described below, choose the correct term to describe the interaction and assign a +, – or 0 for each species involved in the space supplied. Use the completed table above to help you:

Description	Term	Species A	Species B
(a) A tiny cleaner fish picking decaying food from the teeth of a much larger fish (e.g. grouper).	Mutualism	Cleaner fish +	Grouper +
(b) Ringworm fungus growing on the skin of a young child.		Ringworm	Child
(c) Human effluent containing poisonous substances killing fish in a river downstream of discharge.		Humans	Fish
(d) Humans planting cabbages to eat only to find that the cabbages are being eaten by slugs.		Humans	Slugs
(e) A shrimp that gets food scraps and protection from sea anemones, which appear to be unaffected.		Shrimp	Anemone
(f) Birds follow a herd of antelopes to feed off disturbed insects, antelopes alerted to danger by the birds.		Birds	Antelope

Intraspecific Competition

Some of the most intense competition occurs between individuals of the same species (**intraspecific competition**). Most populations have the capacity to grow rapidly, but their numbers cannot increase indefinitely because environmental resources are finite. Every ecosystem has a **carrying capacity** (K), defined as the number of individuals in a population that the environment can support. Intraspecific competition for resources increases with increasing population size and, at carrying capacity, it reduces the per capita growth rate to zero. When the demand for a particular resource (e.g. food, water, nesting sites, nutrients, or light) exceeds supply, that resource becomes a **limiting factor**. Populations respond to resource limitation by reducing their population growth rate (e.g. through lower birth rates or higher mortality). The response of individuals to limited resources varies depending on the organism. In many invertebrates and some vertebrates such as frogs, individuals reduce their growth rate and mature at a smaller size. In some vertebrates, territoriality spaces individuals apart so that only those with adequate resources can breed. When resources are very limited, the number of available territories will decline.

Intraspecific Competition

Scramble competition in caterpillars

Direct competition for available food between members of the same species is called **scramble competition**. In some situations where scramble competition is intense, none of the competitors gets enough food to survive.

Contest competition in wolves

In some cases, competition is limited by hierarchies existing within a social group. Dominant individuals receive adequate food, but individuals low in the hierarchy must **contest** the remaining resources and may miss out.

Display of a male anole

Intraspecific competition may be for mates or breeding sites, as well as for food. In anole lizards (above), males have a bright red throat pouch and use much of their energy displaying to compete with other males for available mates.

Competition Between Tadpoles of *Rana tigrina*

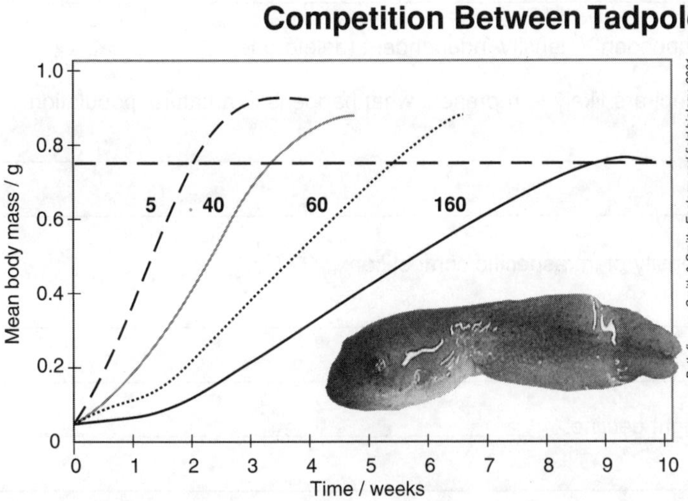

Both figures: Smith & Smith: Ecology and field biology, 2001

Food shortage reduces both individual growth rate and survival, and population growth. In some organisms, where there is a metamorphosis or a series of moults before adulthood (e.g. frogs, crustacean zooplankton, and butterflies), individuals may die before they mature.

The graph (left) shows how the growth rate of tadpoles (*Rana tigrina*) declines as the density increases from 5 to 160 individuals (in the same sized space).

- At high densities, tadpoles grow more slowly, taking longer to reach the minimum size for metamorphosis (0.75 g), and decreasing their chances of successfully metamorphosing from tadpoles into frogs.
- Tadpoles held at lower densities grow faster, to a larger size, metamorphosing at an average size of 0.889 g.
- In some species, such as frogs and butterflies, the adults and juveniles reduce the intensity of intraspecific competition by exploiting different food resources.

1. Using an example, predict the likely effects of **intraspecific competition** on each of the following:

 (a) Individual growth rate: ______________________________

 ____

 ____

 (b) Population growth rate: ______________________________

 ____

 ____

 (c) Final population size: ______________________________

 ____

 ____

Golden eagle breeding territories in Northern Scotland, 1967

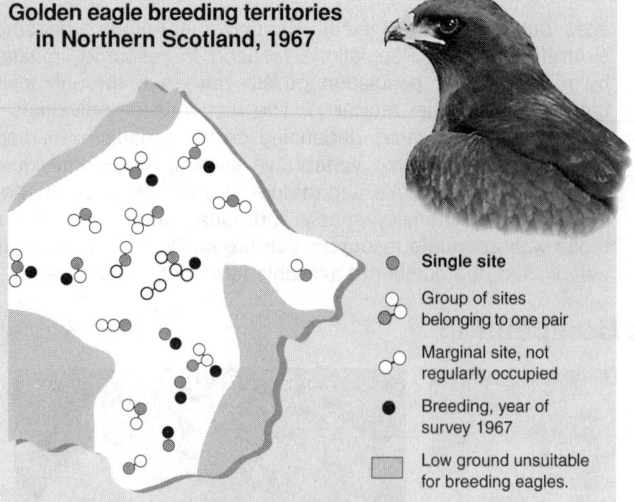

Territoriality in birds and other animals is usually a result of intraspecific competition. It frequently produces a pattern of uniform distribution over an area of suitable habitat, although this depends somewhat on the distribution of resources. The diagram above shows the territories of golden eagles (*Aquila chrysaetos*) in Scotland. Note the relatively uniform distribution of the breeding sites.

Territoriality in Great Tits (*Parus major*)

Six breeding pairs of great tits were removed from an oak woodland (below). Within three days, four new pairs had moved into the unoccupied areas (below, right) and some residents had expanded their territories. The new birds moved in from territories in hedgerows, considered to be suboptimal habitat. This type of territorial behaviour limits the density of breeding animals in areas of optimal habitat.

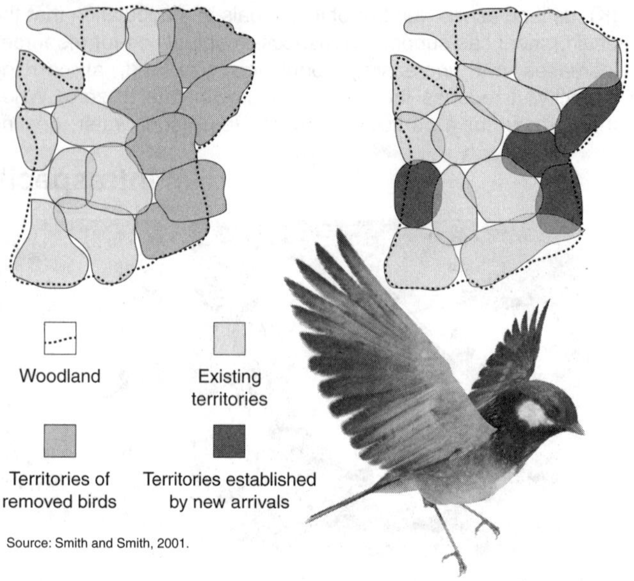

Source: Smith and Smith, 2001.

2. In the tank experiment with *Rana* (see previous page), the tadpoles were contained in a fixed volume with a set amount of food:

   (a) Describe how *Rana* tadpoles respond to resource limitation: ______________________

   ____

   (b) Categorise the effect on the tadpoles as density-dependent / density-independent (delete one).

   (c) Comment on how much the results of this experiment are likely to represent what happens in a natural population:

   ____

   ____

3. Identify two ways in which animals can reduce the intensity of intraspecific competition:

   (a) ______________________

   (b) ______________________

4. (a) Suggest why carrying capacity of an ecosystem might decline: ______________________

   ____

   (b) Predict how a decline in carrying capacity might affect final population size: ______________________

   ____

   ____

5. Using appropriate examples, discuss the role of territoriality in reducing intraspecific competition:

   ____

   ____

   ____

   ____

   ____

   ____

Interspecific Competition

In naturally occurring populations, direct competition between different species (**interspecific competition**) is usually less intense than intraspecific competition because coexisting species have evolved slight differences in their realised niches, even though their fundamental niches may overlap (a phenomenon termed **niche differentiation**). However, when two species with very similar niche requirements are brought into direct competition through the introduction of a foreign species, one usually benefits at the expense of the other. The inability of two species with the same described niche to coexist is referred to as the **competitive exclusion principle**. In Britain, introduction of the larger, more aggressive, grey squirrel in 1876 has contributed to a contraction in range of the native red squirrel (below), and on the Scottish coast, this phenomenon has been well documented in barnacle species (see next page). The introduction of ecologically aggressive species is often implicated in the displacement or decline of native species, although there may be more than one contributing factor. Displacement of native species by introduced ones is more likely if the introduced competitor is also adaptable and hardy. It can be difficult to provide evidence of decline in a species as a direct result of competition, but it is often inferred if the range of the native species contracts and that of the introduced competitor shows a corresponding increase.

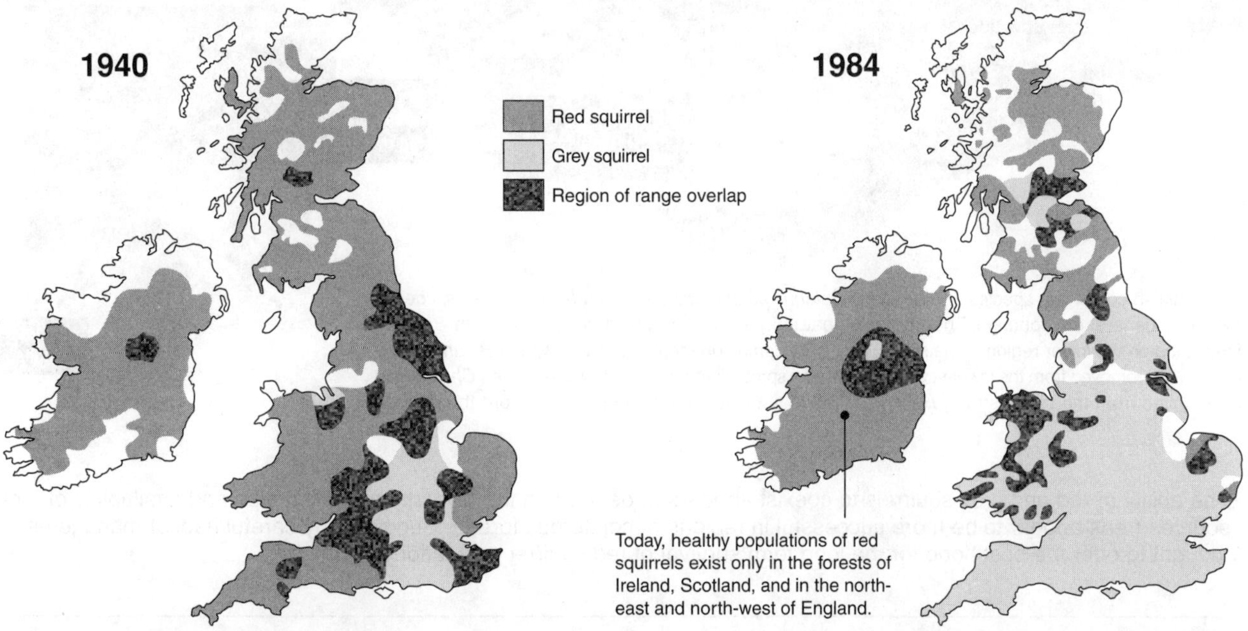

The **European red squirrel**, *Sciurus vulgaris*, was the only squirrel species in Britain until the introduction of the **American grey squirrel**, *Sciurus carolinesis*, in 1876. In 44 years since the 1940 distribution survey (above left), the more adaptable grey squirrel has displaced populations of the native red squirrels over much of the British Isles, particularly in the south (above right). Whereas the red squirrels once occupied both coniferous and broad leafed woodland, they are now almost solely restricted to coniferous forest and are completely absent from much of their former range.

1. Outline the evidence to support the view that the red-grey squirrel distributions in Britain are an example of the competitive exclusion principle:

2. Some biologists believe that competition with grey squirrels is only one of the factors contributing to the decline in the red squirrels in Britain. Explain the evidence from the 1984 distribution map that might support this view:

Competitive Exclusion in Barnacles

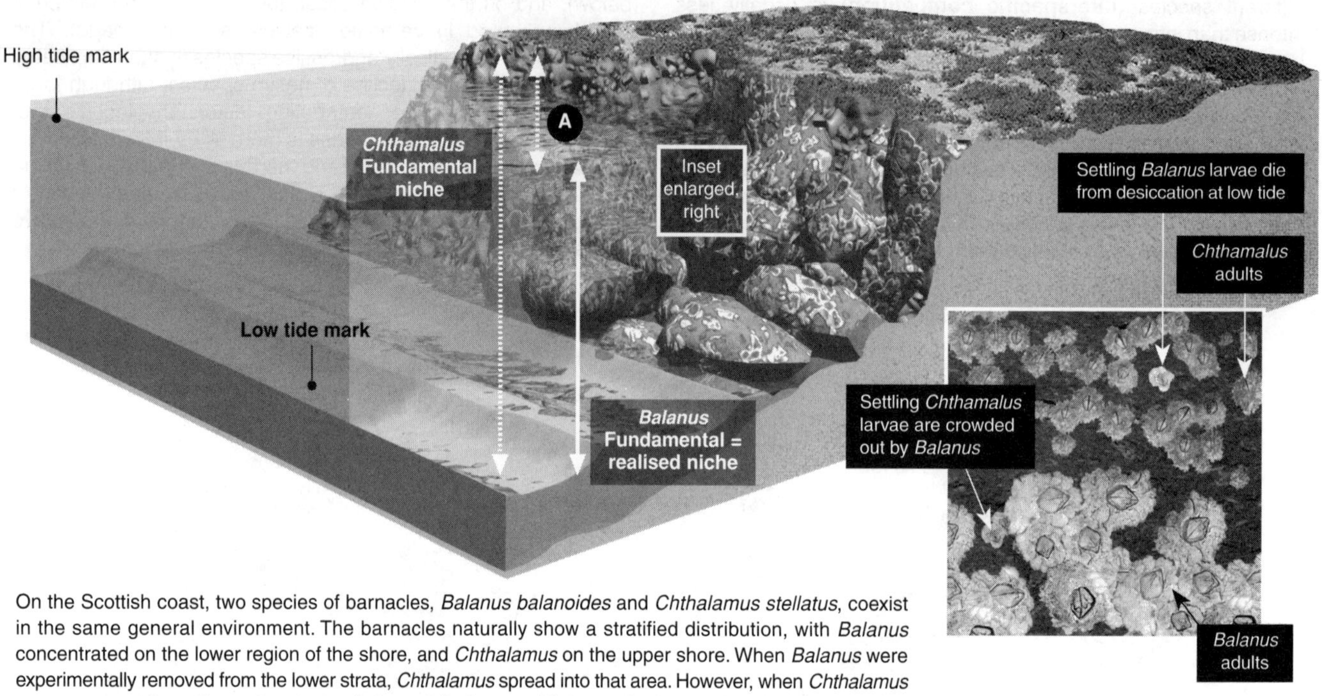

On the Scottish coast, two species of barnacles, *Balanus balanoides* and *Chthalamus stellatus*, coexist in the same general environment. The barnacles naturally show a stratified distribution, with *Balanus* concentrated on the lower region of the shore, and *Chthalamus* on the upper shore. When *Balanus* were experimentally removed from the lower strata, *Chthalamus* spread into that area. However, when *Chthalamus* were removed from the upper strata, *Balanus* failed to establish any further up the shore than usual.

3. The ability of red and grey squirrels to coexist appears to depend on the diversity of habitat type and availability of food sources (reds appear to be more successful in regions of coniferous forest). Suggest why careful habitat management is thought to offer the best hope for the long term survival of red squirrel populations in Britain:

4. Suggest other conservation methods that might aid the survival of viable red squirrel populations:

5. (a) In the example of the barnacles (above), describe what is represented by the zone labelled with the arrow **A**:

   (b) Outline the evidence for the barnacle distribution being the result of competitive exclusion:

6. Describe two aspects of the biology of a named introduced species that have helped its success as an invading competitor:

   Species:

   (a)

   (b)

Niche Differentiation

Interspecific competition is less intense than **intraspecific** competition due to **niche differentiation**. Species with similar needs may reduce competition by exploiting the same region through **microhabitats** or by exploiting the resource at different times of the day or year from other species. In this way they avoid the competition exclusion principle which states *"When different species compete for the same resources in the habitat, one eventually prevails and displaces the other"*.

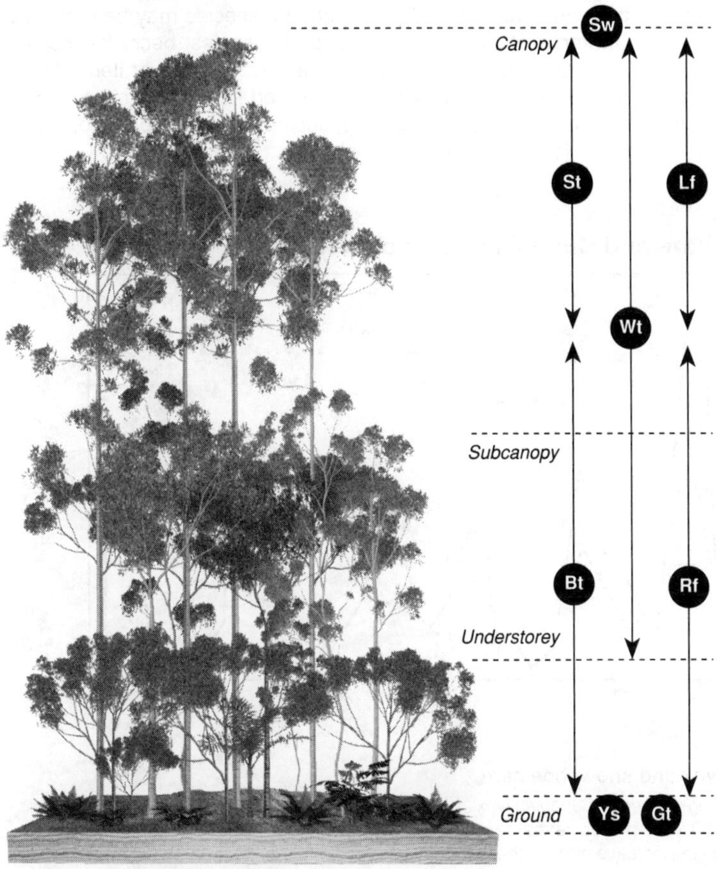

Reducing competition in a eucalypt forest

The diagram on the left shows the foraging heights of birds in an eastern Australian eucalypt forest. A wide variety of food resources are offered by the structure of the forest. Different layers of the forest allow birds to specialise in foraging at different heights. The ground-dwelling yellow-throated scrubwren and ground thrush have robust legs and feet, while the white-throated treecreeper has long toes and large curved claws and the swifts are extremely agile fliers capable of catching insects on the wing.

Key to bird species

Ys Yellow-throated scrubwren	Lf Leaden flycatcher
Bt Brown thornbill	Gt Ground thrush
Sw Spine-tailed swift	Rf Rufous fantail
St Striated thornbill	Wt White-throated treecreeper

Adapted from: Recher *et al.*, 1986. *A Natural Legacy: Ecology in Australia.* Maxwell Macmillan Publishing Australia.

Distribution of ecologically similar fish

The diagram below shows the distribution of ecologically similar damsel fish over a coral reef at Heron Island, Queensland, Australia. The habitat and resource requirements of these species overlap considerably.

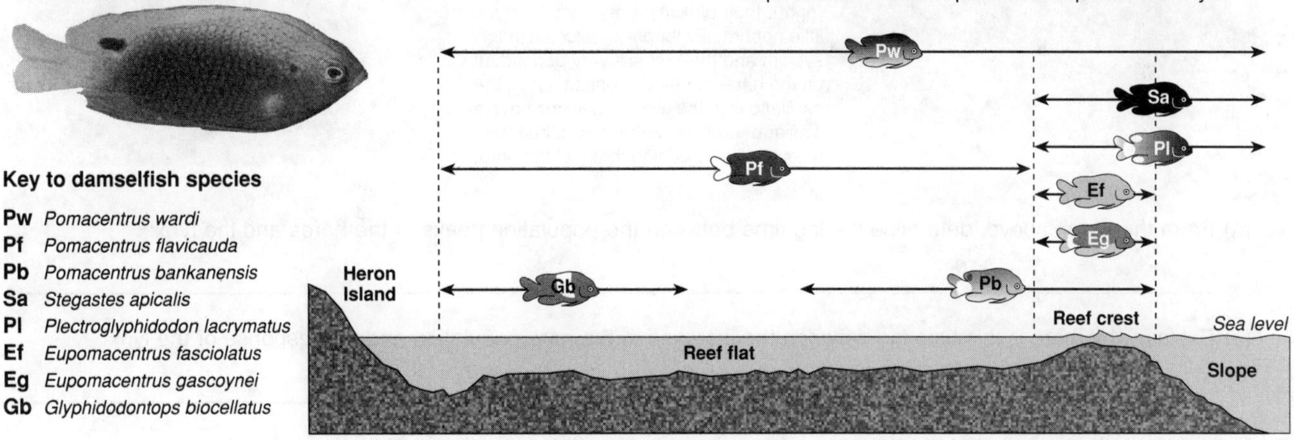

Key to damselfish species

Pw *Pomacentrus wardi*
Pf *Pomacentrus flavicauda*
Pb *Pomacentrus bankanensis*
Sa *Stegastes apicalis*
Pl *Plectroglyphidodon lacrymatus*
Ef *Eupomacentrus fasciolatus*
Eg *Eupomacentrus gascoynei*
Gb *Glyphidodontops biocellatus*

1. Describe two ways in which species can avoid directly competing for the same resources in their habitat:

   (a) ______________________________

   (b) ______________________________

2. Explain how the eight species of bird in the eucalypt forest avoid competitive exclusion: ______________________________

   ____

3. In the example above, damselfish Sa and Pl, and Ef and Eg appear to be exploiting the same area of reef. Explain how they are able to do this:

   ____

   ____

Predator-Prey Interactions

Some mammals, particularly in highly seasonal environments, exhibit regular cycles in their population numbers. Snowshoe hares in Canada exhibit such a cycle of population fluctuation that has a periodicity of 9–11 years. Populations of lynx in the area show a similar periodicity. Contrary to early suggestions that the lynx controlled the size of the hare population, it is now known that the fluctuations in the hare population are governed by other factors, most probably the availability of palatable grasses. The fluctuations in the lynx numbers however, do appear to be the result of fluctuations in the numbers of hares (their principal food item). This is true of most **vertebrate** predator-prey systems: predators do not usually control prey populations, which tend to be regulated by other factors such as food availability and climatic factors. Most predators have more than one prey species, although one species may be preferred. Characteristically, when one prey species becomes scarce, a predator will "switch" to another available prey item. Where one prey species is the principal food item and there is limited opportunity for prey switching, fluctuations in the prey population may closely govern predator cycles.

Oscillations in snowshoe hare and Canadian lynx populations

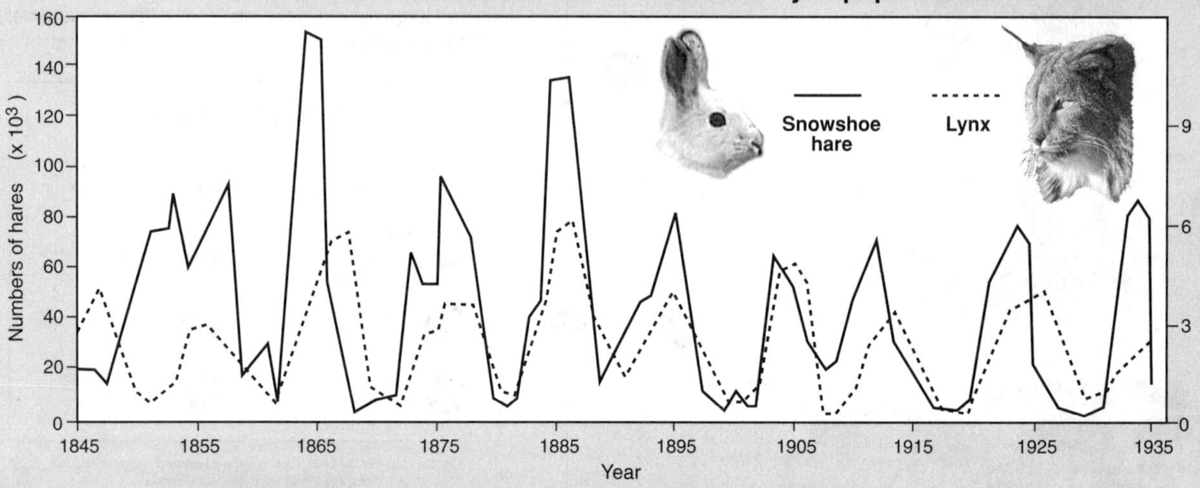

Canadian lynx and snowshoe hare

Regular trapping records of Canadian lynx (left) over a 90 year period revealed a cycle of population increase and decrease that was repeated every 10 years or so. The oscillations in lynx numbers closely matched those of the snowshoe hare (right), their principal prey item. There is little opportunity for prey switching in this system and the lynx are very dependent on the hares for food. Consequently, the oscillations in the two populations have a similar periodicity, with the lynx numbers lagging slightly behind those of the hare.

1. (a) From the graph above, determine the lag time between the population peaks of the hares and the lynx:

(b) Explain why there is this time lag between the increase in the hare population and the response of the lynx:

2. Suggest why the lynx populations appear to be so dependent on the fluctuations on the hare:

3. (a) In terms of birth and death rates, explain how the availability of palatable food might regulate the numbers of hares:

(b) Explain how a decline in available palatable food might affect their ability to withstand predation pressure:

Predator-Prey Strategies

A predator eating its prey is one of the most conspicuous species interactions. In most cases, the predator and prey are different species, though cannibalism is quite common in some species. Predators have acute senses with which to locate and identify prey. Many also have structures such as teeth, claws, and poison to catch and subdue their prey. Animals can avoid being eaten by using passive defences, such as hiding, or active ones, such as rapid escape or aggressive defence.

Predator Avoidance Strategies Among Animals

Batesian mimicry

Harmless prey gain immunity from attack by mimicking harmful animals (called **Batesian mimicry**). The beetle on the right has the same black and yellow colour scheme as the common wasps, which can give a painful sting.

Müllerian mimicry

Many unpalatable species tend to resemble each other; a phenomenon known as **Müllerian mimicry**. The monarch and queen butterflies are both toxic. By looking alike, these mimics present a common image for predators to avoid.

Poisonous

Highly toxic animals, such as arrow poison frogs and lionfish, may advertise this fact with bright colours. The evolution of toxicity may involve kin selection, as the parent may have to die to educate a future predator of its young.

Chemical defence

Some animals can produce offensive smelling chemicals. American skunks squirt a nauseous fluid at attackers.

Hiding

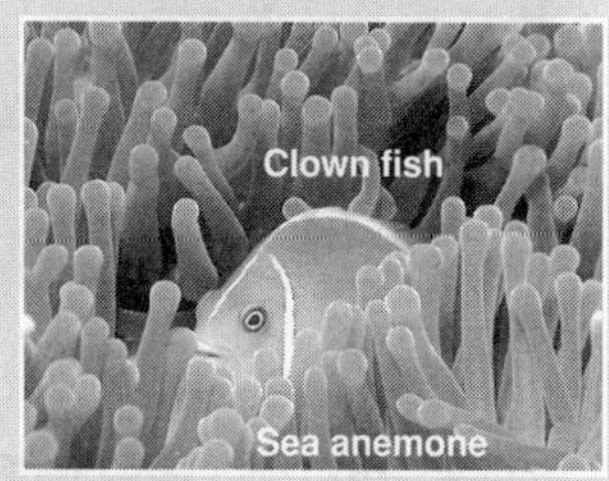

Animals, such as this clown fish, take refuge in the safety provided by animals with more effective defence.

Detection and escape

Some animals, like this grasshopper, are masters of detecting approaching danger and making a rapid escape.

Camouflage

Cryptic shape and colouration allows some animals, such as this leaf insect, to blend into their background.

Startle display

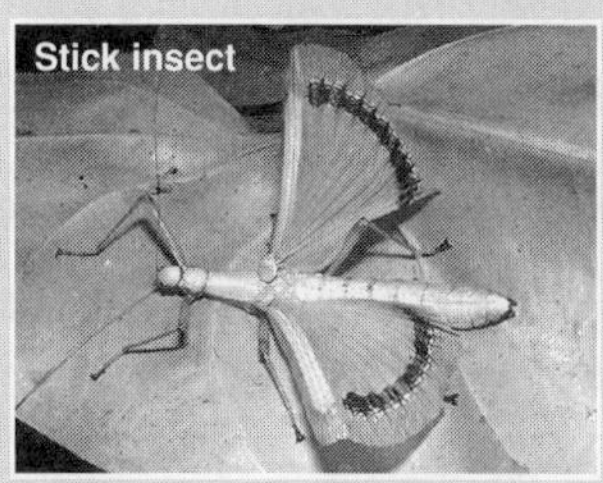

Effective startle displays must come as a surprise. This stick insect will rear up on its hind legs and fan its wings. The frill necked lizard, native to Australia, will rear up suddenly and erect its frill before retreating off at high speed.

Visual deception

Deceptive markings such as large, fake eyes can apparently deceive predators momentarily, allowing the prey to escape. They may also induce the predator to strike at a nonvital end of the prey. Note the fish's real eye is disguised.

Group defence

Fish often swim in large schools, which move together as one mass in a way that confuses predators.

When birds, such as these flamingoes, form large flocks, the risk of predation to each individual is reduced.

Armoured defence

Tough outer cases that hamper predators are common in both vertebrate and invertebrate prey. Almost all molluscs have protective shells built around their sensitive parts. Some animals can coil up to protect vulnerable parts.

Offensive weapons

Offensive weapons are essential if prey are to actively fend off an attack by a predator. Many grazing mammals have sharp horns and can repel attacks by predators. Some animal bodies have spikes that offer passive defence.

Prey Capturing Strategies

Concealment

Some animals camouflage themselves in their surroundings, striking when the prey comes within reach.

Filter feeding

Many marine animals (e.g. barnacles, baleen whales, sponges, manta rays) filter the water to extract tiny plankton.

Lures

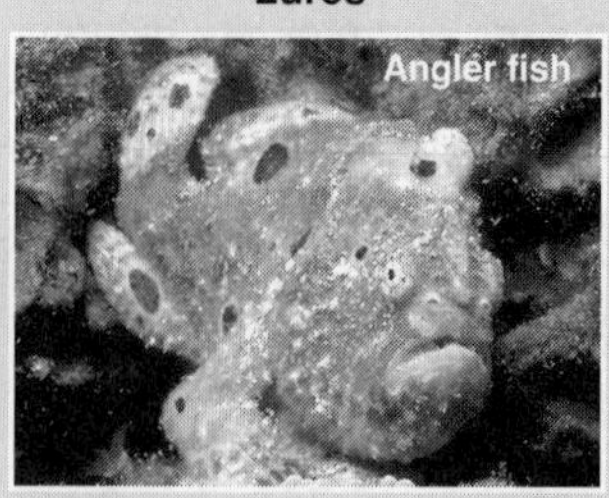

This angler fish, glow worms and a type of spider all use lures to attract prey within striking range.

Traps

Spiders have developed a unique method of trapping their prey. Strong, sticky silk threads trap flying insects.

Tool use

Some animals are gifted tool users. Chimpanzees use carefully prepared twigs to extract termites from mounds.

Stealth

The night hunting ability of some poisonous snakes is greatly helped by the presence of infrared senses.

Speed

Some animals, such as cheetahs and some predatory birds, can simply outrun or outfly their prey.

Group attack

Cooperative group behaviour may make prey capture much easier. Pelicans herd fish into 'killing zones'.

1. Explain why poisonous (unpalatable) animals are often brightly coloured so that they are easily seen: __________

2. Describe the purpose of large, fake eyes on some butterflies and fish: __________

3. Describe a behaviour typical of a (named) prey species that makes them difficult to detect by a predator: __________

4. Describe a behaviour of prey that is actively defensive: __________

5. Describe two behaviours of (named) predators that facilitate prey capture:

   (a) __________

   (b) __________

6. Discuss **Batesian and Müllerian mimicry**, explaining the differences between them and any benefits to the species involved directly or indirectly in the relationship: __________

7. Describe two possible ways in which toxicity could evolve in prey species, given the prey has to be eaten in order for the predator to learn from the experience:

   (a) __________

   (b) __________

Conservation and Sustainability

Conservation is a term describing the management of a resource so that it is maintained into the future. It encompasses resources of all kinds, from plant and animal populations to mineral resources. Resource conservation has become an important theme in the twenty-first century as the rate of resource use by the expanding human population increases markedly. **Sustainability** refers to the management so that the system or resource is replenished at least at same rate at which it is used. Sustainability is based on the idea of using resources within the carrying capacity of the environment. As such, it allows for managed development and resource use. In contrast, **preservation** aims to keep untouched resources or habitats in their pristine state, without human interference.

Conservation

Living systems

Plant conservation

Animal conservation

Habitat conservation

The conservation of living systems focuses heavily on the management of endangered species so that their numbers remain stable or increase over time. Many living systems have no directly measurable economic value but are important for global biodiversity. Many people also support the moral value of conserving as many living systems as possible and that humans do not have the right to exterminate other organisms.

Resources

Energy conservation

Soil conservation

Water conservation

Conservation of resources focuses on the efficient use of resources so that remaining stocks are not wasted. Many of these resources are scarce or economically important so require prudent use. Others are damaging to the environment and it is better to use less of them. In recent decades, there has been a growing acknowledgement that humans cannot afford to continue to waste natural resources.

Sustainability

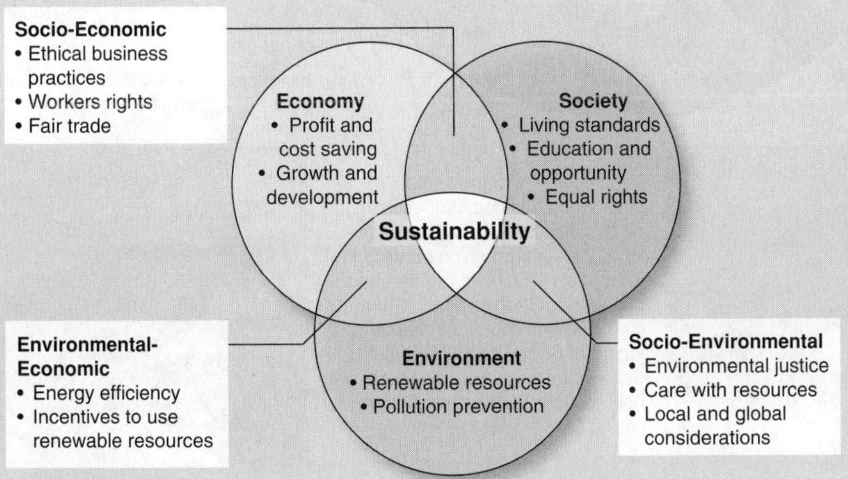

Sustainability can be represented conceptually as the intersection of the environment, society, and economics. Sustainable development must take into account all three of these concepts. The Chinese city of **Shenzhen** was developed to be an example of sustainability. In 1980, it became a special economic zone (SEZ) and, as a result of changes to its boundaries, political ideals, and rapid development, grew from a population of 30,000 to 9 million today. To ensure the new city and SEZ were sustainable, Chinese officials (1) located the new SEZ close to Hong Kong in order to facilitate foreign investment and access to foreign markets, (2) linked many urban areas rather than creating one large one, (3) developed Shenzhen city in the context of the surrounding Pearl River Delta as a whole and (4) shifted the transport infrastructure from a road to a rail-based system.

1. Explain the relationship between conservation and sustainability: ______________________

2. Explain how conservation differs from preservation and describe situations in which each might be appropriate:

3. Discuss the impact of society and economy on the conservation of living systems and resources:

Ecotourism in the Galápagos

Over the last twenty years, **ecotourism** (the specific travelling to regions of ecological significance) has become a major contributor to the economies of many countries. Ideally, ecotourism involves environmental education and has minimal impact to the environment around which it is based. Increasingly though, it involves large groups travelling to sensitive ecological areas with a guide, and the impact of catering to the needs of these tourists can place heavy demands on pristine and fragile systems. The experience of the ecotourism industry in the Galápagos Islands, 97% of which are a National Park, illustrates this well. More than 80 000 people visit the islands each year, and ecotourism has brought costs and benefits to the islands, whose population has more than tripled in the last fifteen years.

Ecotourism to the Galápagos Islands

Benefits

Economic

- Greater development (upgrading of communications and infrastructure)
- Larger population means more sustainable local economy
- More jobs (in both tourism and infrastructure)

Environmental

- Greater local understanding of the importance of the islands
- Development of local wildlife services (National Park Service)
- Greater global awareness of environmental issues to do with the islands

Costs

Economic

- Restrictions placed on local fishing industry because of National Park
- Mass immigration of people looking for jobs
- Most tourist dollars do not go to the Galápagos economy

Environmental

- Issues with rubbish disposal
- Disturbance of plants and animals by tourists
- Increased travel increases the risks of new species introductions

Despite the large impact of the tourist industry on the islands, there has been some progress in the reduction of introduced pests. The island of Santiago has had its population of feral pigs eradicated and the population of feral goats there has also been reduced.

The influx of humans to the Galápagos has had serious impacts on the islands outside the National Park. At least two ships bringing fuel for tourist boats have run aground, one spilling 3 million litres of fuel oil that killed 60% of the marine iguanas on the island of Santa Fe. Sea cucumber populations have also been devastated by more fishermen selling to overseas markets.

1. With reference to the Galápagos Islands, discuss some of the benefits and disadvantages of ecotourism:

2. Describe the impact of human activity on the flora and fauna of the Galápagos with reference to each of the following:

   (a) Increased tourist traffic:

   (b) Higher local population:

   (c) Support for National Park services:

   (d) Greater environmental awareness:

Sustainable Forestry

The goal of sustainable forestry follows acknowledgement of the damage done by unrestricted logging of old growth forests. For forestry to be sustainable, demand for timber must be balanced with the regrowth of seedlings. Sustainable forestry allows timber demands to be met without over-exploiting the timber-producing trees. Different methods for logging are used depending on the type of forest being logged. In the UK, afforestation programmes have increased the area of forest to 12%, with conifers totalling around 1.6 million hectares and broadleaf trees around 1.2 million hectares of land. Restocking of forests and new plantings totalled around 26.4 thousand hectares in 2008. Careful management of these forests has allowed the forested area to double since 1947. However constant management is needed to ensure this resource continues to be used in a sustainable way without destroying the features of the ecosystems in each case.

Clear Cutting

A section of a mature forest is selected (based on tree height, girth, or species), and all the trees are removed. During this process the understorey is destroyed. A new forest of economically desirable trees may be planted. In plantation forests, the trees are generally of a single species and may even be clones. Clear cutting is a very productive and economical method of managing a forest, however it is also the most damaging to the natural environment. In plantation forests, this may not be of concern and may not affect sustainability, but clear cutting of old growth forests causes enormous ecological damage.

Selective Logging

A mature forest is examined, and trees are selected for removal based on height, girth, or species. These trees are felled individually and directed to fall in such a way as to minimise the damage to the surrounding younger trees. The forest is managed in such a way as to ensure continual regeneration of young seedlings and provide a balance of tree ages that mirrors the natural age structure.

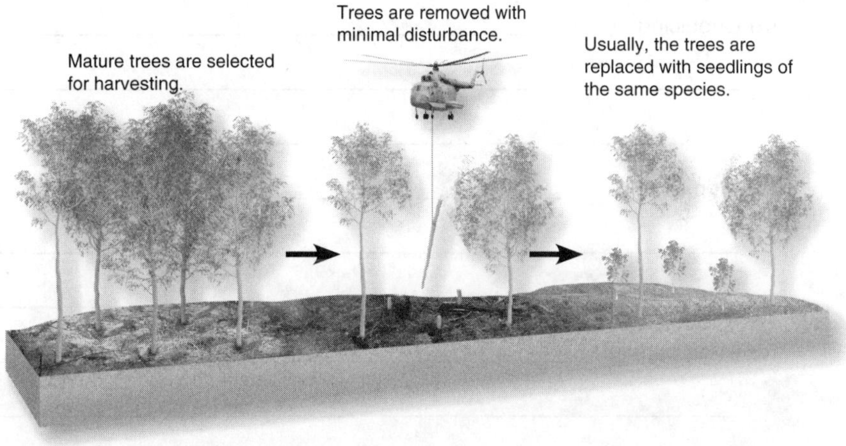

Coppicing

Coppicing is the ancient practice of harvesting wood for weaving, thatching, firewood, or for making charcoal. A selection of deciduous trees is coppiced (cut close to the ground), leaving stumps known as stools. Most deciduous trees have the ability to regrow from their bases when they are cut down. However their growth form changes from a single stem to producing many stems. It is these stems that provide the wood for harvesting in the future. Proper coppicing is skilled, labour intensive work. Well managed, coppiced woodlands are quite open with a diverse understorey that supports a wide range of species. If coppiced woodland is not well managed, the coppice stems grow tall forming a heavily shaded woodland with little ground vegetation. These **overstood** coppices are relatively low diversity because they no longer support open woodland species, but also lack the characteristics of old growth high forest (e.g. trees of different ages).

Strip Cutting

Strip cutting is a variation of clear cutting. Trees are clear cut out of a forest in strips. The strip is narrow enough that the forest on either side is able to reclaim the cleared land. As the cleared forest reestablishes (3-5 years) the next strip is cut. This allows the forest to be logged with minimal effort and damage to forest on either side of the cutting zone, while at the same time allowing the natural reestablishment of the original forest. Each strip is not cut again for around 30 years, depending on regeneration time.

Old growth forests are climax communities. They have remained undisturbed by natural events and human interference for many hundreds of years. Old growth forests are ecologically significant because of their high biodiversity, and they are often home to endangered or endemic species. Larger forests also play a part in climate modification.

Second growth forests result from secondary ecological succession after a major forest disturbance such as fire or logging. At first, these forests may have quite different characteristics from the original community, especially if particular tree species were removed completely by logging. As the forest develops, the trees are often of the same age so that a single canopy develops.

Commercial plantations (tree farms) are specifically planted and grown for the production of timber or timber based products. These forests are virtual monocultures containing a specific timber tree, such as *Pinus radiata* (Monterey or radiata pine). These trees have often been selectively bred to produce straight-trunked, uniform trees that grow quickly and can be easily harvested and milled.

1. Describe the advantages and disadvantages of each of the following methods of logging:

   (a) Coppicing:

   (b) Strip cutting:

   (c) Clear cutting:

   (d) Selective logging:

2. With respect to sustainability, which of the four methods described on the previous page is best suited to:

   (a) Commercial plantations:

   (b) Traditional woodland of hardwood species such as hazel, ash, and oak:

   (c) Second growth forest:

3. Explain which logging method you think best suits the ideals of sustainability and explain your answer:

4. Discuss the role of coppicing as a method of sustainable forestry that also provides a means to conserve biodiversity:

UNIT F215

5.4.1

Plant **Responses**

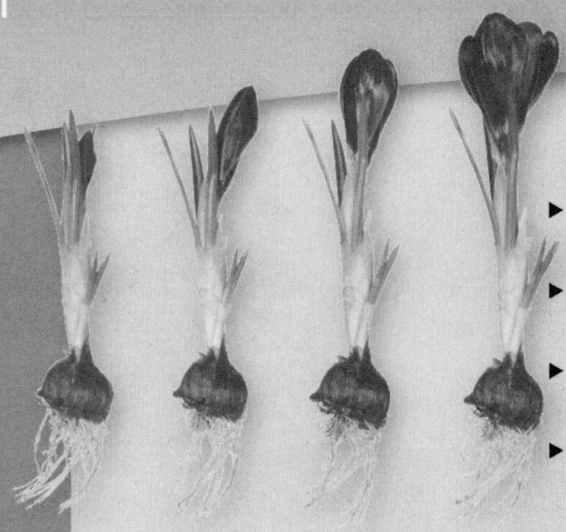

KEY CONCEPTS

- Plant responses to the environment are coordinated by phytohormones.
- Plant responses to hormones are adaptive in helping to avoid predation and abiotic stress.
- Experimental evidence supports the role of plant hormones in growth and developmental responses.
- Plant responses to hormones are exploited in commercial applications.

KEY TERMS

abiotic stress
apical dominance
auxin
cytokinin
ethylene (ethene)
gibberellin
gravitropism
nastic response
phototropism
phytochrome
phytohormone
tropism

OBJECTIVES

□ 1. Use the **KEY TERMS** to help you understand and complete these objectives.

Environment and response

pages 300-308

□ 2. Describe some of the environmental factors that are important to plants. With reference to avoidance of predation and abiotic stress, explain why plants need to respond to the environment.

□ 3. Describe responses in plants and their adaptive role in avoiding predation or minimising abiotic stress. Examples could include:
(a) The role of abscisic acid in the closure of stomata.
(b) The role of ethene (ethylene) in leaf fall.
(c) The role of cytokinins in plant development.
(d) The role of phytochrome in detecting and responding to daylength.
(e) The role of nastic responses of plant leaves to touch.
(f) The responses of plants to temperature changes.

□ 4. Explain what is meant by a **tropism** and distinguish between positive and negative tropisms. Describe **phototropism** and **gravitropism** and explain the role of each in plant growth and development. Recognise thigmomorphogenesis (formerly thigmotropism) in plants as a growth response to a mechanical stimulus.

□ 5. With reference to responses to light, outline the general role of plant hormones in coordinating plant responses to environmental changes.

Plant hormones and their roles

pages 309-312

□ 6. Describe and evaluate the experimental evidence for:
(a) The role of auxins in apical dominance
(b) The role of gibberellins in the control of stem elongation.

□ 7. Describe and explain the role of hormones in leaf loss in deciduous plants, specifically the role of ethylene and its interaction with other plant hormones.

□ 8. With reference to specific examples, describe how plant hormones are used commercially. Some examples (of many) include:
(a) Use of cytokinins in the cut flower industry to delay ageing.
(b) Application of cytokinins and auxins in tissue culture.
(c) Use of auxin to promote rooting in cutting.
(d) Use of gibberellins to increase fruit size in grapes.
(e) Use of gibberellins in the brewing industry to prepare barley malt.
(f) Use of synthetic auxins as weed killers.

□ 9. Appreciate that the role of phytohormones in plant growth and development is often not straightforward; the plant response is often dependent on the interaction between and relative concentrations of two or more hormones.

Periodicals:
Listings for this chapter are on page 343

Weblinks:
www.biozone.co.uk/weblink/OCR-A2-2832.html

Teacher Resource CD-ROM:
Plant Defences

Plant Responses

Even though most plants are firmly rooted in the ground, they are still capable of responding and making adjustments to changes in their external environment, including abiotic stresses and predation pressure. This ability is seen chiefly in changing patterns of growth. Responses may involve relatively sudden physiological changes, such as flowering, or a steady growth response, such as a tropism. Other responses made by plants include nastic movements, photoperiodism, and dormancy.

TROPISMS
Tropisms are growth responses made by plants to directional external stimuli, where the direction of the stimulus determines the direction of the growth response. A tropism may be positive (towards the stimulus), or negative (away from the stimulus). Common stimuli for plants include light, gravity, touch, and chemicals.

LIFE CYCLE RESPONSES
Plants use seasonal changes in the environment as cues for the commencement or ending of particular life cycle stages. Such changes are mediated by **plant growth factors**, such as phytochrome and gibberellin and enable the plant to avoid conditions unfavourable to growth or survival. Examples include flowering and other **photoperiodic responses**, dormancy and germination, and leaf fall.

RAPID RESPONSES TO ENVIRONMENTAL STIMULI
Plants are capable of quite rapid responses. Examples include the closing of **stomata** in response to water loss, opening and closing of flowers in response to temperature, and **nastic responses**. These responses may follow a circadian rhythm and are protective in that they reduce the plant's exposure to abiotic stress or grazing pressure.

PLANT COMPETITION AND ALLELOPATHY
Although plants are rooted in the ground, they can still compete with other plants to gain access to resources. Some plants produce chemicals that inhibit the growth of neighbouring plants. Such chemical inhibition is called **allelopathy**. Plants also compete for light and may grow aggressively to shade out slower growing competitors.

PLANT RESPONSES TO HERBIVORY
Many plant species have responded to grazing or browsing pressure with evolutionary adaptations enabling them to survive constant cropping. Examples include rapid growth to counteract the constant loss of biomass (grasses), sharp spines or thorns to deter browsers (acacias, cacti), or toxins in the leaf tissues (eucalyptus).

1. Identify the stimuli to which plants typically respond and explain their significance: ______

2. Explain how plants benefit by responding appropriately to the environment: ______

3. Describe one adaptive response of plants to each of the following stressors in the environment:

   (a) Low soil water: ______

   (b) Falling autumn air temperatures: ______

   (c) High wind: ______

   (d) Browsing animals: ______

   (e) Low nighttime temperatures: ______

Responses to Temperature in Plants

Plants are capable of marked physiological responses to a wide range of environmental variables, including temperature, light, and water availability. Gardeners are well aware of the seasonal effects of temperature on plant growth and development. Woody plants are able to survive freezing temperatures because of metabolic changes that occur in the plant between summer and winter. This process of **acclimation** involves the production of thicker cell walls and accumulation of growth inhibitors in the plant tissues. Cold hardiness is genetically determined but can be influenced by horticultural practices that mimic seasonal changes. Alternation of periods of growth with periods of **dormancy** allows the plant to survive water shortages and extremes of hot or cold. When dormant, growth will not resume until the right combination of environmental cues are met. Such cues include exposure to cold, dryness, and suitable photoperiod. Annuals produce dormant seeds, whereas in biennials and perennials the shoots may die back while the overwintering structures become dormant. Low temperature stimulation of flowering (**vernalisation**) and seed germination (**stratification**) are common in many species. These temperature responses are usually associated with increased activity in plant growth regulators such as gibberellic acid.

Dormancy is a condition of arrested growth in which the entire plant, or its seeds or buds, do not renew growth without certain environmental cues.

In many plants, after the seeds have taken up water, exposure to a period of low temperature (5°C) will break dormancy. This is called **stratification**.

Bud burst and flowering follow exposure to a cold period in many plants, including bulbs and many perennials. This process is called **vernalisation**.

Daily Rhythm in Tulips

Many flowers, including tulips, show **sleep movements**. In many species, these are triggered by daylength, but in tulips the environmental cue is temperature. This series of photographs show the sleep movements of a single **tulip** flower over one 12 hour period during spring.

7.00 am | 9.30 am | 11.00 am | 5.00 pm | 7.00 pm

All photos: RA

1. Describe three physiological responses of plants to changes in temperature:

   (a) ___

   (b) ___

   (c) ___

2. Explain the adaptive value of **vernalisation** in plants: ___

3. Suggest why evergreen trees have a growth advantage in regions with a very short growing season: ___

4. (a) Describe the sleep movements of tulips in response to temperature: ___

   (b) Suggest how these movements might benefit the plant: ___

Related activities: *Photoperiodism. Apical Dominance, Bolting, and Leaf Loss*

Nastic Responses

As well as relatively slow growth responses, plants are also capable of quite rapid, reversible movements in response to stressors such as touch or changes in temperature. These may be caused by localised turgor changes or the result of rapid cell growth in different parts of the plant. When the direction of the plant response is independent of the stimulus direction, the response is said to be **nastic**. Nastic responses include thermonasty, e.g. the opening and closing of tulip flowers to changes in air temperature, and photonasty e.g. the opening of evening-primrose flowers at dusk. Plant sleep movements, in which plants close their flowers or lower their leaves at night, are specialised photonasties. The rapid collapse of the leaflets in the sensitive plant *Mimosa* (below) is a thigmonasty. The same mechanisms underly the leaf movements of the Venus flytrap.

The sensitive plant (*Mimosa pudica*) has long, compound leaves (leaves composed of small leaflets). When a leaf is touched, it collapses and its leaflets fold together. Strong disturbances cause the entire leaf to droop from its base. This response takes only a few seconds and is caused by a rapid loss of turgor pressure from the cells at the bases of the leaves and leaflets. The message that the plant has been disturbed is passed quickly around the plant by electrical signals (changes in membrane potential). Although the response could be likened to the action potential in animal nervous systems, it is not nearly as rapid. After the disturbance is removed, turgor is restored to the cells, and the leaflets will slowly return to their normal state.

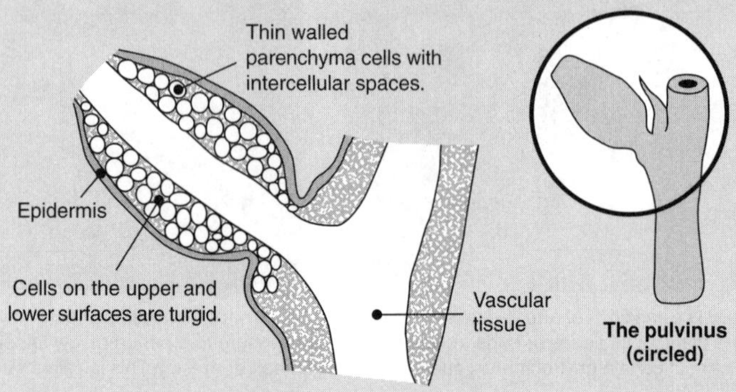

The compound leaves of *Mimosa* has joint-like thickenings, the **pulvini** (*sing.* pulvinus) at the bases of the petioles and also at the bases of each leaflet. These pulvini contain specialised parenchyma cells called **motor cells** which are involved in the rapid leaf movements.

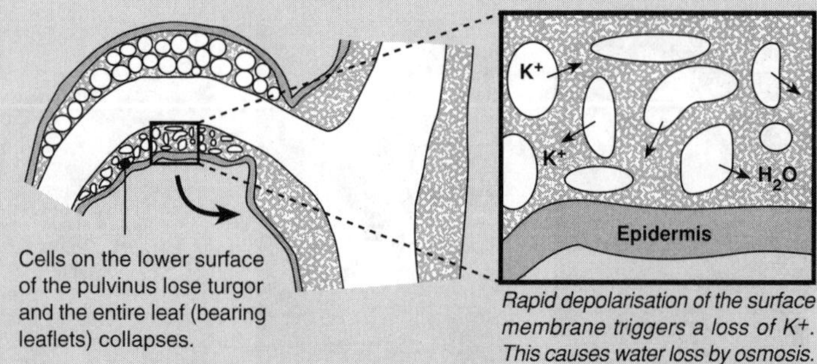

Rapid depolarisation of the surface membrane triggers a loss of K+. This causes water loss by osmosis.

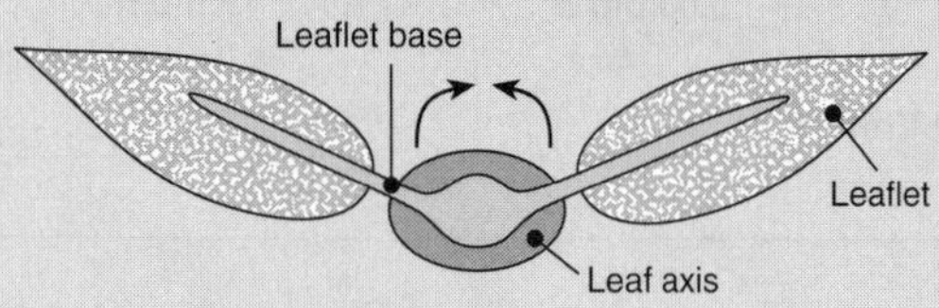

When disturbed, a change in membrane potential of the leaf cells is transmitted to the cells of the pulvinus. These cells respond by actively pumping potassium ions (and tannins) out of the cytoplasm. When water follows osmotically, there is a sudden loss of turgor. **NOTE**: The mechanism outlined above for the leaf bases, also operates at the leaflet bases, except that it is the cells on the **upper surface** of the pulvinus that lose turgor. Consequently, individual leaflets fold upwards, rather than drooping down (left).

1. Describe a possible adaptive advantage of the sensitivity response in plants such as *Mimosa*. Briefly explain your answer (HINT: leaf closure exposes thorns on the stem):

2. Describe how the sudden leaf movements are achieved in *Mimosa*:

3. Some plants use changes in turgor to lower their leaves in the evening and raise them again in the morning (so-called sleep movements). Explain how this behaviour would benefit a plant:

Photoperiodism

Photoperiodism is the response of a plant to the relative lengths of daylight and darkness. Flowering is a photoperiodic activity; individuals of a single species will all flower at much the same time, even though their germination and maturation dates may vary. The exact onset of flowering varies depending on whether the plant is a short-day or long-day type (see next page). Photoperiodic activities are controlled through the action of a pigment called **phytochrome**. Phytochrome acts as a signal for some biological clocks in plants and is also involved in other light initiated responses, such as germination, shoot growth, and chlorophyll synthesis. Plants do not grow at the same rate all of the time. In temperate regions, many perennial and biennial plants begin to shut down growth as autumn approaches. During unfavourable seasons, they limit their growth or cease to grow altogether. This condition of arrested growth is called **dormancy**, and it enables plants to survive periods of water scarcity or low temperature. The plant's buds will not resume growth until there is a convergence of precise environmental cues in early spring. Short days and long, cold nights (as well as dry, nitrogen deficient soils) are strong cues for dormancy. Temperature and daylength change seasonally in most parts of the world, so changes in these variables also influence many plant responses, including germination and flowering. In many plants, flowering is triggered only after a specific period of exposure to low winter temperatures. As described in the previous activity, this low-temperature stimulation of flowering is called **vernalisation**.

Photoperiodism

Photoperiodism is based on a system that monitors the day/night cycle. The photoreceptor involved in this, and a number of other light-initiated plant responses, is a blue-green pigment called **phytochrome**. Phytochrome is universal in vascular plants and has two forms: active and inactive. On absorbing light, it readily converts from the inactive form (**P_r**) to the active form (**P_{fr}**). **P_{fr}** predominates in daylight, but reverts spontaneously back to the inactive form in the dark. The plant measures daylength (or rather night length) by the amount of phytochrome in each form.

Summary of phytochrome related activities in plants

Process	Effect of daylight	Effect of darkness
Conversion of phytochrome	Promotes $P_r \rightarrow P_{fr}$	Promotes $P_{fr} \rightarrow P_r$
Seed germination	Promotes	Inhibits
Leaf growth	Promotes	Inhibits
Flowering: long-day plants	Promotes	Inhibits
Flowering: short-day plants	Inhibits	Promotes
Chlorophyll synthesis	Promotes	Inhibits

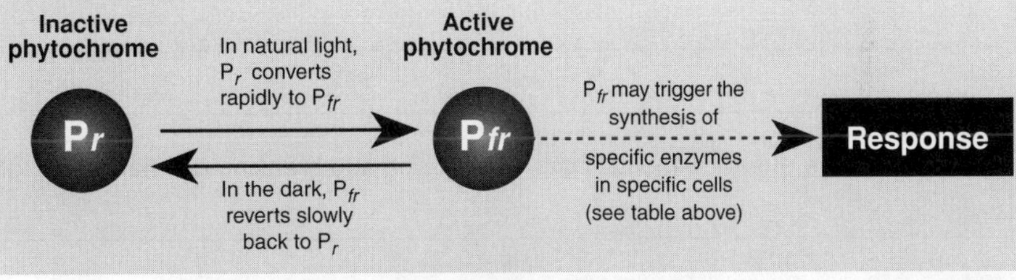

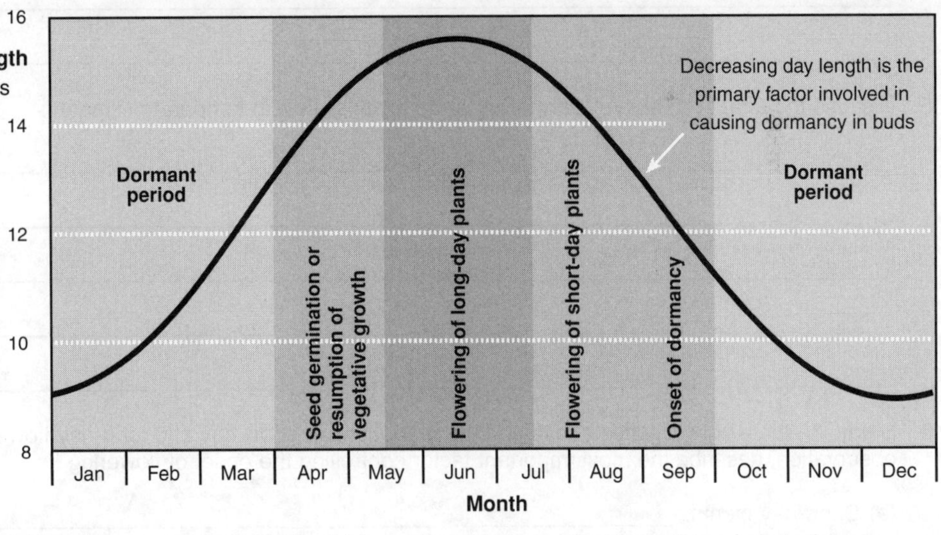

Day length and life cycle in plants (Northern Hemisphere)

The cycle of active growth and dormancy shown by temperate plants is correlated with the number of daylight hours each day (right). In the southern hemisphere, the pattern is similar, but is six months out of phase. The duration of the periods may also vary on islands and in coastal regions because of the moderating effect of nearby oceans.

1. Describe two plant responses, initiated by exposure to light, which are thought to involve the action of phytochrome:

(a) ______________________________

(b) ______________________________

2. Discuss the role of phytochrome in a plant's ability to measure daylength: ______________________________

____

____

____

____

Photoperiodism in Plants

An experiment was carried out to determine the environmental cue that triggers flowering in 'long-day' and 'short-day' plants. The diagram below shows 3 different light regimes to which a variety of long-day and short-day plants were exposed.

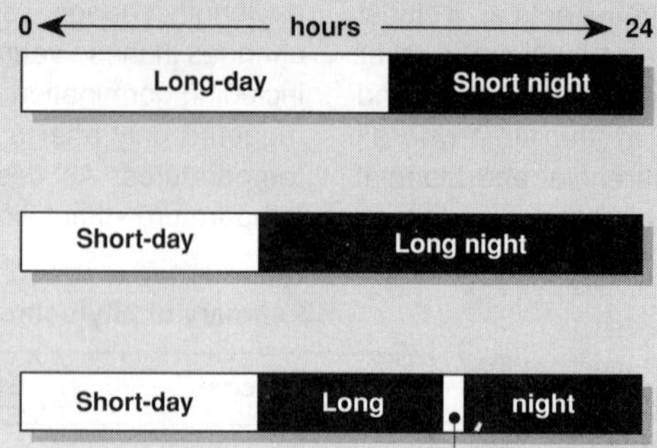

Long night interrupted by a short period exposed to light

Long-day plants

When subjected to the light regimes on the right, the 'long-day' plants below flowered as indicated:

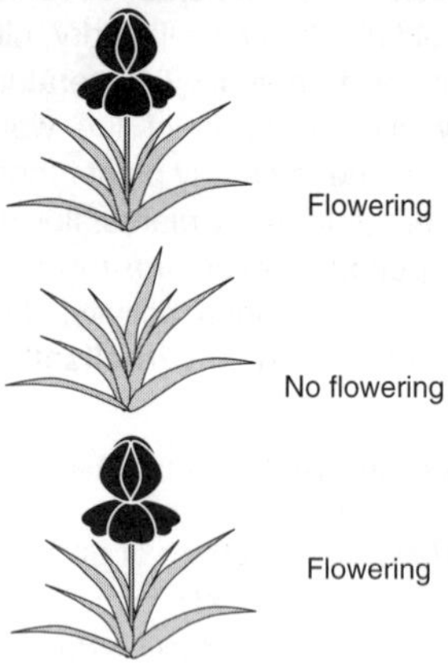

Examples: *lettuce, clover, delphinium, gladiolus, beetscorn, coreopsis*

Short-day plants

When subjected to the light regimes on the left, the 'short-day' plants below flowered as indicated:

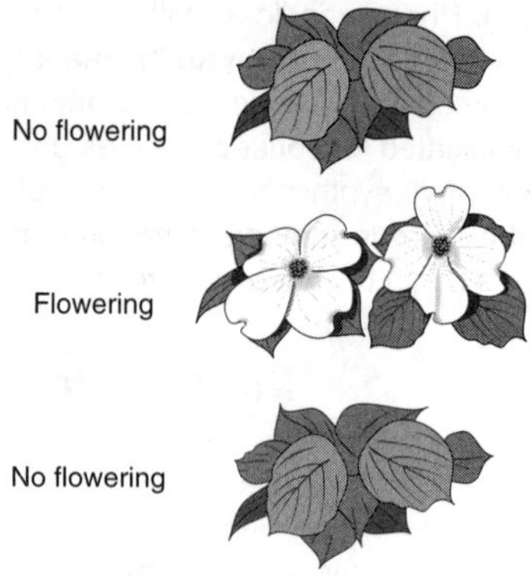

Examples: *potatoes, asters, dahlias, cosmos, chrysanthemums, pointsettias*

3. (a) Identify the environmental cue that synchronises flowering in plants: __________

   (b) Describe one biological advantage of this synchronisation to the plants: __________

4. Discuss the role of environmental cues in triggering and breaking **dormancy** in plants:

5. Discuss the adaptive value of **dormancy** and **vernalisation** in temperate climates:

6. Study the three light regimes above and the responses of short-day and long-day flowering plants to that light. From this observation, describe the most important factor controlling the onset of flowering in:

   (a) Short-day plants: __________

   (b) Long-day plants: __________

7. Using information from the experiment described above, discuss the evidence for the statement "*Short-day plants are really better described as long-night plants.*"

Tropisms and Growth Responses

Tropisms are plant growth responses to external stimuli, in which the stimulus direction determines the direction of the growth response. Tropisms are identified according to the stimulus involved, e.g. photo- (light), gravi- (gravity), hydro- (water), and may be positive or negative depending on whether the plant moves towards or away from the stimulus respectively. A tropism is distinguished from a **nastic response** by the directionality of the stimulus; nastic responses are independent of stimulus direction.

(a) ....

A positive growth response to a chemical stimulus. *Example: Pollen tubes grow towards a chemical, possibly calcium ions, released by the ovule of the flower.*

(b) ....

Stems and coleoptiles grow away from the direction of the Earth's gravitational pull.

(c) ....

Growth response to water. Roots are influenced primarily by gravity but will also grow towards water.

(d) ....

Growth responses to light, particularly directional light. Coleoptiles, young stems, and some leaves show a positive response.

(e) ....

Roots respond positively to the Earth's gravitational pull, and curve downward after emerging through the seed coat.

(f) ....

Growth responses to touch or pressure. Tendrils (modified leaves) have a positive coiling response stimulated by touch.

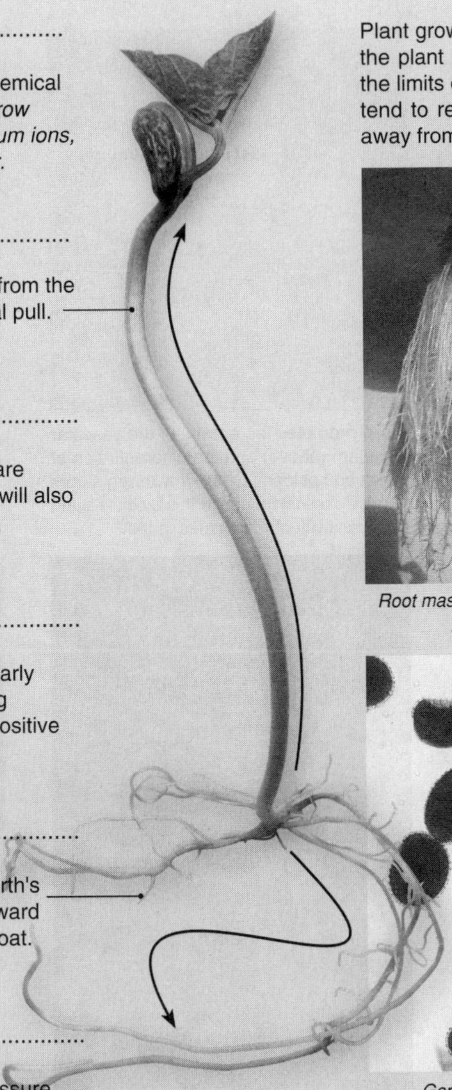

Plant growth responses are adaptive in that they position the plant body in a suitable growing environment, within the limits of the position in which it germinated. They also tend to reinforce each other. For example, shoots grow away from gravity and towards the light.

Root mass in a hydroponically grown plant

Sweet pea tendrils

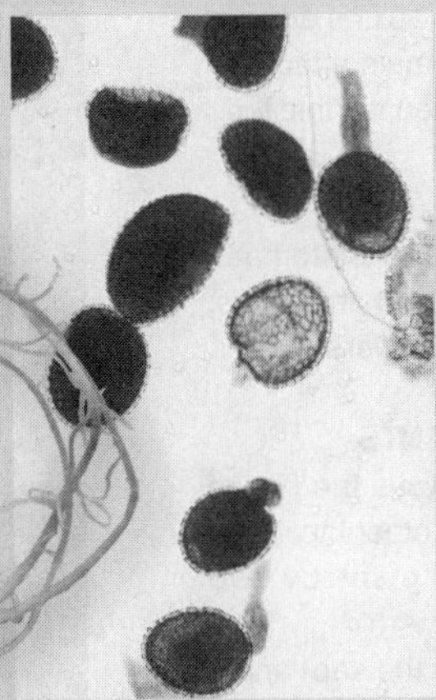

Germinating pollen

Thale cress bending to the light

1. Identify each of the plant tropisms described in (a)-(f) above, including whether the response is positive or negative.

2. Explain the difference between a **tropism** and a **nastic response** (nasty), identifying the adaptive value of each:

___

___

___

3. Describe the adaptive value of the following tropisms:

(a) Positive gravitropism in roots: ___

(b) Positive phototropism in coleoptiles: ___

(c) Positive thigmomorphogenesis in weak stemmed plants: ___

(d) Positive chemotropism in pollen grains: ___

Periodicals: *Sending plants round the bend*

Related activities: *Investigating Phototropism, Investigating Gravitropism* ***Weblinks:*** *Plants in Motion*

Transport and Effects of Auxins

Auxins are phytohormones (plant growth substances) that have a central role in a wide range of growth and developmental responses in vascular plants. **Indole-3-acetic acid** (IAA) is the most potent native auxin in intact plants. It was the first discovered and is the most studied. Although its actions on various aspects of plant growth are well known, it most commonly acts in concert with (or in opposition to) other phytohormones, especially cytokinins and gibberellins. The response of any particular plant tissue to IAA depends on the tissue itself, the concentration of the hormone, the timing of its release, and the presence of other phytohormones. For example, in undifferentiated tissue, the application of IAA and cytokinin in equal concentrations promotes xylem development, but a relatively higher concentration of auxin promotes rooting. Gradients in auxin concentration during growth prompt differential responses in specific tissues and contribute to the plant's organ development and directional growth.

AUXINS IN PLANTS:
The most important auxin produced by plants is **indole-3-acetic acid** (IAA). It plays important roles in a number of plant activities, although its action is often influenced by the presence of other plant growth factors. Auxin is important in:

- apical dominance
- positive phototropic response in stems
- positive gravitropic response in roots
- development of the embryo
- promoting cell elongation and growth in stem length
- promoting cell enlargement and differentiation in cambium (growth of secondary vascular tissues)
- leaf formation and fruit development
- root initiation and development
- delaying the onset of senescence. Young leaves and fruit produce auxins and while they do so, they remain attached to the stem and abscission is inhibited.

PRODUCTION OF AUXIN:
Auxin is synthesised in the meristematic tissues, mainly the root tips and shoot tips, but also in young leaves and flowers.

HOW AUXIN MOVES IN PLANTS:
Synthesis of auxin is not always the site of action so it must be moved to other locations. Auxin moves through the plant by two mechanisms:

- through the phloem (in the sap) and the xylem (in the transpiration stream)
- from cell to cell by diffusion but also via membrane transporters

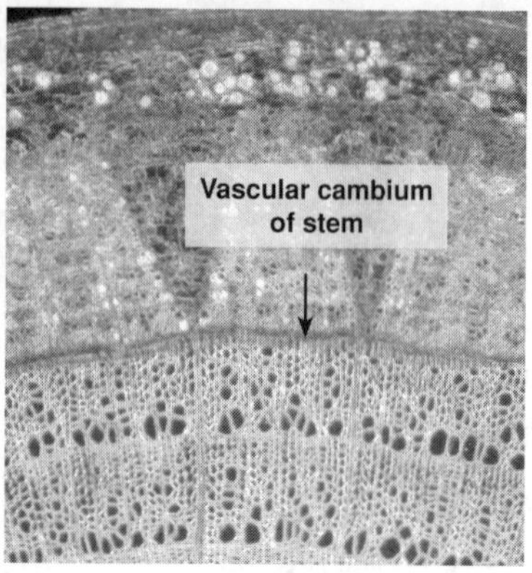

Auxin promotes the activity of the vascular cambium (above) and the differentiation of xylem and phloem. Other growth regulators (e.g. cytokinins) influence this by increasing the sensitivity of the tissues to IAA.

Auxin delays fruit senescence and is required for fruit growth. As the seeds mature, they release auxin, which diffuses to the surrounding flower parts, which develop into the fruit covering the seeds.

Auxins are responsible for apical dominance in shoots. Auxin is produced in the shoot tip and diffuses down to inhibit the development of the lateral buds.

Left: Auxin promotes growth in stem length. The effect is stronger if gibberellins are also present. This photograph shows a healthy *Arabidopsis* plant, next to a stunted auxin signal-transduction mutant.

1. Explain the role of IAA in the following plant growth processes:

   (a) Apical dominance: ______

   (b) Stem growth: ______

   (c) Secondary growth: ______

2. Explain why pruning (removing the central leader) induces bushy growth in plants: ______

3. Explain how IAA can bring about quite different responses in different plant tissues: ______

Investigating Phototropism

Phototropism in plants was linked to a growth promoting substance in the 1920s. A number of classic experiments, investigating phototropic responses in severed coleoptiles, gave evidence for the hypothesis that auxin was responsible for tropic responses in stems. Auxins promote cell elongation. Stem curvature in response to light can therefore result from the differential distribution of auxin either side of a stem. However, the mechanisms of hormone action in plants are still not well understood. Auxins increase cell elongation only over a certain concentration range. At certain levels, auxins stop inducing elongation and begin to inhibit it. There is *some* experimental evidence that contradicts the original auxin hypothesis and the early experiments have been criticised for oversimplifying the real situation. Outlined below are some experiments that investigate plant responses to light, and the role of hormone(s) in controlling these (also see following activities on phytohormones).

1. **Directional light:** A pot plant is exposed to direct sunlight near a window and as it grows, the shoot tip turns in the direction of the sun. If the plant was rotated, it adjusted by growing towards the sun in the new direction.

   (a) Name the hormone that regulates this growth response:

   ____

   (b) Give the full name of this growth response:

   ____

   (c) State how the cells behave to cause this change in shoot direction at:

   Point A: ______________________________

   Point B: ______________________________

   (d) State which side (A or B) would have the highest concentration of hormone:

   ____

   (e) Draw a diagram of the cells as they appear across the stem from point A to B (in the rectangle on the right).

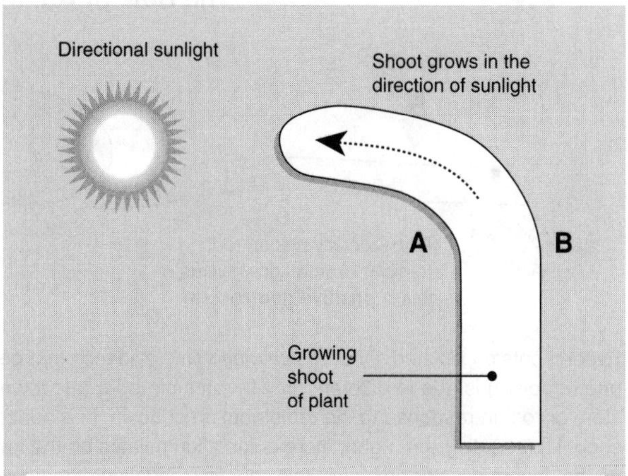

Draw your cells here:

2. **Light excluded from shoot tip:** With a tin foil cap placed over the top of the shoot tip, light is prevented from reaching it. When growing under these conditions, the direction of growth does not change towards the light source, but grows straight up. State what conclusion can you come to about the source and activity of the hormone that controls the growth response:

   ____

   ____

   ____

   ____

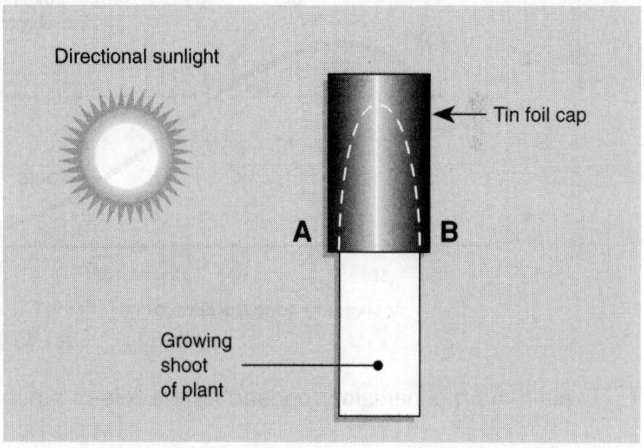

3. **Cutting into the transport system:** Two identical plants were placed side-by-side and subjected to the same directional light source. Razor blades were cut half-way into the stem, thereby interfering with the transport system of the stem. Plant A had the cut on the same side as the light source, while Plant B was cut on the shaded side. Predict the growth responses of:

   Plant A: ______________________________

   ____

   ____

   Plant B: ______________________________

   ____

   ____

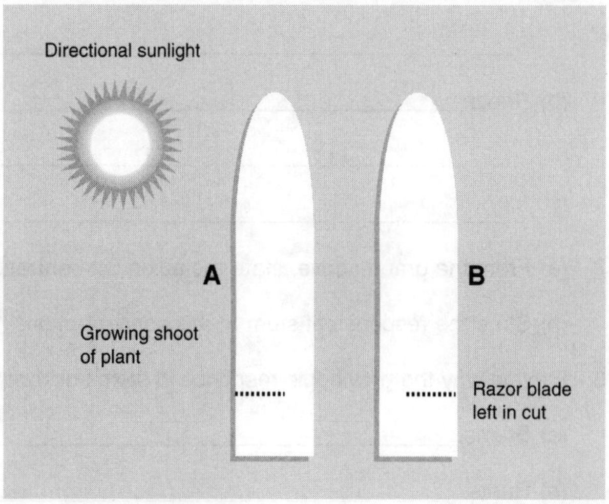

Investigating Gravitropism

Although the response of shoots and roots to gravity is well known, the mechanism behind it is not at all well understood. The importance of auxin as a plant growth regulator, as well as its widespread occurrence in plants, led to it being proposed as the primary regulator in the gravitropic response. The basis of auxin's proposed role in gravitropism (geotropism) is outlined below. The mechanism is appealing in its simplicity but, as noted below, has been widely criticised, and there is not a great deal of evidence to support it. Many of the early plant growth experiments (including those on phototropism) involved the use of coleoptiles. Their use has been criticised because the coleoptile (the sheath surrounding the young shoot of grasses) is a specialised and short-lived structure and is probably not representative of plant tissues generally.

The Role of Auxins in Geotropic Responses

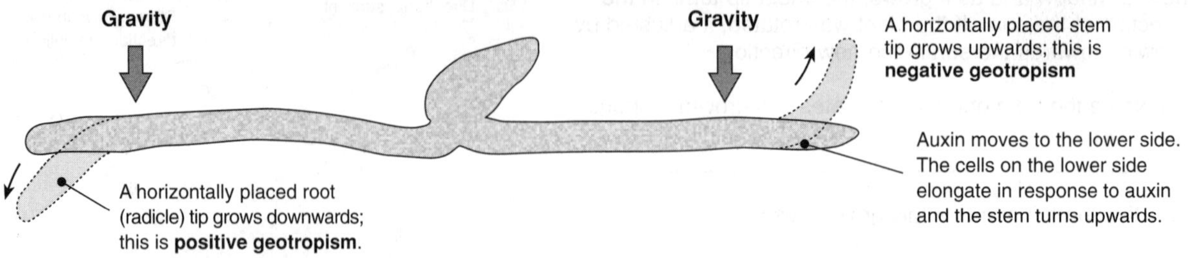

Experiments on isolated shoot tips provide some evidence that geotropism (like phototropism) is due to different growth rates of upper and lower sides of the stem or root in response to the redistribution of auxin. In a horizontally placed shoot tip (see diagram, right), more auxin accumulates on the lower side than on the uppermost side. In stems, this causes elongation of the cells on the lower surface and the stem tip turns up. The root grows down because root elongation is inhibited by the high levels of auxin on the lower surface (see graph below).

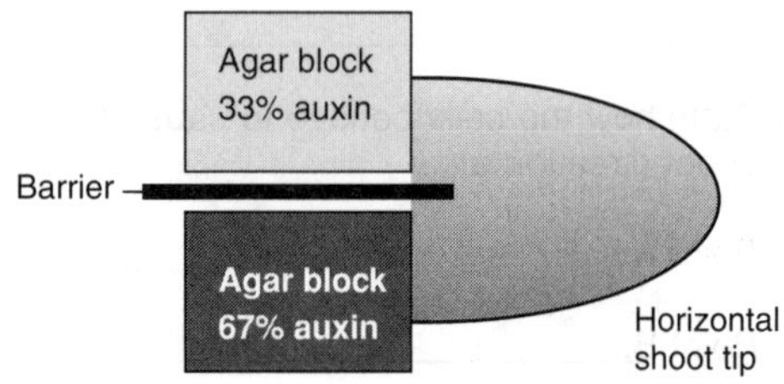

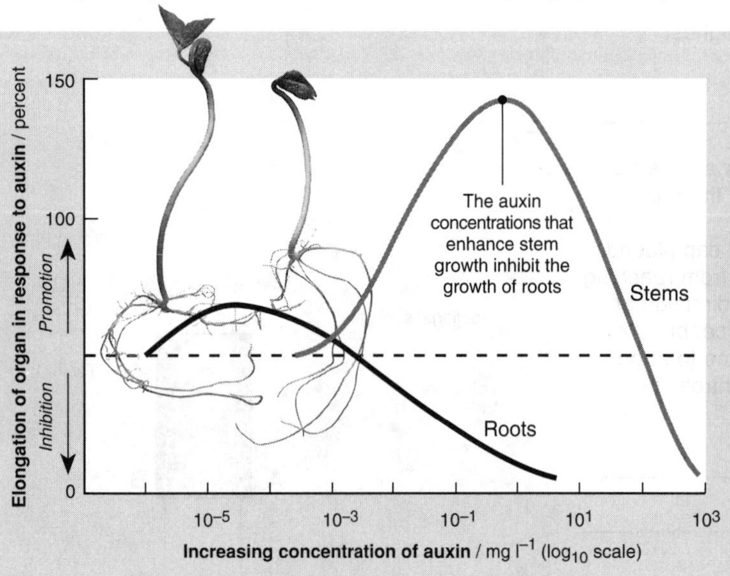

Auxin concentration and root growth

In a horizontally placed seedling, auxin moves to the lower side of the organ in both the stem and root. Whereas the stem tip grows upwards, the root tip responds by growing down. Root elongation is inhibited by the same level of auxin that stimulates stem growth (see graph left). The higher auxin levels on the lower surface cause growth inhibition there. The most elongated cells are then on the upper surface and the root turns down. This simple auxin explanation for the geotropic response has been much criticised: the concentrations of auxins measured in the upper and lower surfaces of horizontal stems and roots are too small to account for the growth movements observed. Alternative explanations suggest that growth inhibitors are also somehow involved in the geotropic response.

1. Explain the mechanism proposed for the role of auxin in the gravitropic response in:

   (a) Shoots (stems): ____________________

   (b) Roots: ____________________

2. (a) From the graph above, state the auxin concentration at which root growth becomes inhibited: ____________________

   (b) State the response of stem at this concentration: ____________________

3. Explain why the gravitropic response in stems or roots is important to the survival of a seedling:

   (a) Stems: ____________________

   (b) Roots: ____________________

Related activities: *Investigating Phototropism*

Apical Dominance, Bolting, and Leaf Loss

A wide variety of plant cells produce hormones to regulate growth and development. Identifying the hormones involved in specific plant processes and understanding their mechanism of action is not always straight forward because a combination of hormones and environmental factors often interact to produce a given response. Understanding these interactions has allowed humans to manipulate plant growth and development (e.g. stimulating growth, inducing fruit fall) to achieve a desired outcome.

Experimental Evidence for the Role of Auxin in Apical Dominance

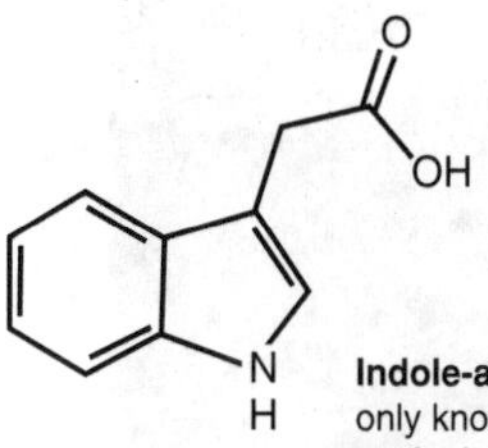

Indole-acetic acid (left) is the only known naturally occurring auxin. It is produced in the apical shoot and young leaves.

Auxin was the first substance to be identified as a plant hormone. Charles Darwin and his son Francis were first to recognise its role in stimulating cell elongation. Frits W. Went isolated this growth-regulating substance, which he called auxin, in 1926. Auxin promotes **apical dominance**, where the shoot tip or apical bud inhibits the formation of lateral (side) buds. As a result, plants tend to grow a single main stem upwards, which dominates over lateral branches.

The effect of auxin on preventing the development of lateral buds can be demonstrated experimentally (right).

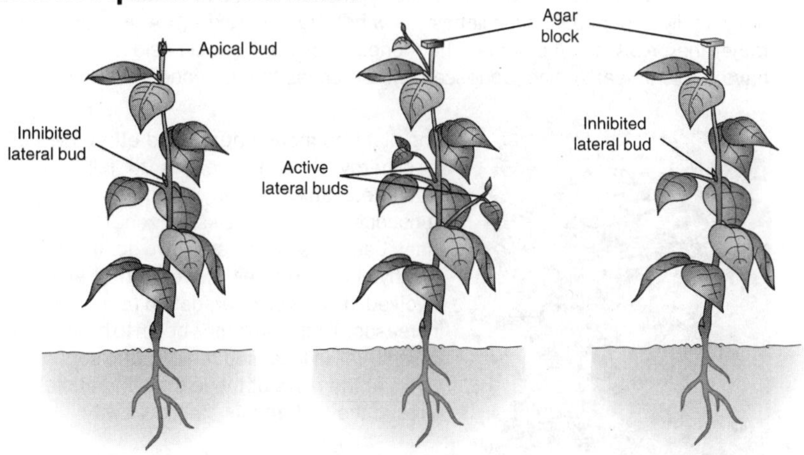

No treatment
Apical bud is left intact.

In an intact plant, the plant stem elongates and the lateral buds remain inactive. No side growth occurs.

Treatment one
Apical bud is removed; no auxin is applied.

The apical bud is removed and an agar block without auxin is placed on the cut surface. The seedling begins to develop lateral buds.

Treatment two
Apical bud is removed; auxin is applied.

The apical bud is removed and an agar block containing auxin is placed on the cut surface. Lateral bud development is inhibited.

Two conclusions can be drawn from this experiment. (1) The apical bud contains a hormone that inhibits lateral growth because its removal promoted lateral growth. (2) The presence of auxin in the apical bud inhibits lateral growth because auxin applied to a cut stem tip could inhibit lateral growth and mimic the effect of an intact apical bud.

Gibberellins and Stem Elongation

Japanese rice farmers documented rapid stem elongation in the 1800s. This process, called **bolting**, resulted in tall, spindly rice plants that set no seed heads. In 1934, two Japanese scientists isolated the plant hormone responsible for the rapid growth. That hormone was **gibberellin**, and it acts by stimulating cell division and cell elongation. Although more than 78 gibberellins have since been identified, scientists believe that only gibberellin A controls stem elongation. The other gibberellins are believed to be intermediate forms of gibberellin A. Under natural conditions, production of gibberellin is triggered by environmental cues such as long days or a period of cold temperatures.

Evidence for Gibberellin's Role in Stem Elongation

Chemical analysis has revealed that bolting plants contain higher levels of gibberellin than non-bolting plants. Experimentally, the link between gibberellin and plant bolting can be tested quite simply by applying gibberellin to one group of plants, and not applying it to another group, which act as the control. Both groups are grown in the same conditions and the differences in stem elongation are measured at the end of set period. The plants treated with gibberellins have longer stems than the plants in the control group.

The use of gibberellin inhibitors have also been important in establishing the link between gibberellins and bolting. When gibberellin was applied to plants they bolted. However, plants in which gibberellin plus a gibberellin inhibitor was applied did not bolt. Because plants given the gibberellin inhibitor did not bolt, it can be assumed that gibberellin is the hormone responsible for this growth response.

Photo, above: Plants treated with gibberellins have longer stems than the control group which had no gibberellins applied during the experimental period.

Leaf Loss in Deciduous Plants

Deciduous plants shed their leaves every year in a process called **abscission**. Leaf abscission usually occurs during the autumn (right), but some plants shed leaves in the presence of a large number of plant pests, such as aphids. During the 1960s, Frederick T. Addicott discovered a substance apparently capable of accelerating abscission in leaves and fruit (which he called abscisin), and which is now called **abscisic acid** (ABA). The hormonal regulation of leaf abscission is not yet fully understood, but scientists now believe that **auxin** (IAA) and **ethylene**, rather than ABA, are the primary hormones involved. Abscisic acid is believed to have a role in leaf ageing (senescence), a process that precedes abscission.

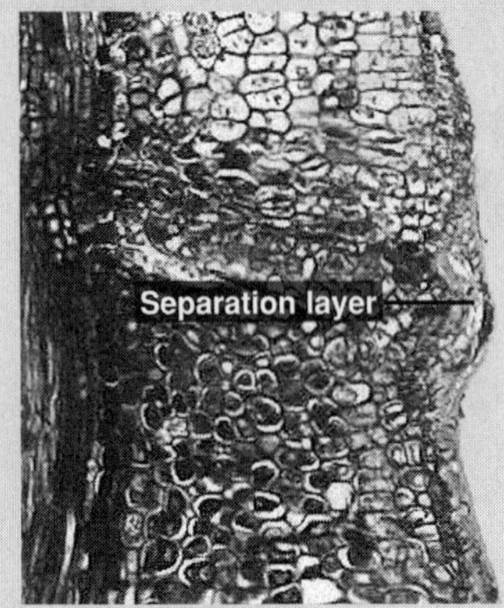

The plant hormones **auxin** and **ethylene** work in synergy to cause leaves to fall. As the leaf ages, auxin levels within the leaf (and subsequently the abscission zone) drop. The plant becomes more sensitive to the effects of ethylene, and gene expression of enzymes involved in cell wall degradation (e.g. cellulase) increases. These enzymes begin to break down the cell wall in localised regions (the separation layer) at the base of the leaf stalk (petiole). As a result the leaf and its stalk fall away.

Photo left: Leaf abscission in an *Asclepia* leaf. Magnification x100.

1. Describe the role of **auxins** in apical dominance: ____________________

2. Describe the role of **gibberellins** in stem elongation: ____________________

3. Outline the experimental evidence supporting:

   (a) The role of **auxins** in apical dominance: ____________________

   (b) The role of **gibberellins** in stem elongation: ____________________

4. (a) Name the two hormones involved in leaf abscission: ____________________

   (b) Describe how these two hormones work synergistically together to cause leaf abscission: ____________________

Plant Hormones and Applications

Like animals, plants use hormones to regulate their growth and development. Plant hormones (**phytohormones**) are organic compounds produced in one part of the plant and transported to another part, where they produce a growth response. Hormones are effective in extremely small amounts. There are five groups of phytohormones: **auxins** (indolacetic acid or IAA), **cytokinins**, **gibberellins**, **ethene**, and **abscisic acid** (ABA). Together they control growth and development of the plant at various stages. Synthetic analogues of IAA have been produced for commercial use and are applied as growth promoters in rooting powders, and as inducers for fruit production. Some analogues (e.g. 2-4-5-T) even act as growth inhibitors and are used as selective herbicides.

Site of Hormone Production

YOUNG LEAVES AND BUDS:
Auxin (IAA)
- Promotes growth in stem length
- Promotes cell enlargement and differentiation in cambium (growth of secondary vascular tissues)
- Responsible for **apical dominance**
- Delays onset of senescence and leaf fall

Gibberellins
- Delay onset of senescence and leaf fall
- Promote elongation in the region just below the shoot tip (subapical region)
- Promote secondary growth (with auxins)

EMBRYO WITHIN SEED
Gibberellins
- Break dormancy in seeds and buds
- Mobilise food stores during germination

DEVELOPING FRUIT
Cytokinins
- Essential for growth of young fruit

RIPE FRUIT
Ethene (ethylene)
- Induces fruit ripening

LEAF CHLOROPLASTS:
Abscisic acid (ABA)
- Growth inhibitor
- Made in response to water stress; acts on guard cells to promote closing of stomata
- Promotes seed dormancy

OLD LEAVES
Ethene (ethylene)
- Promotes leaf fall through the development of the abscission zone

Abscisic acid (ABA)
- Growth inhibitor, promotes seed dormancy

ROOT TIPS
Cytokinins
- Promote cell division
- Keep the shoot and root growth in balance
- Produced in the root tips and travel to the shoots and leaves in the transpiration stream

Auxin (IAA)
- Promotes growth in stem length
- Controls cell enlargement and differentiation

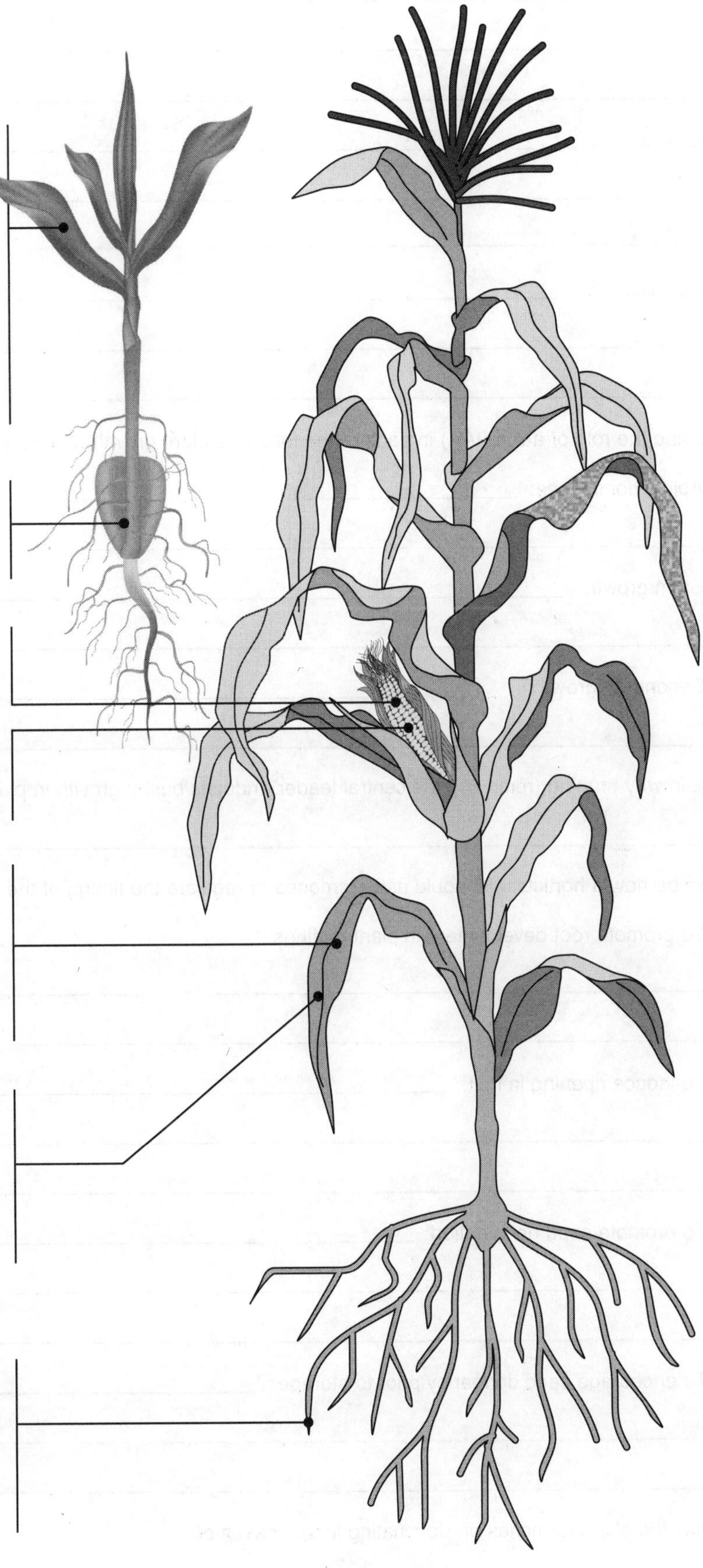

1. Describe one major effect of each of the hormones below, explaining its role in the plant life cycle:

(a) Gibberellins: ______

(b) Cytokinins: ______

(c) Ethene: ______

(d) Abscisic acid: ______

2. Describe the role of auxin (IAA) in each of the following plant growth processes:

(a) Apical dominance: ______

(b) Stem growth: ______

(c) Secondary growth: ______

3. Explain why pruning (removing the central leader) induces bushy growth in plants: ______

4. Describe how a horticulturist could use hormones to regulate the timing of the following life cycle events:

(a) To promote root development in plant cuttings: ______

(b) To induce ripening in fruit: ______

(c) To promote seed germination: ______

(d) To encourage seed dormancy prior to storage: ______

5. Identify the phytohormones predominating in the leaves of:

(a) A young plant: ______ (b) A senescent plant: ______

KEY TERMS: Flash Card Game

The cards below have a keyword or term printed on one side and its definition printed on the opposite side. The aim is to win as many cards as possible from the table. To play the game.....

1) Cut out the cards and lay them definition side down on the desk. You will need one set of cards between two students.
2) Taking turns, choose a card and, BEFORE you pick it up, state your own best definition of the keyword to your opponent.
3) Check the definition on the opposite side of the card. If both you and your opponent agree that your stated definition matches, then keep the card. If your definition does not match then return the card to the desk.
4) Once your turn is over, your opponent may choose a card.

Abiotic stress	Apical dominance	Auxin
Cytokinin	Ethylene (*aka* ethene)	Gibberellin
Gravitropism	Nastic response	Phototropism
Phytochrome	Phyto-hormone	Tropism

When you've finished the game keep these cutouts and use them as flash cards!

A plant hormone responsible for apical dominance, phototropism, and cell elongation.	The inhibitory influence of a shoot tip or apical bud on lateral growth.	Nonliving environmental factors (e.g. lack of water) that can have harmful effects on plants.
A class of plant hormones involved in stem elongation and in breaking seed dormancy.	The plant hormone responsible for inducing fruit ripening.	A plant hormone that is essential for growth in developing fruit.
A growth response in plants to directional light.	A plant response that is independent of the direction of the stimulus.	A directional growth response to gravity in plants.
A directional growth response in plants either towards (positive) or away (negative) from a stimulus.	A plant hormone. A chemical messenger that induces a specific physiological response.	The pigment that controls photoperiodic activities.

UNIT F215

5.4.2 Animal Responses

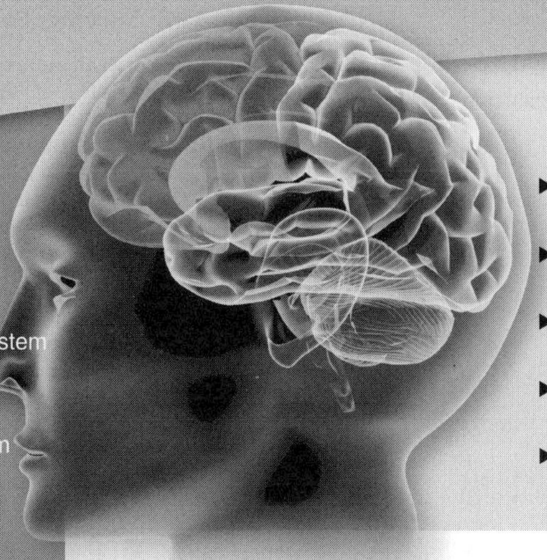

KEY CONCEPTS

- Response to stimuli involves coordination of nervous, hormonal, and muscular systems.
- The structure of the nervous systems enable both voluntary and autonomic responses.
- Voluntary movements occur through the action of skeletal muscle about joints.
- The sliding filament model provides an explanation for the mechanism of muscle contraction.
- Communication between nerves and voluntary muscle occurs at neuromuscular junctions.

KEY TERMS

actin
autonomic nervous system
brain
cardiac muscle
central nervous system
cerebellum
cerebrum
fibre
hypothalamus
involuntary muscle
medulla oblongata
motor division (PNS)
muscle filament (=myofilament)
myofibril
myosin
nervous system
neuromusclar junction
neurone
neurotransmitter
parasympathetic nervous system
peripheral nervous system
sarcomere
sensory division (PNS)
skeletal muscle
sliding filament model
smooth muscle
striated muscle
sympathatic nervous system
synapse
thick filament
thin filament
troponin-tropomyosin complex
voluntary muscle

Periodicals:
Listings for this chapter are on page 343

Weblinks:
www.biozone.co.uk/weblink/OCR-A2-2832.html

OBJECTIVES

☐ 1. Use the **KEY TERMS** to help you understand and complete these objectives.

Nervous systems and response — pages 316-320

☐ 2. Discuss why animals need to respond appropriately to their (internal and external) environment. Recognise that animal responses to environmental change involve nervous, hormonal, and muscular coordination.

☐ 3. Describe the basic structure and organisation of the human nervous system, distinguishing between the **central nervous system** (CNS) and the **peripheral nervous system** (PNS). Recall the role of neurones in carrying electrical impulses rapidly around the body.

☐ 4. Recognise the sensory and motor divisions divisions of the PNS. Know that the motor division is divided into autonomic and **somatic nervous systems**.

☐ 5. Describe the organisation of the **autonomic nervous system** (ANS) into the **sympathetic** and **parasympathetic nervous systems**. Describe the role of each division and recognise that they generally have antagonistic effects.

☐ 6. Using an annotated diagram, describe the gross structure of the human **brain**, including the functions of the **medulla oblongata** (=medulla), **cerebellum**, **hypothalamus**, and **cerebrum** (=cerebral hemispheres).

☐ 7. Describe the role of the nervous system (including the brain) in bringing about and coordinating muscular movement.

Muscles and movement — pages 321-329

☐ 8. Distinguish between **cardiac muscle**, **voluntary muscle**, and **involuntary muscle**, with reference to gross structure, physiology, and functional role.

☐ 9. Explain how coordinated voluntary movement requires the action of skeletal muscles about joints. Use the example of the elbow joint to show how movement is achieved by antagonistic muscle action.

☐ 10. BACKGROUND: Describe the structure of skeletal muscle with reference to the terms **fibres**, **myofibrils**, and **thick** and **thin** (myo)**filaments**. Recognise a **sarcomere** as a complete contractile unit. Describe the relationship between the structure of the sarcomere and the distribution of actin and myosin (thin and thick filaments) within the myofibril.

☐ 11. Use diagrams to explain the **sliding-filament model** of muscle contraction. Identify the role of calcium ions (Ca^{2+}), the **troponin-tropomyosin complex**, and ATP in the cycle of cross-bridge formation.

☐ 12. Explain the role of **ATP** in muscle contraction and the role of **glycogen** and **creatine phosphate** in storing and releasing energy for muscle contraction.

☐ 13. Compare and contrast the action of **neuromuscular junctions** and **synapses**.

☐ 14. Using the example of the "**fight or flight**" response, explain how the nervous and endocrine systems coordinate responses to environmental stimuli.

The Mammalian Nervous System

The **nervous system** is the body's control and communication centre. It has three broad functions: detecting stimuli, interpreting them, and initiating appropriate responses. Its basic structure is outlined below. Further detail is provided in the following pages.

The Human Nervous System

The central nervous system comprises the brain and spinal cord. The spinal cord is a cylinder of nervous tissue extending from the base of the brain down the back, protected by the spinal column. It transmits messages to and from the brain, and controls spinal reflexes.

The **peripheral nervous system** (right, far right) comprises all the nerves and sensory receptors outside the central nervous system.

Below: *cross sections through the spinal cord to show entry and exit of neurones.*

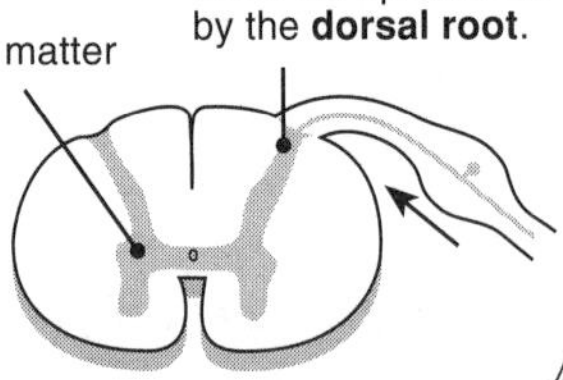

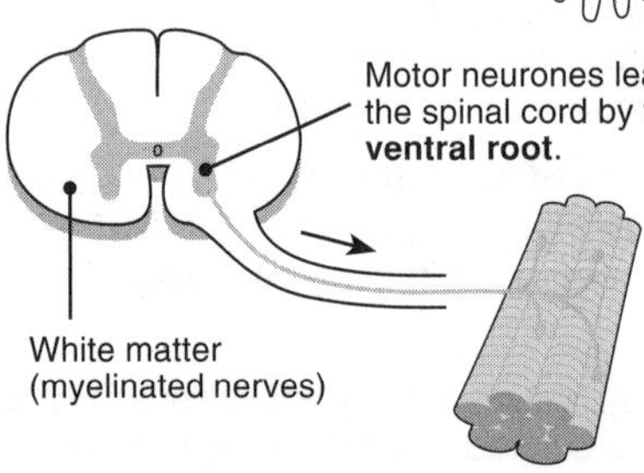

The spinal cord has an H shaped central area of grey matter, comprising nerve cell bodies, dendrites, and synapses around a central canal filled with cerebrospinal fluid. The area of white matter contains the nerve fibres.

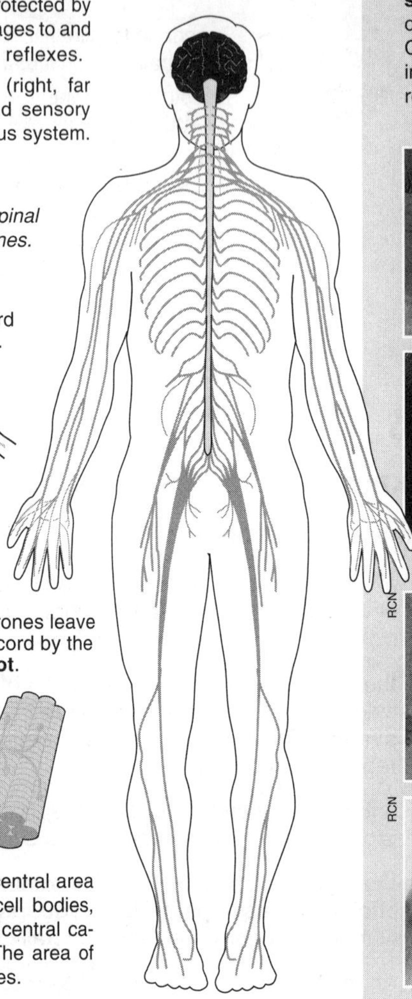

The Peripheral Nervous System (PNS)

The PNS comprises **sensory** and **motor divisions**. Peripheral nerves all enter or leave the CNS, either from the spinal cord (the spinal nerves) or the brain (cranial nerves). They can be **sensory** (from sensory receptors), **motor** (running to a muscle or gland), or **mixed** (containing sensory and motor neurones). Cranial nerves are numbered in roman numerals, I-XII. They include the vagus (X), a mixed nerve with an important role in regulating bodily functions, including heart rate and digestion

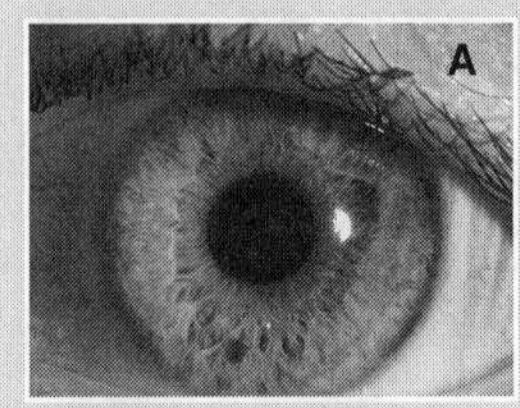

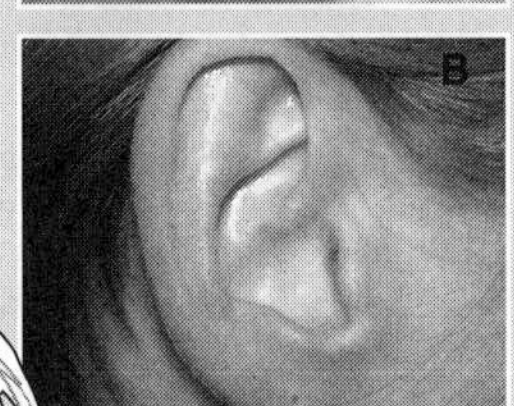

Sensory Division

Sensory nerves arise from **sensory receptors** (left) and carry messages to the central nervous system for processing.

The sensory system keeps the central nervous system aware of the external and internal environments. This division includes the familiar sense organs such as eyes (A), ears (B), and taste buds, and internal receptors that monitor internal state (e.g. body position, thirst, hunger, movement, pain).

RCN

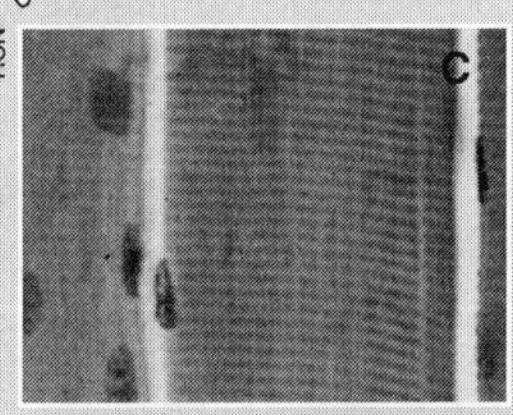

RCN

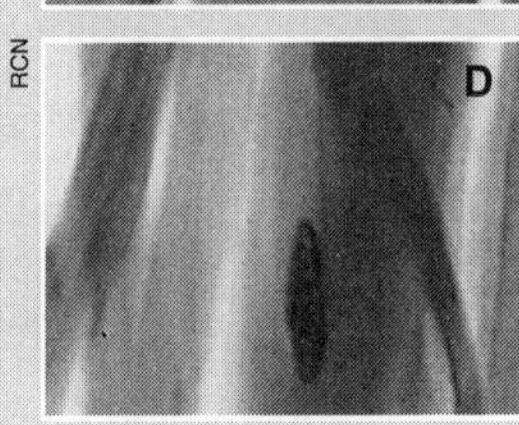

Motor Division

Motor nerves carry impulses from the CNS to **effectors**: muscles (left) and glands. The motor, division comprises the:

Somatic nervous system: the neurones that carry impulses to voluntary (skeletal) muscles (C).

Autonomic nervous system: regulates visceral functions over which there is generally no conscious control, e.g. heart rate, gut peristalsis involving smooth muscle (D), pupil reflex, and sweating.

1. Identify and briefly describe the three main functions of the nervous system:

   (a) ______

   (b) ______

   (c) ______

2. In the human nervous system, briefly explain the structure and role of each of the following:

   (a) The central nervous system: ______

   (b) The peripheral nervous system: ______

3. Explain the significance of the separation of the motor division of the PNS into somatic and autonomic divisions:

   ______

The Autonomic Nervous System

The **autonomic nervous system** (ANS) regulates involuntary visceral functions by means of **reflexes**. Although most autonomic nervous system activity is beyond our conscious control, voluntary control over some basic reflexes (such as bladder emptying) can be learned. Most visceral effectors have dual innervation, receiving fibres from both branches of the ANS. These two branches, the **parasympathetic** and **sympathetic** divisions, have broadly opposing actions on the organs they control (excitatory or inhibitory). Nerves in the parasympathetic division release acetylcholine. This neurotransmitter is rapidly deactivated at the synapse and its effects are short lived and localised. Most sympathetic postganglionic nerves release noradrenaline, which enters the bloodstream and is deactivated slowly. Hence, sympathetic stimulation tends to have more widespread and long lasting effects than parasympathetic stimulation. Aspects of autonomic nervous system structure and function are illustrated below. The arrows indicate nerves to organs or ganglia (concentrations of nerve cell bodies).

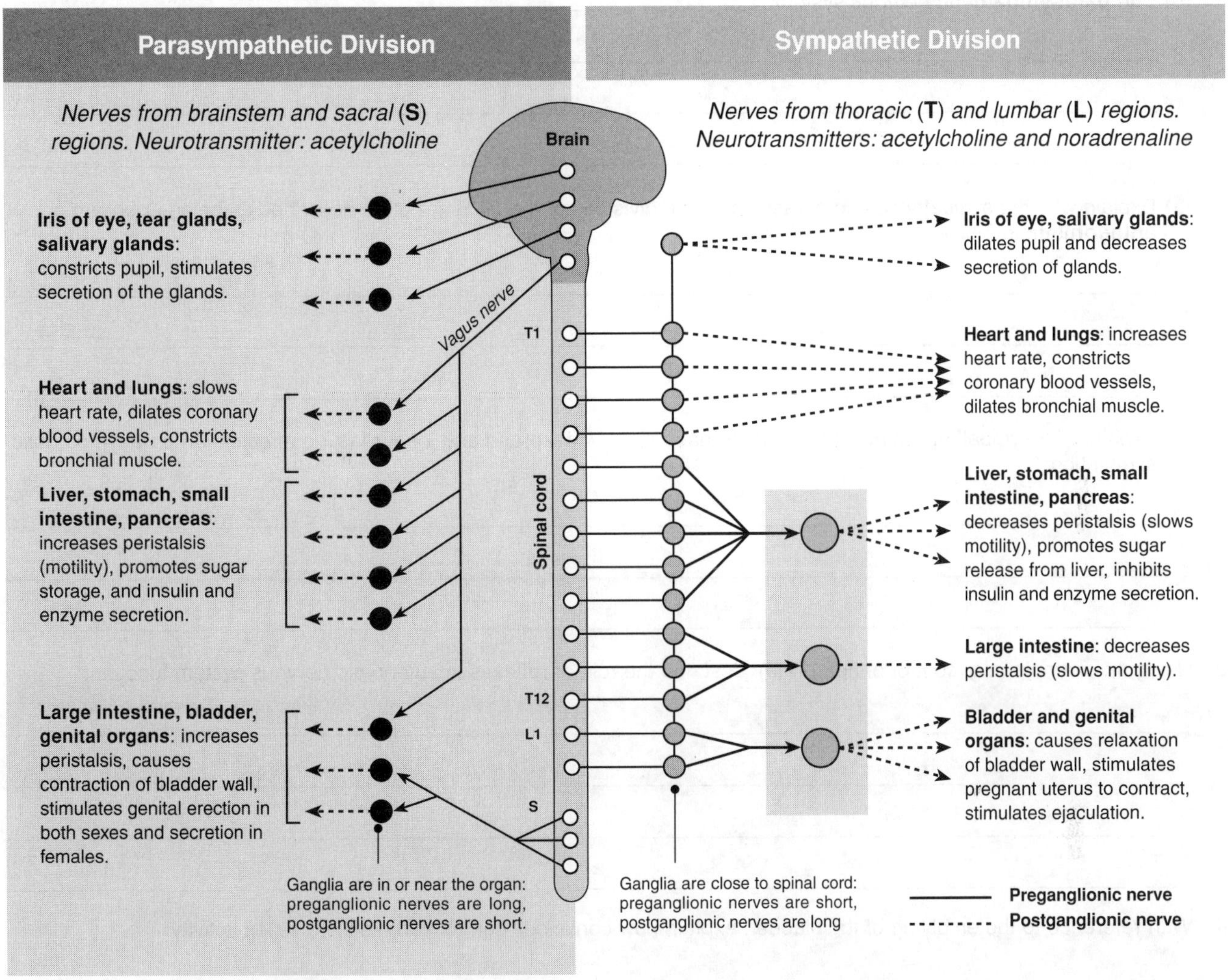

The Effects of the Autonomic Nervous System on the Body

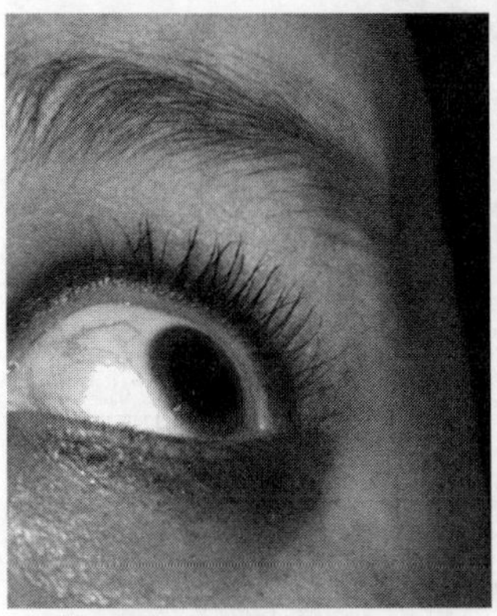

When a person is fearful, their pupils enlarge as a consequence of sympathetic nervous system activity (the fight or flight response). The same response occurs during sexual arousal. Sympathetic stimulation also decreases secretion of the tear (lacrimal) glands.

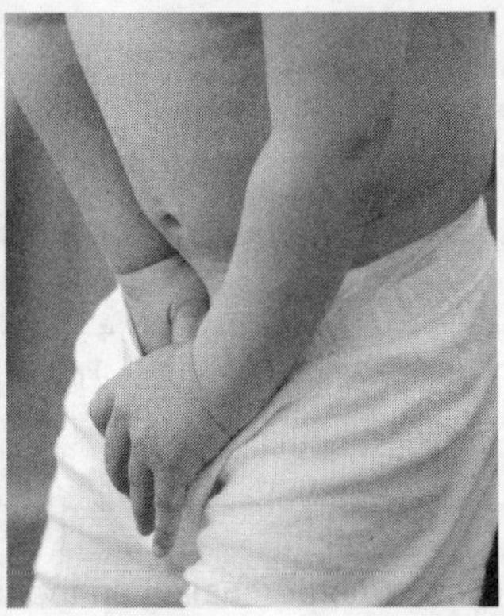

Parasympathetic stimulation is responsible for bladder emptying through contraction of the bladder wall and relaxation of the urethral sphincter. This reflex activity can be inhibited by conscious control, but this ability does not develop until 2-4 years of age.

As part of the fight or flight response, the sympathetic nervous system dilates arteries and increases the rate and force at which the heart contracts.Heart rate is increased when increased blood flow to the heart causes reflex stimulation of the **accelerator** centre.

The **enteric nervous system** (ENS) is a recently recognised, interdependent part of the ANS. The ENS regulates itself but is influenced by sympathetic and parasympathetic nerves which are connected to it. The ENS innervates the gut, pancreas and gall bladder.

1. Explain the structure and role of each of the following divisions of the autonomic nervous system:

   (a) The **sympathetic** nervous system: ______________________

   (b) The **parasympathetic** nervous system: ______________________

2. (a) Explain why the sympathetic and parasympathetic divisions of the ANS are often described as being opposing or **antagonistic** in function:

   (b) Explain why sympathetic stimulation tends to have more widespread and longer lasting effects than parasympathetic stimulation:

3. Using an example (e.g. control of heart rate), describe the role of reflexes in autonomic nervous system function:

4. With reference to the emptying of the bladder, explain how conscious control can modify a reflex activity:

5. Predict how the sympathetic reflexes controlling blood vessels would respond to a sudden decrease in blood pressure:

6. Asthma can be treated by inhaling a drug that mimics the action of noradrenaline on the sympathetic NS. Describe how this drug could be used to target the patient's respiratory system:

The Human Brain

The brain is one the largest organs in the body. It is protected by the skull, the **meninges**, and the **cerebrospinal fluid** (CSF). The brain is the body's control center. It receives a constant flow of sensory information, but responds only to what is important at the time. Some responses are very simple (e.g. cranial reflexes), whilst others require many levels of processing. The human brain is noted for its large, well developed cerebral region, with its prominent folds (**gyri**) and grooves (**sulci**). Each cerebral hemisphere has an outer region of gray matter and an inner region of white matter, and is divided into four lobes by deep sulci or fissures. These lobes: temporal, frontal, occipital, and parietal, correspond to the bones of the skull under which they lie.

Primary Structural Regions of the Brain

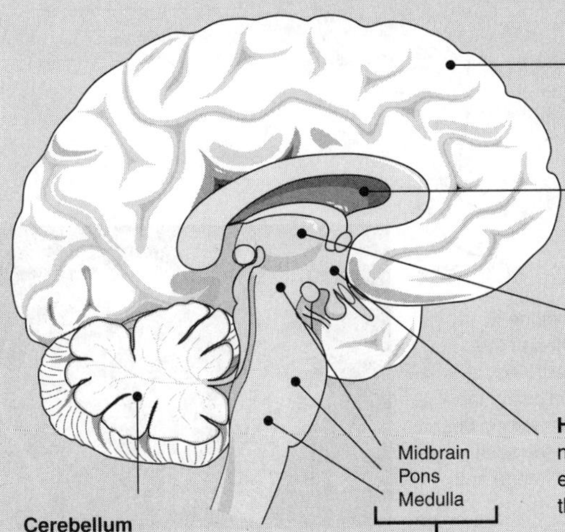

Cerebrum: Divided into two cerebral hemispheres. Many, complex roles. It contains sensory, motor, and association areas, and is involved in memory, emotion, language, reasoning, and sensory processing.

Ventricles: Cavities containing the CSF, which absorbs shocks and delivers nutritive substances.

Thalamus is the main relay centre for all sensory messages that enter the brain, before they are transmitted to the cerebrum.

Hypothalamus controls the autonomic nervous system and links nervous and endocrine systems. Regulates appetite, thirst, body temperature, and sleep.

Cerebellum coordinates body movements, posture, and balance.

Brainstem: Relay centre for impulses between the rest of the brain and the spinal cord. Controls breathing, heartbeat, and the coughing and vomiting reflexes.

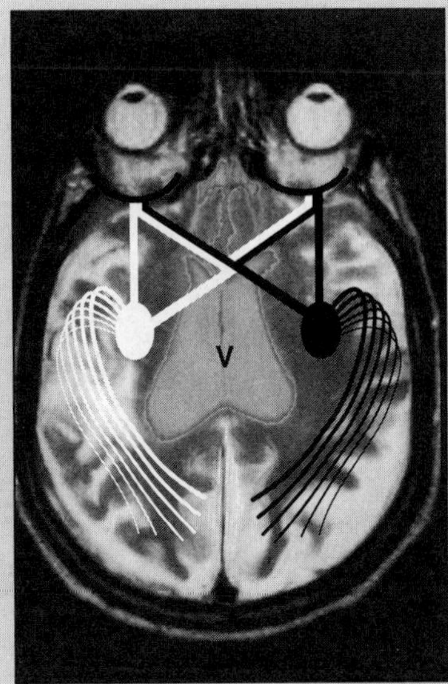

MRI scan of the brain viewed from above. The visual pathway has been superimposed on the image. Note the crossing of some sensory neurons to the opposite hemisphere and the fluid filled ventricles (V) in the centre.

Sensory and Motor Regions in the Cerebrum

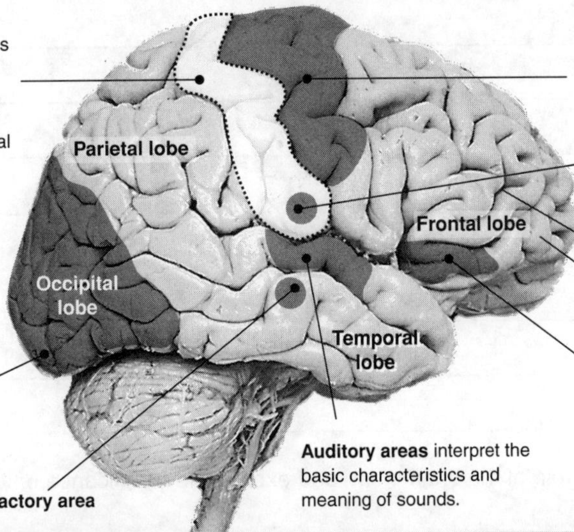

Primary somatic sensory area receives sensations from receptors in the skin, muscles and viscera, allowing recognition of pain, temperature, or touch. Sensory information from receptors on one side of the body crosses to the opposite side of the cerebral cortex where conscious sensations are produced. The size of the sensory region for different body parts depends on the number of receptors in that particular body part.

Visual areas within the occipital lobe receive, interpret, and evaluate visual stimuli. In vision, each eye views both sides of the visual field but the brain receives impulses from left and right visual fields separately (see photo caption above). The visual cortex combines the images into a single impression or **perception** of the image.

Olfactory area

Primary motor area controls muscle movement. Stimulation of a point one side of the motor area results in muscular contraction on the opposite side of the body.

Primary gustatory area interprets sensations related to taste.

Sulci (grooves)

Gyri (elevated folds)

Language areas: The motor speech area (Broca's area) is concerned with speech production. The sensory speech area (Wernicke's area) is concerned with speech recognition and coherence.

Auditory areas interpret the basic characteristics and meaning of sounds.

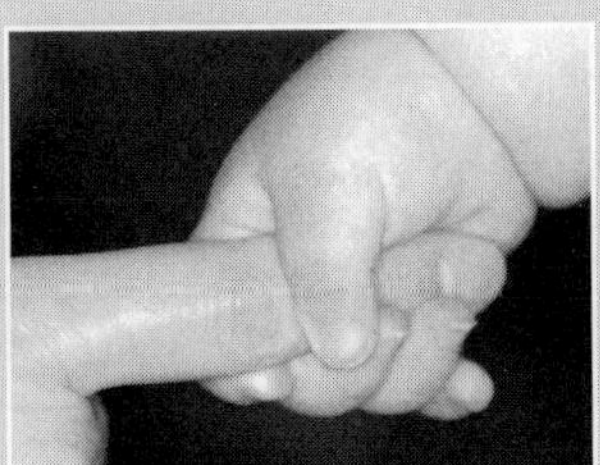

Touch is interpreted in the primary somatic sensory area. The fingertips and the lips have a relatively large amount of area devoted to them.

The hypothalamus regulates many autonomic functions including **appetite**. Hormones are the likely hypothalamic trigger for food intake.

The olfactory tract connects the olfactory bulb with the cerebral hemispheres where olfactory information is interpreted.

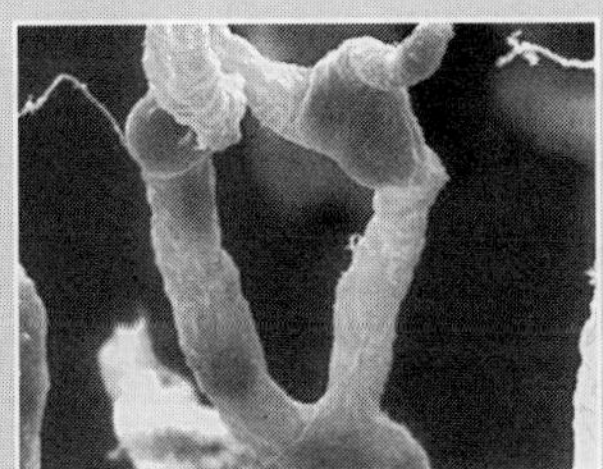

Dan Ferber

The endothelial tight junctions of the capillaries supplying the brain form a protective **blood-brain barrier** against toxins and infection.

The Ventricles and CSF

The delicate nervous tissue of the brain and spinal cord is protected against damage by the **bone** of the skull and vertebral column, the membranes overlying the brain (the **meninges**), and the watery but nutritive **cerebrospinal fluid** (CSF), which lies between the inner two of the meningeal layers. The CSF is formed from the blood by clusters of capillaries on the roof of each of the brain's ventricles (choroid plexuses) and is constantly circulated through the brain's ventricles and into the spinal cord.

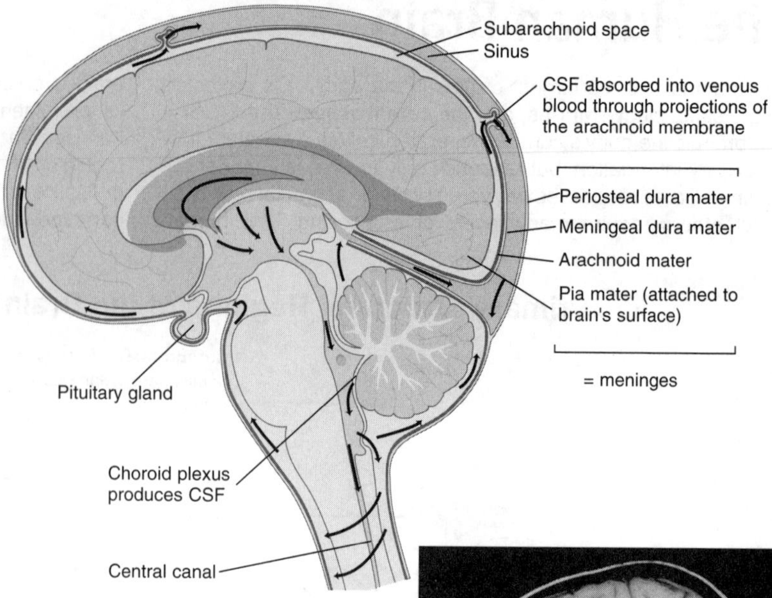

If the passages that normally allow the CSF to exit the brain become blocked, the CSF accumulates within the brain's ventricles causing a condition called hydrocephalus

The accumulated fluid can be seen in this MRI scan.

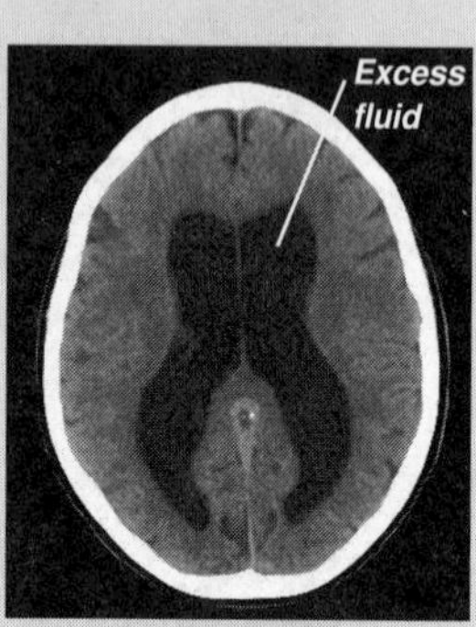

MRI scanning is a powerful technique to visualise the structure and function of the body. It is especially useful in neurological (brain) imaging, especially for indicating the presence of tumors or fluid, and showing up abnormalities in blood supply. In the scan pictured right, the fluid within the lateral and third ventricles is clearly visible.

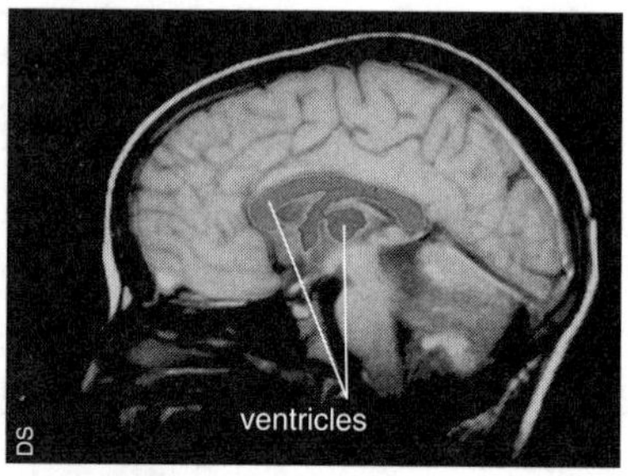

1. For each of the following bodily functions, identify the region(s) of the brain involved in its control:

   (a) Breathing and heartbeat: ______

   (b) Memory and emotion: ______

   (c) Posture and balance: ______

   (d) Autonomic functions: ______

   (e) Visual processing: ______

   (f) Body temperature: ______

   (g) Language: ______

   (h) Muscular movement: ______

2. Explain how the brain is protected against physical damage and infection: ______

3. Describe the structure and role of the brain stem, and explain the significance of its functional position:

4. Using illustrative examples, discuss the pivotal role of the hypothalamus in linking the nervous and endocrine systems:

The Mechanics of Movement

We are familiar with the many different bodily movements achievable through the action of muscles. Contractions in which the length of the muscle shortens in the usual way are called **isotonic contractions**: the muscle shortens and movement occurs. When a muscle contracts against something immovable and does not shorten the contraction is called **isometric**. Skeletal muscles are attached to bones by tough connective tissue structures called **tendons**. They always have at least two attachments: the **origin** and the **insertion**. They create movement of body parts when they contract across **joints**. The type and degree of movement achieved depends on how much movement the joint allows and where the muscle is located in relation to the joint. Some common types of body movements are described below (left panel). Because muscles can only pull and not push, most body movements are achieved through the action of opposing sets of muscles (below, right panel).

The Action of Antagonistic Muscles

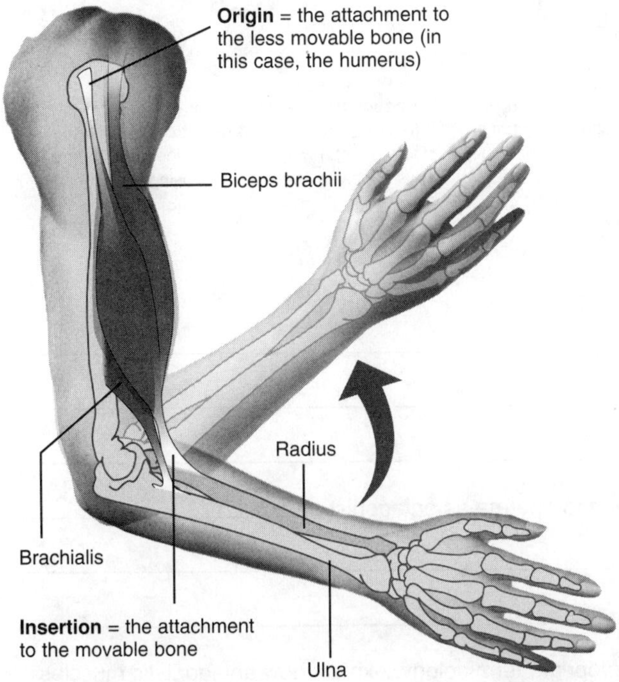

Two muscles are involved in flexing the forearm. The **brachialis**, which underlies the biceps brachii and has an origin half way up the humerus, is the **prime mover**. The more obvious **biceps brachii**, which is a two headed muscle with two origins and a common insertion near the elbow joint, acts as the synergist. During contraction, the insertion moves towards the origin.

The skeleton works as a system of levers. The joint acts as a **fulcrum** (or pivot), the muscles exert the force, and the weight of the bone being moved represents the load. The flexion (bending) and extension (unbending) of limbs is caused by the action of **antagonistic muscles**. Antagonistic muscles work in pairs and their actions oppose each other. During movement of a limb, muscles other than those primarily responsible for the movement may be involved to fine tune the movement.

Every coordinated movement in the body requires the application of muscle force. This is accomplished by the action of agonists, antagonists, and synergists. The opposing action of agonists and antagonists (working constantly at a low level) also produces muscle tone. Note that either muscle in an antagonistic pair can act as the agonist or prime mover, depending on the particular movement (for example, flexion or extension).

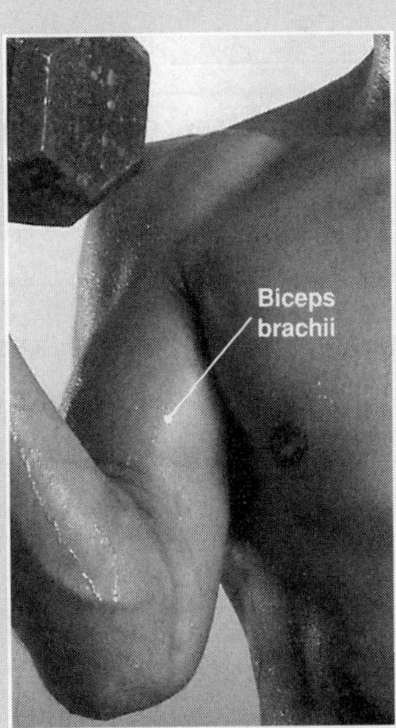

Agonists or prime movers: muscles that are primarily responsible for the movement and produce most of the force required.

Antagonists: muscles that oppose the prime mover. They may also play a protective role by preventing over-stretching of the prime mover.

Synergists: muscles that assist the prime movers and may be involved in fine-tuning the direction of the movement.

During flexion of the forearm (left) the **brachialis** muscle acts as the prime mover and the **biceps brachii** is the synergist. The antagonist, the **triceps brachii** at the back of the arm, is relaxed. During extension, their roles are reversed.

Movement of the upper leg is achieved through the action of several large groups of muscles, collectively called the **quadriceps** and the **hamstrings**.

The hamstrings are actually a collection of three muscles, which act together to flex the leg.

The quadriceps at the front of the thigh (a collection of four large muscles) opposes the motion of the hamstrings and extends the leg.

When the prime mover contracts forcefully, the antagonist also contracts very slightly. This prevents overstretching and allows greater control over thigh movement.

Movement at Joints

The synovial joints of the skeleton allow free movement in one or more planes. The articulating bone ends are separated by a joint cavity containing lubricating synovial fluid. Two types of synovial joint, the shoulder ball and socket joint and the hinge joint of the elbow, are illustrated below.

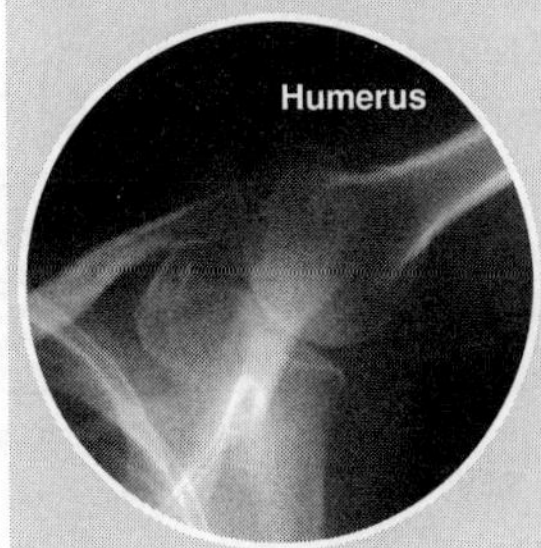

Ball and socket

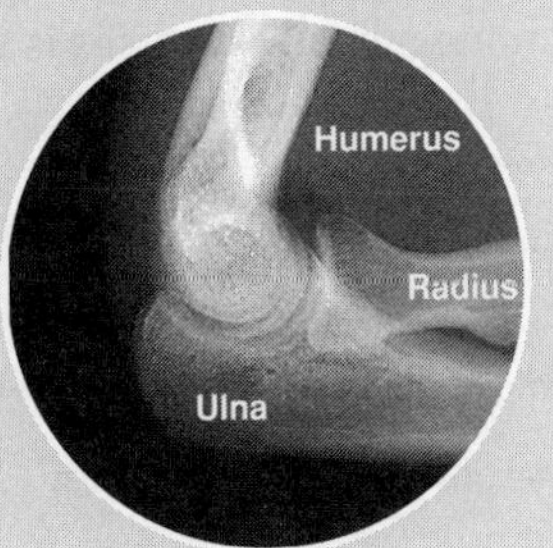

Hinge joint

Types of Body Movement

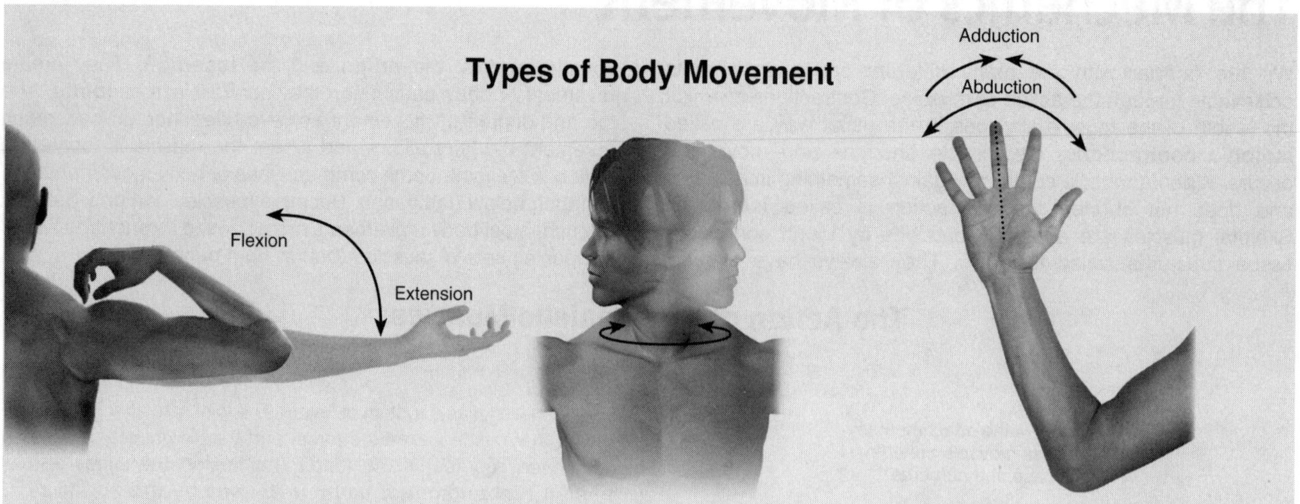

Flexion decreases the angle of the joint and brings two bones closer together. **Extension** is its opposite. Extension more than 180° is called **hyperextension**.

Rotation is movement of a bone around its longitudinal axis. It is a common movement of ball and socket joints and the movement of the atlas around the axis.

Abduction is a movement away from the midline, whereas **adduction** describes movement towards the midline. The terms also apply to opening and closing the fingers.

1. Describe the role of each of the following muscles in moving a limb:

   (a) Prime mover: ______________________

   (b) Antagonist: ______________________

   (c) Synergist: ______________________

2. Explain why the muscles that cause movement of body parts tend to operate as antagonist pairs: ______________________

3. Describe the relationship between muscles and joints Using appropriate terminology, explain how antagonistic muscles act together to raise and lower a limb:

   ____

4. Explain the role of joints in the movement of body parts: ______________________

5. (a) Identify the insertion for the biceps brachii during flexion of the forearm: ______________________

   (b) Identify the insertion of the brachialis muscle during flexion of the forearm: ______________________

   (c) Identify the antagonist during flexion of the forearm: ______________________

   (d) Given its insertion, describe the forearm movement during which the biceps brachialis is the prime mover:

   ____

6. (a) Describe a forearm movement in which the brachialis is the antagonist: ______________________

   (b) Identify the prime mover in this movement: ______________________

7. (a) Describe the actions that take place in the neck when you nod your head up and down as if saying "yes":

   ____

   (b) Describe the action being performed when a person sticks out their thumb to hitch a ride: ______________________

Voluntary Muscle Structure and Function

Voluntary muscle (also called striated or skeletal muscle) is organised into bundles of muscle cells or fibres. Each fibre is a single cell with many nuclei and each fibre is itself a bundle of smaller myofibrils arranged lengthwise. Each myofibril is in turn composed of two kinds of myofilaments (thick and thin), which overlap to form light and dark bands. The alternation of these light and dark bands gives skeletal muscle its striated or striped appearance. The sarcomere, bounded by the dark Z lines, forms one complete contractile unit. Muscle fibres are innervated by the branches of motor neurones, each of which terminates in a specialised cholinergic synapse called the **neuromuscular junction** (or motor end plate). A motor neurone and all the fibres it innervates (which may be a few or several hundred) are called a **motor unit**. Graded responses in the muscle as a whole are achieved by varying the number of motor units active at any one time (recruitment of motor units).

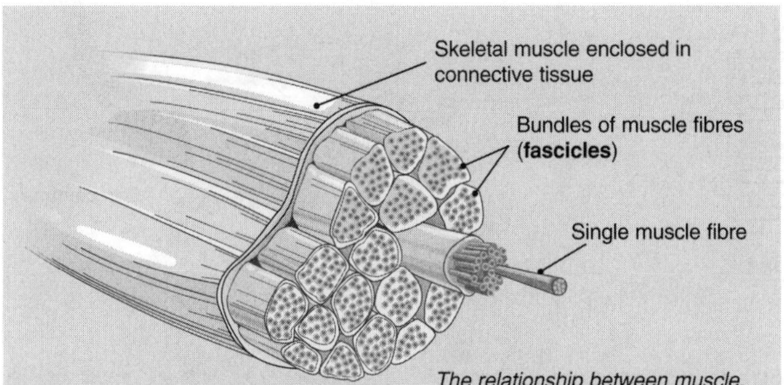

The relationship between muscle, fascicles, and muscle fibres (cells)

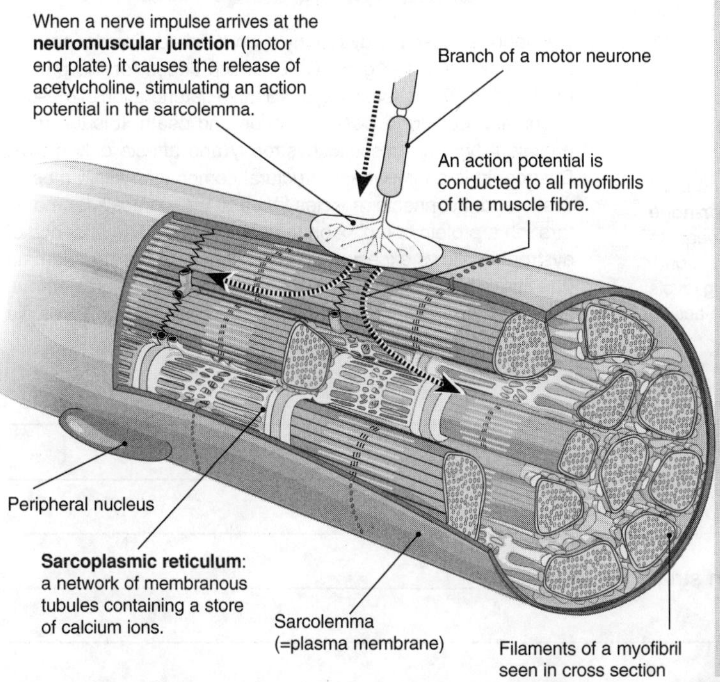

Longitudinal section of a sarcomere

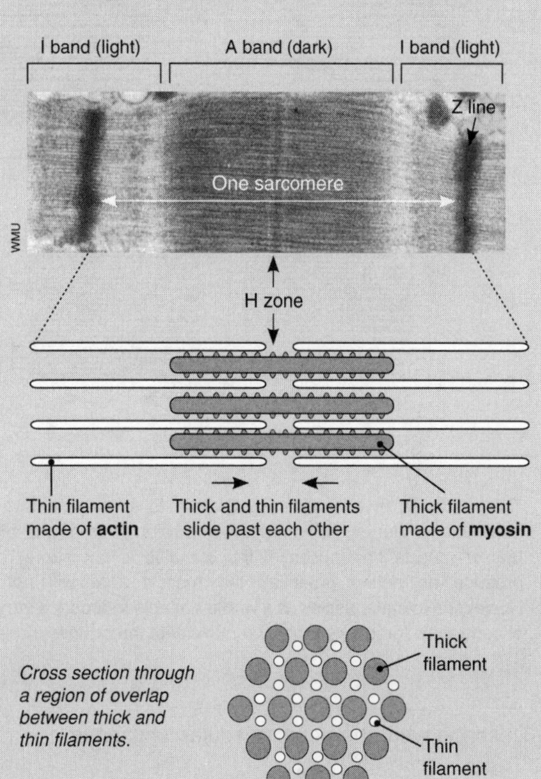

The photograph of a sarcomere (above) shows the banding pattern arising as a result of the highly organised arrangement of thin and thick filaments. It is represented schematically in longitudinal section and cross section.

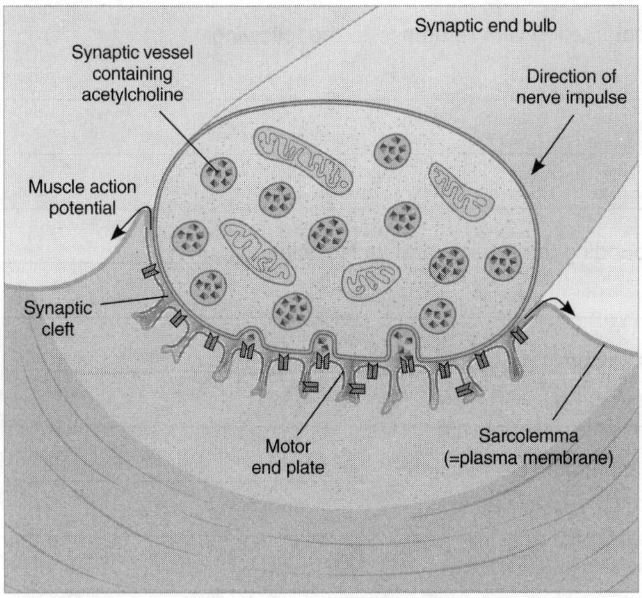

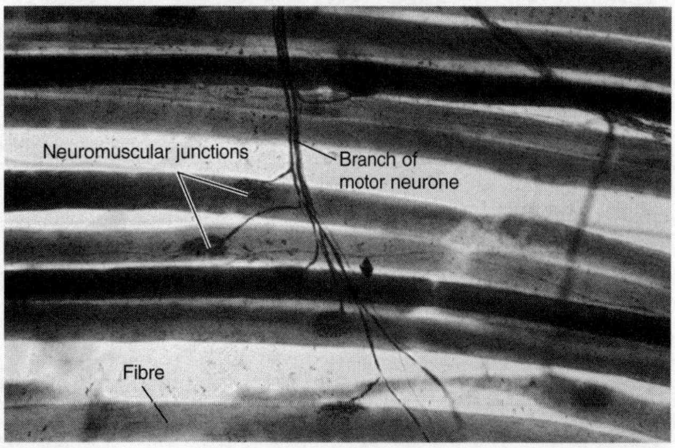

Above: Axon terminals of a motor neurone supplying a muscle. The branches of the axon terminate on the sarcolemma of a fibre at regions called the neuromuscular junction. Each fibre receives a branch of an axon, but one axon may supply many muscle fibres.

Left: Diagrammatic representation of the neuromuscular junction.

The Banding Pattern of Myofibrils

Within a myofibril, the thin filaments, held together by the **Z lines,** project in both directions. The arrival of an action potential sets in motion a series of events that cause the thick and thin filaments to slide past each other. This is called contraction and it results in shortening of the muscle fibre and is accompanied by a visible change in the appearance of the myofibril: the I band and the sarcomere shorten and H zone shortens or disappears (below).

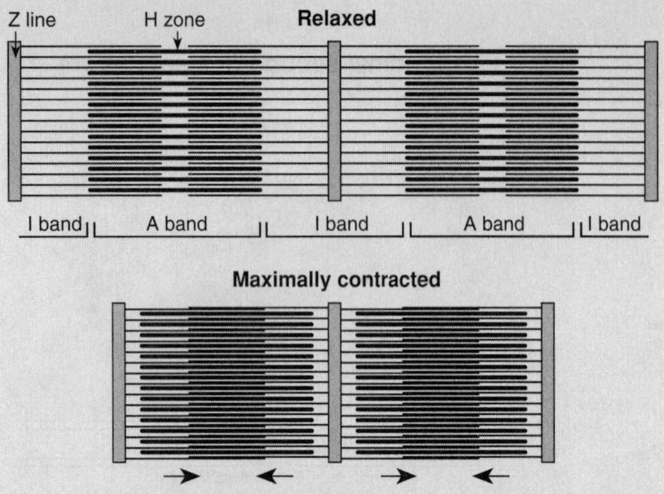

The response of a single muscle fibre to stimulation is to contract maximally or not at all; its response is referred to as the **all-or-none law** of muscle contraction. If the stimulus is not strong enough to produce an action potential, the muscle fibre will not respond. However skeletal muscles as a whole are able to produce varying levels of contractile force by varying the number of motor units that are active.

When Things Go Wrong

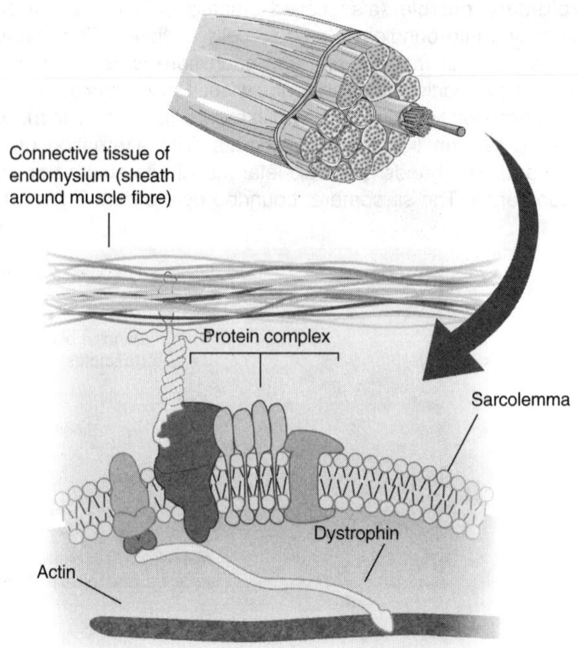

Duchenne's muscular dystrophy is an X-linked disorder caused by a mutation in the gene DMD, which codes for the protein **dystrophin**. The disease causes a rapid deterioration of muscle, eventually leading to loss of function and death. It is the most prevalent type of muscular dystrophy and affects only males. Dystrophin is an important structural component within muscle tissue and it connects muscles fibres to the extracellular matrix through a protein complex on the sarcolemma. The absence of dystrophin allows excess calcium to penetrate the sarcolemma (the fibre's plasma membrane). This damages the sarcolemma, and eventually results in the death of the cell. Muscle fibres die and are replaced with adipose and connective tissue.

1. Describe what the neuromuscular junction is: ______________________________

____

____

2. (a) Explain the cause of the banding pattern visible in striated muscle: ______________________________

____

____

(b) Explain the change in appearance of a myofibril during contraction with reference to the following:

The I band: ______________________________

The H zone: ______________________________

The sarcomere: ______________________________

3. Describe the purpose of the connective tissue sheaths surrounding the muscle and its fascicles: ______________________________

____

4. Explain what is meant by the all-or-none response of a muscle fibre: ______________________________

____

5. Explain why the inability to produce **dystrophin** leads to a loss of muscle function: ______________________________

____

____

The Sliding Filament Model

The previous activity described how muscle contraction is achieved by the thick and thin muscle filaments sliding past one another. This sliding is possible because of the structure and arrangement of the thick and thin filaments. The ends of the thick myosin filaments are studded with heads or **cross bridges** that can link to the thin filaments next to them. The thin filaments contain the protein actin, but also a regulatory protein complex. When the cross bridges of the thick filaments connect to the thin filaments, a shape change moves one filament past the other. Two things are necessary for cross bridge formation: calcium ions, which are released from the **sarcoplasmic reticulum** when the muscle receives an action potential, and ATP, which is hydrolyzed by ATPase enzymes on the myosin. When cross bridges attach and detach in sarcomeres throughout the muscle cell, the cell shortens. Although a muscle fibre responds to an action potential by contracting maximally, skeletal muscles as a whole can produce varying levels of contractile force. These **graded responses** are achieved by changing the frequency of stimulation (**frequency summation**) and by changing the number and size of motor units recruited (**multiple fibre summation**). Maximal contractions of a muscle are achieved when nerve impulses arrive at the muscle at a rapid rate and a large number of motor units are active at once.

The Sliding Filament Model

Muscle contraction requires calcium ions (Ca^{2+}) and energy (in the form of ATP) in order for the thick and thin filaments to slide past each other. The steps are:

1. The binding sites on the actin molecule (to which myosin 'heads' will locate) are blocked by a complex of two protein molecules: tropomyosin and troponin.
2. Prior to muscle contraction, ATP binds to the heads of the myosin molecules, priming them in an erect high energy state. Arrival of an action potential causes a release of Ca^{2+} from the sarcoplasmic reticulum. The Ca^{2+} binds to the troponin and causes the blocking complex to move so that the myosin binding sites on the actin filament become exposed.
3. The heads of the cross-bridging myosin molecules attach to the binding sites on the actin filament. Release of energy from the hydrolysis of ATP accompanies the cross bridge formation.
4. The energy released from ATP hydrolysis causes a change in shape of the myosin cross bridge, resulting in a bending action (the power stroke). This causes the actin filaments to slide past the myosin filaments towards the centre of the sarcomere.
5. (Not illustrated). Fresh ATP attaches to the myosin molecules, releasing them from the binding sites and repriming them for a repeat movement. They become attached further along the actin chain as long as ATP and Ca^{2+} are available.

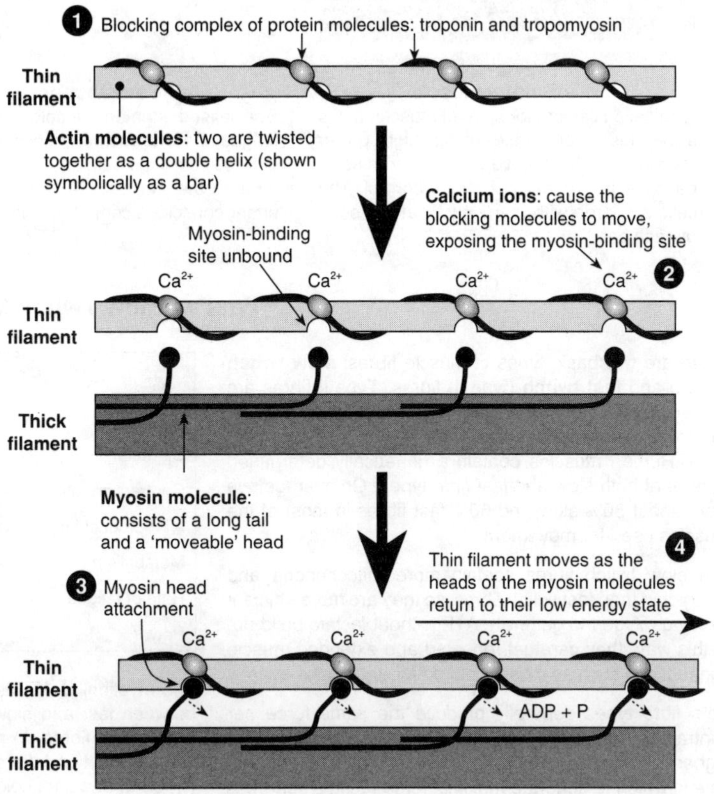

1. Match the following chemicals with their functional role in muscle movement (draw a line between matching pairs):

(a) Myosin	• Bind to the actin molecule in a way that prevents myosin head from forming a cross bridge
(b) Actin	• Supplies energy for the flexing of the myosin 'head' (power stroke)
(c) Calcium ions	• Has a moveable head that provides a power stroke when activated
(d) Troponin-tropomyosin	• Two protein molecules twisted in a helix shape that form the thin filament of a myofibril
(e) ATP	• Bind to the blocking molecules, causing them to move and expose the myosin binding site

2. Describe the two ways in which a muscle as a whole can produce contractions of varying force:

(a) ______________________________

____

(b) ______________________________

____

3. (a) Identify the two things necessary for cross bridge formation: ______________________________

(b) Explain where each of these comes from: ______________________________

____

Types of Muscle

There are three kinds of muscle tissue: **voluntary** (skeletal), **cardiac**, and **involuntary** (smooth) muscle, each with a distinct structure. The muscles used for posture and locomotion are skeletal (voluntary) muscles and are largely under conscious control. Their distinct appearance is the result of the regular arrangement of contractile elements within the muscle cells. Cardiac and smooth muscle are involuntary muscles, and are not under conscious control.

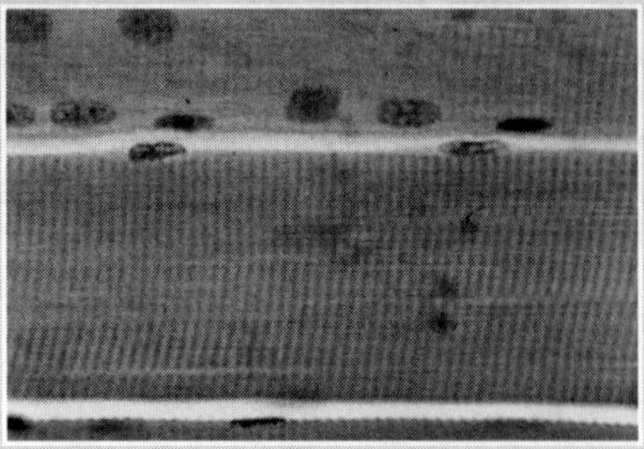
RCN

Voluntary muscle

Also called skeletal or striated muscle. It has a banded appearance under high power microscopy. It is called voluntary muscle because it is under conscious control. The cells are large with many nuclei at the edge of each cell.

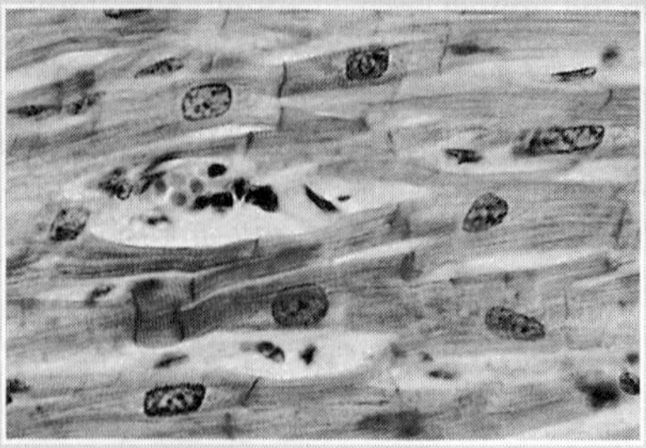

Cardiac muscle

Specialised striated muscle that does not fatigue. Cells branch and connect with each other to assist the passage of nerve impulses through the muscle. Cardiac muscle is not under conscious control (it is involuntary).

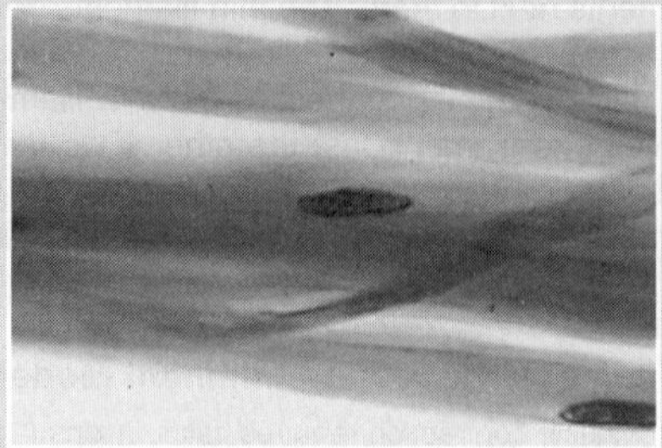
RCN

Smooth muscle

Also called involuntary muscle because it is not under conscious control. Contractile filaments are irregularly arranged so the contraction is not in one direction as in skeletal muscle. Cells are spindle shaped with one central nucleus.

Fast vs Slow Twitch Muscle

There are two basic types of muscle fibres: **slow twitch** (type I) and **fast twitch** (type II) fibres. Type II fibres are further classified (depending on their metabolism) as Type IIa (some oxidative capacity) and Type IIb (fast glycolytic only). Human muscles contain a genetically determined mixture of both slow and fast fibre types. On average, we have about 50% slow and 50% fast fibres in most of the muscles used for movement.

The slow twitch fibres contain more mitochondria and myoglobin than fast twitch fibres, so they are more efficient at using oxygen to generate ATP without lactate build up. In this way, they can fuel repeated and extended muscle contractions such as those required for endurance events.

Both fibre types generally produce the same force per contraction, but fast twitch fibres produce that force at a higher rate, so they are important when there is a limited time in which to generate maximal force (as in a sprint).

Feature	Fast twitch	Slow twitch
Colour	White	Red
Diameter	Large	Small
Contraction rate	Fast	Slow
ATP production	Fast	Slow
Metabolism	Anaerobic	Aerobic
Rate of fatigue	Fast	Slow
Power	High	Low

The myofibrillar ATPase stain is used to distinguish between fast and slow twitch muscle fibres (right). Slow-twitch fibres do not stain as darkly as the two types of fast twitch fibres, which stain an intermediate (type IIa) or a dark colour (type IIb) respectively.

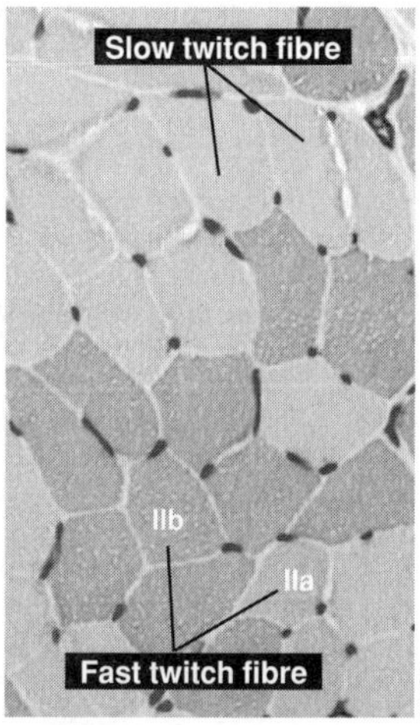

NASA

1. Distinguish between **smooth muscle**, **striated muscle**, and **cardiac muscle**, summarising the features of each type:

2. Contrast the properties of fast and slow twitch skeletal muscle fibres, identifying how these properties contribute to their performance in different conditions:

Related activities: *Voluntary Muscle Structure and Function*

Energy for Muscle Contraction

Muscular contraction places an immediate demand on the body's energy supply systems. During activity, the metabolic rate of the muscles increases by up to 20 times and the body's systems must respond appropriately to maintain homeostasis. The ability to exercise for any given length of time depends on maintaining adequate supplies of ATP to the muscles. There are three energy systems operating to do this: the ATP-CP system, the glycolytic system, and the oxidative system. The ultimate sources of energy for ATP generation in muscle via these systems are glucose, and stores of glycogen and triglycerides. Prolonged intense exercise utilises the oxidative system, and relies on a constant supply of oxygen to the tissues. The **VO_2** is the amount of oxygen (expressed as a volume) used by muscles during a specified interval for cell metabolism and energy production. **VO_2max** is the maximum volume of oxygen that can be delivered and used per minute and therefore represents an individual's upper limit of aerobic metabolism. VO_2max is used as a measure of fitness, and is high in trained athletes. At some percentage of VO_2max (the **anaerobic threshold**) the body is unable to meet its energy demands aerobically and an **oxygen debt** is incurred.

CP provides enough energy to fuel about 10 s of maximum effort (e.g. a 100 m race).

The ATP-CP System

The simplest of the energy systems is the **ATP-CP system**. CP or **creatine phosphate** is a high energy compound that stores enough energy for brief periods of muscular effort. Energy released from the breakdown of CP is not used directly to accomplish cellular work. Instead it rebuilds ATP to maintain a relatively constant supply. This process is anaerobic, occurs very rapidly, and is accomplished without any special structures in the cell. CP levels decline steadily as it is used to replenish depleted ATP levels. The ability of the ATP-CP system to maintain energy levels is limited to 3-15 seconds. Beyond this, the muscle must rely on other processes for ATP generation.

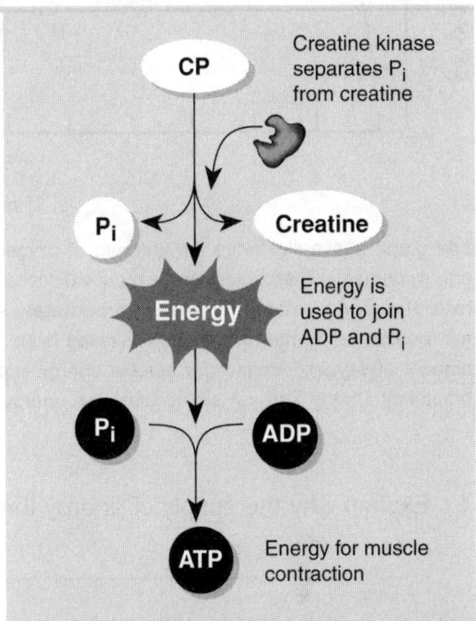

Rugby and other field sports demand brief intense efforts with recovery in-between.

The Glycolytic System

ATP can also be provided by glycolysis: the firstt phase of cellular respiration. The ATP yield from glycolysis is low (net 2ATP per molecule of glucose), but it produces ATP rapidly and does not require oxygen. The fuel for the glycolytic system is glucose in the blood, or glycogen, which is stored in the muscle or liver and broken down to glucose-6-phosphate. Glycolysis provides ATP for a few minutes of full muscular effort. Its main limitation is that it causes lactic acid ($C_3H_6O_8$) to accumulate in the tissues. Indirectly, it is the accumulation of lactic acid that gives the feeling of muscle fatigue. The lactic acid must transported to the liver and respired aerobically. The extra oxygen needed for this is the **oxygen debt**.

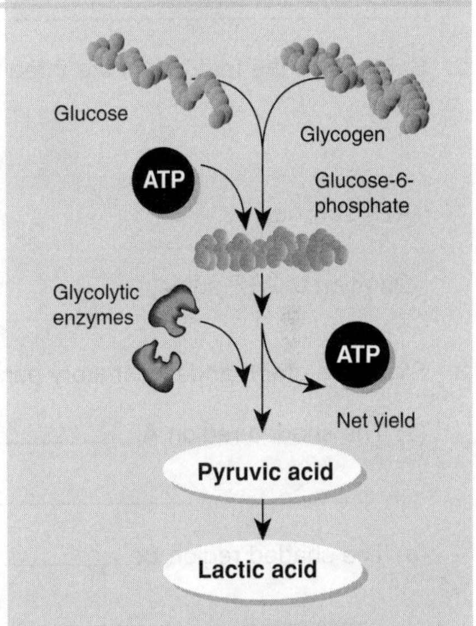

Prolonged aerobic effort (e.g. distance running) requires a sustained ATP supply.

The Oxidative System

In the oxidative system, glucose is completely broken down to yield (about) 36 molecules of ATP. This process uses oxygen and takes place within the mitochondria. Aerobic metabolism has a high energy yield and is the primary method of energy production during sustained high activity. It relies on a continued supply of oxygen and therefore on the delivery of sufficient oxygen to the muscles. The fuels for aerobic respiration are glucose, stored glycogen, or stored triglycerides. Triglycerides provide free fatty acids, which are oxidised in the mitochondria by the successive removal of two-carbon fragments (a process called b-oxidation). These two carbon units enter the Krebs cycle as acetyl coenzyme A (acetyl CoA).

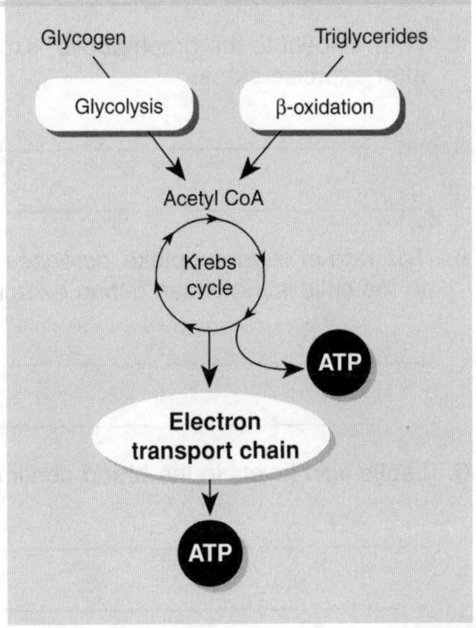

Periodicals:
Lactic acid...who needs it?

Related activities: *Voluntary Muscle Structure and Function*

Oxygen Uptake during Exercise and Recovery

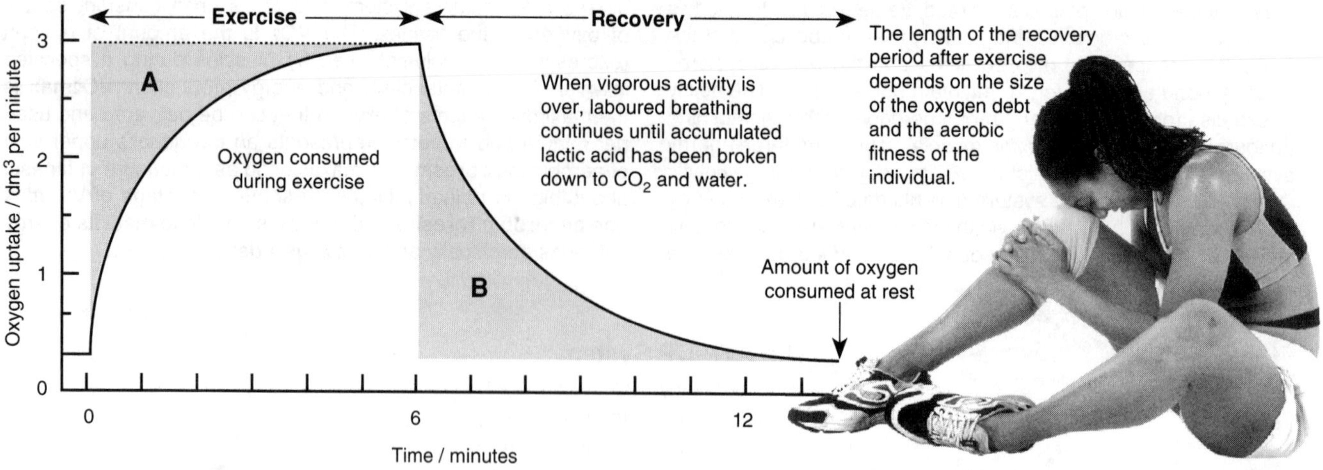

The graph above illustrates the principle of oxygen debt. In the graph, the energy demands of aerobic exercise require 3 dm^3 of oxygen per minute. The rate of oxygen uptake increases immediately exercise starts, but the full requirement is not met until six minutes later. The oxygen deficit is the amount of oxygen needed (for aerobic energy supply) but not supplied by breathing. During the first six minutes, the energy is supplied largely from anaerobic pathways: the ATP-CP and glycolytic systems. After exercise, the oxygen uptake per minute does not drop immediately to its resting level. Extra oxygen is taken in despite the drop in energy demand (the **oxygen debt**). The oxygen debt is used to replace oxygen reserves in the body, restore creatine phosphate, and break down the lactic acid (through various intermediates) to CO_2 and water.

1. Explain why the supply of energy through the glycolytic system is limited:

2. Summarise the features of the three energy systems in the table below:

	ATP-CP system	Glycolytic System	Oxidative system
ATP supplied by:			
Duration of ATP supply:			

3. Study the graph and explanatory paragraph above, then identify and describe what is represented by:

(a) The shaded region **A**:

(b) The shaded region **B**:

4. With respect to the graph above, explain why the rate of oxygen uptake does not immediately return to its resting level after exercise stops:

5. The rate of oxygen uptake increases immediately exercise starts. Explain how the oxygen supply from outside the body to the cells is increased during exercise:

6. Lactic acid levels in the **blood** continue to rise for a time after exercise has stopped. Explain why this occurs:

Fight or Flight

The complex hormonal and nervous interactions of the **hypothalamus, pituitary** and **adrenal glands** are responsible for controlling the body's reactions to stress and regulating many of the body's processes, including digestion, immune function, mood, sexuality, and energy storage and expenditure. The **stress response** is triggered through sympathetic stimulation of the central medulla region of the adrenal glands, in what is popularly know as the **fight or flight syndrome**. This stimulation causes the release of catecholamines (adrenaline and noradrenaline). These hormones help to prepare the body to cope with short-term stressful situations. Continued stress results in release of glucocorticoids (especially **cortisol**) from the outer cortex of the adrenals. These hormones help the body to resist longer term stress. Their secretion is a normal part of what is called the general adaptation syndrome, but continued unrelieved stress can be damaging, or even fatal.

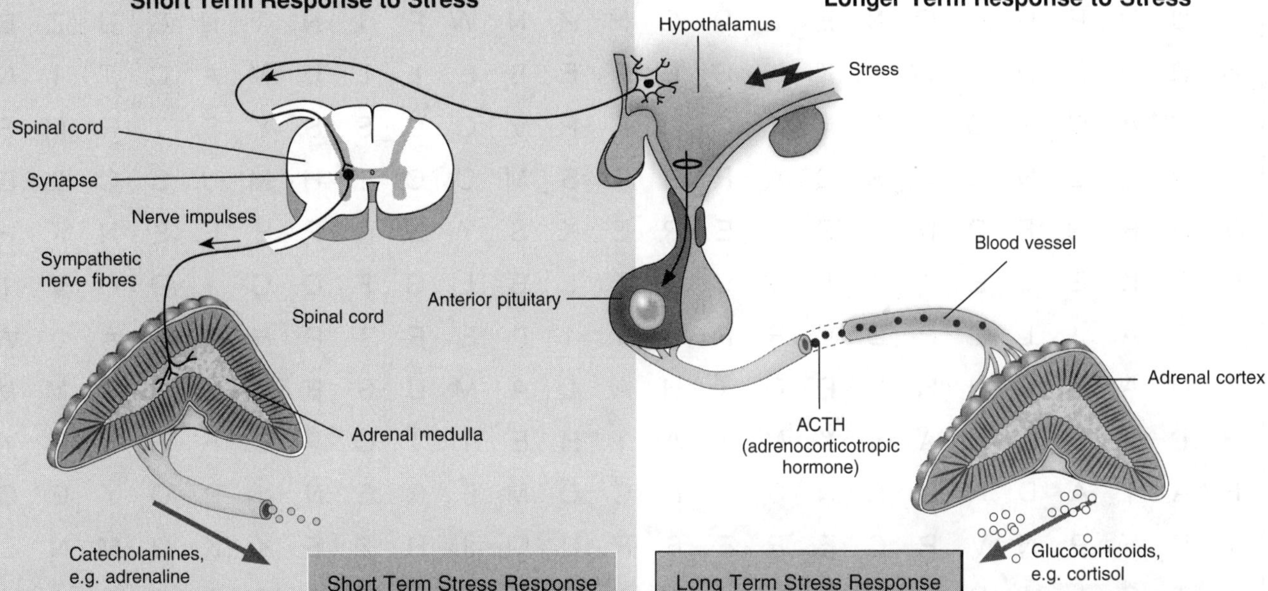

Short Term Stress Response (fight or flight syndrome)

1. Increased heart rate
2. Increased blood pressure
3. Liver converts glycogen to glucose; blood glucose levels increase
4. Dilation of bronchioles
5. Blood flow to gut and kidney reduced

   Blood flow to muscles and brain increased
6. Increased metabolic rate

The physiological changes occurring as part of the short term stress response help us to operate at peak efficiency when endangered, competing, or whenever a high level of performance is required.

Long Term Stress Response (General adaptation syndrome)

1. Proteins and fats converted to glucose of broken down for energy
2. Increased blood sugar
3. Suppression of the immune system

A state of long term unrelieved stress is not normal. The body responds to prolonged periods of stress by making physiological changes to resist the stress (e.g. conserving energy during periods of starvation). If the stress continues unrelieved, the body enters a phase of **exhaustion**, where its resistance to stress is eroded, and the immune system fails and loses its ability to fight disease.

1. Explain how the body's short term response to stress is adaptive: ____________________

____

____

____

2. Explain how nervous and hormonal regulation interact in the body's response to stress: ____________________

____

____

____

____

KEY TERMS: Word Find

Use the clues below to find the relevant key terms in the WORD FIND grid

B	O	I	D	Y	T	S	T	N	E	U	R	O	T	R	A	N	S	M	I	T	T	E	R	S
R	N	F	L	C	A	R	D	I	A	C	M	U	S	C	L	E	W	P	G	J	S	S	S	L
A	E	U	K	D	X	F	C	M	M	E	D	U	L	L	A	O	B	L	O	N	G	A	T	A
I	U	N	E	U	R	O	N	E	L	D	G	M	Z	N	W	P	I	N	I	H	Q	U	Z	B
N	R	P	P	N	C	W	R	K	K	C	E	R	E	B	E	L	L	U	M	A	C	T	I	N
S	O	A	U	T	O	N	O	M	I	C	N	E	R	V	O	U	S	S	Y	S	T	E	M	F
Y	M	Z	G	N	O	L	S	Q	A	R	B	R	S	M	O	O	T	H	M	U	S	C	L	E
M	U	R	G	F	D	N	R	Z	A	E	R	E	X	S	Y	N	A	P	S	E	E	N	K	H
P	S	K	E	L	E	T	A	L	M	U	S	C	L	E	L	G	F	D	G	J	D	O	V	I
A	C	A	J	L	Z	P	D	V	R	R	P	I	I	P	E	R	I	P	H	E	R	A	L	W
T	U	A	Y	U	N	H	Y	P	O	T	H	A	L	A	M	U	S	B	A	S	H	T	M	M
H	L	M	P	A	R	A	S	Y	M	P	A	T	H	E	T	I	C	F	O	F	F	B	R	Y
E	A	Y	A	D	A	D	R	N	S	A	R	C	O	M	E	R	E	N	J	P	O	Y	E	O
T	R	F	P	N	V	P	C	E	R	E	B	R	U	M	J	H	Z	F	K	K	U	M	N	S
I	T	S	L	I	D	I	N	G	F	I	L	A	M	E	N	T	T	S	C	C	C	O	I	I
C	R	U	V	O	L	U	N	T	A	R	Y	M	U	S	C	L	E	B	M	K	F	B	Y	N
C	E	N	T	R	A	L	N	E	R	V	O	U	S	M	Y	O	F	I	B	R	I	L	S	T

The name of the theory for how muscles produce force (2 words).

The lowest half of the brainstem below the pons (2 words).

A cell specialised to transmit electrical impulses.

These chemicals relay signals between a neurone and another cell.

That part of the nervous system comprising all the nerves and sensory receptors outside of the central nervous system.

The gap between neighbouring neurones or between a neurone and an effector.

Another name for striated muscle (2 words).

A complete contractile unit in skeletal muscle.

These are made up of thick and thin myofilaments.

Type of muscle lining the alimentary canal, blood vessels, and many hollow organs (2 words).

Thin filament within the myofibril of striated muscle.

A protein found in the thick myofilaments of the sarcomere of muscle.

A muscle that is under conscious control (2 words).

The junction between a motor neurone and a skeletal muscle fibre is called the _ _ _ _ _ _ _ _ _ _ _ _ _ junction.

A division of the autonomic nervous system, this system causes the fight or flight response in humans.

The region of the brain that coordinates the nervous and endocrine systems.

The portion of the peripheral nervous system that controls visceral functions (3 words).

The system in the human body comprising the brain and spinal cord (2 words).

This is the largest portion of the brain and is divided into two hemispheres. It has many functions including roles in memory, emotion, and language.

Specialised striated muscle found only in the heart. It does not fatigue (2 words).

Region of the brain which coordinates body movements, posture, and balance.

Together with the spinal cord, this organ comprises the central nervous system.

The division of the autonomic nervous system that controls involuntary muscle movement.

UNIT F215

5.4.3

Animal Behaviour

KEY CONCEPTS

- Behaviours, both learned and innate are adaptive.
- Innate behaviours are typically fixed action patterns in response to particular releasers (sign stimuli).
- Learning includes a wide range of behaviours: insight, latent learning, imprinting, habituation, and conditioning.
- Social behaviours facilitate survival in primates.
- A range of human behaviours can be linked to the functioning of chemical receptors in the brain.

KEY TERMS

classical conditioning
conditioned response
conditioned stimulus
critical period
fixed action pattern
habituation
imprinting
innate behaviour
insight learning
kineses (sing. kinesis)
latent learning
learned behaviour
operant conditioning
operant response
Pavlov
reflex behaviour
reinforcement
reward
sign stimulus (=releaser)
Skinner
social behaviour
taxes (sing. taxis)
unconditioned response
unconditioned stimulus

OBJECTIVES

☐ 1. Use the **KEY TERMS** to help you understand and complete these objectives.

Innate behaviour

pages 332-333

☐ 2. Explain what is meant by innate behaviour, and appreciate the role of natural selection in the development of adaptive behaviour patterns.

☐ 3. Explain the adaptive value of **innate behaviour** and describe examples, including **taxes**, **kineses**, and **reflex escape behaviour**. Examples include:

- Taxes: response of *Euglena* toward light, flatworms towards food, and blowfly larvae away from light.
- Kineses: the response of woodlice to humidity and body lice to temperature.
- Escape reflexes: caridoid escape reaction (tail flip) in decapod crustaceans such as crayfish and ink ejection in squid.

Learned behaviour

page 332, 335-338

☐ 4. Explain what is meant by **learned behaviour**, and outline its adaptive role.

☐ 5. Describe examples of learned behaviours, including:

- **Habituation**: Describe the basic characteristics of habituation and its adaptive value. Distinguish habituation from sensory adaptation.
- **Imprinting**: Describe the basic characteristics of imprinting, including reference to the **critical period** in the imprinting behaviour.
- **Classical conditioning**: Explain classical conditioning and the work of Pavlov illustrating this behaviour. Include reference to the **unconditioned** and **conditioned stimuli**, and **unconditioned** and **conditioned response**.
- **Operant conditioning**: Distinguish operant from classical conditioning. Describe the work of Skinner on operant conditioning, including reference to the **operant response**, **reinforcement**, and **reward**. Recognise operant conditioning as the predominant learning process in animals.
- **Latent learning**: Appreciate the difficulty in demonstrating latent learning.
- **Insight behaviour**: Explain the adaptive value of insight to species presented with new problems and associations.

☐ 6. EXTENSION: Explain that behaviour may have both an innate and a learned component and describe an example, e.g. song development in birds.

Primate behaviour

pages 334, 339

☐ 7. Describe an example of social behaviour in non-human primates. Examples could include: dominance hierarchies, social grooming, parental care, imitative learning, and cooperative foraging (including cooperative hunting).

☐ 8. Describe the links between human behaviours (e.g. emotional responses and motivation) and the dopamine receptor (DRD4). Discuss how an understanding of these physiological links contributes to our understanding of human behaviours, including schizophrenia, ADHD, and addiction.

Periodicals:
Listings for this chapter are on page 343

Weblinks:
www.biozone.co.uk/weblink/OCR-A2-2832.html

Teacher Resource CD-ROM: *Communication is Everything*

The Components of Behaviour

Behaviour in animals can be attributed to two components; **innate behaviour** that has a genetic basis, and **learned behaviour**, which results from the experiences of the animal. Together they combine to produce the total behaviour exhibited by the animal. It should also be noted that experience can modify innate behaviour. Animals behave in 'automatic ways' in many situations. The innate behaviour follows a classical pathway called a **fixed-action pattern** (FAP) where an innate behavioural programme is activated by a stimulus or **releaser** to direct some kind of behavioural response. Innate behaviours are generally adaptive and are performed for a variety of reasons. Learning, which involves the modification of behaviour by experience, occurs in various ways.

Innate Behaviours

Reflex behaviour
A stimulus induces an automatic involuntary and stereotyped response. Reflex behaviours are protective, e.g the reflex escape behaviour (caridoid response) of decapod crustaceans.

Kinesis
Random movement of an animal in which the rate of movement is related to the intensity of the stimulus, but not to its direction.

Taxis
A movement in response to the direction of a stimulus. Movements towards a stimulus are positive while those away from a stimulus are negative.

Stereotyped behaviour
Occurs when the same response is given to the same stimulus on different occasions. This behaviour shows fixed patterns of coordinated movements called fixed action patterns.

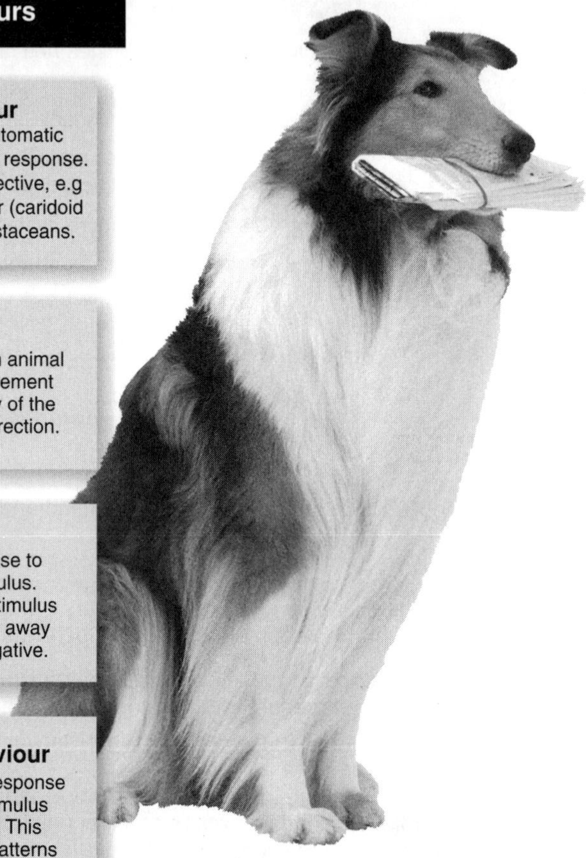

The complex behaviour patterns exhibited by an animal

Learned Behaviours

Classical conditioning
Animals may associate one stimulus with another.

Habituation
Response to a stimulus wanes when it is repeated with no apparent effect.

Insight behaviour
Correct behaviour on the first attempt where the animal has no prior experience.

Imprinting behaviour
During a critical period, an animal can adopt a behaviour by latching on to its first stimulus.

Operant conditioning
Also called trial and error learning; an animal is rewarded or punished after chance behaviour.

Fixed Action Patterns

A releaser (sometimes called a sign stimulus) is a signal that elicits a specific response from members of the same species. The releaser triggers the operation of an **innate releasing mechanism** in the brain that mediates a predictable behavioural response called the **fixed-action pattern** (FAP). FAPs are spontaneous, stereotyped, and indivisible. Once begun, a FAP runs to completion and is independent of learning.

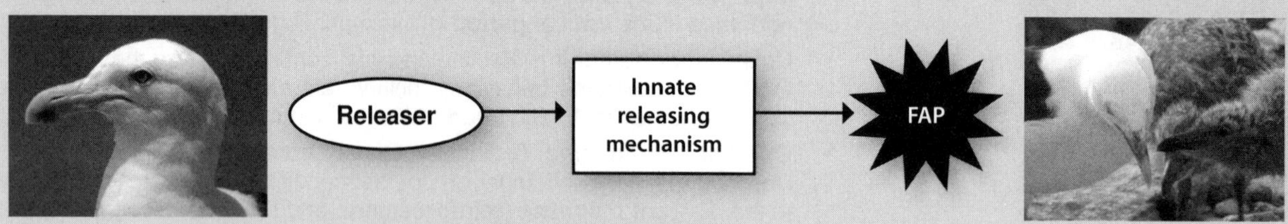

1. Distinguish between innate and learned behaviours: ______________________

____

2. (a) Explain the role of releasers in innate behaviours: ______________________

____

(b) Name a releaser for a fixed action pattern and the animal involved, and describe the behaviour elicited:

____

____

***Related activities:** Simple Behaviours, Learned Behaviour*

Simple Behaviours

Taxes and kineses are adaptive locomotory behaviours and involve movements in response to external stimuli such as gravity, light, chemicals, and temperature. A kinesis (pl. kineses) is a non-directional response to a stimulus in which the speed of movement or the rate of turning is proportional to the stimulus intensity. Kineses do not involve orientation directly to the stimulus and are typical of many invertebrates and protozoa. In contrast, **taxes** involve orientation and movement in response to a directional stimulus or a gradient in stimulus intensity. Taxes often involve moving the head (bearing sensory receptors) from side to side until the sensory input from both sides is equal (a klinotaxic response). Many taxic responses are complicated by a simultaneous response to more than one stimulus. For example, fish orientate dorsal side up in response to both light and gravity. Male moths orientate positively to pheromones but use the wind to judge the direction of the odour source (the female moth).

A

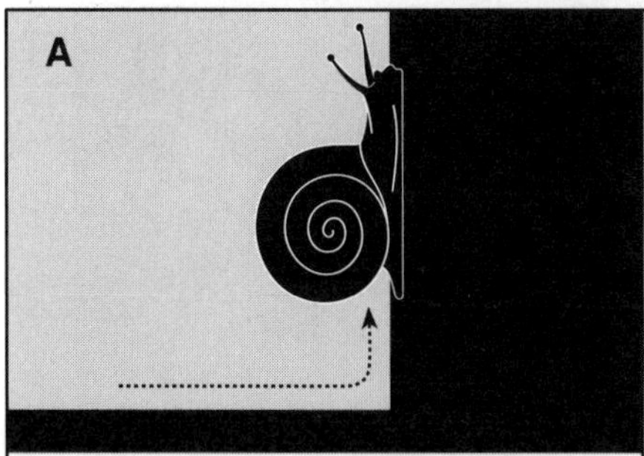

When confronted with a vertical surface, snails will reorientate themselves so that they climb vertically upwards.

B

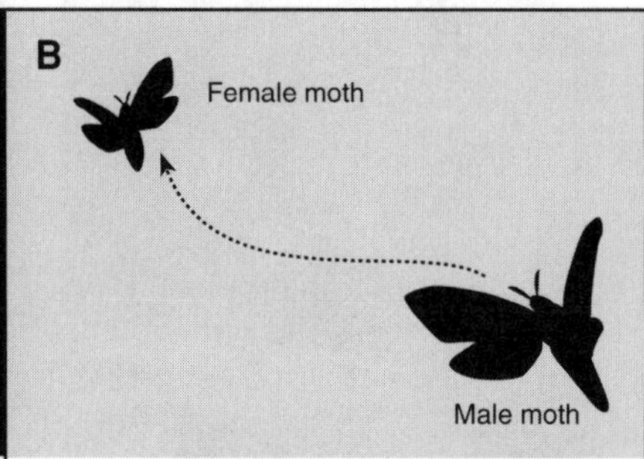

A flying male moth, encountering an odour (pheromone) trail left by a female, will turn and fly upwind until it reaches the female.

C

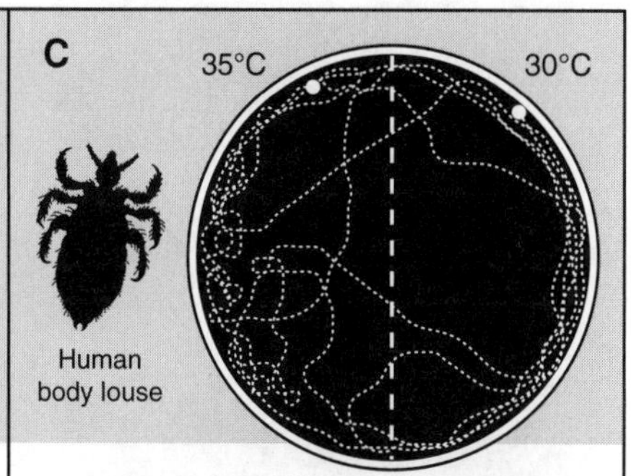

In a circular chamber, lice make relatively few turns at 30°C, but many random turns at 35°C.

D

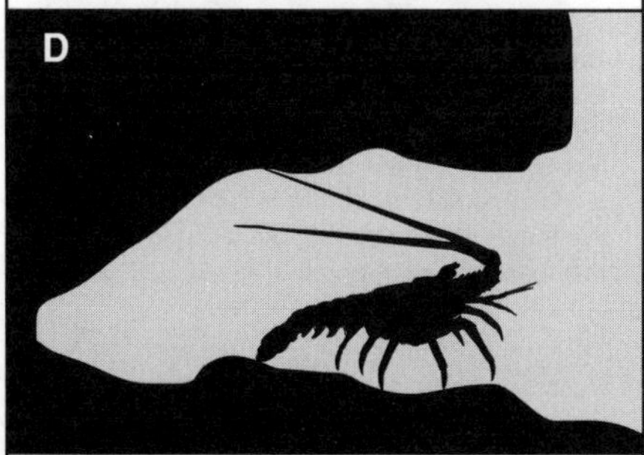

Spiny lobsters will back into tight crevices so that their body is touching the crevice sides. The antennae may be extended out.

E

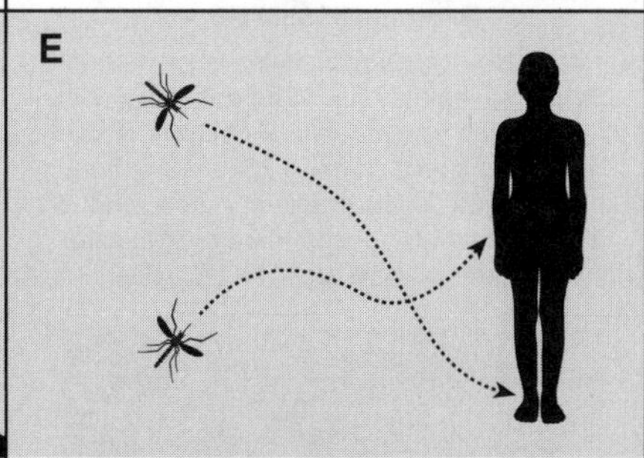

At close range, mosquitoes use the temperature gradient generated by the body heat of a host to home in on exposed flesh.

F

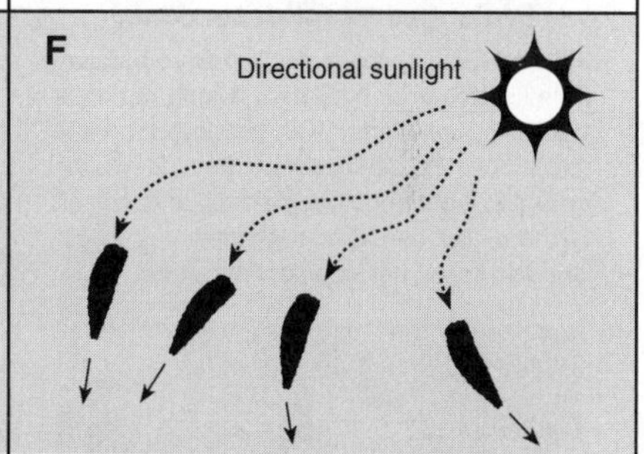

Blowfly maggots will turn and move rapidly away from a directional light source.

1. Distinguish between a **kinesis** and a **taxis**, describing examples to illustrate your answer: ____________________

2. Giving an example, describe the adaptive value of simple orientation behaviours such as kineses: ____________________

3. Name the physical stimulus for each of the following **prefixes** used in naming orientation responses:

(a) Gravi- ______ (b) Hydro- ______ (c) Thigmo- ______

(d) Photo- ______ (e) Chemo- ______ (f) Thermo- ______

4. For each of the above examples (A-F), describe the orientation response. Indicate whether the response is positive or negative (e.g. positive phototaxis):

(a) **A:** ______ (b) **B:** ______

(c) **C:** ______ (d) **D:** ______

(e) **E:** ______ (f) **F:** ______

5. Suggest what temperature body lice "prefer", given their response in the chamber (in C): ____________________

Primate Behaviour

Non-human primates make excellent subjects for observational studies of behaviour. Many of the diurnal species are highly social and they exhibit a large number of behaviours associated with social bonding, dominance, parental care, and learning. Primate behaviour also encompasses locomotory behaviour, signalling and communication, and the specifics of foraging behaviour. These areas are not mutually exclusive of course. In many primates, foraging involves learning as well social interaction and communication. Sociality offers many advantages, including better defence and access to feeding and resting areas.

Prolonged infant dependency

Primate infants (e.g. the infant **olive baboon** with its mother above) have a long period of parental dependency. This provides food and protection, and offers more opportunity for the young to learn from their parents. In apes and humans, the period of dependency is longer and allows the development of culture.

Grooming behaviour

Grooming of other group members is a social behaviour that has little to do with hygiene. It involves the careful removal of flakes of skin and grass seeds. It helps to create a bond between individuals in a family group and is thought to reduce stress. Here two **crab-eater macaques** from Asia are seen grooming.

Visual and olfactory signals

Ring-tailed lemurs are prosimians from the island of Madagascar, off the east coast of Africa. They communicate using a combination of visual signals and scent marks to map out their territory. Their bushy tail with distinctive markings is held erect like a flag for other members of the family group to see.

Learning in macaques

Japanese macaques living in the mountainous areas of Honshu, Japan, survive temperatures below -15 °C by spending much of the winter in naturally heated volcanic hot springs. They are highly intelligent. When researchers presented them with sweet potatoes, one individual washed the food free of sand in the sea. This behaviour was copied by others until all but the very oldest members of the troop were washing their food.

Learning in chimpanzees

Chimpanzees are highly social animals and learned behaviours are an important part of their behavioural repertoire. Tool making and use is common amongst chimps, and learning how to make and use tools is an important part of a chimp's upbringing. For example, wild chimps select and modify sticks to probe termite mounds, and use different tools for different purposes. This chimp has discovered that a broken coconut makes a good drinking vessel.

Group defence in olive baboons

Olive baboons live in troops which have an orderly hierarchy that promotes division of labour and maximises the efficiency with the which the group can search for food and defend itself against predators and other troops. When the troop is on the move, females with young are positioned near the centre for protection. Females in oestrus move in consort with the most dominant males. All other males tend to be positioned on the edges of the group.

1. Describe the benefits of sociality in primates, using an example to illustrate your points: ______________________

Learned Behaviour

Learning describes a relatively permanent modification of behaviour that occurs as a result of practise or experience. Learning is a critical process that affects the behaviour of animals of all ages, across many taxa. Learning behaviours vary widely. The simplest are **habituation** and **imprinting**, when an animal learns to make a particular response only to one type of animal or object. Like most behaviours, they are adaptive in that they enhance survival by ensuring appropriate responses in the given environment. More complex behaviours arise through **conditioning** and observational learning, such as imitation. Latent learning and insight are not readily demonstrated but have been shown experimentally in a range of species.

Filial (Parent) Imprinting

Filial imprinting is the process by which animals develop a social attachment. It differs from most other kinds of learning (including other types of imprinting), in that it normally can occur only at a specific time during an animal's life. This **critical period** is usually shortly after hatching (about 12 hours) and may last for several days. Ducks and geese have no innate ability to recognise mother or even their own species. They simply respond to, and identify as mother, the first object they encounter that has certain characteristics.

Sexual Identity Imprinting

Individuals learn to direct their sexual behaviour at some stimulus objects, but not at others. Termed **sexual imprinting**, it may serve as a species identifying and species isolating mechanism. The mate preferences of birds have been shown to be imprinted according to the stimulus they were exposed to (other birds) during early rearing. Sexual imprinting generally involves longer periods of exposure to the stimulus than filial imprinting (see left).

Digger waso, *Philanthus triangulum*, with prey

© Karen Nichols

Latent Learning

Latent learning describes an association made without reinforcement and expressed later. Tinbergen and Kruyt tested latent learning in predatory digger wasps by providing landmarks around the wasps' nest burrows. On emerging, the wasps survey the area and fly off to forage. If the landmarks were removed or rearranged, the returning wasps became disorientated, supporting the conclusion that the returning wasps use the entire configuration of landmarks as a guide to relocating the burrow.

Habituation

Habituation is a very simple type of learning involving a loss of a response to a repeated stimulus when it fails to provide any form of reinforcement (reward or punishment). Habituation is different to fatigue, which involves loss of efficiency in a repeated activity, and arises as a result of the nature of sensory reception itself. An example of habituation is the waning response of a snail attempting to cross a platform that is being tapped at regular time intervals. At first, the snail retreats into its shell for a considerable period after each tap. As the tapping continues, the snail stays in its shell for a shorter duration, before resuming its travel.

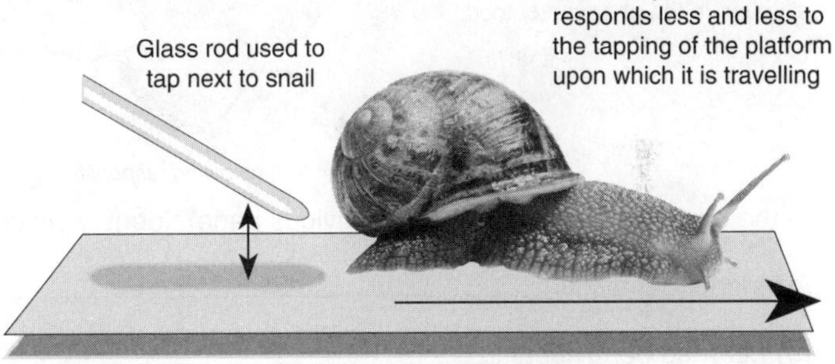

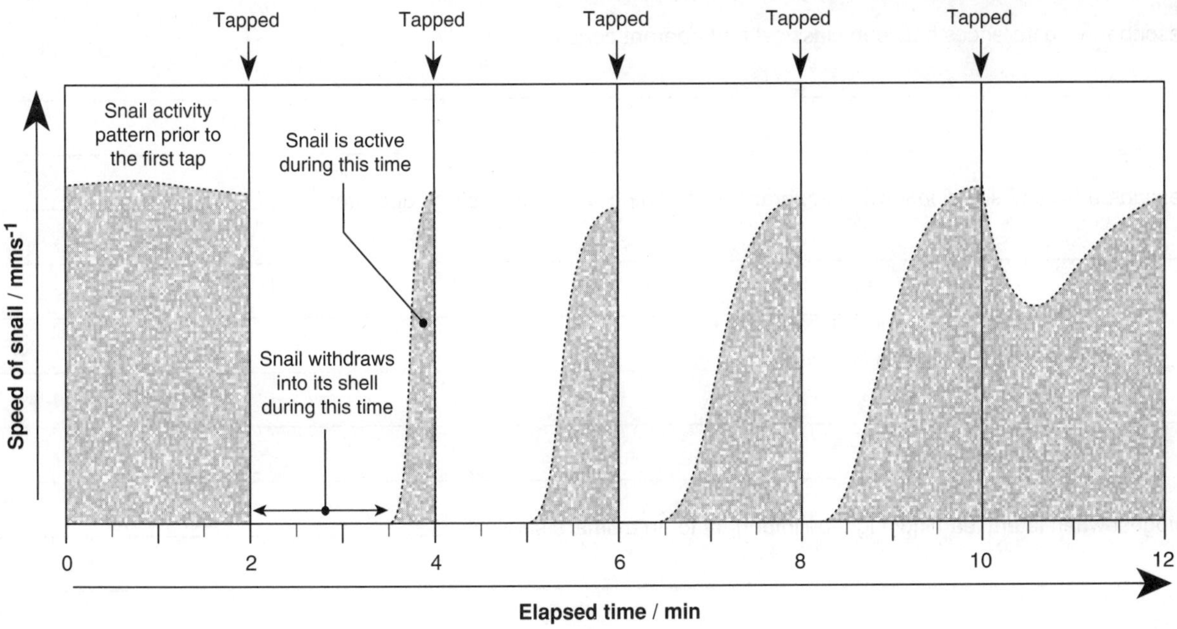

***Related activities:** The Components of Behaviour, Learning to Sing, Insight Behaviour*
***Web links:** Foraging Behaviour, Optimal Foraging*

Classical Conditioning

Classical conditioning, founded by Ivan Pavlov, describes a type of **associative learning** where behaviour that is normally triggered by a certain stimulus comes to be triggered by a substitute stimulus that previously had no effect on the behaviour. Between 1890 and 1900, Pavlov noticed that the dogs he was studying would salivate when they knew they were to be fed. The dogs were alerted by a bell that rung every time the lab door opened. Through experimentation, Pavlov discovered that ringing the bell did not at first cause salivation, but that the dogs could be **conditioned** to relate the bell ringing to food presentation. Eventually the bell caused the same salivation response as food, indicating that the dogs were conditioned to associate the stimuli.

1. Before conditioning an unconditioned stimulus (food) evokes an unconditioned response (salivation).

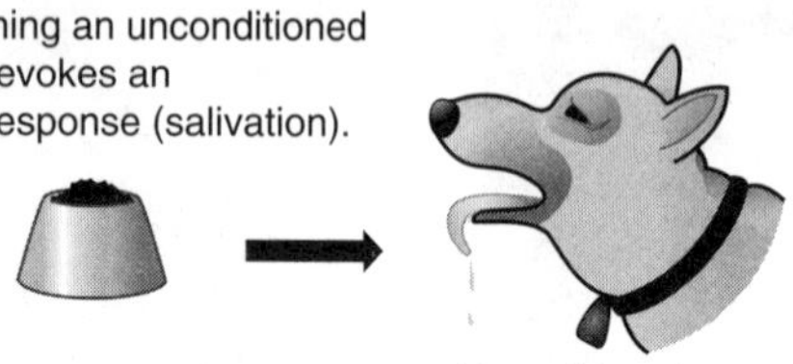

Unconditioned response

2. Before conditioning, a neutral stimulus (bell) evokes no response.

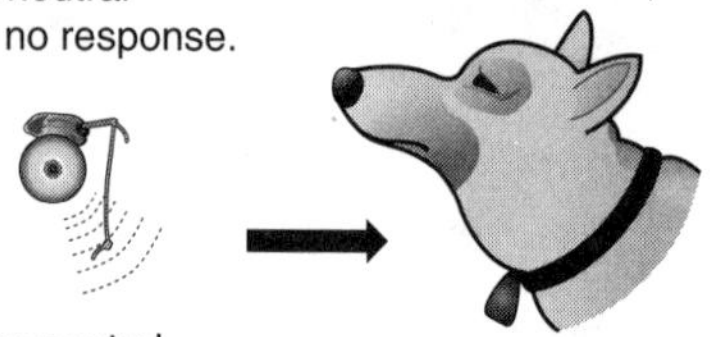

No response

3. During conditioning, the neutral stimulus (bell) is associated with the unconditioned stimulus (food), evoking the unconditioned response.

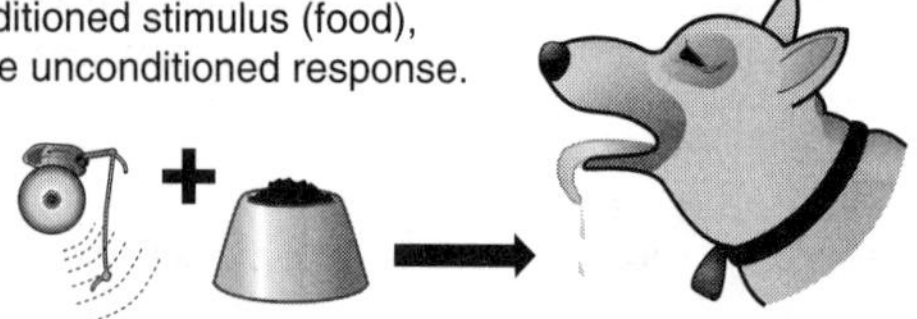

Unconditioned response

4. After conditioning, the (now) conditioned stimulus (bell) evokes the (now) conditioned response, even in the absence of food.

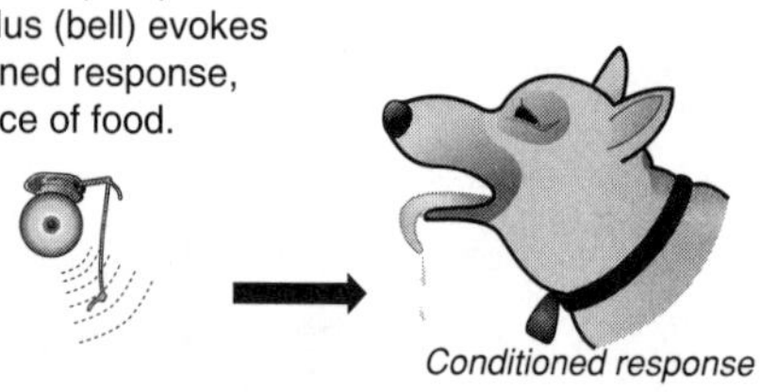

Conditioned response

Operant Conditioning

Operant conditioning describes situations where an animal learns to associate a particular behaviour with a reward. The appearance of the reward is dependent on the appearance of the behaviour. Burrhus Skinner studied operant conditioning using an apparatus he invented called a Skinner box (below). When an animal (usually a pigeon or rat) pushed a particular button it was rewarded with food. The animals learned to associate the pushing of the button with obtaining food (the reward). The behavioural act that leads the animal to push the button in the first place is thought to be generated spontaneously (by accident or curiosity). This type of learning is also called instrumental learning and it is the predominant learning process found in animals.

Operant Learning in Sparrows

Common house sparrows provide a good example of operant conditioning. They have learned to gain access to restaurants and cafés through automatic doors by triggering the motion sensors that control their opening. The birds will flutter in front of the sensor until the door opens, or perch on top of the sensor and lean over until it is triggered. Presumably, after accidentally triggering the sensor and gaining access, the birds learned which behaviours will bring them a reward.

1. In the example of filial imprinting (previous page), identify which parts of the behaviour can be attributed to:

   (a) Innate behaviour: ____________________

   (b) Learned behaviour: ____________________

2. Describe two differences between classical and operant conditioning:

   (a) ____________________

   (b) ____________________

3. Describe a natural situation in which operant conditioning would be likely to operate: ____________________

4. Explain in what way habituation is adaptive: ____________________

5. Suggest when latent learning might be important to an animal's survival: ____________________

Learning to Sing

Song birds use vocalisations (songs and calls) as a way to communicate, establish territories, and attract mates. The characteristics of a song may also be an indicator of fitness, as it has been shown that parasites and disease affect the song produced. While singing is instinctive, learning to sing the correct song is a learned behaviour, and without it, a song bird is unlikely to gain a territory or a mate. Analyses of many bird species show that there are at least two major strategies for song development: (1) imitation of other birds, particularly adults of the same species, and (2) invention or improvisation. These strategies overlie the genetic template for the song learning process. The window during which a song can be learned varies between species. In some species, the inherited song pattern can be modified by learning only during early life. In others, the song is modified according to experience for at least another year, and some (e.g. blackbirds) modify their songs throughout life.

Learning to Sing

The songs of different bird species vary but are generally characteristic of the species. The structure of bird song is studied using a technique called acoustic spectroscopy, a technique which produces a graphical representation of the sounds being made. This enables song patterns to be compared between individuals and has led to experimental work to establish how birds learn song and how much of the song is genetically determined.

Blackbirds modify their songs throughout their life

The sound spectrographs of chaffinch song (below) illustrate how the final song that is produced can be altered by exposure to the songs of same-species individuals during the first three months when the song is learned. The upper trace shows the song of a normal male, while the lower trace is the song of a male reared in isolation from the nest. The isolated male's song is the right pitch and relatively normal in length, but it is simpler and lacks the acoustic 'flourish' at the end (arrow), which is typical of the chaffinch's song.

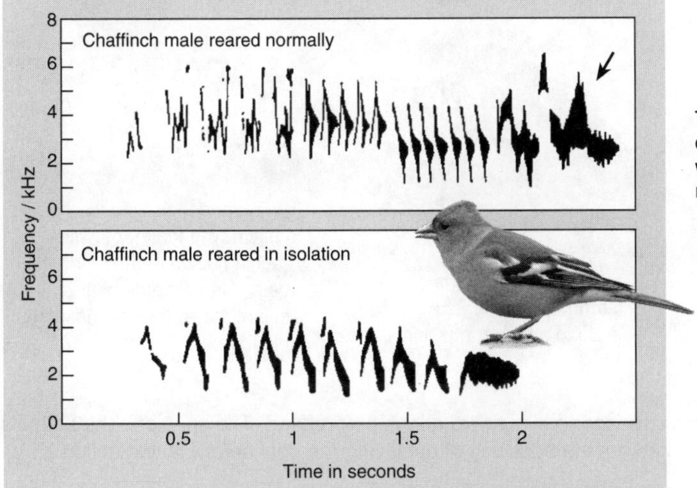

All data modified after A. Manning: An Introduction to Animal Behaviour (1979)

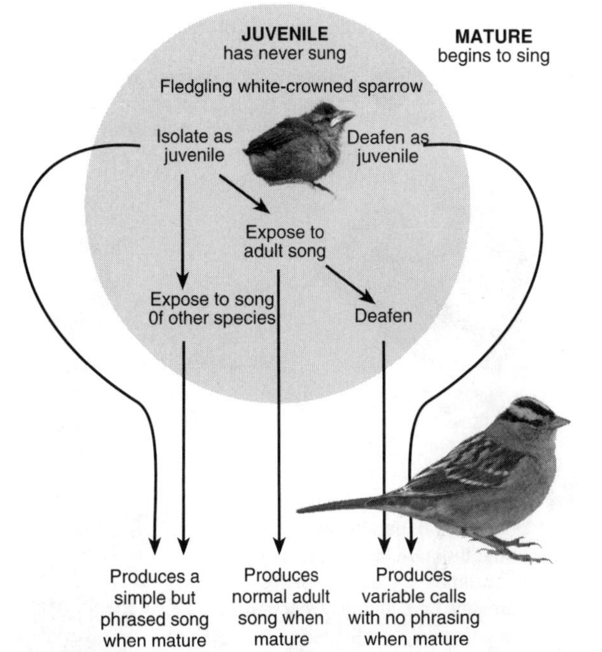

The diagram above summarises experiments investigating song development in white-crowned sparrows. This small finch has a wide range on the Pacific Coast of America and birds from different regions have different song dialects. The experiments found:

- Isolated males will eventually sing similar and simplified versions of the normal song, regardless of which region they come from.
- Isolated males can be trained to sing their own dialect by playing them tape recorded songs of birds from their region.
- After 4 months of age, birds are unreceptive to further learning.
- A bird needs to be able to hear itself in order to produce the normal song. It requires auditory feedback to adjust the notes.
- Once birds have learned their normal adult song, they can continue to sing normally even if deafened.

1. From the studies of song development in white-crowned sparrows, describe the evidence for the following statements:

   (a) The inherited song pattern can be modified by learning only in the early stages of life: ______

   (b) Young birds need to hear themselves sing to produce a normal song as adults: ______

   (c) The song produced by an adult bird is determined by a genetic predisposition and what it hears when it is a juvenile: ______

2. Discuss the possible evolutionary significance of modifying a basic (genetically determined) song pattern by learning: ______

Insight Behaviour

Insight behaviour was described by Wolfgang Kohler in 1917 when observing how chimpanzees solved the problem of retrieving bananas hung out of their reach. Specifically, insight behaviour uses reason to form conclusions or solve a problem that has not before been encountered and is often called "the eureka moment." It is not based on past experiences of a similar problem but does involve linking together isolated experiences from different problems to reach an appropriate response. Insight behaviour appears to be common in higher mammals (such as apes) and, although it is difficult to prove with lower animals, there is good evidence for insight learning in many other animals including dogs, pigeons and ravens.

Demonstrating Insight Behaviour

Chimpanzees (Kohler 1917)

1. Chimps were presented with bananas hung out of reach. They were given various materials to use but not taught what to do with them.

2. After trying a number of times to jump up and reach the bananas, one chimp began to stack boxes under them. Although it took him a few times to stack the boxes correctly, he eventually reached the bananas.

3. On another occasion a different chimp fitted together two sticks in order to reach bananas left outside it cage.

Ravens (Heinrich 1995)

1. Ravens were presented with food placed at the end of a string so it could not be reached from any position the birds could easily alight.

2. Most ravens reached down and gripped the string in their beak.

3. They then pulled the string up, moving the food to a higher position.

4. The ravens then held the string in place with their foot while reaching down to the string again. After repeating this several times, the ravens were able to reach the food.

Importantly, in neither of the examples above were the animals exposed to similar situations beforehand. The solutions the animals used shows they have assessed the situation then mentally worked out the best way of achieving the goal before taking action.

1. Explain the difference between insight learning and learning from experience (trial and error): ______________________

2. Explain why it is difficult to prove conclusively that an animal is using insight learning when solving a given problem:

____

3. Discuss how the use of insight learning can benefit an animal in its natural environment: ______________________

Dopamine and Behaviour

The role of genes in some aspects of human behaviour, although controversial, is becoming more apparent as research is carried out on more genes and their functions. The dopamine receptor D4 (DRD4) has received a lot of research attention, because of its apparent link to substance dependence and sensation seeking. Dopamine pathways are neural pathways in the brain which transmit the neurotransmitter dopamine from one region of the brain to another. Dopamine has many functions in the brain, including important roles in behaviour and cognition, motivation and reward, mood, attention, and learning. In cases of deficiency, dopamine cannot be administered as a drug itself, because it cannot cross the blood-brain barrier.

Dopamine Pathways in the Brain

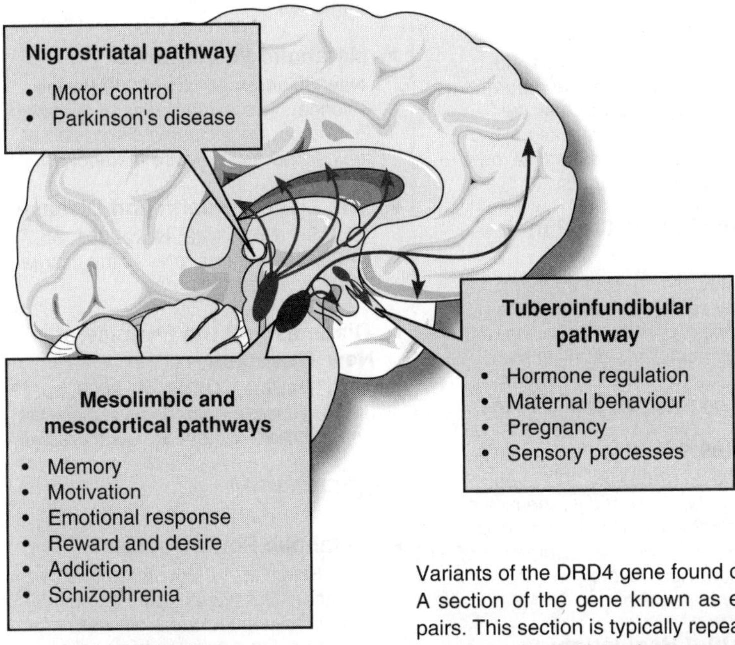

Effects of dopamine in the mesolimbic and mesocortical pathways

Level	Effect
Very low	Inability to focus. Associated with Attention Deficient Hyperactivity Disorder (ADHD).
Low	Addiction: the euphoric feeling caused by certain drugs is similar to the effects of dopamine and can leave the body wanting more.
Normal	Focus constant.
High	Hyperstimulation. Focus becomes narrowed to highly specific objects. Increase in perception of senses.
Very high	Paranoia and hallucination. Extreme situations can lead to schizophrenia.

Variants of the DRD4 gene found of chromosome 11 have been much studied. A section of the gene known as exon III has a repeating section of 48 base pairs. This section is typically repeated between 2 and 10 times. The number of repeats is divided into short repeats (from 2-5 repeats) and long repeats (from 6-10 repeats). Long repeats cause the receptor to be inefficient in binding with dopamine, leaving the body dopamine deficient.

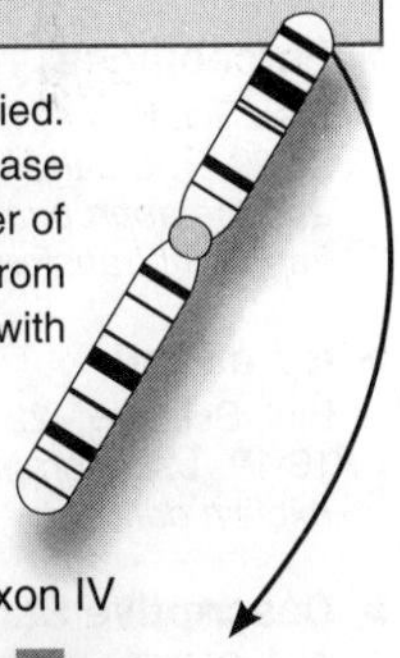

Structure of DRD4 gene

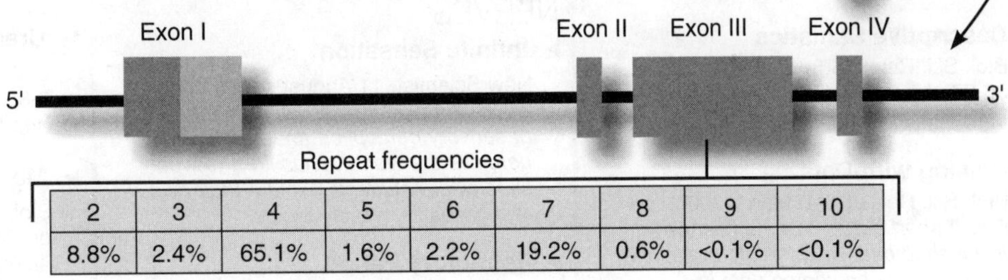

2	3	4	5	6	7	8	9	10
8.8%	2.4%	65.1%	1.6%	2.2%	19.2%	0.6%	<0.1%	<0.1%

The occurrence of long repeats has been linked with higher frequencies of ADHD and risk taking. "DRD4 knock-out" mice (mice without the DRD4 gene) show a deficiency in exploration of novel situations.

1. Explain why it is difficult to attribute behaviour to a single gene:

2. Contrast the effects of various levels of dopamine in the brain on behaviour.

3. Explain the link between the DRD4 gene and behaviour:

4. Discuss how this link helps us understand other aspects of human behaviour:

Appendix

PERIODICAL REFERENCES

PRACTICAL SKILLS IN BIOLOGY 2

- **Experiments**
  Biol. Sci. Rev., 14(3) February 2002, pp. 11-13. *The basics of experimental design and execution: determining variables, measuring them, and establishing a control.*

- **Fieldwork - Sampling Plants**
  Biol. Sci. Rev., 10(5) May 1998, pp. 6-8. *Methodology for sampling plant communities. Includes thorough coverage of quadrat use.*

- **Fieldwork - Sampling Animals**
  Biol. Sci. Rev., 10(4) March 1998, pp. 23-25. *Excellent article covering the appropriate methodology for collecting different types of animals in the field. Includes a synopsis of the mark and recapture technique.*

- **Percentages**
  Biol. Sci. Rev., 17(2) Nov. 2004, pp. 28-29. *The calculation of percentage and the appropriate uses of this important transformation.*

- **It's a Plot!**
  Biol. Sci. Rev., 22 (2) Nov. 2009, pp. 16-19. *Using graphs to evaluate and explain data.*

- **Descriptive Statistics**
  Biol. Sci. Rev., 13(5) May 2001, pp. 36-37. *An account of descriptive statistics using text, tables and graphs.*

- **Dealing with Data**
  Biol. Sci. Rev., 12 (4) March 2000, pp. 6-8. *A short account of the best ways in which to deal with the interpretation of graphically presented data in examinations.*

- **Drawing Graphs**
  Biol. Sci. Rev., 19(3) Feb. 2007, pp. 10-13. *A guide to creating graphs. The use of different graphs for different tasks is explained and there are a number of pertinent examples described to illustrate points.*

- **Estimating the Mean and Standard Deviation**
  Biol. Sci. Rev., 13(3) January 2001, pp. 40-41. *Simple statistical analysis. Includes formulae for calculating sample mean and standard deviation.*

- **The Variability of Samples**
  Biol. Sci. Rev., 13(4) March 2001, pp. 34-35. *The variability of sample data and the use of sample statistics as estimators for population parameters.*

COMMUNICATION AND HOMEOSTASIS

- **Infinite Sensation**
  New Scientist, 11 August, 2001, pp. 24-28. *An examination of the nature of sensory perception and how we perceive the world. It has links to web sites where students explore their own responses to sensory inputs.*

- **Cell Signalling via the P in Protein**
  Biol. Sci. Rev., 17(4) April 2005, pp. 13-16. *How cells communicate: the general principles of cell signalling, and how the extracellular signal interacts with the receptor protein at the cell surface to generate a signal cascade.*

- **Homeostasis**
  Biol. Sci. Rev., 12(5) May 2000, pp. 2-5. *Homeostasis: what it is, the role of negative feedback and the autonomic nervous system, and the adaptations of organisms for homeostasis in extreme environments (excellent).*

- **Temperature Regulation**
  Biol. Sci. Rev., 17(2) Nov. 2004, pp. 2-7. *An account of thermoregulation in animals. It also discusses how animals cope with temperature extremes.*

NERVES

- **Infinite Sensation**
  New Scientist, 11 August, 2001, pp. 24-28. *An examination of the nature of sensory perception and how we perceive the world. It has links to web sites where students explore their own responses to sensory inputs.*

- **Refractory Period**
  Biol. Sci. Rev., 20(4) April 2008, pp. 7-9. *The nature and purpose of the refractory period in response stimuli. The biological principles involved are discussed with in the context of the refractory period of the human heart.*

- **What is a Pacinian Corpuscle?**
  Biol. Sci. Rev., 21(3) Feb. 2009, pp. 11-13. *How these pressure receptors in the skin work to convert a mechanical stimulus into a nervous impulse.*

- **Bridging the Gap**
  Biol. Sci. Rev., 21(2) Nov. 2008, pp. 2-6. *Communication between nerve cells across synapses; the biology of chemical transmission.*

HORMONES

- **The Pancreas and Pancreatitis**
  Biol. Sci. Rev., 13(5) May 2001, pp. 2-6. *The structure of the pancreas and its role in digestion.*

- **Glucose Centre Stage**
  Biol. Sci. Rev., 19(2), Nov. 2006, pp. 14-17. The homeostatic regulation of blood glucose, including the role of hormones.

- **Metabolic Powerhouse**
  New Scientist, 11 Nov. 2000 (Inside Science). *The myriad roles of the liver in metabolism, including discussion of amino acid and glucose metabolism.*

- **The Liver in Health and Disease**
  Biol. Sci. Rev., 14(2) Nov. 2001, pp. 14-20. *The various roles of the liver, a major homeostatic organ.*

- **Diabetes and the Promise of New Therapies**
  Biol. Sci. Rev., 21(2) Nov. 2008, pp. 34-38. *Glucose homeostasis: diabetes and the development of new therapies.*

EXCRETION

- **Metabolic Powerhouse**
  New Scientist, 11 Nov. 2000 (Inside Science). *The myriad roles of the liver in metabolism, including discussion of amino acid and glucose metabolism.*

- **The Liver in Health and Disease**
  Biol. Sci. Rev., 14(2) Nov. 2001, pp. 14-20. *The various roles of the liver, a major homeostatic organ.*

- **Urea**
  Biol. Sci. Rev., 17(4) April 2005, pp. 6-8. *An account of nitrogen balance and how and why urea is formed.*

- **Monoclonals as Medicines**
  Biol. Sci. Rev., 18(4) April 2006, pp. 38-40. *The use of monoclonal antibodies in therapeutic and diagnostic medicine.*

- **The Kidney**
  Bio. Sci. Rev. 16(2) Nov. 2003, pp. 2-7. *The structure and function of the human kidney, including countercurrent multiplication in the loop of Henlé.*

- **Countercurrent Exchange Mechanisms**
  Biol. Sci. Rev., 9(1) September 1996, pp. 2-6. *The diversity and roles of countercurrent multipliers in biological systems including the kidney nephron.*

PHOTOSYNTHESIS

- **The Role of ATP in Cells**
  Biol. Sci. Rev., 19(2) Nov. 2006, pp. 30-33. *Synthesis and uses of ATP.*

- **Photosynthesis...Most Hated Topic?**
  Biol. Sci. Rev., 20(1) Sept. 2007, pp. 13-16. *A useful account documenting key points when learning about processes in photosynthesis.*

Appendix

PERIODICAL REFERENCES

- **Chloroplasts: Biosynthetic Powerhouses**
  Biol. Sci. Rev., 21(4) April 2009, pp. 25-27. *Information and diagrams on the structure and role of chloroplasts in photosynthesis.*

- **Rubisco: The World's Most Important Enzyme**
  Biol. Sci. Rev., 23(4) April 2011, pp. 2-5. *The role of Rubisco in the Calvin cycle, its efficiency as a catalyst, and the significance of photorespiration.*

- **The Double Life of ATP**
  Scientific American, Dec. 2009, pp. 60-67. *ATP the fuel inside living cells, also serves as a molecular messenger that affects cell behaviour.*

- **Fuelled for Life**
  New Scientist, 13 January 1996 (Inside Science). *Energy and metabolism: ATP, glycolysis, electron transport, Krebs cycle, and enzymes and cofactors.*

- **AcetylCoA: A Central Metabolite**
  Biol. Sci. Rev., 20(4) April 2008, pp.38-40. *The role of acetyl coenzyme A in metabolising fat and carbohydrate.*

- **Lactic Acid: Who Needs It?**
  Biol. Sci. Rev., 18(2) Nov. 2005, pp. 6-90. *An account of the biological roles of lactic acid, including its production in anaerobic metabolism in muscle.*

CELLULAR CONTROL

- **Control Centre**
  New Scientist, 17 July 1999, (Inside Science). *An easy to read account of the organisation of DNA in eukaryotic cells, the origin of the nucleus, how genes code for proteins, and the role of ribosomes and RNA in translation.*

- **What is a Gene?**
  Biol. Sci. Rev., 21(4) April 2009, pp. 10-12. *The molecular basis of genes, gene transcription, and production of a functional mRNA by removal of introns.*

- **Gene Structure and Expression**
  Biol. Sci. Rev., 12 (5) May 2000, pp. 22-25. *Gene structure and function, and the basis of gene regulation in eukaryotes and prokaryotes.*

- **The DNA Damage Response**
  Biol. Sci. Rev., 23(4) April 2011, pp. 30-33. *Cells have an emergency response to damage occurring through mutagens or transcription error.*

- **What is a Mutation?**
  Biol. Sci. Rev., 20(3) Feb. 2008, pp. 6-9. *The nature of mutations: causes, timing, and effects. Sickle cell disease is described.*

- **The Price of Silent Mutations**
  Scientific American, June 2009, pp. 34-41. *Small changes to DNA that were once considered silent are proving important in human disease, acting through a variety of mechanisms.*

- **Genetics of Sickle Cell Anaemia**
  Biol. Sci. Rev., 20(4) April 2008, pp. 14-17. *The molecular and physiological basis of sickle cell disease.*

- **Junk DNA and Molecular Evolution**
  Biol. Sci. Rev., 23(4) April 2011, pp. 11-14. *Changes in gene expression through changes in regulatory genes such as Hox gene sequences.*

MEIOSIS AND VARIATION

- **Mechanisms of Meiosis**
  Biol. Sci. Rev., 15(4), April 2003, pp. 20-24. *A clear and thorough account of the events and mechanisms of meiosis.*

- **What is Variation?**
  Biol. Sci. Rev., 13(1) Sept. 2000, pp. 30-31. *The nature of continuous and discontinuous variation. The distribution pattern of traits that show continuous variation is discussed.*

- **Mendel's Legacy**
  Biol. Sci. Rev., 18(4), April 2006, pp. 34-37. *Explores the accuracy of Mendel's laws in light of today's knowledge.*

- **The Y Chromosome: It's a Man Thing**
  Biol. Sci. Rev., 20(4) April 2008, pp. 2-6. *The Y chromosome is at the root of sex determination. This account discusses the nature of the Y chromosome, non-disjunction and Y chromosome disorders and the inheritance of Y linked diseases*

- **The Colour Code**
  New Scientist, 10 March 2002, pp. 34-37. *Researchers are uncovering the five to ten genes responsible for skin pigmentation.*

- **Obesity: Size Matters**
  Biol. Sci. Rev., 20(4) April 2006, pp. 10-13. *Environmental factors appear to have a greater effect on the development of obesity than genetic ones.*

VARIATION AND EVOLUTION

- **The Hardy-Weinberg Principle**
  Biol. Sci. Rev., 15(4), April 2003, pp. 7-9. *An explanation of the basis of the Hardy-Weinberg principle and its uses in estimating genotype frequencies and predicting change in populations.*

- **Evolution at a Snail's Pace**
  Biol. Sci. Rev., 23(2), Nov. 2010, pp. 26-29. *The banded snail provides a perfect case study in phenotypic variation and shifts in allele frequencies in response to changing environments.*

- **Black Squirrels**
  Biol. Sci. Rev., 21(2), Nov. 2008, pp. 39-41. *A look at how squirrel types have changed in Britain over time, and the selection pressures acting on the pigmentation and melanism.*

- **Skin Deep**
  Scientific American, October 2002, pp. 50-57. *This article examines the evolution of skin colour in humans and presents powerful evidence for skin colour ("race") being the end result of opposing selection forces (the need for protection of folate from UV vs the need to absorb vitamin D). Clearly written and of high interest, this is a must for student discussion and a perfect vehicle for examining natural selection.*

- **Fair Enough**
  New Scientist, 12 Oct. 2002, pp. 34-37. *Skin colour in humans: this article examines the argument for there being a selective benefit to being dark or pale in different environments.*

- **The Moths of War**
  New Scientist, 8 Dec. 2007, pp 46-49. *New research into the melanism of the peppered moth reaffirms it as an example of evolution.*

- **Polymorphism**
  Biol. Sci. Rev., 14(1) Sept. 2001, pp. 19-21. *A good account of genetic polymorphism. Examples include the carbonaria gene (Biston), the sickle cell gene, and aphids.*

- **Species and Species Formation**
  Biol. Sci. Rev., 20(3), Feb. 2008, pp. 36-39. *A feature covering the definition of species and how new species come into being through speciation.*

- **Speciation**
  Biol. Sci. Rev., 16(2) Nov. 2003, pp. 24-28. *Species, reproductive isolation, how separated populations diverge, and sympatric speciation. Case examples include the cichlids of Lake Victoria and the founder effect in mynahs.*

- **Listen, We're Different**
  New Scientist, 17 July 1999, pp. 32-35. *An account of speciation in periodic cicadas as a result of behavioural and temporal isolating mechanisms.*

- **What is a Species?**
  Scientific American June 2008, pp. 48-55. *The science of classification; modern and traditional approaches, the value of each, and the importance of taxonomy to identifying and recognising diversity. Excellent.*

Appendix

PERIODICAL REFERENCES

CLONING IN PLANTS AND ANIMALS

► **History of Cloning**
New Scientist, 7 August, 2010, supplement. *An excellent summary of the history of cloning technology: the breakthroughs, applications, and difficulties. Written by Ian Wilmut, the pioneer behind Dolly.*

BIOTECHNOLOGY

► **Growth Industry**
New Scientist, 15 Nov. 1997 (Inside Science). *A special report on biotechnology. Covers fermentation technology, genetic engineering, cloning, and grafting.*

► **The Microbiology of Cheese**
Biol. Sci. Rev., 15(4) April 2003, pp. 37-41. *The microbiology behind cheese-making provides an account of different types of cheeses and how they are made. Included is a discussion of pasteurisation, the microbial cultures, ripening, and microbial fermentation.*

► **Filamentous Fungi as Cellular Factories**
Biol. Sci. Rev., 9(5) May 1997, pp. 7-9. *The uses of fungi in biotechnology especially in enzyme and antibiotic production.*

► **Enzyme Technology**
Biol. Sci. Rev., 12 (5) May 2000, pp. 26-27. *The range and roles of industrial enzymes in modern biotechnology.*

► **Enzymes from Fungi**
Biol. Sci. Rev., 13 (3) Jan. 2001, pp. 19-21. *A discussion of the production and applications of fungal enzymes.*

GENOMES AND GENE TECHNOLOGY

► **DNA Polymerase**
Biol. Sci. Rev., 22(4) April 2010, pp. 38-41. *How DNA polymerase operates during DNA replication in the cell and how the enzyme is used in PCR.*

► **Revolution Postponed**
Scientific American, Oct. 2010, pp. 42-49. *The HGP has failed so far to produce the medical miracles that were promised. Biologists must decide where to go from here.*

► **What is...Genomics?**
Biol. Sci. Rev., 20(2) Nov. 2007, pp. 38-41. *The nature of genome projects and how genomics are being used to study the pathogenicity of bacteria.*

► **The Magic of Microarrays**
Scientific American, Feb. 2002, pp. 34-41. *DNA chips and their use in identifying health and disease, along with implications for drug treatment.*

► **Tailor-Made Proteins**
Biol. Sci. Rev., 13(4) March 2001, pp. 2-6. *Recombinant proteins and their uses in industry and medicine.*

► **Rice, Risk and Regulations**
Biol. Sci. Rev., 20(2) Nov. 2007, pp. 17-20. *The genetic engineering of one of the world's most important cereal crops is an ethical concern for many.*

► **The Engineering of Crop Plants**
Biol. Sci. Rev., 20(4) April 2008, pp. 30-36. *Crop plants can be engineered to increase the nutritional value of foods and to improve non-food crops as sources of raw materials for industry.*

► **Liver Transplantation and Ethical Issues**
Biol. Sci. Rev., 20(3) Feb. 2008, pp. 26-29. *The ethical and technical issues associated with organ transplants (including xenotransplants).*

► **Genes Can Come True**
New Scientist, 30 Nov. 2002, pp. 30-33. *An overview of gene therapy, and a note about future directions.*

► **Secrets of The Gene**
National Geographic, 196(4) Oct. 1999, pp. 42-75. *The nature of genes and the inheritance of particular genetic traits through certain populations.*

► **Birds, Bees, and Superweeds**
Biol. Sci. Rev., 17(2) Nov. 2004, pp. 24-27. *GM crops: their advantages and applications, as well as the risks and concerns associated with their use.*

► **Food / How Altered?**
National Geographic, May 2002, pp. 32-50. *Biotech foods: what are they, how are they made, and are they safe?*

ECOSYSTEMS

► **Ecosystems**
Biol. Sci. Rev., 9(4) March 1997, pp. 9-14. *Ecosystems: food chains & webs, energy flows, nutrient cycles, and ecological pyramids.*

► **Getting to Grips with Ecology**
Biol. Sci. Rev., 22(3), Feb. 2010, pp. 14-16. *A good overview on ecological principles using ladybirds and aphids as example organisms.*

► **The Lake Ecosystem**
Biol. Sci. Rev., 20(3) Feb. 2008, pp. 21-25. *An account of the components and functioning of lake ecosystems.*

► **Plant Succession**
Biol. Sci. Rev., 14 (2) November 2001, pp. 2-6. *Thorough coverage of primary and secondary succession, including the causes of different types of succession.*

► **Microbes and Nutrient Cycling**
Biol. Sci. Rev., 19(1) Sept. 2006, pp. 16-20. *The roles of microorganisms in nutrient cycling.*

POPULATIONS AND SUSTAINABILITY

► **Population Bombshell**
New Scientist, 11 July 1998 (Inside Science). *Current and predicted growth rates in human populations, including analyses of population age distributions.*

► **Logarithms and Life**
Biol. Sci. Rev., 13(4) March 2001, pp. 13-15. *The basics of logarithmic growth and its application to real populations.*

► **Inside Story**
New Scientist, 29 April 2000, pp. 36-39. *Ecological interactions between fungi and plants and animals: what are the benefits?*

► **The Body Snatchers**
New Scientist, 24 July 1999, pp. 42-46. *Parasitic relationships, and the adaptations of parasites that promote their survival.*

► **An Uneasy Eden**
National Geographic, 214(1), July 2008, pp. 144-157. *Predator-prey relationships in marine reef ecosystems.*

► **The Future of Red Squirrels in Britain**
Biol. Sci. Rev., 16(2) Nov. 2003, pp. 8-11. *An account of the impact of the grey squirrel on Britain's native red squirrel populations.*

► **Fish Predation**
Biol. Sci. Rev., 14(1) Sept. 2001, pp. 10-14. *Some fish species in freshwater systems in the UK are important top predators and influence the dynamics of an entire ecosystem.*

► **Predator-Prey Relationships**
Biol. Sci. Rev., 10(5) May 1998, pp. 31-35. *Predator-prey relationships, and the defence strategies of prey.*

► **Ecology and Nature Conservation**
Biol. Sci. Rev., 18(1) Sept. 2005, pp. 11-15. *Further research is needed in order to best restore or manage the natural ecosystems of lowland and upland Britain.*

► **Save those Woods!**
Biol. Sci. Rev., 12 (2) Nov. 1999, pp. 31-35. *Conservation of woodlands involves understanding succession. This article covers primary and secondary succession and discusses the influence of deflecting factors.*

Appendix

INDEX OF LATIN & GREEK ROOTS

PLANT RESPONSES

► **Sending Plants Around the Bend**
Biol. Sci. Rev., 12(4) March 2000, pp. 14-17. *An account of how plants perceive and respond to stimuli around them. Tropisms are fully covered.*

► **How Plants Know Their Place**
Biol. Sci. Rev., 17(3) Feb. 2005, pp. 33-36. *Plant responses to light and the action of phytochromes.*

ANIMAL RESPONSES

► **What is...Neuroscience?**
Biol. Sci. Rev., 23(3) Feb. 2011, pp. 6-8. *The basics of brain structure and disorders of brain function.*

► **The Autonomic Nervous System**
Biol. Sci. Rev., 18(3) Feb. 2006, pp. 21-25. *Description of the structure and roles of the autonomic nervous system.*

► **The Cerebral Cortex**
Biol. Sci. Rev., 21(1) Sept. 2008, pp. 2-6. *The structure, organisation, and many roles of the cerebral cortex.*

► **Human Muscle: Structure and Function**
Biol. Sci. Rev., 19(4) April 2007, pp. 25-29. *The structure and function of muscle in humans: contraction and the mechanics of locomotion.*

► **How Skeletal Muscles Work**
Biol. Sci. Rev., 22(4) April 2010, pp. 10-15. *The structure and function of muscle in humans: contraction, sliding filament theory, and types of muscle.*

► **Lactic Acid: Who Needs It?**
Biol. Sci. Rev., 18(2) Nov. 2005, pp. 6-90. *An account of the biological roles of lactic acid, including its production in anaerobic metabolism in muscle.*

ANIMAL BEHAVIOUR

► **Monkey Business**
New Scientist 5 Nov. 2005. *Examining patterns of primate behaviour, such as the sense of 'fairness' and how monkeys work for mutual benefit.*

► **Wing Tones**
New Scientist 29 March 2008, pp. 33-35. *Adaptability in the songs and behaviour of urban birds as they cope with noise pollution.*

► **Finches with Faulty Talk Gene Fluff Songs**
New Scientist 8 Dec. 2007, p. 17. *Birds with dysfunctional FoxP2 genes are unable to learn and recite their species specific songs properly.*

INDEX OF LATIN AND GREEK ROOTS, PREFIXES, AND SUFFIXES

Many biological terms have a Latin or Greek origin. Understanding the meaning of these components in a word will help you to understand and remember its meaning and predict the probable meaning of new words. Recognizing some common roots, suffixes, and prefixes will make learning and understanding biological vocabulary easier.

The following terms are identified, together with an example illustrating their use in biology.

a(n)- without .... *anoxic*
ab- away from .... *abductor*
ad- towards .... *adductor*
affer- carrying to .... *afferent*
amphi- both .... *amphibian*
amyl- starch .... *amylase*
anemo- wind .... *anemometer*
ante- before .... *antenatal*
anthro- human .... *anthropology*
anti- against, opposite .... *antibiotic*
apo- separate, from .... *apoenzyme*
aqua- water .... *aquatic*
arach- spider .... *arachnoid*
arbor- tree .... *arboreal*
arch(ae/i)- ancient .... *Archaea*
arthro- joint .... *arthropod*
artic- jointed .... *articulation*
artio- even-numbered .... *artiodactyl*
auto- self .... *autologous*
avi- bird .... *avian*
axi- axis .... *axillary*

blast- germ .... *blastopore*
brachy- short .... *brachycardia*
brady- slow .... *bradycardia*
branch- gill .... *branchial*
bronch- windpipe .... *bronchial*
bucca- mouth cavity .... *buccal*

caec- blind .... *caecum*
card- heart .... *cardiac*
cauda- tail .... *caudal*
centi- hundred .... *centimorgan*
ceph(al)- head .... *cephalothorax*
cera(s)(t)- horn .... *ceratopsian*
cerebro- brain .... *cerebrospinal*
cerv- neck .... *cervix*
chrom- color .... *chromoplast*
chym- juice .... *chyme*
cili- eyelash .... *cilia*
cloaca- sewer .... *cloacal*
coel- hollow .... *coelomate*
contra- opposite .... *contraception*
cotyl- cup .... *hypocotyl*
crani- skull .... *cranium*
crypt- hidden .... *crptic*
cyan- blue .... *cyanobacteria*
cyt- cell .... *cytoplasm*

dactyl- finger .... *polydactylic*
deci-(a) ten .... *decibel, decapod*
dendr- tree .... *dendrogram*
dent- tooth .... *edentate*
derm- skin .... *pachyderm*
di- two .... *dihybrid*
dors- back .... *dorsal*
dur- hard .... *dura mater*

echino- spiny .... *echinoderm*
ecto- outside .... *ectoderm*
effer- carrying away .... *efferent*
endo- inside .... *endoparasite*
equi- horse, equal .... *equilibrium*
erect- upright .... *Homo erectus*
erythr- red .... *erthyrocyte*
eu- well, very .... *eukaryote*
eury- wide .... *eurythermal*
ex- out of .... *explant*
exo- outside .... *exoskeleton*
extra- beyond .... *extraperitoneal*

foramen- opening .... *foramen magnum*

gast(e)r- stomach, pouch .... *gastropod*
gymn- naked .... *gymnosperm*

hal- salty .... *halophyte*
haplo- single, simple .... *haploid*
holo- complete, whole .... *holozoic*
hydr- water .... *hydrophyte*
hyper- above .... *hypertonic*
hypo- beneath .... *hypotonic*

infra- under .... *infrared*
inter- between .... *interspecific*
intra- within .... *intraspecific*
iso- equal .... *isotonic*

kilo- thousand .... *kilogram*

labi- lips .... *labial palps*

Appendix and Index

Appendix

INDEX OF LATIN & GREEK ROOTS

lacuna- space ... lacunae
lamella- leaf, layer ... lamellar bone
leuc- white ... leu(k)cocyte
lip- fat ... lipoprotein
lith- stone ... Palaeolithic
lumen- cavity ... lumen
lute- yellow ... corpus luteum
lymph- clear water ... lymphatic

magni- large ... magnification
mamma- breast ... mammal
mat(e)ri- mother ... maternal
mega- large ... megakaryocyte
melan- black ... melanocyte
meso- middle ... Mesolithic
meta- after ... metamorphosis
micro- small ... microorganism
milli- thousand ... millimetre
mirabile- wonderful ... rete mirabile
mono- one ... monohybrid
morph- form ... morphology
motor- mover ... motor nerve
multi- many ... multicellular
myo- muscle ... myofibril

necro- dead ... necrosis
neo- new ... Neolithic
nephr- kidney ... nephro
neur- nerve ... neural
notho- southern ... Nothofagus
noto- back, south ... notochord

oecious- house of ... monoecius
oed- swollen ... oedema
olfact- smelling ... olfactory
opistho- behind ... opisthosoma
os(s/t)- bone ... osteocyte
ovo- egg ... ovoviviparous

pachy- thick ... pachyderm
palae- old ... Palaeocene
pect(or)- chest ... pectoral fin
ped- foot ... quadraped
pent- five ... pentose sugar
per(i)- through, beyond ... peristalsis
peri- around ... periosteum
phaeo- dark ... phaeomelanin
phag- eat ... phagosome
phyll- leaf ... sclerophyll
physio- nature ... physiology
phyto- plant ... phytohormone
pisc- fish ... piscivorous
plagio- oblique ... plagioclimax
pneu(mo/st)- air, lung ... pneumonia
pod- foot ... sauropod
poly- many ... polydactyly
pre- before ... premolar
pro- in front of ... Prokaryote
prot- first ... protandry
pseud- false ... pseudopodia
pter- wing, fern ... Pterophyta
pulmo- lung ... pulmonary

radi- root ... radicle
ren- kidney ... renal
retic- network ... reticulated
rhin- nose, snout ... rhinoceros
rostr- beak, prow ... rostrum

sacchar- sugar ... polysaccharide
schizo- split ... schizocoelomate
scler- hard ... sclerophyll
seba- tallow, wax ... sebaceous
semi- half ... semi-conservative
sept- seven, wall ... septum
soma- body ... opisthosoma, somatic
sperm- seed ... spermatophyte
sphinct- closing ... sphincter
stereo- solid ... stereocilia
stom- mouth ... stoma
strat- layer ... stratification
sub- below ... subtidal
sucr- sugar ... sucrase
sulc- furrow ... sulci
super- beyond ... superior
supra- above ... supracoracoideus
sym- with ... symbiosis
syn- with ... synapsis

tact- touch ... tactile
tachy- fast ... tachycardia
taenia- ribbon ... Taenia (tapeworm)
trans- across ... transmembrane
tri- three ... triploblastic
trich- hair ... trichome

ultra- above ... ultraviolet
un- one ... unicellular
uro- tail ... urodele

vas- vessel ... vascular
ven- vein ... venous
ventr- belly ... ventral
vern- spring ... vernal
visc- organs of body cavity ... viscera
vitr- glass ... in vitro

xanth- yellow ... xanthophyll
xen- stranger ... xenotransplant
xer- dry ... xerophyte
xyl- wood ... xylem
zo- animal ... zoological

MULTIPLES

MULTIPLE	PREFIX	SYMBOL	EXAMPLE
10^9	giga	G	gigawatt (GW)
10^6	mega	M	megawatt (MW)
10^3	kilo	k	kilogram (kg)
10^2	hecto	h	hectare (ha)
10^{-1}	deci	d	decimetre (dm)
10^{-2}	centi	c	centimetre (cm)
10^{-3}	milli	m	milliimetre (mm)
10^{-6}	micro	μ	microsecond (μs)
10^{-9}	nano	n	nanometre (nm)
10^{-12}	pico	p	picosecond (ps)

INTERNATIONAL SYSTEM OF UNITS (SI)

Examples of SI derived units

DERIVED QUANTITY	NAME	SYMBOL
area	square metre	m^2
volume	cubic metre	m^3
speed, velocity	metre per second	ms^{-1}
acceleration	metre per second squared	ms^{-2}
mass density	kilogram per cubic metre	kgm^{-3}
specific volume	cubic meter per kilogram	m^3kg^{-1}
amount-of-substance concentration	mole per cubic meter	$molm^{-3}$
luminance	candela per square meter	cdm^{-2}

Index

Index

